Frommer's

5th Edition

South Pacific

Including Tahiti, Fiji & the Cook Islands

by Bill Goodwin

Macmillan • USA

ABOUT THE AUTHOR

Born and raised in North Carolina, **Bill Goodwin** was an award-winning newspaper reporter before becoming a legal counsel and speech writer for two U.S. senators, Sam Nunn of Georgia and the late Sam Ervin of North Carolina. In 1977 he sailed a 41-foot yacht from Annapolis, Md., to Tahiti; he then spent a year exploring French Polynesia and the rest of the South Pacific. A lawyer and freelance writer, Goodwin is now based in northern Virginia, but returns to paradise as often as possible.

MACMILLAN TRAVEL

A Simon & Schuster Macmillan Company
1633 Broadway
New York, NY 10019

ISBN 0-02-860869-0
ISSN 1044-2367

Editor: Lisa Renaud
Map Editor: Douglas Stallings
Design by Michele Laseau
Digital Cartography by Ortelius Design

SPECIAL SALES

Bulk purchases (10+ copies) of Frommer's travel guides are available to corporations at special discounts. The Special Sales Department can produce custom editions to
be used as premiums and/or for sales promotion to suit individual needs. Existing editions can be produced with custom cover imprints such as corporate logos. For more information write to Special Sales, Simon & Schuster, 1633 Broadway, 6th floor, New York, NY 10019-6785

Manufactured in the United States of America

To my father,
with love, and thanks for the loans.

ACKNOWLEDGMENTS

I wish to thank the many individuals and organizations who helped make this book possible, especially the always friendly and helpful staffs of the South Pacific tourist information offices. I am particularly grateful to Nelson Levy, Maeva Salmon, and Al Keahi in French Polynesia; Isimeli Bainimara, Vili Koyamaibole, Josaia Rayawa, Steve Yaqona, and Isaia Seru in Fiji; Chris Wong and Dianna Clarke in the Cook Islands; Sifuiva Reupena Muagututi'a and Teresa Anastasia Ngau-Chun in Western Samoa; Sinira T. Fuimaono and John Pereira in American Samoa; and Semisi Taumoepeau, Christopher Cocker, Tevita Manu, Sandradee Fonua, Elsie Blake, Nani Bourke, and Suilolo Liolahi in Tonga.

My deep personal thanks go to Mary Anne Gibbons, Nancy Monseaux, Max Parrish, Suzanne McIntosh, Mark Miller, and Curtis and Judy Moore, whose generosity over the years have made this book possible; to my sister, Jean Goodwin Marlowe, who has consistently given much-needed moral support; to Hina Kaptain and all the crew at happy hour on Moorea; and to Dick Beaulieu in Fiji, always a font of information, advice, and cold Stubbies. Everyone should have friends like these.

Contents

List of Maps

An Invitation to the Reader

In researching this book, I discovered many wonderful places—hotels, restaurants, shops, and more. I'm sure you'll find others. Please tell us about them, so we can share the information with your fellow travelers in upcoming editions. If you were disappointed with a recommendation, we'd love to know that, too. Please write to:

Bill Goodwin
Frommer's South Pacific, 5th Edition
Macmillan Travel
1633 Broadway
New York, NY 10019

An Additional Note

Please be advised that travel information is subject to change at any time—and this is especially true of prices. We therefore suggest that you write or call ahead for confirmation when making your travel plans. The authors, editors, and publisher cannot be held responsible for the experiences of readers while traveling. Your safety is important to us, however, so we encourage you to stay alert and be aware of your surroundings. Keep a close eye on cameras, purses, and wallets, all favorite targets of thieves and pickpockets.

What the Symbols Mean

✪ **Frommer's Favorites**

Hotels, restaurants, attractions, and entertainment you should not miss.

⑤ **Super-Special Values**

Hotels and restaurants that offer great value for your money.

The following abbreviations are used for credit cards:

AE	American Express	EU	Eurocard
CB	Carte Blanche	JCB	Japan Credit Bank
DC	Diners Club	MC	MasterCard
DISC	Discover	V	Visa
ER	enRoute		

The Best of the South Pacific

It's no easy task to pick the "best" of an area that has some of the world's most beautiful islands and beaches, a host of remote and romantic resorts, fabulous diving, a storied culture that inspires hedonistic dreams, and a history that has provided fodder for famous books and films. It's virtually impossible, for example, to choose the most friendly South Pacific island, for the Polynesians and Fijians are among the friendliest people on earth. Their big smiles and genuine warmth are prime attractions everywhere in the South Pacific.

Personally, I like all the islands and all the islanders, which further complicates my chore to no end. Nevertheless, I will attempt in this chapter to point out the best of the best—not necessarily to pass qualitative judgment, but to help you choose among many options.

Your own choice obviously will depend on why you are going to the islands. You can scuba dive to exhaustion, or just sit on the beach with a trashy novel. You can share a 300-room hotel with package tourists, or get away from it all at a tiny resort on a remote island. Even out there, you can be left alone with your lover, or join your fellow guests at lively dinner parties. You can totally ignore the Pacific Islanders around you, or enrich your own life by learning about theirs. You can listen to the day's events on CNN, or see what the South Seas were like a century ago. Those decisions are all yours.

For a brief sketch of each South Pacific country, see "The Islands Today" in Chapter 2, "Introducing the South Pacific."

1 The Most Beautiful Islands

"In the South Seas," Rupert Brooke wrote in 1914, "the Creator seems to have laid himself out to show what He can do." How right the poet was, for all across the South Pacific lie some of the world's most dramatically beautiful islands. In my opinion, the best of the lot have jagged mountain peaks plunging into aquamarine lagoons. Here are some you see on the travel posters and in the brochures:

- **Moorea, French Polynesia:** Personally, I think Moorea is the most beautiful island in the world. Nothing to my mind compares with its sawtooth ridges and the great dark-green hulk of Mount Rotui separating glorious Cook's and Opunohu Bays. The view from Tahiti of Moorea's dinosaurlike skyline is unforgettable. See Chapter 6, "Moorea."

- **Bora Bora, French Polynesia:** James Michener thinks that Bora Bora is the most beautiful island in the world. Although tourism has turned this gem into sort of an expensive South Seas Disneyland since Michener's day, development hasn't altered the incredible beauty of Bora Bora's basaltic tombstone towering over a lagoon ranging in color from yellow to deep blue. See Chapter 7, "Bora Bora & Other Islands."
- **Tutuila, American Samoa:** The one good reason to go to American Samoa these days is to see the physical beauty of Tutuila and its magnificent harbor at Pago Pago. If you can ignore the tuna canneries and huge stacks of shipping containers, this island is right up there with Moorea. See Chapter 14, "American Samoa."
- **Ovalau, Fiji:** The sheer cliffs of Ovalau kept the town of Levuka from becoming Fiji's modern capital, but they create a dramatic backdrop to an old South Seas town little changed in the past century. Ovalau has no good beaches, which means it has no resorts to alter its landscape. See Chapter 11, "Suva & Levuka."
- **The Yasawa Islands, Fiji:** Unspoiled is the best description for this chain of long, narrow islands off the northwest coast of Viti Levu, Fiji's main island. Blue Lagoon Cruises goes out there, and the hilly islands have a few small resorts, but mostly the Yasawas are populated by Fijians who live in traditional villages beside some of the region's great beaches. See "Resorts off Nadi" and "Blue Lagoon Cruises" in Chapter 10, "Nadi & Viti Levu."
- **Qamea, Matagi, and Laucala Islands, Fiji:** These little jewels off the northern coast of Taveuni are lushly beautiful, with their shorelines either dropping precipitously into the calm surrounding waters or forming little bays with idyllic beaches. See "Resorts off Taveuni" in Chapter 12, "Northern Fiji."
- **Vava'u, Tonga:** One of the South Pacific's best yachting destinations, hilly Vava'u is shaped like a jellyfish, with small islands instead of tentacles trailing off into a quiet lagoon. Waterways cut into the center of the main island, creating the picturesque and perfectly protected Port of Refuge. See "Vava'u" in Chapter 15, "Tonga."
- **Aitutaki, Cook Islands:** A junior version of Bora Bora, a small island sits at the apex of Aitutaki's shallow, colorful lagoon, which from the air looks like a turquoise carpet laid on the deep blue sea. See "Aitutaki" in Chapter 8, "Rarotonga & the Cook Islands."
- **Savai'i, Western Samoa:** One of the largest Polynesian islands, this great volcanic shield slopes gently on its eastern side to a chain of gorgeous beaches. There are no towns on Savai'i, only traditional Samoan villages, which add to its unspoiled beauty. See "Savai'i" in Chapter 13, "Western Samoa."
- **Rarotonga, Cook Islands:** The capital of the Cook Islands is like a small version of Tahiti, but without the development. See Chapter 8, "Rarotonga & the Cook Islands."

2 The Best Beaches

Since all but a few South Pacific islands are surrounded by coral reefs, there are few surf beaches in the region. Tahiti has some, but they all have heat-absorbing black volcanic sand. Otherwise, most islands (and all but a few resorts) have bathtub-like lagoons lapping on coral sands draped by coconut palms. Fortunately for the environmentalists among us, some of the most spectacular beaches are on remote islands and are protected from development by the islanders' devotion to their cultures and villages' land rights. Here are a few that stand out from the crowd.

- **Huahine, French Polynesia:** My favorite resort beach is at Relais Mahana, a small hotel near Huahine's south end. Trees grow along the white beach, which slopes into a lagoon deep enough for swimming at any tide. The resort's pier goes out to a giant coral head, a perfect and safe place to snorkel, and the lagoon here is protected from the trade winds, making it ideal for sail- and paddleboats. See "Huahine" in Chapter 7, "Bora Bora & Other Islands."
- **Yasawa Island, Fiji:** One of the most spectacular beaches I've ever seen is on the northern tip of Yasawa Island, northernmost of the gorgeous chain of the same name. This long expanse of deep sand is broken by a teapot-like rock outcrop, which also separates two Fijian villages, whose residents own this land. Blue Lagoon Cruises and oceangoing cruise ships stop here; otherwise, the Fijians keep it all to themselves. There are other good beaches on Yasawa, however, all within reach of the Yasawa Island Lodge resort. See "Resorts off Nadi" and "Blue Lagoon Cruises" in Chapter 10, "Nadi & Viti Levu."
- **Yacata Island, Fiji:** Remote, hat-shaped Yacata shares a gorgeous small lagoon with Kaibu Island, which means the only way to get there is to stay at the very expensive Kaimbu Island Resort. If you can afford that, then you'll have access to Yacata's five miles of perfect beaches, all of them deserted and backed by coconut palms and fronted by the incredibly clear lagoon. See "Resorts off Taveuni" in Chapter 12, "Northern Fiji."
- **Upolu, Western Samoa:** The main island of Western Samoa has three outstanding beaches. Return to Paradise Beach is an idyllic stretch of white sand and black rocks where the 1953 Gary Cooper movie of that name was filmed. Surf actually pounds on the rocks. On eastern Upolu, the lagoon beaches of Aleipata all face a group of small islets offshore, and on a clear day you can see American Samoa. And at the village of Vavau, you can actually swim in the shade in a tidal pool formed by two outcrops. See "Seeing Upolu" in Chapter 13, "Western Samoa."
- **Horseshoe Bay, Matagi Island, Fiji:** Home of one of the region's best small resorts, Matagi is an extinct volcano whose crater fell away on one side and formed picturesque Horseshoe Bay. The half-moon beach at its head is one of the finest in the islands, but you will have to be on a yacht or a guest at Matagi Island Resort to enjoy it. See "Resorts off Taveuni" in Chapter 12, "Northern Fiji."
- **Matira Beach, Bora Bora, French Polynesia:** Beginning at the Hotel Bora Bora, this fine ribbon of sand stretches around skinny Matira Point, which forms the island's southern extremity, all the way to the Club Med. The eastern side has views of the sister islands of Raiatea and Tahaa. In addition to being shared by most of Bora Bora's high-priced resorts, Matira Beach is home to one of the region's best hostels. See Chapter 7, "Bora Bora & Other Islands."
- **Moorea, French Polynesia:** The northwest and northeast corners of Moorea are bordered by unnamed but uninterrupted beaches. The Club Med and several other hotels are on the northwest beach, where they have great sunsets. Around the Hotel Sofitel Ia Ora on the northeast, the beach is enhanced by a view of Tahiti across the Sea of the Moon. See "Where to Stay" in Chapter 6, "Moorea."
- **Muri Beach, Rarotonga, Cook Islands:** Wrapping for eight miles around Rarotonga's southeastern corner, Muri Beach faces little islets out on the reef

and the island's best lagoon for boating. The sand rather than the road serves as the main avenue among the Muri Beach resorts and restaurants. See "Seeing Rarotonga" in Chapter 8, "Rarotonga & the Cook Islands."

- **Natadola Beach, Viti Levu, Fiji:** Although Fiji's main island of Viti Levu doesn't have the high-quality beaches found on the country's small islands, Natadola is an exception. Until recently this long stretch was spared development, but hotels and restaurants are coming. So far the locals haven't permitted buildings right on the beach. See "The Coral Coast" in Chapter 10, "Nadi & Viti Levu."
- **Malololailai Island, Fiji:** The western end of Malololailai Island, in Fiji's Mamanuca Group off Nadi, trails off to a point bordered by an archetypical South Seas beach, with coconut palms hanging over the curving sand. See "Resorts off Nadi" in Chapter 10, "Nadi & Viti Levu."
- **Naitasi Resort, Fiji:** Of the resorts in the Mamanuca Islands off Nadi, Naitasi has a lovely beach with deep, soft sand and a lagoon that is deep enough for swimming and boating at all tides. See "Resorts off Nadi" in Chapter 10, "Nadi & Viti Levu."

3 The Best Honeymoon Destinations

Whether you're on your honeymoon or not, the South Pacific is a marvelous place for romantic escapes. After all, romance and the islands have gone hand-in-hand since the early explorers were given rousing welcomes by the barebreasted young women of Tahiti.

Two choices are especially appealing in this respect. One is a thatch-roof bungalow built on stilts over the lagoon, with a glass panel in its floor for viewing fish swimming below you and steps leading from your front porch into the warm waters below. The second is a small, relatively remote island offering as much privacy as you are likely to find at a modern resort. These little establishments would also fall into another category: The Best Places to Get Away from It All.

A friend of mine says that her ideal wedding would be to rent an entire small resort in Fiji, take her wedding party with her, get married in Fijian costume beside the beach, and make the rest of her honeymoon a diving vacation. Most resorts covered in this book are well aware of such desires, and they offer wedding packages complete with traditional ceremony and costumes. Choose your resort, then contact the management for details about their wedding packages.

Meantime, here's what the two best honeymoon destinations have to offer:

- **French Polynesia:** The resorts here have the region's only over-water bungalows (more protective of their environments and aware that hurricanes could wash them into the lagoon, the other island countries prohibit over-water bungalows altogether). Invariably these are the most expensive style of accommodation in French Polynesia. The **Hotel Bali Hai Moorea** was the first resort to have them, and if it hasn't been sold and turned into a super-deluxe facility by the time you marry, it will be the least expensive choice. Although a time-share operation without a beach, Moorea's **Club Bali Hai** has bungalows over Cook's Bay; facing the jagged peaks surrounding this magnificent body of water, they have the most photographed view of all. The more modern **Moorea Beachcomber Parkroyal** has bungalows partially built over the lagoon. See "Where to Stay" in Chapter 6, "Moorea."

On Huahine, the **Hotel Sofitel Heiva** has six bungalows with views of the mountainous main part of that island. On Rangiroa, the **Kia Ora Village** has them over the world's second-largest lagoon. See "Huahine" and "Rangiroa" in Chapter 7, "Bora Bora & Other Islands."

Even on Tahiti, which most visitors now consider a way station to the other islands, the **Tahiti Beachcomber Parkroyal** has over-water bungalows facing the dramatic outline of Moorea across the Sea of the Moon. See "Where to Stay" in Chapter 5, "Tahiti."

But it's on Bora Bora that the over-water bungalow dominates. Some of those at the **Hotel Bora Bora** look directly out to tombstone-like Mount Otemanu rising across the famous lagoon; along with Cook's Bay on Moorea, this is one of the most photographed scenes in the entire South Pacific. They also sit right on the edge of the clifflike reef, making for superb snorkeling right off your front porch. The new **Bora Bora Lagoon Resort** has 50 bungalows over its reef, some with great views of Bora Bora's other peak, the more rounded Mount Pahia. Those at the **Moana Beach Parkroyal** are the most luxurious; the glass tops of their coffee tables come off so that you can feed the fish, and they sit so far out on a pier that room service is canoe-borne. Those at the **Hotel Sofitel Marara** may be the least expensive on Bora Bora, but they have views of Raiatea and Tahaa sitting on the horizon. See "Bora Bora" in Chapter 7, "Bora Bora & Other Islands."

An alternative in French Polynesia is **Hana Iti Resort** on Huahine. Instead of being over the water, or even beside the beach, most of Hana Iti's huge bungalows sit atop a ridge, thus commanding terrific views from the spa pools built into their decks. The units are very widely spaced, offering the ultimate in privacy. The "downside" is that you can't just stroll over to the beach. See "Huahine" in Chapter 7, "Bora Bora & Other Islands."

• **Fiji:** For the remote island experience, Fiji has one of the world's finest collection of small offshore resorts. These little establishments have two advantages over their French Polynesian competitors. First, they have only 3 to 15 bungalows each, instead of the 40 or more found at the French Polynesian resorts. Second, they are on islands all by themselves. Together, these two advantages multiply the privacy factor severalfold.

Movie stars and others with the bucks retreat to top-of-the-line resorts such as **Kaimbu Island Resort,** in the remote Lau Group off Taveuni. Kaimbu has only three bungalows, of which the honeymoon unit has a deck overlooking the beautiful lagoon surrounding Kaimbu, its hat-shaped sister island Yacata, and several small islets where you can escape for private champagne picnics on gorgeous, deserted beaches. The unit even has an outdoor hammock completely surrounded by tropical foliage. Guests are made to feel like houseguests of the Kaimbu's young American owners. This same houseguest theme prevails at **Fiji Forbes Laucala Island,** the Northern Fiji retreat of the late publisher Malcolm S. Forbes, Sr., where seven bungalows are widely spaced in a coconut grove. The staff will bring your meals anywhere on the island, including a romantic tree house at its own private beach. See "Resorts off Taveuni" in Chapter 12, "Northern Fiji."

In central Fiji off Suva, **The Wakaya Club** has eight of the largest bungalows in Fiji, and a staff that leaves the guests to their own devices. See "Resorts off Suva" in Chapter 11, "Suva & Levuka."

Off Nadi, the atmosphere at the 15-bungalow **Vatulele Island Resort** and the 14-unit **Turtle Island Lodge** is more active, with guests given the choice of dining alone in their bungalows or at lively dinner parties hosted by the engaging owners. **Yasawa Island Lodge** sits on one of the prettiest beaches and has a very low-key, friendly ambience. It has 16 very large bungalows, but be sure to reserve one of the newer units, since a communal pathway runs just outside the bedroom windows of the older bungalows. See "Resorts off Nadi" in Chapter 10, "Nadi & Viti Levu."

In the moderate range, the 11 bungalows and stunning central building at **Qamea Beach Club** off Taveuni in Northern Fiji are my favorites. The 52-foot-high thatch roof of the main building is romantically lighted by kerosene lanterns, and each bungalow has its own hammock strung across the front porch. Qamea is oriented toward couples. Nearby **Matagi Island Resort** is one of the region's best family vacation spots, but its 11 bungalows are more widely spaced than Qamea's, and one is even built 20 feet up in a Pacific almond tree (it's reserved for honeymooners). See "Resorts off Taveuni" in Chapter 12, "Northern Fiji."

Moody's Namena is the most remote of all moderately priced resorts, with five bungalows on a dragon-shaped island all by itself in the Koro Sea off Savusavu. There's no electricity on Tom and Joan Moody's island, so gaslights provide a romantic mood. The hexagonal units are perched tree-house-like on a ridge, providing both privacy and stunning sea views. See "A Resort off Savusavu" in Chapter 12, "Northern Fiji."

4 The Best Family Vacations

Unless you consider the entire region to be a South Seas theme park, there are no Disney Worlds or other such attractions in the islands. That's not to say that children won't have a fine time here, but they will enjoy themselves more if they like being around the water. Any family can vacation in style and comfort at large resorts like the Sheraton Fiji, the Regent Fiji, or Shangri-la's Fijian Resort, but here are some of the best smaller establishments that welcome families with children.

- **Matagi Island Resort, Northern Fiji:** Born as a hard-core dive base, this low-key, family-run resort has adjusted to divers who want to bring the youngsters along. Parents do their two dives—or go snorkeling—in the morning, while the other mothers help the staff keep the kids busy building sand castles. The children have their own mealtimes, but everyone is welcome to make visits to Fijian villages, go on picnics to the fabulous Horseshoe Bay, or hike up to Bouma Falls on Taveuni. See "Resorts off Taveuni" in Chapter 12, "Northern Fiji."
- **Bora Bora Lagoon Resort, French Polynesia:** In addition to a fine and attended beach, this super-deluxe hotel has the largest and most attractive swimming pool area in French Polynesia. It also has satellite TVs in every unit, great for parking the kids on rainy days. See Chapter 7, "Bora Bora & Other Islands."
- **Moorea Beachcomber Parkroyal, French Polynesia:** The most modern resort on Moorea, the Beachcomber has an attractive swimming pool, a calm lagoon, and the widest selection of water sports in French Polynesia. See "Where to Stay" in Chapter 6, "Moorea."
- **Castaway Island Resort, Fiji:** One of Fiji's oldest resorts but recently refurbished, Castaway has plenty to keep both adults and children occupied, from

a wide array of water sports to a kid's playroom and a nursery. There's even a nurse on duty. See "Resorts off Nadi" in Chapter 10, "Nadi & Viti Levu."

- **Naitasi Resort, Fiji:** In addition to one of the best beaches in the Mamanuca Islands off Nadi, Naitasi has large—if somewhat dated—two-bedroom villas equipped with kitchens, and there's a small store on the premises selling groceries. It's very popular with New Zealand families. See "Resorts off Nadi" in Chapter 10, "Nadi & Viti Levu."
- **Muri Beachcomber, Cook Islands:** There are several good family choices on Rarotonga in the Cook Islands, including the villas at the nearby Pacific Resort, but the Muri Beachcomber offers one-bedroom apartments facing a swimming pool, so the folks can keep a sharp eye on the kids taking a dip. The lagoon here is peaceful and shallow. There is no restaurant on the premises, but the Pacific Resort, the Rarotonga Sailing Club, and the very fine Flame Tree restaurant are short walks away along lovely Muri Beach. See "Where to Stay" in Chapter 8, "Rarotonga & the Cook Islands."
- **Aggie Grey's Hotel, Western Samoa:** The grand dame of South Pacific hotels, family-owned Aggie's is not on a beach, but the complex surrounds a courtyard whose swimming pool has a coconut palm sitting on its own little island. Although the clientele is primarily adult, the friendly Samoan staff is adept at taking care of children. See "Where to Stay" in Chapter 13, "Western Samoa."

5 The Best Cultural Experiences

The South Pacific Islanders are justly proud of their ancient Polynesian and Fijian cultures, and they eagerly inform anyone who asks about both their ancient and modern ways. Here are some of the best ways to learn about the islanders and their lifestyles.

- **Rarotonga, Cook Islands:** In addition to offering some of the most laid-back beach vacations, the people of Rarotonga go out of their way to let visitors know about their unique Cook Islands way of life. A morning spent at the Cook Islands Cultural Village and on a cultural tour of the island is an excellent educational experience. For a look at flora and fauna of the island, and their traditional uses, Pa's Nature Walks cannot be topped. See "Cultural Experiences" in Chapter 8, "Rarotonga & the Cook Islands."
- **Tongan National Centre, Nuku'alofa, Tonga:** Artisans turn out classic Tongan handcrafts, and a museum exhibits Tongan history, including the robe worn by Queen Salote at the coronation of Queen Elizabeth II in 1953, and the carcass of Tui Malila, a Galápagos turtle that Capt. James Cook reputedly gave to the King of Tonga in 1777, and which lived until 1968. The center also has island-night dance shows and feasts of traditional Tongan food. See "Seeing Tongatapu" in Chapter 15, "Tonga."
- **Village Visits, Fiji:** Many tours from Nadi and from most offshore resorts include visits to traditional Fijian villages, whose residents stage welcoming ceremonies (featuring the slightly narcotic drink kava) and then show visitors around and explain how the old and the new combine in today's villages. See "Sightseeing Tours" in Chapter 10, "Nadi & Viti Levu."
- **Tiki Theatre Village, French Polynesia:** Built to resemble a pre-European Tahitian village, this cultural center on Moorea has demonstrations of handcraft making and puts on a daily dance show and feast. It's a bit commercial, and the staff isn't always fluent in English, but this is the only place in French Polynesia

where one can sample the old ways. See "Seeing Moorea" in Chapter 6, "Moorea."

- **Western Samoa:** The entire country of Western Samoa is a cultural storehouse of *fa'a Samoa,* the old Samoan way of doing things. Most Western Samoans still live in villages featuring oval *fales,* some of which have stood for centuries (although tin roofs have replaced thatch). The island of Savai'i is especially well preserved. See Chapter 13, "Western Samoa."
- **Visiting a Tongan Family:** The Tonga Visitors Bureau will arrange for overseas visitors to visit a local family to see how Tongans live today. They will even find families whose members are engaged in a particular profession or trade. At least a day's notice is required. See "Seeing Tongatapu" in Chapter 15, "Tonga."
- **Touring Savai'i, Western Samoa:** A highlight of any visit to Savai'i should be a tour with Warren Jopling, a retired Australian geologist who has lived on Western Samoa's largest island for many years. Not only does he know the forbidding lava fields like the back of his hand, everyone on Savai'i knows him, which helps make his cultural commentaries extremely informative. See "Savai'i" in Chapter 13, "Western Samoa."

6　The Best of the Old South Seas

Many South Pacific islands are developing rapidly, with modern, fast-paced cities replacing what were sleepy backwater ports at Papeete in French Polynesia and Suva in Fiji. There still are many remnants of the Old South Sea days of coconut planters, beachbums, and missionaries.

- **Levuka, Fiji:** No town has remained the same after a century as has Levuka, Fiji's first European-style town and its original colonial capital in the 1870s. The dramatic cliffs of Ovalau Island hemmed in the town and prevented growth, so the government moved to Suva in 1882. Levuka looks very much as it did then, with a row of clapboard general stores along picturesque Beach Street. See Chapter 11, "Suva & Levuka."
- **Neiafu, Vava'u, Tonga:** Although Nuku'alofa, the capital of Tonga on the main island of Tongatapu, still has a dusty, 19th-century ambience, the little village of Neiafu on the sailor's paradise of Vava'u has remained untouched by development. Built by convicted adulteresses, the Road of the Doves still winds above the dramatic Port of Refuge, just as it did in 1875. See "Vava'u" in Chapter 15, "Tonga."
- **Apia, Western Samoa:** Despite a seawall along what used to be a beach, and two large high-rise buildings built on reclaimed land, a number of clapboard buildings and 19th-century churches make Apia look much as it did when German, American, and British warships washed ashore during a hurricane here in 1889. See "Seeing Apia & Upolu" in Chapter 13, "Western Samoa."
- **Aitutaki, Cook Islands:** Noted for its crystal-clear lagoon, the little island of Aitutaki is very much Old Polynesia, with most of its residents still farming and fishing for a living. There's not a paved road on the island. See "Aitutaki" in Chapter 8, "Rarotonga & the Cook Islands."
- **Huahine, French Polynesia:** Of the French Polynesian islands frequented by visitors, Huahine has been the least affected by tourism. As on Aitutaki, agriculture still is king on Huahine, which makes it the "Island of Fruits." There are ancient marae temples to visit, and the only town, tiny Fare, is little more than a collection of Chinese shops fronting the island's wharf, which comes

to life when ships pull in. See "Huahine" in Chapter 7, "Bora Bora & Other Islands."

- **Savai'i, Western Samoa:** One of the largest of all Polynesian islands, this great volcanic shield also is one of the least populated, with the oval-shaped houses of traditional villages sitting beside freshwater bathing pools fed by underground springs. See "Savai'i" in Chapter 13, "Western Samoa."
- **Taveuni, Fiji:** Like Savai'i, Fiji's third-largest and most lush island has changed little since Europeans started coconut plantations there in the 1860s. With the largest remaining population of indigenous plants and animals of any South Pacific island, Taveuni is a nature lover's delight. See "Taveuni" in Chapter 12, "Northern Fiji."

7 The Best Food

You won't be stuck eating island-style food cooked in an earth oven (see "The Islanders," in Chapter 2), nor will you be limited to the rather bland tastes of New Zealanders and Australians, which predominate at most restaurants. Wherever the French go, fine food and wine are sure to follow, and French Polynesia is no exception. The East Indians brought curries to Fiji, and chefs trained there have spread those spicy offerings to the other islands. Many chefs in Tonga are from Germany and specialize in their own "native" food. Chinese cuisine of varying quality can be found everywhere. And a Kenyan and a Canadian have brought exotic tastes to the Cook Islands.

Wine connoisseurs will have ample opportunity to sample the vintages from nearby Australia, where abundant sunshine produces renowned full-bodied, fruit-driven varieties, such as chardonnay, semillon, Riesling, shiraz, hermitage, cabernet sauvignon, and merlot. New Zealand wines also are widely available, including distinctive whites, such as chenin blanc, sauvignon blanc, and soft plummy merlot. Freight and import duties drive up the cost of wine, so expect slightly higher prices than at home.

That having been said, there are few outstanding restaurants or hotel dining rooms in the South Pacific. If you want to dine on gourmet fare every meal, then pick any expensive French Polynesian or Fijian resort mentioned under "Best Honeymoon Destinations," above. They all have cuisines to match their rates, but unfortunately for us less-well-heeled, we can't walk in and have a meal without staying there.

Otherwise, the best restaurants in the islands are Papeete's **Auberge du Pacifique** (see "Where to Dine" in Chapter 5); Moorea's **Te Honu Iti** and **Le Pêcheur** (see "Where to Dine" in Chapter 6); Bora Bora's **Yacht Club** (see "Where to Dine" in Chapter 7); Rarotonga's **The Flame Tree** (see "Where to Dine" in Chapter 8); Nadi's **Chefs The Restaurant** and **Ports O' Call,** the latter in the Sheraton Fiji Resort (see "Where to Dine in Nadi" in Chapter 10); and Suva's **Swiss Tavern** (see "Where to Dine" in Chapter 11).

8 The Best Island Nights

Don't come to the South Pacific islands expecting opera and ballet. Other than "pub crawling" to bars and nightclubs with music for dancing, evening entertainment here consists primarily of island nights, which invariably feature feasts of island foods followed by traditional dancing.

In the cases of French Polynesia and the Cook Islands, of course, their hip-swinging traditional dances are world famous. They are not as lewd and lascivious as they were in the days before the missionaries arrived, but they still have plenty of suggestive movements to the beat of primordial drums. By contrast, dancing in Fiji, Tonga, and the Samoas is much more reserved, with graceful movements, terrific harmony, and occasional action in a war or fire dance.

- **The Cook Islands:** Although the Tahitians are more famous for their dancing, many of their original movements were quashed by the missionaries in the early 19th century. When the French took over and allowed dancing again, the Tahitians had forgotten much of the old movements. They turned to the Cook Islands, where dancing was—and still is—the thing to do when the sun goes down. The costumes tend to be more natural and less colorful than in the Tahitian floor shows, but the movements tend to be more active, suggestive, and genuine. There's an island night show every evening except Sunday on Rarotonga. The best troupes usually perform at the Edgewater Resort and the Rarotongan Resort, but ask around. The best public performances are during the annual Dancer of the Year contest in April and the Constitution Week celebrations in August. See "Island Nights" in Chapter 8, "Rarotonga & the Cook Islands."

- **French Polynesia:** Hotels are the places in which to see Tahitian dancing here, with the best troupe usually at the Hyatt Regency Tahiti. Elsewhere, the resorts rely on village groups to perform a few times a week. The very best shows are during the annual *Heiva Tahiti* festival in July; the winners then tour the other islands in August for minifestivals at the resorts. See "Island Nights" in Chapter 5, "Tahiti"; Chapter 6, "Moorea"; and Chapter 7, "Bora Bora & Other Islands."

- **Western Samoa:** Among the great shows in the South Pacific are *fiafia* nights in the magnificent main building at Aggie Grey's Hotel in Apia. This tradition was started in the 1940s by the late Aggie Grey, who at the show's culmination personally danced the graceful *siva*. That role is now played by daughter-in-law Marina Grey, and the show has been expanded to include a rousing fire dance around the adjacent swimming pool. See "Island Nights" in Chapter 13.

- **Tonga:** The weekly shows at the Tongan National Centre are unique, for this museum provides expert commentary before each dance, explaining its movements and their meanings. That's a big help, since all songs throughout the South Pacific are in the native languages. See "Island Nights" in Chapter 15.

9 The Best Buys

Take some extra money along, for there are many things to spend it on throughout the islands, especially handcrafts, black pearls, and tropical clothing. For locations of the best shops, see "Best Buys" in the country chapters.

- **Handcrafts:** Locally produced handcrafts are the South Pacific's best buys. The most widespread are hats, mats, and baskets woven of pandanus or other fibers, usually made by the local women, who have maintained this ancient art to a high degree. Tonga has the widest selection of woven items, although Western Samoa and Fiji have made comebacks in recent years. The finely woven mats made in Tonga and the Samoas are still highly valued as ceremonial possessions and are seldom for sale to tourists.

Before the coming of European traders and printed cotton, the South Pacific islanders wore garments made from the beaten bark of the paper mulberry tree. The making of this bark cloth, widely known as *tapa,* is another preserved art in Tonga, Western Samoa, and Fiji (where it is known as *masi*). The cloth is painted with dyes made from natural substances, usually in geometric designs whose ancestries date back thousands of years. Tapa is an excellent souvenir, since it can be folded and brought back in a suitcase.

Woodcarvings are also popular. Spears, war clubs, knives made from sharks' teeth, canoe prows, and cannibal forks are some examples. Many carvings, however, tend to be produced for the tourist trade and often lack the imagery of bygone days, and some may be machine-produced today. Carved tikis are found in most South Pacific countries, but many of them resemble the figures of the New Zealand Maoris rather than figures indigenous to those countries. The carvings from the Marquesas Islands of French Polynesia are the best of the lot today.

Note: Some governments restrict the export of antique carvings and other artifacts of historic value. If the piece looks old, check before you buy.

Jewelry made of shells and of pink or black coral is available in many countries, as is scrimshaw. Black pearls are produced in the atolls of French Polynesia and the Cook Islands.

- **Clothing:** Colorful hand-screened, hand-blocked, and hand-dyed fabrics are very popular in the islands for making dresses or the wraparound skirt known as *pareu* in Tahiti and Rarotonga, *lavalava* in the Samoas and Tonga, and *sulu* in Fiji. Heat-sensitive dyes are applied by hand to gauzelike cotton, which is then laid in the sun for several hours. Flowers, leaves, and other designs are placed on the fabric, and as the heat of the sun darkens and sets the dyes, the shadows from these objects leave their images behind on the finished product.

10 The Best Diving & Snorkeling

All the islands have excellent scuba diving and snorkeling, and all but a few of the resorts either have their own dive operations or can easily make arrangements with a local company. Here are the best:

- **Fiji:** With nutrient-rich waters welling up from the Tonga Trench offshore and being carried by strong currents funneling through narrow passages, Fiji is famous for some of the world's most colorful soft corals. This is especially true of the Somosomo Strait between Vanua Levu and Taveuni in Northern Fiji, home of the Rainbow Reef and the Great White Wall. The Beqa Lagoon and Astrolabe Reef also are famous for plentiful soft corals. See Chapter 12, "Northern Fiji."

- **French Polynesia:** Like those surrounding most populated islands, many lagoons in French Polynesia have been "fished out" over the years. That's not to say that diving in such places as Moorea and Bora Bora can't be world class, but the best now is at Rangiroa and Manihi in the Tuamotu Archipelago, both famous more for their abundant sea life, including sharks, than colorful soft corals. See "Rangiroa" and "Manihi" in Chapter 7, "Bora Bora & Other Islands."

- **Tonga:** The north shore of the main island of Tongatapu fronts a huge lagoon, where the government has made national parks of the Hakaumama'o and

Malinoa reefs. The best diving in Tonga, however, is around unspoiled Vava'u. See "Island Excursions, Water Sports & Other Outdoor Activities" and "Vava'u" in Chapter 15, "Tonga."

11 The Best Golf & Tennis

While many resorts have tennis courts, both tennis and golf are secondary to water sports in the South Pacific. Except for Fiji, the countries in this book just don't have enough land for golf courses. In the Cook Islands, for example, the very flat courses on both Rarotonga and Aitutaki run under the guy wires of the local radio stations, making for some interesting obstacles but not particularly challenging golf. In Tonga, the only course is a flat nine holes where the highlight may be playing behind the crown prince.

The best links in the South Pacific are those designed by Robert Trent Jones at **Pacific Harbor Golf and Country Club,** on Fiji's main island of Viti Levu. Unfortunately, they are in Viti Levu's "rain belt," which caused the early demise of the original Pacific Harbor real estate development. See "Golf, Tennis & Other Outdoor Activities" in Chapter 11, "Suva & Levuka."

Across the road from the Sheraton Fiji and The Regent of Fiji resorts, **Denarau Golf & Racquet Club** has Fiji's most popular course. It's also the region's only tennis facility. See "Cruises, Island Escapes & Outdoor Activities" in Chapter 10, "Nadi & Viti Levu."

French Polynesia has only one course, and it's on the south shore of Tahiti, an hour's drive from Papeete. If you stay on Moorea, Bora Bora, or another island, leave your clubs at home. See "Golf, Water Sports & Other Outdoor Activities" in Chapter 5, "Tahiti."

12 The Best Sailing

One would think that the South Pacific is a yachting paradise, and it certainly gets more than its share of cruising boats on holiday from Australia and New Zealand or heading around the world (the region is on the safest circumnavigation route). The reefs in most places, however, make sailing a precarious undertaking, so yachting is not that widespread. It only recently has gained a toehold in Fiji. Here are the only places where you can charter a yacht:

- **Raiatea, French Polynesia:** The Moorings and a French firm have charter fleets based in Raiatea in the Leeward Islands of French Polynesia. Raiatea shares a lagoon with Tahaa, a hilly island indented with long bays that shelter numerous picturesque anchorages. Boats can be sailed completely around Tahaa without leaving the lagoon, but both Bora Bora and Huahine are just 20 miles away over blue water. See "Raiatea & Tahaa" in Chapter 7, "Bora Bora & Other Islands."

- **Vava'u, Tonga:** The second-most-popular yachting spot, Vava'u is virtually serrated by well-protected bays like the nearby Port of Refuge. Chains of small islands trail off the south side of Vava'u like the tentacles of a jellyfish, creating large and very quiet cruising grounds. Many anchorages are off deserted islands with their own beaches. See "Vava'u" in Chapter 15, "Tonga."

- **Musket Cove, Fiji:** The Moorings recently moved into Musket Cove Resort in Fiji's Mamanuca Islands, inside the Great Sea Reef off Nadi. Although a local guide is required, skippers can tour the Mamanuca resorts and explore the undeveloped Yasawas. See "Cruises, Island Escapes & Outdoor Activities" in Chapter 10, "Nadi & Viti Levu."

13 The Best Hiking

The islands aren't the Rocky Mountains or the Southern Alps of New Zealand, but there are a few walks that stand out.

- **Cross-Island Track, Rarotonga, Cook Islands:** It takes less than half a day to scale Rarotonga's central mountain and go coast to coast via this famous track, the highest point of which skirts the bottom of The Needle, the island's thumblike trademark. See "Scuba Diving, Kayaking & Other Outdoor Activities" in Chapter 8, "Rarotonga & the Cook Islands."
- **Pa's Nature Walk, Rarotonga, Cook Islands:** A blond, dreadlocked Cook Islander named simply Pa has become famous for leading these hikes into Rarotonga's interior, stopping to explain wild plants, such as the candlenut and the shampoo plant, and their uses in the old days. He even visits a cave used by ancient Cook Island warriors. See "Cultural Experiences" in Chapter 8, "Rarotonga & the Cook Islands."
- **Bouma Falls and Lavena Coastal Track, Fiji:** Both on Taveuni's northeastern corner, these two tracks have recently been upgraded under an environmental project funded by the government of New Zealand. The Bouma track goes to three waterfalls. The Lavena Coastal Track starts at Lavena village, on one of Fiji's most picturesque beaches, then follows the coast and up a creek to a waterfall. See "Taveuni" in Chapter 12, "Northern Fiji."
- **The Bélvèdere, Moorea, French Polynesia:** A paved road leads up to this lookout, which commands one of the South Pacific's great views back over Cook's and Opunohu Bays, flanking the dramatic Mount Rotui. A restored Tahitian temple in a nearby chestnut grove makes it doubly worthwhile. See "Seeing Moorea" in Chapter 6, "Moorea."
- **Viti Levu Highlands:** You will need a guide, but several hikes lead from Nadi up into the rolling hills and mountains of Fiji's main island. They all pass Fijian villages, which welcome visitors with kava ceremonies. One organized hike takes several days to cross the island. See "Cruises, Island Escapes & Outdoor Activities" in Chapter 10, "Nadi & Viti Levu."
- **Across Tahiti:** Another walk requiring a guide, this one follows a jeep track up the Papenoo Valley, through the sheer walls of Tahiti's old volcanic crater, via a water supply tunnel, and down past the island's only lake. See "Golf, Water Sports & Other Outdoor Activities" in Chapter 5, "Tahiti."

14 The Best Off-Beat Experiences

Some cynics might say that a visit to the South Pacific itself is an off-beat experience, but there are a few things to do that are even more unusual.

- **Worshipping with the King in Tonga:** It's not every day you get to see a real-life king, but you can in Tonga. In fact, you can even go to church with him on Sunday, or perhaps watch him go by on his bicycle other days of the week. See Chapter 15, "Tonga."
- **Getting Asked to Dance, Everywhere:** Personally, I've seen so many traditional South Pacific dance shows that I now stand by the rear door, ready to beat a

quick escape before those lovely young women in grass skirts can grab my hand and force me to make a fool of myself trying to gyrate my hips up on the stage. It's part of the tourist experience at all resorts, and all in good fun. See "Island Nights" in all the destination chapters.

- **Swimming with the Sharks in Bora Bora:** A key attraction in Bora Bora's magnificent lagoon is to snorkel with a guide, who actually feeds a school of sharks as they thrash around in a frenzy. I prefer to leave this one to the Discovery Channel. See Chapter 7, "Bora Bora & Other Islands."

- **Cave Swimming in Vava'u & Tonga:** Boats can go right into Swallows Cave on one of the small islands that make up beautiful Vava'u, but you have to don masks and snorkels and follow a guide underwater into Mariner's Cave, whose only light comes from the passage you just swam through. See "Vava'u" in Chapter 15, "Tonga." You also have to swim underwater into the Piula Cave Pool in Western Samoa. See "What to See & Do in Apia & Upolu" in Chapter 13, "Western Samoa."

- **Riding the Rip in Rangiroa, French Polynesia:** Snorkelers will never forget the flying sensation as they ride the strong currents ripping through a pass into Rangiroa, the world's second-largest lagoon. See "Rangiroa" in Chapter 7, "Bora Bora & Other Islands."

Introducing the South Pacific

Few places have had such a romantic impact on the Western imagination as have the South Pacific islands. The magical names of Tahiti, Fiji, Tonga, Rarotonga, and Samoa have conjured up hedonistic images of an earthly paradise since European explorers brought home tales of their tropical splendor and uninhibited people more than two centuries ago. The South Pacific was the home of Rousseau's "noble savages," living guilt-free lives beside crystal-clear lagoons; of missionaries struggling to save their heathen souls; of Fletcher Christian, a man so obsessed by a Tahitian *vahine* that he committed the world's most famous mutiny; of besotted beachbums adrift on deserted isles; of traders swapping guns and whiskey for sea cucumbers and coconuts. These images found fertile ground in the imaginations of such literary giants as Herman Melville, Robert Louis Stevenson, W. Somerset Maugham, and James A. Michener. The great characters were brought to life on the silver screen by the likes of Clark Gable and Mel Gibson (both portraying Fletcher).

Despite the inroads of modern materialism and the moral fervor of Christian fundamentalism, the travel posters still come to life in these languid islands. Palm-draped beaches beckon us to get away from it all. Blue lagoons and colorful reefs offer some of the world's best diving and snorkeling. Roaring rivers provide white-water rafting. Steep mountain valleys await hikers to visit islanders who live much as their ancestors did centuries ago. And uninhabited islands beg to be explored under sail.

Above all, the proud and friendly Pacific Islanders stand ready to welcome visitors to their shores and to explain their ancient customs and traditions. If the enormous beauty of their islands doesn't charm you, then the islanders' highly infectious smiles surely will.

1 The Islands Today

In the old days, islanders throughout the South Pacific lived in an environment that required little in the way of clothes, shelter, or effort to gather food, which grew abundantly on trees or could be found in the lagoons surrounding their islands. Even today, a perpetually warm climate, rich volcanic soils on most islands, and the islanders' strong communal family system mean that hunger and homelessness are virtually nonexistent. The islanders' extended

> ### ❓ Did You Know?
>
> - The countries in this book occupy a total area larger than the United States, but they have less dry land than half of Florida.
> - When you reach a point in the South Pacific Ocean some 1,650 miles east of the Marquesas Islands, you are as far away from land as you can get.
> - Except for Antarctica, Polynesia was the last part of the earth to be settled by humans.
> - Because of emigration and European diseases, Polynesia's population of some 1.1 million is about the same as when Captain Cook explored the islands in the 1770s.
> - Twice as many Samoans reside in the United States as live in American Samoa.
> - Rather than have a commoner in the family, King Taufa'ahau Tupou of Tonga annulled the marriage of his niece; later, one of his own sons married a commoner.
> - There are no dogs on Aitutaki in the Cook Islands; legend says the people ate them all, but it isn't true.
> - Toads were brought to American Samoa and Fiji to control insects; now both insects and toads are pests.
> - In pre-European days, Fijians practiced cannibalism and infanticide, strangled widows, and used live humans as rollers to launch new canoes.
> - The total cost of a funeral and related activities in the Cook Islands can exceed 10 years of annual per capita income.

family system is a testament to their strong sense of tradition, for they consciously are blending their old lifestyles with what they view as the best of Western culture and amenities. While television and automobiles are a fact of life in all the main islands, so are many of the ancient customs, which adds a cultural richness to any visit to the area.

The islands covered in this book are variations on an overall cultural theme, for most are part of the great Polynesian Triangle extending across the Pacific from Hawaii to Easter Island to New Zealand. Each has carved its own identity, yet each is fundamentally Polynesian. Only Fiji is significantly different. Living on the border between Polynesia and the Melanesian islands to the west, the indigenous Fijians look more like African-Americans than like their Polynesian neighbors. Their distinctly Fijian culture blends elements from both Polynesia and Melanesia. The Fijians also share their islands with East Indians, who add a starkly contrasting culture to the mix.

Let's make a quick tour to see what each island country or territory contributes to this fascinating smorgasbord of geography, peoples, history, and cultures.

French Polynesia   If there is a "major league" of dramatically beautiful islands, then Tahiti and its French Polynesian companions dominate it. This is especially true of Moorea and Bora Bora, which surely must provide Hollywood with many of its choice "stock shots" of glorious tropical settings. Bora Bora's central peak leaps out of a deep blue lagoon, while Moorea's jagged mountains serrate the horizon like the back of some primordial dinosaur resting on the sea just 12 miles (20km) west of Tahiti. The sunsets over those shark's-teeth ridges are deservedly some of the most photographed in the world.

As the name states, this part of Polynesia is French, and the Gallic *joie de vivre* is a mere overlay on the Tahitians' laid-back lifestyle, one of the most storied—and studied—in all Polynesia. The Tahitians' easygoing attitude about most things captivated Europeans of the 1770s, who saw in them the perfect example of Jean-Jacques Rousseau's noble savage, who lived in harmony with nature without artificial restraints. More than any South Pacific peoples, the French Polynesians—and their cousins in the nearby Cook Islands—have maintained some semblance of this easygoing, relatively unrestrained lifestyle.

Papeete, the storied capital, is a busy little city overrun by cars, trucks, and motor scooters. A building boom has drastically changed its face in the past 25 years, and the town has lost much of its old charm. So I will say from the outset: To find Polynesia, put your sights on Moorea and Tahiti's other companion islands.

The Cook Islands The Cook Islands, about 500 miles west of Tahiti, have much in common with French Polynesia. Barely 20 miles (32km) around, Rarotonga is a miniature Tahiti in terms of its mountains, beaches, and reefs. No other South Pacific destination has so many hotels, restaurants, daytime activities, and night-clubs packed into so small a space as does Rarotonga. Unlike Papeete, however, the Cook Islands' capital of Avarua remains a quiet little backwater, a picturesque village without a stoplight. Among the outer islands, Aitutaki bears the same relationship to Rarotonga as Bora Bora does to Tahiti, with a small central island surrounded by an aquamarine lagoon.

The Cook Islanders share with the Tahitians a fun-loving lifestyle, many of the old Polynesian legends and gods, and about 60% of their native language. Since the Cooks were a New Zealand territory from 1901 until 1965 and still are associated with New Zealand, most Cook Islanders also speak English fluently. Consequently, language is no barrier for English-speaking travelers, who can take advantage of the South Pacific's most informative cultural tours and exhibits.

Fiji Because its international airport at Nadi is the major regional hub, Fiji is a prime place with which to begin or end a trip to the South Pacific. In fact, twice as many people of every income bracket visit Fiji each year as visit any other South Pacific island destination. And with good reason, for there is something for everyone to do in Fiji—from lying on some of the region's best beaches to scuba diving on some of the world's most colorful reefs, from cruising to intriguing outer islands to hiking into the mountainous interior.

Fiji's accommodations are just as varied. The island has one of the finest collections of romantic getaway resorts in the world. While some of them charge more than $600 a couple a night, backpackers' hostels at the other extreme fetch just $5 for a bed. In between wait a variety of fine establishments, affordable for all. Fiji also has many inexpensive restaurants, offering excellent value.

Although known for its rainy climate, Fiji's cosmopolitan capital city, Suva, gives a glimpse of the bygone era when Great Britain ruled these 300-plus islands. Suva's citizenry reflects Fiji's fascinating mix of extraordinarily friendly peoples. About half of the nation's population is made up of easygoing Fijians, most of whom still live in traditional villages surrounded by vegetable gardens. The other half is mostly industrious East Indians whose ancestors came to work Fiji's sugarcane plantations—which make Fiji one of the richest South Pacific countries—and stayed to

The South Pacific

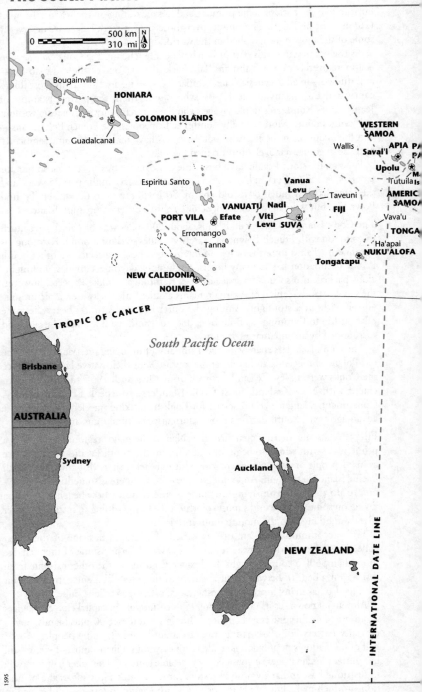

0   500 km
0   310 mi

N

Bougainville

HONIARA

SOLOMON ISLANDS

Guadalcanal

WESTERN SAMOA

Wallis

APIA   P/

Savai'i   P/

Upolu   M

Tutuila Is

AMERIC SAMO/

Espiritu Santo

Vanua Levu

Taveuni

VANUATU   **Nadi**

FIJI

PORT VILA   Efate

Viti Levu

SUVA

Erromango

Vava'u

TONGA

Tanna

Ha'apai

NUKU'ALOFA

NEW CALEDONIA

Tongatapu

NOUMEA

TROPIC OF CANCER

South Pacific Ocean

Brisbane

AUSTRALIA

Sydney

Auckland

NEW ZEALAND

INTERNATIONAL DATE LINE

1595

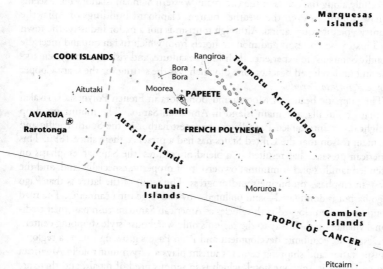

Pukapuka

South Pacific Ocean

Marquesas Islands

COOK ISLANDS

Rangiroa

Bora Bora

Moorea

Aitutaki

PAPEETE

Tahiti

Tuamotu Archipelago

AVARUA

Rarotonga

FRENCH POLYNESIA

Austral Islands

Tubuai Islands

Moruroa

Gambier Islands

TROPIC OF CANCER

Pitcairn

JAPAN

Tokyo

U.S.

Pacific Ocean

Los Angeles

Hawaii

Tahiti–Los Angeles 4,100 miles

Fiji

Tahiti

AUSTRALIA

Sydney

Auckland

Tahiti–Sydney 3,800 miles

NEW ZEALAND

found a class of intellectuals and merchants. Although this stark contrast in cultures has resulted in political strains, including two military coups in 1987 (the government, however, soon returned to civilian control), it also makes Fiji an interesting place in which to get into a conversation.

The Samoas   The heart of Polynesia, independent Western Samoa is like a cultural museum, especially when compared with its much smaller cousin, American Samoa. The peoples of the two Samoas are related by family and tradition, if not politics. While Samoan culture still exists in the American islands, it is preserved to a remarkable degree in Western Samoa, relatively unchanged by modern materialism. Traditional Samoan villages, with their turtle-shaped houses, rest peacefully along the coasts of the two main Western Samoan islands. Time seems to have forgotten even the weather-beaten, clapboard buildings of Apia, the country's picturesque capital. Although tourism is not a major industry, the town has a luxury beach resort and modern hotels from which to fan out and meet the friendly Samoans, to experience their unique culture, and visit their truly remarkable and undeveloped beaches, one of which was the setting for the Gary Cooper movie *Return to Paradise.*

The dramatic beauty of Moorea and Bora Bora in French Polynesia is rivaled by that of Tutuila, the main island in American Samoa. The mountains drop straight down into fabled Pago Pago, the finest harbor in the South Pacific and the main reason that the United States has had a presence there since 1890. This American presence has resulted in a blend of cultures: the Samoan emphasis on extended families and communal ownership of property, especially land, and the Western emphasis on business and progress. The result of the latter is that Pago Pago harbor is dominated—and polluted—by two large tuna canneries. The road around it is often clogged with vehicles as American Samoans rush past their traditional villages on their way to the region's only warehouse-style shopping center.

Despite its economic development and Pago Pago's growing role as a regional transportation and shipping center, tourism plays a very minor role in American Samoa. There is only one hotel, which is in serious need of repair, and there are few quality restaurants.

Tonga   South of Samoa lies Tonga, Polynesia's only surviving kingdom and the only country in the region never controlled by a European power. From his Victorian palace in Nuku'alofa, King Taufa'ahau Tupou IV—all 300-plus pounds of him—rules over a nobility that carries European titles but is in reality a pure Polynesian system of high chiefs. Despite considerable grumbling among his commoner subjects in recent years, he and the nobles control the government and all the land, of which they are obligated to give $8^1/2$ acres to every Tongan adult male.

Tonga is the heart of the South Pacific "Bible Belt." While things are slow on Sunday in most island countries, they stop completely in Tonga—for picnics at the beautiful beaches and escapes to resorts on tiny islets offshore.

Impressions

I wish I could tell you about the South Pacific. The way it actually was. The endless ocean. The infinite specks of coral we call islands. Coconut palms nodding gracefully toward the ocean. Reefs upon which waves broke into spray, the inner lagoons, lovely beyond description.

—James A. Michener, 1947

Impression

All the time our visits to the islands have been more like dreams than realities: the people, the life, the beachcombers, the old stories and songs I have picked up, so interesting; the climate, the scenery, and (in some places) the women, so beautiful.

—Robert Louis Stevenson, 1889

While the relatively flat Tongatapu, the main island, offers little in the way of dramatic scenic beauty, the adjacent lagoon provides excellent boating, snorkeling, fishing, and diving. By contrast, hilly Vavau'u in the north presents long and narrow fjords and a plethora of deserted islands, which make it one of the South Pacific's leading yachting centers. Neiafu, the only town on Vavau'u, is a reminder of the old days of traders and beachbums.

2   A Look at the Past

The islanders had been living on their tiny outposts for thousands of years before Europeans had the foggiest notion that the Pacific Ocean existed. And even after Vasco Nuñez de Balboa crossed the Isthmus of Panama and discovered this largest of oceans in 1513, more than 250 years went by before Europeans paid much attention to the islands that lay upon it.

In the meantime, the Pacific was the domain of a few Spanish and Portuguese explorers. Beginning with Ferdinand Magellan's monumental voyage around Cape Horn and across the Pacific in 1521, their goal was to find a route from Europe (and later from Peru) to the rich Spice Islands, now Indonesia and the Philippines. Magellan stumbled upon few Pacific islands, and none below the equator. Alvaro de Medaña discovered some of the Solomon, Cook, and Marquesas islands in 1568 and 1595, respectively, and in 1606 Pedro Fernández de Quirós happened upon some of the Tuamotu, Cook, and New Hebrides (now Vanuatu) islands. Otherwise, the Spanish missed the South Pacific islands.

The Dutch took a turn in 1642, when Abel Tasman discovered and explored much of Australia, New Zealand, Tonga, and Fiji. The Dutch did nothing to exploit his discoveries, nor did they follow up on those of Jacob Roggeveen, who found Easter Island and Samoa in 1722.

Terra Australis Incognita   A theory came into vogue in Europe during the latter half of the 18th century that an unknown southern land—a *terra australis incognita*—lay somewhere in the southern hemisphere. It had to exist, the theory went, for

Dateline

- 30,000 B.C. Australoid peoples settle in Southwest Pacific.
- 7,000–3,500 B.C. Papuans arrive from Southeast Asia.
- 3,000–1,000 B.C. Austronesians arrive from Asia, push eastward.
- 1,000 B.C. Polynesians migrate eastward to Samoa and Tonga.
- 1513 Balboa discovers the Pacific Ocean.
- 1521 Magellan crosses the Pacific.
- 1568 Medaña discovers the Marquesas and some of Cook and Solomon Islands.
- 1606 De Quirós discovers islands in the Tuamotus, Cooks, and the New Hebrides (Vanuatu).
- 1642 Abel Tasman explores western Pacific, finds Tonga and Fiji.
- 1722 Roggeveen happens upon Easter Island and Samoa.
- 1764 Byron fails to find Terra Australis Incognita.
- 1767 Wallis discovers Tahiti.
- 1768 Bougainville also discovers Tahiti.

continues

- 1769–71 Captain Cook observes transit of Venus from Tahiti, explores South Pacific.
- 1772–74 On second voyage, Cook finds New Caledonia, Norfolk Island, more of the Cook Islands, and Fiji.
- 1778–79 Cook explores northwest America, dies in Hawaii.
- 1789 Fletcher Christian leads mutiny on the *Bounty.*
- 1797 First missionaries arrive in Tahiti.
- 1800–1810 Whalers, merchants, and sandalwood traders flock to islands, bring guns and whiskey.
- 1808 Last *Bounty* mutineer discovered on Pitcairn.
- 1820–50 *Bêche-de-mer* trade flourishes; Western-style towns founded in Tahiti, Samoa, Tonga, Fiji.
- 1842 France annexes Tahiti; Herman Melville arrives in Papeete the same day.
- 1848 Tonga captures eastern Fiji.
- 1858 Fiji asks to become a British colony.
- 1865 First Chinese brought to Tahiti to harvest cotton.
- 1874 Britain accepts Fiji as a colony.
- 1879 First Indians brought to Fiji.
- 1884 International Dateline established.
- 1888 Britain, foiling France, declares protectorate over the Cook Islands.
- 1889 Unrest in Western Samoa; hurricane destroys U.S., British, and German

continues

otherwise the unbalanced earth would wobble off into space. King George III of Great Britain took great interest in the idea and in 1764 sent Capt. John Byron (the poet's grandfather) on a mission to the Pacific in H.M.S. *Dolphin.* The mission, however, was unsuccessful, but King George, not discouraged, immediately dispatched Capt. Samuel Wallis in the *Dolphin.* Wallis had no better luck finding the unknown continent, but it was on this trip, in 1767, that he stumbled upon Tahiti; he was given a rousing welcome by the islanders.

Venus Discovered   Less than a year later, the French explorer Louis Antoine de Bougainville was given a similar welcome by Tahitians when he visited their island. Bougainville claimed Tahiti for France and named it New Cythère—after the Greek island of Cythera, associated with the goddess Aphrodite (Venus)—so enchanted was he by the Venus-like quality of Tahiti's women. And when he returned home, he brought with him a young Tahitian as living proof of Rousseau's theory that man at his best lived an uninhibited life as a noble savage.

Bougainville discovered several islands in Samoa and explored the Solomon Islands, of which the island of Bougainville—now part of Papua New Guinea—still bears his name. So does the bright tropical shrub known as bougainvillea. He was the first Frenchman to circumnavigate the globe and was treated to a rousing reception when he returned home in 1769.

Capt. James Cook   A year earlier, shortly after Wallis had sailed back to England, the Lords of the Admiralty put a young lieutenant named James Cook in command of a converted collier and sent him to Tahiti. Like Rousseau and Bougainville, Cook was a product of the Age of Enlightenment. A master navigator, he was also a mathematician, astronomer, and practical physician who became the first captain of any ship to prevent scurvy among his crewmen by feeding them fresh fruits and vegetables. His ostensible mission was to observe the transit of the real Venus—the planet, that is—across the sun, an astronomical event that would not occur again until 1874, but which, if measured from widely separated points on the globe, would enable scientists for the first time to determine longitude on the earth's surface. Cook's second, highly secret mission was to find the still-unknown southern continent.

Cook's measurements proved to be somewhat less than useful, but his observations of Tahiti, made during a stay of six months, were of immense importance in understanding the "noble savages" who lived there.

Cook then sailed southeast to carry out the secret part of his mission. He discovered the Society Islands northwest of Tahiti and the Australs to the south, and then fully explored the coasts of New Zealand and eastern Australia, neither of which had been visited by Europeans since Tasman's voyage in 1642. After nearly sinking his ship on the Great Barrier Reef, he left the South Pacific through the strait between Australia and Papua New Guinea, which he named for his converted collier, the *Endeavor*. He returned to London in 1771.

Cooks' Other Voyages   Nine months later, Cook was dispatched again to find the unknown southern continent, this time with two ships, the *Resolution* and the *Adventure*. During this three-year voyage, he visited Tonga and discovered several other islands, among them what now are Fiji, the Cook Islands, Niue, New Caledonia, and Norfolk Island. His ships were the first to sail below the Antarctic Circle; although he failed to sight Antarctica, he put to rest the theory that a large land mass lay in the tropical South Pacific.

In 1778–79, Cook sailed on a third voyage, to find a northwest passage between the Atlantic and the Pacific. After visiting Tahiti and discovering the Hawaiian Islands, he explored the northwest coast of North America until Bering Strait ice turned him back. He returned to the Big Island of Hawaii, where, on February 14, 1779, he was killed during a petty skirmish with the islanders.

With the exception of the Hawaiians who smashed his skull, Captain Cook was revered throughout the Pacific. Although he claimed many of the islands for Britain, he hoped they never would be colonized. He treated the islanders fairly and respected their traditions. The Polynesian chiefs looked upon him as one of their own. Today, you'll find a Cook's Bay, a Cooktown, a Cook Strait, any number of Captain Cook's landing places, and an entire island nation named for this giant of an explorer.

warships at Apia. Robert Louis Stevenson settles in Apia.

- 1890 Germany takes Western Samoa, U.S. gets Eastern Samoa, Britain claims protectorate over Tonga.
- 1891 Paul Gauguin arrives in Tahiti.
- 1894 Robert Louis Stevenson dies in Samoa.
- 1901 Paul Gauguin dies in French Polynesia.
- 1915 During World War I, German Admiral von Spee shells Papeete.
- 1917 Count von Luckner captured in Fiji after his German raider runs aground in the Cook Islands.
- 1933 Charles Nordhoff and James Norman Hall publish *Munity on the Bounty*, a bestseller.
- 1935 *Mutiny on the Bounty*, starring Clark Gable and Charles Laughton, is a smash box-office hit.
- 1941 Japanese bomb Pearl Harbor in Hawaii, begin advance into the South Pacific.
- 1942–44 Allied forces strike Guadalcanal in Solomon Islands, use other islands as bases for attacks on Japanese.
- 1947 James A. Michener's *Tales of the South Pacific* is published; gives rise to musical and movie *South Pacific*.
- 1959–60 International airports open at Tahiti and Fiji.
- 1960 MGM remakes *Mutiny on the Bounty*, starring Marlon Brando.

continues

- 1962 Western Samoa becomes independent.
- 1965 Cook Islands gain local autonomy in association with New Zealand.
- 1966 France explodes first nuclear bomb in Tuamotus.
- 1970 Fiji gains independence from Britain.
- 1978 Solomon Islands become independent.
- 1980 New Hebrides become independent Vanuatu.
- 1985 Treaty of Rarotonga declares South Pacific to be a nuclear-free zone.
- 1987 Fiji's military overthrows elected government.
- 1990 U.S. President George Bush and island leaders meet at summit conference.
- 1992 France halts nuclear testing in Tuamotus; Fiji elects civilian government.
- 1994 South Pacific countries send joint peacekeeping force to Bougainville in Papua New Guinea.
- 1995 French resume limited nuclear testing.

Mutiny on the *Bounty*   Based on reports by Cook and others, a group of West Indian planters asked King George III to transport breadfruit trees from Tahiti to Jamaica as a cheap source of food for their slaves. Captain William Bligh, who had been one of Cook's navigators, was put in command of H.M.S. *Bounty* in 1787 and sent to do just that. One of his officers was a former shipmate named Fletcher Christian.

Their story is one of history's great sea yarns. Christian and the crew frolicked on Tahiti for six months. On the way home, they overpowered Bligh off Tonga, on April 28, 1789. Accompanied by their Tahitian wives and six Tahitian men, Christian and eight other mutineers disappeared with the ship, after having set the captain and his loyalists adrift. The latter miraculously rowed the *Bounty's* longboat some 3,000 miles to the Dutch East Indies, where they hitched a ride back to England. The Royal Navy then rounded up the *Bounty* crewmen left on Tahiti, of whom three were later hanged.

Christian's whereabouts remained a mystery until 1808, when an American whaling ship discovered the last surviving mutineer on remote Pitcairn Island. The mutineers, after landing there in 1789, had burned and sunk the *Bounty* (the ship's rudder has been recovered and now is on display at the Fiji Museum in Suva). Their descendants still live on Pitcairn and elsewhere in the South Pacific.

Whalers, Traders, and Beachbums   The American ship that found the mutineers' retreat at Pitcairn was one of many whalers roaming the South Pacific in the early 1800s. Their ruffian crews made dens of iniquity of many ports, such as Lahaina and Honolulu in Hawaii, Papeete and Nuku Hiva in Polynesia, and Levuka in Fiji. Many crewmen jumped ship and lived on the islands, some of them even casting their lots—and their guns—with rival chiefs during tribal wars. With their assistance, some chiefs were able to extend their domain over entire islands or groups of islands.

One such deserter who jumped ship in the Marquesas Islands and later went to Tahiti, in the early 1820s, was Herman Melville. He returned to New England and

Impressions

From the moment the boat slid into the glassy water near shore it had seemed that all my plugs had been pulled.

—John Dyson, 1982

wrote two books, *Typee* and *Omoo,* based on his South Pacific exploits. They were the start of his literary career.

Along with the whalers came traders. Some of them sailed from island to island in search of sandalwood, pearls, shells, and the sea slugs known as *bêches-de-mer,* which they traded for beads, cloth, whiskey, and guns and then sold at high prices in China. Others established stores that became the catalysts for Western-style trading towns. The merchants brought more guns and alcohol to people who had never used them before. They also put pressure on local leaders to coin money, which introduced a cash economy where none had existed before. Guns, alcohol, and money had far-reaching effects on the easygoing, communal traditions of the Pacific Islanders.

Diseases brought by the Europeans and Americans were even more devastating. The Polynesians had little, if any, resistance to such ailments as measles, influenza, tuberculosis, pneumonia, typhoid fever, and venereal disease. Epidemics swept the islands and killed the majority of their inhabitants.

While the traders were building towns, other arrivals were turning the bush country into plantations: cotton in Tahiti, sugar in Fiji, coconuts everywhere. With the native islanders either disinclined to work or unable to do so, Chinese indentured laborers were brought to a cotton plantation in Tahiti in the 1860s. After it failed, some of them stayed and became farmers and merchants. Their descendants now form the merchant class of French Polynesia. The same thing happened in Fiji, where East Indians were brought to work the sugar plantations. Again, many stayed behind, and today almost half of Fiji's citizens and the overwhelming majority of its merchants and business leaders are of Indian descent.

The Missionaries   The reports of the islands by Cook and Bougainville may have brought word of noble savages living in paradise to some people in Europe; to others, they heralded heathens to be rescued from hell. So while alcohol and diseases were destroying the islanders' bodies, a stream of missionaries arrived on the scene to save their souls.

The "opening" of the South Pacific coincided with a fundamentalist religious revival in England, and it wasn't long before the London Missionary Society (LMS) was on the scene in Tahiti. Its first missionaries, who arrived in the LMS ship *Duff* in 1797, were the first Protestant missionaries to leave England for a foreign country. They chose Tahiti because there "the difficulties were least."

Polynesians, already believing in a supreme being at the head of a hierarchy of lesser gods, quickly converted to Christianity in large numbers. As an act of faith, the puritanical missionaries demanded the destruction of all *tikis,* which they regarded as idols (as a result, today most Polynesian tikis carved for the tourist souvenir trade resemble those of New Zealand, where the more liberal Anglican missionaries were less demanding). The missionaries in Polynesia also insisted that the heathen temples (known as *maraes*) be torn down. Many now have been restored, however, and can be visited in the islands.

"Island Time"

There's an old story about a 19th-century planter who promised a South Pacific islander a weekly wage and a pension if he would come to work on his copra plantation. Copra is dried coconut meat, from which oil is pressed for use in soaps, cosmetics, and other products. Hours of back-breaking labor are required to chop open the coconuts and extract the meat by hand.

When the planter approached the islander, the latter was sitting in the shade of his breadfruit tree, eating the fruit he had gathered while hauling in one fish after another from the lagoon.

"Do I understand correctly?" asked the islander. "You want me to break my back working for you for 30 years, at the end of which time you'll pay me a pension so that I can spend the rest of my life doing what I am doing now—sit under my breadfruit tree and eat my fruit while fishing in the lagoon?"

The islander's response reflects an attitude that still prevails in the South Pacific. For here life has a different rhythm from what it has elsewhere; everything, you'll notice, moves on "island time"—that is, at an unhurried pace. For example, the service rendered in most hotels and restaurants is not slothful inattention; it's just the way things are done. Your drink will come in due course. Why rush? If you must have it immediately, order it at the bar. Otherwise, relax with your friendly hosts and enjoy their charming company.

Roman Catholic missionaries made less puritanical progress in Tahiti after the French took over in the early 1840s, but for the most part the South Pacific was the domain of rock-ribbed Protestants. The LMS extended its influence west through the Cook Islands and the Samoas, and the Wesleyans had luck in Tonga and Fiji. Today, thanks to those early missionaries, Sunday is a very quiet day throughout the islands.

Colonialism   Although Captain Cook laid claim to many islands, Britain was reluctant to burden itself with such far-flung colonies, beyond those it already had—Australia and New Zealand. Accordingly, colonialism was not a significant factor in the history of the South Pacific islands until the late 19th century. The one exception was France's declaring a protectorate over Tahiti in 1842.

The situation changed half a century later, when imperial Germany colonized the western islands of Samoa in the 1890s (at the same time that novelist Robert Louis Stevenson arrived to live there). Britain took over Fiji and agreed to protect the Kingdom of Tonga from takeover by another foreign power; France moved into New Caledonia; and the United States stepped into the eastern Samoan islands, which became known as American Samoa. Britain also claimed the Cook Islands, but they were later annexed by newly independent New Zealand. Thus, within a period of 30 years, every South Pacific island group except Tonga became a colony.

Impressions

It would have been far better for these people never to have known us.
—Captain James Cook, 1769

Impressions

Missionaries, traders, and broken white folk living on the bounty of the natives, are to be found in almost every isle and hamlet.

—Robert Louis Stevenson, 1889

After World War I, New Zealand took over in Western Samoa when Germany was stripped of its colonies. Otherwise, the colonial structure in the South Pacific remained the same, politically, until the 1960s.

Economically, the islands came under the sphere of Australia and, to a somewhat lesser extent, New Zealand. Large Australian companies, such as Burns Philp and Carpenters, built up trading and shipping empires based on the exchange of retail goods for copra and other local produce, and Australian and New Zealand banks came to dominate finance in most islands outside the French and American territories.

World War I Thousands of Pacific Islanders went off to fight with their colonial rulers during World War I. The islands themselves, however, escaped action, with two exceptions.

First, a small German naval force under Admiral Graf von Spee sped across the Pacific during 1915, sinking Allied merchant ships and shelling the town of Papeete.

Two years later, the colorful Count von Luckner brought his German raider *Seeadler* into the Pacific to hunt for merchant prey. After three months' prowling, which netted only three small sailing vessels, the *Seeadler* was swept onto the reef at Mopelia atoll in the remote northern Cook Islands. Von Luckner and five crewmen set out in the ship's launch for Rarotonga to commandeer another ship. He could have captured the town of Avarua but steered away when he saw a "ship" in port—in reality, a wreck sitting upright on the reef. He then headed for Fiji, where, deceived as to the actual British force on the island, he surrendered to one armed policeman and five unarmed constables sent to investigate.

World War II The South Pacific leaped onto the front pages in World War II. Within weeks after the bombing of Pearl Harbor, in December 1941, the Japanese drove south to New Guinea and the Solomon Islands, where, in July 1942, they began constructing an airfield on Guadalcanal. The U.S. Marines invaded Guadalcanal and nearby Tulagi on August 8, and during the next six months one bloody jungle skirmish and sea battle after another took place. By February 1943, with Guadalcanal entirely in U.S. hands, the Japanese advance in the southwestern Pacific had been stopped. The stage was soon set for the Allied counteroffensive that would island-hop its way toward Japan.

Although the South Pacific fighting took place only in Papua New Guinea and the Solomon Islands, many other islands played significant supporting roles. Airstrips and training bases were built all over the South Pacific (many of the airfields are still in use today). Out-of-the-way islands, such as Bora Bora and Aitutaki, became refueling stops on transpacific flights, and the Samoas and Fiji were invaded by thousands of U.S. Marines and GIs preparing for the fighting farther west and north. Entire communities with modern infrastructures were built in weeks—only to be abandoned almost overnight when the war ended.

The war's effect on the islanders was profound. The profusion of new things that arrived on their islands, and the wages paid them for working on the Allied bases,

Impressions

Travel writers—and travel agents—may continue to popularize the Pacific as a place of great sensuality, but my impression of those islands is of churches and cholesterol, of Christianity and canned corned beef, of tubby evangelists Bible-thumping to an almost deafening degree.

—Paul Theroux, 1991

brought a wave of Western influence. The experience was so overwhelming on some Melanesian islands that local "cargo cults" began worshipping Americans or the airplanes with which they brought "mana from heaven."

The soldiers, sailors, and marines also left behind another legacy: thousands of mixed-race children.

Modern Governments   Colonialism began to crumble in the South Pacific when New Zealand granted independence to Western Samoa in 1962 and, three years later, gave complete local autonomy to the Cook Islands. Fiji became independent of Great Britain in 1970. Elsewhere, Britain left the Solomon Islands in 1978, and in 1980 Britain and France gave up their condominium government in the New Hebrides, which became the independent Republic of Vanuatu.

All these young nations have governments based on the Westminster parliamentary system, with wrinkles tailored to fit the traditions of their citizenries. Almost everywhere there is a council of chiefs to advise the modern-style governments on custom and tradition. In a modern vestige of the old chiefly system, the national governments tend to have strong individuals at the helm. Elections in these small countries, where everyone seems to know everyone else, often are hard fought and sometimes bitter. Usually, the victors take office, while the vanquished keep on grouching until the polls open again. Fiji's bloodless military coup of 1987, which overthrew that country's first Indian-dominated government, was a shock to observers, since it was directly opposed to this democratic tradition. Fiji has since adopted a constitution providing for an elected parliament, albeit one with a permanent Fijian majority.

Of the old colonial powers, only the United States and France remain. But American Samoans are not clamoring for independence—and see no reason why they should be. As American nationals, they are eligible for U.S. passports and most U.S. federal aid programs; moreover, except for Washington's control of their budget, they already have almost complete say over their domestic affairs.

Nuclear-Free Movement   After independence, the countries of the South Pacific had to deal with a major regional problem that threatened their relations with the West: the problem of nuclear testing as posed by France. Between 1966 and 1992, France exploded 210 nuclear weapons in the Tuamotu Archipelago, first in the air and then underground. The tests were vociferously opposed, especially by New Zealand, where French secret agents sank the Greenpeace protest ship *Rainbow Warrior* in 1985. That year, the regional heads of government, including the prime ministers of New Zealand and Australia, adopted the Treaty of Rarotonga, calling for the South Pacific to become a nuclear-free zone. The call, however, found no appeal in Paris. In 1995, French President Jacques Chirac decided, after a lull, to resume underground testing, a move which set off worldwide protests and a day of rioting in Tahiti (but not in the rest of French Polynesia).

Land Rights   Underlying many political issues in the South Pacific is the fundamental question of land rights. There isn't much land in the islands, and the indigenous peoples want to maintain their customary ownership of it. Thus, when Vanuatu became independent in 1980 it abolished freehold property and returned all land to its customary owners. Similarly, when it appeared in Fiji that the Indian-dominated government would rewrite the laws protecting Fijian land rights, the military staged a coup.

Violence, however, is not the usual way in which islanders try to solve their problems, whether political or personal. They prefer what they call the "Pacific way": discussion, compromise, and consensus, often achieved during all-night kava-drinking sessions. And their way seems to be working, as I concluded on my recent travels through the region. For the islands continue to be a peaceful and thoroughly enchanting part of the world to visit.

The Environment   Just as the islanders are protective of their land, so they're concerned about the surrounding ocean. For example, the Pacific island states have opposed drift-net fishing; it not only kills dolphins and other sealife unnecessarily, they argue, but also strips them of a vital natural resource. The islanders also are involved in efforts to reduce pollution of the oceans. Many of them see a looming threat in the greenhouse effect: an increase in world temperatures could raise the world's sea level by melting part of the polar ice caps, thus endangering many of the low-lying islands.

Another concern has been the announced plan by the United States to destroy its stockpile of chemical weapons at Johnston Atoll, south of Hawaii. To allay the islanders' worries, U.S. President George Bush met in Honolulu, in 1990, with the leaders of most of the Pacific island states. The summit was the first of its kind, demonstrating growing U.S. awareness of the region and its needs; to foster closer ties between the United States and the island states, the conference set up a joint trade commission.

3 The Islanders

The early European explorers were astounded to find the far-flung South Pacific islands inhabited by peoples who shared similar physical characteristics, languages, and cultures. How had these people—who lived a late–Stone Age existence and had no written languages—crossed the vast Pacific to these remote islands long before Europeans had the courage to sail out of sight of land on the Atlantic? Where had they come from? Those questions baffled the early European explorers, and they continue to intrigue scientists and scholars to this day.

THE FIRST SETTLERS

Thor Heyerdahl drifted in his raft *Kon Tiki* from South America to French Polynesia in 1947 to prove his theory that the Polynesians came from the Americas,

Impressions

Sentimentalists who moan against natives improving their diet with refrigerators and can openers—"Why, they live on Chinese bread, Australian beef and American pork and beans"—could complain with equal logic that dear old ladies in Boston no longer dip tallow candles because they prefer electricity.

—James A. Michener, 1951

but most experts now believe that the Pacific islanders have their roots in Southeast Asia. The generally accepted view is that during the Ice Age a race of early humans known as Australoids migrated from Southeast Asia to Papua New Guinea and Australia, when those two countries were joined as one land mass. Another group, the Papuans, arrived from Southeast Asia between 5,000 and 10,000 years ago. Several thousands of years later, a lighter-skinned race known as Austronesians pushed the Papuans inland and out into the more eastern South Pacific islands.

Lapita Pottery   The most tangible remains of the early Austronesians are remnants of pottery, the first shards of which were found during the 1970s in Lapita, a village in New Caledonia. Probably originating in Papua New Guinea, Lapita pottery spread as far east as Tonga. Throughout the area it was decorated with geometric designs similar to those used today on Tongan tapa cloth.

Lapita was the only type of pottery in the South Pacific for a millennium. Apparently, however, the Lapita culture died out some 2,500 years ago. By the time European explorers arrived in the 1770s, gourds and coconut shells were the only crockery used by the Polynesians, who cooked their meals underground and ate with their fingers off banana leaves. Of the islanders covered in this book, only the Fijians still make pottery using Lapita methods.

MELANESIANS

The islands settled by the Papuans and Austronesians are known collectively as Melanesia, which includes Papua New Guinea, Solomon Islands, Vanuatu, and New Caledonia. Fiji is the melting pot of the Melanesians to the west and the Polynesians to the east.

The name Melanesia is derived from the Greek words *melas,* "black," and *nesos,* "island." The Melanesians in general have negroid features—brown-to-black skin, flat or hooked noses, full lips, and wiry hair—but the interbreeding among the successive waves of migrants resulted in many subgroups with varying racial characteristics. That's why the Fijians look more African-American than Polynesian. Their culture, on the other hand, has many Polynesian elements, brought by interbreeding and conquest.

POLYNESIANS

The Polynesians' ancestors did not stop in Fiji on their migration from Southeast Asia but pushed on into the eastern South Pacific. Archaeologists now believe that they settled in Tonga and Samoa more than 3,000 years ago and then slowly fanned out to colonize the vast Polynesian triangle.

These extraordinary mariners crossed thousands of miles of ocean in large, double-hulled canoes capable of carrying hundreds of people, animals, and plants. They navigated by the stars, the wind, the clouds, the shape of the waves, and the flight pattern of birds—a remarkable achievement for a people who on land used no metal tools and gave up the use of pottery of any kind thousands of years before.

Most Polynesians have copper skin and black hair that is straight or wavy rather than fuzzy. A well-built, athletic people, many have become professional football and rugby players in the United States, Australia, and New Zealand. Their ancestors fought each other with war clubs for thousands of years, and it stands to reason that the biggest, strongest, and quickest survived. The notion that all Polynesians are fat is incorrect. In the old days, body size did indeed denote wealth and status, but obesity today is more likely attributable to poor diet. On the other hand, village chiefs still are expected to partake of food and drink with anyone who visits to discuss a problem; hence, great weight remains an unofficial marker of social status.

Polynesian Society The Polynesians frequently experienced wars among their various tribes. Generally, however, the wars were not as bloody as those in Fiji. Nor were they followed as often by a cannibalistic orgy at the expense of the losers.

Polynesians developed highly structured societies, and to this day they place great emphasis on hereditary bloodline when choosing leaders. Most members of the modern Western Samoan parliament, for example, must hold the inherited title of *matai*. Strong and sometimes despotic chiefdoms developed on many islands. The present king of Tonga carries on a line of central leaders who were so powerful in the 1700s that they conquered much of Fiji, where they installed many Polynesian customs, including their tradition of hereditary chiefs. Just to make sure, the victorious Tongans forced the conquered Fijian chiefs to take Tongan wives. As a result, today Tongan blood flows in the veins of many Fijian chiefs, some whom have the Polynesian title *tui*.

In some places, such as Tahiti, the Polynesians developed a rigid class system of chiefs, priests, nobility, commoners, and slaves. Their societies emphasized elaborate formalities, and even today ceremonies featuring kava—a slightly narcotic drink—play important roles in Samoa, Tonga, and Fiji. Everyday life was governed by a system based on *tabu*, a rigid list of things a person could or could not do, depending on his or her status in life. *Tabu* and its variants *(tapu, tambu)* are used throughout the South Pacific to mean "do not enter"; from them derives the English word *taboo*.

Western principles of ownership have made their inroads, but by and large everything in both Polynesia and Fiji—especially land—is owned communally by the family. In effect, the system is pure communism at the family level. If your brother has a crop of taro and you're hungry, then some of that taro belongs to you. The same principle applies to a can of corned beef sitting on a shelf in a store, which helps explain why islander-owned grocery shops often teeter on the edge of bankruptcy.

While many islanders would be considered poor by Western standards, no one in the villages goes hungry or sleeps without a roof over his or her head. Most of

Impressions

Now the cunning lay in this, that the Polynesians have rules of hospitality that have all the force of laws; an etiquette of absolute rigidity made it necessary for the people of the village not only to give lodging to the strangers, but to provide them with food and drink for as long as they wished to stay.

—W. Somerset Maugham, 1921

Sex and the Single Polynesian

The puritanical Christian missionaries who arrived in the early 19th century convinced the islanders that they should clothe their nearly naked bodies. They had less luck, however, when it came to sex. To the islanders, sex was as much a part of life as any other daily activity, and they uninhibitedly engaged in it with a variety of partners from adolescence until marriage.

Even today, there exists a somewhat laissez-faire attitude about premarital sex. Every child, whether born in or out of wedlock, is accepted into one of the extended families that are the bedrock of Polynesian society. Mothers, fathers, grandparents, aunts, uncles, and cousins of every degree are all part of the close-knit Polynesian family. Relationships sometimes are so blurred that every adult woman within a mile is known as a child's "auntie"—even the child's mother.

Male transvestism, homosexuality, and bisexuality are facts of life in Polynesia, where young boys are often reared as girls by families with a shortage of female offspring. Some of these youths grow up to be heterosexual; others become homosexual or bisexual and, often appearing publicly in women's attire, actively seek out the company of tourists. In Tahitian, these males are known as *mahus;* in Samoan, *magus;* and in Tongan, *fakaleitis.*

the thatch roofs in Polynesia today are actually bungalows at the resort hotels; nearly everyone else sleeps under tin.

It's little wonder, therefore, that visitors are greeted throughout the islands by friendly, peaceable, and extraordinarily courteous people.

Polynesian Religions   Before the coming of Christian missionaries in the 1800s, the Fijians believed in many spirits in the animist traditions of Melanesia. The Polynesians, however, subscribed to a supreme spirit, who ruled over a plethora of lesser deities who, in turn, governed the sun, fire, volcanoes, the sea, war, and fertility. *Tikis* were carved of stone or wood to give each god a home (but not a permanent residence) during religious ceremonies, and great stone *maraes* were built as temples and meeting places for the chiefs. Sacrifices—sometimes human—would be offered to the gods, and cannibalism was not unknown in Polynesia, although it was not as widely practiced there as it was in Fiji and Melanesia.

LANGUAGES

Traced by linguists to present-day Taiwan, the Austronesian family of languages are spoken across a wide area, extending from Madagascar, off the coast of Africa, through Indonesia, Malaysia, the Philippines, and parts of Vietnam, to the South Pacific as far as Easter Island, off the coast of South America. No other group of ancient languages spread to so much of the earth's surface.

Today, the Polynesian islanders still speak similar languages from one major island group to another. For example, the word for "house" is *fale* in Tongan and

Impressions

A low ribbon of reef and sand encircling a lagoon, an atoll is the very soul of Pacific romance.

—John Dyson, 1982

Samoan, *fare* in Tahitian, *'are* in Cook Islands Maori, *hale* in Hawaiian, and *vale* in Fijian. Without ever having heard the other's language, Cook Islanders say they can understand about 60% of Tahitian, and Tongans and Samoans can get the gist of each others' conversations.

Thanks to the American, British, New Zealand, and Australian colonial regimes, English is an official language in the Cook Islands, both Samoas, and Fiji. It is spoken widely in Tonga. French is spoken alongside Tahitian in French Polynesia, although English is understood among most hotel and many restaurant staffs.

ISLAND FEASTS

Before the Europeans arrived, the typical South Pacific diet consisted of bananas, coconuts, and other fruits. Staples were starchy breadfruit and root crops, such as taro, arrowroot, yams, and sweet potatoes. The reefs and lagoons provided abundant fish, lobsters, and clams to augment the meats provided by domesticated pigs, dogs, and chickens. Taro leaves and coconut cream served as complements. Corned beef has replaced dog on today's menu; otherwise, these same ingredients still make up what is commonly called an "island feast."

Like their ancestors, today's islanders still prepare their major meals in an earth oven, known as *himaa* in Tahiti, *lovo* in Fiji, and *imu* or *umu* elsewhere. Individual food items are wrapped in leaves, placed in the pit on a bed of heated stones, covered with more leaves and earth, and left to steam for several hours. The results are quite tasty, with the steam spreading the aroma of one ingredient to the others.

When the meal has finished cooking, the islanders uncover the oven, unwrap the food, and, using their fingers, set about eating their feast of *umukai* (island food) in a leisurely and convivial manner. Then they dance the night away.

The umu still is widely used on special occasions and for big family meals after church on Sunday. If you're lucky enough to be invited, don't miss a family feast. Otherwise, many restaurants, especially those at the resort hotels, prepare traditional "island night" feasts for their guests. Don't worry: You can use knives and forks instead of your fingers.

4 The Islands & the Sea

A somewhat less than pious wag once remarked that God made the South Pacific islands on the sixth day of creation so He would have an extraordinarily beautiful place to relax on the seventh day. Modern geologists have a different view, but the fact remains that the islands and the surrounding sea are possessed of heavenly beauty and a plethora of life forms.

HIGH, LOW & IN BETWEEN

The Polynesian islands were formed by molten lava escaping upward through cracks in the earth's crust as it has crept slowly northwestward over the eons, thus building great seamounts. Many of these—called "high islands"—have mountains soaring into the clouds. In contrast, pancake-flat atolls were formed when the islands sank back into the sea, leaving only a thin necklace of coral islets to circumscribe their lagoons and mark their original boundaries. In some cases, geologic forces have once again lifted the atolls, forming "raised" islands whose sides drop precipitously into the sea. Still other, partially sunken islands are left with the remnants of mountains sticking up in their lagoons.

Impressions

The South Pacific is memorable because when you are in the islands you simply cannot ignore nature. You cannot avoid looking up at the stars, large as apples on a new tree. You cannot deafen your ear to the thunder of the surf. The bright sands, the screaming birds, and the wild winds are always with you.

—James A. Michener, 1951

The islands of Tonga and Fiji, on the other hand, were created by volcanic eruptions along the collision of the Indo-Australian and Pacific tectonic plates. Although the main islands are quiet today, they are part of the volcanically active and earthquake-prone "Ring of Fire" around the Pacific Ocean.

FLORA & FAUNA

Most species of plants and animals native to the South Pacific originated in Southeast Asia and worked their way eastward across the Pacific, by natural distribution or in the company of humans. The number of native species diminishes the farther east one goes. Very few local plants or animals came from the Americas, the one notable exception being the sweet potato, which may have been brought back from South America by voyaging Polynesians.

Plants In addition to the west-to-east difference, flora changes according to each island's topography. The mountainous islands make rain from the moist tradewinds and thus possess a greater variety of plants. Their interior highlands are covered with ferns, native bush, or grass. The low atolls, on the other hand, get sparse rainfall and support little other than scrub bush and coconut palms.

Ancient settlers brought coconut palms, breadfruit, taro, paper mulberry, pepper (kava), and bananas to the isolated midocean islands because of their usefulness as food or fiber. Accordingly, they are generally found in the inhabited areas of the islands and not so often in the interior bush.

With a few indigenous exceptions, such as the *tiare Tahiti* gardenia and Fiji's *tagimaucia,* tropical flowers also worked their way east in the company of humans. Bougainvillea, hibiscus, allamanda, poinsettia, poinciana (the flame tree), croton, frangipani (plumeria), ixora, canna, and water lilies all give colorful testament to the islanders' love for flowers of every hue in the rainbow. The aroma of the white, yellow, or pink frangipani is so sweet it's used as perfume on many islands.

Animals The fruit bat, or "flying fox," and some species of insect-eating bats are the only mammals native to South Pacific islands. Dogs, chickens, pigs, rats, and mice were introduced by early settlers. There are few land snakes or other reptiles in the islands. The notable exceptions are geckos and skinks, those little lizards that seem to be everywhere. Don't go berserk when a gecko walks upside-down across the ceiling of your bungalow. They are harmless and actually perform a valuable service by eating mosquitoes and other insects.

Birds The number and variety of species of birdlife also diminishes as you go eastward. Most land birds live in the bush away from settlements and the accompanying cats, dogs, and rats. For this reason the birds most likely to be seen are terns, boobies, herons, petrels, noddies, and others that earn their livelihoods from the sea. Of the introduced birds, the Indian myna is the most numerous. Brought to the South Pacific early in this century to control insects, the myna quickly became a noisy nuisance in its own right.

THE SEA

The tropical South Pacific Ocean virtually teems with sea life, from colorful reef fish to the horrific Great White sharks featured in *Jaws,* from the paua clams that make tasty chowders in the Cook Islands to the deep-sea tuna that keep the canneries going at Pago Pago.

Coral Reefs   More than 600 species of coral created the great reefs that make the South Pacific a divers' mecca, 10 times the number found in the Caribbean. Billions of tiny coral polyps build their own skeletons on top of those left by their ancestors, until they reach the level of low tide. Then they grow outward, extending the edge of the reef. The old skeletons are white, while the living polyps present a rainbow of colors; they grow best and are most colorful in the clear, salty water on the outer edge or in channels, where the tides and waves wash fresh seawater along and across the reef. A reef can grow as much as two inches a year in ideal conditions. Although pollution, rising seawater temperature, and a proliferation of crown-of-thorns starfish have greatly hampered reef growth—and beauty—in parts of the South Pacific, there still are many areas where the color and variety of corals are unmatched.

Most island countries have tough laws protecting their environment, so *don't deface the reef.* You could land in the slammer for breaking off a gorgeous chunk of coral to take home as a souvenir.

Sea Life   The lagoons are like gigantic aquariums filled with a plethora of tropical fish and other marine life, including whales, which migrate to Tonga and Fiji from June to October, and sea turtles, which lay their eggs on some beaches from November through February. Nearly every main town has a bookstore with pamphlets containing photographs and descriptions of the creatures that will peer into your face mask.

Most South Pacific countries restrict the use of spearguns, so ask before you go in search of the catch of your life. Sea turtles and whales are on the list of endangered species, and the importation of their shells, bones, and teeth is prohibited by many countries, including the United States.

Some Warnings   By and large, the South Pacific's marine creatures are harmless to humans, but there are some to avoid. Always seek local advice before snorkeling or swimming in a lagoon away from the hotel beaches. Most diving operators conduct snorkeling tours. If you don't know what you're doing, go with them.

Wash and apply a good antiseptic or antibacterial ointment to all coral cuts and scrapes as soon as possible. Since coral cannot grow in fresh water, the flow of rivers and streams into the lagoon creates narrow channels known as passes through the reef. Currents can be very strong in the passes, so stay in the protected, shallow water of the inner lagoons.

Sharks are curious beasts attracted by bright objects such as watches and knives, so be careful what you wear in the water. Don't swim in areas where sewage or edible wastes are dumped, and never swim alone if you have any suspicion that sharks might be present. If you do see a shark, don't splash in the water or urinate. Calmly retreat and get out of the water as quickly as you can without creating a disturbance.

Those round things on the rocks and reefs that look like pin cushions are sea urchins, whose calcium spikes can be more painful than needles. If you get stuck with one, soak the injury in hot water, vinegar, or urine for about 15 minutes. That will stop the pain. If you can't get it out, the spike will dissolve and disappear on its own in about two weeks.

Jellyfish stings can hurt like the devil but seldom are life-threatening. Adolph's Meat Tenderizer is a great antidote; otherwise, use rubbing alcohol to swab the affected areas, not water or any petroleum-based compound.

The stone fish is so named because it looks like a piece of stone or coral as it lies buried in the sand on the lagoon bottom with only its back and 13 venomous spikes sticking out. Its venom can cause paralysis and even death. You'll know by the intense pain if you're stuck. Serum is available, so get to a hospital at once. Sea snakes, cone shells, crown-of-thorns starfish, moray eels, lionfish, and demon stingers also can be painful if not deadly. The last thing any of these creatures wants is to tangle with a human, so keep your hands to yourself.

5   Recommended Books & Films

BOOKS

Rather than list the hundreds of books about the South Pacific, I have picked some of the best that are likely to be available in the United States and Canada, either in bookstores or at your local library. Many other tomes, especially scholarly works, have been published in Australia, New Zealand, and the islands themselves (notably by the University of the South Pacific in Suva, Fiji, and by Vava'u Press in Tonga). Libraries in those countries may have much wider South Pacific selections than do their counterparts in North America.

A number of out-of-print island classics have been reissued in paperback by Mutual Publishing Company, Mezzanine B, 1127 11th Ave., Honolulu, HI 96816 (tel. 808/732-1709, fax 808/734-4094). In some cases, I give a book's original publisher and date of publication, followed by the recent Mutual edition and its date.

If you have time to read only one South Pacific book, *The Lure of Tahiti* (Mutual, 1986) should be it. Editor A. Grove Day includes 18 short stories, excerpts of other books, and essays; there is a little here from many of the writers mentioned below, plus selections from Captains Cook, Bougainville, and Bligh.

General   The National Geographic Society's book *The Isles of the South Pacific* (1971), by Maurice Shadbolt and Olaf Ruhen, and Ian Todd's *Island Realm* (Angus & Robertson, 1974) are somewhat out-of-date coffee-table books but have lovely color photographs. *Living Corals* (Clarkson N. Potter, 1979), by Douglas Faulkner and Richard Chesher, shows what you will see under water.

For reference purposes, *The South Pacific: An Introduction* (Univ. of the South Pacific, 1989), by Ron Crocombe, provides a wealth of political and economic data, as does *Pacific Islands Yearbook* (Fiji Times, 1995), eds. Norman and Ngaire Douglas; both are published in Suva, Fiji.

History & Politics   Several of the early English and French explorers published accounts of their exploits, but *The Journals of Captain James Cook* stand out as the most exhaustive and even-handed. Edited by J.C. Beaglehole, they were published

Impressions

I have often been mildly amused when I think that the great American novel was not written about New England or Chicago. It was written about a white whale in the South Pacific.

—James A. Michener, 1951

in three volumes (one for each voyage) by Cambridge University in 1955, 1961, and 1967. A. Grenfell Price edited many of Cook's key passages and provides short transitional explanations in *The Explorations of Captain James Cook in the Pacific* (Dover, 1971). Modern prose accounts are given by Lynne Withey in *Voyages of Discovery: Captain Cook and the Exploration of the Pacific* (Morrow, 1987) and by Richard Hough in *Captain James Cook: A Biography* (Norton, 1995).

The explorers' visits and their consequences in Tahiti, Australia, and Antarctica are the subject of Alan Moorehead's study *The Fatal Impact: The Invasion of the South Pacific, 1767–1840* (Harper & Row, 1966), a colorful tome loaded with sketches and paintings of the time.

Three other very readable books trace Tahiti's post-discovery history. *Tahiti: Island of Love* (Pacific Publications, 1979), by Robert Langdon, takes the island's story up to 1977. *Tahiti: A Paradise Lost* (Penquin, 1985), by David Howarth, covers more thoroughly the same early ground covered by Langdon but stops with France's taking possession in 1842. *The Rape of Tahiti* (Dodd, Mead, 1983), by Edward Dodd, covers the island from prehistory to 1900.

Mad about Islands (Mutual, 1987), by A. Grove Day, follows the island exploits of literary figures Herman Melville, Robert Louis Stevenson, Jack London, and W. Somerset Maugham. Also included are Charles Nordhoff and James Norman Hall, co-authors of the so-called "Bounty Trilogy" and other works about the islands (see "Fiction," below). *In Search of Paradise* (Mutual, 1987), by Paul L. Briand, recounts the Nordhoff and Hall story in detail. *A Dream of Islands* (Norton, 1980), by Gavan Dawes, tells of the missionary John Williams as well as of Melville, Stevenson, and painter Paul Gauguin.

For descriptions of the islands during the 1950s, see Eugene Burdick's *The Blue of Capricorn* (Houghton Mifflin, 1961; Mutual, 1986). In *Tales from Paradise* (BBC Publications, 1986), June Knox-Mawer tells charming yarns of the final years of British rule in Fiji and the Solomons, as seen by a colonial official's wife.

Former *New York Times* reporter Robert Turnbull traveled the islands in the 1970s and reported his findings in *Tin Roofs and Palm Trees* (Univ. of Washington Press, 1977). Scott L. Malcolmson did the same in the late 1980s; his somewhat opinionated views of the political situations in Fiji and French Polynesia are in *Tuturani: A Political Journey in the Pacific Islands* (Poseidon, 1990).

For a political document, order a copy of *Problems in Paradise: United States Interests in the South Pacific* (U.S. House of Representatives, 1990) from the U.S. Government Printing Office in Washington, D.C. It's an excellent report by a 1989 congressional delegation that toured the islands.

Peoples and Cultures   Peter Bellwood's *The Polynesians: Prehistory of an Island People* (Thames & Hudson, 1987) examines the Polynesians' history before the coming of Europeans and explains the various island cultures existing at the time. The book contains sketches of island life by the early explorers and photographs of ancient handcrafts that have been unearthed or preserved.

In *We, the Navigators* (Univ. of Hawaii, 1972), Professor David Lewis tells how the islanders managed to sail great distances over open ocean without modern navigation tools.

Some of the most interesting accounts of island life were written by persons who lived among the islanders and then wrote about their experiences. Perhaps the most famous is *Coming of Age in Samoa* (1928), in which Margaret Mead tells of her year studying promiscuous adolescent girls in the Manu'a islands of American Samoa. The book created quite a stir when it was published in a more modest time than the present. Her interpretation of Samoan sex customs was taken to task by New Zealander Derek Freeman in *Margaret Mead and Samoa: The Making and Unmaking of an Anthropological Myth* (1983).

Bengt Danielsson, a Swedish anthropologist who has lived in Tahiti since arriving there on Thor Heyerdahl's *Kon Tiki* raft in 1947, paints a much broader picture of Polynesian sexuality in *Love in the South Seas* (Mutual, 1986). He finds that some of the old ways have gone, while others are still hanging on.

Heyerdahl tells his tale and explains his theory of Polynesian migration (since debunked) in *Kon Tiki* (Rand McNally, 1950; translated by F.K. Lyon). In 1936, Heyerdahl and his wife lived for a year in the Marquesas. The resulting book, *Fatu-Hiva: Back to Nature* (Doubleday, 1975), provides an in-depth look at Marquesan life at the time.

Two Americans give unscholarly but entertaining accounts of Polynesian island life during the 1920s. Robert Dean Frisbe spent several years as a trader in the Cook Islands and tells about it charmingly in *The Book of Puka-Puka* (1928; Mutual, 1986). Robert Lee Eskridge spent a year on Mangareva in French Polynesia; his equally charming book is titled, appropriately, *Manga Reva* (Bobbs-Merrill, 1931; Mutual, 1986).

In recent times, noted conservationist Joana McIntyre Varawa married Fijian Male Varawa, half her age, and moved from Hawaii to his home village. In *Changes in Latitude* (Atlantic Monthly Press, 1989), she writes of her experiences, providing many insights into modern Fijian culture.

Travel   Although Robert Louis Stevenson lived in Western Samoa for several years, he composed very little fiction about the South Pacific. But he wrote articles and letters about his travels and about events leading up to Germany's acquisition of the islands in 1890. Many of them are available in two collections: *In the South Seas* (1901) and *Island Landfalls* (Cannongate, 1987). The latter also includes three Stevenson short stories with South Seas settings: "The Bottle Imp," "The Isle of Voices," and "The Beach at Falesá."

Sir David Attenborough, the British director and documentary producer, traveled to Papua New Guinea, Vanuatu, Fiji, and Tonga in the late 1950s to film, among other things, Tongan Queen Salote's royal kava ceremony. Sir David entertainingly tells of his trips in *Journeys to the Past* (Penguin, 1983).

John Dyson rode inter-island trading boats throughout the South Pacific and wrote about his experiences in *The South Seas Dream* (Little, Brown, 1982). It's an entertaining account of the islands and their more colorful inhabitants. Julian Evans tells of a more recent trading-boat trip to Fiji, the Samoas, and Tonga in *Transit of Venus* (Pantheon, 1992).

The noted travel writer and novelist Paul Theroux took his kayak along for a tour of the South Pacific and reported on what he found in *The Happy Isles of Oceania: Paddling the Pacific* (Putnam's, 1992). The book is a fascinating yarn, full of island characters and out-of-the-way places.

Few travelogues dedicated to particular island countries are readily available outside of the South Pacific. One of the best is Ronald Wright's enjoyable book *On Fiji Islands* (Penquin, 1986). It's packed with insights about the Fijians and Indians.

Fiction   Starting with Herman Melville's *Typee* (1846) and *Omoo* (1847)— semifictional accounts of his adventures in the Marquesas and Tahiti, respectively—the South Pacific has spawned a wealth of fiction. (Melville's 1851 classic, *Moby-Dick*, though set in the South Pacific Ocean, does not tell of the islands.)

After Melville came Julian Viaud, a French naval officer who fell in love with a Tahitian woman during a short sojourn in Tahiti. Under the pen name Pierre Loti, he wrote *The Marriage of Loti* (1880; KPI, 1986), a classic tale of lost love.

W. Somerset Maugham's *The Moon and Sixpence* (1919) is a fictional account of the life of Paul Gauguin. Maugham changed the name to Charles Strickland and made the painter English instead of French. (Gauguin's own novel, *Noa Noa*, was published in English in 1928, long after his death.) Maugham also produced a volume of South Pacific short stories, *The Trembling of a Leaf* (1921; Mutual, 1985). The most famous is "Rain," the tragic story of prostitute Sadie Thompson and the fundamentalist missionary she led astray in American Samoa. My personal favorite is "The Fall of Edward Bernard," about a Chicagoan who forsakes love and fortune back home for "beauty, truth, and goodness" in Tahiti.

Next on the scene were the aforementioned Charles Nordhoff and James Norman Hall (more about them in Chapters 4 and 5). Together they wrote the most famous of all South Pacific novels, *Mutiny on the Bounty* (1932). They immediately followed that enormous success with two other novels: *Men Against the Sea* (1934), based on Bligh's epic longboat voyage after the mutiny; and *Pitcairn's Island* (1935), about the mutineers' sorry demise on their remote hideaway.

Nordhoff and Hall later wrote *The Hurricane* (1936), a novel that has been made into two movies (see "Films," below). Hall also wrote short stories and essays, collected in *The Forgotten One* (Mutual, 1986).

The second most famous South Pacific novel appeared just after World War II—*Tales of the South Pacific* (Macmillan, 1947), by James A. Michener. A U.S. Navy historian, Michener spent much of the war on Espiritu Santo, in the New Hebrides (now Vanuatu), which is the setting for most of the book. Richard Rodgers and Oscar Hammerstein turned the novel into the musical *South Pacific,* one of the most successful Broadway productions ever; it was later made into a movie (see "Films," below).

Michener toured the islands a few years later and wrote *Return to Paradise* (Random House, 1951), a collection of essays and short stories. The essays are particularly valuable, since they describe the islands as they were after World War II but before tourists began to arrive via jet aircraft—in other words, near the end of the region's backwater, beachcomber days. His piece on Fiji predicts that country's Fijian-Indian problems.

FILMS

Just as authors and book publishers have thrived on South Pacific yarns, so has Hollywood. In fact, most of the well-known novels about the region have been turned into movies.

The most famous are two *Mutiny on the Bounty* films based on the novel by Charles Nordhoff and James Norman Hall. The 1935 version starred Clark Gable as Fletcher Christian and Charles Laughton as a tyrannical Captain Bligh. (It actually was the second film to be based on the *Bounty* story; the first was an Australian production, starring Errol Flynn in his first movie role.) Although the 1935 version contained background shots of 40 Tahitian villages, most of the movie was filmed on Santa Catalina, off the California coast; neither Gable nor Laughton visited Tahiti. The 1962 remake, however, with Marlon Brando and Trevor Howard in the Gable-Laughton roles, was actually filmed on Tahiti; it was the beginning of Brando's tragic real-life relationship with Tahiti. A 1984 version, *The Bounty,* not based on Nordhoff and Hall, was filmed on Moorea and featured Mel Gibson as Christian and Anthony Hopkins as a more sympathetic Bligh.

The Hurricane, another Nordhoff and Hall novel, also was made into two films. The 1937 version starred Jon Hall, a Tahiti-born second cousin of James Norman Hall. He went on to lesser roles, but the film launched the sarong-clad career of Dorothy Lamour. A 1979 remake, filmed on Bora Bora, starred Mia Farrow; it was a flop. Another hurricane was featured in *The Silent One,* a 1984 New Zealand production about a Polynesian village's hostility toward a mute boy.

Several W. Somerset Maugham stories have been turned into movies. His short story "Rain" was first filmed in 1928 by Gloria Swanson, who changed the title to *Miss Sadie Thompson* after the Motion Picture Association declared the story to be blasphemous. A 1932 version, starring Joan Crawford and Walter Huston, kept Maugham's title, but a 1953 remake, with Rita Haworth and José Ferrer, came out as *Miss Sadie Thompson.* Other Maugham-based movies are *The Moon and Sixpence,* with George Stevens, and *The Beachcomber,* with Charles Laughton.

Herman Melville's *Typee* was filmed in 1958 as *Enchanted Island,* starring Jane Powell as the Polynesian maiden. The movie version of his *Moby-Dick,* with Gregory Peck, was a box-office bomb.

James Michener's World War II novel *Tales of the South Pacific* was turned into the blockbuster musical *South Pacific,* which was filmed in Hawaii in 1958. The 1953 movie version of his *Return to Paradise,* starring Gary Cooper, was filmed in Western Samoa. It was based on "Mr. Morgan," one of that book's short stories about a beach bum who runs afoul of missionaries while falling in love with a local lass.

Jean Simmons played a teenage girl shipwrecked with a boy on a deserted island in the 1949 version of *The Blue Lagoon.* The 1980 version helped launch the career of Brooke Shields, then 14 years old. Both movies were shot in Fiji's Yasawa islands. A 1991 sequel, *Return to the Blue Lagoon,* was made on Taveuni, also in Fiji.

The most recent movie set in the South Pacific is *Love Affair,* a 1994 tear-jerking flop with Warren Beatty and real-life wife Annette Bening. Filmed on Moorea and aboard the freighter-cruise ship *Aranui* in French Polynesia, it is a remake of *An Affair to Remember* (1957), starring Cary Grant and Deborah Kerr.

Planning a Trip to the South Pacific

3

Since the South Pacific can hold some surprises, wise planning is essential to get the most out of your time and money spent in this vast and varied modern paradise.

Each of the six small countries covered in this book has its own sources of information, entry requirements, currency, government, customs, laws, internal transportation, styles of accommodation, and food. They also have many things in common. This chapter tells you how to plan a trip to the South Pacific islands in general. It augments, but is not a substitute for, the information contained in the individual chapters that follow.

1 Visitor Information & Entry Requirements

VISITOR INFORMATION

For general information about the South Pacific, contact the **Pacific Asia Travel Association (PATA),** 1 Montgomery Street, West Tower, Suite 1000, San Francisco, CA 94104 (☎ 415/986-4646; fax 415/986-3458). PATA's South Pacific Regional Office, P.O. Box 645, Kings Cross, NSW 2001, Australia (☎ 02/332-3599, fax 02/331-6592), directly handles the island countries. PATA has a home page on the Internet, with information about member countries. The address is **http://www.singapore.com/pata/**

The U.S. Department of State maintains a 24-hour **Travel Advisory** (☎ 202/647-5225) to keep you abreast of political or other problems throughout the world.

See the "Visitor Information & Entry Requirements" and "Money" sections in the individual chapters for the address of each country's tourist information office.

ENTRY REQUIREMENTS

All South Pacific countries require new arrivals to have a **passport** that will be valid for the duration of the visit, and an onward or return airline ticket. Your passport should be valid for six months beyond the date you expect to return home.

U.S. citizens and nationals can obtain passport applications (form DSP-11) from the U.S. Passport Agency (☎ 202/647-0518), which has offices in Boston, Chicago, Honolulu, Houston, Los Angeles,

Miami, New Orleans, New York, Philadelphia, San Francisco, Seattle, Stamford, Conn., and Washington, D.C. Applications also are accepted by some 3,500 post offices and federal courthouses around the U.S.

Visas usually are not required of citizens of the United States, Canada, New Zealand, Japan, and the European Community countries for stays of 30 days or less (see "Visitor Information & Entry Requirements" and "Money" in each country chapter). The initial stay in Fiji is four months. Australians *must* have visas before arriving in French Polynesia. Extensions of up to three months usually are granted to visitors who still have their return tickets and enough money—and who behave themselves.

If you fall in love with (or in) the South Pacific and start thinking about emigrating there, think some more. These small countries make it difficult for foreigners to live there on a permanent basis. Write to each country's immigration department for its stringent regulations. Foreign ownership of land is equally restricted—not impossible, but difficult.

Marriages are relatively simple, on the other hand, and most resorts have wedding packages that include a traditional Polynesian or Fijian ceremony. They will tell you the documents you need to bring and what local formalities will need to be executed before your wedding.

Vaccinations The only shot required to enter the South Pacific countries is for yellow fever, and then only if you're coming from an infected area of South America or Africa. It's a good idea, however, to have your tetanus, typhoid fever, polio, diphtheria, and hepatitis-A vaccinations up to date.

Driver's Licenses Valid home country driver's licenses are recognized throughout the South Pacific, although you will need to get a local license in the Cook Islands and Tonga. No new test will be administered; it's just a way for these two countries to raise a little revenue. I have never found an international driver's license to be useful.

2 Money

CURRENCIES

American Samoa uses U.S. dollars. French Polynesia uses the French Pacific franc, the value of which is pegged directly to the regular French franc. Local and New Zealand dollars circulate side by side in the Cook Islands. Otherwise, each South Pacific country has its own currency. The Cook Islands, Western Samoan, and Tongan currencies are virtually worthless outside those countries.

U.S., Australian, and New Zealand dollars are accepted widely in the islands, and the local banks will change most other major currencies. Accordingly, don't bother changing currency before leaving home.

Getting Local Currency Banks in all the main towns will cash, and most major hotels, resorts, restaurants, and car-rental firms will accept, traveler's checks issued by American Express, Thomas Cook, VISA, Bank of America, Citicorp, and MasterCard. You won't necessarily be able to cash them on many outer islands with limited, if any, banking facilities.

Holders of VISA and MasterCard can get cash advances at Westpac Bank and ANZ Bank, and at automated teller machines (ATMs) in Tahiti and Fiji. Make sure you get a 4-digit personal identification number (PIN) from your bank in order to use the ATMs. Between them, Westpac and ANZ have offices in every

South Pacific country, including Western Samoa, where they have major stakes in the local banks. The American Express agents in Tahiti and Fiji will cash cardmembers' personal checks.

CREDIT CARDS

Most hotels, car-rental companies, and many restaurants and large shops accept VISA and MasterCard, less so American Express. Diners Club is present but not as widespread. Always ask first, and when you're away from the main towns, don't count on putting anything on plastic.

American Express American Express has full-service representatives in Tahiti and Fiji. If you lose your American Express credit card or traveler's checks in the Cook Islands, American Samoa, or Tonga, have the international operator place a collect call to American Express's number in your home country. United States cardholders should phone collect 910/333-3211.

WHAT WILL IT COST?

There is a common misconception that the South Pacific is a terribly expensive place to visit. Even with a decrease in airfares in recent years, it still costs a fair sum to cross the thousands of miles of ocean to get there from North America or Europe. Still, this reputation is now a bum rap, for many destinations—including Hawaii—have caught up with the South Pacific. Although some resorts in French Polynesia and Fiji can set a couple back more than $700 a day, and a beer in some Tahitian nightclubs can run more than $10, cost-conscious travelers can get excellent value throughout the islands.

How much you spend a day depends both on where you go and on the standard of living you desire. The South Pacific has a wide range of hotels, in both quality and price. Even in French Polynesia, dining out will be no more expensive than in most American cities, provided you eat somewhere other than in the big resort hotels, whose restaurants and dining rooms charge a premium for food. There are no fast-food chain restaurants such as McDonald's in the islands, but you can keep costs down by eating at local snack bars, which serve the same purpose.

Tipping is considered contrary to both the Polynesian and Melanesian traditions of hospitality and generosity. That's not to say that some small gratuity isn't in order for truly outstanding service, or that you won't get that "Where's-my-tip?" look from a porter as he sheepishly delays leaving your room. But American-style tipping officially is discouraged throughout the South Pacific. Nor will you be socked with a service charge on your hotel and restaurant bills. So forget that hidden 15% or more your vacation could cost elsewhere.

The following chapters contain tables giving precise price information for each country and territory. As you will see, prices vary from island to island. If cost is a factor, compare this information before deciding which islands to visit.

Prices in this book are given in local currency, with the U.S. dollar equivalent in parentheses, based on the rate of exchange at the time of writing. **The dollar sign ($) used alone denotes U.S. dollars.**

The **price ranges** for restaurants include the costs of main courses. As a general rule, doubling the cost of a main course will yield the price of a full meal.

Inflation alert: I have done my best to report prices accurately, but they may vary from those given in this book. Inflation is as much a fact of life in the South Pacific as anywhere else. The island countries import much of what is consumed by the local tourism industry and all of their petroleum, and they impose duties on virtually everything brought in. Accordingly, prices depend on the exchange value of the local currency, the price of crude oil, and the amount of duty imposed by the customs departments.

3 When to Go

THE CLIMATE

The South Pacific islands covered in this book lie within the tropics. Compared to the pronounced winters and summers of the temperate zones, there is little variation from one island group to the next: They are warm and humid all year. Local residents, however, recognize two distinct seasons, which may bear on when you choose to visit.

A somewhat cooler and more comfortable **dry season** occurs during the austral winter from May though October. The winter trade wind blows fairly steadily during these months, bringing generally fine tropical weather throughout the area. Rain usually is limited to brief showers. Daytime high temperatures reach the delightful upper 70s (24°C to 27°C) to low 80s (28°C to 30°C) in French Polynesia, Samoa, and Fiji, with early morning lows in the high 60s (18°C to 20°C). Rarotonga in the Cook Islands and Tongatapu in Tonga are farther from the equator and see cooler temperatures, with the highs in the 60s or low 70s (15°C to 23°C). Breezy wintertime nights can feel downright chilly in those islands.

The austral summer from November through April is the warmer and more humid **wet season.** Daytime highs climb into the upper 80s (30°C to 33°C) throughout the islands, with nighttime lows about 70°F (21°C). Low-pressure troughs and tropical depressions can bring several days of rain at a time, but usually it falls during heavy showers followed by periods of very intense sunshine. This is also the season for cyclones (hurricanes), which can be devastating and should never be taken lightly. Fortunately, they usually move fast enough that their major effect on visitors is a day or two of heavy rain and wind. If you're caught in one, the hotels are experts on knowing what to do to ensure your safety.

Bear in mind that the higher the altitude, the lower the temperature. If you're going up in the mountains, be prepared for much cooler weather.

HOLIDAYS

The busiest tourist season in the South Pacific is the austral winter months of July and August. That's when Australians and New Zealanders head for the islands to escape the cold back home. It's also when residents of Tahiti head off to their own outer islands in keeping with the traditional July–August holiday break in France. Many Europeans also visit the islands during this time.

There also are busy mini-seasons at school holiday time in Australia and New Zealand. These periods vary, but in general they are from the end of March through the middle of April, two weeks in late May, two more weeks at the beginning of July, two more in the middle of September, and from mid-December until mid-January.

With a few exceptions, South Pacific hoteliers do not raise their rates during any of the busy periods.

From Christmas through the middle of January is a good time to get a hotel reservation in the South Pacific, but airline seats can be hard to come by, since thousands of islanders fly home from overseas jobs and schools.

SPECIAL EVENTS

The chapters of this book list each country's festivals and special events, which can change the entire nature of a visit to the South Pacific. The annual *Heiva I Tahiti* (or *Tiruai*) in French Polynesia, the King's Birthday in Tonga, and the week of Constitution Day in Rarotonga are just three examples, and every country has at least one such major celebration. These are the best times to see traditional dancing, arts, and sporting events. Be sure to make your reservations well in advance, however, for hotel rooms and airline seats can be in short supply.

4 The Active Vacation Planner

Scuba diving is far and away the South Pacific's most widely available form of adventure, primarily because the diving is some of the world's best, especially in Fiji. Every major island now has at least one diving operation.

Sailors can charter yachts and explore many islands in French Polynesia, Tonga, and Fiji.

Fiji has white-water rafting and hiking expeditions into the mountains, plus organized overnight trips to Fijian villages in the highlands.

Your travel agent should know of adventure travel companies that have trips to the South Pacific. For example, **All Adventure Travel** (☎ 800/537-4025), an agency that represents operators in more than 60 countries, recently offered a bicycle expedition to Tahiti and Moorea.

5 Health & Insurance

STAYING HEALTHY

Facilities   Hospitals and clinics are widespread in the South Pacific, but the quality varies a great deal from place to place. You can get a broken bone set and a coral scrape tended, but treating more serious ailments likely will be beyond the capability of the local hospital everywhere except in Tahiti. For this reason, it's a good idea to buy a travel insurance policy that includes medical evacuation (see "Health Insurance," below).

Pharmacies are numerous, but their prescription and over-the-counter medications likely will be from France, New Zealand, or Australia and thus unfamiliar to most Americans and Canadians. Only the Lyndon B. Johnson Medical Center in American Samoa dispenses American-made medications. Take an adequate supply of any prescription medications you may need, and carry them in your hand luggage. Ask your pharmacist for the generic names—not the brand names—of your medications, and keep these with your passport. Eyeglasses are not easily replaced, so carry spares.

Potential Problems   The South Pacific islands covered in this book pose no major health problem for most travelers. If you have a chronic condition, however, you should check with your doctor before visiting the islands. Among minor illnesses, the islands have the common cold and occasional outbreaks of influenza and conjunctivitis ("pink eye").

Also present from time to time is dengue fever, a viral disease borne by the *Aëdes aegypti* mosquito, which lives indoors and bites only during daylight hours. It usually starts with a sudden high fever, excruciating frontal headache, and muscle and joint pain so severe that dengue also is known as "breakbone fever." Many victims also get a measleslike rash that can spread from torso to arms, legs, and face. The symptoms usually go away within 7 to 10 days, but complete recovery can take several weeks or even months. There is no vaccine, and treatment is strictly for the symptoms, with heavy emphasis on drinking lots of fluids and replenishing vitamins. Aspirin is not recommended. Dengue seldom is fatal in adults, but take extra precautions to keep children from being bitten by mosquitoes if the disease is present.

Malaria is not present in the islands covered in this book. If you're going on to Vanuatu and Solomon Islands, check with your doctor well in advance of departure so that you can start anti-malarial medication a week before you arrive.

Cuts, scratches, and all open sores should be treated promptly in the tropics. I always carry a tube of antibacterial ointment and a package of adhesive bandages such as Band-Aids.

Special precautions should be taken if you are traveling with children. See "Tips for Special Travelers," below.

Insects   The Aitutaki Lagoon Resort in the Cook Islands has this notice posted in its guest bungalows: "You will find that we Cook Islanders are among the friendliest people in the South Pacific. Amongst all the friendly people we also have the friendliest ants, roaches, geckos, crabs, and insects, who are all dying to make your acquaintance."

Indeed, every South Pacific island has more than its share of mosquitoes, roaches, and ants. Some beaches and swampy areas also have those invisible sand flies—the dreaded "no-seeums" or "no-nos"—which bite the ankles around daybreak and dusk. Insect repellent is widely available in the South Pacific shops. Good local brands are Dolmix Pic in French Polynesia and Rid, an excellent Australian brand sold elsewhere. American brands such as Off also are widely available. The most effective skin repellents contain "deet" (N,N-diethyl-m-toluamide).

I keep a "mosquito coil" burning in my non-air-conditioned rooms at night. I have found the Fish brand to work best. You can buy them in shops throughout the islands.

AIDS   As pointed out elsewhere in this book, sexual mores in the South Pacific are often quite different from those in Western countries. Sexual relations before marriage—heterosexual, homosexual, and bisexual—are more or less accepted behavior. Further, both male and female prostitution is common in the larger towns, such as Papeete and Suva. Because of these more relaxed sexual mores, and because the Acquired Immune Deficiency Syndrome (AIDS) virus has been detected in the South Pacific Islands, visitors are advised to exercise *at least* the same caution in choosing their sexual partners, and in practicing "safe sex," as they would at home.

Smoking   Cigarette smoking is still widespread in the islands. Although the airlines are smoke-free, non-smoking sections are scarce in restaurants, and only a few of the largest hotels have no-smoking rooms. Inquire when you make a reservation whether non-smoking rooms are available.

Tap Water   Except in Apia, Western Samoa, tap water in the main towns is safe to drink, and bottled spring water can be bought in most grocery stores.

More Information   The U.S. Centers for Disease Control in Atlanta, Georgia, provides up-to-date overseas health information on its International Traveler's

Hotline (☎ 404/332-4559, or 404/647-3000 for automatic fax service). You can also call the U.S. State Department's Citizen's Emergency Center (☎ 202/647-5225) for advisories pertaining to health as well as crime and politics in foreign countries.

American Express has a "Global Assist" service, which provides emergency medical referrals and legal advice to its members who are traveling. Card members can call collect 202/554-2639 from overseas.

INSURANCE

Many travelers buy insurance policies providing health and accident, trip cancellation and interruption, and lost-luggage protection. The coverage you need will depend on the extent of protection contained in your existing policies. Some credit card companies also insure their customers against travel accidents if the tickets were purchased with their cards. Read your policies and credit card agreements over carefully before purchasing additional insurance.

Many health insurance companies and health maintenance organizations provide coverage for illness or accidents overseas, but you may have to pay the foreign provider up front and file for a reimbursement when you get home. You will need adequate receipts, so collect them at the time of treatment. Some traveler's health insurance policies will pay the local provider directly, saving you this hassle.

Since many medical facilities in the South Pacific are not up to Western standards, I always buy a traveler's health policy providing evacuation in case of medical necessity. Evacuation by air ambulance is very expensive, so I get a policy that provides this service regardless of how much it costs.

Trip cancellation insurance covers your loss if you have made non-refundable deposits, bought airline tickets that provide no or partial refunds, or if you have paid for a charter flight and for some good reason you can't travel. Trip interruption insurance, on the other hand, provides refunds in case an airline or tour operator goes bankrupt or out of business.

Lost-luggage insurance covers your loss over and above the limited amounts for which the airlines are responsible, and some policies provide instant payment so that you can replace your missing items on the spot.

Your travel agent should know of a company that offers traveler's insurance. Here are some American companies:

Travel Assistance International (TAI) (☎ 202/347-2025, or 800/821-2828). The American agent for Europ Assistance Worldwide Services, Inc., TAI has no limit on the cost of evacuation in case of medical necessity.

Travel Guard International (☎ 715/345-0505, or 800/782-5151).

Access America (☎ 804/285-3300, or 800/284-8300).

Health Care Abroad (Wallach & Co., Inc) (☎ 703/687-3166, or 800/237-6615).

Divers Alert Network (DAN) (☎ 919/684-2948, or 800/446-2671).

6 Tips for Special Travelers

FOR TRAVELERS WITH DISABILITIES

Unfortunately, the same sensibilities that have led to ramps, handles, accessible toilets, automatic opening doors, telephones at convenient heights, and other helpful aids in Western countries have not made serious inroads in the islands.

There may be a cultural reason why the South Pacific lags behind in this respect: Usually shy anyway, the islanders traditionally have felt ashamed when something was "wrong" with them and were dreadfully afraid of being made fun of because of it. Even today, many islanders will stay home from work rather than have anyone know they have anything as simple as pink eye. This may explain the lack of political support in most island countries to provide programs and facilities for the disabled.

That's not to say that some hoteliers haven't taken it upon themselves to provide rooms specially equipped for the disabled. Such improvements are ongoing; I have pointed out a few of them in this book, but inquire when making a reservation whether such rooms are available.

The airlines make special arrangements for disabled persons. Be sure to tell them of your needs when you make your reservation.

FOR SENIORS

Just as children are cared for communally in the South Pacific's extended family systems, so are senior citizens. In fact, most islanders live with their families from birth to death. Consequently, the local governments don't provide programs and other benefits for persons of retirement age. You won't find many senior citizen discounts. Children get them; you don't.

You might, however, be able to take advantage of special group tours put together by senior citizens' organizations, which can mean big savings on airfares, hotels, and meals. Check with the **American Association of Retired Persons (AARP)** (☎ 202/872-4700). **Elderhostel** (☎ 617/426-7788) has fun, low-priced overseas courses for seniors, some to the South Pacific islands.

FOR SINGLES

Having traveled alone through the South Pacific for more years than I care to admit, I can tell you it's a great place to be unattached. After all, this is the land of smiles and genuine warmth to strangers. The attitude soon infects visitors: all I've ever had to do to meet my fellow travelers is wander into a hotel bar, order a beer, and ask the persons next to me where they are from and what they have done in Fiji, Tahiti, and so on.

The islands have three playgrounds especially suited to singles. Two are the **Club Méditerranées** on Moorea and Bora Bora in French Polynesia. The other is rocking **Beachcomber Island Resort** in Fiji.

FOR WOMEN TRAVELING ALONE

The South Pacific islands are relatively safe for women traveling alone; however, women should exercise the same precautions as they would if they were in the U.S. or anywhere else in the world, for that matter. Don't let the charm of warm nights and smiling faces lull you into any less caution than you would exercise at home.

FOR FAMILIES

Infants and young children are adored by the islanders, but childhood does not last as long in the South Pacific as it does in our Western societies. As soon as they are capable, children are put to work, first caring for their younger siblings and cousins and helping out with household chores, later tending the village gardens. It's only as teenagers, and then only if they leave their villages for town, that they know unemployment in the Western sense. Accordingly, few towns and villages have children's facilities, such as playgrounds, outside school property.

With their love of children, the islanders are very good at babysitting; however, make sure you get one who speaks English. The hotels can take care of this for you.

Some hotels, such as Matagi Island Resort in Fiji, welcome children and have special programs to keep them safely occupied while their parents go diving. Others do not accept children at all. I point those out in the establishments listings, but you may want to ask to make sure. Also inquire whether the hotel can provide cribs, bottle warmers, and other needs.

Disposable diapers, cotton swabs (known as Buds, not Q-Tips), and baby food are sold in many main-town stores, but you should take along a supply of such items as children's aspirin, a thermometer, adhesive bandages, any special medications, and such. Make sure their vaccinations are up to date before leaving home. If your children are very small, perhaps you should discuss your travel plans with your family doctor.

Remember to protect youngsters with ample sunscreen.

Some other tips: Some tropical plants and animals may resemble rocks or vegetation, so teach your youngsters to avoid touching or brushing up against rocks, seaweed, and other objects. If your children are prone to swimmer's ear, use vinegar or preventive drops before they go swimming in freshwater streams or lakes. Have them shower soon after swimming or suffering cuts or abrasions.

Rascals in Paradise, 650 Fifth St., San Francisco, CA 94107 (☎ 415/978-9800 or 800/872-7225), specializes in organizing South Pacific tours for families with kids, including visits with local families and school children.

7 Getting There

A few cruise ships visit the islands, but today more than 98% of all visitors to the islands arrive by plane. Since the distances are great and the populations small, flights are not nearly as frequent in the islands as we Westerners are accustomed to at home. There may be only one flight a week between some countries, and flights that are scheduled today may be wiped off the timetables tomorrow. Most of the outer-island airports are unlighted, so there are few connecting flights after dark. Accordingly, it's always wise to consult a travel agent or contact the airlines to see what's happening at present.

THE AIRPORTS

With the exception of Fiji, where **Nadi** is the major airport and a few international flights also arrive at **Suva,** all other island countries have just one international airport each. These are **Papeete** on Tahiti in French Polynesia; **Rarotonga** in the Cook Islands; **Pago Pago** in American Samoa; **Apia** in Western Samoa; and **Tongatapu,** the main island in Tonga. Nadi (pronounced and sometimes spelled "Nandi") is the regional hub.

Always **reconfirm your return flight** as soon as you arrive on an outer island, primarily so that the local airline will know where to reach you in case of a schedule change. Avoid booking a return flight from an outer island on the same the day your international flight is due to leave for home; give yourself plenty of leeway in case the plane can't get to the outer island on schedule.

BY PLANE

Here are the airlines serving the South Pacific islands, with their North American telephone numbers:

Air New Zealand (☎ 310/615-1111 in the Los Angeles area or 800/262-1234 elsewhere), consistently one of the world's top-rated airlines, has the most extensive network to and from the islands. It has several flights a week directly from Los Angeles to Tahiti, Fiji, the Cook Islands, Western Samoa, and Tonga, with service continuing on to its home base in Auckland. From there, the system fans out to serve Tonga, Western Samoa, and several Australian cities, which means that Australians can reach most of the South Pacific islands through Auckland. From Europe, Air New Zealand has nonstop flights from Frankfurt and London's Heathrow Airport to Los Angeles, where connections can be made to the islands. From Asia, it flies between Japan and Fiji, and it links both Singapore and Hong Kong to Auckland.

Air Pacific (☎ 800/227-4446), Fiji's international airline, has at least two nonstop flights a week from Los Angeles to its base in Nadi, including one on Saturday. From there it offers several flights per week to Tonga and Western Samoa, and it goes west to Vanuatu and Solomon Islands. It also links Nadi to Sydney, Brisbane, and Melbourne in Australia. To New Zealand, it has nonstop service to Auckland, Wellington, and Christchurch. It also provides nonstop service between Fiji and both Tokyo and Osaka in Japan. Given its frequent flights and special deals for visitors from North America and Europe (see "Airfares," below), traveling on Air Pacific is one of the most convenient and economical ways to get around the South Pacific.

AOM French Airlines (☎ 800/892-9136) flies several times a week between Paris, Los Angeles, and Papeete. The company often offers cut-rate fares to Tahiti, especially in connection with air-hotel packages offered by Tahiti Vacations (see "Package Tours," below).

Air France (☎ 800/237-2747) flies to Tahiti from Paris, Los Angeles, and Tokyo.

Canadian Airlines International (☎ 800/426-7000) shares service with Air New Zealand from Canada to Fiji. You get on Canadian in Vancouver or Toronto and change to an Air New Zealand or Qantas plane in Honolulu.

Corsair Airlines (☎ 800/677-0720), a French carrier, flies to Tahiti from Paris via Los Angeles and San Francisco. Although primarily a charter airline, individuals can buy seats, though not necessarily at the charter price.

Hawaiian Airlines (☎ 808/838-1555 in Honolulu or 800/367-5320 in the continental U.S., Alaska, and Canada) flies from Los Angeles, San Francisco, Portland, and Seattle to Tahiti and Pago Pago, connecting in Honolulu.

Lan-Chile Airlines (☎ 800/735-5526) flies weekly between Santiago, Chile, and Tahiti by way of Easter Island.

Polynesian Airlines (☎ 22-737; fax 20-023 in Western Samoa) connects Apia to New Zealand, Australia, Tonga, Rarotonga, and Fiji. It's Polypass fare (see below) is a bargain for Aussies and Kiwis. It has offices in Sydney, Melbourne, Auckland, Wellington, and Christchurch. Some of its flights are on Air New Zealand aircraft.

Qantas Airways (☎ 800/227-4500) had a weekly flight between Los Angeles and Tahiti as we went to press, but it may be discontinued by the time you plan your trip. Qantas shares seats on Air Pacific between Los Angeles and Fiji (which means you actually will fly on Air Pacific if you buy a Qantas ticket). The same is true of all Qantas flights between Australia and Fiji.

Royal Tongan Airlines (☎ 23-414 in Tonga) connects its home country to Auckland and Nadi. It has offices in Auckland and Sydney.

Samoa Air (☎ 699-9106 in American Samoa) flies its small planes between Pago Pago and Vava'u in Tonga.

AIRFARES

The Pacific Ocean hasn't shrunk since it took 10 days and more than 83 hours in the air for Charles Kingsford Smith to become the first person to fly across it in 1928. Even though you can now board a jetliner in Los Angeles in the evening and be strolling under the palm trees of Tahiti or Fiji by the crack of dawn, the distances still run into the thousands of miles. Consequently, transportation costs may be the largest single expense of your trip to the South Pacific.

Be sure to shop all the airlines mentioned above to see who has the best deals. Keep calling if no attractive fare is available at first, since wholesalers and groups often reserve blocks of low-cost seats in advance but release some of them near the date of departure. Occasionally a carrier will hold a last-minute sale to get rid of unused seats, so always ask for the *lowest* fare.

Seasonal Fares   Depending on the carrier, the South Pacific has four airfare seasons: High or "peak" season is from December through February. One "shoulder" season includes March and April; a second runs from September through November. Low or "basic season" is from May through August. Fares can change as much as 25%, depending on the season. When I checked recently, for example, Air New Zealand's regular mid-week round-trip coach fare from Los Angeles to Fiji was about $1,200 in peak season. It dropped to $900 in the low season.

The less expensive time to fly usually is during the Northern summer months of May, June, July, and August. That's also when the weather is at its finest in the islands.

Special Fares   The airlines set aside a certain number of seats for discounted promotional sale, which usually are the cheapest available and must be purchased from two weeks to a month in advance. Always inquire what special deals the airlines are offering when you want to fly.

Several special fares offer savings if you're going to more than one South Pacific country, and if you can live with the restrictions that apply to each (always ask about restrictions).

One good deal is Air New Zealand's **Coral Route fare,** which includes stops at Tahiti, the Cook Islands, and Fiji (one of my recommended itineraries) as well as Honolulu. When I asked recently, this ticket cost about $1,700 in peak season and $1,400 during low season, but special discounts may be available when you plan your trip.

Air Pacific offers a **Pacific Air Pass** to North American and European travelers, which permits trips from Nadi to Apia, Tonga, and Vanuatu for $449 coach class and $749 business class. The Pacific Air Pass must be bought in North America or Europe. Air Pacific primarily flies "spoke" routes among the islands; like the spokes of a wheel, most of its planes fly from Nadi or Suva to another country, then turn around and come back.

Air Pacific also participates in a **Pacific Triangle Fare** in conjunction with Royal Tongan Airlines. It's good for direct travel between Fiji, Tonga, and Western Samoa, eliminating the need to backtrack to Fiji. It costs $448 and can be purchased in the South Pacific.

Australians and New Zealanders can save with Polynesian Airlines' **Polypass,** permitting unlimited travel for 30 days among Western Samoa, American Samoa, Fiji, Tonga, and Rarotonga, plus one round trip to the islands from Sydney or

Auckland. A Polypass costs $999 for adults, $500 for children under 12 years old, and $100 for children under two.

Feeder Fares   If you don't live in a city where flights to the South Pacific originate, then you will have to pay to get there in order to make a connection. Most carriers offer "feeder" or "add-on" fares to cover the connecting flights. Be sure to ask about them.

Discounters and Consolidators   Some travel agents will actively discount fares and hotel rooms by buying wholesale and then passing on some of their commissions to you. Discover Wholesale Travel, Inc. (☎ 714/883-1136 or 800/576-7770), owned by Mary Anne Cook, widow of legendary South Pacific tourism pioneer Ted Cook, is one of the few discount firms specializing in the islands. When I called recently, Mary Anne was offering round-trip Los Angeles–Tahiti tickets on Corsair Airlines for $538, a savings of $115 off the lowest regular fare at the time. She also discounts hotel rooms. By all means give this firm a ring.

Sometimes called "bucket shops," consolidators are discount firms that sell seats on the major international carriers which otherwise would go unfilled, especially during the slow seasons. Some discount firms run small ads in the Sunday travel sections of newspapers, and you should look into the fares they offer. Generally, however, it's best to go through a travel agent. Ask the agent to comparison shop for you, but always compare the deals he or she comes up with to those offered directly by the airlines.

Consolidator deals can be riskier than direct buys from a carrier, since the agent will deal with a middleman. On the other hand, they can result in substantial savings on tickets that have fewer restrictions than you would get with an advance purchase ticket bought from an airline. In any event, inquire as to any and all restrictions there may be.

Some American consolidators are: **UniTravel Corp.** (☎ 314/569-0900 or 800/325-2222); **Euram Tours** (☎ 202/789-2255 or 800/848-6789); **Council Charter** (☎ 212/661-0311); **Access International, Inc.** (☎ 800/333-7280); **C.L. Thompson, Inc.** (☎ 415/398-2535 or 800/833-4258); **Air Brokers** (☎ 415/397-1383 or 800/883-3273); **C&H International** (☎ 800/833-8888); and **1-800-FLY-ASAP** (☎ 602/956-6414 or 800/359-2727).

PACKAGE TOURS

Quite often a package tour will result in savings, not just on air fares but on hotels and other activities as well. You pay one price for a package that varies from one tour operator to the next. Air fare, transfers, and accommodations are always covered, and sometimes meals and specific activities are thrown in. The costs are kept down because wholesale tour operators (known as "wholesalers" in the travel industry) can make volume bookings on the airlines and at the hotels. The packages usually are then sold through retail travel agents, although some wholesalers will deal directly with the public. It's worth a phone call to find out.

There are some drawbacks: The least expensive tours may put you up at a bottom-end hotel. And since the lower costs depend on volume, some more expensive tours could send you to a large, impersonal property. You may find that once you're in the islands, you want to shift to that cozy bungalow down the road; if you do, you may lose the accommodation portion of the money you've already paid. Some hoteliers will endorse your vouchers to another property if you're unhappy with theirs; others will not. And since the tour prices are based on double occupancy, the single traveler is almost invariably penalized. You could end up traveling with strangers who become friends for life; they also could be loud-mouthed bores.

Most tour companies require payment to be made well in advance of travel. If possible pay by credit card, which will give you some protection in case the company doesn't come through with the tour. Also consider buying both trip cancellation and trip interruption insurance (see "Health & Insurance," above).

If you decide to go, read the fine print carefully. You may not want all the "extras" that are included, such as all meals (why pay in advance for all meals in places like French Polynesia, where dining out can be a major extracurricular activity?). And don't think the free manager's welcoming party is any big deal; you may be invited anyway, whether you're on the tour or not.

Here are some companies that specialize in the islands:

Brendan Tours (☎ 818/785-9696 or 800/421-8446) provides packages to Fiji for Air Pacific Holidays. Some of its recent off-season packages have started as low as $800 for a week, including air and hotel.

Hawaiian Sunspots (☎ 503/666-3893 or 800/334-5623) is expert on the Cook Islands and Samoa— despite its name—and will arrange an itinerary for you anywhere else in the islands.

Islands in the Sun (☎ 310/536-0051 or 800/828-6877) is the largest whole-saler offering packages to all the islands. Started in the 1960s by the late Ted Cook, this firm is now owned by Accor, the French firm that manages the Sofitel hotels in French Polynesia.

Island Vacations (☎ 714/476-6380 or 800/745-8545) has economical pack-ages to Tahiti, the Cook Islands, and Fiji.

Tahiti Nui's Island Dreams (☎ 206/216-2910 or 800/359-4359) is a branch of Tahiti Nui Travel, one of French Polynesia's largest agencies. It shares quarters and phone numbers with **Destinations Pacific,** which specializes in the Cook Islands and Fiji, so it sells packages to all three destinations.

Tahiti Vacations (310/337-1040 or 800/553-3477) offers packages to French Polynesia, the Cook Islands, and Fiji. Some of its one-week tours to Tahiti have cost as little as $700 in recent years, including air and hotel. The company is a subsidiary of Air Tahiti, French Polynesia's domestic airline. It also is the North American agent for AOM French Airlines, on which it often provides its least expensive packages to Tahiti.

BAGGAGE ALLOWANCES

A "weight system" applies on international flights except to or from the United States and its territories (such as American Samoa). First-class and business-class passengers are limited to 30kg (66 lbs.) of checked baggage and economy-class passengers to 20kg (44 lbs).

A "piece system" applies to all flights to or from the United States and its territories. All passengers are limited to two checked bags without regard to weight but with size limitations: when added together, the three dimensions (length, height, depth) of any one first- or business-class bag must not exceed 158cm (62 in.) in length. Economy-class passengers may check two bags whose total measurements do not exceed 270cm (106 in.), with the larger of the two not more than 158cm (62 in.).

For example, if you fly Los Angeles–Papeete–Fiji–Honolulu–Los Angeles, the piece system applies only on the Los Angeles–Papeete, Fiji–Honolulu, and

Honolulu–Los Angeles segments. The weight system applies to Papeete–Rarotonga and Rarotonga–Fiji. In other words, pack according to the weight restrictions.

In addition to a small handbag or purse, all international passengers are permitted one carry-on bag with total measurements not exceeding 115cm (45 in.).

Most domestic air carriers in the islands limit their baggage allowance to 10kg (22 lbs.). Check with the individual airlines to avoid showing up at the check-in counter with too much luggage. Most hotels in the main towns have storage facilities where you can safely leave your extra bags during your side trips.

JET LAG

Flying the long distances to the South Pacific islands invariably translates into jet lag. There are probably as many theories about what to do for this condition as there are travelers. Some people advise trying to adjust to destination time before leaving home by getting up early or sleeping late. Others say you shouldn't eat or drink alcoholic beverages on the plane. Still others advise not sleeping during the flight. Air New Zealand says you should drink lots of nonalcoholic fluids to counter dehydration that takes place at high altitudes, eat lightly, and exercise occasionally by walking up and down the aisle (all those fluids probably will send you to the rear of the plane whether you're in the mood to exercise or not).

Since I live in Virginia, I try to break my transpacific trips by stopping in either Los Angeles or Honolulu for at least one good night's sleep. I also make every effort to schedule flights during the daylight hours (I sometimes think the airlines' schedulers must be a bunch of sadists, since so many transpacific flights are overnighters). When I have no choice but to fly overnight, I eat lightly, put on my inflatable neck cushion, and try to sleep as much as possible, comforted by visions of lazing the next morning away on a South Pacific beach.

BY SHIP

Although the days of the great ocean liners are long gone, occasionally it may be possible to cross the Pacific on a cruise ship making an around-the-world voyage or being repositioned, say, from Alaska to Australia. Most of them, however, steam through the islands for a week or two at a time from a home port such as Papeete or Sydney. They are usually underway at night, with visits to the islands during the day.

Passengers fly to the home port, enjoy the cruise, and fly home, which means that cruises are no longer only for the idle rich with time on their hands. The cruise companies usually offer some form of reduced air fares on these "fly-and-cruise" vacations, so you'll save over the cost of booking the air and cruise separately. Many operators also offer land packages that enable their passengers to stay over for a few days or a week at a hotel at or near the home port, usually for a reduced rate.

The cruise price ordinarily includes all meals and double-occupancy stateroom or cabin, although their fares vary with the size and position of the quarters. You can save money by booking one of the smaller interior cabins on the lower decks. You won't have a porthole, but I can tell you from having served in the U.S. Navy that the lower amidship cabins tend to ride more smoothly than those on the outside of the upper decks.

Three very popular cruises operate in French Polynesia and Fiji: the *Windsong* and *Club Med 2* out of Papeete, and the six vessels of Blue Lagoon Cruises out of Lautoka, Fiji. See Chapters 4 and 13.

Most other South Pacific cruise ships sail from ports in Australia and New Zealand, and visit the islands in the western South Pacific such as Vanuatu, Fiji, and Tonga. Their itineraries tend to change from season to season, and there's not space here to describe every possibility and price. For more information, contact a travel agent or the following companies that operate cruise ships in the South Pacific:

Princess Cruises (☎ 310/553-1770 or 800/421-0522); **Royal Cruise Line** (☎ 415/956-7200 or 800/227-4534); **Royal Caribbean Cruise Line** (☎ 305/539-6000 or 800/327-6700); **Cunard Line** (☎ 212/880-7500 or 800/221-4770), whose ships include the *Queen Elizabeth II*; **Abercrombie and Kent** (☎ 708/954-2944 or 800/323-7308), which specializes in nature- and culture-oriented cruises; **Orient Lines** (☎ 305/527-6660 or 800/333-7300); and **Holland America Line** (☎ 205/281-3535 or 800/258-7245).

8 Suggested Itineraries

People often ask where I would go on a vacation in the South Pacific. It's a difficult question for me to answer. I am fond of the dramatic, breathtaking scenery of French Polynesia, the liveliness of the Cook Islanders, the ancient cultures of Western Samoa and Tonga, the great variety of things to do in Fiji, and the enormously friendly people everywhere.

If you want to see it all, give yourself several busy months of island hopping. If you have only one week, then your time will best be spent in just one island country. Several companies offer attractively priced packages to individual countries, so you will save that way. If you have two or three weeks, here are some suggestions to consider.

FIJI–RAROTONGA–TAHITI

One of the easier and less expensive ways to sample the South Pacific is to fly with Air New Zealand over its "Coral Route," from Tahiti to Rarotonga to Fiji, or vice versa. Air New Zealand pioneered this route in the days of flying boats, and one of its jumbo jets now does it once a week, leaving Auckland early in the morning and ending in Papeete about midnight. The plane turns around and returns by the same route the following day, so it's possible to do this trip in either direction.

Since the Coral Route is a once-a-week proposition, you will have to spend seven days in the Cook Islands. For a three-week trip, add to that a week in Fiji and another in French Polynesia. Depending on flight connections, you can shorten your stays in Fiji and Tahiti. As a variation, you can cut out Tahiti altogether and reduce your time in the Cook Islands by flying directly to Rarotonga from Los Angeles, Honolulu, or Auckland. See the section on airline fares, above, for information about Air New Zealand's excellent excursion fare over this route.

I highly recommend this itinerary because it gives a good sampling of Melanesia and the transplanted Indian culture in Fiji, of English-speaking Polynesia in the Cook Islands, and of Polynesia with a French overlay in Tahiti and its islands.

THE SAMOAS AND TONGA

A tour through the "Bible Belt" of Polynesia includes Western Samoa, nearby American Samoa, and the Kingdom of Tonga, the last of the South Pacific's monarchies. All three are very conservative, but by being so, they have maintained their traditional Polynesian cultures.

You can tour American Samoa in a day, so make your base in Western Samoa with its relatively unchanged Polynesian way of life. Tonga is worth a visit just to see all 300-plus pounds of King Tupou IV. His friendly subjects will see that you enjoy your time in the realm.

Air New Zealand flies directly to Western Samoa and Tonga from Los Angeles via Honolulu, or you can go on Air Pacific's Pacific Pass or on the Triangle Fare using Air Pacific and Royal Tongan Airlines.

FIJI–TONGA–THE SAMOAS

These three countries offer diversity, friendly people, fine beaches, reefs, and tropical scenery. Fiji is by far the larger of the countries, so give yourself more time there.

Air Pacific's Pacific Pass, and the Triangle Fare using Air Pacific to Tonga or Apia and Royal Tongan Airlines between the two, make visits combining Fiji, Tonga, and Western Samoa attractive, as do each country's reasonably priced accommodations and restaurants. The most expeditious routing is Fiji–Tonga on Air Pacific, Tonga–Apia on Royal Tongan Airlines or Polynesian Airlines, and Apia–Fiji on Air Pacific.

THE BACKPACKING TRAIL

Backpackers will have lots of company while traveling the islands on a shoe-string, just as I did back in the 1970s: Young Australians and New Zealanders frolicking on school breaks, Canadians going or coming from work Down Under, Europeans out to see the world. Except in Fiji, which is well equipped for low-budgeteers, the number of low-end properties is limited. The result: a narrow "trail" of backpackers traveling through the islands. Once on the trail, you very quickly will meet fellow travelers coming from the opposite direction who will clue you in on which places are clean and friendly, who's offering the best scuba diving prices, and so on.

The most popular low-budget journey is from Tahiti to Rarotonga to Fiji, or vice versa, the itinerary I describe above. Because Tahiti is the most expensive South Pacific destination from a backpacker's standpoint, most people spend less time there before moving on for a week or two in the Cooks, then on for a longer stay in Fiji, where prices for food and transportation, as well as for accommodation, are more reasonable.

Another popular route includes stops in the Samoas and Tonga between the United States and New Zealand or Australia.

9 Saving on Hotels

The South Pacific has a wide range of accommodations, from deluxe resort hotels on their own islands to mom-and-pop guesthouses and dormitories with bunk beds.

TYPES OF ROOMS

My favorite type of hotel accommodates its guests in individual bungalows set in a coconut grove beside a sandy beach and quiet lagoon. In French Polynesia some of these super-romantic bungalows actually stand on stilts out over the reef. Others are as basic as a tent. In between they vary in size, furnishings, and comfort. In all, you enjoy the privacy of your own place, one usually built or accented with thatch and other native materials but containing most of the modern conveniences. Few of these accommodations are air conditioned, but they do have ceiling fans. Hotels of this style are widespread in the South Pacific.

With the exception of French Polynesia, the major tourist markets for the island countries are Australia and New Zealand. Accordingly, the vast majority of hotels are tailored to Aussie and Kiwi tastes, expectations, and uses of the English language.

Unlike the usual American hotel room, which likely has two humongous beds, the standard "Down Under" room has a double bed and a single bed that also serves as a settee. The room may or may not have a bathtub but always has a shower. There may be no washcloths (bring your own), but there will be tea and instant coffee and an electric "jug" to heat water for same. Televisions are becoming more numerous but are not yet common, but most hotels have radios whose selections are limited to the one, two, or three stations on the island.

Rooms are known to South Pacific reservation desks as "singles" if one person books them regardless of the number and size of beds they have. Singles are slightly less expensive than other rooms. Units are "doubles" if they have a double bed and are reserved for two persons who intend to sleep together in that bed. On the other hand, "twins" have two twin beds; they are known as "shared twins" if two unmarried people book them and don't intend to sleep together. Third and fourth occupants of any room usually are charged an additional few dollars on top of the double or shared twin rates.

Some hotel rooms, especially in Rarotonga and the Cook Islands, have kitchenettes equipped with a small refrigerator (the "fridge"), hotplates (the "cooker"), pots, pans, crockery, silverware, and cooking utensils. Establishments with cooking facilities but no restaurants often call themselves "motels" rather than hotels, especially in the Cook Islands. Having the kitchenette can result in quite a saving on breakfasts and light meals.

MONEY-SAVING TIPS

You can save on many hotel rooms by booking them through the airlines. One example is **Hotpac,** an Air New Zealand subsidiary that offers savings at a number of establishments everywhere that airline goes. You book and pay for the rooms ahead through Air New Zealand's offices and agents. Ask Air New Zealand for one of its Hotpac brochures listing the hotels and rates.

The rates quoted in this book are known in the hotel industry as "rack" or "published" rates, that is, the maximum a property charges for a room. Hotels pay travel agents and wholesalers as much as 30% of these rack rates for sending clients their way. If business is slow, some hotels may give you the benefit of at least part of this commission if you book directly instead of going through an airline or travel agent. Most also have "local" rates for islanders, which they may extend to visitors during slow periods. It never hurts to ask politely for a discounted or local rate.

Some less expensive hotels that take credit cards may reduce their rates if you offer to pay cash. If you're going to spend a week or more at one hotel, ask about long-term rates or discounts.

Also ask how much the hotel charges for local and long-distance calls, for surcharges can more than double the cost. If so, make your calls at a post office or pay phone.

Most South Pacific countries charge a room tax—or in the case of Fiji, a value added tax (VAT). Inquire whether these taxes are included in the quoted rate. The "Fast Facts" in the country chapters give the amount of tax charged.

4 Introducing French Polynesia

Perhaps more than any other South Pacific island, Tahiti is associated with the magical image of an idyllic tropical paradise. Such has been the case since canoeloads of young Tahitian *vahines* gave uninhibited, barebreasted receptions to the European explorers of the late 1700s. Today Tahiti is the largest and most heavily populated island in French Polynesia, and its name often is used synonymously with this overseas territory of France.

Some visitors may be surprised to find the territory's capital of Papeete to have grown from a legendary, languid little backwater port into a busy city clogged with cars and scooters. Papeete's sleazy bars and stage-set wooden Chinese stores have been replaced by chic bistros and high-rise shopping centers, and its cheap waterfront hotels by the glass and steel of luxury resorts out on the edge of town.

Beyond Papeete, the awesome beauty of these islands is unsurpassed anywhere in the world. On Moorea, Bora Bora, Huahine, and Tahiti's other companion islands, today's visitors will witness the other-worldly mountain peaks, multihued lagoons, and palm-draped beaches that have come to symbolize the South Pacific.

1 French Polynesia Today

French Polynesia sprawls over an area of two million square miles in the eastern South Pacific. That's about the size of Europe, excluding the former Soviet Union, or about two-thirds the size of the continental United States. The 130 main islands, however, consist of only 1,500 square miles, an area smaller than Rhode Island, with a population of 200,000 or so.

The Islands Within this huge area lie five major archipelagos that differ in terrain, climate, and to a certain extent, people. With the exception of the Tuamotus, an enormous chain of low coral atolls northeast of Tahiti, all but a few are high islands, the mountainous tops of ancient volcanoes that have been eroded into jagged peaks, deep bays, and fertile valleys. All have fringing or barrier coral reefs and blue lagoons worthy of postcards.

The most strikingly beautiful and most frequently visited are the **Society Islands,** so named by Capt. James Cook because they lay relatively close together. These include **Tahiti** and its nearby companion **Moorea,** which also are known as the Windward Islands

What's Special About French Polynesia

Great Towns/Villages
- Papeete, Tahiti's storied port, now a bustling little city.
- Huahine's main village, Fare, full of old South Seas charm.

Ancient Monuments
- Polynesian *marae,* temples of rock and stone that hauntingly evoke the old religion.

Museums
- Museum of Tahiti and Her Isles, one of the South Pacific's best.
- The Gauguin Museum, which doesn't contain many of the great painter's works but captures his time in Polynesia.

Events
- *Heiva I Tahiti,* Bastille Day turned into a rollicking, month-long good time, with incredible dancing.

Natural Spectacles
- The mountains on Moorea and Bora Bora: Green-shrouded ridges and jagged peaks soar to the clouds.
- The lagoons of Bora Bora and Rangiroa—water shouldn't be this clear or colorful.
- There's surf on Tahiti's black beaches; waves lap white sand elsewhere.

Shopping
- A wide selection of the world's best black pearls, produced in the Tuamotu Islands.
- Tropical clothing drapes every body with a rainbow of colors.

After Dark
- Tahitian dance shows—find out why there was a mutiny on the *Bounty.*

because they sit to the east, the direction of the prevailing trade wind. To the northwest lie **Bora Bora, Huahine, Raiatea, Tahaa, Maupiti,** and several smaller islands. Because they are downwind of Tahiti, they also are called the Leeward Islands.

To James A. Michener's eye, Bora Bora is the most beautiful island in the world. Others give that title to Moorea in a close race. It's all a matter of degree, for the Society Islands definitely are the world's most dramatically beautiful collection of islands.

One of the world's largest collections of atolls, the 69 low-lying **Tuamotu Islands** run for 720 miles on a line from northwest to southeast, across the approaches to Tahiti from the east. The early European sailors called them the "Dangerous Archipelago" because of their tricky currents and because they virtually cannot be seen until a ship is almost on top of them. Even today they are a wrecking ground for yachts and inter-island trading boats. Two of them, Moruroa and Fangataufa, are used by France to test its nuclear weapons. Others provide the bulk of Tahiti's well-known black pearls. **Rangiroa,** the world's second-largest atoll and the territory's best scuba diving destination, is the most frequently visited.

It is no exaggeration to say, that to a European of any sensibility, who, for the first time, wanders back into these valleys—away from the haunts of the natives—the ineffable repose and beauty of the landscape is such, that every object strikes him like something seen in a dream; and for a time he almost refuses to believe that scenes like these should have a commonplace existence.

—Herman Melville, 1847

The **Marquesas,** a group of 10 high islands, sit beyond the Tuamotus some 750 miles northeast of Tahiti. They are younger than the Society Islands, and protecting coral reefs have not enclosed them. As a result, the surf pounds on their shores, there are no encircling coastal plains, and the people live in a series of deep valleys that radiate out from central mountain peaks. The Marquesas have lost their once-large populations to 19th-century disease and the 20th-century economic lure of Papeete; today their sparsely populated, cloud-enshrouded valleys have an almost haunted air about them.

The **Austral Islands** south of Tahiti are part of a chain of high islands that continues westward into the Cook Islands. The people of the more temperate Australs, which include Rurutu, Raivavae, and Tubuai (where the Bounty mutineers tried to settle), once produced some of the best art objects in the South Pacific, but these skills have passed into time.

Far on the southern end of the Tuamotu Archipelago, the **Gambier Islands** are part of a semisubmerged, middle-aged high island similar to Bora Bora. The hilly remnants of the old volcano are scattered in a huge lagoon, which is partially enclosed by a barrier reef marking the original outline of the island before it began to sink. The largest of these remnant islands is Mangareva.

Government French Polynesians elect 30 members of a Territorial Assembly, which in turns selects its own president, the territory's highest-ranking local official (who often is referred to as the President of French Polynesia). The Assembly and its Council of Ministers decide most issues affecting the territory, while the metropolitan French government decides matters of defense, justice, national police, and foreign affairs. The voters also cast ballots in French presidential elections and choose two elected deputies and a senator to the French parliament in Paris.

Metropolitan France also plays a significant role in law enforcement. The city of Papeete and a few other *communes* have their own police forces, but French *gendarmes* are in control of many parts of the territory. The man wearing the round de Gaulle hat who stops you for riding a motorbike without a helmet is more likely to be from Martinique than from Moorea.

There is a small but active movement that would like to see the territory free of France. The village of Faaa surrounding the airport on Tahiti is a hotbed of such pro-independence sentiment. You'll also see more English used in Faaa than anywhere else, as evidenced by stores with American-sounding English names, such as "Cash and Carry," "Magic City," and "Kiddy Shop."

Economy The territory's major industries are tourism and black pearls. Otherwise, very little is produced or grown locally, including most foodstuffs. The territory would be bankrupt were it not for billions of francs poured in by the French government.

The Society Islands

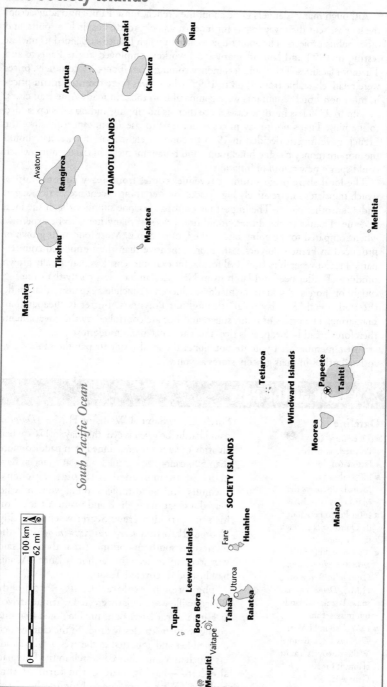

Although many islanders gripe about the French, most Tahitians readily accept the largesse sent their way to pay for modern schools, roads, hospitals, airports, and other public projects. The good times took a hit when France suspended its nuclear testing in 1992 and laid off many local workers employed at the Papeete and Tuamotu facilities. The result: less money coming from France. Accordingly, prices were relatively stable from 1988 to 1995 (when I was there recently, menu prices in most non-hotel restaurants were comparable to those in many American cities, and up to 23% less in some cases since there is no tipping and no sales tax added to the bill). That's not to say prices won't start to rise again, especially since the French government decided in 1995 to conduct eight more tests. That should mean more money chasing hotel rooms and restaurant meals in the territory, which could spur a new round of inflation.

The local share of government revenues comes from heavy customs duties, which translates into relatively high prices for everything except bread, rice, sugar, and a few other basics. The import tax on tobacco alone supplies 7% of the local revenue. Thanks to the duties, you'll find prices of many items to be expensive when compared to the going rate in the United States. Most foodstuffs grown or produced in French Polynesia are more expensive than their imported counterparts. Frozen vegetables from California, for example, cost less than locally grown produce. Tender beef and lamb from New Zealand are less costly than the fish caught offshore and sold in the markets. Chicken is much less expensive than pork, the traditional "Sunday meal" throughout Polynesia. Butter is cheaper than margarine. The prices of flour, sugar, and rice are controlled by the government; therefore, bread is cheap, as is rice, the Tahitians' main modern staple.

Just remember that you are not alone; the local residents pay the same duty-inflated prices in their grocery stores as you will.

2 A Look at the Past

Dateline

- 6th century A.D. Polynesians arrive (estimated time).
- 1595 Alvaro de Medadā discovers the Marquesas Islands.
- 1606 Pedro Fernández de Quirós sails through the Tuamotus.
- 1765 Searching for *terra australis incognita*, Capt. John Byron on H.M.S. *Dolphin* finds some Tuamotu islands but misses Tahiti.
- 1767 Also in H.M.S. *Dolphin*, Capt. Samuel Wallis discovers Tahiti, claims it for King George III.

continues

Surely Capt. Samuel Wallis of H.M.S. *Dolphin* could hardly believe his eyes that day in 1767 when an army of large brown-skinned men paddled more than 500 canoes across the lagoon at Matavai Bay, many of them loaded with pigs, chickens, coconuts, fruit, and topless young women "who played a great many droll and wanton tricks" on his scurvy-ridden crew. Secretly sent by King George III to find *terra australis incognita*—the mysterious southern continent that theorists said was necessary to keep the earth in balance—Wallis had instead discovered Tahiti.

The French explorer Louis Antoine de Bougainville was similarly greeted when he arrived at Hitiaa a year later. Bougainville noted that one young woman "carelessly dropped the cloth which covered her and appeared to the eyes of all beholders much as Venus showed herself to the Phrygian shepherd—having indeed the form of that goddess." With visions of Aphrodite, the Greek goddess of love, Bougainville promptly named his discovery New Cythère in honor of her hometown. It has ever since been known as The Island of Love.

Bougainville stayed at Hitiaa only 10 days, but he took back to France a young Tahitian named Ahutoru, who became a sensation in Paris as living proof of Jean-Jacques Rousseau's theory that man was at his best a "noble savage." Indeed, Bougainville and Ahutoru gave Tahiti a hedonistic image that has survived to this day.

The real Venus played a role in Tahiti's history when Capt. James Cook arrived in 1769 on the first of his three great voyages of discovery to the South Pacific. Cook's job was to measure the transit of the planet across the face of the sun, which if successful would enable navigators for the first time to accurately measure longitude on the earth's surface. Cook set up an observation point on a sandy spit on Tahiti's north shore, a locale he appropriately named Point Venus. His measurements were of little use, but Cook remained in Tahiti for six months. His studies of the island contributed greatly to the world's understanding of Polynesian cultures.

Cook used Tahiti as a base during his two subsequent voyages, during which he disproved the southern continent theory, discovered numerous islands, and charted much of the South Pacific.

The Breadfruit Mutiny   Capt. William Bligh, one of Cook's navigators, returned to Matavai Bay in 1788 in command of H.M.S. *Bounty* on a mission to procure breadfruit as cheap food for plantation slaves in Jamaica. One of Bligh's handpicked officers was a former shipmate, Fletcher Christian.

Delayed by storms off Cape Horn, Bligh missed the breadfruit season and had to wait on Tahiti for six months until his cargo could be transplanted. Christian and some of the crew apparently didn't want to leave, so much had they enjoyed the island's women and easygoing lifestyle. For whatever reason, the *Bounty's* 1,015 breadfruit plantings made it only to Tonga before Christian staged a mutiny on April 28, 1789. He set Bligh and 18 of his loyal officers and crewmen adrift in a longboat with a compass, a cask of water, and a few provisions.

Christian sailed the *Bounty* back to Tahiti, where he put ashore 25 other crew members who were loyal to Bligh. After searching unsuccessfully for a hiding place, the mutineers returned to Tahiti for the last time. Christian, eight mutineers,

- 1768 French Capt. Antoine de Bougainville discovers Tahiti.
- 1769 Capt. James Cook arrives to observe the transit of Venus on the first of his three voyages of discovery.
- 1788 H.M.S. *Bounty* under Capt. William Bligh arrives to take breadfruit to the Caribbean.
- 1789 Lt. Fletcher Christian leads the mutiny on the *Bounty*.
- 1797 London Missionary Society emissaries arrive looking for converts.
- 1827 Queen Pomare IV succeeds to the throne.
- 1837 Protestants deny French Catholic priests permission to land. Irate France demands full reparations.
- 1838 Queen reluctantly signs ultimatum of French Adm. du Petit-Thouars.
- 1841 French traders trick Tahitian chiefs into asking for French protection. They later disavow it.
- 1842 Tahiti becomes a French protectorate. Herman Melville jumps ship, spends time in the *Calaboosa Beretane* (British jail). He later writes *Omoo* about his adventures.
- 1844–48 Tahitians wage guerilla war against the French.
- 1847 Queen Pomare acquiesces to full French protection.
- 1862 Irish adventurer William Stewart starts a cotton plantation at Atimaono.
- 1865 The first 329 Chinese arrive from Hong Kong to work Stewart's plantation. It fails, but most of them stay.

continues

- 1872 Pierre Loti (Julian Viaud) spends several months on Tahiti. His *The Marriage of Loti* is published eight years later.
- 1877 Queen Pomare IV dies at age 64.
- 1880 King Pomare V abdicates in return for pensions for him, his family, and mistress. Tahiti becomes a French colony.
- 1888 Robert Louis Stevenson spends two months at Tautira on Tahiti Iti.
- 1891 "Fleeing from civilization," the painter Paul Gauguin arrives.
- 1903 Paul Gauguin dies at Hiva Oa in the Marquesas, apparently of syphilis. All of eastern Polynesia becomes one French colony.
- 1914 Two German warships shell Papeete, sink the French navy's *Zélée*.
- 1917 W. Somerset Maugham spends several months on Tahiti.
- 1933 *Mutiny on the Bounty* is published, becomes a best-seller.
- 1935 Clark Gable and Charles Laughton star in the movie *Mutiny on the Bounty*.
- 1942 U.S. Marines build the territory's first airstrip on Bora Bora.
- 1960 Faaa International Airport opens, turning Tahiti into a jet-set destination. Marlon Brando arrives to film a second movie version of *Mutiny on the Bounty*.
- 1963 France chooses Mururoa as its nuclear testing site.
- 1966 France explodes the first nuclear bomb above ground at Mururoa.

continues

their Tahitian wives, and six Tahitian men then disappeared.

In one of the epic open-boat voyages of all time, Bligh and his crew miraculously made it back to England via the Dutch East Indies, thence to England, whereupon the Royal Navy sent H.M.S. *Pandora* to Tahiti to search for the *Bounty*. It found only the crewmen still there. Four eventually were acquitted. Three were convicted but pardoned, including Peter Heywood, who wrote the first English-Tahitian dictionary while awaiting court martial. Three others were hanged.

The captain of an American whaling ship that happened upon remote Pitcairn Island in 1808 was astonished when some mixed race teenagers rowed out and greeted him not in Tahitian but in perfect English. They were the children of the mutineers, only one of whom was still alive.

Bligh collected more breadfruit on Tahiti a few years later, but his whole venture went for naught when the slaves on Jamaica insisted on rice.

The Fatal Impact The discoverers brought many changes to Tahiti, starting with iron, which the Tahitians had never seen, and barter, which they had never practiced. The Tahitians figured out right away that iron was much harder than stone and shells, and that they could swap pigs, breadfruit, bananas, and the affections of their young women for it. Iron cleats, spikes, and nails soon took on a value of their own, and so many of them disappeared from the *Dolphin* that Wallis finally restricted his men to the ship out of fear it would fall apart in Matavai Bay. A rudimentary form of monetary economy was introduced to Polynesia for the first time. The English word "money" soon entered the Tahitian language as *moni*.

Wars were fought hand-to-hand with sticks and clubs until the *Bounty* mutineers hiding on Tahiti loaned themselves and their guns to rival chiefs, who for the first time were able to extend their control beyond their home valleys. With the mutineers' help, chief Pomare II came to control half of Tahiti and all of Moorea.

A much more devastating European import were diseases such as measles, influenza, pneumonia, and syphilis, to which the islanders had no resistance. Captain Cook estimated Tahiti's population at some 200,000 in 1769. By 1810 it had dropped to less than 8,000.

Converts and Clothes   The first missionaries sent to Tahiti by the London Missionary Society arrived on March 5, 1797, aboard the ship *Duff*. They toiled for 15 years before making their first convert, and even that was only accomplished with the help of Chief Pomare II. The missionaries thought he was king of Tahiti, but in reality Pomare II was locked in battle to extend his rule and to become just that. He converted to Christianity primarily to win the missionaries' support, and with it, he quickly gained control of the entire island. The people then made the easy intellectual transition from their primary god Taaroa to the missionaries' supreme being. They put on clothes and began going to church.

- 1973 Infamous Quinn's Bar closes, is replaced by a shopping center.
- 1977 France grants limited self-rule to French Polynesia.
- 1984 Local autonomy statute enacted by French parliament.
- 1992 France halts nuclear testing, hurting local economy.
- 1995 Conservative French President Jacques Chirac plans eight more nuclear tests.

The Protestant missionaries had a free hand on Tahiti for almost 30 years. There were few ordained ministers among them, for most were tradesmen sent to Tahiti to teach the natives useful Western skills, which the London Missionary Society considered essential for the Tahitians' successful transition to devout, industrious Christians in the mold of working-class Englishmen and women. Some of the missionaries stayed and went into business on their own (some island cynics say they "came to do good and stayed to do well").

The Tricked Queen   The Protestant monopoly ended when the first Roman Catholic priests arrived on the scene from France in the 1830s. The Protestants immediately saw a threat, and in 1836 they engineered the interlopers' expulsion by Queen Pomare IV, the illegitimate daughter of Pomare II, who by then had succeeded to the throne created by her father.

When word of this outrage reached Paris, France sent a warship to Tahiti to demand a guarantee that Frenchmen would thereafter be treated as the "most favored foreigners" in Tahiti. Queen Pomare politely agreed, but as soon as the warship left Papeete, she sent a letter to Queen Victoria asking for British protection. Britain declined to interfere, which opened the door for a Frenchman to trick several Tahitian chiefs into signing a document requesting that Tahiti be made a protectorate of France. The French were in fact interested in a South Pacific port, and when word of the document reached Paris, a ship was dispatched to Papeete. Tahiti became a French protectorate in 1842.

Unaware of the document signed by the chiefs, Queen Pomare continued to resist. Her subjects launched an armed rebellion against the French troops, who surrounded her Papeete palace and forced her to retreat to Raiatea. The fighting continued until 1846, when the last Tahitian stronghold was captured and the remnants of their guerrilla bands retreated to Tahiti Iti, the island's eastern

Impressions

The reputation of Pomaree is not what it ought to be. She, and also her mother, were, for a long time, excommunicated members of the Church; and the former, I believe, still is. Among other things, her conjugal fidelity is far from being unquestioned. Indeed, it was upon this ground, chiefly, that she was excluded from the communion of the Church.
—Herman Melville, 1847

Sexy Skin

America isn't the only home of trendy tattoos. With their increasing interest in the ancient Polynesian ways, many young Tahitian men and women are getting theirs—but not with the modern electric needles used elsewhere.

Tattooing was unknown in Europe when the 18th-century explorers arrived in Tahiti. They were shocked, therefore, to find many Polynesians on Tahiti and throughout the South Pacific to be covered from face to ankle with a plethora of geometric and floral designs. In his journal, Capt. James Cook described in detail the excruciatingly painful tattoo procedure, in which natural dies are hammered into the skin by hand. The repetitive tapping of the mallet gave rise to the Tahitian word *tatau*, which became tattoo in English.

Any Tahitian with plain old skin was rejected by members of the opposite sex, which may explain why members of Cook's crew were so willing to endure the torture to get theirs. At any rate, they began the tradition of the tattooed sailor.

Appalled at the sexual aspects of tattoos, the missionaries stamped out the practice on Tahiti in the early 1800s. Although the art continued in the remote Marquesas and in Samoa, by 1890 there were no tattooed natives left in the Society Islands.

When a British anthropologist undertook a study of tattooing in 1900, the only specimen he could find was in the Royal College of Surgeons. It had been worn by a Tahitian sailor, who died in England in 1816. Before he was buried, an art-loving physician removed his skin and donated it to the college.

peninsula. A monument to the fallen Tahitians now stands beside the round-island road near the airport at Faaa, the village still noted for its strong pro-independence sentiment.

Giving up the struggle in 1847, the queen returned to Papeete and ruled as a figurehead until her death 30 years later. Her son, Pomare V, who liked the bottle more than the throne, ruled three more years until abdicating in return for a sizable French pension for him, his family, and his mistress. Tahiti then became a full-fledged French colony. In 1903 all of eastern Polynesia was consolidated into a single colony known as French Oceania, which it remained until 1957, when its status was changed to the overseas territory of French Polynesia.

A Blissful Backwater   Except for periodic invasions by artists and writers, French Polynesia remained an idyllic backwater from the time France took complete possession until the early 1960s.

French painter Paul Gauguin gave up his family and his career as a Parisian stockbroker and arrived in 1891; he spent his days reproducing Tahiti's colors and people on canvas until he died in 1903 on Hiva Oa in the Marquesas Islands. Stories and novels by writers such as W. Somerset Maugham, Jack London, Robert Louis Stevenson, and Rupert Brooke added to Tahiti's romantic reputation during the early years of this century. In 1932 two young Americans—Charles Nordhoff and James Norman Hall—published *Mutiny on the Bounty,* which quickly became an enormous bestseller. Three years later MGM released an even more successful movie version with Clark Gable and Charles Laughton in the roles of Christian and Bligh, respectively.

The book and movie brought fame to Tahiti, but any plans for increased tourism were put on hold during World War II. Local partisans sided with the Free French, who gave permission for the United States to use the islands in the war against Japan. In 1942 some 6,000 U.S. sailors and marines quickly built the territory's first airstrip on Bora Bora and remained there throughout the war. A number of mixed-race Tahitians are descended from those American troops.

Movies and Bombs   Even after the war, the islands were too far away and too difficult to reach to attract more than the most adventurous or wealthy travelers who arrived by ocean liner or by seaplane. Then two early 1960s events brought rapid changes to most of French Polynesia.

First, Tahiti's new international airport opened at Faaa in late 1960. Shortly thereafter, Marlon Brando and a movie crew arrived to film a remake of *Mutiny on the Bounty*. This new burst of fame, coupled with the ability to reach Tahiti overnight on the new long-range jets, transformed the island into a jet-set destination, and hotel construction began in earnest.

Second, France established the *Centre d'Experimentation du Pacifique,* its nuclear testing facility in the Tuamotus, about 700 miles southeast of Tahiti. A huge support base was constructed on the outskirts of Papeete.

Together, tourism and the nuclear testing facility brought a major boom to Tahiti almost overnight. Thousands of Polynesians flocked to Papeete to take the new construction and hotel jobs, which enabled them to earn good money and experience life in Papeete's fast lane.

In addition, some 15,000 French military personnel and civilian technicians swarmed into the territory to man the new nuclear testing facility, all of them with money and many with an inclination to spend it on the local girls. The Tahitian men struck back, brawls erupted, and for a brief period in the 1960s the island experienced one of its rare moments of open hostility between the Tahitian majority and the French.

That's not to say there weren't hard feelings all along. An independence movement had existed since the guerrilla skirmishes of the 1840s, and by the 1970s it forced France to choose between serious unrest or granting the territory a much larger degree of control over its internal affairs. In 1977 the French parliament created an elected Territorial Assembly with powers over the local budget. The vice president of the Assembly was the highest elected local official. A High Commissioner sent from Paris, however, retained authority over defense, foreign affairs, immigration, the police, civil service, communications, and secondary education. This system lasted until 1984, when the French Parliament set up the present system.

3 The Islanders

About 70% of French Polynesia's population of 200,000 are Polynesian. About 4% are of Asian descent (primarily Chinese), and some 14% are of mixed races. The rest are mostly French and a few other Europeans, Americans, Australians, and New Zealanders.

Members of the Polynesian majority are known as Tahitians, although persons born on the other islands do not necessarily consider themselves to be "Tahitians" and sometimes gripe about this overgeneralization. They all are called Tahitians, however, because more than 70% of the territory's population live on Tahiti, and because the Polynesian language originally spoken only on Tahiti and Moorea has become the territory's second official language (French is the other).

Of the approximately 150,000 persons who live on Tahiti, some 90,000 reside in or near Papeete. No other village in the islands has a population in excess of 4,000.

THE TAHITIANS

Many Tahitians now refer to themselves as *Maohi* (the Tahitian counterpart of *Maori)*, a result of an increasing awareness of their unique ancient culture. Their ancestors came to Tahiti as part of a great Polynesian migration that fanned out from Southeast Asia to much of the South Pacific. These early settlers brought along food plants, domestic animals, tools, and weapons. By the time Capt. Samuel Wallis arrived in 1767, Tahiti and the other islands were lush with breadfruit, bananas, taro, yams, sweet potatoes, and other crops. Most of the people lived on the fertile coastal plains and in the valleys behind them, each valley or district ruled by a chief. Wallis counted 17 chiefdoms on Tahiti alone.

Society Tahitians were highly stratified into three classes: chiefs and priests, landowners, and commoners. Among the commoners was a subclass of slaves, mostly war prisoners. One's position in society was hereditary, with primogeniture the general rule. In general, women were equal to men, although they could not act as priests.

A peculiar separate class of wandering dancers and singers, known as the *Arioi*, traveled about the Society Islands performing ritual dances and shows—some of them sexually explicit—and living in a state of total sexual freedom. The children born to this class were killed at birth.

The Polynesians had no written language, but their life was governed by an elaborate set of rules that would challenge modern legislators' abilities to reduce them to writing. Most of these rules were prohibitions known as *tabu*, a word now used in English as "taboo." The rules differed from one class to another.

Religion The ancient Tahitians worshiped a hierarchy of gods. At its head stood Taaroa, a supreme deity known as Tangaroa in the Cook Islands and Tangaloa in Samoa. Below him was Tane, the god of all good and the friend of armies, and Tu, who was more or less the god of the status quo. *Mana*, or power, came down from the gods to each human, depending on his or her position in society. The highest chiefs had so much mana that they were considered godlike, if not actually descended from the gods. They lived according to special rules and spoke their own vocabularies. No one could touch them other than high-ranking priests, who cut their hair and fed them. If a high chief set foot on a plot of land, that land automatically belonged to him or her; consequently, servants carried them everywhere they went. If they uttered a word, that word became sacred and was never used again in the everyday language. When the first king of Tahiti

Impressions

I was pleased with nothing so much as with the inhabitants. There is a mildness in the expression of their countenances which at once banishes the idea of a savage, and an intelligence which shows that they are advancing in civilization.

—Charles Darwin, 1839

Impressions

He had once landed there [the Marquesas], and found the remains of a man and a woman partly eaten. On his starting and sickening at the sight, one of Moipu's young men picked up a human foot, and provocatively staring at the stranger, grinned and nibbled at the heel.

—Robert Louis Stevenson, 1890

decided to call himself Pomare, which means "night cough," the word for night— *po*—became tabu for a time. It isn't anymore.

The Tahitians worshipped their gods on *marae* built of stones and rocks. Every family had a small marae, which served the same functions as a chapel would today, and villages and entire districts—even islands—built large marae that served not only as places of worship but also as meeting sites. Elaborate religious ceremonies were held on the large central marae. Priests prayed that the gods would come down and reside in carved tikis and other objects during the ceremonies (the objects lost all religious meaning afterward). Sacrifices were offered to the gods, sometimes including humans, most of whom were war prisoners or troublemakers. Despite the practice of human sacrifice, cannibalism apparently was never practiced on Tahiti, although it was fairly widespread in the Marquesas Islands.

The souls of the deceased were believed to be taken by the gods to Hawaiki, the homeland from which their Polynesian ancestors had come. In all Polynesian islands, Hawaiki always lay in the direction of the setting sun, and the souls departed for it from the northwest corner of each island.

Sex The sexual freedom that intrigued the early European explorers permeated Tahitian society, although it was not without its limits. Except for the nobility, sex was restricted to one's own class. Teenagers generally were encouraged to have as many partners as they wanted from puberty to marriage so that they would learn the erotic skills necessary to make a good spouse. Even within marriage there was a certain latitude. Married men and women, for example, could have extramarital affairs with their sisters-in-law and brothers-in-law, respectively. Since first cousins were considered brothers and sisters, the opportunities for licensed adultery were numerous.

The old rules have disappeared, and sexual relations in Tahiti today are governed by a mishmash of morals. The coming of Christianity and its ethics has left Tahitians with as much guilt over adultery as anyone else. On the other hand, the European moral code was not accepted as readily as was the belief in God, and premarital sex has continued to be practiced widely in French Polynesia. Prostitution, which was unknown before the coming of the Europeans and their system of sex-for-nails, is widespread in Papeete's cash economy.

As in other Polynesian societies, homosexuality was accepted among a class of transvestites known as *mahu*, a fact that startled the early explorers and shocked the missionaries who followed. Mahus still abound in Papeete, especially at the nightclubs that cater to all sexual preferences and at the resort hotels, where the mahus perform as women in some dance reviews. Women were not considered equal in this respect in ancient times, however, and lesbianism was discouraged.

Note that the Acquired Immune Deficiency Syndrome (AIDS) virus is present in French Polynesia. Accordingly, visitors should exercise at least the same degree of caution and safe sex practices as they would at home.

THE CHINESE

The outbreak of the American Civil War in 1861 resulted in a worldwide shortage of cotton. In September 1862 an Irish adventurer named William Stewart founded a cotton plantation at Atimaono, Tahiti's only large tract of flat land. The Tahitians weren't the least bit interested in working for Stewart, so he imported a contingent of Chinese laborers. The first 329 of them arrived from Hong Kong in February 1865.

Stewart ran into difficulties, both with finances and with his workers. At one point, a rumor swept Tahiti that he had built a guillotine, practiced with it on a pig, and then executed a recalcitrant Chinese laborer. That was never proved, although a Chinese immigrant, Chim Soo, was the first person to be executed by guillotine in Tahiti. Stewart's financial difficulties, which were compounded by the drop in cotton prices after the American South resumed production after 1868, led to the collapse of his empire.

Nothing remains of his plantation at Atimaono (a golf course now occupies most of the land), but many of his Chinese laborers decided to stay. They grew vegetables for the Papeete market, saved their money, and invested in other businesses. Their descendants and subsequent immigrants from China now influence the economy far in excess of their numbers. They run nearly all of French Polynesia's grocery and general merchandise stores, which in French are called *magasins chinois,* or Chinese stores.

4 Language

The official languages in the territory are French and Tahitian. English is also taught as a second language in the schools, so communication is usually not a problem in shops, hotels, and restaurants. Once you get away from the beaten path, however, some knowledge of French or Tahitian is very helpful.

Tahitian is the language spoken in most homes in the Society Islands, although the old local dialects are used on a daily basis in the far outer islands. With the exception of some older Polynesians, everyone speaks French. Only after the Tahitians gained control over their own internal affairs in 1984 was their native tongue taught in the schools. This is one reason many pro-independence Tahitians view French as a symbol of colonial control over their islands.

TAHITIAN PRONUNCIATION

No Polynesian language was written until Peter Heywood jotted down a Tahitian vocabulary while awaiting trial for his part in the mutiny on the *Bounty.* The early missionaries who later translated the Bible into Tahitian decided which letters of the Roman alphabet to use to approximate the sounds of the Polynesian languages.

These tended to vary from place to place. For example, they used the consonants *t* and *v* in Tahitian. In Hawaiian, which is similar, they used *k* and *w*. The actual Polynesian sounds are somewhere in between.

The consonants used in Tahitian are *f, h, m, n, p, r, t,* and *v*. There are some special rules regarding their sounds, but you'll be understood if you say them as you would in English.

The Polynesian languages, including Tahitian, consist primarily of vowel sounds, which are pronounced in the Roman fashion—that is, *ah, ay, ee, oh,* and *ou,* not *ay, ee, eye, oh,* and *you,* as in English. Almost all vowels are sounded separately. For example, Tahiti's airport is at Faaa, which is pronounced Fah-ah-ah, not Fah. Papeete is Pah-pay-*ay*-tay, not Pa-pee-tee. Paea is Pah-*ay*-ah.

Westerners have had their impact, however, and today some vowels are run together. Moorea, for example, technically is Moh-oh-*ray*-ah, but nearly everyone says Mo-*ray*-ah. The Punaauia hotel district on Tahiti's west coast is pronounced Poo-*nav*-i-a.

Look for *Say It in Tahitian* (Pacific Publications, 1977), by D.T. Tryon, in the local bookshops and hotel boutiques. This slim volume will teach you more Tahitian than you can use in one vacation.

Useful Words

To help you impress the local residents with what a really friendly tourist you are, here are a few Tahitian words you can use on them:

English	Tahitian	Pronunciation
hello	ia orana	ee-ah oh-*rah*-na (sounds like "your honor")
welcome	maeva	mah-*ay*-vah
goodbye	parahi	pah-*rah*-hee
good	maitai	*my*-tie
very good	maitai roa	*my*-tie-*row*-ah
thank you	maruru	mah-*roo*-roo
thank you very much	maruru roa	mah-*roo*-roo *row*-ah
good health!	manuia	mah-*new*-yah
woman	vahine	vah-*hee*-nay
man	tane	*tah*-nay
sarong	pareu	pah-*ray*-oo
small islet	motu	*moh*-too
take it easy	hare maru	*ha*-ray *mah*-roo
fed up	fiu	few

5 Visitor Information & Entry Requirements

VISITOR INFORMATION

Other than this guide, your best source of information is **Tahiti Tourisme,** B.P. 65, Papeete, French Polynesia (☎ 50.57.00, fax 43.66.19). The main Papeete office is in Fare Manihini, the Polynesian-style building on the waterfront at the foot of rue Paul Gauguin on boulevard Pomare. The staff members all speak English and are very helpful to visitors, especially in providing such information as when trading boats will leave for the distant island groups. Hours are 7:30am to 5pm Monday to Friday, 8am to noon on Saturday. Other Tahiti Tourisme offices to contact are:

United States: 300 N. Colorado Blvd., Suite 180, El Segundo, CA 90245 (☎ 310/414-8484, fax 310/414-8490). There's a second office at 444 Madison Ave., 16th Floor, New York, NY 10022 (☎ 212/832-8780 or fax 212/838-7855).

Australia: 620 St. Kilda Rd., Suite 301, Melbourne, Vic. 3004 (☎ 03/ 521-3877, fax 08/521-3867).

New Zealand: 172 Wellesley St., P.O. Box 5, Auckland (☎ 09/373-2649, fax 09/373-2415).

France: 28 bd. Saint Germain, 75005 Paris (☎ 16/46.34.50.59, fax 16/ 46.33.82.54).

Germany: Haingasse 22, D-61348 Bad Hamburg v.d. H. (☎ 61/722-1021, fax 61/726-9048).

Low-budget travelers can request lists of all the territory's less expensive "unclassified" hotels, pensions, and campgrounds. These are compiled by island, so ask for the lists applicable to your specific destinations. Most owners of these establishments don't speak English, so some French on your part will be very helpful if you stay with them.

Local tourism committees have information booths on Moorea and Bora Bora.

ENTRY REQUIREMENTS

Most visitors are required to have a valid **passport** and a return or ongoing ticket. The immigration official may ask to see both. No **vaccinations** are required unless you are coming from a yellow fever, plague, or cholera area.

Visas valid for one month are issued upon arrival to visitors from the U.S., Canada, European Community countries, New Zealand, and Japan. Australians need to get a visa before leaving home. French embassies and consulates overseas can issue visas valid for stays of between one and three months, and they will forward applications for longer visits to the local immigration department in Papeete. There are French consulates in Boston, Chicago, Detroit, Houston, Los Angeles, New York, San Francisco, New Orleans, and Honolulu. Residents of those cities are required to apply there. If there is no French consulate in your hometown, contact the Embassy of France, 4102 Reservoir Road NW, Washington, DC 20007 (☎ 202/944-6000).

As a practical matter, your initial visa can be extended to six months if you still have your return air ticket, sufficient funds, aren't employed in French Polynesia, and have kept your nose clean. Applications for extensions must be made at the immigration office in the Faaa International Airport terminal building. Work and residency permits are difficult to obtain unless you are a French citizen.

Customs allowances are 200 cigarettes or 50 cigars, 2 liters of spirits or two liters of wine, 50 grams of perfume, 2 still cameras and 10 rolls of unexposed film, one video camera, one cassette player, and sports and camping equipment. Narcotics, dangerous drugs, weapons, ammunition, and copyright infringements (that is, pirated video and audio tapes) are prohibited. Pets and plants are subject to stringent regulations.

MONEY

French Polynesia uses the French Pacific franc (CFP), which is pegged directly to the French franc (5.5 CFP per franc) and comes in coins up to 100 CFP and in colorful notes ranging from 500 CFP into the millions. No decimals are used, so prices at first can seem staggering.

Although the dollar has fluctuated on either side of 100 CFP in recent years, I have used the rate of **$1 = 100 CFP** to compute the equivalent U.S. dollar prices given in parentheses after the CFP prices in this book. To find out approximately how many CFP you will get for one U.S. dollar, look in the financial section of your hometown newspaper, locate the number of French francs per dollar, and multiply that amount by 18.18. (Example: $1 = 5.5 francs × 18.18 = 100 CFP.)

Helpful Hint: Think of 100 CFP as $1, 1,000 CFP as $10, and so on (that is, drop the last two zeros, and you have the approximate amount of U.S. dollars), then add or subtract the percentage difference between the actual rate and 100 CFP.

Don't bargain, for to haggle over a retail price is to offend the integrity of the seller, especially if he or she is a Polynesian.

How to Get Local Currency Westpac, Banque de Polynésie, Banque de Tahiti, and Banque Socredo have offices on the main islands. For specific locations and banking hours, see "Fast Facts" in the following chapters. All banks charge between 350 CFP and 450 CFP ($3 and $4.50) for each transaction, regardless of the amount, so you may want to change large amounts each time to miminize this bite.

Cash advances using Visa and MasterCard can be obtained at Banque Socredo's automatic teller machines (ATMs) at Faaa International Airport and in front of its offices on boulevard Pomare along the Papeete waterfront.

You probably will get a better rate if you change your money in French Polynesia rather than before leaving home.

Credit Cards MasterCard and Visa are widely accepted on the most visited islands, and American Express and Diners Club cards are taken by most hotels and car rental firms, and by many restaurants.

The CFP & the Dollar

At this writing, $1 = approximately 100 CFP, the rate of exchange used to calculate the U.S. dollar prices given in this chapter. This rate has fluctuated widely and may not be the same when you visit. Accordingly, use the following table only as a guide.

CFP	U.S. $	CFP	U.S. $
100	1	1,000	10
150	1.50	1,500	15
200	2	2,000	20
300	3	3,000	30
400	4	4,000	40
500	5	5,000	50
600	6	6,000	60
700	7	7,000	70
800	8	8,000	80
900	9	9,000	90
1,000	10	10,000	100

What Things Cost in French Polynesia	U.S. $
Taxi from airport to Papeete (at night)	25.00
Local phone call	.50
Ride on *le truck*	1.20
Overwater bungalow at Hotel Bora Bora (deluxe)	750.00
Room at Hotel Le Royal Tahitien (moderate)	150.00
Bungalow at Moorea Village (inexpensive)	80.00
Dormitory bed at Village Pauline (budget)	20.00
Lunch at Restaurant Te Honu Iti (moderate)	15.00
Lunch at Snack Fare Hotu (budget)	8.00
Dinner without wine at Auberge du Pacific (expensive)	60.00
Dinner without wine at Lou Pescadou (moderate)	30.00
Dinner without wine at *les roulettes* (inexpensive)	10.00
Beer (at a hotel bar)	3.50
Coca-Cola (in a snack bar)	1.50
Roll of ASA 100 Kodacolor film, 36 exposures	10.00

6 When to Go—Climate, Holidays & Events

There is no bad time to go to French Polynesia, but some periods are better than others. For the best combination of weather and availability of hotel rooms, the months of May, June, September, and October are best.

CLIMATE

Tahiti and the Society Islands have a balmy tropical climate. November through April is the summer **wet season,** when the average maximum daily temperature is 86°F and rainy periods can be expected. Nighttime lows are about 72°F. May through October is the austral winter **dry season,** when midday maximum temperatures average a delightful 82°F, with early-morning lows of 68°F often making a blanket necessary. Some winter days, especially on the south side of the islands, can seem quite chilly when a strong wind blows from Antarctica. Tropical showers can pass overhead at any time of the year. Humidity averages between 77% and 80% throughout the year.

The central and northern Tuamotus have somewhat warmer temperatures and less rainfall. Since there are no mountains to create cooling night breezes, they can experience desertlike hot periods between November and April. The Marquesas are closer to the equator, and temperatures and humidity tend to be slightly higher than in Tahiti. The climate in the Austral and Gambier islands is more temperate.

French Polynesia is on the far eastern edge of the South Pacific cyclone (hurricane) belt.

HOLIDAYS

Public holidays are New Year's Day, Good Friday and Easter Monday, Ascension Day, Whitmonday, Assumption Day, Missionary Day (March 5), Labor Day (May 1), Bastille Day (July 14), Internal Autonomy Day (September 8), All Saints Day (November 1), Armistice Day (November 11), and Christmas Day.

The dance competitions—and other events of the Heiva festival—are unexpectedly tourist-free, a genuine people's celebration on which it is a privilege to eavesdrop.
—Ron Hall, 1991

From a visitor's standpoint, July is the busiest month because of the *Heiva i Tahiti* festival (see "Calendar of Events," below). Hotels on the outer islands are at their fullest during August, the traditional French vacation month, when many Papeete residents do their own version of getting away from it all.

Tahiti Tourisme publishes an annual list of the territory's leading special events (see "Visitor Information," "Entry Requirements," and "Money," above).

FRENCH POLYNESIA CALENDAR OF EVENTS

January
- **Chinese New Year.** Parade, musical performances, demonstrations of martial arts, Chinese dances, and handcrafts. Between mid-January and mid-February.

February
- **Moorea International Marathon.** Prizes worth up to $15,000 entice some of the world's best runners to trot 42km around Moorea. Third Saturday.
- **Cultural Exhibitions.** Demonstrations of traditional tattooing, medicine, massages, basket weaving, and flower-crown making. At Place Vaiete, Papeete. Mid-February to mid-March.

March
- **Arrival of First Missionaries.** Gatherings on Tahiti commemorate arrival of the London Missionary Society. March 5.
- **National Women's Day.** French Polynesia's own version of Mother's Day. Second Sunday in March.
- **Week of the Fish.** A gastronomical extravaganza as several restaurants create special menus using the territory's catch. Last week in March.

April
- **International Triathlon.** A smaller version of the famous Hawaii Iron Man Classic includes swimming, cycling, running competition. Venue changes from year to year. Mid-April.
- **Maohi Sports Festival.** A chance to see traditional Polynesian sports, including outrigger canoe races (French Polynesia's national sport), fruit carriers' races, stone lifting, and javelin-throwing. Late April.

May
- **Taputapuatea Inaugural Ceremony.** Traditional outrigger canoes gather at Taputapuatea Marae on Raiatea. Early May.
- **Tahiti Black Pearl Festival.** Gala evening features the best jewelry, auctions, fashion shows. Late May.

June
- **World Environment Day.** Program at Point Venus emphasizes campaign to clean up the islands. Guided hikes to Fautaa and Papenoo valleys, Lake Vaihiria, summit of Mt. Aroai. Early June.

- **Maire Fern Day.** Celebrates the many uses of the sweet-scented Maire Fern. Concludes with a ball. Late June.
- **Miss Tahiti Contest.** A dozen candidates from around the islands vie to win the title. Mid-June.
- **Horue International Pro-Am Surfing Open.** Competition on Taharu'u Beach in Papara is dedicated to *horue*, the sport that began in French Polynesia. Late June to early July.
- **International Pro-Open.** Golfers vie for $40,000 in prizes at Olivier Bréaud Golf Course at Atimaono. End of June to early July.

July

✪ *Heiva i Tahiti.* The festival to end all festivals in French Polynesia. It originally was a celebration of Bastille Day on July 14, but the islanders have extended the shindig into a month-long blast (it is commonly called *Tiurai*, the Tahitian word for July). They pull out all the stops, with parades, outrigger canoe races, javelin-throwing contests, fire walking, games, carnivals, festivals, and reenactments of ancient Polynesian ceremonies at restored marae. Highlight for visitors: An extraordinarily colorful contest to determine the best Tahitian dancing troupe for the year—never do the hips gyrate more vigorously. Airline and hotel reservations are difficult to come by during July, so book early and take your written confirmation with you. Contact the Tahiti Tourisme for details (see "Visitor Information," "Entry Requirements," and "Money," above).

August

- **Mini Fêtes.** Winning dancers and singers from the Heiva i Tahiti perform at hotels on the outer islands. All month.
- *Te Aito.* Paddles fly at the Marathon Outrigger Canoe races, starting at Point Venus. Early August.

September

- **Floralies Day.** In the biggest flower show of the year, the Territorial Assembly Hall is bedecked in flowers and tropical plants in honor of Harrison W. Smith, the American who created the botanical gardens next to the Gauguin Museum in Papeari. Mid-September.
- **World Tourism Day.** Islanders pay homage to overseas visitors, who get discounts. Late September.

October

- **Stone Fishing Ceremony.** A four-day celebration on an outer island includes sports, song and dance, speedboat and sailing races around the island, fire walking, and a stone fishing festival, climaxed by a huge island feast on a small islet. First half of October.

November

- **All Saints Day.** Flowers are sold everywhere to families who put them on graves after whitewashing the tombstones. November 1.
- *Hawaiki Nui.* Local and international outrigger canoe teams race from Tahiti to the Leeward Islands. Early November.

December

- **Tiare Tahiti Days.** Everyone on the streets of Papeete and in the hotels receives a *tiare Tahiti*, the fragrant gardenia that is indigenous to Tahiti. First week in December.

⭐ Frommer's Favorite French Polynesia Experiences

Sunset over Moorea. I was born to see sights, and no matter how many times I visit French Polynesia, I never tire of its incredible natural beauty. I always spend sunset of my first day on Tahiti's west coast, burning up film as the sun paints another glorious red and orange sky over Moorea's purple ridges.

View from the Belvédère. If the view from Le Belvédère Restaurant on Tahiti doesn't thrill me enough, the scene from the Moorea lookout of the same name certainly does. I never tire of standing there at the base of that cliff and watching dramatic Mt. Rotui separate the deep blue fingers of Cook's and Oponohu Bays.

View of Tahiti. My neck strains every time I cross the hill behind Moorea's Hotel Sofitel Ia Ora, for there across the Sea of the Moon sits Tahiti in all its green glory. Whenever possible I stop and reflect on what amazement the early explorers must have felt when those mountains appeared over the horizon.

Happy Hour at Club Bali Hai. The other worldly mountains and deep blue waters of Cook's Bay on Moorea are at their haunting best as the setting sun changes their colors from green against the blue sky to a mystical black against grey. The waterside bar has a Tahitian string band and half-price drinks from 6 to 7pm Tuesday and Friday, a balm for the pocketbook.

Bora Bora Lagoon. Shining with every hue on the blue end of the color spectrum, this watery playground is one of my favorite snorkeling spots. The Hotel Bora Bora has bungalows sitting right on the edge of a reef that drops precipitously to dark depths. I experience the exhilaration of flying when I glide out over that underwater cliff.

7 Getting There & Getting Around

Several airlines fly to French Polynesia, and internal transportation is modern and reliable, with fast ferries operating between the most frequently visited destinations. The territory also has a number of inter-island trading boats, descendants of the "copra schooners" that plied these waters in the days of sail.

Always **reconfirm your return flight** as soon as you reach an island.

GETTING TO FRENCH POLYNESIA

Major airlines flying to French Polynesia are **Air New Zealand** (☎ 310/642-0196 in Los Angeles or 800/262-1234); **AOM French Airlines** (☎ 800/892-9136); **Air France** (☎ 212/247-0100 in New York City or 800/237-2747); **Corsair Airlines** (☎ 800/677-0720); **Qantas Airways** (☎ 800/227-4500); **Hawaiian Airlines** (☎ 808/838-1555 in Honolulu or 800/367-5320 in the continental United States, Alaska, and Canada); and **Lan Chile** (☎ 800/735-5526).

All arrive at Faaa International Airport on Tahiti's northwest corner, about seven miles from downtown Papeete. For details about the airport and local transportation, see "Getting There & Getting Around" in the Tahiti chapter.

GETTING AROUND
BY PLANE

To Moorea Shuttle service is provided between Faaa Airport and Moorea by **Air Moorea** (☎ 86.41.41), whose small planes leave Faaa on the hour and half hour from 6 to 9am and from 4 to 6pm daily. From Moorea, they depart at

15 minutes before and after the hour. There are no flights after dark or before dawn. Air Moorea does not take reservations. Its little terminal is on the east end of Faaa airport (that's to the left as you come out of Customs).

Air Tahiti (☎ 86.42.42) has service between Papeete and Moorea a few days a week, going on to Huahine and Bora Bora. Air Tahiti's terminal is on the west end of Faaa airport—that's to the right as you exit Customs.

The **fare** is 2,750 CFP ($27.50) one way on both Air Tahiti and Air Moorea.

The **baggage limit** on both airlines is **10kg** (22 lbs.) per person. You may get around that limit by booking Air Tahiti as a connection to your international flight, in which case the limit is 20kg (44 lbs.). Otherwise, you may have to leave some extra belongings in the storage room at your hotel or at Faaa Airport (see "Getting There & Getting Around" in the chapter on Tahiti).

To the Other Islands   With a monopoly, **Air Tahiti** (☎ 86.42.42) provides service to more than 40 islands beyond Moorea. It has several daily flights between Papeete and Bora Bora. Flights to the other islands are less frequent. In other words, reserve as early as possible.

Air Tahiti's central reservations office in Papeete is on the second level (the French call it the first floor, or *premier étage)* of Fare Tony, the building just west of the Vaima Centre on boulevard Pomare. Its airport ticketing booth is in the west end of Faaa airport. Air Tahiti is represented in Los Angeles by its subsidiary, Tahiti Vacations (☎ 310/337-1040, or 800/553-3477).

One-way Air Tahiti fares on the usual visitor's circuit (double the fare for round trips between any two islands) are the following:

Papeete to Huahine	8,600 CFP ($86)
Huahine to Raiatea	4,300 CFP ($43)
Raiatea to Bora Bora	5,000 CFP ($50)
Bora Bora to Papeete	12,100 CFP ($121)
Bora Bora to Rangiroa	20,700 CFP ($207)
Rangiroa to Papeete	13,300 CFP ($133)

Visitors can save by buying **"Passes"** over the popular routes. For example, one version permits travel over the popular Papeete–Moorea–Huahine–Raiatea–Bora Bora–Papeete route for 30,500 CFP ($305), or 2,750 CFP ($27.50) less than the full fares. Rangiroa can be added for a total of 45,500 CFP ($455). Other passes permit travel to the Marquesas and Austral Islands. Restrictions apply.

An alternative to taking Air Tahiti's scheduled flights is to charter a plane and pilot from **Air Moorea** (☎ 86.41.41), or a helicopter and pilot from **Pacific Helicoptère Service** (☎ 83.16.80) or **Tahiti Helicoptère** (☎ 83.34.26). When the total cost is split among a large enough group, the price per person could be less than the regular air fare.

BY SHIP

To Moorea   Three ferries make about five runs daily from the Papeete waterfront opposite the Hotel Royal Papeete (which everyone calls the "Moorea Ferry Docks") to Vaiare, a small bay 12 miles away on Moorea's southeast coast. In general, they depart Papeete about 7am, 9am, noon, 3pm, and 5pm, with extra voyages on Friday and Monday (Moorea is a popular weekend retreat for Papeete's residents). Pick up printed schedules at the ferries' booths at the dock.

The *Aremiti II* (☎ 42.88.88 on Tahiti, 56.31.10 on Moorea), a sleek, air-conditioned catamaran, takes less than 20 minutes to cross the Sea of the

Moon. The somewhat larger *Tamarii Moorea II* (☎ 45.00.30 on Tahiti, 56.13.92 on Moorea) takes slightly longer. Both have bars selling snacks and libations. Adult fare is 800 CFP ($8) one way, 1,400 CFP ($14) round trip on both ferries. Children pay half. Reservations are not accepted by either.

The automobile–passenger ferry *Tamarii Moorea* (☎ 45.00.30 on Tahiti, 56.13.92 on Moorea) takes one hour to reach Vaiare. One-way fares are 700 CFP ($7) for adults, half that for children. You can take your Budget rental car to Moorea from Papeete for 2,000 CFP ($20) one way, plus 700 CFP ($7) for your own passage. Reservations are required only for automobiles.

The ferries have buses waiting at Vaiare to take you to your hotel or other destination for 200 CFP ($2). They take about one hour to reach the Club Med area on the opposite side of Moorea.

To the Leeward Islands   Two ferries provide service from Papeete to the Leeward Islands of Bora Bora, Huahine, Raiatea, and Tahaa. Even if you don't ride one of these between Papeete and the Leewards, consider a shorter journey between Huahine, Raiatea, or Bora Bora. The voyage between Raiatea and Bora Bora is absolutely beautiful, since the ships pass through the lovely Tahaa lagoon and then provide a gorgeous view of Bora Bora as they approach.

The fast, jet-powered passenger ferry *Ono Ono* (☎ 45.35.35) makes three voyages a week, usually leaving Papeete at 9am on Monday and Wednesday and at 4:30pm on Friday. Return voyages are the following days. It takes just over three hours for the Papeete–Huahine run and about an hour between each of the Leewards. One-way fares are 4,300 CFP ($43) from Papeete to Huahine and 5,800 CFP ($58) to Bora Bora. Each leg between the Leewards costs 1,600 CFP ($16). The Papeete ticket office is in a booth on boulevard Pomare at the foot of rue Paul Gauguin.

The *Raromatai Ferry* (☎ 43.19.88) takes considerably longer to carry both passengers and vehicles over this same route. Usually it departs Papeete at 6pm on Tuesday and at 4:30pm on Friday. It arrives in Huahine after midnight, then goes on to Raiatea and Bora Bora. Return journeys are the next days. One-way fare between Papeete and Bora Bora is 3,800 CFP ($38). Each inter-Leeward leg costs 1,000 CFP ($10).

The *Vaeanu* and the *Toporo VI* carry both cargo and passengers between Papeete and the Leewards. Both leave the inter-island shipping wharf in Motu Uta on Monday, Wednesday, and Friday just before dark. They arrive at Huahine in the middle of the night, do their loading, and depart for the short passage to Raiatea. Most passengers bring their own food, drinks, blankets, and rain gear, and sleep on deck. Fares from Papeete to Bora Bora are about 1,700 CFP ($17) on deck and 20,000 CFP ($200) for your own cabin. Tahiti Tourisme publishes their schedules and fares. For more information about the *Vaeanu*, contact Société Coopérative ouvrière de production Ihitai Nui (☎ 41.25.35). *Toporo VI* is operated by Compagnie Française Maritime de Tahiti (☎ 42.63.93).

To the Outer Islands   There are more than 20 ships that journey to the Tuamotu, Marquesas, Gambier, and Austral groups. They keep schedules in terms of weeks or even months, not days. Their primary mission is trade—retail goods for fresh produce and copra (dried coconut meat)—with passenger traffic a secondary source of income. Accordingly, they leave an island when the cargo is loaded, not necessarily when their schedules dictate. They also are at the mercy of the weather and mechanical breakdowns.

There is a charm to riding these small ships. The sea will be an incredible shade of royal blue, and the sun setting through the clouds will split the horizon into colors spanning the spectrum. Your fellow passengers will be the salt of the Polynesian earth, with straw sleeping mats and cardboard suitcases. On the other hand, many passengers (perhaps even you) will spend the entire voyage with seasick heads slung over the rail. You will often experience choking diesel fumes, and you will seldom escape the acrid stench coming from sacks of copra. Your shipmates may include cockroaches seemingly large enough to steal the watch off your wrist, and some of the cabins—if you can get one—could pass for outhouses. In other words, you'll need lots of flexible time, tolerance born of adversity, and the patience of Job.

If you're still interested, ask Tahiti Tourisme for a list of inter-island schooners, their fares, and approximate schedules. Tickets should be purchased at least a day in advance of scheduled departure. Make sure you have obtained a three-month visa to stay in French Polynesia. I once met a young Australian who took a boat to Rapa in the Austral Islands, expecting to return with it in a few weeks to Papeete. The ship broke down and went into the repair yard on Tahiti, stranding him for three months on Rapa, where he survived on coconuts and the generosity of the local residents.

BY CRUISE

One island trading boat not only is reliable but provides one of the best experiences of French Polynesia: the ✪ *Aranui*. Comfortably outfitted for 90 passengers, this 343-foot freighter makes regular 15- to 16-day round trips from Papeete to 6 of the 10 Marquesas Islands, with stops at Rangiroa and Takapoto in the Tuamotus. Passengers engage in picnics, snorkeling expeditions, and other activities ashore while the ship loads its cargo. Accommodation is in five air-conditioned deluxe cabins with their own showers and toilets, 40 air-conditioned first-class cabins (some of which share shower and toilets), or on 20 mats laid on a covered deck. Showers are provided for the deck-class passengers. The ship has a restaurant and bar, boutique, library, video lounge, and swimming pool. Fares for the complete voyage range from about 160,000 CFP ($1,160) for deck passage to 400,000 CFP ($4,000) for deluxe cabins, including all meals. For more information or reservations, contact Compagnie Polynésienne du Transport Maritime, B.P. 220, Papeete, Tahiti (☎ 42.62.40 or fax 43.48.89 in Papeete; ☎ 415/541-0674 or 800/972-7268 in the U.S.).

The 440-foot, four-masted sail cruiser *Wind Song* carries up to 148 passengers in 74 spacious cabins on one-week voyages from Papeete to Huahine, Raiatea, Bora Bora, and Moorea. This unusual vessel provides all the amenities of a luxury yacht. Guests won't get their hands chaffed hauling lines, however, for all sails are set mechanically. The ship also spends most nights in port, giving guests ample time to explore the islands. Double-occupancy rates for the one-week cruises range from about $3,200 to $3,500 per person. Add another $140 port fees per person. For more information or reservations, contact Windstar Cruises (☎ 206/281-3535 or 800/258-7245 in the United States and Canada).

Another option is the 617-foot *Club Med 2*, which spends most of each year voyaging from Papeete to Moorea, Huahine, Raiatea, Tahaa, Bora Bora, and Rangiroa. Like the *Wind Song,* this luxury vessel uses huge sails as well as diesel engines to move at up to 16 knots. She can carry 392 passengers in 191 cabins on six decks, has two restaurants, five bars, a nightclub and casino, a sauna, and a beauty spa. Air-conditioned cabins are equipped with phones, TVs, and minibars. Activities have a heavy emphasis on water sports (a stern platform drops to make its own marina). There's also a golf simulator and gym on board. The ship normally does seven-day cruises. Rates range from $810 to $2,240 per person, depending on length of cruise, season, and location of cabin, plus $140 port fees per person. For more information, contact Club Med (☎ 800/453-7447).

BY CHARTERED YACHT

Boating enthusiasts can charter their own yacht—with or without skipper and crew—and knock around some of the French Polynesian islands as the wind and their own desires dictate.

The Moorings (☎ 66.35.93, or 800/535-7289 in the U.S. and Canada) operates a fleet of sailboats based on Raiatea, which shares the same lagoon with Tahaa and is within sight of Huahine and Bora Bora, all of which are within the approved "cruising grounds." Boats up to 51 feet in length are available. Weekly bare-boat rates (that is, you rent the "bare" boat without skipper or crew) range from $2,900 to $6,500 per boat. Provisions are extra. The agency will check you out to make sure you and your party can handle sailboats of these sizes; otherwise, you must pay extra for a skipper.

Stardust Marine (☎ 66.23.18, or 800/634-8822 in the U.S. and Canada) has a fleet of yachts based at Faaroa Bay on Raiatea. Its bare-boat rates range from about $2,300 to $7,200 a week, depending on the size of boat and season, plus provisions and skipper and hostess if you need them.

BY RENTAL CAR

The major car-rental firms (*locations de voiture* in French) have licensees on Tahiti, Moorea, and Bora Bora. Reputable local firms operate on Tahiti, Moorea, Bora Bora, Huahine, and Raiatea. Not all rental firms permit their cars to be taken on the inter-island ferries; check with them before doing it.

Valid **driver's licenses** from your home country will be honored in French Polynesia.

Gasoline (*essence* in French) costs about 110 CFP ($1.10) per liter (that's about $4.20 per U.S. gallon). Total and Mobil are the major brands. Service stations are fairly common on Tahiti, but only in the main villages on the other islands.

Driving Rules   *Driving is on the right-hand side of the road,* as in North America and continental Europe.

All persons in a vehicle **must wear seat belts.**

Helmets (*casques,* pronounced "casks") are mandatory if you drive or ride on a scooter or motorbike.

Speed limits are 40kmph (24 m.p.h.) in the towns and villages and 80kmph (48 m.p.h.) on the open road. The limit is 60kmph (36 m.p.h.) for eight kilometers on either side of Papeete. The general rule on the Rte. 5 freeway between Papeete and Punaauia, on Tahiti's west coast, is 90kmph (54 m.p.h.), although there is one short stretch going down a hill where it's officially 110kmph (66 m.p.h.).

Drivers on the main rural roads have the right of way. In Papeete, priority is given to vehicles entering from the right side, unless an intersection is marked with a traffic light or a stop or yield sign. This rule differs from those of most other countries, so be especially careful at all intersections, especially those marked with a *priorité à droite* (priority to the right) sign, and give way accordingly.

Drivers are required to stop for pedestrians on marked crosswalks, but on busy streets, don't assume that drivers will politely stop for you when you try to cross.

Traffic lights in Papeete may be difficult to see, since some of them are on the far left-hand side of the street instead of on the driver's side of the intersection.

SUGGESTED ITINERARIES

If You Have 1 Day

Some visitors have a one-day layover between flights. If this is your case, spend at least half of it on Moorea. Head into downtown Papeete for breakfast and an early morning look at the Municipal Market. Take the 9am ferry to Moorea. Tour Moorea (including a trip to the Belvédère overlook) by rental car or scooter, or simply by riding the bus from the ferry landing to the Club Méditerranée area. Return to Papeete on an afternoon plane. Make a walking tour of downtown, with some shopping thrown in. Ride a late afternoon le truck to the Tahiti Beachcomber Parkroyal for sunset over Moorea. Catch a Tahitian dance show in the evening.

If You Have 2 Days

Day 1   Take an early-morning ferry to Moorea. Drive or take a tour around the island, including the Belvédère overlook. After lunch and some beach time, have a sunset drink at the Club Bali Hai, where the views of Cook's Bay are unparalleled. Overnight on Moorea.

Day 2   Return to Papeete on an early ferry or flight and go straight to the *Marché Municipale* (Municipal Market). After breakfast make a walking tour of downtown. Have lunch, then spend the afternoon on a tour around Tahiti, either by car or with an organized tour. End the day by watching the sunset over Moorea from a hotel on the west coast, then attending a Tahitian dance show.

If You Have 7 Days (Leisurely)

Day 1   Tour Tahiti on the first day, following the one-day suggestions above.
Days 2, 3, and 4   Spend these three full days on Moorea. There's plenty to do.
Days 5 and 6   Fly to Bora Bora on the morning of your fifth day. Stay there two days. Be sure to tour the island and take a trip on the lagoon.
Day 7   Return to Papeete in time for your international flight.

If You Have 7 Days (Busy)

Day 1 and 2   Tour Tahiti and Moorea, as suggested above.
Day 3   Spend an extra day on Moorea.
Day 4   Fly to Huahine. Tour the island and its historical maraes in the afternoon. Spend some time looking around the village of Fare; it has lots of old South Seas charm.
Day 5   Fly to Raiatea. Tour the island, including the great Taputapuatea marae, and Uturoa, French Polynesia's second-largest town.
Day 6   Fly to Bora Bora. Tour the island and take a trip on the lagoon.
Day 7   Return to Papeete for your flight home.

FAST FACTS: French Polynesia

American Express   The territory's one full-service representative is in Papeete. See "Fast Facts" in the "Tahiti" chapter.

Area Code   The international country code for French Polynesia is 689. There are no domestic area codes.

Bookstores   Only Tahiti and Moorea have well-stocked bookstores (for locations, see the "Fast Facts" in the following chapters). Many hotel boutiques sell colorful picture books of the islands.

Business Hours   Although some shops stay open over the lunch period, general shopping and business hours are from 7:30 to 11:30am and from 2 to 5pm Monday to Friday, 8am to noon on Saturday. In addition to regular hours, most small general stores also are open from 2 to 6pm Saturday and from 6 to 8am on Sunday.

Camera/Film   Photographic film and color-print processing are widely available but expensive. You can bring 10 rolls with you duty-free.

Clothing   Evening attire for men is usually a shirt and slacks; and for women, a long, brightly colored dress. Topless sunbathing is the norm at most beaches. Shorts are acceptable during the day almost everywhere. Outside Papeete, the standard attire for women is the colorful wraparound sarong known in Tahitian as a *pareu,* which can be tied in a multitude of ways into dresses, blouses, or skirts.

Crime   See "Safety," below.

Doctor   Highly qualified specialists practice on Tahiti, where some clinics possess state-of-the-art diagnostic and treatment equipment; nevertheless, public hospitals tend to be crowded with local residents, who get their care for free. Most visitors use private doctors or clinics. English-speaking physicians are on call by larger hotels. Each of the smaller islands has at least one infirmary. American health insurance plans are not recognized, so remember to get receipts at the time of treatment.

Drug Laws   Possession and use of dangerous drugs and narcotics are subject to heavy fines and jail terms.

Electricity   Electrical power is 220 volts, 50 cycles, and the plugs are the French kind with two round, skinny prongs. Most hotels have 110-volt outlets for shavers only, so you will need a converter and adapter plugs for your other appliances. Some hotels, especially those on the outer islands, have their own generators, so ask at the reception desk what voltage is supplied.

Embassies/Consulates   Austria, Chile, Denmark, Finland, Italy, South Korea, Monaco, Norway, the Netherlands, Sweden, the United Kingdom, and West Germany have honorary consulates in Papeete. Tahiti Tourisme has their phone numbers. The nearest full-service U.S. embassy is in Suva, Fiji.

Emergencies   If you are in a hotel, contact the staff. Otherwise, the emergency phone number is 17 throughout the territory.

Etiquette   Even though many women go topless and wear the skimpiest of bikini bottoms at the beach, the Tahitians have a sense of propriety that you find in any Western nation. Don't offend them by engaging in behavior that would be impermissible at home.

Firearms All weapons except bush knives (machetes) and BB guns are prohibited, but don't try to bring either into the territory.

Gambling Some hotels in Papeete have small gambling casinos. You can also play "Lotto," the French national lottery.

Hitchhiking Thumbing rides is possible in the rural parts of Tahiti and on the outer islands. Women traveling alone should be extremely cautious (see "Safety," below).

Insects There are no dangerous insects in French Polynesia. The only real nuisances are mosquitoes and tiny, nearly invisible sand flies known locally as "no-nos." If you forget to bring insect repellent along, look for the Off or Dolmix Pic brands at the pharmacies.

Liquor Laws Regulations about where and when you can drink are liberal, and some bars stay open until the very wee hours on weekends.

Mail Airmail postage from French Polynesia to the United States and Canada is 110 CFP ($1.10) for letters and 92 CFP (92¢) for postcards. Letters usually take about a week to 10 days to reach overseas destinations in either direction.

Mailing addresses in French Polynesia consist of post office boxes *(boîtes postales* in French, or B.P. for short) but no street numbers or names.

Maps Tahiti Tourisme distributes free maps of each island. Most useful is that of downtown Papeete. Each weekly edition of the free *Tahiti Beach Press* carries artistic island and Papeete maps. Librairie Vaima, a large bookstore in Papeete's Vaima Centre, carries several *cartes touristiques.* The most detailed map is *Tahiti: Archipel de la Société,* published by the Institut Géographique National. It shows all the Society Islands in detail, including all roads and topographic features, and costs about 1,000 CFP ($10). The full-color *Tahiti et ses Isles: 39 Cartes Touristiques* shows the precise locations of all hotels and pensions. It also costs about 1,000 CFP ($10) and is a useful tool if you're hunting for cheap hotels.

Newspapers/Magazines The *Tahiti Beach Press,* an English-language weekly tabloid devoted to news of Tahiti's tourist industry, runs features of interest to tourists and advertisements for hotels, restaurants, real estate agents, car-rental firms, and other businesses that cater to tourists and have English-speaking staffs. It is given away free by the establishments that buy ads in it. The daily newspapers, *La Dépêche de Tahiti* and *Les Nouvelles,* are in French. Le Kiosk in front of the Viama Centre on boulevard Pomare in Papeete carries the *International Herald Tribune, Time,* and *Newsweek.*

Pets Your pet will be placed in quarantine.

Police The emergency number for police is 17.

Radio/TV French Polynesia has one government-operated AM radio station with programming in French and Tahitian. Several private AM and FM stations in Papeete play as many American and British musical numbers as they do those from France. The announcers, however, speak French. The one government-owned television station broadcasts two channels entirely in French and Tahitian. The government-owned radio and TV stations can be received throughout the territory via satellite. Papeete also has two private satellite television operators, which are similar to cable systems elsewhere.

Safety   French Polynesia has seen increasing property theft in recent years, including break-ins of hotel rooms and resort bungalows. Fortunately street crimes against tourists still are rare, but you nevertheless should stay alert whenever you're out at night. Women should not wander alone on deserted beaches, since some Polynesian men may still consider such behavior to be an invitation for instant amorous activity.

Taxes   All hotel bills will have an 8% government tax added to them. There are no sales or other direct taxes.

Telephone/Telex/Fax   Direct international dialing is available to all telephone and fax numbers in French Polynesia. The international country code is 689.

International calls can be placed through your hotel, though with a surcharge, which can more than double the fee. It's less expensive to make them from a post office or even a pay phone (see below). In the post offices, place your call at the desk and wait for it to come through to one of the booths across the room.

The minimum charge for calls to North America is about 400 CFP ($4) per minute. Local calls on Tahiti cost 50 CFP (50¢) for the first five minutes. Calls to Moorea cost 50 CFP (50¢) per minute. Calls to the other islands cost at least 100 CFP ($1) a minute.

Calls within French Polynesia and to overseas can be dialed direct without going through a long-distance operator. To call overseas, dial 00, then the country code (1 for the U.S. and Canada), followed by the area code and phone number. The international operator is at 19. The emergency *(secours)* police number is 17. For directory information *(service des renseignements)*, dial 12.

Public pay phones are located at all post offices and are fairly numerous elsewhere on Tahiti. They sit in large glass-and-metal booths with black lettering on a yellow background.

Most pay phones take only a *télécarte,* a credit card sold at all post offices and by many shops. They come in 1,000 CFP, 2,000 CFP, and 5,000 CFP ($10, $20, and $50) sizes. The disadvantage is that you can't just walk up and put in a coin; the advantage is that you don't have to stand there and feed the machine's voracious appetite while calling home. Since most public phones take only *télécartes,* I buy a 1,000 CFP or 2,000 CFP version and keep it with me during my visit.

Some phones still take coins. Most are equipped with digital displays instead of coin stacks. You put your money in the slot on top, listen for a dial tone, then *composez* (dial) your number on the push-button pad. The readout tells you how many francs you have used and will give you a 12-second warning before your money is exhausted. In other words, keep an eye on the display, or your party may be unceremoniously cut off in midsentence.

A few public phones are like the older ones used in France: that is, you lift the receiver, listen for the dial tone, deposit your coins in the slots across the top of the phone (which match the size of the coins), watch them stack up behind the glass window under each slot, dial your number, and start talking when the party answers. A light on the upper left-hand front of the phone will flash 12 seconds before the last of your coins drops from behind the glass.

Time   Local time in the most visited islands is 11 hours behind Greenwich mean time. I find it easier to think of it as five hours behind U.S. eastern standard time or two hours behind pacific standard time. Translated: When it's noon pacific standard time in California, it's 10am in Tahiti. When it's noon eastern standard time on the East Coast, it's 5am in Tahiti. Add one hour for daylight saving time.

The Marquesas Islands are 30 minutes ahead of the rest of the territory.

French Polynesia is on the west side of the international date line; therefore, Tahiti has the same date as the U.S., the Cook Islands, and the Samoas, and is one day behind Australia, New Zealand, Fiji, and Tonga.

Tipping Despite inroads made by uninformed American tourists, tipping is considered contrary to the Polynesian custom of hospitality. In other words, tipping is not expected unless the service has been truly beyond the call of duty. Some hotels accept contributions to the staff Christmas fund.

Water Although the tap water on most of the main islands is considered safe to drink, it is untreated and can become muddy during heavy rains. Bottled mineral water is available at every grocery and is served by restaurants. Eau Royale, derived from a spring on Tahiti, is the least expensive brand. Well water in the Tuamotus tends to be brackish; rainwater is used there for drinking.

Weights/Measures French Polynesia is on the metric system.

Tahiti 5

Tahiti's status as a large and abundant island centrally located in the eastern South Pacific made it a gateway and natural base for the early European explorers. It was from Tahiti that most of the rest of the South Pacific was explored and added to the world maps in the 18th century. In later years, Papeete became a major shipping crossroads.

Vehicles of every sort now race along Papeete's waterfront and the four-lane freeway linking it to the trendy suburban district of Punaauia on the west coast. Indeed, suburbs have crept up the mountains overlooking the city and sprawled for miles along the coast in both directions. Some visitors are invigorated by Papeete's frantic pace, chic shops, busy Municipal Market, and lively mix of French, Polynesian, and Chinese cultures. Others aren't so charmed and leave immediately for Moorea, Bora Bora, or another island.

Whether you are enchanted or disenchanted with Papeete, you will have to spend at least a few hours on Tahiti, since all international flights land there. So let's make the most of this legendary and still very beautiful island.

1 Getting There & Getting Around

Tahiti is shaped like a figure eight lying on its side. The "eyes" of the eight are two extinct, eroded volcanoes joined by the flat Isthmus of Taravao. The larger western part of the island is known as Tahiti Nui ("Big Tahiti" in Tahitian), while the smaller eastern section beyond the isthmus is named Tahiti Iti ("Little Tahiti"). Together they comprise about 416 square miles, about two-thirds the size of the island of Oahu in Hawaii.

Tahiti Nui's volcano has been eroded over the eons so that now long ridges, separating deep valleys, march down from the crater's ancient rim to the coast far below. The rim itself is still intact, except on the north side where the Papenoo River has cut its way to the sea. The highest peaks, Mount Orohena (7,353 feet) and Mount Aora (6,817 feet), tower above Papeete. Another peak, known as the Diademe (4,360 feet), can be seen from the eastern suburb of Pirae but not from downtown.

With the exception of the east coast of Tahiti Iti, where great cliffs fall into the lagoon, and a few places where the ridges end abruptly at the water's edge, the island is skirted by a flat coastal plain. Tahiti's residents live on this plain or in the valleys, or on the hills adjacent to it.

GETTING THERE

Faaa International Airport sits on the northwest corner of Tahiti, 7km (4 miles) west of downtown Papeete. Most overseas flights arrive in the middle of the night. Once through Immigration and Customs, you will see a booth straight ahead staffed by **Tahiti Tourisme.** Start there for maps and other information. Group tour operators will be holding signs announcing their presence. A branch of **Westpac Bank** is to the left; in addition to its regular daytime hours, it opens one hour before an international flight is due to arrive or depart and stays open until the last passengers have changed enough money to get to their hotels. To the right, **Banque Socredo** has an ATM machine where you can get local currency using your VISA or MasterCard.

A snack bar to the right opens for all night flights.

Unless you are on a package tour or your hotel has made arrangements, your only choice of transportation to your hotel between 10pm and 6am will be a taxi. A large board mounted near the taxi area gives the official fares. From 8pm to 6am they are 1,500 CFP ($15) to the hotels on the west coast; 2,500 CFP ($25) to downtown; and 3,900 CFP ($39) to the Hyatt Regency Tahiti. Add 100 CFP ($1) for each bag. They drop by at least 30% between 6am and 8pm.

If you arrive any other time, you can haul your baggage across the parking lot in front of the terminal, climb the stairs to the main road, and flag down *le truck* (see "Getting Around," below).

If you are driving a rental car, watch for the Rte. 5 signs directing you to the freeway that connects Papeete to the west coast. You can take it or Rte. 1, the old road that runs along the inland side of the airport.

To the right of the Air Tahiti terminal, the airport's **baggage storage room** is open Monday to Saturday from 8am to 5pm, Sunday from 6am to noon and from 2 to 6pm, and two hours before every international flight departs. Charges range from 180 CFP ($1.80) per day for regular-size bags to 600 CFP ($6) for large items such as surfboards and bicycles. The hotels will keep your baggage for free.

Check-in time for departing flights is 90 minutes before flight time. There is no airport departure tax.

GETTING AROUND

The island's highway system consists primarily of a paved two-lane road running for 72 miles around Tahiti Nui and halfway down each side of Tahiti Iti. From the isthmus, a road partially lined with trees wanders up to the high, cool Plateau of Taravao, whose pastures and pines give it an air more of provincial France than of the South Pacific.

BY *LE TRUCK*   Although it may appear from the number of vehicles scurrying around Papeete that everyone owns a car or scooter, the average Tahitian gets around by *le truck.* These colorful vehicles are called trucks instead of buses because the passenger compartments are gaily painted wooden cabins mounted on the rear of flatbed trucks. Each compartment has a padded bench and Plexiglass windows that slide up when it's raining. Some also have at least one monstrous

Tahiti

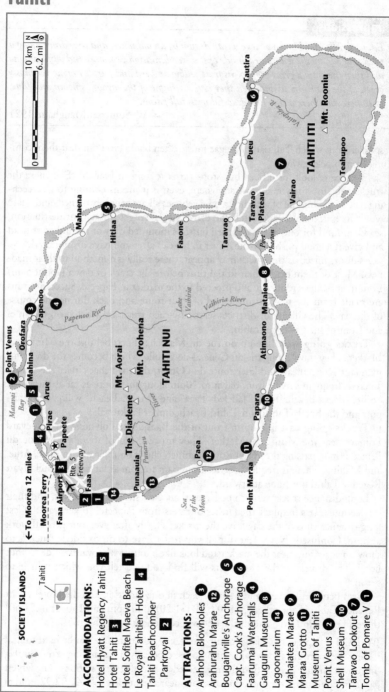

SOCIETY ISLANDS

Tahiti

ACCOMMODATIONS:

Hotel Hyatt Regency Tahiti **5**
Hotel Tahiti **3**
Hotel Sofitel Maeva Beach **1**
Le Royal Tahitien Hotel **4**
Tahiti Beachcomber Parkroyal **2**

ATTRACTIONS:

Arahoho Blowholes **3**
Arahurahu Marae **12**
Bougainville's Anchorage **5**
Capt. Cook's Anchorage **6**
Faarumai Waterfalls **4**
Gauguin Museum **8**
Lagoonarium **14**
Mahaiatea Marae **9**
Maraa Grotto **11**
Museum of Tahiti **13**
Point Venus **2**
Shell Museum **10**
Taravao Lookout **7**
Tomb of Pomare V **1**

Ferry – – –

1597

Impressions

Edward called for him in a rickety trap drawn by an old mare, and they drove along a road that ran by the sea. On each side of it were plantations, coconut and vanilla; now and then they saw a great mango, its fruit yellow and red and purple among the massy green of the leaves, now and then they had a glimpse of the lagoon, smooth and blue, with here and there a tiny islet graceful with tall palms.

—W. Somerset Maugham, 1921

speaker from which Tahitian or reggae music often blares (you can hear them coming from blocks away).

In Papeete, look for official bus stops *(arrêt le truck* in French). Elsewhere the trucks will stop for you almost anywhere, even if it means coming to a screeching halt in the middle of rush hour. The vehicles all are privately owned, and a fare won't be missed. Wave to catch the driver's eye. To get off at your destination, search around for one of the doorbell buttons mounted over or behind your head and give it a good push. Pay the driver in his cab after you have dismounted.

As disorganized as the trucks may appear, there really is a method to their madness. Most of them begin their initial runs before the crack of dawn (about 5am) from their owner's residence and proceed to the market in Papeete. Successive runs are made from the market to the end of their route and back during the course of the day. The villages or districts served by each truck are written on the sides and front of the passenger cabin.

Trucks going west line up on rue du Maréchal-Foch behind the Municipal Market. They travel along rue du Général-de-Gaulle, which becomes rue du Commandant-Destremeau and later route de-l'Ouest, the road that circles the island. There is frequent service from dawn to 10pm along this route as far as the Hotel Sofitel Maeva Beach. Trucks labeled "Faaa" and "Maeva Beach" will pass the airport and the hotels Tahiti and Tahiti Beachcomber Parkroyal.

Trucks going east line up in front of the Banque de Polynésie on boulevard Pomare near the Municipal Market. They proceed out of town via avenue du Prince-Hinoi, passing the Hotel Royal Tahitien cutoff on their way to Pirae, Arue, and Mahina. There is frequent service from 6am to 5pm as far as the Hotel Hyatt Regency Tahiti but none afterward.

Long-distance trucks tend to be larger than their short-haul cousins, and their service much less frequent the farther one gets from Papeete. In general, the last long-distance runs of the day leave the market shortly after everyone gets off work at 5pm. Confused? Never fear, for all you really have to do to ride le truck is to show up at stations near the market and look like a tourist who wants a ride to your hotel. The drivers or their assistants will find you and tell you which vehicle to get in.

Fares between Papeete and Maeva Beach in one direction and the Hotel Hyatt Regency Tahiti in the other are 120 CFP ($1.20) until 6pm and 150 CFP ($1.50) thereafter. A trip to the end of the line will cost about 500 CFP ($5).

BY TAXI   Papeete has a large number of taxis, although they can be hard to find during the morning and evening rush hours, especially if it's raining. You can flag one down on the street or find them gathered at one of several stations. The largest gathering points are on boulevard Pomare near the market (☎ 42.02.92) and at the Vaima Centre (☎ 42.98.35). Most taxi drivers understand some English.

Taxi fares are set by the government, and all cabs should have meters. Be sure the driver turns it on, or that you and he have agreed on a fare before you get in. Note that *all fares are increased by at least 30% from 8pm to 6am.* A trip anywhere within downtown Papeete during the day will start at 800 CFP ($8) and go up 120 CFP ($1.20) for every kilometer after the first one. As a rule of thumb, the fare from the Papeete hotels to the airport or vice versa is about 1,500 CFP ($15) during the day; from the west coast hotels to the airport, about 1,000 CFP ($10); from the Hotel Hyatt Regency Tahiti to Papeete, about 1,500 CFP ($15); and from the Hyatt Regency Tahiti to the airport, about 2,800 CFP ($28). A trip to the Gauguin Museum on the south coast will cost 6,500 CFP ($65) one way. The fare for a journey all the way around Tahiti is about 15,000 CFP ($150). Drivers may charge 100 CFP ($1) per bag of luggage.

BY RENTAL CAR   Budget (☎ 43.80.79 or 800/527-0700) offers its smallest cars for about 2,000 CFP ($20) a day plus 35 CFP (35¢) a kilometer. Add the cost of gasoline and 1,100 CFP ($11) a day for full insurance coverage. The unlimited kilometer rate of 6,150 CFP ($61.50) a day represents a savings if you are driving around the island and intend to wander off on Tahiti Iti. Ask about special half-day rates, applicable between 11am and 5pm, and three-day weekends for the price of two days. Budget's main office is at the end of rue des Remparts in Fare Ute, and it has toll-free phones at Faaa Airport, downtown at boulevard Pomare and rue Jeanne-d'Arc opposite the Vaima Centre, and in the lobbies of the Tahiti Beachcomber Parkroyal and Hotel Le Mandarin. Office hours are Monday to Friday from 7:30am to noon and 1:30 to 5pm. The English-speaking staff also answers the phone 24 hours a day on Saturday and Sunday. They will deliver to any hotel in and around Papeete.

Other international firms on Tahiti are **Avis** (☎ 42.96.49 or 800/331-1212); **Hertz** (☎ 42.48.62 or 800/654-3001); and **Europcar** (☎ 45.24.24 or 800/227-7368), which is known as National Car Rental/Interent in the United States. **Pacificar** (☎ 41.93.93) is a local firm that usually undercuts the big companies.

Driving Hints   In Papeete priority is given to vehicles entering an intersection from the right side. This rule does not apply on the four-lane boulevard Pomare along the waterfront, but be careful everywhere else because drivers on your right will expect you to yield the right of way at intersections where there are no stop signs or traffic signals. Outside of Papeete, priority is given to vehicles already on the round-island road.

Parking   Finding a parking space can be difficult in downtown Papeete. Some large buildings, such as the Vaima Centre, have garages in their basements. I usually resort to the lots on the waterfront by the Moorea Ferry docks, especially in front of the Royal Papeete Hotel. The spaces there are not metered, but many are reserved at night for the food wagons that gather there in the evenings (see "Where to Dine," below). Be safe and find a space close to boulevard Pomare.

FAST FACTS: Tahiti

American Express   The full-service American Express representative is Tahiti Tours, on rue Jeanne-d'Arc (☎ 54.02.50), across from the Vaima Centre in downtown Papeete. The mailing address is B.P. 627, Papeete, Tahiti, French Polynesia.

Bookstores   Librairie Vaima (☎ 45.57.57), on the second level of the Vaima Centre, has a wide selection of books on French Polynesia, many of them in English, and a few English-language novels and other paperback books. In addition, they sell the excellent *Carte Touristique,* or Tourist Map, published by the Institut Géographique Nationale, showing geographical features (in topographical relief) and the system of roads and trails on all the Society Islands. Le Kiosk in front of the Vaima Centre sells the *International Herald Tribune*, *Time*, and *Newsweek.*

Business Hours   Although some shops stay open over the long lunch break, most businesses are open from 8 to 11:30am and 2 to 5pm, give or take 30 minutes. Saturday hours are 8 to 11:30am, although some shops in the Vaima Centre stay open Saturday afternoon. The Papeete Municipal Market is a roaring beehive from 5 to 7am on Sunday, and many of the nearby general stores are open during those hours. Except for some small groceries, most other stores are closed on Sunday.

Camera/Film   Film and one-hour color print processing are available at several stores in downtown Papeete. One of the best is Tahiti Photo in the Vaima Centre (they speak English).

Currency Exchange   Westpac Bank, Banque de Polynésie, Banque de Tahiti, and Banque Socredo all have at least one branch on boulevard Pomare and in many suburban locations. They all charge a fee for each transaction. You can get cash advances against your Visa or MasterCard at Banque Socredo's automatic teller machines at Faaa Airport and in front of its offices on boulevard Pomare (one is in the block west of the Vaima Centre; another is near the Municipal Market).

Banking hours on Tahiti generally are 8am to 3:30pm Monday through Thursday, to 4:30pm on Friday. A Banque de Tahiti branch on the second level of the Vaima Centre is open Saturday from 8 to 11:30am.

Drugstores   Pharmacie du Port (☎ 42.00.69) is on Boulevard Pomare at rue Paul Gauguin, opposite Tahiti Tourisme. Pharmacies rotate night duty, so ask your hotel staff to find out which one is open after dark.

Emergencies   Consult with your hotel staff. The emergency police telephone number is 17, but don't expect the person on the other end of the line to speak English.

Eyeglasses   Optique Surdité (☎ 42.77.52).

Hairdressers/Barbers   Staffs of the beauty salons in the Sofitel Maeva Beach, Tahiti Beachcomber Parkroyal, and Hyatt Regency Tahiti speak English.

Hospitals   Both Clinque Cardella (☎ 42.80.10), on rue Anne-Marie-Javouhey, and Clinic Paofai (☎ 43.77.00) on boulevard Pomare have highly trained specialists and some state-of-the-art equipment.

Libraries   The *Office Territorial D'Action Culturelle* (Territorial Cultural Center) on boulevard Pomare, west of downtown Papeete (☎ 42.88.50), has a small library of mostly French books on the South Pacific and other topics. Hours are 8am to 5pm Monday to Friday, except on Wednesday when it closes at 4pm.

Police   The emergency number is 17. Otherwise, contact the Central Gendarmerie (☎ 42.02.02), at the inland terminus of avenue Bruat.

Post Office   The main post office, on boulevard Pomare a block west of the Vaima Centre, is open from 7am to 3pm Monday through Friday. The postal clerks are on the second floor; take the escalators. Mail may be picked up at the *poste restante* counter on the ground floor next to the international telephone counter (there's a small fee for each letter and newspaper received). The branch post office at the Faaa airport terminal is open from 5 to 9am and 6 to 10pm Monday through Friday, and from 6am to 10am on Saturday and Sunday.

Telephone/Telex/Fax   The telephone, telegraph, and telex office on the second floor of the main post office on boulevard Pomare is open Monday to Friday from 7am to 6pm and Saturday from 8 to 11am. Place your call at the desk and wait for it to come through to one of the booths across the room. Out of town, check with the local post office. See "Fast Facts" in Chapter 4 for more information about pay phones and international calls.

2 What to See & Do

SEEING PAPEETE

Located on the flat coastal plain on the northwest corner of Tahiti, Papeete curves around one of the South Pacific's busiest harbors. There wasn't even a village here until the 1820s, when Queen Pomare set up headquarters along the shore and merchant ships and whalers began using the harbor in preference to the less protected Matavai Bay to the east. A claptrap town of stores, bars, and billiard parlors sprang up quickly, and between 1825 and 1829 it was a veritable den of iniquity. It grew even more after the French made it their headquarters upon taking over Tahiti in 1842. A fire nearly destroyed the town in 1884, after which thatch was outlawed as a building material. Waves churned up by a cyclone did severe damage in 1906, and in 1914 two German warships shelled the harbor and sank the French navy's *Zélée*.

Papeete was well known for Quinn's, a waterfront establishment whose reputation as the quintessential South Seas bar has survived its demise. For many, the watershed in Papeete's transition from a backwater port to a modern city was not the building of the airport or the nuclear testing facility in the early 1960s; it was the tearing down of Quinn's and its replacement by modern retail stores in 1973.

WALKING TOUR
Papeete

Start: Tahiti Tourisme
Finish: Papeete Town Hall
Time: 2 hours

Best Time: Early morning or late afternoon
Worst Time: Midday, or Sunday when most establishments are closed

Begin at Tahiti Tourisme's information office at the foot of rue Paul Gauguin and stroll westward along Boulevard Pomare. Opposite the tuna boat dock stands

1. **Vaima Centre,** whose chic shops are a mecca for Papeete's French and European communities (the Municipal Market still attracts most Tahitians and Chinese). Quinn's Bar stood in the block east of the Viama Center, where the Noa Noa boutique is now. The Vaima Centre takes its name from the Vaima Restaurant, everyone's favorite eatery in those days, which it replaced.

Across the four-lane boulevard from the Vaima is

2. **The Quay,** where cruising yachts from around the world congregate from April to September, resident boats all year.

Beyond them on the other side of the harbor is **Motu Uta,** once a small natural island belonging to Queen Pomare but now home of the wharves and warehouses of Papeete's shipping port. The reef on the other side has been filled to make a breakwater and to connect Motu Uta by road to **Fare Ute,** the industrial area and French naval base to the right. The inter-island boats dock alongside the filled-in reef, and their cargoes of copra (dried coconut meat) are taken to a mill at Fare Ute, where coconut oil is extracted and later shipped overseas to be used in cosmetics.

Walk west along the waterfront past the main post office, next to which you come to

3. **Bougainville Park,** a shady block named for the French explorer who found Tahiti a little too late to get credit for its discovery. Two naval cannons hang over the sidewalk: The one nearest the post office was on the *Seeadler,* Count von Luckner's infamous World War I German raider, which ran aground in the Cook Islands after terrifying the British and French territories of the South Pacific. The other was on the French navy's *Zélée.* Bougainville's statue stands between the guns.

On the waterfront a block farther along boulevard Pomare, at the end of avenue Bruat, stands the

4. **Pacific Battalion Monument,** a tribute to the French Polynesians who fought with General Charles de Gaulle's Free French forces during World War II. The territory quickly went over to the free French side after the fall of France to Nazi Germany in 1940, and it permitted the Allies to build an airstrip on Bora Bora in 1942. Later, the majority of French Polynesians supported de Gaulle as president of France, and the conservative Gaullist party has been an important force in local politics ever since.

Keep going west along the waterfront to rue l'Arthémise, where you can't miss the impressive steeple of

5. **Eglise Evangélique,** the largest Protestant church in French Polynesia. The local evangelical sect grew out of the early work by the London Missionary Society. Today the pastors are Tahitian. Sleek outrigger racing canoes are kept on the shady black sand beach across the boulevard. They can be seen cutting the harbor during lunchtime and in the late afternoons (canoe racing is Tahiti's national sport). Imbedded in the stone gateway are the twin hulls of the *Hokule'a,* a traditional voyaging canoe that toured the South Pacific in the 1980s, setting off a wave of Polynesian pride.

Walking Tour—Papeete

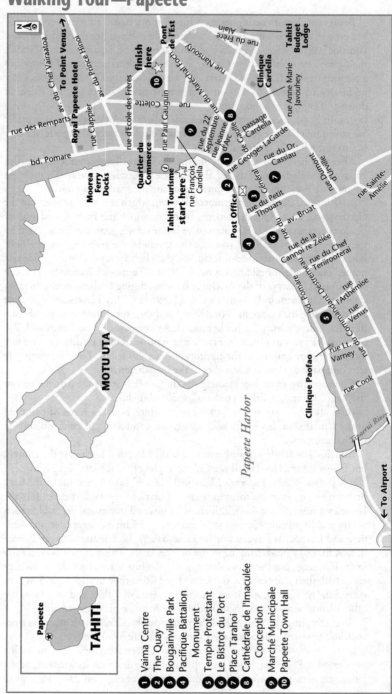

1. Vaima Centre
2. The Quay
3. Bougainville Park
4. Pacifique Battalion Monument
5. Temple Protestant
6. Le Bistrot du Port
7. Place Tarahoi
8. Cathédrale de l'Imaculée Conception
9. Marché Municipale
10. Papeete Town Hall

TAHITI
Papeete

MOTU UTA

Papeete Harbor

Moorea Ferry Docks

Quartier du Commerce

Tahiti Tourisme start here

Post Office

Royal Papeete Hotel

finish here

Pont de l'Est

Tahiti Budget Lodge

Clinique Cardella

Clinique Paofao

To Point Venus →

← To Airport

Fautaua River

rue des Remparts
bd. Pomare
av. du Chef Vairaatoa
av. du Prince Hinoi
rue Clappier
rue d'Ecole des Frères
rue Paul Gauguin
Colette
rue du Maréchal Foch
rue Nansouty
rue du Frère Alain
rue Anne Marie Javouhey
rue du 22 Septembre
rue Jeanne d'Arc
rue de Crulle
passage Cardella
rue François Cardella
rue Georges LaGarde
rue du Dr. Cassiau
rue du Général
rue du Petit Thouars
av. Bruat
rue du
rue de la Cannoi re Zélée
rue Destrenneau
rue du Chef Teriirooterai
bd. Pomare
rue du Chef Commandant
rue Lt. Varney
rue Cook
rue Venus
rue Arthémise
rue Dumont d'Urville
rue Sainte-Amélie

Boulevard Pomare continues west for six more blocks, the canoes and harbor on one side and a few remaining stately old colonial homes on the "mountain side" of the street. Near its end, on the banks of Tipaerui Stream, stands the *Office Territorial d'Action Culturelle,* Tahiti's cultural center and library. It's a pleasant stroll to this quiet enclave, but we will turn around and backtrack east on boulevard Pomare to the corner of avenue Bruat. When you get there, sit down and enjoy a refueling stop at

6. **Bistro du Port,** one of the city's largest sidewalk cafes. Although the noisy traffic has stolen much of the charm of French-style outdoor cafes in Papeete, it's easy to imagine what the quieter days were like.

After you have recovered, walk up the shady, tree-lined avenue Bruat, turn left at the stoplight, and proceed along rue de Général-de-Gaulle. To the right as you walk back toward the Vaima Centre are the spacious grounds of

7. **Place Tarahoi,** Papeete's governmental center, which was royal property in the old days and site of Queen Pomare's mansion, which the French used as their headquarters after 1842. Her impressive home is long gone but is replicated by the Papeete Town Hall. As you face the grounds, the buildings on the right house the French government, including the High Commissioner's office and home. The modern building on the left is the Territorial Assembly. You can walk around hallways of the Assembly building during business hours. In front stands a monument to Pouvanaa a Oopa (1895–1977), a Tahitian who became a hero fighting for France in World War I and then spent the rest of his life battling for independence for his homeland. At one point in the 1960s and '70s he spent 15 years in prison in France but returned home in time to see more local autonomy granted to the territory. In fact, his fellow Tahitians promptly sent him back to Paris as a member of the French Senate.

Continue two more blocks along rue du Général-de-Gaulle past the rear of the Vaima Centre to Tahiti's oldest Catholic church,

8. **Cathédrale de L'Immaculée Conception,** which houses a series of paintings of the Crucifixion. It's a very cool, quiet, and comforting place to worship or just to contemplate.

Rue du Général-de-Gaulle becomes rue du Maréchal-Foch past the church, but follow it for a block until rue Colette angles off to the left. Take it to

9. **Marché Municipale,** Papeete's Municipal Market. Take a stroll under the large tin pavilion and examine the multitude of fruits and vegetables offered for sale. Unwritten rules dictate that Tahitians sell fruits and traditional vegetables, such as taro and breadfruit, Chinese sell European and Chinese vegetables, and Chinese and Europeans serve as butchers and bakers. If your stomach can handle it, look for hogs' heads hanging in the butcher stalls. The market is busiest early in the mornings, but the local fishermen set off a new wave of activity when they arrive with their daily catch about 4pm. The busiest time of all is from 5 to 7am every Sunday, when people from the outlying areas of Tahiti, and even from the other islands, arrive to sell their produce. By 8am the pickings are slim.

After sampling the market and the marvelous handcraft stalls along its sidewalk and upstairs, walk along rue Colette two more blocks to

10. **Papeete Town Hall,** a magnificent replica of Queen Pomare's mansion, which once stood at Place Tarahoi. This impressive structure, with its wraparound veranda, captures the spirit of the colonial South Pacific. This *Hôtel de Ville* or

Fare Oire (French and Tahitian, respectively, for town hall) was dedicated in 1990 by French President François Mitterand during an elaborate celebration. It's worth a walk up the grand entrance steps and to catch a cool breeze from its broad balconies.

THE CIRCLE ISLAND TOUR

✪ Known locally as the Circle Island Tour, a drive around Tahiti is a popular way to see the island's outlying sights, and a bit of old Polynesia away from Papeete's bustle. It takes less than a day and can be done even if you're staying on Moorea (take an early-morning ferry over and a late-afternoon boat back to Moorea).

Several companies offer tours around the coastal road. Expect to pay about 4,500 CFP ($45). Optional buffet lunches at the Restaurant du Musée Gauguin are an additional 2,000 CFP ($20) per person (you can order à la carte for less). The major circle island tour operators are **Paradis Tours** (☎ 42.49.36), **Tahiti Tours** (☎ 42.78.70), **Tahiti Nui Travel** (☎ 42.68.03), and **Marama Tours** (☎ 82.08.42). They have reservations desks in several hotels.

If you drive yourself, proceed clockwise from Papeete on the road skirting the shore. On the land side of the road are red-topped concrete markers (*postes kilomètres* in French, or "PK" for short), which tell the distance in kilometers between Papeete and the isthmus of Taravao. The end of each kilometer is marked with a PK. The markers give the distance from Papeete to Taravao in each direction—not the total number of kilometers around the island. The large numbers facing the ocean are the number of kilometers from Papeete; the numbers facing you as you drive along are the number of kilometers you have to go, either to Papeete or Taravao, depending on your direction. Distances between the PKs are referred to in tenths of kilometers; for example, PK 35.6 would be 35.6 kilometers from Papeete. Once you've mastered these facts, they make handy frames of reference.

The road around the island is 114km (72 miles) long, not counting side trips on Tahiti Iti. It's 54km (32 miles) from Papeete to Taravao along the east coast and 60km (40 miles) back along the west coast. If your car has an odometer, reset it to zero; if not, make note of the total kilometers at the outset.

No le truck goes all the way around the island, but you can make a circle island tour by taking one from Papeete to Taravao, Vairao, or Teahupoo on the west side. Get off at Taravao, walk across the isthmus, and catch a truck returning to Papeete in midafternoon. There are no set schedules, but if you get stranded, it's relatively easy for tourists to hitch a ride back to Papeete.

For a detailed description of the tour, buy a copy of Bengt Danielsson's *Tahiti: Circle Island Tour Guide.* It's available in the local bookstores.

Impressions

The air was full of that exquisite fragrance of orange blossom and gardenia which is distilled by night under the thick foliage; there was a great silence, accentuated by the bustle of insects in the grass, and that sonorous quality, peculiar to night in Tahiti, which predisposes the listener to feel the enchanting power of music.

—Pierre Loti (Julien Viaud), 1880

THE NORTH AND EAST COASTS

First you have to find your way out of town. The broad **avenue du Prince-Hinoi,** which runs off Boulevard Pomare at the Hotel Prince Hinoi on the waterfront, is the start of the road that eventually circles the island. Therefore, turn at the Prince Hinoi and go straight.

Loti's Pool   At PK 2.5, a road goes right into the Fautaua Valley and the Bain Loti, or Loti's Pool. Julien Viaud, the French merchant mariner who wrote under the pen name Pierre Loti, used this pool as a setting for his novel, *The Marriage of Loti,* which recounted the love of a Frenchman for a Tahitian woman. Now part of Papeete's water-supply system, the pool is covered in concrete and is not worth a side trip. The road goes into the lower part of the valley and terminates at the beginning of a hiking trail up to the **Fautaua Waterfall,** an arduous three-hour walk away.

Tomb of Pomare V   At PK 4.7 turn left at the sign and drive a short distance to a Protestant churchyard commanding an excellent view of Matavai Bay to the right. The tomb with a Grecian urn on top was built in 1879 for Queen Pomare. Her remains were removed a few years later by her son, King Pomare V, who abdicated in return for a French pension and later died of too much drink. Now he is buried there, and tour guides like to say the urn is not an urn at all but is a liquor bottle, which makes it a monument not to Pomare V but to the cause of his death.

Home of James Norman Hall   At PK 5.4, on the mountain side of the road just east of the small bridge stands the now-overgrown home built by James Norman Hall, coauthor with Charles Nordhoff of *Mutiny on the Bounty.* Nordhoff and Hall served together in World War I, moved to Tahiti to write, and produced three novels on the mutiny *(Men Against the Sea* and *Pitcairn's Island)* and several more books about French Polynesia. Hall died in 1951 and is buried on the hill above his home. A poem he wrote is engraved on the gravestone: "Look to the Northward, stranger/Just over the hillside there/Have you in your travels seen/A land more passing fair?" The house belongs to the territorial government. It is not open to the public.

✪ Point Venus   At PK 10, turn left at Super Marché Venus Star and drive to Point Venus, Tahiti's northernmost point. The low, sandy peninsula covered with casuarina trees is about two kilometers from the main road. Captains Wallis, Cook, and Bligh landed here from their ships, which they anchored behind the reef in Matavai Bay offshore. Captain Cook made his observations of the transit of Venus across the sun in 1769 from a point between the black-sand beach and the meandering river cutting the peninsula in two. The beach and the parklike setting around the tall white lighthouse, which was completed in 1868 (notwithstanding the 1867 date over the door), are popular for picnics. There are a snack bar, souvenir and handcraft shop, and toilets.

A good refreshment stop is **Chez Kennedy,** a small snack bar on the main road opposite the Point Venus turnoff. Its juicy, Australian-style hamburgers are among Tahiti's best.

Orofara Leper Colony   At PK 13.2 begins the entrance to Orofara Valley, which the French colonial administration made a leper colony in 1914. Leprosy once was a fairly common disease throughout Polynesia, and until then, those afflicted were sent into the hills. Today leprosy is curable with sulfa drugs, and victims can remain at home with their families.

Papenoo Valley   At PK 17.1, Tahiti's longest bridge crosses its longest river at the end of its largest valley at one of its largest rural villages—all named Papenoo. The river flows down to the sea through the only wall in Tahiti Nui's old volcanic crater. Four-wheel-drive vehicles go up the valley on their excursions across the island (see "Safari Tours," below).

The Arahoho Blowholes   At PK 22, the surf pounding against the headland at Arahoho has formed overhanging shelves with holes in them. As waves crash under the shelves, water and air are forced through the holes, resulting in a geyserlike phenomenon. An overlook with free parking and toilets is west of the sharp curve.

✪ Faarumai Waterfalls   At PK 22.1, a sign on the right just past the blowhole marks a paved road that leads 1.3km up a small valley to the Cascades de Faarumai, Tahiti's most accessible waterfalls. Park near the stand of bamboo trees and follow the signs. Vaimahuta falls are an easy walk; Haamaremare Iti and Haamaremarerahi falls are a 45-minute climb up a more difficult trail. Vaimahuta falls plunge straight down several hundred feet from a hanging valley into a large pool. Bring insect repellent.

Mahaena Battlefield   At PK 32.5, the Tahitian rebellion came to a head on April 17, 1844, when 441 French troops charged several times and many poorly armed Tahitians dug in near the village of Mahaena. The Tahitians lost 102 men and the French, 15. It was the last set battle of the rebellion.

Bougainville's Landing   At PK 37.6, a plaque mounted on a rock on the northern end of the bridge at Hitiaa commemorates Bougainville's landing. The French explorer anchored just offshore when he arrived in Tahiti in 1768. The two small islands on the reef, Oputotara and Variararu, provided slim protection against the prevailing trade winds, and Bougainville lost six anchors in 10 days trying to keep his ships off the reef. One was recovered by the Tahitians, who gave it to the high chief of Bora Bora, who in turn gave it to Captain Cook in 1777.

Faatautia Valley   At PK 41.8 begins a view of Faatautia Valley, which looks so much like those in the Marquesas that in 1957 director John Huston chose it as a location for a movie version of *Typee*, Herman Melville's novelized account of his ship-jumping adventures among the Marquesans in the 1840s. The project was scrapped after another of Huston's Melville movies, *Moby Dick*, bombed at the box office. **Vaiharuru Waterfall** cascades into the uninhabited valley, which must look much today as it did a thousand years ago.

Taravao   At PK 53, after passing the small-boat marina, the road climbs up onto the Isthmus of Taravao. At the top are the stone walls of Fort Taravao, which the French built in 1844 to bottle up what was left of the rebellious Tahitians on the Tahiti Iti peninsula. Germans stuck on Tahiti during World War II were interned there. It is now used as a French army training center. The village of Taravao with its shops, suburban streets, and churches has grown up around the military post. Its snack bars are a good place for a refueling stop.

TAHITI ITI

Taravao joins the larger Tahiti Nui to its smaller Siamese twin, the peninsula of Tahiti Iti. The latter is much more sparsely populated, and paved roads dead-end about halfway down its north and its south sides. A series of cliffs plunges into the sea on Tahiti Iti's rugged east end.

The Taravao Plateau   If you have to chose one of three roads on Tahiti Iti, take the one that dead-ends high up into the rolling pastures of the Taravao Plateau. It begins at the traffic signal on the north coast road to Tautira and runs up through cool pastures reminiscent of rural France, with huge trees lining the narrow paved road. From there you'll have a spectacular view of the entire isthmus and down both sides of Tahiti Nui. At more than 1,200 feet high, the plateau is blessed with a refreshing, perpetually springlike climate.

The North Coast   The road on the north coast of Tahiti Iti goes for 18km (11 miles) to the sizable village of **Tautira,** which sits on its own little peninsula. Captain Cook anchored in the bay off Tautira on his second visit to Tahiti in 1773. His ships ran aground on the reef while their crews were partying one night. He managed to get them off but lost several anchors in the process. One of them was found in 1978 and is now on display at the Museum of Tahiti and Her Islands, which we will come to on the west side of the island.

A year after Cook landed at Tautira, two Franciscan priests were put ashore there by the *Aguila,* a Spanish ship from Peru, whose captain claimed the island for Spain. It was the third time Tahiti had been claimed for a European power. The *Aguila* returned a year later, but the priests had had enough of Tahiti and sailed back to Peru.

As far as anyone knows, Tautira's next famous visitor was Robert Louis Stevenson, who spent two months there in 1888 working on *The Master of Ballantrae,* a novel set not in Tahiti but in Scotland. Stevenson's mother was with him in Tautira. After she returned to London, she sent the local Protestant church a silver communion service, which is still being used today.

The South Coast   The picturesque road along the south coast of Tahiti Iti skirts the lagoon, passing through small settlements. Novelist Zane Grey had a deep-sea-fishing camp from 1928 to 1930 at PK 7.3, near the village of Toahotu. In 1930 he caught a silver marlin that was about 14 feet long and weighed more than 1,000 pounds—even after the sharks had had a meal on it while Grey was trying to get it aboard his boat. He wrote about his adventures in *Tales of Tahitian Waters.*

According to Tahitian legends, the demi-god Maui once made a rope from his sister Hina's hair and used it to slow down the sun long enough for Tahitians to finish cooking their food in their earth ovens (a lengthy process). He accomplished this feat while standing on the reef at a point 8.5km (5 miles) along the south coast road, and his footprints are still there. Beyond Maui's alleged footprints, the Bay of Tapueraha provides the best natural harbor on Tahiti and was used as a base by a large contingent of the French navy during the aboveground nuclear tests at Moruroa atoll in the 1960s. Some of the old mooring pilings still stand just offshore.

THE SOUTH COAST OF TAHITI

As you leave Taravao, heading back to Papeete along Tahiti's south coast, note the PK markers begin to decrease the nearer to Papeete you get. The road rims casuarina-ringed Port Phaeton, which cuts nearly halfway across the isthmus. Port Phaeton and the Bay of Tapueraha to the south are Tahiti's finest harbors, yet European settlement and most development have taken place on the opposite side of the island, around Papeete.

The Moon & Six Million

In 1891 a marginally successful Parisian painter named Paul Gauguin left behind his wife and six children and sailed to Tahiti. He wanted to devote himself to his art, free of the chains of civilization.

Instead of paradise, however, Gauguin found a world that suffered from some of the same maladies as did the one from which he fled. His decade in the islands was marked by poverty, sickness, and frequent disputes with church and colonial officials. He had syphilis, a bad heart, and an addiction to opium.

Gauguin disliked Papeete and spent his first two years in the rural Mataiea district, on Tahiti's south coast, where a village woman asked what he was doing there. Looking for a girl, he replied. The woman immediately offered her 13-year-old daughter Tehaamana, first of Gauguin's early-teenage Tahitian mistresses. One of them bore him a son in 1899.

Tehaamana and the others figured prominently in Gauguin's impressionistic masterpieces, which brought fame to Tahiti but did little for his own pocketbook. After 649 paintings and a colorful career, immortalized by W. Somerset Maugham in *The Moon and Sixpence,* Gauguin died penniless in 1903.

At the time of his death, apparently of a drug overdose, in the Marquesas Islands, a painting by Gauguin sold for 150 French francs. Today, on the rare occasion when one comes on the market, it fetches at least $6 million.

Papaeari   At PK 52 stands Tahiti's oldest village. Apparently the island's initial residents recognized the advantages of the south coast and its deep lagoons and harbors, for word-of-mouth history says they came through the Hotumatuu Pass in the reef and settled at Papeari sometime between A.D. 400 and 500. Robert Keable, author of *Simon Called Peter,* a best-selling novel about a disillusioned clergyman, lived here from 1924 until he died in 1928 at the age of 40. Now a private residence, his home stands at PK 55. Today Papeari is a thriving village whose residents often sell fruit and vegetables at stands along the road.

✪ **Gauguin Museum**   At PK 51.2 is the entrance to the museum-memorial to Paul Gauguin, the French artist who moved to the nearby Mataiea district from 1891 until 1893. The museum owns one of his minor paintings and some of his sculptures, wood carvings, engravings, and a ceramic vase. It has an active program to borrow his major works, however, and one might be on display during your visit. Otherwise, the exhibits are dedicated to his life in French Polynesia. It's best to see them clockwise, starting at the gift shop, which sells excellent reproductions of his works. The museum is open daily from 9am to 5pm. Admission is 450 CFP ($4.50) for adults and 250 CFP ($2.50) for children.

The museum sits in lush **Harrison Smith Botanical Gardens**, which were started in 1919 by Harrison Smith, an American who left a career teaching physics at the Massachusetts Institute of Technology and moved to Tahiti. He died here in 1947. His gardens, which now belong to the public, have a plethora of tropical plants from around the world.

Restaurant du Musée Gauguin   At PK 50.5, the circle island tour buses stop for lunch at this lagoonside restaurant. Owner Roger Gowan, a transplanted Englishman, offers a buffet for 2,000 CFP ($20) per person. A la carte main courses featuring shrimp and mahi mahi range from 1,000 CFP to 1,800 CFP ($10 to $18). Sandwiches are available for less. The restaurant is open daily from noon to 3pm. For reservations, phone 57.13.80.

Vaihiria River   At PK 48, the main road crosses the Vaihiria River. An unpaved jeep track beside the bridge leads inland to Lake Vaihiria. At 1,500 feet above sea level, Tahiti's only lake is noted for its freshwater eels. Cliffs up to 3,000 feet tall drop to the lake on its north side.

Atimaono   At PK 41 begins the largest parcel of flat land on Tahiti, site of Olivier Bréaud International Golf Course, French Polynesia's only links. Irishman William Stewart started his cotton plantation here during the American Civil War. Nothing remains of the plantation, but it was Stewart who brought the first Chinese indentured servants to Tahiti.

Mahaiatea Marae   At PK 39.2, a road goes left through a residential area to the beach and a huge overgrown pile of boulders that was once Tahiti's most imposing Polynesian temple, the Mahaiatea Marae. Capt. James Cook described its dimensions as about 100 yards long, 30 yards across, and 15 yards high. One reason it's no longer that large today is that William Stewart apparently raided it for stones to use on his cotton plantation.

Dorence Atwater's Grave   At PK 36 stands a Protestant church in whose yard is buried Dorence Atwater, American consul to Tahiti after the Civil War. Atwater had been a Union Army soldier held as a prisoner of war by the Confederates. He was assigned to a Southern hospital, where he recorded the names of Union soldiers who died while in captivity. He later escaped and brought his lists to the federal government, thus proving that the Confederacy was keeping inaccurate records. His action made him a hero in the eyes of the Union Army. He later moved to the south coast of Tahiti, married the daughter of a chief of the Papara district, and at one time invested in William Stewart's cotton venture.

Papara village also is home to the *Musée de Coquillage* (Seashell Museum). It has a collection of polished shell collages and dried sea snakes, sea-turtle shells, and crabs—many of which are for sale as well as for viewing. The museum is open Tuesday to Friday from 8am to 5pm, and Saturday and Sunday from 9am to noon and from 1 to 5pm. Admission is 300 CFP ($3) for adults and 200 CFP ($2) for children.

Maraa Grotto   At PK 28.5, on Tahiti's southwest corner, the road turns sharply around the base of a series of headlands, which drop precipitously to the lagoon. Deep into one of these cliffs goes the Maraa Grotto, also called the Paroa Cave. It usually has a lake inside and goes much deeper into the hill than appears at first glance. The mouth of the cave is clearly visible from the road. Park in the parking lot, not along the road.

THE WEST COAST

North of Maraa the road runs through the Paea and Punaauia suburbs of Papeete. The west coast is the driest part of Tahiti, and it's very popular with Europeans, Americans, and others who have built homes along the lagoon and in the hills overlooking it and Moorea.

✪ **Arahurahu Marae**   At PK 22.5 a small road on the right of Magasin Laut leads to a narrow valley, on the floor of which sits the Arahurahu Marae. This particular temple apparently had no special historical importance, but it was restored in 1954, complete with exhibit boards explaining the significance of each part. For example, the stone pens near the entrance were used to keep the pigs to be sacrificed to the gods. This is the only marae in all of Polynesia that has been fully restored, and it is maintained like a museum. Arahurahu is used during the Tiurai celebrations for the reenactment of old Polynesian ceremonies.

✪ **Tahiti Museum**   At PK 15.1, turn left at the gas station and follow the signs through a residential area to the lagoon and the *Musée de Tahiti et Ses Isles* (Museum of Tahiti and Her Islands), one of the best in the South Pacific. It has displays of the geological history of the islands; their sea life, flora, and fauna; and the history and culture of their peoples. There are exhibits devoted to traditional weaving, tapa-cloth making, early tools, body ornaments, tatooing, fishing and horticultural techniques, religion and maraes, games and sports, warfare and arms, deaths and funerals, writers and missionaries. Most, but not all, of the display legends are translated into English. The museum is open from 9:30am to 5:30pm Tuesday through Sunday; admission is 500 CFP ($5).

Lagoonarium   At PK 11.4, the Captain Bligh Restaurant and Bar has a terrific view of Moorea and is home to the *Le Lagoonarium de Tahiti,* an underwater viewing room surrounded by pens containing reef sharks, sea turtles, and many tropical fish. Admission is 500 CFP ($5) for adults and 300 CFP ($3) for children under 12. The Lagoonarium and the restaurant's bar is open Tuesday to Sunday from 9am to 9pm.

The road becomes four lanes soon after the Lagoonarium, and passes shopping centers and marinas in Punaauia. Just before the Hotel Sofitel Maeva Beach, it divides. The left lanes feed into the Rte. 5 freeway, which roars back to Papeete. The right lanes will take you along Rte. 1, the old road that goes past the west coast hotels and the Faaa airport before returning to town.

SAFARI EXPEDITIONS

So-called safari expeditions into Tahiti's interior offer a very different view of the island. They follow narrow, unpaved roads up over the mountains from one coast to the other, usually via the breathtaking Papenoo Valley, through a tunnel cut through the island's steep interior ridge, and down a steep track to Lake Vaihiria. On the way down they follow the Vaihiria River and stop for a refreshing swim. These trips fall into the "soft adventure" category, since you ride in the back of four-wheel-drive vehicles over some very rough roads. The views are spectacular, however, and the cool temperatures at the higher elevations are refreshing. William Leeteg of **Adventure Eagle Tours** (☎ 41.37.63) lends his experiences growing up on the island to his commentaries. Patrice Bordes's **Tahiti Safari Expedition** (☎ 42.14.15) and French-led **Tahiti Ata Mou'a Safari Tours** (☎ 41.99.00) also are informative. All three charge about 5,500 CFP ($55) per person. Reservations may be made at most hotel activities desks.

It's far from inexpensive, but a spectacular way to see Tahiti's interior mountains, valleys, and waterfalls is by helicopter with **Tahiti Helicoptères**

Impressions

It came upon me little by little. I came to like the life here, with its ease and its leisure, and the people, with their good-nature and their happy smiling faces.
—W. Somerset Maugham, 1921

(☎ 83.34.26) or **Pacific Helicoptère Service** (☎ 83.16.80). Pick a day when clouds aren't hanging around the mountain tops. Early morning usually is the clearest time.

3 Where to Stay

Two of Tahiti's large resort hotels are on the northwest coast, facing Moorea, while the Hotel Hyatt Regency Tahiti and Le Royal Tahitien Hotel are both east of town. These establishments have more of a beachside resort atmosphere than do the businesslike hotels in Papeete, which provide the convenience of being close to restaurants, shops, nightclubs, and a quick escape on the Moorea ferries. Another thing to consider in making your choice of hotel is public transportation, since le trucks go as far west as the Sofitel Maeva Beach until 10pm but stop running to the Hyatt and Le Royal Tahitien after 5pm.

There is a huge difference in quality between Tahiti's moderate and inexpensive accommodations, which are very basic, roof-over-your-head establishments. No establishment in the entire territory is comparable in price or quality to the inexpensive motels so common in the United States, Canada, Australia, and New Zealand.

Tahiti Tourisme has a list of pensions, private homes, and camping facilities. See "Visitor Information & Entry Requirements" and "Money," in the previous chapter.

EXPENSIVE

Hotel Hyatt Regency Tahiti

B.P. 1015, Papeete, Tahiti (Mahina, 8km [5 miles] east of Papeete). ☎ **48.11.22** or 800/ 228-9000. Fax 45.25.44. 200 rms. A/C MINIBAR TEL. 27,000 CFP–31,500 CFP ($270–$315). AE, DC, MC, V. Take one of the Mahina trucks, which do not run after 5pm.

Referred to locally as the Tahara'a, its former name, the Hyatt virtually hangs off the steep headland Captain Cook named One Tree Hill, with the reception and other public areas on top. From this clifflike perch, the entire complex has a breathtaking view over Matavai Bay, Tahiti's north coast, and Moorea, a vista shared by each room's bougainvillea-draped terrace. The view is the prime reason to stay here, however, for this hotel is not as well maintained as the Tahiti Beachcomber Parkroyal. Nor is there a beach directly on the premises, although a free "beach buggy" shuttles between reception and a black-sand beach at the bottom of the hill. To make up for this shortcoming, there's a snazzy hilltop pool area with waterfall, its own imported white-sand sunning area, and adjacent restaurant and bar. Americans will feel right at home here, since all units have combination tub-showers and two double beds.

Dining/Entertainment: Both indoor and outdoor seating are available at the Mahana Café, which specializes in European and Japanese cuisine and hosts the *Grande Revue du Pacifique,* one of Tahiti's top dance shows, on Saturday evening.

Services: Laundry; baby-sitting; downtown shopping shuttle.

Facilities: Shops; swimming pool; two tennis courts; spa and fitness center; car rental, tour, and activities desks; beauty salon.

Hotel Sofitel Maeva Beach

B.P. 6008, Papeete, Tahiti (Punaauia, 7.5km [4 miles] west of Papeete). ☎ **42.80.42** or 800/ 763-4835. Fax 41.05.05. 230 rms. A/C MINIBAR TV TEL. 18,500 CFP–25,000 CFP ($185–$250). AE, DC, MC, V. Take any Faaa or Mahina Truck.

Designed like a modern version of a terraced Mayan pyramid, this high-rise building sits beside Maeva Bay and a half-moon, black-sand beach of the same name. Unfortunately the murky lagoon off the beach isn't as good for swimming and snorkeling as for anchoring numerous cruising yachts, whose masts slice the hotel's view of Moorea. Rooms on the upper floors on the beach overlook Moorea from their balconies, while those on the garden side look south along Tahiti's west coast.

Dining/Entertainment: The open-air Restaurant L'Amiral de Bougainville, under a large thatch roof on the ground level next to the pool, serves three meals a day, while the indoor Sakura Restaurant has appropriate blond-wood, paper-wall decor for its tappanyaki-style Japanese dishes cooked by your table. Nighttime entertainment features Tahitian dance shows.

Services: Laundry, baby-sitting.

Facilities: Boutique; car rental, tour, and activities desks; swimming pool; tennis courts and pro; golf driving range; water sports equipment (see "Golf, Water Sports & Other Outdoor Activities," below).

✪ Tahiti Beachcomber Parkroyal

B.P. 6014, Faaa, Tahiti (Faaa, 7km [4 miles] west of Papeete). ☎ **86.51.10** or 800/835-7742. Fax 86.51.30. 182 rms, 32 bungalows. A/C MINIBAR TV TEL. 28,500 CFP–44,000 CFP ($285–$440). AE, DC, MC, V. Take any Faaa or Maeva Beach truck.

Known locally as "The Beachcomber," this extraordinarily well-maintained property sits at Tataa Point on Tahiti's northwest corner. In the old pre-Christian days, souls leaped from this point on their journey to the ancient homeland. Today's guests get one of Tahiti's best views of Moorea, especially from romantic over-water bungalows. Each of the Beachcomber's Australian-style hotel rooms has a private patio or balcony with Moorea view through the coconut palms dotting the property. This hotel was born a Travelodge, so don't expect the largest rooms in Tahiti (the Hyatt has those). Although it has the best beach of the three expensive Tahiti hotels, the Beachcomber's white sand was imported, and the lagoon here isn't as clear as those on the outer islands.

Dining/Entertainment: Beside the lagoon and its own pool with swim-up bar, Le Lotus Restaurant provides gourmet lunches and dinners. In the main building, the open-air Te Tiare Restaurant serves breakfast, lunch, and dinner; it opens to a second pool. Tahitian string bands play nightly in Le Tiare Bar (open 24 hours a day), and Le Tiare Restaurant has Tahitian dance shows several nights a week.

Services: Laundry service, baby-sitting.

Facilities: Tennis courts; boutique; beauty salon; tour and car-rental desks; water sports equipment (see "Golf, Water Sports & Other Outdoor Activities," below).

MODERATE

⑤ Hotel Royal Papeete

B.P. 919, Papeete, Tahiti (blvd. Pomare opposite Moorea Ferry docks). ☎ **42.01.29** or 800/421-0000. Fax 43.79.09. 85 rms. A/C TEL. 10,500 CFP–12,000 CFP ($105–$120). AE, DC, MC, V.

This is one of my bases of operations, primarily because of its proximity to the Moorea Ferry docks and the inexpensive, mobile snack bars that gather there at night (see "Where to Dine," below). Presiding over a cozy lobby, the friendly veteran staff is adept at helping both business and vacation travelers, many of them Americans who find the rooms here more like home than tropical (even the plumbing fixtures were made in the U.S.A). Avoid rooms 221 through 227 and 321 through 327, which are subject to the weekend beat of La Cave nightclub downstairs and the whine of Papeete's diesel-powered generating plant next door. Le Gallieni Restaurant serves the most reasonably priced cooked breakfasts in town, plus French and Continental lunches and dinners. Its cozy bar is a popular watering hole for Moorea residents waiting for the ferry.

Hotel Tahiti

B.P. 416, Papeete, Tahiti (round-island road 1.6km [1 mile] west of downtown). ☎ **82.95.50** or 800/421-0000). Fax 81.31.51. 92 rms. and bungalows. A/C TEL. 9,000 CFP ($90) room; 10,000 CFP–11,000 CFP ($100–$110) bungalow. AE, DC, MC, V. Take any Faaa or Maeva Beach truck.

Time has taken its toll on this venerable establishment, the island's premier hotel before the Sofitel Maeva Beach was built in the 1960s. Nevertheless, it still has considerable old South Seas charm, especially under the huge thatch roofs over its public areas. The guest bungalows are the choice here. If you opt for a colonial-style hotel room, ask for one away from the main road along the rear of some of the buildings. There is no beach, but a lagoonside pool has partial views of Moorea. The bar features live Tahitian entertainment several nights a week, and an overwater restaurant serves French, American, and Polynesian meals. Because of its large public areas, the Tahiti is a popular venue for local gatherings.

❸ Le Royal Tahitien Hotel

B.P. 5001, Pirae, Tahiti (Pirae, 4km [2¹/₂ miles] east of downtown). ☎ **42.81.13** or 818/843-6068 in U.S. Fax 41.05.35. 40 rooms. A/C TEL. 15,000 CFP ($150). AE, DC, MC, V. Take a Mahina truck or follow avenue Prince Hinoi to Total and Mobil stations opposite each other; turn left, follow lane to Maire de Pirae, then into parking lot.

Another of my favorites, the Royal Tahitien is the island's only moderately priced hotel with its own beach, a stretch of deep black sand from which its suburban neighbors fish and swim. Contemporary two-story wood and stone buildings look like an American condominium complex, and their spacious rooms have a Scandinavian ski lodge ambiance, with Danish-style furniture and stonelike brick walls. The tropics are in abundance outside, however, for each room looks onto an expansive lawn and lush garden traversed by a small stream. Tropical ambience also pervades a beachside restaurant covered by a 1937-vintage thatch ceiling. Both the restaurant and adjacent bar are popular with local businesspeople, since they are one of the few such beachside establishments on Tahiti. The menu features good, moderately priced French cuisine—another draw. The rooms have coffee- and teamaking facilities, which those at the Hotel Tahiti and the Royal Papeete don't. There is no swimming pool.

HOSTELS

Tahiti Budget Lodge

B.P. 237, Papeete, Tahiti (rue du Frère Alain at the end of rue Edouard Ahnne). ☎ **42.66.82.** 7 rms (3 with bath). 12 bunks. FAN. 3,800 CFP–4,800 CFP ($38–$48) room; 1,800 CFP ($18) bunk. MC, V. From boulevard Pomare near market, go inland five blocks on rue du 22 Septembre, which becomes rue Edouard Ahnne.

This low-slung hostel is a quiet respite on the edge of Papeete's business district. Of the small, very basic but clean rooms, the best are those at the rear, away from an al fresco communal kitchen and TV lounge. Dormitory beds are in four rooms with three bunks each. Windows are not screened. A snack bar serves inexpensive fare. Laundry facilities and baggage storage are available for a fee. The hostel provides free airport transfers for guests with reservations.

4 Where to Dine

Visitors face a dilemma when choosing where to dine in Tahiti, for the island has a plethora of excellent French, Italian, and Chinese restaurants. The restaurants recommended below are but a few of many on Tahiti; don't hesitate to strike out on your own.

Ma'a Tahiti   The Tahitians have adopted many Western and Chinese dishes, but *ma'a Tahiti* (Tahitian food) remains highly popular. Like their Polynesian counterparts elsewhere, Tahitians still cook meals in an earth oven, known here as an *himaa*. Pork, chicken, fish, shellfish, leafy green vegetables such as taro leaves, and root crops such as taro and yams are wrapped in leaves, placed on a bed of heated stones, covered with more leaves and earth, and left to steam for several hours. When all is done, the earth is removed, the food unwrapped, and everyone proceeds to eat with his or her fingers. Results of the himaa are quite tasty, since the steam spreads the aroma of one ingredient to the others, and liberal use of coconut cream adds a sweet richness.

Tahiti's three big resort hotels usually have at least one *tama'ara'a* (Tahitian feast) a week; phone them to see when one will be offered. They usually run about 5,000 CFP to 6,000 CFP ($50 to $60) a head, but most include a Tahitian dance show after the meal (see "Evening Entertainment," below).

Many individual Tahitian dishes are offered by restaurants whose cuisine may otherwise be French, Italian, or Chinese. One you will see on almost every menu is *poisson cru,* French for "raw fish"; it's a Tahitian-style salad of fresh tuna or mahi mahi marinated in lime juice, cucumbers, onions, and tomatoes, all served in coconut cream. Another is local freshwater shrimp sautéed and served in a sweet sauce of curry and coconut cream.

Money-Saving Tips   Take advantage of *plats du jour* (daily specials), especially at lunch, and *prix-fixe* (fixed priced) menus, sometimes called "tourist menus" by Tahiti's restaurants. These three- or four-course offerings usually are made from fresh produce direct from the market and represent a significant savings over ordering from the menu.

Patronize restaurants subscribing to the government's "tourist rates" on alcoholic beverages; beer and wine in these establishments cost significantly less than elsewhere. And order *vin ordinaire* (table wine) served in a carafe. The chef buys good-quality wine in bulk; you get the savings.

Be Your Own Chef   Another method of saving on food is to make your own snacks or perhaps a picnic lunch to enjoy at the beach. Every village has a Chinese grocery, and Le Défi supermarket is in the heart of Papeete, in Fare Tony on the west side of the Vaima Centre. Fresh sticks of French bread are very inexpensive, and the markets carry cheeses, deli meats, vegetables, and other sandwich makings, many imported from France.

Locally brewed Hinano beers sell for about 125 CFP ($1.25) in grocery stores, versus 350 CFP ($3.50) or more at the hotel bars, and bottles of decent French wine cost a fraction of restaurant prices. The least expensive wines are Margot and Faragui, both Algerian and Moroccan vintages shipped in bulk to Tahiti and bottled in plastic containers (they are jokingly referred to as "Château Plastique"). Add a little water to make them more palatable.

✪ Les Roulettes   The best food bargain in Papeete literally rolls out every night on the Moorea Ferry docks: *les roulettes.*

These portable meal wagons have assigned spaces in the waterfront parking lots. Some owners set up charcoal grills behind their trucks and small electric generators in front to provide plenty of light for the diners, who sit on stools along either side of the vehicles. The entire waterfront takes on a carnival atmosphere as young French soldiers and sailors squire their beautiful Tahitian vahines among the trucks, sampling this and that.

The normal menu includes charbroiled steaks or chicken with french fries (known, respectively, as *steak frites* and *poulet frites),* familiar Cantonese dishes, and poisson cru for 700 CFP to 900 CFP ($7 to $9) per plate. Glassed-in display cases along the sides of some trucks hold actual examples of what's offered at each (not exactly the most appetizing exhibits, but you can just point to what you want rather than fumbling in French). Other trucks specialize in crepes, pizzas, couscous, and waffles *(gaufres).* Even if you don't eat an entire meal at les roulettes, stop for a crepe or waffle and enjoy the scene.

FRENCH RESTAURANTS

⊛ Acajou Restaurant
Bd. Pomare in Fare Tony (opposite the west side of Vaima Centre on the Papeete waterfront). ☎ **42.87.58.** Reservations recommended at dinner. 1,000 CFP–1,800 CFP ($10–$18). AE, DC, MC, V. Mon–Sat 5am–9:30pm. FRENCH.

The flagship of chef Acajou's empire (he goes only by this nickname), this is consistently the most popular French restaurant on Tahiti. The food is excellent, the prices very reasonable, and the setting alongside the Quay and Vaima Center convenient. A sidewalk terrace faces the yachts moored along the Quay; a more formal dining room re-creates the atmosphere of a French country inn. The sidewalk terrace is a nice place to have a cool beer or a mixed drink after a day of shopping in Papeete. All the waiters speak English. Acajou's fabulous freshwater shrimp with coconut-curry sauce is as good as this mouth-waterer gets.

✪ Auberge du Pacifique
PK 11.2, Punaauia (3.7km [2.2 miles] south of Hotel Sofitel Maeva Beach on the round-island road; the Paea trucks go by it during the day; take a taxi at night). ☎ **43.98.30.** Reservations recommended, especially on weekends. 1,600 CFP–3,000 CFP ($16–$30); special tourist menu 4,000 CFP ($40). AE, MC, V. Wed–Mon 11:30am–2pm and 6:30–9:30pm. FRENCH, TAHITIAN.

This lagoonside restaurant has been Tahiti's finest since 1974. Owner Jean Galopin was named a Maître Cuisinier (Master Chef) de France in 1987, in large part because of his unique blending of French and Tahitian styles of cooking. His *fafa* (chicken and taro leaves steamed in coconut milk) is in marked contrast with what comes out of a local himaa on Sunday afternoon. Jean has shared many of his techniques in a popular cookbook, *La Cuisine de Tahiti et des Iles.* The roof over his main dining room opens to reveal the twinkling stars above, while a second, air-conditioned salon sports a mural by noted local artist François Revello. Guests are welcome to visit Tahiti's only air-conditioned wine cellar and choose from among excellent French vintages. A special tourist menu features poisson cru and main courses such as a light mahi mahi soufflé.

Le Belvédère

Fare Rau Ape Valley (perched high on a ridge overlooking Papeete and Moorea; transportation provided by restaurant from your hotel). ☎ **42.73.44.** Reservations imperative. 4,200 CFP ($45) per person, including full meal, wine, and ride. AE, MC, V. Thurs–Tues 11:30am–2pm and 6–9:30pm. FRENCH.

Dinner at Le Belvédère is a highlight of Tahiti for many visitors who don't stay at the Hyatt, for this innlike establishment has a spectacular view of the city and Moorea from its perch 2,000 feet up in the cool hills above Papeete. The restaurant provides free round-trip transportation from your hotel up the narrow, one-lane, winding, switchback road that leads to it (I don't encourage anyone to attempt this drive in a rental car). Le Belvédère's truck makes several trips for lunch or dinner. The 5pm pickup reaches the restaurant in time for a sunset cocktail. The specialty of the house is fondue bourguignonne served with six sauces. Other choices are mahi mahi grilled with butter, steak in green-pepper sauce or "any way you like it," shish kebab, and chicken with wine. Unfortunately the quality of the cuisine doesn't match the view, so treat the evening as a sightseeing excursion, not as a fine dining experience.

Captain Bligh Restaurant and Bar

PK 11.4, Punaauia, at the Lagoonarium (3.9km [2.3 miles] south of Hotel Sofitel Maeva Beach on the round-island road; the Paea trucks go by it during the day; take a taxi at night). ☎ **43.62.90.** Reservations recommended on weekends. 1,500 CFP–2,900 CFP ($15–$29); set tourist menu 3,500 CFP–4,500 CFP ($35–$45). AE, V. Tues–Sun 11:30am–2pm; Tues–Sat 7–9pm; bar Tues–Sat 9am–9pm. FRENCH.

One of Tahiti's most unusual restaurant settings, this large thatch-roofed building extends over the lagoon (you can toss bread crumbs to the fish swimming just over the railing), or you can stroll along a pier to a tiny man-made island and dine al fresco under the stars. The pier goes on out to the Lagoonarium, an underwater viewing room (see "The Circle Island Tour," earlier in this chapter). Specialties of the house are grilled steaks and lobster plus a few seafood dishes, such as curried shrimp and mahi mahi under a creamed pepper sauce. The Captain Bligh usually stages Tahitian dance shows Friday and Saturday at 8:45pm.

ITALIAN RESTAURANTS

L'Api'zzeria

Bd. Pomare, west of av. Bruat (west of the Vaima Centre and post office, on the waterfront). ☎ **42.98.30.** Reservations not accepted. Pizzas and pastas 400 CFP–1,300 CFP ($4–$13); meat courses 1,500 CFP–1,900 CFP ($15–$19). MC, V. Mon–Sat 11:30am–10pm. ITALIAN.

This small building sitting among a grove of trees across from the harbor resembles an Elizabethan waterfront tavern. The exposed-beam Tudor interior has been accented with nautical relics, such as a ship's brass compass in one corner and a large pilot wheel used as a table divider. The food, on the other hand, is definitely Italian. Both pizzas and steaks are cooked in a wood-fired oven. The menu features spaghetti, fettuccine, lasagna, steak milanese, veal in white or marsala wine sauce, and grilled homemade Italian sausage. You can dine inside or outside under large shade trees beside boulevard Pomare.

⑤ Lou Pescadou

Rue Anne-Marie Javouhey at passage Cardella (take narrow passage Cardella, a one-block street that looks like an alley, directly behind the Vaima Centre). ☎ **43.74.26.** Reservations not accepted. Pizzas and pastas 500 CFP–1,300 CFP ($5–$13); meat courses 1,300 CFP–1,600 CFP ($13–$16). No credit cards. Daily 11:30am–2pm and 6:30–11pm. ITALIAN.

Ambience is one reason this cozy establishment draws a lively young professional clientele: red-and-white-checked tablecloths, dripping candles on each table, Ruffino bottles hanging from every nook and cranny, a backlit stained-glass window, ceiling fans circulating the aroma of garlic and oregano, shuttered windows thrown open so passersby can look in, friendly waiters running hither and yon carrying pizzas. Good Italian fare at reasonable prices is another reason it's one of Papeete's most popular eateries (come prepared to wait for a table). The individual-size pizzas are cooked in a wood-fire oven range, and the pasta dishes include spaghetti, fettuccine, and lasagna.

CHINESE RESTAURANTS

Acajou Numera Hoe

Rue François-Cardella (just off bd. Pomare, opposite the Municipal Market). ☎ **43.19.22.** Breakfast 400 CFP–700 CFP ($4–$7); lunch 750 CFP–1,000 CFP ($7.50–$10). No credit cards. Daily 4am–5pm. CANTONESE.

Not to be confused with the Acajou French restaurant mentioned above, this establishment has the same owner who insists on offering quality food, hearty portions, and reasonable prices. Here his selections are Cantonese-style dishes such as chow mein, which can be prepared in bulk and displayed cafeteria-style. The wait staff delivers your selection to your table.

La Jade Palace

Bd. Pomare in the Vaima Centre (east side street level of Vaima Centre). ☎ **42.02.19.** Reservations recommended. 1,000 CFP–1,500 CFP ($12–$22). AE, V. Mon–Fri 11am–1:40pm; Mon–Sat 6:30–9:40pm. CANTONESE.

The most elegant of Papeete's Chinese restaurants, La Jade Palace serves a relatively limited number of excellent Cantonese dishes, with emphasis on soups, chicken, and beef. Best of the seafood dishes are the crystal prawns (actually local freshwater shrimp), which are served almost raw with flavorings of ginger and spicy peppers. Limited outdoor seating is available.

Le Mandarin

Rue des Ecoles, near rue Collette (near the Town Hall, in the heart of Papeete, two blocks from bd. Pomare). ☎ **42.99.03.** Reservations not necessary. 1,000 CFP–2,400 CFP ($10–$24); tourist menu 2,100 CFP–3,150 CFP ($21–$31.50). MC, V. Daily 11am–1:30pm and 6–9:30pm. CANTONESE.

A good moderate choice, Le Mandarin and the hotel of the same name (it's just around the corner on rue Collette) share the same owners and are joined by a passageway. Chinese decor disguises the storefront location of the dining rooms. A wide-ranging menu lists vegetable, chicken, duck, beef, pork, and seafood dishes. Special tourist menus are prepared for two persons or more.

Polyself

Rue Paul-Gauguin, in Banque de Polynésie Building (¹⁄₂ block off bd. Pomare, near the Municipal Market). ☎ **43.75.32.** 700 CFP–900 CFP ($7–$9). No credit cards. Daily 5am–1:30pm. CANTONESE.

Chinese dishes such as chow mein, sweet and sour pork, and fried rice are displayed in a stainless-steel counter in this air-conditioned establishment. No English is necessary; just point to what you want. Dim sim dumplings augment such traditional French breakfast fare as croissants and coffee.

SNACK BARS

You won't find a McDonald's or any other international fast-food chain in French Polynesia. Their places are taken here by a plethora of snack bars, or simply "snacks." Most offer hamburgers, but their most popular item is the *casse-croûte*, a sandwich made from a crusty French baguette and slivers of such ingredients as ham, tuna, lettuce, tomatoes, cucumbers, and even spaghetti. They usually cost about 150 CFP ($1.50) or less.

D. Hillaire Patissier

Rue du Général-de-Gaulle in the Vaima Centre (at street level, rear side of Vaima Centre). ☎ **42.68.22.** Pastries and sandwiches 150 CFP–500 CFP ($1.50–$5). No credit cards. Mon–Fri 5am–6pm; Sat 5am–noon. PATISSERIE.

One of several patisseries in Papeete, this spotless, air-conditioned establishment has been my favorite breakfast haunt since the late 1970s. Order at the cash register, then sit down. The staff will bring your selections to your table. The strong French coffee is dear at 250 CFP ($2.50) a cup but worth it.

L'Oasis du Vaima

Rue Général-de-Gaulle at rue Jeanne d'Arc (corner of Vaima Centre, opposite Cathédrale de l'Immaculée Conception). ☎ **45.45.01.** Sandwiches, burgers, small pizzas 200 CFP–950 CFP ($2–$9); meals 1,000 CFP–1,350 CFP ($10–$13.50). No credit cards. Mon–Sat 5am–6pm. SNACK BAR.

In addition to dishing out ice cream and milk shakes to passersby at a sidewalk counter, this kiosklike building has a covered dining terrace to one side where it serves up a variety of goodies, from crispy casse-croûtes to two delicious plats-du-jour selections each day. A special treat for Papeete: You can make a light meal from the salad bar for 850 CFP ($8.50).

Le Retrot

Bd. Pomare, front of Vaima Centre, on waterfront. ☎ **42.86.83.** Sandwiches and burgers 400 CFP–750 CFP ($4–$7.50); pizza and pastas 600 CFP–1,200 CFP ($6–$12); main courses 1,650 CFP–2,100 CFP ($16.50–$21.50). Daily 6am–midnight. FRENCH/ITALIAN/SNACKS.

Although this Parisian-style sidewalk cafe has full French- and Italian-style meals, I include it under snack bars because it's a popular place to grab a quick bite while on the run, or just sit and laze away the day while watching the world pass along the Quay. The menu is large and diverse, with an excellent selection of salads, pizzas, and pasta getting most attention from the cafe crowd. There's also an excellent pastry and ice cream bar in the back corner.

Snack Epi d'Or

Rue du Maréchal-Foch near rue Edouard-Ahnne (behind the Municipal Market, same block as Te Hoa Chinese restaurant). ☎ **43.07.13.** 150 CFP–250 CFP ($1.50–$2.50). No credit cards. Mon–Sat 4am–2pm; Sun 3am–10am. SNACK BAR.

The casse-croûtes don't get any crispier than at Epi d'Or because this establishment is actually an upstairs bakery. Stand on the sidewalk in front of the carryout counter (there's no place to sit here), and watch the hot sticks of French bread come down the dumbwaiter. You can buy baguettes by themselves or as sandwiches. Note the unusual hours on Sunday.

5 Golf, Water Sports & Other Outdoor Activities

GOLF   The 18-hole, 6,950-yard Olivier Bréaud International Golf Course, PK 40.2, Atimaono (☎ 57.40.32), sprawls over the site of William Stewart's cotton plantation. A clubhouse, pro shop, restaurant, bar, locker rooms, showers, swimming pool, spa pool, and driving range are on the premises. Greens fees are 3,000 CFP ($30), or 11,000 CFP ($110), including fees, clubs, cart, and transportation from Papeete.

HIKING   Tahiti has a number of hiking trails, such as the cross-island Papenoo Valley–Lake Vaihiria route. Another ascends to the top of Mount Aorai. None of these should be undertaken without the proper equipment and a guide. Downpours can occur in the higher altitudes, swelling the streams that most trails follow, and the nights can become bitterly cold and damp. The "rainy side" of the island can shift from one day to the next, depending on which way the wind blows. In addition, the quick-growing tropical foliage can quickly obscure a path that was easily followed a few days before. Permits are required to use some trails that cross government land. With all this in mind, check with the Tahiti Tourisme for the names of guides and hiking clubs.

HORSEBACK RIDING   Tropical Ranch (☎ 45.34.34), in Punaauia above the Hotel Sofitel Maeva Beach, has horses for rent at 2,500 CFP ($25) an hour. Tahiti Tourisme provides a list of local equestrian clubs.

SAILING   Mer et Loisirs (☎ 43.97.99), in a floating office on the Quay across from the main post office, is agent for several charter sail- and powerboats. Most of these come with or without a skipper and rent for at least 60,000 CFP ($600) a day. Day trips or weekend voyages to Marlon Brando's Tetiaroa atoll, about 30 miles north of Papeete, cost 12,000 CFP ($120) if you bring your own picnic, 16,000 CFP ($160) if they provide lunch. Weekend excursions to Tetiaroa cost 26,000 CFP ($260), including meals and drinks.

SPORTS CLUBS   The Matavai Hotel, Resort & Sports Centre (☎ 42.67.67), in the Tipaerui Valley on the west side of downtown, has a minigolf course, billiards, table tennis, darts, swimming pool, and snack bar. It's open daily 8am to 11pm. Admission is 1,000 CFP ($10), including one drink.

TENNIS   Visitors are not encouraged to use Tahiti's public tennis courts, so if you're a tennis buff, stay at a hotel with courts available for its guests.

WATER SPORTS   Owned and operated by Richard Johnson, an American marine biologist who has lived in French Polynesia for a number of years, Tahiti Aquatique (☎ 41.08.54) offers a comprehensive list of water sports activities at the Hotel Sofitel Maeva Beach. Some sample prices (per person, unless otherwise indicated): scuba diving, per dive including equipment and a guide, 5,000 CFP ($50); introductory dive, 8,000 CFP ($80); fin, mask, and snorkel rental, 800 CFP ($8); glass-bottomed-boat tour, 1,900 CFP ($19); waterskiing, per 15 minutes, 1,900 CFP ($19); sport-fishing charters, 45,000 CFP ($450) for a half day or 65,000 CFP ($650) for a full day, per boat; and windsurfers, 1,500 CFP ($15) per hour per boat. Tahiti Aquatique also operates the water sports shack at the Hotel Tahiti Beachcomber Parkroyal (☎ 82.51.10, ext. 5610).

6 Shopping

THE SHOPPING SCENE

There's no shortage of things to buy in Tahiti, especially in Papeete: black pearls, both French and Tahitian fashions, and handcrafts. The selection and prices on some items may be better on Moorea.

Duty-free shopping is very limited, with French perfumes the best deal. **Duty Free Tahiti** (☎ 42.61.61), on the street level, water side of the Vaima Centre, is the largest duty-free shop. Its specialties are Seiko, Lorus, and Cartier watches and Givenchy, Yves St. Laurent, Chanel, and Guerlain perfumes. The **airport departure lounge** has four duty-free shops.

BEST BUYS
BLACK PEARLS

French Polynesia is the world's largest producer of cultured black pearls, most of which are grown at pearl farms in the clear, clean lagoons of the Tuamotu Archipelago east of Tahiti. Pearls are cultured by implanting a small nucleus into the shell of a live oyster, which then coats it with nacre, the same lustrous substance that lines the mother-of-pearl shell. The nacre of the oysters used in French Polynesia, the *Pinctada margaritifera,* produces dark pearls that are known as "black" but whose actual color ranges from black with shades of rose or green, which are the rarest and most valuable, to slightly grayer than white. The bulk of the crop is black with bluish or brownish tints. Most range in size from 10mm to 17mm (slightly less than half an inch to slightly less than three-quarters of an inch).

A pearl's value is determined by its size, color, luster, lack of imperfections, and shape. No two are exactly alike, but the most valuable are the larger ones that are most symmetrical, have few dark blemishes, and whose color is dark with the shades of a peacock showing through a bright luster. A high-quality pearl 13mm or larger will sell for $10,000 or more, but there are thousands to choose from in the $400 to $1,000 range. Some small, imperfect-but-still-lovely pearls cost much less.

The *National Geographic* carried a very informative article on cultured pearls in its August 1985 issue, so dig it out of the attic before heading off to Tahiti.

With most tourists now spending minimum time on Tahiti in favor of the other islands, you may find pearl prices in Papeete to be less than on Moorea and Bora Bora. That's not always the case, so you should look in **Island Fashion Black Pearls** and the other shops on Moorea before making a purchase in Papeete.

Even in Papeete, it pays to shop around. The city has scores of *bijouteries* (jewelry shops) carrying black pearls in a variety of settings. Most are in or around the Vaima Centre or along boulevard Pomare.

Start at ✪ **Tahiti Perles Center** (☎ 42.46.44) on boulevard Pomare next to the Protestant Temple. This shop not only has a fine selection but also a museum explaining the history of pearls back to antiquity, the method by which they are cultured, and the things to look for when making your selection. The center carries only excellent-quality pearls and uses only 18-karat gold for its settings, so the prices tend to be high.

Now walk along boulevard Pomare to the Vaima Centre. At the street level, check out **Tahiti Perles** (☎ 45.05.05), a branch of Tahiti Perles Center. On the second level, look around **Or et Perles Création Centre** and **World of Pearls** (both ☎ 41.36.34), which carry the jewelry line of Didier Sibani, one of the pioneers of the local industry.

When finished, walk east along boulevard Pomare, then turn right on rue Jean Gilbert (between Banque Socredo and Tahiti Sport) in the Quartier du Commerce. A block inland, look for **Pai Moana Perles** (☎ 43.31.10), a little shop owned by Peter Ringland, a Canadian whose Pai Moana pearl farm at Manihi in the Tuamotus directly supplies this shop as well as outlets on Moorea. (*Advisory:* Pai Moana may move all its operations to Moorea and close this Papeete shop during the life of this edition.)

HANDCRAFTS

Economic hard times in recent years have had one salutary effect: Strapped for income, many local residents began producing a wide range of jewelry made from seashells, homemade quilts, rag dolls, needlework, and straw hats, mats, baskets, and handbags.

The most popular item by far, however, is the cotton *pareu*, or wraparound sarong, which is screened, blocked, or printed by hand in the colors of the rainbow. The same material is made into other tropical clothing and various items, such as bedspreads. Pareus are sold virtually everywhere a visitor might wander.

✪ **Papeete Municipal Market** is the place to shop. It has stalls both upstairs and on the surrounding sidewalk, where local women's associations offer a wide selection of handcrafts at reasonable prices. The market is one of the few places where you can regularly find pareus for 1,000 CFP ($10), bedspreads made of the colorful tie-dyed and silk-screened pareu material, and *tivaivai*, the colorful appliqué quilts stitched together by Tahitian women as their great-grandmothers were shown by the early missionaries. By and large, cloth goods are sold at the sidewalk stalls; those upstairs have a broader range of shell jewelry and other items.

Tahitian women also operate handcraft and flower stalls on the Quay at the foot of rue Paul-Gauguin, where cruise ships dock.

For finer-quality handcrafts, such as woodcarvings from the Marquesas Islands, shell chandeliers, tapa lamp shades, or mother-of-pearl shells, try **Manuia Curios** (☎ 42.04.94) on place Notre Dame opposite the Catholic cathedral. Manuia Curios carries some artifacts from several South Pacific countries, including large basket masks from the Sepik River area of Papua New Guinea, and jade and porcelain from China. **Tamara Curios** (☎ 42.54.42), on rue Général-de-Gaulle in Fare Tony, has a wide range of quality shell jewelry, wood carvings, place mats, and local pineapple jam made with rum.

Impressions

It's a comfort to get into a pareu when one gets back from town . . . I should strongly recommend you to adopt it. It's one of the most sensible costumes I have ever come across. It's cool, convenient, and inexpensive.

—W. Somerset Maugham, 1921

TROPICAL CLOTHING

You've arrived in Tahiti and you notice that everyone under the sun is wearing print sun dresses or flowered aloha shirts. Where do you go to get yours?

Each hotel has at least one boutique carrying tropical clothing, including pareus. The prices there reflect the heavy tourist traffic, but they aren't much worse than at the stores in Papeete. Clothing, to put it bluntly, is dear in French Polynesia.

On boulevard Pomare, stop in **Marie Ah You** (☎ 42.03.31) and **Aloha Boutique** (☎ 42.87.52), both in the block west of the Vaima Centre. Their selections for women are trendy and a bit expensive. In the Vaima Centre, **Anemone** (☎ 43.02.66) has an unusual combination of quality T-shirts and chocolates.

Tahiti Art (☎ 42.97.43), in Fare Tony on boulevard Pomare just west of the Vaima Centre, specializes in block-printed traditional designs (as opposed to the swirls and swooshes with leaves and flowers popular on most pareus). Its designs are the most unique in town.

Tahiti Beach (☎ 42.24.34), on rue Emile Martin a block inland from boulevard Pomare, has Papeete's widest selection of colorful men's aloha shirts in traditional flowered patterns, plus hand-designed T-shirts, dresses, tablecloths, and beach towels. It's a good place to find children's sizes, and you can shop over the lunch break (it's open from Monday to Friday from 8am to 5pm and on Saturday, from 8am to noon).

7 Island Nights

A 19th-century European merchant once wrote of the Tahitians, "Their existence was in never-ending merrymaking." In many respects this is still true, for once the sun goes down Tahitians like to make merry as much today as they did in the 1830s, and Papeete has lots of good choices for visitors who want to join in the fun.

✪ **Tahitian Dancing**   Like all Polynesians—the Hawaiians and their hula are one example—Tahitians are renowned for their dancing. Before the Europeans came, they would stage dancing entertainments known as *heivas* for almost any reason, from blessing the harvest to celebrating a birth. After eating meals cooked in their earth ovens, they would get out the drums and nose flutes and dance the nights away. As described by Captain Cook and other early European visitors, some of the dances involved elaborate costumes, while others were quite lasciviously and explicitly danced in the nude or seminude, which only added to Tahiti's reputation as an island of love.

The puritanical Protestant missionaries managed to get laws enacted in the early 1820s to end all dancing. Of course, strict prohibition never works, and Tahitians—including a young Queen Pomare—would sneak into the hills to do what

Impressions

The young girls when ever they can collect 8 or 10 together dance a very indecent dance which they call Timorodee singing most indecent songs and useing most indecent actions in the practice of which they are brought up from their earlyest Childhood. . . .

—Capt. James Cook, 1769

Impressions

They have several negative comments on the beachcombing life in Tahiti: Not much cultural life. No intellectual stimulus. No decent library. Restaurant food is disgraceful . . . But I noticed that Saturday after Saturday they turned up at Quinn's with the most dazzling beauties on the island. When I reminded them of this they said, "Well that does compensate for the poor library."

—James A. Michener, 1951

came naturally. Only after the French took over in 1842 was dancing permitted again, and then only with severe limitations on what the dancers could do and wear. A result of these various restrictions was that most of the traditional dances performed by the Tahitians prior to 1800 were totally forgotten within a period of 100 years.

You'd never guess that Tahitians ever stopped dancing, for after tourists started coming in 1961 they went back to the old ways—or so it would seem. Today traditional dancing is a huge part of their lives—and of every visitor's itinerary. No one goes away without vivid memories of the elaborate and colorful costumes, the thundering drums, and the swinging hips of a Tahitian *tamure* in which young men and women provocatively dance around each other.

The tamure is one of several dances performed during a typical dance show. Others are the *o'tea,* in which men and women in spectacular costumes dance certain themes, such as spear throwing, fighting, or love; the *aparima,* the hand dance, which emphasizes everyday themes, such as bathing and combing one's hair; the *hivinau,* in which men and women dance in circles and exclaim *"hiri haa haa"* when they meet each other; and the *pata'uta'u,* in which the dancers beat the ground or their thighs with their open hands. It's difficult to follow the themes without understanding Tahitian, but the color and rhythms (which have been influenced by faster, double-time beats from the Cook Islands) make the dances thoroughly enjoyable—and leave little doubt as to the temptations that inspired the mutiny on the *Bounty.*

As mentioned in the listings under "Where to Stay," above, traditional dance shows usually are staged along with Tahitian feasts at Tahiti's big resort hotels: the **Hyatt Regency Tahiti** (☎ 48.11.22); the **Sofitel Maeva Beach** (☎ 42.80.42); and the **Tahiti Beachcomber Parkroyal** (☎ 86.51.30). Although there is no le truck service to the Hyatt after 5pm, its *Grande Revue du Pacifique* is consistently the best show. For many years the Sofitel Maeva Beach has had a midday feast and show on Sunday. The **Hotel Tahiti** (☎ 82.95.50) may also have a performance. Call to find out when the feasts and dance shows are scheduled.

In addition to the hotels, the **Captain Bligh Restaurant and Bar** (☎ 43.62.90) usually has shows on Friday and Saturday at 8:45pm.

Gambling   Three small gambling casinos beckon visitors to wager at bacarat, roulette, blackjack tables, and a Chinese wheel-of-fortune game known as *pau.* They are in **Hotel Royal Papeete** (☎ 42.09.29), **Hotel Kon Tiki Pacific** (☎ 43.72.82), and **Hotel Prince Hinoi** (☎ 42.33.66), all within a block of each other on boulevard Pomare, opposite the Moorea Ferry docks. All are open daily from 2pm to 2am. Although they technically are private clubs (local residents must pay dues), overseas visitors get in free (tell the doorman you're a tourist). Dress codes are smart casual: slacks for men, dresses for women.

Pub Crawling   Papeete has a nightclub or watering hole to fit anyone's taste, from upscale private (*privé*) discotheques to down-and-out bars and dance halls where Tahitians strum on guitars while sipping on large bottles of Hinano beer. If you look like a tourist, you'll be allowed into the private clubs. Generally, everything gets to full throttle after 9pm (except on Sunday, when most are closed). None of the clubs is inexpensive. Expect to pay 1,000 CFP ($10) or more cover charge, which will include your first drink. After that, beers cost at least 500 CFP ($5), with most mixed drinks in the 1,000 CFP–1,500 CFP ($10–$15) range.

Before you head out, stroll down boulevard Pomare near the Tahiti Tourisme's office. There you will find Tahitian women weaving flower crowns, traditional headgear for Papeete's female merrymakers. Buy one if you want to look the part. The Tahitians will love you for it; everyone else will think you're a silly tourist.

The Hotel Royal Papeete (☎ 42.01.29), on boulevard Pomare, is home to two popular nightspots: The **Tamure Hut** is one of the city's few clubs designed for visitors as well as locals. The decor evokes the earlier period when Quinn's Bar dominated Papeete's nightlife scene. Live bands crank out various styles of dance music, from Tahitian to 1950s rock-and-roll. It's open Saturday from 9pm to 3am. **La Cave** has loud Tahitian music for dancing on Friday and Saturday from 9pm to 3am. It's dark inside and popular with mahus, so one cannot always be sure at first glance of every stranger's gender.

The narrow rue des Ecoles is the heart of Papeete's mahu district, where male transvestites hang out. The **Piano Bar** (☎ 42.88.24) is the most popular of the "sexy clubs" along this street, especially for its late-night strip shows featuring female impersonators. When you've seen enough, go next door to **Lido Nightclub** (☎ 42.95.84). Both are open daily from 3pm to 3am.

6 Moorea

Across the Sea of the Moon from Tahiti beckons the haunting, dinosaur-like outline of Moorea, an island so stunningly beautiful that Hollywood often uses "stock shots" of its jagged mountains, deep bays, and emerald lagoons to create a South Seas setting for movies that don't even take place in French Polynesia. It also is a peaceful island where a hint of old Polynesia coexists with modern resort hotels and fine restaurants. It's with very good reason, therefore, that most visitors to French Polynesia head to Moorea.

Geologists attribute Moorea's beauty to a great volcano, the northern half of which either fell into the sea or was blown away in a cataclysmic explosion, leaving the heart-shaped island we see today. The remaining rim of the old crater has eroded into the jagged peaks and spires that give the island its unique profile. Cathedral-like Mount Mouaroa—Moorea's trademark "Shark's Tooth"—shows up on innumerable postcards and on the 100-CFP coin. Mount Tohiea has a hole in its thumblike top, made by the legendary hero Pai. When the god of thieves attempted to steal Mount Rotui in the middle of the night, the legend goes, Pai threw his spear from Tahiti and pierced the top of Mount Tohiea. The noise woke up Moorea's roosters, who alerted the citizenry to put a stop to the dastardly plan.

Mount Rotui stands alone in the center of the ancient crater, its black cliffs and stovepipe buttresses dropping dramatically into Cook's Bay and Opunohu Bay, two blue fingers cutting deep into Moorea's interior. If not the world's most gorgeous bodies of water, these mountain-shrouded bays are certainly among the most photographed.

A paved road climbs to the base of the cliffs of the crater's wall to the Belvédère overlooking both bays, Mount Rotui, and the jagged old crater rim curving off to left and right. It is one of the South Pacific's most awesome views.

An offshore coral reef around Moorea encloses a calm blue lagoon, making the island ideal for swimming, boating, snorkeling, and diving. Unlike the black sands of Tahiti, white beaches stretch for miles on Moorea.

There are no towns on Moorea, which adds to its charm. Most of the island's 10,000 or so residents live on its fringing coastal plain, many of them in small settlements where lush valleys meet the

Impressions

From Tahiti, Moorea seems to have about forty separate summits: fat thumbs of basalt, spires tipped at impossible angles, brooding domes compelling to the eye. But the peaks which can never be forgotten are the jagged saw-edges that look like the spines of some forgotten dinosaur.

—James A. Michener, 1951

lagoon. Vanilla was the island's big crop early in the 20th century, and clapboard "vanilla houses" built with the profits still stand, surrounded by wide verandas trimmed with Victorian fretwork. Tourism is the base of Moorea's economy today, but vegetables, pineapples, and copra are still grown and are shipped to market in Papeete. Compared to the noisy city 12 miles away, Moorea is a rural paradise.

1 Getting Around

The ferries from Papeete land at Vaiare, a small bay 5km (3 miles) south of the airport on Moorea's east coast. Trucks and buses meet each ferry at Vaiare to carry its passengers to their final destinations on Moorea. Tell the drivers where you're going; they will show you which vehicle is going to your hotel. The trip from Vaiare to the end of the line at the Club Med, on Moorea's northwest corner, takes about one hour. These trucks also return to Vaiare prior to each departure, starting at the Club Med. They stop at the hotels and can be flagged down along the road elsewhere. The one-way fare is 200 CFP ($2) regardless of direction or length of the ride.

BY BUS   Although the island has no Tahitian-style le truck service, there is a *service de transport public:* two buses that run in opposite directions along the north shore between the large Chez Toa supermarket in Vaiare and Magasin Haapiti on the west coast. One bus leaves each store Monday to Saturday at 8am, 9am, 11am, 1pm, 3pm, 5pm, 7pm, and 9:30pm (they pass each other en route). The hotel reception desks should know the approximate time they will pass, or call 56.12.54 for the present schedule. The buses stop for passengers who flag them down (look for their "Transport Public" markings). One-way fare is 200 CFP ($2) for adults and 100 CFP ($1) for children.

BY TAXI   Moorea's taxis are owned by individuals who don't run around looking for customers. The only **taxi stands** are at the airport (☎ 56.10.18) and Club Med (☎ 56.33.10). The airport stand is manned daily from 6am to 6pm. The hotel desks can call one for you, or phone **Pero Taxis** (☎ 56.14.93) or **Albert Tours** (☎ 56.13.53). Make advance reservations for service between 6pm and 6am.

Fares are 600 CFP ($6) at flag fall plus 110 CFP ($1.10) per kilometer. They double from 8pm to 6am. Expect to pay about 3,500 CFP ($35) one way from the airport or Cook's Bay to the Club Med area, less for stops along the way. Be sure that you understand what the fare will be before you get in.

BY RENTAL CAR & SCOOTER   International car-rental firms on Moorea are **Avis** (☎ 56.12.58 or 800/331-1212) and **Europcar** (☎ 56.34.00 or 800/227-7368). Europcar is the less expensive of the two, with daily rates starting at 2,000 CFP ($20) plus 32 CFP (32¢) per kilometer. Unlimited kilometer rates begin at 4,300 CFP ($43) for half a day. The local firms **Pacificar** (☎ 56.11.03) and **Albert Rent-a-Car** (☎ 56.13.53) have unlimited mileage rates starting at 4,000 CFP ($40) for half a day. Add insurance and gasoline to all rates.

Pacificar also rents scooters and mopeds at 3,100 CFP to 3,500 CFP ($31–$35) for a full day, including gasoline, full insurance, and unlimited kilometers. If you rent a scooter, make sure that the brakes, headlight, and horn work before you drive off. None of the companies like to rent their scooters overnight, since local youths can easily jump-start them and go for joy rides.

Reservations are a very good idea, especially on weekends, when many Tahiti residents come to Moorea for a day or two.

BY BICYCLE The 60km (36-mile) road around Moorea is relatively flat. The two major hills are on the west side of Cook's Bay and just behind the Hotel Sofitel Ia Ora (which has a stupendous view of Tahiti). **Paradise Bikes** (☎ 56.31.97) provides mountain bikes to the hotels on the northwest coast. Contact the activities desks. **Pacificar** (☎ 56.11.03) and **Albert Rent-a-Car** (☎ 56.13.53) also both rent bicycles at their numerous locations. They cost about 1,000 CFP ($10) per day, more if you keep them overnight.

FAST FACTS: Moorea

Bookstores Kina Maharepa (☎ 56.22.44) in the Maharepa shopping center has English novels and magazines. Supersonics (☎ 56.14.96) in Le Petit Village shopping center opposite the Club Med carries some English-language magazines.

Currency Exchange Banque Socredo, Banque de Tahiti, and Banque de Polynésie have offices in or near the Maharepa shopping center near the Hotel Bali Hai. Westpac Bank is in Le Petit Village opposite the Club Med. Banque Socredo is open Monday to Friday from 7am to 3pm. The others are open Monday to Friday from 8am to noon and 1:30 to 4:30pm. Cash advances can be had using Visa and MasterCard at Banque Socredo's ATM machine at the Vaiare ferry docks.

Doctor Dr. Christian Joinville (☎ 56.32.32) has an office in Centre Noha, opposite the post office in Maharepa. He has lived on Moorea many years, speaks English fluently, and has treated many visitors, including me.

Drugstores Pharmacie Tran (☎ 56.10.51) is in Maharepa. The owner, Tran Thai Thanh, is a Vietnamese refugee who speaks English. Open Monday to Friday from 7:30am to noon and 2 to 5pm; Saturday from 7:30am to noon; and Sunday and holidays from 8 to 11am. In case of emergency, knock on the door.

Emergencies The telephone number for the Gendarmerie in Cook's Bay is 56.13.44. Local police have offices at Pao Pao (☎ 56.13.63) and at Haapiti (☎ 56.10.84) near the Club Med.

Hairdressers/Barbers Harmony Coiffure (56.18.04) is in Centre Noha in Maharepa. Vaitiare Coiffure (☎ 56.18.04) is opposite the Club Med in Haapiti.

Hospitals The island's infirmary, which has an ambulance, is at Afareaitu on the southwest coast (☎ 56.24.24).

Information The local Comité du Tourisme, B.P 531, Maharepa, Moorea (☎ 56.29.09), has an information office at Le Petit Village shopping center opposite the Club Med. Hours are Monday to Saturday from 8am to 5pm. The

Moorea

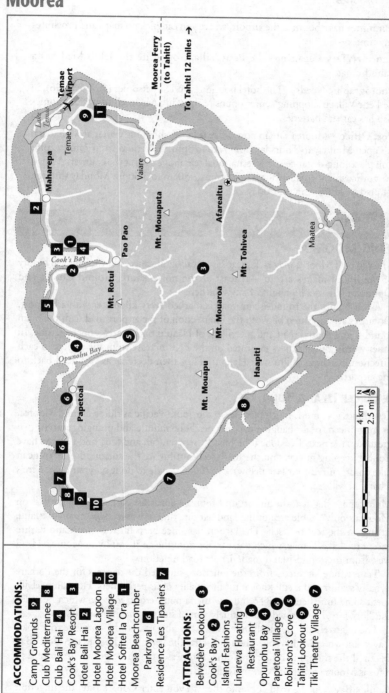

ACCOMMODATIONS:

Camp Grounds 9
Club Mediterranee 8
Club Bali Hai 4
Cook's Bay Resort 3
Hotel Bali Hai 2
Hotel Moorea Lagoon 5
Hotel Moorea Village 10
Hotel Sofitel Ia Ora 1
Moorea Beachcomber Parkroyal 6
Residence Les Tipaniers 7

ATTRACTIONS:

Belvédère Lookout 3
Cook's Bay 2
Island Fashions 1
Linareva Floating Restaurant 8
Opunohu Bay 4
Papetoai Village 6
Robinson's Cove 5
Tahiti Lookout 9
Tiki Theatre Village 7

Ferry - - -

committee has a booth at the airport, where you can pick up maps and brochures any time.

Laundry/Dry Cleaning   Le Petit Village opposite the Club Med has a Laundromat.

Photographic Needs   The hotel boutiques and Supersonics (☎ 56.14.96), in Le Petit Village shopping center opposite the Club Med, sell film. Supersonics also has camera batteries.

Post Office   Moorea's main post office is in the shopping center at Maharepa. It's open Monday to Thursday from 7am to 3pm, and Friday from 7am to 2pm. You place long-distance and international telephone calls at the counter. A small post office in Papetoai village is open from 7:30am to 3:30pm Monday through Thursday, to 2:30pm on Friday.

2 What to See & Do

SEEING MOOREA

The sights of Moorea may lack great historical significance, but the physical beauty of the island makes a tour—at least of the north shore, around Cook's and Opunohu bays—a highlight of any visit here.

As on Tahiti, the round-island road is marked every kilometer with a PK post. Distances are measured between the intersection of the airport road with the main round-island coastal road and the village of Haapiti on Moorea's opposite side. In other words, the distances indicated on the PKs increase from the airport in each direction, reaching 30km near Haapiti. They then decrease as you head back to the airport.

THE CIRCLE ISLAND TOUR

Few things give me as much pleasure in the South Pacific as riding around Moorea, its magnificent peaks hanging over my head one minute and plunging into its two great bays the next. I've done it by bicycle, scooter, car, and foot, and I always have trouble keeping my eyes on the road, so beautiful are the surroundings. You can take an organized tour (see below), but if you decide to do it on your own, here's what you will see.

Maharepa   Begin at the airport on Moorea's northeast corner. The airstrip is on Moorea's only sizable area of flat land. At one time it was a *motu,* or small island, sitting on the reef by itself. The lagoon has since been filled by man and nature except for Lake Temae, which you can see from the air if you fly to Moorea. Head west from the round-island road/airport road junction.

Temae, one kilometer from the junction, supplied the dancers for the Pomare dynasty's court and is still known for the quality of its performers. Herman Melville spent some time here in 1842 and saw the famous, erotic *upaupa,* which he called the "lory-lory," performed clandestinely, out of sight of the missionaries.

The relatively dry north shore between the airport and the entrance to Cook's Bay is known as **Maharepa.** The road skirts the lagoon and passes the Hotel Bali Hai and the shopping center and other businesses that have grown up around it. This is Moorea's primary commercial district.

Cook's Bay   As the road curves to the left, you enter **Cook's Bay,** the fingerlike body of water virtually surrounded on three sides by the jagged peaks lining the semicircular "wall" of Moorea. **Mount Tohiea** is the large thumb with a small hole in its top made by Pai's spear. **Mount Mouaroa,** the "Shark's Tooth," is the cathedral-like mountain buttressed on its right by a serrated ridge. It comes into view as you drive farther along the bay.

On your right is the ✪ **Aquarium de Moorea** (☎ 56.24.00), an experimental pearl farm founded by the noted jewelry designer and artisan Teva Yrondi. Tanks inside the main thatch-roofed building contain an amazing variety of sea life, from luminescent reef fish to ominous moray eels to phosphorescent corals. Out on a pier stand Teva's experimental tanks, where he is attempting to grow black pearls outside the natural environment of a lagoon. A staff member's brief demonstration of the process is one of the best ways to learn how black pearls are cultured, since you see how it's done in live oysters. The aquarium is open daily from 9am to noon and 2 to 5:30pm. Admission is 500 CFP ($5) for adults and 250 CFP ($2.50) for children.

The village of **Pao Pao,** huddled along the curving beach at the head of the bay, is one of Moorea's economic centers. The *Marché Municipale* (Municipal Market) is open Monday to Saturday from 5am to 5pm and Sunday from 5 to 8am. Unlike Papeete's market, this one has slim pickings. The paved road that seems to run through the school next to the bridge cuts through the valley between Cook's Bay and Opunohu Bay. Its surface soon turns to dirt, but it intersects with the main road between Opunohu Bay and the Belvédère lookout.

A small **Catholic church** sits on the shore on the west side of Cook's Bay, at 10 kilometers from the airport. Inside is a large mural painted by artist Peter Heyman in 1946 and an altar decorated with mother-of-pearl. Beyond the church, near the mouth of the bay, the **Moorea Distillery and Fruit Juice Factory** (☎ 56.22.33) turns the island's produce into the Rotui juices sold throughout the territory.

Opunohu Bay   Towering over you is **Mount Rotui,** the huge green-and-black rock separating Moorea's two great bays. Unlike Cook's Bay, Opunohu is virtually devoid of development, a testament to efforts by local residents to maintain the natural beauty of their island (notice how little litter lines Moorea's roads). As soon as the road levels out, watch for pathways through the woods on the right. These lead a few feet to **Robinson's Cove,** one of the world's most photographed yacht anchorages.

For the 1983 production of *The Bounty,* starring Mel Gibson and Anthony Hopkins, the curving beach backed by shade trees and the valley at the head of Opunohu Bay were turned into Matavai Bay on Tahiti. The replica canoes made for the film were sold to local hotels and residents. A few can still be seen around Moorea today. They look remarkably like dugout log canoes but in reality are fiberglass.

The Belvédère   The paved road to the left runs up the central valley through pastures before climbing steeply to the **Titiroa Marae** and the ✪ **Belvédère** lookout,

Impressions

Seen for the first time by European Eyes, this coast is like nothing else on our workaday planet; a landscape, rather, of some fantastic dream.
                                                    —Charles Nordhoff and James Norman Hall, 1933

with its remarkable view of the valley and both bays. The restored marae was part of a concentration of temples and other structures, including an archery platform used for competition (archery was a sport reserved for high-ranking chiefs and was never used in warfare in Polynesia). The remains of these structures can be seen by taking a short stroll among the towering Tahitian chestnut trees that have grown up around and through them.

Haapiti　Back on the coastal road, the village of **Papetoai,** which has more than its share of "vanilla houses," was the retreat of the Pomare dynasty in the 1800s and the base from which Pomare I launched his successful drive to take over all of Tahiti and Moorea. It also was headquarters for the London Missionary Society's work throughout the South Pacific, and the road to the right by the post office leads to an octagonal **Temple Protestant** built on the site of a marae dedicated to Oro, son of the supreme Taaroa and the god of war. The original church was constructed in the 1820s, and although advertised as the oldest European building still in use in the South Pacific, the present structure dates to the late 1880s.

From Papetoai, the road runs through the Haapiti hotel district on the northwest corner and then heads south through the rural parts of Moorea. The 300-bungalow Club Med and the businesses it has generated, including Le Petit Village shopping center across the road, dominate the northwest corner of the island.

The Club Med area is your last chance to stop for refreshment before you travel the sparsely populated southern half of Moorea. My favorite stop is **Snack Michel** west of the Club's entrance. See "Where to Dine," below, for details.

Two kilometers beyond the Club, look for the **Tiki Theatre Village,** a cultural center consisting of thatch huts on the coastal side of the road. It's the only place to see what a Tahitian village looked like when Captain Cook arrived, so pull in. See "Cultural Experiences," below, for details and admission fees.

When those first Europeans arrived, the lovely village of **Haapiti** was home of the powerful Marama family, which was allied with the Pomares. It became a center of Catholic missionary work after the French took over the territory and is one of the few villages whose Catholic church is as large as its Protestant counterpart.

The South Coast　South of Haapiti, just as the road curves sharply around a headland, is a nice view of a small bay with the mountains towering overhead. In contrast to the more touristy north shore, the southeast and southwest coasts have retained an atmosphere of old Polynesia.

The village of **Afareaitu,** on the southwest coast, is the administrative center of Moorea, and the building that looks like a charming hotel across from the village church actually is the island's *mairie,* or town hall. Farther up the coast is the small bay of **Vaiare,** a beehive of activity when the ferries pull in from Papeete.

The road then climbs a hill just past the Hotel Sofitel Ia Ora, and from the top is the **Tahiti Overlook:** a magnificent view of the hotel, the green lagoon flecked with brown coral heads, the white line of the surf breaking on the reef, the deep blue of the Sea of the Moon, and all of Tahiti rising on the horizon. There's a parking area at the overlook, so stop and burn up some film.

ORGANIZED TOURS

Circle Island　The hotel activities desks offer tours around Moorea and up to the Belvédère lookout in the interior. **Albert's Tours** (☎ 56.13.53), **Moorea Transports** (☎ 56.12.86), and **Billy Transports** (☎ 56.12.64) all have half-day round-island tours including the Belvédère for about 2,000 CFP ($20) per person.

Nothing on Tahiti is so majestic as what faces it across the bay, for there lies the island of Moorea. To describe it is impossible. It is a monument to the prodigal beauty of nature.
—James A. Michener, 1951

The tour buses all stop at one black pearl shop or another (guess who gets a commission when you buy the pearl of your dreams!). I suggest you look at more than one establishment before making your purchase, since quality, settings, and prices vary from shop to shop (see "Best Buys," below).

Safari Tours   Alex and Gheslaine Haamatearii, owners of **Inner Island Safari Tours** (☎ 56.20.09), take passengers into the interior of the island in their air-conditioned, four-wheel-drive vehicles. One tour goes through the mountains to vanilla and fruit plantations and the other to a waterfall in the hills behind Afareaitu. Prices vary depending on the number of passengers. They operate from Sunday to Friday. Other operators are **Moorea Safari Tours** (☎ 56.35.80) and **Albert's Tours** (☎ 56.13.53). Albert's Tours charges 3,500 CFP ($35) a person.

CULTURAL EXPERIENCES

The best cultural experience on Moorea—in all of French Polynesia, for that matter—is at **Tiki Theatre Village,** 2km (1.2 miles) south of Club Med (☎ 56.18.97). Built in the fashion of ancient Tahitian villages, this cultural center stages various demonstrations of traditional Polynesian lifestyles. The main "show" takes place at noon each day, but guides will lead you through the village Tuesday to Sunday from 11am to 4pm. Included are examples of house construction, handcraft making, tattooing, and food preparation.

They even will arrange traditional beachside wedding ceremonies. The bride is massaged with flowery *monoi* oil like a Tahitian princess, while the groom is tattooed (with a pen). Both wear traditional costumes.

A guided tour including noontime show costs 1,000 CFP ($10). Lunch is another 2,000 CFP ($20). For a total of 4,000 CFP ($40), they will come as far as the Moorea Beachcomber Parkroyal to get you in an outrigger canoe, lead you around the village, let you watch the show at noon, and feed you lunch. Children between 3 and 12 years old pay half of all fees. Reservations are required for lunch.

The village also has an evening Tahiti feast several times a week (see "Island Nights," below).

3 Where to Stay

Most of Moorea's hotels and restaurants are huddled in or near Cook's Bay or in the Haapiti district on the northwest corner of the island. With the exceptions of the Hotel Bali Hai and Sofitel Ia Ora hotels, those in or near Cook's Bay do not have the best beaches on the island, but their views of the mountains are unsurpassed in the South Pacific. Those on the northwest corner, on the other hand, have fine beaches, lagoons like giant swimming pools, and unobstructed views of the sunset, but not of Moorea's mountains. The two areas are relatively far apart, so you may spend most of your time near your hotel unless you rent transportation or otherwise make a point to see the sights. An alternative is to split your stay between the two areas.

All Moorea hotels provide water sports activities, Tahitian string bands nightly and dance shows at least one night a week, activities desks, and laundry and baby-sitting services. Unless otherwise noted below, the resorts have swimming pools. All rooms and bungalows are equipped with ceiling fans.

HOTELS IN COOK'S BAY

Club Bali Hai

B.P. 26, Maharepa, Moorea (Cook's Bay, near Pao Pao). ☎ **56.13.68** or 800/282-1402 in California, 800/282-1401 in rest of U.S. Fax 56.19.22. 19 bungalows, 20 rms. A/C. 9,500 CFP ($95) room; 18,000 CFP–22,500 CFP ($180–$225) bungalows. AE, DC, MC, V.

This time-share operation deep in Cook's Bay has an incredible view of Moorea's ragged mountains across the water, a scene that epitomizes the South Pacific. Bungalows and rooms are frequently full of American time-share owners, but they are rented out if not claimed (expect a polite sales pitch). Thirteen over-water bungalows have the best views, but those from six beachside units are almost as good. Somewhat removed are 20 rather ordinary but comfortable hotel rooms. All units have kitchens, and there's a guest Laundromat.

A highlight here is the outdoor bar under its own thatch pavilion right on Cook's Bay and within hailing distance of a bayside swimming pool with waterfall (there is no sand beach here). Tuesday and Friday happy hours are popular with local residents (see "Island Nights," below). The dining room under a large thatch roof specializes in seafood and steaks of moderate price and quality. All units have kitchens, and several restaurants are nearby.

Hotel Bali Hai Moorea

B.P. 26, Maharepa, Moorea (between Cook's Bay and airport). ☎ **56.13.59** or 800/282-1402 in California, 800/282-1401 in rest of U.S. Fax 56.19.22. Telex 331. 54 rms, 9 over-water bungalows. $9,500 CFP ($95) room; 14,000 CFP–32,000 CFP ($140–$320) bungalow. AE, DC, MC, V.

Opened in 1961, this is the flagship of the small hotel chain founded by Moorea's legendary Bali Hai Boys (see box), who were actively trying to sell their properties when I was there recently. If they are successful, new owners may not retain all of the existing structures, which are dated by today's standards but still have their charms. The Bali Hai was the first hotel to have bungalows (nine of them) standing on pilings over the lagoon. The other rooms sit in a coconut grove, although a few have porches extending over a decent beach to the water. There are beachfront bungalows and garden bungalows, a few of which have two or more units in them. All have thatch-covered roofs, tiled shower-only baths, small fridges, double and single beds, and tea- and coffee-making facilities.

A central building on the beach contains a dining room and bar. The *Liki Tiki,* a pontoon boat with its own thatch roof, offers snorkeling, picnics, and sunset cruises. A swimming pool has a waterfall on one end and a swim-up bar on the other.

Cook's Bay Resort Hotel

B.P. 30, Maharepa, Moorea (east side of Cook's Bay). ☎ **56.10.50.** Fax 56.29.18. 76 rooms, 24 bungalows. A/C TEL. 8,400 CFP–9,900 CFP ($84–$99) room; 9,600 CFP–14,200 CFP ($96–$142) bungalow. AE, DC, MC, V.

Local owners took over two adjoining hotels a few years ago and turned them into this economy-priced version of a Club Med. Most guests pay far less than the rates quoted above, since this hotel usually is the least expensive package-tour accommodation in French Polynesia. Accordingly, it's often full; if not, you could get a greatly reduced rate by bargaining a little. Don't expect luxury if you do. The main two-story, L-shaped, colonial-style building has small motel-style rooms with twin beds, shower-only baths, and either ceiling fans or air conditioners. They look out on a bayside courtyard with pool and small beach. The bungalows are about 100 yards away across an open field. Five moderately priced food outlets offer snacks, tacos, pizzas, and French dishes. Guests are treated to Tahitian dance shows three times a week but must pay for tours, picnics, and cruises on the rusty *Fat Cat* pontoon boat. Bring your own snorkeling gear.

Hotel Moorea Lagoon

B.P. 11, Maharepa, Moorea (between Cook's Bay and Opunohu Bay). ☎ **56.14.68.** Fax 56.26.25. 45 bungalows. 12,000 CFP–17,000 CFP ($120–$170) double. AE, DC, MC, V.

This establishment halfway between Cook's and Opunohu Bays attracts couples seeking a more isolated setting, since no other hotels or restaurants are within an easy walk. A bulkhead holds the lagoon away from most of the property, since recent storms have eliminated all but a small patch of beach. Lagoonfront bungalows, with the water virtually at their front porches, are the choice. Those in the garden are shaded by a few palms or other trees. All identical, the bungalows have thatch roofs, rattan furnishings, and double beds. There are no screens on the windows or doors. The dining room under a large, beachside thatch roof could offer more variety, but unless you intend to rent a car or scooter to get to distant restaurants, consider buying a modified American plan at 3,600 CFP ($36) per person a day. A string band plays during happy hour and dinner. Facilities include a swimming pool, tennis court, and water sports equipment.

✪ Hotel Sofitel Ia Ora Moorea

B.P. 28, Maharepa, Moorea (Temae, on northeast coast, facing Tahiti). ☎ **56.12.90,** 41.04.04 in Papeete, or 800/763-4835. Fax 41.05.05. 80 bungalows, 1 suite. 21,500 CFP–24,500 CFP ($215–$145) bungalow; 36,500 CFP–48,000 CFP ($365–$480) suite. AE, DC, MC, V.

Situated alone on the island's northeast coast south of the airport, this venerable collection of thatch-roofed buildings enjoys one of the island's most picturesque lagoons and a long, lovely beach over which grape-leaf and casuarina trees hang. It's also the only hotel on Moorea with a view of Tahiti, whose green, cloud-topped mountains seem to climb out of the horizon beyond the reef. Most of the Ia Ora's luxurious bungalows face this vista from a coconut grove; a few have unobstructed views of Tahiti from a ridge above the trees. A few suite-size bungalows have two separate bedrooms. A restaurant sitting on a long pier over the lagoon was closed during my recent visit, awaiting repairs after being damaged by a freak storm. Meantime, French cuisine was being served in a large thatch building overlooking lily ponds, a venue usually reserved for dinner only.

HOTELS ON THE NORTHWEST COAST

⑤ Club Méditerranée Moorea

B.P. 575, Papeete, Tahiti (Haapiti, on island's northwest corner). ☎ **56.15.00,** 42.96.99 in Papeete, or 800/528-3100 in U.S. Fax 42.16.83. 350 bungalows. 14,300 CFP ($143) per person, including all meals with wine. AE, DC, MC, V.

One of the oldest Club Meds, this huge playground is the center of activity on the northwest corner of Moorea (17 miles from the airport). The setting is exceptional, with an azure lagoon lying between the beach and a private motu on the reef offshore, which the club's guests can use for sunbathing in the buff (the skimpiest of bottoms are required on the main beach). The club is such a world unto itself that it even marches to its own clock, set an hour earlier than Moorea's in order to give the guests extra time in the sun. You pay one price for everything, including meals with wine and a wide range of mile-a-minute activities. The only extras are drinks at the bar, scuba diving, tours of the island, and a snorkeling extravaganza to Marlon Brando's Tetiaroa atoll.

The club's 350 bungalows are a cross between traditional and colonial styles: shingled roofs, tongue-in-groove plank walls, polished hardwood floors, and brass-trimmed ceiling fans and mirrors. Each has two oversize twin beds; if you don't have a roommate, one of the same sex may be assigned. Honeymooners may prefer the quarters at the Club Med on Bora Bora, which are newer and provide more privacy (see the following chapter).

Although good, the food is better known for its substantial quantity than quality. Breakfasts and lunches are all-you-can-eat buffets and dinners are sit-down affairs. The staff performs nightclub-style several nights a week.

✪ Moorea Beachcomber Parkroyal

B.P. 1019, Papetaoi, Moorea (between Papetaoi and Haapiti). ☎ **56.19.19** or 800/421-0536. Fax 56.18.88. 102 bungalows, 52 rms. A/C (rooms only) MINIBAR TV TEL. 28,000 CFP ($280) room; 34,000 CFP–38,000 CFP ($340–$380) bungalow. AE, DC, MC, V.

Although relatively isolated about three miles east of the Club Med area, Moorea's top-rated and best-managed resort has plenty to keep its guests busy, since it has the widest range of water sports activities on the island—all of them available to the non-guests (see "Horseback Riding, Water Sports & Other Outdoor Activities," below). A large, airy central building with a shingle roof built at several angles houses the hotel's reception and indoor activities areas. It opens to a large pool area surrounded by an ample sunning deck. Most of the Beachcomber's bungalows extend partially over the water from unpainted concrete supports anchored on manmade islands (the hotel has won environmental awards for restoring the reef around these islets). They are of European construction, but mat walls and rattan furnishings lend tropical ambience. Wood frame doors open to porches, but only small windows in the rear of each unit give ventilation. The air-conditioned hotel rooms are in a curving two-story building. They all have combination tub-shower baths, a rarity on Moorea. In the main building, an open-air dining room offers French cuisine in a tropical setting under a large thatch roof. A more formal restaurant provides gourmet-quality dinners.

Hotel-Résidence Les Tipaniers

B.P. 1002, Papetaoi, Moorea (in Haapiti, east of Club Med). ☎ **56.12.67** or 800/521-7242. Fax 56.29.25. 22 bungalows. 9,800 CFP–12,500 CFP ($98–$125) double with kitchenette. AE, DC, MC, V.

This pleasant establishment sits in a coconut grove beside the same sandy beach as the Club Med. The thatch bungalows are set back from the edge of the beach, which gives the small complex an open, airy atmosphere. The bungalows are comfortable if simple, and the flowered-print bedspreads and sofa covers give them an authentic Tahitian feel. Newer, larger units have kitchenettes. A pleasant restaurant with a deck over the beach serves breakfast and lunch, and snacks after 2pm. The hotel is also home of the excellent Les Tipaniers restaurant, which is known for its Italian fare (see "Where to Dine," below). There is no swimming pool here.

Ⓢ Hotel Moorea Village

P.O. Box 1008, Papetoai, Moorea (in Haapiti, west of the Club Med). ☎ **56.10.02.**
Fax 56.22.11. 65 bungalows. 8,000 CFP–10,500 ($80–$105). AE, MC, V.

One of Moorea's better values, and my long-standing favorite for the money, this comfortable establishment has 65 bungalows situated on a grassy lawn under coconut palms within walking distance of the Club Med and nearby restaurants and shops. Recently refurbished, the simply furnished bungalows consist of one room and a bath under a peaked thatch roof that extends out over a front porch. The more expensive units are beside the lagoon. Like them, the restaurant-bar is perched on a bank next to the beach, while one side opens to a swimming pool. Breakfast, lunch, and libations are served on a long porch hanging over the sand along the lagoon side of the restaurant. Evening meals indoors emphasize both French and Chinese cooking at moderate prices.

HOSTELS & CAMPING

Chez Nelson et Josiane's Backpackers' Club

PK 27.1, Papetoai, Moorea (in Haapiti, near Club Med). ☎ **56.15.18.** 2 bungalows, 15 bunks. 700 CFP–1,000 ($7–$10) per camper; 1,000 CFP–1,200 CFP ($10–$12) dorm bed; 2,500 CFP–3,000 CFP ($25–$30) per person small bungalow; 5,000 CFP–6,000 CFP ($50–$60) per large bungalow. No credit cards.

Josiane and Nelson Flohr have a roaring campground and hostel business in a beachside coconut grove about 200 yards west of the Club Med. All guests share adequate toilets, cold-water showers, and communal kitchen facilities. The Flohrs have seven very small bungalows for couples, a block of 10 tiny dorm rooms (two bunks each) that looks like it might belong in a migrant labor camp, and two other thatch-roofed hostel bungalows down the road (and still on the beach). Each of the latter has a kitchen, modern bathroom, and porch. A beachside restaurant offers inexpensive Chinese and other fare plus wine and beer.

Moorea Camping (Backpackers' Paradise)

PK 27.5, Papetoai, Moorea (in Haapiti, west of Club Med). ☎ **56.14.47.** 5 bungalows, 8 rooms, 20 beds, 20 tent sites. 500 CFP–800 CFP ($5–$8) per camper; 800 CFP–1,000 CFP ($8–$10) dorm bed; 2,000 CFP–2,500 CFP ($29–$25) per person in rooms; 4,000 CFP ($40) per bungalow. No credit cards.

This establishment in a coconut grove has considerably less shade and space but a better beach for swimming than at Chez Nelson and Josiane's Backpackers' Beach Club (see above). A beachside pavilion covers picnic tables and a communal kitchen. Two long plywood houses—actually little more than permanent tents—contain eight rooms with foam mattresses. One bungalow can accommodate up to four persons. The higher rates apply if you stay just one night.

4 Where to Dine

Restaurants have a way of coming and going on Moorea; therefore, I hesitate to tell you much more than where to find the ones that were operating during my recent visit. As on Tahiti, you can save by eating at snack bars for breakfast, lunch, or an early dinner. Moorea has several excellent choices, which fortunately have tended to stick around longer than many of its restaurants.

Tahitian Feasts   Most hotels stage Tahitian feasts, followed by traditional dance shows, at least one evening a week. Call to find out their schedules.

My favorite is the Sunday feast at **Hotel Moorea Village** (☎ 56.10.02) in Haapiti. You can watch the dirt being removed from atop the *himaa* shortly after noon, then sit down about 1pm at long tables in the beachside dining room. The succulent food is served in the traditional Tahitian way, family-style without silverware. That's right. You eat with your fingers. Dancers from a nearby village put on a short show after the feast. It's a bargain at 3,800 CFP ($38) per person, which includes wine. It's a popular event with locals, some of whom hang around after the show to drink at the bar. They reportedly can become rowdy later in the afternoon.

If you can't make it to Haapiti on Sunday, the **Hotel Bali Hai** (☎ 56.13.29) in Maharepa also has a midday feast and dance show.

RESTAURANTS IN COOK'S BAY

Alfredo's

Pao Pao, near Club Bali Hai. ☎ **56.17.71.** Reservations recommended. Main courses 950 CFP–1350 CFP ($9.50–$13.50). MC, V. Tues–Sun 11am–2:30pm and 5:30–9pm. ITALIAN/FRENCH.

Charming host Syd Pollack has a habit of starting excellent restaurants and then selling them (Le Pêcheur, below, is one of his creations). If he hasn't sold it, then Alfredo's should be one of the better Italian eateries in the islands, as it was during my recent visit. Its quarters once were a Chinese grocery store, but today the first floor is an open-air terrace whose white patio furniture and green-and-red table cloths present the colors of Italy. The wonderfully sweet tomato sauce used on pizzas and pastas is the result of Syd's insisting the chef add local honey to his recipe. Syd also offers French dishes and daily specials, such as his luscious marinated lamb stew simmered in herbs and tomatoes.

✪ Le Pêcheur

Maharepa, west of Hotel Bali Hai. ☎ **56.36.12.** Reservations recommended. Main courses 1,400 CFP–2,100 CFP ($14–$21). AE, MC, V. Tues–Sun 11:30am–2:30pm and 6–9:30pm. SEAFOOD.

Bernard Procureur's seafood emporium is Moorea's most popular eatery with local residents, who pack the place on Saturday evenings for fine food and live entertainment featuring Bernard on the guitar. Fishnets and traps hanging from a thatch roof set the scene for seafood, such as island-style shrimp—a concoction of local shrimp cooked with pineapple and papaya in a sweetly rich yet spicy vanilla sauce. The fisherman's platter provides a broiled taste of three fresh local fish, shrimp, scallops, and a small lobster tail.

✪ Te Honu Iti (Chez Roger)

Pao Pao, north of Municipal Market. ☎ **56.19.84.** Reservations recommended. Main courses 1,000 CFP–2,000 CFP ($10–$20); sandwiches and burgers 400 CFP–600 CFP ($4–$6). MC, V. Wed–Mon 11:30am–2pm; Wed–Sun 6:30–9:30pm. CLASSICAL FRENCH.

Owner-chef Roger Iqual won the *Concours National de la Poêle d'Or* (Golden Pot Contest) in Cannes for a sea bass concoction, and his specialties here are fresh seafood prepared in the classical French fashion but with some delightful twists, such as his lightly smoking sashimi-thin slices of yellow-fin tuna and serving them over a piquant potato salad. Roger's chalkboard menu often features his delicate mahi mahi mousse, a local favorite. A thatch-roofed dock on Cook's Bay provides a scenic setting worthy of Roger's cuisine, which is among the very best in all French Polynesia. There's nothing pretentious here, since Te Honu Iti (The Little Turtle) started as a snack bar before Roger bought it, and it still has its old relaxed atmosphere. He offers sandwiches and burgers at lunch only.

SNACK BARS IN COOK'S BAY

La Crêperie

Pao Pao, opposite Club Bali Hai. ☎ **56.12.06.** Reservations not accepted. Crepes and waffles 250 CFP–500 CFP ($2–$5); burgers and meals 500 CFP–1,000 CFP ($5–$10). V. Tues–Sun 10am–8pm. SNACK BAR/CREPES.

Jean-Philippe and France Reymond's clean little front-porch establishment specializes in sweet crepes filled with eggs, curry, cheese, ham, or other stuffings. They also serve waffles, burgers, omelets, steak with french fries, fish of the day, and other platters. Their smooth ice creams provide relief from the midday heat.

Le Sylesie Patisserie

Maharepa, next to post office. ☎ **56.15.88.** Reservations not accepted. Snacks and light meals 350 CFP–900 CFP ($3.50–$9); breakfasts 450 CFP–750 CFP ($4.50–$7). MC, V. Daily 6:30am–6pm. PATISSERIE/SNACKS.

This newest and largest of the Le Sylesie branches has a wider selection of pastries, crepes, pizzas, salads, omelets, ice cream, sundaes, and other goodies than its sister in Haapiti. The patio tables here are set in a cool, shady spot for a full, American-style breakfast or tasty lunch, but you can get sunburned while eating outside in the late afternoon.

✪ Snack Fare Hotu

Pao Pao, north of Club Bali Hai. ☎ **56.39.86.** Reservations not accepted. Sandwiches and burgers 150 CFP–500 CFP ($1.50–$5); meals 800 CFP–1,100 CFP ($8–$11). No credit cards. Sun–Fri 9am–3pm. TAHITIAN/SNACKS.

Edwin White's very clean snack bar is on the mountain side of the road next to Super Marché Pao Pao, but it still enjoys a view of Cook's Bay from the seven tables on its covered patio. His is one of the best places in the territory for visitors to try *ma'a tinito,* the Tahitian version of Chinese food: diced chicken, Chinese noodles, red beans, and rice (definitely enough starch to last a Westerner a week). Other local goodies include fresh poisson cru and Edwin's tasty version of coconut curry shrimp. For lighter fare, order salads, hamburgers, fish burgers, hot dogs, or casse-croûte sandwiches.

Snack Rotui

Pao Pao, west of bridge at head of Cook's Bay. ☎ **56.18.16.** Reservations not accepted. Sandwiches 150 CFP ($1.50); plate lunches 500 CFP ($5). No credit cards. Tues–Sun 7am–6pm. ECLECTIC.

Located on the shore of Cook's Bay, this is run by a Chinese family, and for 350 CFP ($3) you can get a casse-croûte sandwich, a soft drink, and a slice of delicious homemade cake topped with chocolate pudding. Daily plate lunches, usually a Chinese dish with rice, are prepared earlier in the day and served without refrigeration. A few tables under a roof beside the beach catch the breezes off the bay.

RESTAURANTS ON THE NORTHWEST COAST

✪ L'Aventure Restaurant

Haapiti, west of Club Med. ☎ **56.23.36.** Reservations recommended. Main courses 1,500 CFP–2,000 CFP ($15–$20). AE, DC, MC, V. Wed–Sun noon–2pm; Tues–Sun 6:30–9pm. CLASSICAL FRENCH.

Chef Bernard Frerot uses all fresh ingredients at this roadside restaurant, which shares quarters with co-owner Carole Stiehi's boutique (see "Best Buys," below), so his menu changes according to what's available at the markets. I started with a herring salad during my recent visit, followed by a substantial portion of mahi mahi under toasted almonds and a rich butter sauce. Local French residents consider Bernard's classical cuisine to be right up there with Roger Iqual's at Te Honu Iti in Cook's Bay (see above).

Le Dauphin Restaurant-Pizzeria

Haapiti, in Petit Village, opposite Club Med. ☎ **56.29.53.** Reservations accepted. Main courses 950 CFP–1,900 CFP ($9.50–$19). MC, V. Daily 8am–10pm. ITALIAN/FRENCH.

Sharing quarters with Tropical Iceberg snack bar and ice cream parlor, this establishment with a pink ceiling over green plants offers more pizza toppings than any restaurant in French Polynesia, from spicy sausage to syrupy pineapple. Also on the extensive menu are pastas and a mix of Italian and French meat and seafood offerings. Omelets and continental breakfasts are served from 8 to 11am.

✪ Linareva Floating Restaurant and Bar

Haapiti, 7km (4 miles) south of Club Med. ☎ **56-15-35.** Reservations recommended for dinner. Main courses 1,900 CFP–2,250 CFP ($19–$22.50). MC, V. Daily 11:30am–5pm and 6–9pm. SEAFOOD.

This restaurant and bar holds title to Moorea's most unusual home: the hull of the original *Tamarii Moorea*, the first ferry to ply between Papeete and Moorea. Owner Eric Lussiez completely rebuilt the old vessel (twice, actually, for it sank at its dock due to a plumbing error after the job was finished). He outfitted the dining room with polished wood, large windows, and plenty of bright brass and other nautical decor. The menu changes with availability of local produce, but house specialties feature whatever fresh seafood is available, most prepared with traditional French sauces. Transportation from as far away as the Moorea Beachcomber Parkroyal is available to guests with reservations. Round-trip rides cost 400 CFP ($4) per person.

Restaurant Les Tipaniers

Haapiti, at Hotel-Résidence Les Tipaniers, east of Club Med. ☎ **56-12-67.** Reservations recommended. Pasta and pizza 950 CFP–1,050 CFP ($9.50–$10.50); main courses 1,600 CFP–1,900 CFP ($16–$19). AE, DC, MC, V. Wed–Mon 7–9:30pm. ITALIAN/FRENCH.

This romantic, thatch-roof restaurant is popular with both visitors and Moorea's permanent residents, who come here for pizzas with a variety of toppings and homemade spaghetti, lasagna, and fettuccine served with bolognese, carbonara, or napoletana sauce. Year-round features include popular French dishes such as pepper steak and filets of mahi mahi in pepper sauce or spiced butter. Transportation is available for guests staying as far west at the Hotel Moorea Lagoon.

SNACK BARS ON THE NORTHWEST COAST

Le Sylesie Patisserie

Haapiti, west of Club Med. ☎ **56.20.45.** Snacks and light meals 350 CFP–900 CFP ($3.50–$9); breakfasts 450 CFP–750 CFP ($4.50–$7.50). MC, V. Daily 6:30am–6pm. SNACKS/BREAKFAST.

A sister of Le Sylesie in Maharepa (see above), this little shop serves some of the same croissants-and-coffee or full American-style breakfasts, burgers, sandwiches, snacks, and pastries. The low-slung building has a few tables under cover in front, but it's primarily a carryout establishment.

✪ Snack Michel

Haapiti, walking distance west of Club Med. No phone. Reservations not accepted. Salads and burgers 350 CFP–650 CFP ($3.50–$6.50); meals 600 CFP–950 CFP ($6–$9.50). No credit cards. Wed–Mon 8:30am–7pm. ECLECTIC.

This clean, extraordinarily friendly little establishment near Haapiti's campgrounds is run by Swiss-born Michel Rauber and his Tahiti-born wife Julienne. They offer sandwiches, burgers, and meals at reasonable prices. I am particularly fond of their filling daily specials, served over rice. Eat inside or outside. Every expatriot I know on this end of Moorea does.

5 Horseback Riding, Water Sports & Other Outdoor Activities

Most hotels have active water sports programs for their guests, such as glass-bottomed-boat cruises and snorkeling in or sailing on Moorea's beautiful lagoon. Of the resort hotels, the Sofitel Ia Ora and the Club Med have the best lagoons for water sports.

By far the most extensive array of sporting activities is at the **Moorea Beach-comber Parkroyal** (☎ 56.19.19), whose facilities can be used by visitors willing to pay. These include parasailing, waterskiing, sailboarding, scooting about the lagoon on motor-powered wave runners, viewing coral and fish from Aquascope boats, dolphin-watching excursions, and sailing on the *Manu,* a 38-foot catamaran moored at the resort's dock. Non-guests can also pay to use the pool, snorkeling gear, and tennis courts, and to be taken over to a small islet. Call the hotel for details and prices. The jet skis at **Hotel Sofitel Ia Ora** (☎ 56.22.87) can be rented by the public.

If you must play golf, stay on Tahiti, which has the territory's only course. Moorea also has no public tennis courts.

HORSEBACK RIDING   Landlubbers can go horseback riding with **Tiahura Ranch** (☎ 56.28.55), west of the Club Med in Haapiti, or with **Pegasus Ranch** (☎ 56.34.11) in Maharepa. Rates are about 1,500 CFP ($15) for one hour and 2,000 CFP ($20) for 90 minutes.

LAGOON EXCURSIONS   Based at the Hotel Bali Hai in Maharepa, Hiro Kelley's **Moorea Tours** (☎ 56.13.59) has snorkeling, picnic trips to a small island, and glass-bottom-boat excursions, including one trip all the way around Moorea inside the reef. Hiro is the son of Hugh Kelley, a cofounder of the Bali Hai Hotels (see "Where to Stay," above). Call for his schedule and prices.

SCUBA DIVING   Although Moorea's lagoon is not in the same league with those at Rangiroa and Bora Bora, its outer reef has some decent sites for viewing coral and sealife. The island's oldest diving operator is Philippe Molle's **Moorea Underwater Scuba-diving Tahiti (M.U.S.T.)** (☎ 56.17.32), whose office is on the dock next to the Cook's Bay Resort Hotel Philippe; his instructors take up to five divers out to the reef. The Beachcomber Parkroyal is home to **Bathy's Club Moorea** (☎ 56.19.19, ext. 1139), and Résidence Les Tipaniers is host to **Scubapiti Moorea** (☎ 56.30.38), both on the northwest coast. All charge about 5,000 CFP ($50) for one dive, including equipment. Lessons cost about 6,500 CFP ($65).

SPORT FISHING   Chris Lilley, an American who has won several sports fishing contests, takes guests beyond the reef in search of big game on his **Tea Nui**

(☎ 56.15.08). You can go out for half a day for 45,000 CFP ($450) and a whole day for 75,000 CFP ($750). In keeping with South Pacific custom, you can keep the little fish you catch; he sells the big ones. If Chris doesn't answer the phone, look for him or leave word at the Club Bali Hai dock.

6 Shopping

THE SHOPPING SCENE

Moorea has a number of boutiques and other shops. I mention those that have been in business for many years and which I have found to give good value for your money.

Every village has at least one Chinese grocery store. Chez Toa supermarket at Vaiare is by far the island's largest. All the staff speak English at Chez Are, a modern establishment on Cook's Bay on Pao Pao.

A one-stop place to shop are the neocolonial buildings of **Le Petit Village,** opposite the Club Med in Haapiti. **Vanille Boutique** has hand-silkscreened pareus and a small collection of handcrafts and souvenirs. **Lagon Bleu** is an upscale shop featuring jewelry of black pearls, shark's teeth, black coral, and scrimshaw. **Supersonics** carries film, watch and camera batteries, stamps, magazines, and other items. Upstairs, **Tiki Pearls** and **Atoll** both have expensive black pearls and other jewelry. **Tahiti Parfum** sells French perfumes. **Arts Polynésiens** is an outlet for the reproductions of Tahiti's Gauguin Museum and for Moorea's Galerie A.P.I. (see separate listing below).

BEST BUYS

✪ Island Fashion Black Pearls
Cook's Bay, 200 yards north of Cook's Bay Resort Hotel. ☎ **56.11.06.**

Ron Hall sailed from Hawaii to Tahiti with the actor Peter Fonda in 1974; Peter went home, Ron didn't. Now Ron runs this air-conditioned Moorea retail outlet, which he decorated with old photos of Tahiti, including one of the infamous Quinn's Bar, and an original Leeteg painting of a Tahitian vahine (Ron's wife Josée was herself a championship Tahitian dancer when they met in the 1970s). In 15 minutes of "pearl school," Ron will show you the basics of picking a pearl. He also will have your selection set in a mounting of your choice, and his prices are fair (don't hesitate to bargain politely). In addition to stylish pearls, Island Fashions has one of Moorea's best selections of bathing suits, aloha shirts, and T-shirts. Open Monday to Saturday from 9am to 6pm.

Pai Moana Pearls
Haapiti, at Linerava Floating Restaurant and Bar. ☎ **56.25.25.**

This was the main outlet for Canadian Peter Ringland's Pai Moana pearl farm when I was on Moorea recently, but he was planning to move into new quarters opposite the Club Med. He may also open a new shop in Cook's Bay. Peter's operation markets very aggressively, so you probably will hear about the new locations. The sales personnel always speak English (some are expatriot Americans). Hours at the Linerava shop were Monday to Friday from 9am to 6pm, Saturday and Sunday from 9am to 4pm.

Teva's Moorea Perles Centre

Cook's Bay, opposite Club Bali Hai. ☎ **56.13.13.**

In a low-slung, V-shaped building, Hervé Peltier carries some large black pearls, finely polished seashells, and very wellmade handcrafts, especially shell necklaces and mother-of-pearl earrings fashioned by the noted designer Teva Yrondi. Open Monday to Saturday from 8am to noon and 2 to 5pm.

SHOPPING A TO Z

ART & ANTIQUES

Arts Polynésiens

Haapiti, opposite Club Med in Le Petit Village. ☎ **56.39.42.**

This shop represents both the Gauguin Museum on Tahiti and Moorea's Galerie A.P.I. (see below). From the museum come reproductions of Gauguin's paintings as well as such souvenir items as coasters and T-shirts bearing his works. Galerie A.P.I. supplies paintings, tapa cloth, and Marquesan wood carvings. Also for sale are paintings and ceramics by local artists. Open Monday to Saturday from 9am to noon and 2 to 6pm, Sunday from 9am to noon.

Galerie A.P.I.

Haapiti, east of Club Med. ☎ **56.13.57.**

Take the dirt road on the eastern edge of the Club Med to find Patrice Bredel's beachside art gallery and home. A long-time Moorea resident, he has exclusive rights to sell works by noted local artists François Ravello and Michelle Dallet. One museumlike room displays such artifacts as 18th-century stone carvings from the Marquesas, ancient hair decorations made of human bone, and intricately carved canoe paddles from the Austral Islands. Open Monday to Saturday from 9:30am to noon and 2:30 to 5:30pm.

Galerie Baie de Cook

Cook's Bay, near Club Bali Hai. ☎ **56.12.67.**

Chantel Cowan's art gallery features paintings of Polynesia by the likes of William Alister MacDonald, Peter Heyman, and Leeteg (William Edgar), plus intricate woodcarvings and sennit weavings by some of the most skilled artisans still at work in French Polynesia. She also displays *Vaamotu,* a sailing canoe built in the traditional Polynesian fashion by her husband Francis Cowan, a noted student of the old ways. It's not for sale. Open daily from 9am to 6pm. Admission is 100 CFP ($1).

Galerie van der Heyde

Cook's Bay, 150 yards north of Cook's Bay Resort Hotel. ☎ **56.14.22.**

Dutch artist Aad van der Heyde has lived and worked on Moorea since 1964. One of his bold, impressionist paintings of a Tahitian woman was selected for French Polynesia's 100-CFP postage stamp in 1975. Aad will sell you a lithograph of the painting for 8,900 CFP ($89) and will autograph it for free. Some of his paintings are displayed in the gallery's garden. He also has a small collection of pearls, wood carvings, tapa cloth, shell and coral jewelry, and primitive art from Papua New Guinea. Aad's hours are somewhat irregular.

CLOTHING & SOUVENIRS

Carole Boutique
Haapiti, west of Club Med. ☎ **56.16.06.**

Carole Stiehi has been in business at this little shop, which shares space with Restaurant l'Aventure, for more than 20 years. She carries wood carvings, straw baskets, books about the islands, shirts and dresses, tablecloths, black pearls, and excellent shell jewelry. Open Monday to Saturday from 9am to 5:30pm.

⑤ Heimata Boutique
Pao Pao, Cook's Bay, near Municipal Market. ☎ **56.18.51.**

Seamstress Micheline Tetuanui's shop has reasonable prices on pareus and souvenir items, such as soap made with tiare-scented monoi oil and Hinano beer glasses, and its prices on books about French Polynesia are the best to be found anywhere. It also has a good selection of tablecloths and napkins printed with tapa designs. You may find Micheline sewing away on a fine selection of tropical fashions, many of them in traditional Tahitian fabrics and styles. Open Monday to Saturday from 8am to noon and 2 to 5 pm.

La Maison Blanche (The White House)
Mararepa, near Hotel Bali Hai. ☎ **56.13.26.**

This whitewashed vanilla planter's house with railing enclosing a magnificent front veranda is now home to this shop carrying an array of pareus, tropical dresses, bathing suits, T-shirts, shell jewelry, and other handcrafts. Prices reflect the high quality of the merchandise. Open Monday to Saturday from 8:30am to 5pm.

The Bali Hai Boys

Californians Jay Carlisle, Don "Muk" McCallum, and Hugh Kelley gave up their budding business careers as stockbroker, lawyer, and sporting goods salesman, respectively, and in 1960 bought an old vanilla plantation on Moorea. Much to their chagrin, the vanilla boom had gone bust in the 1920s. Simply put, there was no money to be made in vanilla.

Not wanting to go bankrupt, they refurbished an old beachfront hotel that stood on their property. Taking a page from James A. Michener's *Tales of the South Pacific,* they renamed it the Bali Hai and opened for business in 1961. With construction of Faaa International Airport across the Sea of the Moon that same year, their timing couldn't have been better. With Jay managing the money, Hugh doing the building, and Muk overseeing the entertainment, they quickly had a success on their hands. Travel writers soon dubbed them the Bali Hai Boys.

Supplies and fresh produce weren't easy to come by in those days, so they put the old vanilla plantation to work producing chickens, eggs, and milk. It was the first successful poultry and dairy operation on the island.

In addition, we can thank the Bali Hai Boys for over-water bungalows—cabins sitting on pilings over the lagoon with glass panels in their floors so that we can watch the fish swim below us. Once a novelty, their romantic invention now sets French Polynesia's top resorts apart from all others in the South Pacific.

7 Island Nights

Unfortunately, the One Chicken Inn, Moorea's colorful version of Quinn's infamous Tahitian-style bar in Papeete, is long gone. No one now goes to Moorea just for its nightlife. Most of the island's evening entertainment now is limited to the hotels, with a few notable exceptions.

Remember that the hotels' schedules change, so do your detective work. Call ahead before striking out. Most charge 4,500 CFP to 5,500 CFP ($45 to $55) per person for dinner and a Tahitian dance show.

Tiki Theatre Village (☎ 56.18.97) in Haapiti, 2km (1.2 miles) west of the Club Med, stages the island's most authentic feast and dance show on Tuesday, Thursday, and Saturday. The feast starts at 6:30pm each night and the dance show at 9pm. Transportation is provided from all Moorea hotels (by canoe from those on the northwest coast). The dinner and show cost 5,800 CFP ($58) per person. Add 1,000 CFP ($10) for transportation.

Le Manu Manu, opposite the Club Med in Haapiti (☎ 56.16.90), is as close as Moorea has to a supper club. Dinner is followed by a Parisian-style cabaret show performed by local expatriot residents. There's one show nightly Monday to Thursday at 9pm, and two on Friday and Saturday at 9:15 and 10:45pm. Main courses at dinner cost about 1,500 CFP ($15).

Le Pêcheur restaurant in Maharepa (☎ 56.36.12) has live entertainment on Saturday evenings, all for the price of a meal. Local performers are joined by owner Bernard Procureur, who sings and plays the guitar.

Chez Billy (no phone), on the beach west of Hotel Moorea Village in Haapiti, offers a chance to dance, drink, and occasionally fight with the locals on Friday and Saturday nights. Billy kicks off at 8pm and roars on into the wee hours. Expect to pay a 1,000 CFP ($10) cover charge, 350 CFP ($3.50) and up for drinks.

Among the hotels, **Club Méditerranée** (☎ 56.14.09) has nightly skits, floor shows, and other entertainment for its guests. When business is slow, it may open its doors to outsiders.

Hotel Sofitel Ia Ora (☎ 56.12.90) has Tahitian dance shows at 8pm on Saturday and several nights a week, depending on the number of guests on hand.

Moorea Beachcomber Parkroyal (☎ 56.19.19) has a barbecue and Tahitian dance show twice a week and a dinner-dance on Saturday evening.

Hotel Moorea Village (☎ 56.10.02) has a barbecue with a pareu fashion show on Saturdays at 7:30pm.

Hotel Bali Hai (☎ 56.13.59) has its show on Wednesday night, followed by a barbecue.

✪ **Club Bali Hai** (☎ 56.13.68) has a very popular happy hour Tuesday and Friday from 6 to 7pm; most of the island's English-speaking expatriot residents show up to take advantage of half-price drinks. It's one of my favorite French Polynesian experiences.

7 Bora Bora & Other Islands

Many visitors to French Polynesia go on from Tahiti and Moorea to see the dramatic, tombstone-like central mountain and incredibly beautiful lagoon of Bora Bora, whose sing-song name has come to symbolize the ultimate escape from civilization. Bora Bora is the most famous of the Leeward Islands, whose lovely mountainous members offer a glimpse into old Polynesia, or, as they say in these parts, "The way Tahiti used to be." This is especially true of Huahine, Raiatea, and Tahaa, where agriculture still far outweighs tourism. In contrast, Bora Bora is French Polynesia's most expensive destination, a playground for the rich and famous. Go to Bora Bora for its beautiful scenery, great lagoon, and luxury resorts, not for a Polynesian cultural experience.

Still other visitors venture to the low-lying atolls of the Tuamotu Archipelago, where Rangiroa offers extraordinary diving and snorkeling in the world's second-largest lagoon, and where Manihi provides both diving and tours of its famous black pearl farms, the territory's second-largest industry.

1 Bora Bora

As you arrive, you'll appreciate why James A. Michener wrote that this half-atoll/half-mountain is the world's most beautiful island. Lying 143 miles northwest of Tahiti, Bora Bora is one of those middle-aged islands consisting of a high center completely surrounded by a lagoon enclosed by coral reef. What makes it so beautiful is the combination of sand-fringed motus sitting on the outer reef, the multihued lagoon cutting deep bays into the central high island, and the basaltic tombstone known as Mount Otemanu towering over it all.

Be first to board the plane, for all this will be visible from the left side of the aircraft as you fly up from Papeete and descend to the island's airport on Motu Mute, a flat island on the northern edge of the barrier reef. Beyond Motu Mute the lagoon turns deep blue because it's deep—deep enough for the U.S. Navy to have used Bora Bora as a way station during World War II. The airstrip you land on is another legacy of that war, built by the U.S. Navy as part of Operation Bobcat, during which 6,000 American sailors and soldiers were stationed on this tiny island. Bora Bora never saw combat

Bora Bora

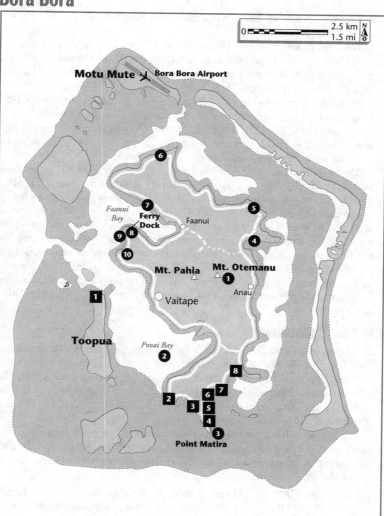

Motu Mute ✈ **Bora Bora Airport**

🔵6

Faanui Bay

🔵7
Ferry Dock

Faanui ○

🔵5

🔵9 🔵8

🔵4

🔵10

Mt. Pahia △

Mt. Otemanu △
🔵1

○ Vaitape

Anau ○

■1

Toopua

Povai Bay
🔵2

■8

■2

🔵6 🔵7

■3

🔵5

🔵4

🔵3

Point Matira

0 ▬▬▬▬ 2.5 km
1.5 mi

N

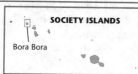

SOCIETY ISLANDS

Bora Bora

ACCOMMODATIONS:
Beach Club Bora Bora ■6
Bora Bora Lagoon Resort ■1
Club Med ■8

Hotel Bora Bora ■2
Hotel Matira ■3
Moana Beach Parkroyal ■4
Sofitel Marara ■7
Village Pauline ■5

ATTRACTIONS:
Aehautai Marae 🔵4
Mareotetini Marae 🔵8
Matira Beach 🔵3

Mt. Otemanu 🔵1
Old Hyatt Site 🔵6
Povai Bay 🔵2
Revatua Club 🔵5
U.S. Wharf 🔵7
U.S. Guns 🔵10
Yacht Club 🔵9

during World War II, but it was a major refueling base on the America-to-Australia supply line.

You'll get to see the lagoon close up soon after landing, for all passengers are ferried across it from the airport, some directly to their hotels but most to Vaitape, the main village on the west coast, sitting opposite Teavanui Pass, the only entrance through the reef into the lagoon.

As is the case on Tahiti and Moorea, a road runs around the shoreline of Bora Bora, cutting in and out of the bays and skirting what seem like a thousand white-sand beaches lapped by the waters of the lagoon. The best of the beaches—in fact, one of the best in French Polynesia—stretches for more than two miles around a flat, coconut-studded peninsula known as Matira Point.

The island is so small that the road around it covers only 27km (17 miles) from start to finish. All the 4,500 or so Bora Borans live on a flat coastal strip that quickly gives way to the mountainous interior. The highest point on the island is the unusual slab, Mount Otemanu (2,379 feet), Bora Bora's trademark. Next to it is the more normal Mount Pahia (2,165 feet). These two mountains never quite seem the same from any two different viewpoints. Mount Otemanu can look like a tombstone from one direction, a needle from another. Because these mountains are relatively low, Bora Bora doesn't get as much rain as the taller Tahiti, Moorea, or Raiatea. Water shortages can occur, especially during the drier months from June through September (consequently, most hotels have their own desalinization facilities).

GETTING AROUND

Le trucks going to the hotels meet Air Tahiti's ferries when they land at Vaitape. The *Ono Ono, Raromatai Ferry,* and the inter-island freighters dock about two miles north of Vaitape at the entrance to Faanui Bay, where le truck drivers also wait to take passengers to the hotels. Get in the one with the name of your hotel painted on the side. Fares to the Matira Point hotel district are 300 CFP ($3) from Vaitape and 500 CFP ($5) from Faanui Bay.

There is no le truck type of public transportation system on Bora Bora. The larger hotels get their guests to town and back, but the frequency can vary depending on how many tourists are on the island. Some restaurants will pick up dinner guests who call for reservations.

BY RENTAL CAR, SCOOTER & BICYCLE   The only car-rental firm is Europcar (☎ 67.70.15, or 800/227-7368), which also rents scooters and bicycles. Cars begin at 7,000 CFP ($70) for 24 hours, including unlimited kilometers and insurance; there's a 100,000 CFP ($100) deductible for any damages. Scooters cost 5,500 CFP ($55) for a day. Bicycles go for 2,000 CFP ($20). Europcar has booths on the main road, opposite the Vaitape wharf and at the hotels.

The 17-mile-long road around Bora Bora is paved for only about two-thirds of the way. Most of it is flat, but be very cautious on the steep hill on the east side of the island above the Club Med. Also watch out for pedestrians and dogs; always drive or ride slowly and carefully.

By Taxi   For a taxi, call Otemanu Tours (☎ 67.70.49), Jeanine Buchin (☎ 67.74.14), or Jacques Isnard (☎ 67.72.25). Fares between Vaitape and the Matira hotel district are at least 1,000 CFP ($10) from 6am to 6pm, 1,500 CFP ($15) from 6pm to 6am.

FAST FACTS: BORA BORA

Baby-sitters   Contact Robin Teraitepo at Chez Ben's (☎ 67.74.54).

Bookstores   Librairie Vaite (☎ 67.62.02) in the shopping center just north of the Vaitape wharf has some English books.

Camera/Film   Boutique Beach Club (☎ 67.71.16) opposite the Bora Bora Beach Club in Matira carries film and offers one-day processing of color print film.

Currency Exchange   Banks are located in Vaitape; all are open Monday through Friday from 8 to 11am and from 2 to 4pm, but beyond that, each has its own business hours.

Doctor   An infirmary (☎ 67.70.77) and both a doctor and dentist are available in Vaitape.

Drugstores   A pharmacy north of the town wharf in Vaitape is open Monday through Friday from 8 to noon and 3:30 to 6pm, Saturday from 8 to noon and 5 to 6pm, and Sunday from 9 to 9:30 am.

Information   The Bora Bora Comité du Tourisme (☎ 67.76.36) has an office in the large building on the north side of Vaitape wharf. Hours are Monday to Friday from 7:30am to noon and 1:30 to 4pm, Saturday from 8 to 11:30am. The address is B.P. 144, Vaitape, Bora Bora.

Police   The gendarmerie is opposite the Vaitape wharf (☎ 67.70.58).

Post Office   The post office in Vaitape is open on Monday from 8am to 3pm, Tuesday through Friday from 7am to 3pm, and on Saturday from 7 to 9am.

WHAT TO SEE & DO

✪ **The Circle Island Tour**   Since the island is only 17 miles around, many visitors see it on bicycles (give yourself at least four hours), by scooter, by car, or by an organized tour (see below). If you do it yourself, begin at the wharf in Vaitape, where there's a monument to French yachtsman Alain Gerbault, who sailed his boat around the world between 1923 and 1929 and lived to write about it (thus adding to Bora Bora's fame).

From the wharf, head south (counterclockwise) around the island. The road soon curves along the shore of Povai Bay, where Mounts Otemanu and Pahia tower over you. Take your time along this bay; the views are the best on Bora Bora. When you reach the area around the Bamboo House Restaurant, stop for a look back across the water at Mount Otemanu.

The road climbs the small headland at the Hotel Bora Bora on Raititi Point, then runs smoothly along curving Matira Beach, one of the South Pacific's best. Just off the end of the beach closest to the hotel, you can do some good snorkeling. When the road curves sharply to the left, look for a narrow paved road to the right. This leads to Matira Point, the low, sandy, coconut-studded peninsula that extends out from Bora Bora's south end. Down this track about 50 yards is a public beach area on the west side of the peninsula, opposite Moana Beach Parkroyal. The lagoon is shallow all the way out to the reef at this point, but the bottom is smooth and sandy. When I first came to Bora Bora in 1977, I camped a week on Matira Point; the Moana is only one of many structures in what was then a deserted coconut grove completely surrounded by unspoiled beach.

Up the east coast, you'll pass the Beach Club Bora Bora and the Hotel Sofitel Marara before climbing a steep hill above the Club Méditerranée (get off and walk your bicycle over it, or go very slowly if on a scooter). A trail cuts off to the right on the north side of the hill and goes to the Aehautai Marae, one of several old temples on Bora Bora. This particular one has a great view of Mount Otemanu and the blue outlines of Raiatea and Tahaa islands beyond the motus on the reef.

You will go through a long stretch of coconut plantations before entering Anau, a typical Polynesian village with a large church, a general store, and tin-roofed houses crouched along the road. The east-coast road beyond Anau is unpaved and can be treacherous. Except for a few native homes and the Revatua Club (☎ 67.71.67), which makes an excellent refueling stop, the northwest coast is deserted. Here you ride through several miles of coconut plantations pockmarked by thousands of holes made by the land crabs known as *tupas*. After turning at the northernmost point, you pass a group of over-water bungalows and another group of houses, which climb the hill. Some of these are expensive condominiums; the others are part of defunct project that was to have been a Hyatt resort. Across the lagoon are Motu Mute and the airport.

Faanui Bay was used during World War II as an Allied naval base. It's not marked, but a wharf on the north shore was built by the U.S. Navy's Seabees as a seaplane ramp. At the head of the bay, a road cuts off into the Faanui valley, from which an unmarked hiking trail leads over the saddle to Bora Bora's east coast.

Just beyond the main shipping wharf at the point on the south side of Faanui Bay is the restored Marotetini Marae, which in pre-European days was dedicated to navigators. In his novel *Hawaii*, James Michener had his fictional Polynesians leave this point to discover and settle the Hawaiian Islands. Nearby are tombs in which members of Bora Bora's former royal family are buried. If you look offshore at this point, you'll see the only pass into the lagoon; a path up to two of the American guns that guarded it begins near the Club Med. Ask around for directions.

Near the end of your round-island tour you will pass Magasin Chin Lee, a major gathering place for local residents. It's a good place to soak up some local culture while having a soft drink or, if you have been riding a bike, a cold bottle of Eau Royale. Opposite the store is a modern shopping center with a patisserie, bookstore, hairdresser, and a branch of Sibani Perles.

Sightseeing Tours   Not everything on Bora Bora has been included in the tour described above, and even some of those sights I mentioned may not be all that easy to find. Accordingly, consider taking a guided sightseeing tour around the island. Every hotel activities desk offers one. Alfredo Doom's **Bora Bora Tours** (☎ 67.70.28) operates from the Hotel Bora Bora. Paul Desmet's **Otemanu Tours** (☎ 67.70.49) has its base north of Vaitape but will pick up at the hotels.

While the regular tours stick to the shoreline, Dany Leverd's **Tupuna Four-Wheel Drive Expeditions** (☎ 67.75.06) and Vincent Soustrot's **Bora Bora Jeep Safari** (☎ 67.70.34) head into the hills in Land Rovers for panoramic views and visits to old U.S. Navy gun sites. The mountain roads are mere ruts in places, so you could get stuck if it has been raining.

WHERE TO STAY

Bora Bora has three of the South Pacific's finest—and most expensive—resorts. As I said earlier, this is a playground for the rich and famous (and Japanese honeymooners, who are enamored of the island's fine selection of over-water bungalows), and Bora Bora lacks quality establishments in the moderate-price range. Except at the Club Med, guests pay extra for everything except their rooms.

VERY EXPENSIVE

✪ Bora Bora Lagoon Resort

B.P. 175, Vaitape, Bora Bora (on Motu Toopa, 1 mile off Vaitape). ☎ **60.40.00** or 800/ 223-6800. Fax 60.40.01. 80 bungalows. MINIBAR TV TEL. U.S. $520–$690 bungalow; U.S. $760 suite. AE, DC, MC, V.

The venerable but rebuilt Hotel Bora Bora (see below) got some stiff competition when this Japanese-owned resort opened in 1994 on Motu Toopa, a hilly island facing the rounded peak of Mount Pahia (not Mount Otemanu's tombstone). Locals without permission aren't allowed on the resort's launches, which shuttle from Vaitape 23 times a day. Nor will you see many Polynesian faces in key jobs here, for management has imported expatriot staff in order to maintain the highest level of service in the islands (when I stayed here, a redheaded Englishwoman greeted diners, and a blonde Australian lass picked up towels at the beach).

The property, on the other hand, is very Polynesian. The main building, under three interlocking thatch roofs, holds reception, bar, reading and media room, an underground disco, and gourmet restaurant. The end facing Mount Pahia actually protrudes over the lagoon. To the rear, French Polynesia's largest swimming pool is surrounded by an expansive stone deck. Sailboats, canoes, windsurfers, and other equipment are parked on a white-sand beach, where an activities shack provides scuba diving, snorkeling, fishing, and other outdoor activities.

Piers with hand-carved railings lead to 50 over-water bungalows, and 30 more sit ashore in tropical gardens. All of the 528-square-foot units are identical: peaked thatch roofs over polished wood floors and walls, which evoke a ship's cabin; floor-to-ceiling jalousie windows on one side, doors sliding to porches or decks on another; sofas and easy chairs with ottomans; armoires hiding TVs with CNN, ESPN, movies, and other satellite programming; spacious baths with telephones, glass-door showers, and double sinks (which leave little space for toiletries). As luxurious as they are, the units are so close together you can overhear your neighbor's favorite TV show, and cross-ventilation could be better, given the lack of air conditioning and the amount of space to be churned by a lone ceiling fan.

Dining/Entertainment: With widely spaced tables all facing the lagoon, the main dining room excellently presents gourmet Asian-accented cuisine (dresses for women, trousers and collared shirts for men required at dinner). Informal dress is permitted at the lounge-bar, which serves light meals. Tahitian dance shows are featured two nights a week. The underground Club Heiva has disco dancing or karaoke until after midnight.

Services: Turndown with ice; laundry; baby-sitting; limited room service; *New York Times Fax* delivered to rooms daily.

Facilities: Lighted tennis courts; game room and library; boutique; activities desk; two rooms equipped for disabled guests.

✪ Hotel Bora Bora

B.P. 1, Vaitape, Bora Bora (Matira Point, 4.4 miles from Vaitape). ☎ **60.44.60** or 800/421-1490. Fax 60.44.66. 55 bungalows. MINIBAR TEL. 39,500 CFP–70,000 CFP ($395–$700). AE, DC, MC, V.

The American manager and many of his Tahitian staff have been at this grand hotel since it opened in the early 1960s as French Polynesia's premier resort. Thanks to recent renovations, the bungalows have been completely rebuilt, but left alone was the thatch-roofed central building that has been a key part of this resort's charm since its beginning. It sits atop a low headland overlooking the start of magnificent Matira Beach, whose coral gardens provide some of the best snorkeling off any hotel in the territory. Down below, one of the most charming beach bars in the South Pacific rests right on those white sands and adjacent to a lagoonside swimming pool. The entire complex faces west, presenting glorious sunsets over the lagoon and hilly Motu Toopua.

The comfortable Tahitian-style bungalows are among the palm trees on the flat shoreline on either side of the headland. On the north, some of the 15 over-water bungalows are actually perched right on the reef's edge, where coral gives way to a deep blue lagoon (snorkeling off their porches is like flying off a canyon wall). Some also enjoy views of Mount Otemanu's tombstone across Povai Bay. None of the bungalows are as large as those at Bora Bora Lagoon Resort, but the hotel's huge new L-shaped villas are. They all have separate bedrooms, and the garden versions even have their own small swimming pools surrounded by rock walls for privacy. The villas and over-water bungalows all have four-poster king size beds with romantic mosquito nets. Furnishings throughout are top-of-the-line, with some Oriental antique pieces here and there. All units have stereo sound systems and oak-trimmed, claw-footed bath tubs in addition to showers. Three units are air conditioned and have Jacuzzis.

The only serious drawback here is the neighboring round-island road, which can send the noise of Bora Bora's innumerable scooters into some units at the crack of dawn. Signs at each end of the property ostensibly keep intruders out, but that's not to say anyone can't wander onto the premises.

Dining/Entertainment: Offering a mix of continental and Polynesian fare, the hotel's dining room overlooks the lagoon on three sides. You can have your lunch brought to the pool- and beachside bar. A second bar adjoins the restaurant, and Tahitians strum their guitars and sing there every evening, when a dress code is in effect (no shorts, tank tops, or shower sandals). Traditional dance shows occur at least two nights a week.

Services: Turndown; laundry; baby-sitting; twice-daily shuttle to Vaitape; afternoon tea; *New York Times Fax* delivered to rooms daily.

Facilities: Lighted tennis courts; water sports, including scuba diving; bicycles; boutique; convenience store; games bungalow with satellite-fed TV (CNN and ESPN), table tennis, and billiards; activities and car-rental desks.

✪ Moana Beach Parkroyal

B.P. 156, Vaitape, Bora Bora (east side of Matira Point). ☎ **67.73.73** or 800/346-6262. Fax 67.71.41. 41 bungalows. MINIBAR TEL. 43,300 CFP–59,700 CFP ($433–$597). AE, DC, MC, V.

Although this deluxe resort lacks the history of the Hotel Bora Bora and the snap-to service of the Bora Bora Lagoon Resort, it stands out for its exquisitely crafted 30 over-water bungalows. You can remove the tops of their glass coffee tables and actually feed the fish swimming in the turquoise lagoon below. A Japanese-style sliding wall separates the king-size bed from the lounge area; the bath has two sinks and an American-size tub; and you can sunbathe in the buff on a private deck with steps leading down to the lagoon. Bedside tables have built-in stereo tape players. Ashore on Point Matira, 11 beachside bungalows are less enchanting, but like the over-water units, they have Raiatea and Tahaa in their lagoon views, which neither the Hotel Bora Bora nor Bora Bora Lagoon Resort can boast. Also beside the beach, four thatch-roofed buildings, which surround a small courtyard, house the reception area, a lounge complete with a TV equipped to play any type of videotape, and the bar and restaurant (with outdoor seating).

Dining/Entertainment: The airy, beachside dining room offers very fine French selections, with emphasis on seafood. A Tahitian string band entertains every evening.

Services: Laundry; baby-sitting; room service (delivered to over-water bungalows by canoe turndown).

Facilities: Swimming pool; water sports, including scuba diving and waterskiing; activities and car-rental desks; boutique.

EXPENSIVE

Hotel Sofitel Marara Bora Bora

B.P. 6, Bora Bora (north of Matira Point on east side). ☎ **67.70.46**, 41.04.04 in Papeete or 800/763-4835 in U.S. Fax 67.74.03. 64 bungalows. MINIBAR TEL. 27,000 CFP–50,000 CFP ($270–$500). AE, DC, MC, V.

Known locally as "The Marara," this hotel may lack the traditions of the Hotel Bora Bora, but it has its own history: Italian movie producer Dino De Laurentis built it in 1977 to house star Mia Farrow and the crew working on his box-office bomb *Hurricane.* It is the least charming—and least expensive—of the "Big Four" resorts on the island, but it does have 43 bungalows facing a curving beach of white sand, the lagoon, and Raiatea and Tahaa on the horizon. A long pier joins another 21 over-water models to the shore.

A beehive-shaped central building houses the restaurant and bar, both of which open to a swimming pool sunken into a deck built out over the beach and lagoon. Open on three sides to the lagoon, the restaurant features French and Chinese cuisines, with many meals served buffet style. Guests are taken on picnics to a small island offshore. Evening entertainment features a Tahitian string band every night, and a traditional dance show, which is held once a week, usually Saturday evening. Services include turndown, laundry, baby-sitting, and a shuttle bus to Vaitape. On the beach, guests enjoy extensive water sports, including scuba diving and parasailing. Facilities include tennis courts, a boutique, and activities and car rental desks.

MODERATE

Beach Club Bora Bora

B.P. 252, Bora Bora (north of Matira Point on east side). ☎ **67.71.16**, 43.08.29 in Papeete. Fax 41.09.28. 36 rms. A/C. 23,000 CFP–29,000 CFP ($230–$290). AE, DC, MC, V.

Originally an Ibis hotel but now locally managed, this motel-like property has shown need of refurbishment during each of my visits going back several years, and is a prime candidate for a complete overhaul. Were it not on Bora Bora, its rates would be less than half those quoted above (and often are, when purchased as part of a package tour). Nevertheless, it is one of only two moderately priced hotels on the island, not counting the Club Med, and for this reason is mentioned here. Its saving grace is a location just a short stroll along beautiful Matira Beach to the Hotel Sofitel Marara. Nine shingle-roof buildings each hold four motel-style rooms; like those in most Ibis hotels, they are on the small side. Each has a private terrace. Twenty of the rooms are in a coconut grove next to a U-shaped central building, which houses a mediocre restaurant and bar next to the beach. Some units are air conditioned; others have ceiling fans. The hotel provides some water sports equipment.

⑤ Club Méditerranée Bora Bora

B.P. 34, Vaitape, Bora Bora (north of Point Matira on east side). ☎ **60.46.04**, 42.96.99 in Papeete, or 800/258-2633. Fax 42.16.83. 150 units. A/C TEL. 143,000 CFP ($143) per person (including all meals). AE, DC, MC, V.

Lush tropical gardens provide the setting for this Club Med, which opened in 1994 beside the northeastern end of Matira Beach. Behind it, the round-island road climbs up the interior hills, which provide a backdrop. The focus of attention is a large thatch-roofed beachside pavilion housing reception, bar, dining room, and nightclub. Guests pay extra for scuba diving, but all meals and a wide range of water sports activities are included in the rates, which makes the Club a bargain considering the prices elsewhere on Bora Bora. There's a pool, two lighted tennis courts, an archery range, and a place to practice your golf swing. Accommodation is in a mix of stand-alone and duplex bungalows and two-story, motel-style buildings. The beachfront bungalows are preferable here, especially for honeymooners and others seeking a degree of privacy. The rooms are comfortably if minimally furnished (their most interesting feature: lights shining up from their tile floors). If you don't have a roommate, one of the same sex may be assigned.

Hotel Matira

B.P. 31, Bora Bora (on Matira Beach, south of Hotel Bora Bora). ☎ **67.70.51**. Fax 67.77.00. 28 bungalows. 9,500 CFP–26,000 CFP ($95–$260). AE, MC, V.

The reception desk is just inside Matira Restaurant and Bar (see "Where to Dine," below), which serves as headquarters for this collection of bungalows on and near the beach. In the past, you basically got your own cottage and daily maid service here, but the owners are replacing all their older units with more modern bungalows and adding activities for their guests. Accordingly, all rates may be at the higher end of the range by the time you get there. Whether new or old, all units have thatch roofs, porches on the front, shower-only baths, refrigerators, and a double bed or two singles. Some of the older units have kitchens, but the new ones will not. About half are on Matira Point, while the others are about 500 yards away next to the restaurant. Preferable are the more expensive units directly on the beach.

HOSTELS & CAMPING

✪ Village Pauline

B.P. 215, Vaitape, Bora Bora (north of Matira Point between Moana Beach and Sofitel Marara hotels). ☎ **67.72.16**. Fax 67.78.14. 4 bungalows, 9 beach cabins (none with bath), 12 rooms (none with bath), 10 dorm beds, 20 tent sites. 1,600 CFP ($16) tent site; 2,000 CFP ($20) bunk in hostel; 5,000 CFP ($50) beach cabin or private room; 9,000 CFP ($90) bungalow (higher rates apply to one-night stays). MC, V.

Pauline Youseff has a variety of no-frills accommodations at her very popular place, one of the great hostels in the South Pacific. For a fraction of the price, her guests enjoy the same beach as those at the island's far more expensive establishments. On the other hand, her one-bedroom cabins built of plywood and thatch give basic shelter, but they are right on Matira Beach. Her private rooms are in motel-like blocks across the road, where she also has her dormitory and tent sites. The one-bedroom bungalows have kitchens and baths with hot and cold water, but occupants of the rooms, beach bungalows, dorm, and tents share communal toilets, showers, and kitchen facilities. Bookings should be made at least a month in advance for bungalows. There's a snack bar on the premises, and the staff arranges activities at less cost than do the big hotels.

WHERE TO DINE
EXPENSIVE

Bamboo House
Matira, 1 mile north of Hotel Bora Bora. ☎ **67.76.24**. Reservations advised. Main courses 1,400 CFP–2,600 CFP ($14–$26). AE, MC, V. Daily 11:30am–2pm and 6:30–8:30pm. FRENCH/SEAFOOD.

That's exactly what this little establishment is: a bamboo house, and a charming one at that. The entire building is made of varnished split bamboo, and lots of dried bamboo leaves are stacked or hung here and there to render a jungly effect. Japanese lanterns provide subdued lighting. Prime tables are on a small front porch. The menu depends on what seafood is caught in local waters but usually features parrot fish, tuna, and shrimp, all well prepared in French sauces. This French-operated establishment's cuisine is considered second best on the island, right behind the Yacht Club Bora Bora (see below). Free transportation is provided from the hotels by reservation.

Bloody Mary's Restaurant & Bar
Matira, around the bend from Hotel Bora Bora. ☎ **67.72.86**. Reservations recommended. Pizzas 750 CFP–1,100 CFP ($7.50–$11); main courses 2,300 CFP–4,000 CFP ($23–$40). MC, V. Mon–Sat 11am–3pm and 6:30–9:30pm. SEAFOOD.

You won't be on Bora Bora long before you hear of Bloody Mary's, but don't expect fine cuisine here: this essentially is a barbecued seafood restaurant with California ambience and Bora Bora prices. Some of your fellow readers have said it's a tourist trap; others have had a wonderful evening. In any event, Bloody Mary's is worth at least a drink to soak up its extraordinary tropical decor. A floor of fine white sand is covered by a large thatch roof from which hang ceiling fans, colored spotlights, and stalks of dried bamboo. The butcher-block tables are made of coconut-palm lumber, and the seats are sections of palm trunks cut into stools. Bloody Mary's is operated by Americans, which explains the "Hi, I'm Rick" greeting you will receive as you are shown the seafood laid out on a bed of ice. Your choice will be charbroiled and served on large round plates covered with banana leaves, with a sauce on the side if you want. The fish is fresh from the lagoon; some other items are imported. Guests get free transportation from hotels if they reserve by 5pm. The lunch menu consists solely of pizzas, which are not served at dinner.

✪ Yacht Club Bora Bora
Faanui, on the lagoon, 1 mile north of Vaitape. ☎ **67.70.69**. Reservations strongly advised. Burgers and sandwiches 1,000 CFP–1,100 CFP ($10–$11); main courses 2,100 CFP–3,100 CFP ($21–$31). MC, V. Daily 7–10:30am, noon–2pm, and 6:30–9pm (bar daily noon–9pm). FRENCH.

This establishment isn't a club but a small French-owned hotel with what is consistently the finest restaurant on Bora Bora. Juicy burgers are available for lunch, but everyone comes here for the fresh seafood specials served under a variety of wonderful French sauces. If you missed them at Acajou's in Papeete, shrimps are served here in one of the most delicious coconut-curry sauces in the islands. The open-air, thatch-roofed dining room is open at one end to a dock where passing yachties come ashore. If your credit cards can stand it, make a point of eating here. Free transportation for 7pm seating if reservations are made by 5pm.

MODERATE

☉ Chez Ben's

Matira, between Hotel Bora Bora and Matira Point. ☎ **67.74.54**. Sandwiches, salads, pizzas 1,000 CFP–1,250 CFP ($10–$12.50); meals 1,000 CFP–1,800 CFP ($10–$18). AE, MC, V. Fri–Wed 11am–8pm. SNACK BAR/PIZZA.

Bora Bora–born Ben Teraitepo and Oklahoma-born wife Robin hold fort just across the road from a shady portion of Matira Beach. They serve sandwiches, unusually spicy poisson cru, and lasagna. Ben's fresh tuna salad sandwiches and Robin's American-style pizzas are delicious.

Matira Bar and Restaurant

In Hotel Matira, 1 mile south of Hotel Bora Bora. ☎ **67.70.51**. Reservations required. Main courses 900 CFP–1,500 CFP ($9–$15). AE, MC, V. Daily 7–10am; Tues–Sun 11am–2pm and 6–9pm. CANTONESE.

Literally hanging over the beach, this Chinese restaurant is an excellent place to have a lagoonside lunch or sunset drink before dinner. The menu offers a selection of beef, pork, chicken, duck, and seafood dishes done in the Cantonese fashion, with Hakka overtones (Tahiti's first Chinese immigrants came from the Hakka region of the mainland).

INEXPENSIVE

Bora Bora Burgers

Vaitape, next to post office. No phone. Reservations not accepted. Meals 350 CFP–800 CFP ($3.50–$8). No credit cards. Mon–Sat 7:30am–5pm. FAST FOOD.

This counter with coconut poles as stools and a few tables on the sidewalk has reasonably priced sandwiches, burgers, and hot dogs, making it one of Bora Bora's few real food bargains. It calls itself the "3B."

LAGOON OUTINGS AND OTHER WATER SPORTS

✪ **LAGOON OUTINGS**   Bora Bora has one of the world's most beautiful lagoons, and getting out on it, snorkeling and swimming in it, and visiting the islands on its outer edge are absolute musts. Your hotel or pension can recommend one of several guides for lagoon trips. Mike Henry of **Poeiti Tours** has an all-day outrigger canoe tour including lunch on a motu for 5,000 CFP ($50) per person. Book at any hotel desk or at Chez Ben's (☎ 67.74.54).

Most tours include shark-feeding demonstrations (the guide actually feeds reef sharks while you watch from nearby while snorkeling). Some go to the Bora Bora Lagoonarium, a fenced-in underwater area where you can swim with the manta rays and observe sharks (they are on the other side of the fence here).

Another way to see the lagoon is on the *Vehia,* a 46-foot catamaran owned by American expatriate Richard Postma. The name *Vehia* comes from a legendary woman surfer who defeated her much stronger men competitors in a royal match; one of the last Polynesian families to oppose French rule symbolically took the

Marlon's Mana

Marlon Brando did more than star in the remake of *Mutiny on the Bounty* when he came to Tahiti in 1962. He fell in love with his beautiful Tahitian co-star, Tarita, who became his wife and the mother of two of his children. He also fell for Tetiaroa, an atoll 30 miles north of Papeete.

In the old days, this cluster of 12 flat islets surrounding an aquamarine lagoon was the playground of Tahiti's high chiefs, who frequently were joined by the *Ariori*, those traveling bands of sexually explicit entertainers and practioners of infanticide. High-ranking women would spend months on Tetiaroa, resting in the shade to lighten their skins and gouging on starchy foods to broaden their girths. Chiefly men and women were said to possess *mana*, and the bigger the body, the more the mana.

For a time Tetiaroa was owned by an American dentist who married into the royal family, but it was abandoned when Brando bought it in 1966. He turned one of his islets into a refuge for Tetiaroa's thousands of seabirds. He built a retreat for himself on a second islet and a small, rather rustic resort on a third.

Guests at the resort would seldom see the great actor, on whose waistline Tetiaroa worked its expansive magic. During the day he would stay at home in the shade, playing with his radios and computers. At night he would go fishing and lobstering.

A series of hurricanes blew most of his resort away in 1983, and Brando's relationship with Tahiti turned to human disaster a decade later when his son Christian shot and killed his sister's Tahitian boyfriend in Hollywood. Marlon's distraught daughter later committed suicide on Tahiti.

Ex-wife Tarita still operates what's left of the resort, which is once again a local playground. For information, contact Hotel Tetiaroa, B.P. 2418, Papeete, Tahiti (☎ 82.63.02, fax 85.00.51).

---

name. The *Vehia* is docked at the Hotel Bora Bora and goes on picnic cruises three days a week and sunset cruises on the other days. The all-day picnic cruise costs 7,000 CFP ($70) per person; the sunset cruise is 2,500 CFP ($25) per person. Reservations can be made at the Hotel Bora Bora's activities desk (☎ 60.44.05) or by calling Richard direct (☎ 67.77.79).

SCUBA DIVING   Scuba divers can swim among the coral heads, sharks, and fishes. Michel and Anne Condesse's **Bora Bora Diving Center** (☎ 67.71.84), adjacent to the Hotel Bora Bora, gives a 30-minute introductory course for 5,000 CFP ($50). One-tank dives cost 6,000 CFP ($60), or 7,500 CFP ($75) at night.

SPORT FISHING   For excellent deep-sea game fishing, contact Kirk Pearson, an American whose **Mokalei II** is based at the Hotel Bora Bora (☎ 67.74.93). Kirk charges 48,000 CFP ($480) for half a day's fishing and 80,000 CFP ($800) for all day, including drinks. As is the case throughout the South Pacific, you catch all the fish you can, but you keep only as much as you can eat. Take your camera.

For combined sailing and fishing, Richard Postma's **Tara Vana** (☎ 67.77.79, or 714/650-7175 in the U.S.) is the world's first sail-powered luxury game fishing boat. This 50-footer is available for day trips or for overnight charters to the other Leeward Islands. A day's sailing or fishing costs 80,000 CFP ($800) for up to eight persons. Cruises range from 150,000 CFP ($1,500) for one day to 1,050,000 CFP ($10,500) for a week, including food but not alcoholic beverages. Among Richard's first guests on the *Tara Vana* were actors Dennis Quaid and Meg Ryan.

OTHER WATER SPORTS You don't have to stay there to use the water sports equipment and facilities at the **Hotel Sofitel Marara** (☎ 67.70.46), but you will have to pay. These include waterskiing, sailing on Hobie Cats, paddling canoes, and getting a bird's-eye view of the lagoon while hanging below a parasail.

You can rent your own speedboat from Frank Sachsse's **Moana Adventure Tours** (☎ 60.44.70), at the Hotel Bora Bora.

SHOPPING

Compared with those on Tahiti and Moorea, the pickings on Bora Bora are relatively slim and the prices rather high for black pearls, most handcrafts, silk-screened pareus, and clothing. However, the following are worth examining.

Local artisans display their straw hats, pareus, and other handcraft items at **Bora Bora I Te Fanau Tahi** (no phone), in the large hall at the Vaitape wharf. It's always open when the *Windsong*, *Club Med 2*, or other cruise ships are in the lagoon. The local Tourism Committee (☎ 67.70.10) has its offices on the waterfront side of the building and can tell you when that will be.

Boutique Gauguin (☎ 67.76.67), in a white house one mile north of Hotel Bora Bora, offers a selection of handcrafts, clothing, and black pearls in addition to curio items such as ashtrays and coasters featuring the works of Paul Gauguin. Some of its pareus are particularly artistic. Hours are Monday to Saturday from 8:30am to 6pm and Sunday from 9:30am to 4:30pm.

Matira Pearls (☎ 67.79.14), at Matira Point, is operated by Steve Fearon, whose family once owned a piece of the Hotel Bora Bora. Steve designed his air-conditioned shop to resemble his friend Ron Hall's successful Island Fashion Black Pearls on Moorea. Set and loose black pearls start at $100, and his simple settings are designed to emphasize the pearl, not the gold. He also has a selection of bathing suits, aloha shirts, and T-shirts. Steve has another small outlet at Bloody Mary's Restaurant and Bar (see "Where to Dine," above).

Moana Arts (☎ 67.70.33), virtually next to the Hotel Bora Bora, is where noted photographer Erwin Christian sells some of his dramatic works, which you will inevitably see in numerous books and on many postcards. He also has a selection of designer resort wear. Open Monday to Saturday from 9am to noon and 2 to 6pm.

Pokalola Boutique (☎ 67.71.82), over Bora Bora Burger in Vaitape, has the island's largest selection of T-shirts, pareus, tropical clothing, wood carvings, black pearls, shell jewelry, and curios such as Hinano beer glasses. Open Monday to Saturday from 8am to 6pm.

Sibani Perles (☎ 67.72.49), opposite Magasin Chin Lee in Vaitape, offers the designs of Didier Sibani, one of the pioneers of the black pearl industry. His elegant and pricey designs are displayed in bamboo cases.

ISLAND NIGHTS

Like Moorea, things are really quiet on Bora Bora after dark. You may want to listen to a Tahitian band playing at sunset or watch the furious hips in a Tahitian dance show. If so, you will be limited to whatever is going on at **Hotel Bora Bora**

(☎ 60.44.60), **Hotel Sofitel Marara** (☎ 67.70.46), and **Club Méditerranée** (☎ 67.72.57). See "Where to Stay," above, for their general entertainment schemes. Remember that schedules change; call ahead.

La Récife Discothèque (no phone), about two miles north of Vaitape, is the island's one nightclub, and it opens only on Fridays and Saturdays at 11pm (that's right, 11pm) and closes sometime around dawn the following mornings. The clientele are mostly Tahitians between 18 and 24 years old, and fights have been known to break out at that late hour. Admission is about 500 CFP ($5). Beers cost at least 500 CFP ($5) each.

2 Huahine

The first of the Leeward Islands northwest of Tahiti, mountainous Huahine is notable for its serrated coastline, long beaches, ancient maraes, picturesque main town, and independent-spirited residents whose main livelihood is farming. As the least developed of the islands with luxury hotels and comfortable hostels, Huahine offers one of the territory's best opportunities to observe Polynesian life relatively unchanged by fast-paced Western civilization.

Pronounced *Wa-ee-nee* by the French and *Who-a-hee-nay* by the Tahitians, Huahine actually is two islands enclosed by the same reef and joined by a bridge. About 4,000 people live on the two islands, and most of them earn a living growing cantaloupes and watermelons and harvesting copra for the Papeete market. Huahine was not annexed by France until 1897—more than 50 years after Tahiti was taken over—and its people are still independent in spirit. At the time the first Europeans arrived, Huahine was governed as a single chiefdom and not divided into warring tribes as were the other islands, and this spirit of unity is still strong. Pouvanaa a Oopa, the great leader of French Polynesia's independence movement, was born on Huahine.

The ancient chiefs built a series of maraes on the shores of Maeva Lake, which separates the north shore from a long, motu-like peninsula, and on Matairea Hill above the lakeside village of Maeva. These have been restored and are some of the most impressive in French Polynesia.

The main village of Fare, hardly more than a row of Chinese stores opposite a quay, is nestled alongside the lagoon on the northwest shore, opposite the main pass in the reef. When the inter-island boats put in from Papeete, Fare comes to life before the crack of dawn—or long before. Trucks and buses arrive from all over Huahine with passengers and cargo bound for the other islands. The rest of the time, however, Fare lives at the lazy, slow pace of the South Seas of old as a few people amble down its tree-lined main street and browse through the Chinese general stores facing the town wharf.

GETTING AROUND

The airport is on the peninsula paralleling the north side of the island, 3km (2 miles) from Fare. Unless you have previously reserved a rental car or are willing to walk into Fare, take your hotel minibus or **Enite's Taxi** (☎ 68.82.37), the only cab authorized to pick up tourists arriving by air. The fare into Fare (no pun intended, since Fare is pronounced *Fah-ray*) is 400 CFP ($4), 500 CFP ($5) to the Hotel Sofitel Heiva, and 600 CFP ($6) to Relais Mahana on Huahine's south end.

Pacificar (☎ 68.81.81) and **Kake Rent-a-Car** (☎ 68.82.59) both have offices on the town wharf. They charge the same prices, starting at 5,500 CFP ($55) for an overnight rental. Scooters start at 2,500 CFP ($25) for four hours. Add 800 CFP ($8) for insurance plus the cost of the gasoline you use. Bicycles run 1,000 CFP ($10) for 24 hours.

Only part of Huahine's roadways are paved, but the rest should be in reasonably good shape—except for the *traversière,* which traverses the mountains from Maroe Bay to Faie Bay on the east coast. Other than during periods of heavy rain, this road is passable but is very steep and rough; travelers have died trying to ride bicycles down it. The island's only gasoline stations are in the center of Fare.

Each district has its le truck, which runs into Fare at least once a day, but the schedules are highly irregular. If you take one from Fare to Parea, for example, you may not be able to get back on the same day.

FAST FACTS: HUAHINE

Currency Exchange   Banque Socredo is in Fare, on the road that parallels the main street and bypasses the waterfront. Banque de Tahiti and most other businesses are along Fare's waterfront.

Doctor   The government infirmary is in Fare (☎ 68.82.48).

Drugstore   The pharmacist at the drugstore opposite the town wharf speaks English (☎ 68.80.90). Open Monday to Saturday from 7:30 to 11:30am and 2:30 to 5:30pm.

Information   The local tourism committee has a booth at the airport, but it seldom is staffed. Check the brochures and other materials posted there for information.

Police   The phone number of the gendarmerie in Fare is 68.82.61.

Post Office   The post office is in Fare, on the bypass road opposite the Hotel Bali Hai entrance. Hours are Monday to Thursday from 7am to 3pm, Friday from 7am to 2pm.

Safety   Campers have reported thefts from their tents on Huahine, so don't camp.

WHAT TO SEE & DO

✪ **Touring the Maraes**   A tour of the many 16th-century maraes near the village of Maeva can be made on your own or arranged through your hotel. Start east of Maeva village, where the large, reed-sided meetinghouse sits over Maeva Lake. The stones sitting at the lake's edge and scattered through the adjacent coconut grove were family maraes. More than 200 stone structures have been discovered between there and Matairea Hill, which looms over Maeva, including some 40 maraes (the others were houses, paddocks, and agricultural terraces). Of six maraes and other structures on Matairea Hill, some were built as fortifications during the 1844–48 French-Tahitian war. The track up the hill can be muddy and slippery during wet weather, and the steep climb is best done in early morning or late afternoon.

A large marae that is easier to reach stands on the beach about half a mile across the bridge on the east end of Maeva. To find it, follow the left fork in the dirt road after crossing the bridge. The setting is impressive.

From the bridge you will see several stone fish traps, which were restored by Dr. Yoshiko H. Sinoto, the chairman of the anthropology department of the Bernice P. Bishop Museum in Honolulu and the man responsible for restoring many maraes throughout Polynesia. They work as well today as they did in the 16th century, trapping fish as the tide ebbs and flows in and out of the narrow passage separating the lake from the sea.

When construction began on the Hotel Bali Hai Huahine (see below) in 1973, workers discovered some old artifacts while excavating the lily ponds. Dr. Yoshiko just happened to be on the island and took charge of further excavations. During the next two years the diggers uncovered adzes, fishhooks, and ornaments that had been undisturbed for more than 1,000 years, according to radiocarbon dating of a whale bone found with the other items. So far it's the earliest evidence of habitation found in the Society Islands. Some of the artifacts are exhibited in the hotel's public areas.

Sports & Outdoor Recreation   La Petite Ferme ("The Little Farm," ☎ 68.82.98), on the main road north of Fare, just before the airport turnoff, has Marquesas-bred horses that can be ridden with English or western saddles. Prices start at 4,000 CFP ($40) for half a day. They also organize two- and three-day horseback camping trips into Huahine's interior.

Huahine Land will take you on a photo safari into the island's mountainous interior by more modern means: a four-wheel-drive vehicle. This half-day venture costs 4,000 CFP ($40). Book at any hotel activities desk.

Matairea Cruise (☎ 68.83.79) offers a day of reef-walking excursions, a tour of Huahine's magnificent bays, and a picnic at Parea on the south coast, all in a speedy outrigger canoe equipped with a 70-horsepower outboard motor. Prices are 4,000 CFP ($40).

Moana Tropicale operates the *Terei'a Nui II,* a 35-foot deep-sea-fishing vessel that takes guests along on half-day outings for 48,000 CFP ($480), or full-day trips for 78,000 CFP ($780). The owner fishes for a living, so he keeps the catch. Also available are lagoon picnic excursions for 5,000 CFP ($50) per person. Book at your hotel activities desk.

Pacific Blue Adventures (☎ 68.87.21), the local scuba dive operator whose office is on the town wharf, charges 5,000 CFP ($50) for a one-tank dive and will take snorkelers along for 1,500 CFP ($15) each. The guide often feeds the sharks and pets the moray eels.

Kayaks can be rented at the souvenir shop on the town wharf next door to Chez Guynette (Club Bed) for 500 CFP ($5) for two hours.

WHERE TO STAY
RESORTS

Hana Iti Resort
B.P. 185, Fare, Huahine (near Haapu, 15 minutes from airport). ☎ **68.85.05** or 800/ 225-4255. Fax 68.85.04. 22 bungalows. MINIBAR TEL. U.S. $630–$730 AP. AE, MC, V.

American Tom Kurth made a fortune by inventing the chemical process that makes meat taste smoked when it isn't, then spent most of it developing this unusual, super-deluxe resort on Huahine's west coast. Unfortunately, he ran out of money, the property was slow opening, and some exterior areas already showed need of renewed varnish and other upkeep during my recent visit. Rather than placing his enormous, highly unusual bungalows near the beach, he built them atop a ridge enclosing this 70-acre, amphitheater-like site. Most have great sea views from their isolated perches, which along with their outdoor Jacuzzis make them suited for totally secluded romantic getaways. On the other hand, it's a stiff walk up and down steep, often muddy dirt roads to the dining room, beach, and pool (guests not up to these strenuous strolls can call for the hotel's small version of le truck). Frankly, this somewhat eccentric resort should be at most a two- or three-night stopover on the way to Bora Bora, unless you want maximum privacy, enjoy being a hefty hoof from the beach, and appreciate Balinese as opposed to Polynesian styles.

Swaybacked thatch roofs cover the beachside restaurant and bar as well as most of the bungalows, and most furnishings have an Indonesian rather than Tahitian flair. Natural materials were used whenever possible, such as knurled tree trunks and limbs supporting most roofs, and spiral staircases made of coconut palms. A few bungalows were designed by a noted French woodcarver and look something akin to airport control towers built of tree limbs. Most units have two large buildings. One holds the living room and the other, the bedroom and spacious bath. A man-made waterfall cascades down from a 100-foot-high clifftop lookout to a recreation area containing a pool, Jacuzzi, and game room. Guests also have use of snorkeling gear, sailboats, and canoes; and they can pay extra to scuba dive, game fish, and ride.

Dining/Entertainment: Gourmet meals are served in the dining room next to a lily pond romantically lighted at night (the American Plan is optional but strongly advised at this isolated property). The staff entertains nightly by strumming guitars and singing island songs.

Services: Laundry; room service for continental breakfast only.

Facilities: Swimming pool, tennis court, game room, water sports equipment.

⊖ Hotel Bali Hai Huahine

B.P. 26, Maharepa, Moorea (1/2 mile north of Fare). ☎ **68.84.77,** 56.13.59 on Moorea, or 800/282-1401 in the U.S. Fax 56.19.22. 10 rms, 33 bungalows. 9,500 CFP–17,000 CFP ($95–$170). AE, DC, MC, V.

Like the Bali Hai on Moorea, this creation of Moorea's "Bali Hai Boys" is dated but charming (it also was for sale during my recent visit). It sits beside a fine little beach; enjoys a great view west, with Raiatea, Tahaa, and Bora Bora on the horizon; and is a short walk to town. The soaring thatch roof of the beachside main building covers reception, tour desk, restaurant, and bar. Seven bungalows are on the beach, while 11 others have porches extending over a series of lily ponds that dot the coconut groves on the grounds (the ancient Polynesian artifacts uncovered when the ponds were excavated in 1973 are on display in the reception foyer). In addition, 10 motel-like rooms stand near a swimming pool. The shower-only baths in each unit are surrounded by planters and opaque walls. Guests can use canoes and windsurfers and go on various excursions. The weekly Tahitian feast and dance show was the thing to do in Fare on Friday nights during my recent visit.

✪ Hotel Sofitel Heiva

B.P. 38, Fare, Huahine (on Maeva Motu, 10km [6 miles] from airport). ☎ **68.85.86,** 41.04.04 in Papeete, or 800/763-4835. Fax 41.05.05. 22 rms., 2 suites, 29 bungalows. MINIBAR TEL. 21,000 CFP–60,000 CFP ($210–$600). AE, DC, ME, V.

This luxury hotel sits at the end of Maeva Motu where a pass lets the sea into Maeva Lake. The flat almost-island is joined to the mainland by a one-lane bridge. A large, airy, thatch-roofed building holds reception, dining room, and bar-lounge with glass doors opening to adult and children's swimming pools between which water pours from a giant clam shell. White-sand beaches and bungalows flank this central complex. The spacious bungalows are tastefully furnished with comfortable bamboo chairs and tables, ceiling fan, polished wooden floors, and bath with large shower. Each has sliding doors opening to a covered porch. In addition, the six over-water models—joined to the shore by a curving pier—have glass panels for fish watching and balconies with steps to the lagoon. Although in long buildings, the rooms are as spacious as the bungalows.

Dining/Entertainment: The dining room, known as the Omai Restaurant in honor of the Tahitian who went to London with Capt. James Cook, specializes in French cuisine and offers abundant buffets twice a week when the staff performs traditional Tahitian dances.

Services: Laundry, baby-sitting.

Facilities: Children's and adults' swimming pools, water sports equipment, scuba diving, double-hull canoe with glass bottom for lagoon excursions, TV-video lounge, boutique, small library.

⑤ Relais Mahana

B.P. 30, Fare, Huahine (on Avera Bay near Huahine's south end). ☎ **68.81.54**. Fax 68.85.08. 22 bungalows. 16,000 CFP–18,000 CFP ($160–$180). AE, DC, MC, V.

This pleasant but relatively remote property offers one of the best beach-lagoon combinations in the entire South Pacific, for it sits right on the long white beach stretching down the peninsula on Huahine's south end. A pier from the Mahana's main building runs out over a giant coral head, around which fish and guests swim. The peninsula blocks the brunt of the southeast trade winds, so the lagoon is usually as smooth as glass. Just climb down off the pier and step right in or go for a ride on a paddleboat or Hobie Cat.

The French-operated Mahana has bungalows on the beachfront and bungalows with views of the water; all have shingle roofs, one double or two single beds, baths with showers (very hot water), and porches. Excellent French-style meals on the Modified American plan (breakfast and dinner) are 3,500 CFP ($35) per person a day and should be purchased unless you rent a car (Pacificar is on the premises). Friday evenings usually feature Tahitian entertainment; reservations are essential. Facilities include a swimming pool with bar, video lounge, Laundromat, tennis court, table tennis, rental bikes, and water sports equipment (including kayaks, canoes, paddleboats, and Windsurfers).

HOSTELS

Chez Guynette (Club Bed)

B.P. 87, Fare, Huahine (opposite the town wharf). ☎ **68.83.75**. 6 rooms (all with bath), 7 bunks. 1,200 CFP–1,500 CFP ($12–$15) dorm bed; 2,000 CFP–3,000 CFP ($20–$30) room (higher rates apply to one-night stays). MC, V.

Alain and Helen Guerineau (he's French, she's French Canadian) bought this friendly establishment in 1991, and in a play on Club Med, added Club Bed to the name. They gave it a good painting and cleaning, too, and have kept it spic-and-span. A corridor runs down the center of the building to a communal kitchen and lounge at the rear. The simple rooms and dorms flank the hallway to either side. The rooms have baths with cold-water showers. The Guerineaus offer breakfast and lunch.

WHERE TO DINE

Huahine's version of *les roulettes* gather on the Fare wharf when boats are in port. A wagon serving crepes permanently resides on the waterfront near Chez Guynette (Club Bed).

Restaurant Orio

Fare, south end of town wharf. ☎ **68.83.03**. Reservations not accepted. Meals 850 CFP–1,600 CFP ($8.50–$16). MC, V. Tues–Sun 10:30am–2pm and 6–9pm. FRENCH/CHINESE.

Polynesian charm permeates Jacqueline Itchner's lagoonside eatery and bar. Coconut logs support a thatch roof, which covers a crushed coral floor inside as well as a plank deck right over the harbor. You can dine at booths inside or at tables on the deck while watching the fishing boats come in. In keeping with its name (Orio is the Tahitian god of the sea), the emphasis here is on what comes off the boats—usually fish in French sauces—plus plain Cantonese fare such as chow mein.

Restaurant Tiare Tipanie

Fare, north end between wharf and bypass road. ☎ **68.80.52**. Reservations accepted. Burgers and omelets 350 CFP–550 CFP ($3.50–$5.50); main courses 1,000 CFP–1,200 CFP ($10–$12). MC, V. Tues–Sun 7:30am–2pm and 6:30–8:30pm. FRENCH/PASTRIES.

The Pommier family started out running a pastry shop but now have a small restaurant on their hands. In addition to their pastries (excellent for breakfast) they serve omelets, sandwiches, hamburgers, salads, and main courses such as steak in bordelaise sauce and smoked salmon with eggs, plus a daily plat du jour. The original carry-out counter is still there, but guests now sit at tables on a pleasant veranda.

Restaurant Te Marara

Fare, north end of the wharf. ☎ **68.89.31**. Reservations accepted. Main courses 900 CFP–1,800 CFP ($9–$18). MC, V. Mon–Thurs 9am–2:30pm and 6–9:30pm; Fri 9am–2:30pm; Sat–Sun 8–11:30am. FRENCH.

This pleasant waterside establishment is another fine place to have a drink or meal while listening to the lagoon lap the shore or watching another tremendous tropical sunset. The menu is mostly French but with some interesting local variations, such as shrimp or fish with fruit and coconut milk sauce. Other than the Hotel Bali Hai, this is the only place in town with evening entertainment: local string bands start playing at 5pm Saturday and Sunday.

3 Raiatea & Tahaa

The mountainous clump of land you can see on the horizon from Huahine or Bora Bora is actually two islands, Raiatea and Tahaa, which are enclosed by a single coral reef. There are no beaches on either Raiatea or Tahaa, and tourism is not considered an important part of their economies, which are based on agricultural produce and, in the case of Raiatea, government salaries.

Raiatea, the largest island in the Leeward Group, is by far the more important of the two, both in terms of the past and the present. In the old days Raiatea was the religious center of all the Society Islands, including Tahiti. Polynesian mythology has it that Oro, the god of war and fertility, was born in Mount Temahani, the extinct flat-top volcano that towers over the northern part of Raiatea. Taputapuatea, on its southeast coast, was at one time the most important marae in the islands. Legend also has it that the great Polynesian voyagers who discovered and colonized Hawaii and New Zealand left from there. Archaeological discoveries have substantiated the link with Hawaii.

Today Raiatea (pop. 7,000) is still important as the economic and administrative center of the Leeward Islands. Next to Papeete, the town of Uturoa (pop. 3,500) is the largest settlement and most important transportation hub in French Polynesia.

Tahaa (pronounced "Tah-ah-ah") is much smaller than Raiatea in terms of land area, population (about 1,500), and the height of its terrain. It's a lovely island, with a few very small villages sitting deep in bays that cut into its hills. Although sailors can circumnavigate it without leaving the lagoon, most visitors see it on day trips from Raiatea.

GETTING AROUND

The Raiatea airstrip is 3km (2 miles) north of Uturoa. You will have to take a taxi, for there is no regular public transportation system on Raiatea and no public transport whatsoever on Tahaa. Nor is there an airport on Tahaa.

The *Uporu* (☎ 65.67.10) runs between Uturoa and Tahaa's west coast, with departures from Uturoa from Monday to Saturday, usually at 7:45am, 11am, 1:45pm, and 5pm. Water-taxi service is available at **Apooiti Marina** (☎ 65.61.01).

There are no regular le trucks on Raiatea, but some leave the outlying villages for Uturoa at the crack of dawn and return in the afternoon. They gather around the market on the waterfront in the heart of town. Asking around is the only way to find out when they leave, where they go, and when (and whether) they return to Uturoa.

Raiatea Location (☎ 66.34.06), on the main street in the heart of Uturoa, rents cars for 5,500 CFP ($55) for 8 hours and 6,000 CFP ($60) for 24 hours, including insurance and unlimited kilometers but not gasoline.

Raiatea Safari Tours (☎ 66.37.10), at Hotel Chez Marie-France, rents bicycles for 1,000 CFP ($10) a day.

There is a taxi stand near the market in Uturoa, or contact **René Guilloux** (☎ 66.31.40), **Marona Teanini** (☎ 66.34.62), or **Apia Tehope** (☎ 66.36.41). Fares are 600 CFP ($6) from the airport to town and 1,200 CFP ($12) to the Hotel Hawaiki Nui.

FAST FACTS: RAIATEA & TAHAA

Bookstores   Librairie d'Uturoa (☎ 66.30.80) on the inland side of the main street, in the center of town, carries French books and magazines. Polycentre (☎ 66.31.13) next door has picture books about French Polynesia.

Currency Exchange   French Polynesia's four banks have offices on Uturoa's main street. There is no bank on Tahaa.

Drugstores   Pharmacie de Raiatea (☎ 66.34.44) in Uturoa carries French products.

Emergencies   See "Police," below.

Hospitals   The hospital at Uturoa (☎ 66.32.92) serves all the Leeward Islands. Tahaa has an infirmary at Patio (☎ 65.63.31). Private physicians and dentists practice in Uturoa; ask your hotel for a recommendation.

Information   The local tourism committee has a tourist information office in Uturoa at the corner of the city park nearest the waterfront. The friendly, English-speaking staff is quite helpful. Hours vary from day to day, but they are usually there Monday to Friday from 8 to 11am.

Police   The telephone number of the Uturoa gendarmerie is 66.31.07. On Tahaa, the gendarmerie is at Patio, the administrative center, on the north coast (☎ 65.64.07).

Post Office   The post and telecommunications office is in a modern building north of Uturoa on the main road (as opposed to a new road that runs along the shore of reclaimed land on the north side of town) and is open Monday to Thursday from 7am to 3pm and Friday from 7am to 2pm.

WHAT TO SEE & DO

Highlights of a visit to Raiatea include day trips to and around Tahaa, picnics on small islands on the outer reef, canoe adventures up the Faaroa River (French Polynesia's only navigable river), and hikes into the mountains to see the *tiare apetahi,* a one-sided white flower found nowhere else on earth. Legend says that the five delicate petals are the fingers of a beautiful Polynesian girl who fell in love with a prince but couldn't marry him because of her low birth. Just before she died heartbroken in her lover's arms, she promised to give him her hand to caress each day throughout eternity. At daybreak each morning, accordingly, the five petals pop open.

✪ **Taputapuatea Marae**   On the outskirts of Opoa village 35km (21 miles) south of Uturoa, the Taputapuatea Marae is one of the most sacred locations in all of Polynesia, for legend says Opoa Pass offshore was the departure point for the discovery and settlement of both Hawaii and New Zealand. The large marae on the site actually was built centuries later by the Tamatoa family of chiefs. Vying for supremacy, the Tamatoas mingled religion with politics by creating Oro, the ferocious god of war and fertility supposedly born on Mount Temehani, and by spreading his cult. It took almost 200 years, but Oro eventually became the most important god in the region. Likewise, the Tamatoas became the most powerful chiefs. They were on the verge of conquering all of the Society Islands when the missionaries arrived in 1797. With the Christians' help, Pomare I became king of Tahiti, and the great marae the Tamatoas built for Oro was soon left to ruin, replaced by the lovely Protestant church nearby in Opoa village.

The marae was restored once in the 1960s, and the Tahiti Museum began an even more extensive rehabilitation in 1994. The museum's archaeologists have discovered human bones under some of the structures, apparently the remains of sacrifices to Oro. The marae's huge *ahu,* or raised altar of stones for the gods, is more than 50 yards long, 10 yards wide, and 3.5 yards tall. Flat rocks, used as backrests for the chiefs and priests, still stand in the courtyard in front of the ahu. The entire complex is in a coconut grove on the shore of the lagoon, opposite a pass in the reef, and legend says that bonfires on the marae guided canoes through the reef at night.

Taputapuatea is worth a visit, not only for the marae itself but for the scenery there and along the way. The road skirts the southeast coast and follows Faaroa Bay to the mouth of the river, then back out to the lagoon.

Seeing Uturoa   A stroll through Uturoa will show you what Papeete must have been like a few generations ago. A number of Chinese stores line the main street, which parallels the waterfront a block inland, but Raiatea is not the place to shop except for handcrafts made on Tahaa (check the vendors' stalls on the harbor side of the city park for pareus and handcrafts, including brassieres made of two polished coconut shells). The market on the waterfront is busiest when the interisland boats arrive.

The road beside the gendarmerie, just north of downtown Uturoa, leads to a trail that ascends to the television towers atop 970-foot-tall **Papioi Hill**. The view from the top includes Uturoa, the reef, and the islands of Tahaa, Bora Bora, and Huahine. Another trail begins with a jeep track about 200 yards south of the bridge, at the head of Pufau Bay on the northwest coast. It leads up to the plateau atop **Mount Temehani**. The mountain itself actually is divided in two by a deep gorge.

If you're curious about undersea life but don't want to go underwater, have a look at the extensive collection at **Na Te Ara Museum** (☎ 66.27.00) at Apooti Marina, north of the airport. Admission is 300 CFP ($3) for adults and 150 CFP ($1.50) for children. A boutique sells polished shells and shell jewelry. February-to-October hours are Monday to Saturday from 9am to noon and 2 to 5:30pm; and from November to January, Monday to Saturday from 8am to noon.

Seeing Raiatea   American Bill Kolans of ○ **Almost Paradise Tours** (☎ 66.23.64) has lived on Raiatea since sailing his boat down from Hawaii in 1979. He leads road expeditions to Taputaputea and other archaeological sites, and provides very informative commentary. (Bill lectures on the *Wind Song* when it's in port each week. His three-hour island tour by minibus costs 3,000 CFP [$30] per person.)

Patrice Philip of **Raiatea Safari Tours** (☎ 66.37.10), the touring part of Hotel Chez Marie-France (see below), has a half-day tour of Raiatea's highlights by four-wheel-drive vehicle. It costs 4,000 CFP ($40) per person. A two-hour trip to Taputaputea Marae costs 2,500 CFP ($25).

Seeing Tahaa   You can easily go to Raiatea's sister island of Tahaa on the *Uporu* (see "Getting Around," above), on which you can carry a bicycle or scooter, but once there you will be on your own. Tahaa may be much smaller than Raiatea, but it's almost cut through by a series of lovely bays, which means its actual circumference (and the distance around its circle island road) is deceptively long. A much easier way to explore Tahaa is on a day tour to **Marina Iti** (☎ 65.63.87), Philippe and Marie Robin's pleasant little hotel and yacht club on the island's southwest corner. Marie is an excellent chef, and Philippe rents boats, cars, and mountain bikes. You also can take a tour around the island, by either four-wheel-drive vehicle or boat. Round-trip transportation from Raiatea by speedboat costs 2,000 CFP ($20). You will have to pay for lunch and everything else once you get there, so call ahead for prices and reservations.

WHERE TO STAY
HOTELS

Hotel Chez Marie-France
B.P. 272, Uturoa, Raiatea (2km [1.2 miles] south of town). ☎ **66.37.10**. Fax 66.26.25. 14 rms. TV TEL. 9,000 CFP–10,000 CFP ($90–$100). MC, V.

Hosts Marie-France and Patrice Philip, who run Raiatea Safari Tours, keep improving their little establishment tucked between the main road and the lagoon. Once a pension popular with backpackers, it's now a small hotel with four rooms in a shingle-roof building sitting perpendicular to the lagoon (one end unit opens to the lagoon and the other to a small pool). These units all have TVs, phones, minimal cooking facilities, small shower-only baths, and sleeping lofts, but they lack adequate closet space and places to sit other than on their beds. Ten other rooms near the road have their own baths but no kitchenettes, TVs, or phones. A small restaurant-bar offering French fare has a mix of European and tropical furnishings and decor. Raiatea Plongée has its dive shop here, and Raiatea Safari Tours' boats depart from the pier.

✪ Hotel Hawaiki Nui

B.P. 43, Uturoa, Raiatea (2km [1.2 miles] south of town). ☎ **66.20.23**. Fax 66.20.20. 12 rms., 20 bungalows. TV TEL. 10,500 CFP–26,000 CFP ($105–$260). AE, DC, MC, V.

The Hotel Bali Hai Raiatea used to occupy this narrow site wedged between the road and lagoon, but local interests bought it after the main building burned down in 1992. They rebuilt the waterfront restaurant and bar, and completely gutted and upgraded all rooms and bungalows. Today it not only has a new name, it's like a new luxury hotel, and a very well-managed one, too. The friendly and helpful staff all speak English, but the ambience is definitely more French than when the American-owned Bali Hai stood here. Like everywhere else on Raiatea, there is no beach, but eight over-water bungalows extend out over the clifflike reef face. The other bungalows, some of which have two units under their thatch roofs, are either along the seawall or in the gardens beyond. A pier extends out to a dock from which you can climb into the water and get the sensation of flying as you snorkel along the face of the reef. Opening to a lagoonside pool, the dining room offers excellent French cuisine. Facilities include tennis courts, snorkeling gear, table tennis, and an activities desk that will arrange scuba diving, and lagoon and historical tours.

⑤ Sunset Beach Motel

B.P. 397, Uturoa, Raiatea (in Apooiti, 5km [3 miles] northwest of Uturoa). ☎ **66.33.47**. Fax 66.33.08. 20 bungalows, 25 campsites. TV. 7,500 CFP–8,500 CFP ($75–$85) bungalow; 1,000 CFP ($10) per person campsite (higher rates for stays of one night). MC, V.

One of the best values in French Polynesia for guests wanting to do their own cooking, this property occupies a coconut grove on a skinny peninsula sticking out west of the airport. The bungalows sit in a row just off a palm-draped beach. The lagoon here is very shallow, but the beach enjoys a gorgeous westward view toward Bora Bora. The lagoon excursion companies pick up their guests off a long pier that stretches to deep water (guests can paddle canoes or waterski from it). Although of European construction rather than Polynesian, the modern bungalows are spacious, comfortably furnished, and have fully equipped kitchens and TVs with the local French-language channels. Each has a large front porch with lagoon view. Solar panels provide hot water for cleaning and showering. Part of the grove is set aside for campers, who have their own building with toilets, showers, and kitchen. Manager-owner Eliane Boubée speaks English.

HOSTELS & CAMPING

Pension Manava

B.P. 559, Uturoa, Raiatea (6km [3¹/₂ miles] south of town). ☎ **66.28.26**. 4 bungalows (all with bath), 2 rms (none with bath). 3,000 CFP ($30) room; 4,000 CFP ($40) bungalow with kitchen; 5,000 CFP ($50) bungalow without kitchen. No credit cards.

Roselyne and Andrew Brotherson rent two rooms in their house and have four simple bungalows on their front lawn, across the road from the lagoon. Both rooms share a bath and the Brotherson's kitchen. The bungalows have thatch roofs, pandanus mat-lined walls, louvered windows, double and single beds, and large baths with hot-water showers. Two also have kitchens. Roselyne will cook breakfast and dinner on request.

Peter's Place

Avera, Raiatea (6km [3.7 miles] south of Uturoa). ☎ **66.20.01**. 8 rms. 1,200 CFP–1,400 CFP rooms; 700 CFP ($7) campsite per person (higher rates for stays of one night). No credit cards.

Backpackers will find a home in Peter Brotherson's simple and basic rooms in a plywood building, or they can pitch a tent in his expansive front yard across the road from the lagoon. Everyone shares communal toilets, showers, and a kitchen under its own thatch roof. Peter organizes hiking expeditions to a plantation and waterfall in a valley behind his place.

WHERE TO DINE

Raiatea's version of Papeete's *les roulettes* congregate after dark in the park on the south end of Uturoa's business district. They stay open past midnight on Friday and Saturday.

⊛ Le Gourmet Patisserie

Main street, Uturoa (in Westpac Bank Building). ☎ **66.21.51**. Reservations recommended for lunch. Pastries 150 CFP–400 CFP ($1.50–$4); salads and burgers 300 CFP–500 CFP ($3–$5); meals 1,100 CFP–1,200 CFP ($11–$12). No credit cards. Mon–Thurs 6am–6pm, Fri–Sat 6am–6pm and 7–10pm; lunch served Mon–Fri 11am–1pm. PASTRIES/FRENCH/ITALIAN.

This little bakery has excellent breads and pastries for breakfast, and plats du jour such as steak with vegetables for lunch on weekdays. The baked goodies are on display in a case; point and order. Friday and Saturday are pizza and spaghetti nights, with meals ranging from 700 CFP to 1,200 CFP ($7 to $12).

Jade Garden Restaurant

Main street, Uturoa. ☎ **66.34.40**. Reservations recommended on weekends. Main courses 1,000 CFP–1600 CFP ($10–$16). V. Wed–Sat 11am–1pm and 6:30–9pm. CANTONESE.

On first impression, this appears to be just another family-run Chinese restaurant, but those who try it are in for a pleasant surprise. My most recent meal here consisted of ginger beef, chicken with fresh water chestnuts, and pork with cashew nuts. All three dishes were delicately seasoned in the Cantonese style and were worthy of the more sophisticated Chinese restaurants in Papeete. The upstairs dining room is more pleasant than the one on the street level. Both are air conditioned.

Restaurant le Quai des Pêcheurs

Waterfront, Uturoa. ☎ **66.36.86**. Reservations recommended weekend evenings and Sunday lunch. Main courses 1,600 CFP–2,200 CFP ($10–$25). MC, V. Daily 7am–10pm. SEAFOOD.

Lea Constant, who was a Miss Tahiti back when we both were young, operates this somewhat-less-than-gourmet yet pleasant restaurant on the quay where the fishing boats land. Usually right off the boat, the seafood selections are best, especially the poisson cru. Eat them on the veranda right by the dock. At 10pm on Friday and Saturday, the restaurant becomes Disco Quaidep, one of Uturoa's two nightspots.

✪ Restaurant Moana

Main street, Uturoa (upstairs in Léogite Building, opposite market). ☎ **66.35.33**. Reservations recommended weekend evenings. Main courses 900 CFP–1,800 CFP ($9–$18). AE, MC, V. Tues–Sun 10:30am–1:30pm and 6–9:30pm. CHINESE.

Proprietor Alphonse Léogite lived in the United States for 15 years before returning home to Raiatea and opening this excellent establishment in Uturoa's business district. He uses chrome chairs, potted plants, and linen tablecloths to set an appropriate ambience for some of the finest—and most unusual—Chinese cuisine in the South Pacific. Most items on the menu will be familiar, but you can ask for sea cucumber steamed with ginger and served with pork and vegetables. If that's not on hand, try seafood prepared with shredded taro. The restaurant undergoes a metamorphosis and becomes Club Zenith Discothèque at 10pm on Friday, Saturday, and Sunday.

Snack Moemoea

Waterfront, Uturoa (in Toporo Building). ☎ **66.39.84**. Sandwiches 250 CFP–400 CFP ($2–$4); main courses 1,000 CFP–1,500 CFP ($10–$15). No credit cards. Mon–Fri 6am–5pm, Sat 6am–1pm. SNACK BAR.

While there are several snack bars open for breakfast and lunch near the Uturoa market, this is the most pleasant of the lot. The old corner storefront has tables both outside on the sidewalk and inside on the ground floor or on a mezzanine platform. The menu includes casse-croûte sandwiches and fine hamburgers, poisson cru, grilled fish, and steaks.

SAFARI TOURS & OTHER OUTDOOR ACTIVITIES

If you can put together your own group (because a minimum of four persons is required), you can take a variety of **Lagoon Tours** and see firsthand the Raiatea-Tahaa lagoon, one of the most beautiful in French Polynesia. All trips include snorkeling, and most include picnics on tiny islets sitting on the outer reef; unlike the mainland part of Raiatea, they have beautiful white-sand beaches.

Raiatea Safari Tours (☎ 66.37.10) has several boat trips, including one by canoe up the Faaroa River. A full-day trip to Tahaa includes snorkeling over a coral garden, a visit to a fish park, and stops at white-sand beaches on two deserted islets. Prices range from 2,500 CFP to 7,500 CFP ($25 to $75). For 800 CFP ($6) the company will take you to a motu off Hotel Chez Marie-France, its base (see "Where to Stay," above). Bring your own supplies.

The Moorings (☎ 66.35.93) and **Stardust Marine** (☎ 66.23.18), charter sailboat operators, are based on Raiatea (see "Getting Around by Ship," in Chapter 4, "Introducing French Polynesia"). If a boat is available, it can be chartered on a daily basis. Arrangements for longer charters ordinarily should be made before leaving home. Tahaa is the only French Polynesian island that can be circumnavigated without the boat actually putting out to sea.

Raiatea may not have beaches, but the reef and lagoon are excellent for scuba diving. Based at Hotel Chez Marie-France, **Raiatea Plongée** (☎ 66.37.10) takes divers on one-tank excursions for 5,000 CFP ($50).

Kaoha Nui (☎ 66.25.46) offers horseback riding into the interior, starting at 3,000 CFP ($30) per person for 1$^1/_2$ hours.

ISLAND NIGHTS

Except for string bands playing each evening at the Hotel Hawaiki Nui (see "Where to Stay," above), only weekend nights come alive in Uturoa, and that's only because **Restaurant Moana** (☎ 66.35.33) and **Restaurant Le Quai des Pêcheurs** (☎ 66.36.86) turn themselves into Club Zenith and Disco Quaidep, respectively, at 10pm on Fridays and Saturdays. Cover charges are 1,000 CFP ($10) at both. Drinks cost 500 CFP ($5) and up. See "Where to Dine," above, for more about these restaurants and their business hours.

4 Rangiroa

The largest and most often visited of the great chain of atolls known as the Tuamotu Archipelago, Rangiroa lies 312km (194 miles) northeast of Tahiti. It consists of a chain of low, skinny islets that enclose a tadpole-shaped lagoon more than 46 miles long and 14 miles wide. This means that when you stand on one side of the lagoon, you cannot see the other. In fact, the entire island of Tahiti could be placed in Rangiroa's lagoon, with room left over.

The islets are so low—never more than 10 feet above sea level, not including the height of the coconut palms growing all over them—that ships cannot see them until they're a few miles away. For this reason, Rangiroa and its sisters in the Tuamotus are also known as the Dangerous Archipelago. Hundreds of yachts and ships have been wrecked on the reefs, either unable to see them until it was too late or dragged ashore by tricky currents. Rangiroa has two navigable passes into its interior lagoon, and currents of up to six knots race through them as the tides first fill the lagoon and then empty it during their never-ending cycle. Even at slack tide, watching the coral rocks pass a few feet under your yacht is a tense experience. Once inside the lagoon, however, you anchor in a huge bathtub whose crystal-clear water is stocked with an incredible amount and variety of sea life (including a multitude of sharks).

Most visitors come to Rangiroa primarily for the territory's best scuba diving and snorkeling. Others venture across the lagoon to Rangiroa's islets, where they can literally get away from civilization at two very remote resorts.

GETTING AROUND

Rangiroa's airstrip and most of its hotels and pensions lie on a perfectly flat, seven-mile-long island on the north side of the lagoon. The airport is about equidistant from the village of Avatoru on the west end and Tiputa Pass on the east. The hotels and pensions send somebody to meet their guests. Most hotels and pensions rent scooters and bicycles to their guests. There are no taxis or car-rental agencies on Rangiroa.

FAST FACTS: RANGIROA

Currency Exchange   Banque de Tahiti has a branch in Avatoru.

Drugstores   Avatoru also has a small pharmacy.

Hospitals   There are infirmaries at Avatoru (☎ 96.03.75) and across the pass at Tiputa (☎ 96.03.96).

Photographic Needs   For film, check the boutique at the Hotel Kia Ora Village or the pharmacy in Avatoru.

Post Office   Ask your hotel staff when the small post office in Avatoru is open.

Water   The tap water is brackish. Don't drink it.

WHAT TO SEE & DO

Except for walks around Avatoru and Tiputa, typical Tuamotuan villages with white-washed churches and stone walls lining the main streets, plan on either doing nothing or enjoying the fantastic lagoon. The hotels and pensions either have or can arrange outings by boat. One favorite destination is the so-called Blue Lagoon, an area of colorful corals and plentiful sea life.

For scuba diving, **Raie Manta Club**, B.P. 55, Avatoru, Rangiroa (☎ 96.04.80), operates from the Hotel Kia Ora Village or from a base near Avatoru. **Rangiroa Paradive** (☎ 96.05.55) is based at Chez Glorine pension at Tiputa Pass. Any of the hotels or pensions can arrange dives, which cost 5,000 CFP ($50), including all equipment. Divers must be certified in advance and bring a medical certificate.

WHERE TO STAY

There are no restaurants on Rangiroa outside the hotels, so the rates below include the American Plan or *pension complet* (three meals). Modified American or *demi pension* plans (breakfast and dinner) are available if you want to take one meal a day at another establishment.

A knowledge of French will be helpful outside the hotels on Rangiroa.

Kia Ora Sauvage

B.P. 706, Papeete, Tahiti (hotel is 1-hour boat ride from airport). ☎ **96.02.22**, or 800/763-4845. Fax 96.02.02. 5 bungalows. U.S. $320 AP. AE, DC, MC, V.

As with Village Sans Souci on the other side of the lagoon (see below), this outpost offers one of the South Pacific's most remote Robinson Crusoe–like escapes. Guests are transferred by a one-hour speedboat ride every other day from Hotel Kia Ora Village, which manages this retreat. Once there, you will find a thatched main building, where the Tahitian staff cooks up the day's catch, often caught during the guests' lagoon excursions. Accommodation is in five comfortable bungalows built entirely of native materials. They have their own modern baths. Round-trip boat transfers cost $150 per person.

Kia Ora Village

B.P. 706, Papeete, Tahiti (3km [2 miles] east of airport, near east end of island). ☎ **96.02.22**, or 800/763-4835. Fax 96.02.02. 45 bungalows. U.S. $400–$550 AP. AE, DC, MC, V.

This romantic, first-class establishment has been Rangiroa's premier hotel for two decades. Its thatch-roofed buildings look like a Polynesian village set in a coconut grove directly on the lagoon. White sand has been hauled over from the ocean side of the island, but the beach still is a bit rocky; however, a long pier reaches out into deep water for excellent swimming and snorkeling. The beachside main building features an open-air dining room, and a bar sitting over the lagoon provides spectacular sunsets. Ten bungalows sit over the reef; they have considerably more space than those ashore, including separate bedrooms. All units have plaited exteriors, modern baths, refrigerators, ceiling fans, and sliding opaque doors to decks or porches.

Excellent French cuisine in the dining room features local fish and meats imported from New Zealand. Depending on the number of guests, local villagers stage Tahitian dance shows. A wide range of water sports equipment and activities is available, including a wild ride in snorkeling gear on the riptide through Tiputa Pass. The hotel also arranges boat trips to Tiputa village across the pass, and tours to Avatoru. Lagoon excursions range from 4,000 CFP to 12,000 CFP ($40 to $120) per person. Rental bikes and scooters are available on the premises.

Raira Lagoon

B.P. 87, Avatoru, Rangiroa (5 minutes from airport). ☎ **96.04.23**. Fax 96.05.86. 9 bungalows. 9,000 CFP ($90) AP. AE, MC, V.

Hinano Chardon was born and raised in Papeete, went to high school in California, and then with French-born husband Bruno bought this pleasant establishment, the pick of Rangiroa's pensions. The Chardons have nine small but
comfortable thatch-roofed bungalows equipped with ceiling fans, tiled baths with
cold-water showers, reading lights, and front porches with chairs. A beachside
thatch pavilion has a restaurant and bar, whose furniture once graced the Hyatt
Regency Tahiti in Papeete.

Village Sans Souci

B.P. 22, Avatoru, Rangiroa (45 minutes by boat from Avatoru). ☎ **42.49.36** in Papeete. Fax
42.48.62. 15 bungalows. 25,000 CFP ($250) AP. AE, V.

American Sara Nantz has 15 very basic, thatch-roofed bungalows at her establishment on a remote islet on the western edge of Rangiroa's lagoon. All are set near
the beach and have their own veranda, but guests share communal toilets and
showers. A central restaurant specializes in French preparation of the lagoon's
abundant seafood. There's not much to do out here except relax and swim, snorkel, and fish in the lagoon, but the setting is idyllic. Electricity is 12 volts supplied
by solar panels, and there's no phone on the islet. Sara's booking agent is Paradis
Tours in Papeete. She makes the 45-minute boat ride to Avatoru twice a week, so
a three-night minimum stay is required. Round-trip boat transfers cost 13,000
CFP ($130) for one person and 16,000 CFP ($160) for two.

5 Manihi

Known for its black pearl farms, Manihi lies 520km (312 miles) northeast of
Tahiti in the Tuamotus. Although not nearly as large as Rangiroa, it sports a clear
lagoon filled with tropical sea life and colorful coral.

The only hotel is the **Hotel Kaina Village**, B.P. 2560, Papeete, Tahiti
(☎ 42.75.53, or 800/346-6262 in the U.S.; fax 43.46.94). This lagoonside
establishment has a restaurant and bar and 12 modern, over-water bungalows on
the main islet near the airport. Rates including three meals are 28,600 CFP ($286)
single and 31,000 CFP ($310) double. American Express, Diners Club,
MasterCard, and Visa cards are accepted. Free activities include a visit to a pearl
farm, windsurfing, snorkeling both in the lagoon and with the strong current
through one of the passes in the reef, fishing, reef walking, and visits to a native
village by speedboat. You pay to rent a boat or be taken to a remote island for a
picnic. Gilles Petre's **Manihi Blue Nui Dive Center** is located at the hotel. He
charges about 5,000 CFP ($50) per dive.

8 Rarotonga & the Cook Islands

Perhaps it's the rugged beauty, rivaling that of the more famous Tahiti. Maybe it's the warmth and friendliness of a proud Polynesian people who love to talk about their islands, and do so in English. It could be the old South Seas charm of a small island nation whose little capital is like Papeete was a very long time ago. Whatever the reason, there are few old South Pacific hands who aren't absolutely enraptured with Rarotonga and the other Cook Islands. As soon as you get there, you'll see why the local tourist authority wasn't far wrong in calling the country "Heaven on Earth."

The Cook Islanders have more than beautiful islands in common with the people of French Polynesia, some 900km (550 miles) to the east. They share with the Tahitians about 60% of their native language, and their lifestyles and religions were similar in the old days. Like many Tahitians, they have a keen interest in their eastern Polynesian past, but they are better at showing it off, at explaining to visitors both the old ways and the new.

They also enjoy having a good time, and this lust for happiness very quickly rubs off on visitors. With tourism their primary industry, the Cook Islanders offer a surprising lot to do in their very small islands, from swimming in the lagoon to climbing to the top of the rocky outcrop known as "The Needle" to crawling from one charming pub to another.

With so much to offer, it's little wonder that Rarotonga has become a popular vacation spot in recent years. Thanks to a stronger New Zealand dollar, the Cooks aren't as inexpensive as they used to be, but there are still good values here. And an awful lot of fun, too.

1 The Cook Islands Today

Rarotonga and the other 14 Cook Islands are tiny specks scattered between Tahiti and Samoa in an ocean area about a third the size of the continental United States, yet all together they comprise only 93 square miles of land. Rarotonga is by far the largest, with 26 of those square miles, yet it is only 32km (20 miles) around. A microcosm of modern Polynesia, Rarotonga has enough island activities to satisfy almost anyone, whether it's snorkeling, shopping, sightseeing, scuba diving, or several other pastimes. Its cultural tours are the best in the South Pacific.

What's Special About the Cook Islands

Beaches/Natural Spectacles
- Muri Beach, with white sands stretching eight miles around one corner of Rarotonga.
- Aitutaki Lagoon: Shallow but colorful and stocked with sea life, it's one of the South Pacific's best.

Events/Festivals
- Constitution Week; Cook Islands dancing at its hip-swinging best.
- Island Dance Festival, another week of drums and hips.

Great Towns/Villages
- Avarua, evoking the South Seas era of traders and beachbums.

After Dark
- Cook Islands dancers make Tahiti look tame.
- Pub crawling into the wee hours.

Shopping
- Black pearls at less than you pay in French Polynesia.
- Bring home a Tangaroa tiki to shock your mother.

Sunday Selections
- Church services—you'll never hear such lovely, unpracticed harmony anywhere else.

The Natural Environment   The Cook Islands are divided both geographically and politically into a Southern and a Northern Group. Most of the nine islands of the Southern Group, including Rarotonga, are volcanic, with lush mountains or hills. The islands of the remote Northern Group, except Nassau, are typical atolls, with circles of reef and low coral islands enclosing central lagoons. The sandy soil and scarce rainfall support coconut palms, scrub bush, and a handful of people. Although they can be reached by air, the remote Northern Group receives few visitors.

Rarotonga, the only high, mountainous island, in many ways is a miniature Tahiti: It has jagged peaks and steep valleys surrounded by a flat coastal plain, white sandy beaches, an azure lagoon, and a reef about a quarter of a mile offshore. In most places the shoreline consists of a slightly raised sandy bar backed by a swampy depression, which then gives rise to the valleys and mountains. Before the coming of missionaries in 1823, Rarotongans lived on the raised ground beyond the swampy flats, which they used for growing taro and other wet-footed crops. They built a remarkable road, actually paved in part with stones, from village to village almost around the island. That "back road" still exists, although the paved

Impressions

If I could vacation on only one Pacific island I would choose Rarotonga. It's as beautiful as Tahiti, much quieter, much stuffier and the food is even worse. But the climate is better and the natives are less deteriorated.

—James A. Michener, 1951

round-island road now runs near the shore. The area between the two roads appears to be bush but is in fact heavily cultivated with a plethora of crops and fruit trees.

While Rarotonga masquerades as a small version of Tahiti, **Aitutaki** plays the role of Bora Bora in the Cook Islands. Although lacking the spectacular mountains that Bora Bora has, little Aitutaki is nearly surrounded by a large, shallow lagoon whose multihued beauty and abundant sea life rival those of its French Polynesian counterpart and make this charming, atoll-framed outpost the second most-visited of the Cooks.

The vegetation of the southern islands is typically tropical: The mountains and hills are covered with native brush, while the valley floors and flat coastal plains are studded with coconut and banana plantations and a wide range of flowering trees and shrubs.

Government   The Cook Islands have a Westminster-style parliament with 24 elected members led by a prime minister chosen by members of the majority party. Parliament meets twice a year, in February and March and from July to September. There is also a House of Ariki (hereditary chiefs), which advises the government on matters of traditional custom and land tenure. Each island has an elected Island Council and a Chief Administrative Officer, who is appointed by the prime minister.

Economy   The economy is based on tourism and agriculture, mainly tropical fruit and fruit juices. Some revenue is derived from the Cook Islands' status as a tax-free haven. Without New Zealand aid and the money earned from tourism, however, the country would be in serious financial trouble. In fact, it ran into a great deal of difficulty recently when the government failed to back its local currency with adequate New Zealand dollars, thus rendering the local money worthless (overseas traders insisted on being paid in New Zealand dollars, which the local banks promptly rationed). The problem was unresolved at presstime, but the local currency could be withdrawn and New Zealand dollars used exclusively again (see "Visitor Information & Entry Requirements" and "Money," below).

2 A Look at the Past

Dateline

- A.D. 1200 First Polynesians arrive.
- 1595 Mendaña discovers Pukapuka.
- 1606 De Quirós finds Rakahanga.
- 1773–77 Capt. James Cook discovers more islands, names them the Hervey Islands.
- 1789 Capt. Bligh finds Aitutaki shortly before mutiny on the *Bounty*.
- 1790 *Bounty* mutineers probably visit Rarotonga.

continues

Legend says that the first Polynesians arrived in the Cook Islands by canoe from the islands of modern-day French Polynesia about A.D. 1200, although anthropologists think the first of them may have come much earlier. In any event, they discovered the Cook Islands as part of the great Polynesian migrations that settled all of the South Pacific long before the Spanish explorer Alvaro de Mendaña laid the first European eyes on any of the Cook Islands when he discovered Pukapuka in 1595.

The Spanish at that time were more interested in getting from Peru to the riches of Manila than in general exploration. Thus, except for Rakahanga, which was discovered by Pedro Fernández de Quirós during a voyage along the same general route in 1606, the islands did not appear on European maps for another 170 years.

And then, as happened in so many South Pacific island groups, along came Capt. James Cook, who stumbled onto some of the islands during his voyages in 1773 and 1777; he named them the Hervey Islands. In 1824 the name was changed to the Cook Islands by the Russian cartographer John von Krusenstern.

Captain Cook sailed around the Southern Group but missed Rarotonga, which apparently was visited first by the mutineers of H.M.S. *Bounty,* under Fletcher Christian. There is no official record of the visit, but oral history on Rarotonga has it that a great ship arrived offshore about the time of the mutiny. A Cook Islander visited the ship and was given some oranges, the seeds of which became the foundation for the island's citrus industry.

When the first Europeans arrived, the local Polynesians were governed by feudal chiefs, who owned all the land within their jurisdictions and held life-and-death power over their subjects. Like other Polynesians, they believed in a hierarchy of gods and spirits, among them Tangaroa, whose well-endowed carved image is now a leading handcraft item.

More Missionaries   The man who claimed to have discovered Rarotonga was the same man who brought Christianity to the Cook Islands, the Rev. John Williams of the London Missionary Society. Williams had come from London to Tahiti in 1818 as a missionary, and he soon set up a base of operations on Raiatea in the Society Islands, from which he intended to spread Christianity throughout the South Pacific. He set his sights on the Hervey Islands after a canoeload of Polynesians from there was blown by a storm to Raiatea. They were receptive to Williams's teachings and asked that missionaries be sent to the Herveys.

In 1821 Williams went to Sydney and on the way dropped two teachers at Aitutaki. One of them was a Tahitian named Papeiha. By the time Williams returned two years later, Papeiha had converted the entire island. Pleased with this success, Williams and a new missionary named Charles Pitman headed off in search of Rarotonga. It took a few weeks, during which Williams stopped at Mangaia, Mauke, Mitiaro, and Atiu, but he eventually found it in July 1823. Until the day he died years later in a cannibal's earth oven in Vanuatu, Williams insisted he had discovered Rarotonga—never mind the inconvenient fact that the *Bounty*

- 1814 American sandalwood trader discovers Rarotonga.
- 1821 Tahitian missionaries convert Aitutaki to Christianity.
- 1823 Rev. John Williams rediscovers Rarotonga, lands missionaries.
- 1824 Missionaries divide Rarotonga into five villages.
- 1863 William Marsters starts unique family with three wives on Palmerston Island.
- 1888 Residents on Manihiki trick French warship into turning away; Britain declares protectorate.
- 1901 Cook Islands included in boundaries of newly independent New Zealand.
- 1942 U.S. troops build airstrip on Aitutaki.
- 1965 Cook Islands become independent in association with New Zealand. Sir Albert Henry elected first prime minister.
- 1974 Queen Elizabeth II dedicates new Rarotonga International Airport. Islands opened to tourists.
- 1978 Sir Albert Henry indicted, stripped of knighthood.
- 1990 Rarotonga gets television.
- 1992 Rarotonga hosts South Pacific Arts Festival, adding public buildings and infrastructure.
- 1994 Sheraton Hotel project goes bust.
- 1995 Cook Islands dollar becomes virtually worthless in New Zealand.

mutineers were there or that an American sandalwood trader almost certainly stopped on the island in 1814.

Williams, Pitman, and Papeiha were joined in 1824 by Aaron Buzacott, another missionary. Pitman soon left for the village of Ngatangiia on the east coast, Papeiha went to Arorangi in the west, and Buzacott took over in Avarua in the north. Williams spent most of the next four years using forced native labor to build a new ship, *The Messenger of Peace,* and eventually sailed it west in search of new islands and more converts.

Meanwhile, the missionaries quickly converted the Cook Islanders. They overcame the powerful feudal chiefs, known as *ariki,* whose titles but not their power have been handed down to their present-day heirs. On Rarotonga, the missionaries divided the island into five villages and split the land into rectangular parcels, one for each family. Choice parcels were set aside for the church buildings and rectories. Rarotongans moved down from the high ground near their gardens and became seaside dwellers for the first time.

The religion the missionaries taught was rock-ribbed and puritanical. They blamed the misdeeds of the people for every misfortune, from the epidemics of Western diseases that came with the arrival of more Europeans to the hurricanes that destroyed crops. They preached against sexual permissiveness and cut off the hair of wayward women. The Rarotongans took it all in stride. Whenever the missionaries would shear a woman's locks, she would appear in public wearing a crown of flowers and continue on her merry way. For the most part, however, the transition to Christianity was easy, since in their old religion the Rarotongans, like most Polynesians, believed in a single, all-powerful Tangaroa, who ruled over lesser gods.

Out of the seeds planted by Williams and the London Missionary Society grew the present-day Cook Islands Christian Church, to which about 60% of all Cook Islanders belong. The churches, many of them built by the missionaries in the 19th century, are the center of life in every village, and the Takamoa College bible school that the missionaries established in 1837 still exists in Avarua. The Cook Islands Christian Church still owns the land under its buildings; the churches of other denominations sit on leased property.

Coming of the Kiwis   It was almost inevitable that the Cook Islands would be caught up in the wave of colonial expansion that swept across the South Pacific in the late 1800s. The French, who had established Tahiti as a protectorate, wanted to expand their influence west, and in 1888 a French warship was sent to Manihiki in the Northern Group of the Cooks. The locals quickly sewed together a British Union Jack and ran it up a pole. The French ship turned away. Shortly thereafter the British declared a protectorate over the Cook Islands, and the Union Jack went up officially.

The islands were small and unproductive, and in 1901 Britain gladly acceded to a request from New Zealand's Prime Minister, Richard Seddon, to include the Cook Islands within the boundaries of his newly independent country. In

Impressions

People here honor the Sabbath even more virtuously than Scottish Highlanders, but they also honor Tangaroa, ancient god of fertility, whose well-endowed figure appears on their own one-dollar coin.

—Lawrence Millman, 1990

All in the Family

The missionaries weren't the only Englishmen to have a lasting impact on the Cook Islands.

In 1863 a farmhand from Gloucester named William Marsters accepted the job as caretaker of tiny, uninhabited Palmerston Island, an atoll sitting all by itself northwest of Rarotonga. He took his Cook Islander wife and her sister with him. They were joined by a Portuguese sailor and his wife, who was a first cousin of Mrs. Marsters.

The Portuguese sailor skipped the island within a year, leaving his wife behind. Marsters then declared himself a minister of the Anglican church and married himself to both his wife's sister and to her first cousin.

Marsters proceeded to start three families, one with each of his three wives. Within 25 years he had 17 children and 54 grandchildren. He divided the island into three parts, one for each clan, which he designated the "head," "tail," and "middle" families. He prohibited marriages within a clan (in a twist of logic, he apparently thought sleeping with your half-brother or half-sister apparently wasn't incest).

Obviously there was a lot of marrying outside the clans, for today there are uncounted thousands of Marsters in the Cook Islands and New Zealand. All trace their roots to Palmerston Atoll, although only 50 or so live there.

William Marsters died in 1899 at the age of 78. He is buried on Palmerston near his finely crafted homestead.

addition to engineering the transfer, Seddon is best remembered in the Cook Islands for his vehement hatred of the Chinese. He instituted the policy that has effectively barred the Chinese—and most other Asians, for that matter—from the Cook Islands to this day.

Otherwise, New Zealand, itself a former colony, was never interested in becoming a colonial power, and the Kiwis never did much to exploit—or develop—the Cook Islands or Western Samoa (over which they exercised a League of Nations trusteeship from the end of World War I until 1962). For all practical purposes, the Cook Islands remained a South Seas backwater for the 72 years of New Zealand rule, with a brief interlude during World War II when U.S. troops built and manned an airstrip on Aitutaki.

Sir Albert Gets the Boot   The situation began to change after 1965, when the Cook Islands became self-governing in association with New Zealand. Under this arrangement, New Zealand provides for the national defense needs of the islands and renders substantial financial aid. There is an official New Zealand "representative" in Avarua, not an ambassador or consul. For all practical purposes, the Cook Islands are independent, although the paper ties with New Zealand deprive them of a seat in the United Nations. The Cook Islanders hold New Zealand citizenship, which means they can live there. New Zealanders, on the other hand, are not citizens of the Cook Islands.

The first prime minister of the newly independent government was Sir Albert Henry, one of the South Pacific's most colorful modern characters. He ruled for a controversial 13 years, during which the Cook Islands were put back on the map.

That came in 1974. Using aid from New Zealand, which wanted to provide an independent source of revenue for its former colony, the government enlarged Rarotonga's airport. Queen Elizabeth II was on hand for the new strip's grand opening. Three years later the Rarotongan Resort Hotel opened, and the Cook Islands became an international destination.

Sir Albert ruled until the national elections in 1978. Even though his party won a majority, he and it were indicted for bribery. Allegedly, government funds had been used to pay for charter flights that ferried his party's voters home from New Zealand on election day. The chief justice of the High Court agreed, and Sir Albert and his party were booted out of power. Queen Elizabeth then stripped him of his knighthood. He remained highly popular with his supporters, however, and many Cook Islanders still refer to him as "Sir Albert." When he died in 1981, his body was taken around Rarotonga on the back of a pickup truck; the road was lined with mourners.

Money, Money, Money Sir Albert was succeeded by Dr. Tom Davis, who had worked in the United States for the National Aeronautics and Space Administration until returning home. To avoid a repetition of the scandal that caught Sir Albert, he added a seat in Parliament for voters living overseas. The constitution also was amended to include a bill of rights. Davis ruled until 1987, when his own party deposed him in favor of Dr. Pupuke Robati.

The premiership returned to Henry hands in 1989 with the victory of Sir Geoffrey Henry, Sir Albert's cousin. Sir Geoffrey's tenure has been marked by scandal, first when a long-planned and almost-completed Sheraton Hotel project was caught up in a Mafia scandal in Italy. The hotel's unfinished buildings look hauntingly like ancient ruins-in-the-making. More recently, Sir Geoffrey allowed too much Cook Islands currency to be printed, which left it valueless outside the country, and he caught severe criticism for signing letters guaranteeing billions of dollars in loans that the Cook Islands didn't make and can never repay. The man everyone calls simply "Geoff" was still in office as we went to press.

3 The Islanders

Population About half of the 20,000 or so people who live in the Cook Islands reside on Rarotonga, and of these 10,000 people, about 4,000 live on the north coast in Avarua, the only town in the country. Some 80% to 85% of the entire population is pure Polynesian. In culture, language, and physical appearance, this great majority is closely akin to both the Tahitians and the Maoris of New Zealand. Only on Pukapuka and Nassau atolls to the far northwest, where the residents are more like the Samoans, is the cultural heritage significantly different.

Culture Modern Cook Islanders have maintained much of the old Polynesian way of life, including the warmth, friendliness, and generosity that characterize Polynesians everywhere. Like their ancestors, they put great emphasis on family life. Within the extended family it's share and share alike, and no one ever goes without a meal or a roof over his or her head. In fact, they may be generous to a fault, since many of the small grocery stores they run reputedly stay on the verge of bankruptcy.

Although not a matriarchy, Cook Islands culture places great responsibility on the wife and mother. The early missionaries divided all land into rectangular plots (reserving choice parcels for themselves and their church buildings, of course), and women are in charge of the section upon which their families live. They decide which crops and fruit trees to plant, they collect the money for household expenses, and, acting collectively and within the churches, they decide how the village will be run. The land cannot be sold, only leased, and when the mother dies, it passes jointly to her children. Since many women prefer to build simple homes so as not to set off squabbles among their offspring when they pass away, most houses provide basic shelter and are not constructed with an eye to increasing value. In fact, when a woman dies, the house occasionally is left vacant by succeeding generations.

The burial vaults you will see in many front yards are the final resting places of the mothers who built the houses. Their coffins are sealed in concrete vaults both for sanitary reasons and because to shovel dirt on a woman's dead body is to treat her like an animal. (Likewise, striking a live woman is the quickest way for a Cook Islands man to wind up in prison.) The survivors care only for the graves of persons they knew in life, which explains the many overgrown vaults. Eventually, when no one remembers their occupants, the tops of the old vaults will be removed and the ground plowed for a new crop.

Cook Islanders have also retained that old Polynesian tradition known as "island time." The clock moves more slowly here, as it does in other South Pacific Islands. Everything will get done in due course, not necessarily now. So service is often slow by Western standards, but why hurry? You're on vacation.

In addition to those who are pure Polynesian, a significant minority are of mixed European-Polynesian descent. There are also a number of New Zealanders, Australians, Americans, and Europeans, most of whom live on Rarotonga and seem to move to the beat of "island time," too. There are very few Chinese or other Asians in the Cook Islands—thus the relative scarcity of Asian cuisine here.

4 Language

Nearly everyone speaks English, the official language. All signs and notices are written in it. The everyday language for most people, however, is Cook Islands Maori, a Polynesian language similar to Tahitian and New Zealand Maori. A little knowledge of it is helpful, particularly since nearly all place names are Maori.

Cook Islands Maori has eight consonants and five vowels. The vowels are pronounced in the Roman fashion: *ah, ay, ee, oh, oo* instead of *a, e, i, o, u* as in English. The consonants used are *k, m, n, p, r, t,* and *v.* These are pronounced much as they are in English. There also is *ng,* which is pronounced as the *ng* in "ring." The language is written phonetically; that is, every letter is pronounced. If there are three vowels in a row, each is sounded. The name of Mangaia Island, for example, is pronounced "Mahn-gah-ee-ah."

More than likely, Cook Islanders will speak English to all Europeans, but here are some helpful expressions with suggested pronunciations.

English	Maori	Pronunciation
hello	kia orana	*kee*-ah oh-*rah*-nah
good-bye	aere ra	ah-*ay*-ray rah
thank you	meitaki	may-ee-*tah*-kee
how are you?	peea koe	*pay*-ay-ah *ko*-ay
yes	ae	*ah*-ay
no	kare	*kah*-ray

English	Maori	Pronunciation
good luck	kia manuia	*kee*-ah mah-*nu*-ee-ah
European person	Papa'a	pah-*pah*-ah
wrap-around sarong	pareu	pah-*ray*-oo
keep out	tapu	*tah*-poo
small island	motu	*moh*-too

5 Visitor Information & Entry Requirements

VISITOR INFORMATION

The helpful staff at the **Cook Islands Tourist Authority** will provide information upon request. The address is P.O. Box 14, Rarotonga, Cook Islands, South Pacific (☎ 29-435, fax 21-435). The main office and visitors center is just west of the traffic circle in the heart of Avarua. Other offices are:

North America: 6033 W. Century Blvd., Suite 690, Los Angeles, CA 90045 (☎ 310/216-2872 or 800/624-6250; fax 310/216-2868).

New Zealand: 330 Parnell Rd., P.O. Box 37391, Auckland (☎ 09/379-4140, fax 09/309-1876).

Australia: 1/177 Pacific Hwy., North Sydney, NSW 2060 (☎ 02/955-0446, fax 02/955-0447).

United Kingdom: 2 Cinnamon Row, Plantation Wharf, York Place, London SW11 3TW (☎ 071/978-5222; fax 071/924-3171).

Germany: Romanplatz 10, 80639 München (☎ 89/178-2941; fax 89/178-2811).

Hong Kong: Pacific Leisure, Tung Ming Building, 40 Des Voeux Rd., Central, Box 2382, Hong Kong (☎ 524-7065).

Once you get to Rarotonga, visit the authority and pick up copies of their lists of current activities and nightlife, which give their prices, and brochures describing the Cross-Island Track and the natural flora and fauna of the island.

The authority also should have copies of *What's On In The Cook Islands* and *Cook Islands Sun,* two free tourist publications full of facts and advertisements. The daily *Cook Islands News* carries radio and TV schedules, weather forecasts, shipping information, and advertisements for island nights and other entertainment.

If you're heading to the outer islands, check the bookstores for Elliott Smith's *Cook Islands Companion,* a guide packed with information.

ENTRY REQUIREMENTS

Visitors with valid passports, onward or return air tickets (they will be examined at the immigration desk upon arrival), and sufficient funds are allowed to stay for 31 days. Extensions are granted on a month-to-month basis for up to five months beyond the initial 31-day visa upon application to the Immigration Department near the airport in Avarua. Visitors intending to stay more than six months must apply from their home country to the Principal Immigration Officer, Ministry of Labour and Commerce, P.O. Box 61, Rarotonga, Cook Islands.

At one time the government required all visitors to have a confirmed hotel reservation before arrival. Although this is no longer the case, the Cooks are a very popular destination, so advance reservations are strongly advised.

   Customs allowances are two liters of spirits or wine, 200 cigarettes or 50 cigars, and NZ$250 ($175) in other goods. Arriving passengers can purchase items from the duty-free shop and change money before clearing Immigration. Firearms, ammunition, and indecent materials are prohibited. So are live animals, including pets (they will be placed in quarantine until you leave the country). Personal effects are not subject to duty. All food and other agricultural products must be declared and will be inspected.

6 Money

The New Zealand dollar is the medium of exchange, although the Cook Islands government has been printing its own colorful notes and also mints unusual coins (too many of them, given their lack of value outside the country). The triangular $2 piece and the famous Tangaroa dollar make fine souvenirs. The latter bears the likeness of Tangaroa—well-defined private part and all—on one side and Queen Elizabeth II on the other (the Queen reportedly was not at all pleased about sharing the coin with Tangaroa in all his glory). So both the New Zealand and Cook Islands currencies are used and have the same values, but the Cook Islands currency cannot be exchanged outside the islands.

   At the time of this writing, the New Zealand dollar was worth about U.S. 70¢, give or take a few cents. The exchange rate is carried in the business sections of most daily newspapers.

How to Get Local Currency   Two banks operate on Rarotonga, and both are open from 9am to 3pm Monday through Friday. **Westpac Bank** has its main office west of the traffic circle on the main road in Avarua, as well as a branch in Arorangi on the west coast. **ANZ Bank** has an office at the rear of the first-floor shopping arcade in the C.I.D.C. House, the large modern structure west of the traffic circle in Avarua (it has wooden stairs ascending in front).

   You can get cash advances against your MasterCard and Visa cards at the banks. There were no ATM machines in the Cook Islands during my recent visit.

   On the outer islands, you can cash traveler's checks at the local post offices.

Credit Cards   American Express, MasterCard, and Visa are widely accepted by hotels and restaurants on Rarotonga and Aitutaki, Diner's Club less so.

7 When to Go

THE CLIMATE

The islands of the Southern Group, which are about as far south of the equator as the Hawaiian Islands are north, have a very pleasant tropical climate. Even during the summer months of January and February, the high temperatures on Rarotonga average a comfortable 29°C (84°F), and the southeast trade winds usually moderate even the hottest day. The average high drops to 25°C (77°F) during the winter months, from June to August, and the ends of Antarctic cold fronts can bring a few downright chilly nights during those months. It's a good idea to bring a light sweater or jacket for evening wear anytime of the year.

   December through April is both the cyclone (hurricane) and rainy season. There always is a chance that a cyclone will wander along during these months, but most of the rain comes in short, heavy cloudbursts that are followed by sunshine. Rain

What Things Cost in the Cook Islands	U.S. $
Hotel bus from airport to Avarua	5.50
Local phone call	.14
Ride on The Bus	2.10
Room at Manuia Beach Hotel (expensive)	263.00
Room at Rarotongan Sunset Motel (moderate)	95.00
Room at Kii Kii Motel (inexpensive)	47.00
Lunch for one at Ronnie's (moderate)	11.00
Lunch for one at Cook's Corner Cafe (budget)	7.00
Dinner for one, without wine, at The Flame Tree (expensive)	35.00
Dinner for one, without wine, at Kaena Restaurant (moderate)	20.00
Dinner for one, without wine, at Metua's Cafe (inexpensive)	11.00
Beer	2.50
Coca-Cola	1.05
Roll of ASA 100 Kodacolor film, 36 exposures	7.00

The New Zealand & U.S. Dollars

At this writing, NZ$1 = approximately $.70, the rate of exchange used to calculate the U.S. dollar prices given in this chapter. This rate may change by the time you visit, so use the following table only as a guide.

NZ $	U.S. $	NZ $	U.S. $
.25	.18	15	10.50
.50	.35	20	14.00
.75	.53	25	17.50
1	.70	30	21.00
2	1.40	35	24.50
3	2.10	40	28.00
4	2.80	45	31.50
5	3.50	50	35.00
6	4.20	75	52.50
7	4.90	100	70.00
8	5.60	125	87.50
9	6.30	150	105.00
10	7.00	200	140.00

clouds usually hang around Rarotonga's mountain peaks, even during the dry season, from June to August.

In short, there is no bad time weatherwise to visit the Cook Islands, although the "shoulder" months of April, May, September, and October usually provide the best combination of sunshine and warmth. Frankly, I much prefer cool and dry Rarotonga in July and August to the hot and steamy mid-Atlantic state where I live.

HOLIDAYS & SEASONS

Legal **holidays** are New Year's Day, Anzac (Memorial) Day (April 25), Good Friday, Easter Monday, the Queen's Birthday (in June), Constitution Day (August 4), Christmas Day, and Boxing Day (December 26).

The busiest season used to be July and August when New Zealanders and Australians escaped their own winters; however, more and more Americans and Canadians have been visiting in recent years, which means that all year is fairly busy, especially for the smaller hotels and motels. Make your hotel reservations early. Many Cook Islanders live in New Zealand and come home for Christmas; airline seats may be hard to come by during that holiday season.

THE COOK ISLANDS CALENDAR OF EVENTS

February

- **Arts & Crafts Exhibition.** Original paintings, wood and shell carvings, and coral stone sculptures are featured at this annual show. Second week in February.

April

- ✪ **Dancer of the Year Contest.** Features one of the South Pacific's great traditional dance competitions; villages from all over the country send their young people to Rarotonga to compete for the coveted Dancers of the Year award. Last week in April.
- **Anzac Day.**   Cook Islanders killed in the two World Wars are honored with parades and church services. April 25.

August

- ✪ **Constitution Week/Cultural Festival Week.** Honoring the attainment of self-government on August 4, 1965, this biggest Cook Islands celebration is highlighted by a weeklong Polynesian dance contest. The dancing is at its purest and most energetic as each village's team vies for the title of best in the country. There are also parades and sporting events. Begins last Friday in July and runs for 10 days.

September

- **Cook Islands Art Exhibition Week.** Works of local artists and sculptors are displayed at a variety of exhibitions. Second week in September.

October

- **Cook Islands Fashion Week.** Local fashions and accessories are featured at various displays and shows. Third week in October.
- **Gospel Day.**   Honors the arrival of the first missionaries and features outdoor religious plays known as *nuku*. Last Sunday in October.

November

- **Round Rarotonga Road Run.** Marathoners race completely around Rarotonga—all 32km (20 miles) of it. First week in November.
- **Tiare Floral Week.** Shops and offices are ablaze with fresh arrangements, each leading up to a grand finale parade of flower-covered floats. Fourth week of November.

8　Getting There & Getting Around

GETTING THERE

Air New Zealand has direct service from Los Angeles to Rarotonga via Honolulu. It also has weekly service to Rarotonga from Tahiti and Fiji on its Coral Route. In addition, Air New Zealand has several flights a week between Auckland and Rarotonga. Polynesian Airlines connects Rarotonga to New Zealand and Australia via Apia. For more information, see "Getting There" in Chapter 3.

Arriving　The small terminal at **Rarotonga International Airport,** the country's only gateway, is 2.2km (1.3 miles) west of Avarua. Westpac Bank's terminal office is open one hour before and after all international flights; it has windows both inside and outside the departure lounge. Small shops in the departure lounge sell handcrafts, liquor, cigarettes, and stamps. Arriving passengers can purchase duty-free items before clearing Immigration. Air New Zealand and the other airlines have their Rarotonga offices in the terminal.

Transportation from the airport is by hotel bus, taxi, or rental car. Most hotels tack from NZ$6 to NZ$12 ($4 to $8.50) per person to your hotel bill for the round-trip transfer. In general, taxi fares are NZ$2 ($1.50) per kilometer. See "By Taxi," below.

A **departure tax** of NZ$25 ($17.50) for adults and NZ$12.50 ($9) for children between the ages of 2 and 12 is payable in New Zealand or Cook Islands currency; check in at the airline counter first, then pay at the window beside the entrance to Immigration. No tax is imposed for domestic departures.

GETTING AROUND
BY PLANE

Air Rarotonga (☎ 22-888) has three flights a day (except Sunday) to Aitutaki and one a day to Atiu, Amuke, Mangaia, and Mitiaro. Round-trip fares are about NZ$285 ($200) to Aitutaki, the most visited island, slightly less to the others in the Southern Group. Air Rarotonga will also book hotels and most activities on the other islands free of charge. You can save as much as NZ$100 ($70) by buying a package of air fare and accommodations.

Don't forget to reconfirm your return flight.

BY SHIP

"Adventures in Paradise," the 1950s television series, may have glorified the South Pacific "copra schooners" that plied the South Seas trading corned beef and printed cotton for copra, but today's ships operating in the Cook Islands have experienced anything but glory in recent years. In fact, several of them have run aground; one even stopped working while at sea and drifted several hundred miles before being

Impressions

For my taste, there are few approaches anywhere on this planet more exhilarating than when your plane sweeps down out of the clouds and, suddenly, miraculously, you see the lush green mountains of Rarotonga rising out of the sea like a landscape from a childhood fairy tale, like a lost world.

—Lawrence Millman, 1990

Rarotonga

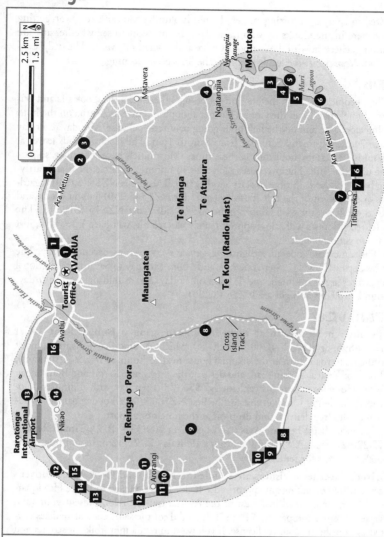

ACCOMMODATIONS:
Are-Renga Motel **11**
Edgewater Resort **13**
Kii Kii Motel **2**
Lagoon Lodges **9**
Little Polynesian Motel **7**
Manuia Beach Hotel **12**
Moana Sands Hotel **6**
Muri Beachcomber Motel **5**
Oasis Village **15**
Paradise Inn **1**
Puaikura Reef Lodges **10**
Rarotongan Resort Hotel **8**
Rarotongan Sunset Motel **14**
Sokala Village **3**
The Pacific Resort **4**
Tiare Village Dive Hostel **16**

ATTRACTIONS:
Arorangi **10**
Black Rock **12**
Christian Church **1**
Cultural Village **11**
Marae Arai-Te-Tonga **2**
Mt. Raemaru **9**
Muri Beach **6**
Ngatangiia **4**
Parliament **13**
Sailing Club **5**
The Needle **8**
Tereora College **14**
Titikaveka **7**
Tupapa Stream **3**

Information ⓘ

1091

towed to safety by a passing tanker. To put it bluntly, you can't count on getting anywhere in the Cooks by ship these days. If you want to see whether any are running, check in with the Harbour Office at the wharf in Avatiu. The daily *Cook Islands News* prints the local shipping schedules each morning.

BY BUS

When people say "catch the bus" on Rarotonga, they mean the Cook's Island Bus (no phone) that leaves the Cook's Corner shopping center in Avarua on the hour going clockwise and on the half hour going counter-clockwise, Monday to Friday from 7am to 4pm and Saturday from 8am to 1pm. The clockwise bus leaves at 25 minutes past the hour during these times. Most hotels have schedules, so pick one up to be sure. The two buses each take 50 minutes to circle the island, arriving back in Avarua in time to start another trip. The fare is NZ$3 ($2.10) regardless of the length of the ride, but day passes for NZ$5 ($3.50) let you get on and off as often as you wish. Books good for 10 rides cost NZ$15 ($10.50). The hotel receptionists will know approximately when a bus will pass. Elsewhere, just wave to get on board.

The same buses operate a nighttime service every evening except Sunday. The buses depart Cook's Corner at 6, 7, 9, and 10pm Monday to Saturday. Additional departures are at midnight and 1:30am on Friday, and at midnight on Saturday. Round-trip fares at night are NZ$4 ($2.80).

BY RENTAL CAR

I usually rent from Winton Pickering and the gang at **Budget Rent-A-Car** (☎ 20-895, or 800/527-0700 in the U.S.), which has an office in Avarua a block off the main road (turn at the colonial house next to Ronnie's Bar & Restaurant), a booth on Avarua's main road, and desks at the Edgewater Resort and Rarotongan Resort Hotel. Small sedans rent for NZ$50 ($35) per day with unlimited kilometers. The renter is responsible for the first NZ$600 ($420) of any damage. Budget provides free delivery and drop-off at the hotels or airport.

The other firms here are **Avis** (☎ 21-901, or 800/331-1212); **Tipani Rentals** (☎ 22-327 or 22-328); and **Rarotonga Rentals** (☎ 22-326). In addition, some hotels have cars for rent.

Driver's Licenses   Visitors are required to have a valid Cook Islands driver's license before operating any motorized vehicle. To get one, go to Police Headquarters (on the main road just west of the Avarua traffic circle), present your valid overseas license, and pay NZ$10 ($7). It's valid for the same class of vehicles covered by your home-country license. If you want to rent a motorbike or scooter and you aren't licensed to drive them at home, you will have to take a driving test and pay an additional NZ$2 ($1.40). All drivers must be at least 21 years old. (The laminated license with your photo makes a nice souvenir.)

Driving Rules   *Driving is on the left side of the road.* The speed limit is 50kmph (30 m.p.h.) in the countryside and 25kmph (15 m.p.h.) in Avarua and the villages. Gasoline (petrol) is available from service stations in Avarua and at some village shops. During my recent visit, petrol cost about NZ$1.00 (70¢) a liter, or about $2.60 for an American-size gallon. The road around the island is paved but somewhat rough, and drivers must be on the alert at all times for dogs, chickens, potholes, and pigs.

BY SCOOTER & BICYCLE

Cook Islanders are as likely to travel by motorbike or scooter as they are by automobile. **Polynesian Bike Hire Ltd.** (☎ 20-895) and **Tipani Rentals** (☎ 22-327) both rent them on a daily or weekly basis. Rates start at NZ$20 ($14) per day. Polynesian Bike Hire Ltd. and Budget Rent-A-Car share offices (see above).

There are no hills on the round-island road, so touring by bicycle (or "push bikes," as they're called in the Cook Islands) is a pleasure. Several hotels have bicycles available for their guests to use. **Polynesian Bike Hire Ltd.** (☎ 20-895) and **Tipani Rentals** (☎ 22-327) have them for NZ$10 ($7) per day.

BY TAXI

There are a number of cars and minibuses scurrying around Rarotonga with "taxi" signs on top. Service is available daily from 7am to midnight and whenever international flights arrive. As a rule of thumb, taxi fares should be about NZ$2 ($1.40) per kilometer. To call a taxi, phone either 27-021, 23-510, 20-213, 21-773, or 22-238.

DISTANCES

Here are some distances from the traffic circle in Avarua.

Going East (Clockwise)	Km	Miles
Kii Kii Motel	2.8	1.6
Sailing Club/Pacific Resort	10.7	6.4
Muri Beachcomber Motel	10.9	6.5
Little Polynesia Motel	14.1	8.5
Moana Sands Hotel	14.3	8.6

Going West (Counterclockwise)	Km	Miles
Airport terminal	2.2	1.3
Parliament	3.2	1.9
Golf course	5.1	3.0
Rarotongan Sunset Motel	6.3	3.8
Edgewater Resort	6.8	4.1
Dive Rarotonga	7.2	4.3
Manuia Beach Hotel	8.0	4.8
Are-Renga Motel	8.5	5.1
Puaikura Reef Lodges	11.5	6.9
Lagoon Lodges	13.1	7.8
The Rarotongan Resort	13.5	8.1
Sheraton hotel project	15.0	9.0

FAST FACTS: Rarotonga

American Express   There is no American Express representative in the Cook Islands. See "Visitor Information & Entry Requirements" and "Money" in Chapter 3 for how to report lost or stolen American Express credit cards or traveler's checks. The local banks may be able to assist in reporting lost checks.

Area Code   The international country code for the Cook Islands is 682.

Baby-sitters   Contact your hotel reception desk.

Baggage Storage   There are 12 storage lockers just outside the arrivals concourse at the airport. Cost is NZ$3 ($2.10). Most hotels and motels will keep your bags for free.

Bookstores   **The Bounty Book Shop,** in the high-rise C.I.D.B. Building in Avarua, and the **Cook Islands Trading Corporation (C.I.T.C.),** on the waterfront, both sell paperback novels, maps of Rarotonga and Aitutaki, and books about the Cook Islands and the South Pacific in general. The Bounty Bookshop also carries the international editions of *Time* and *Newsweek,* the latter incorporated into the *Bulletin,* an Australian newsmagazine.

Business Hours   Most shops on Rarotonga are open from 8am to 4pm weekdays and from 8 to noon on Saturday. Some small grocery stores in the villages are open in the evenings and for limited hours on Sunday.

Camera/Film   A reasonable selection of color-print film is available at many shops in Avarua. One-hour processing of color-print film is available at Rarotonga Pharmacy Ltd. in the Cook Islands Trading Corporation (C.I.T.C.) shopping center in Avarua. Cocophoto, next to South Seas Duty Free near Avatiu harbor, offers a four-hour developing service. Color slides are sent to New Zealand for processing.

Clothing   Dress in the Cook Islands is informal. Shorts of respectable length (that is, not of the short-short variety) are worn during the day by both men and women, but beach attire should stay at the beach. Nude or topless sunbathing is not permitted anywhere (although some European tourists do it anyway). The colorful wraparound pareu is popular with local women. Evenings from May to September can be cool, so trousers, skirts, light jackets, sweaters, or wraps are in order after dark. The only neckties to be seen are at church on Sunday.

Crime   See "Safety," below.

Currency Exchange   See "Visitor Information & Entry Requirements" and "Money," earlier in this chapter.

Dentist   Ask at your hotel desk for the name of a private practitioner, or go to the Tupapa Outpatient Clinic on the east end of Avarua. Hours are Monday to Friday from 8am to 4pm.

Doctor   Medical care in the Cook Islands is relatively good by South Pacific standards but by no means sophisticated. Most doctors and dentists were trained in New Zealand, and several of them are in private practice. See "Hospitals," below.

Drug Laws   Dangerous drugs and narcotics are illegal; possession can land you in a very unpleasant jail for a very long time.

Drugstores   **Rarotonga Pharmacy** (☎ 29-292), in the C.I.T.C. shopping center west of the traffic circle, and **Cook Islands Pharmacy** (☎ 27-577), in the Vanwil Building east of the traffic circle, both dispense prescription medications and carry toiletries. The clinics on the outer islands have a limited supply of prescription medications.

Electricity   Electricity is 230 volts, 50 cycles, so converters are necessary in order to operate American appliances. The plugs, like those of New Zealand and

Australia, have two-angled prongs, so an adaptor will also be needed. If your appliances or the table lamps in your room don't work, check to see whether the switch on the wall outlet is turned on.

Embassies and Consulates   No foreign government maintains an embassy or consulate in the Cook Islands. In case of a problem, seek advice from the travel facilitation and consular officer in the Ministry of Foreign Affairs (☎ 20-507). The New Zealand government has a representative, whose office is at the traffic circle in Avarua. The U.S. embassy in Wellington, New Zealand, has jurisdiction.

Emergencies   The emergency number for the police is 999; for an ambulance or the hospital, 998; for fire, 996.

Eyeglasses   Nev Pearson (☎ 25-477) can make repairs to frames and possibly replace a lens.

Firearms   Don't even think about it—they're illegal.

Gambling   There are no gambling casinos in the Cook Islands, but you can bet on the Australian and New Zealand lotteries at the C.I.T.C. shopping center.

Hairdressers/Barbers   Top Shape Hairdressers (☎ 21-254) is in the Top Shape Gym, east of the traffic circle. Paradise Hair & Beauty (☎ 22-774) is on the main road in Arorangi.

Hitchhiking   Technically, hitchhiking is frowned upon by the government.

Hospitals   The hospital (☎ 22-664, or 998 in case of emergency) is located behind the golf course. For minor problems, go to the Tupapa Outpatient Clinic on the east end of Avarua; it's open Monday to Friday from 8am to 4pm.

Insects   There are no poisonous insects in the Cook Islands. Mosquitoes are plentiful, especially during the summer months and in the inland areas, so bring a good repellent. Mosquito coils can be bought at most village shops.

Laundry/Dry Cleaning   **Sunbird Laundry** has facilities at Avarua, behind the Empire Theatre building and in Arorangi. They will wash, dry, and fold a load for NZ$8 ($5.50).

Libraries   The Cook Islands Library and Museum is open Monday to Saturday from 9am to 1pm. The library has a fine collection of works on the South Pacific, including many hard-to-find books.

Liquor Laws   When it's open during regular business hours (see "Business Hours" above), the government-owned Cook Islands Liquor Supplies has a corner on sales of beer, wine, and liquor by the bottle. Some village shops sell beer when it's closed. Bars and nightclubs close promptly at midnight Saturday. The hotel bars can sell alcoholic beverages to their guests all day Sunday, and the restaurants can resume service on Sunday at 6pm.

Mail   The Chief Post Office is located at the traffic circle in Avarua and is open Monday to Friday from 8am to 4pm. There's a branch post office opposite Titikaveka College on Rarotonga's south coast, which is open Monday to Friday from 8am to noon and 1 to 3:30pm. Each of the other islands has a post office. The international airmail rate for letters is NZ$1.05 (74¢); postcards and airgrams are NZ85¢ (60¢). There is no mail delivery, so all addresses include a post office box.

Maps   The two tourist publications, *What's On In The Cook Islands* and the *Cook Islands Sun,* both contain maps of Rarotonga and the town of Avarua. Get copies at the Tourist Authority's office or at most hotels. Pacific Supplies near Avatiu Harbour sells excellent topographic maps prepared by the New Zealand surveyor general.

Newspapers/Magazines   The *Cook Islands News* is published Monday through Saturday. It contains local, regional, and world news; radio and TV schedules; shipping schedules; a weather map for the South Pacific; and notices of local events, including advertisements for "island nights" at the hotels. It even has two comic strips. Copies are available at the Bounty Bookshop and the large Cook Islands Trading Corporation (C.I.T.C.) store in the center of Avarua.

Police   See "Safety," below.

Radio/TV   Rarotonga has one AM and one FM radio station; both broadcast Polynesian and Western music, and most programming is in English. International news from Radio Australia and Radio New Zealand is broadcast several times a day, beginning at 8am. One TV channel broadcasts entertainment programs daily from 5 to 11pm. Television New Zealand news usually comes on at 9:30pm.

Safety   Property thefts have been increasing in the Cook Islands, so don't leave valuables in your hotel room or your belongings untended elsewhere.

Taxes   In addition to the NZ$25 ($17.50) airport departure tax, a 10% tax is included in all hotel, restaurant, and car-rental bills.

Telephone/Telex/Fax   Direct dialed calls can be made into the Cook Islands from most parts of the world. The country code is 682.

International telephone calls, telegrams, and telex messages can be made or sent from most hotels or from Cook Islands Telecom, on the street between the Cook Islands Trading Corp. and the Cook's Corner shopping centers in Avarua. The Telecom office is open 24 hours a day, including Sunday.

There is a minimum charge of about NZ$18.50 ($13) for the first three minutes of all calls to North America. Each additional minute costs about NZ$6.20 ($4.35). Payment is made after the call is completed, in cash or by MasterCard.

International and local calls can be dialed directly from Phonecard public phones outside most post offices. Buy the credit cards inside at the desk.

Old-fashioned red public telephones are at the post offices, and in booths in many villages. To operate, lift the receiver, listen for a dial tone, deposit a New Zealand or Cook Islands 20-cent coin, and dial the local number. Dial 010 for local directory assistance, 015 for international calls, and 020 for calls to the outer islands. Emergency numbers are listed above.

Time   Local time is 10 hours behind Greenwich mean time. Translated, that's two hours behind California during standard time, three hours behind during daylight saving time. The Cook Islands are on the east side of the international date line, which puts them in the same day as the U.S. and a day behind New Zealand and Australia.

Tipping   Tipping is considered contrary to the Polynesian way of life and is frowned upon.

Water   Generally, the water on Rarotonga is safe to drink from the tap, although it can become slightly muddy after periods of heavy rain. Many hotels have their own filtration systems. If in doubt, boil it in the electric "jug" in your hotel room. The tap water on Aitutaki is not safe to drink.

Weights and Measures The Cook Islands are on the metric system.

9 What to See & Do

SEEING RAROTONGA

The Cook Islands' capital can be seen on foot, since this picturesque little South Seas town winds for only a mile or so along the curving waterfront between its two harbors. Virtually every sight and most of the shops sit along or just off the main around-the-island road, which for this mile serves as Main Street.

If you tire along the way, hop on the **carriage rides** operated by the Beachcomber, an upscale pearl and crafts shop. Drawn by Clydesdale horses, the carriage runs along the waterfront from the Beachcomber to Avatiu Harbour and back during business hours. They cost NZ$2 ($1.40) per ride.

WALKING TOUR OF AVARUA

Let's start at the **traffic circle** in the heart of town at the old harbor, which is both the beginning and end of the round-island road. The clapboard government buildings once stood on the vacant lot on the southeast side of the circle, but they were destroyed by fire a few years ago. The entire area around the circle, and the small boat harbor across the main road, may someday be developed into a marina-dining-shopping complex. The rusty carcass on the reef offshore belonged to the **S.S. Maitai,** a trading ship that went aground here in 1916. To the west, the low-slung building with a large veranda used to be the **Banana Court Bar,** one of the South Pacific's most famous drinking holes. The building actually began life as a hotel.

From the traffic circle, walk east. On your right is **Vanwil's,** one of the few remaining old South Seas–style trading stores. Its dark, dusty shelves carry everything from fishhooks to flashlights to fresh vegetables. About 200 yards farther on the main road stands its present-day counterpart, the modern **Beachcomber Ltd.** This pearl and handcraft shop occupies a coral-block building erected in 1843 as a school for missionary children. The local legislative council met here from 1888 to 1901, but by 1968 it was condemned as unsafe. It sat roofless and weed-infested until owners Joan Rolls and David Gragg beautifully renovated it in 1992.

In a shady parklike setting across the road stands **Taputapuatea,** the restored "palace" of Queen Makea Takau Ariki. Don't enter the grounds without permission, for they are tabu to us commoners. Queen Makea is long dead, but when she was around in the 19th century, the palace reputedly was a lively place.

Facing the palace grounds across the road running inland is the tall, white **Cook Islands Christian Church,** which was built in 1855. Just to the left of the main entrance is the grave of Albert Henry, the late prime minister. A bust of Sir Albert sits atop the grave, complete with shell lei, crown, and his reading glasses. Robert Dean Frisbie, the American-born writer and colorful South Seas character, is buried in the inland corner of the graveyard, next to the road. (See "Recommended Books" in the second chapter of this book.)

To the right, near the end of the road, is the **Cook Islands Library and Museum Society.** The museum is small but worth a visit. It has excellent examples of Cook Islands handcrafts; a canoe from Pukapuka built in the old style, with planks lashed together; the island's first printing press (brought to Rarotonga by the London Missionary Society in the 1830s and used until the 1950s by the government printing office); and the bell and compass from the *Yankee,* a world-famous yacht that in 1964 wrecked on the reef behind the Beachcomber, where its forlorn skeleton rusted away for 30 years. No admission fee is charged, but there is a box for donations. The library and museum are open Monday to Saturday from 9am to 1pm.

Farther up the inland road past the Avarua Primary School stands **Takamoa Theological College,** opened in 1842 by the London Missionary Society. The original Takamoa Mission House still sits on the campus.

Now walk a block along the street in front of the library and museum to the **Sir Geoffrey Henry National Cultural Centre** (also known as Te Puna Korero), the country's showplace built in time for the 1992 South Pacific Festival of the Arts. The large green building houses the **Civic Auditorium,** while the long yellow structures contain government offices as well as the **National Museum** and **National Library.** Exhibits at the National Museum feature contemporary and replicated examples of ancient crafts. It's open Monday to Friday from 8am to 4pm. Admission is by donation.

Opposite the national museum is the **Tupapa Sports Ground.** Like other South Pacific islanders formerly under New Zealand or Australian rule, the Cook Islanders take their rugby seriously. Although much of the action has shifted to the stadium at Tereora College behind the airport, Tupapa may still see a brawl or two on Saturday afternoons.

Now walk back to the main road, turn left at the Paradise Inn, and head to downtown. You can take a break at one of the restaurants or snack bars along the way. From the traffic circle west to Avatiu Harbour is a lovely stroll, either by the storefronts or along the seafront promenade known as Te Ara Maire Nui. At the west end of town, stroll through **Avatiu Market.** Vendors sell clothing and souvenirs here, and caravans offer take-away food that you can munch at picnic tables under the shade of casuarinas whispering in the wind.

We end our tour at Avatiu Harbour, which is Rarotonga's commercial port (Avarua is strictly a small-boat refuge). Tere's Bar, under a large thatch cabana at the harbor, is the perfect place to recover with ice-cold refreshment.

THE CIRCLE ISLAND TOUR

Traveling completely around Rarotonga and seeing the sights should take about four hours—with the help of a motor. Some of the tour operators mentioned in "Cultural Experiences," below, go around the island while explaining the cultural and historical aspects of Rarotonga. A tour can also be made independently by car or motorbike. I would give myself all day to do it on a bicycle.

Let's travel in a clockwise direction from Avarua.

North Coast　About 1km past the Kii Kii Motel, signs mark a small dirt road to the right. It leads to the **Marae Arai-Te-Tonga,** one of the most sacred spots

<hr>

Impressions

I have hunted long for this sanctuary. Now that I have found it, I have no intention, and certainly no desire, ever to leave it again.

—Robert Dean Frisbie, 1928

on the island. Before the coming of Europeans, these stone structures formed a *koutu,* or royal court. The investiture of high chiefs took place here amid much pomp and circumstance; also, offerings to the gods and the "first fruits" of each season were brought here and presented to the local *ariki,* or chief. The basalt investiture pillar, the major remaining structure, stands slightly offset from a rectangular platform about 12 feet long, 7 feet wide, and 8 inches high. Such temples, or maraes, still are considered sacred by some Cook Islanders, so don't walk on them.

The ancient Ara Metua road crosses by Arai-Te-Tonga and leads south a few yards to a small marae on the banks of **Tupapa Stream.** A trail follows the stream up to the peaks of Mounts Te Ikurangi, Te Manga, and Te Atukura, but these are difficult climbs; it's advisable to make them only with a local guide.

East Coast　Back on the main road, **Matavera** village begins about 2km (1¹/₄ miles) beyond Tupapa Stream. Notable for the picturesque Cook Islands Christian Church and graveyard on the mountain side of the road, it's worth a stop for a photograph before continuing on to historic **Ngatangiia** village. Legend has it that a fleet of canoes left Ngatangiia sometime around A.D. 1350 and sailed off to colonize New Zealand, departing from a point across the road from where the Cook Islands Christian Church now stands in the center of the village. Offshore is **Ngatangiia Passage,** between the mainland and Motutapu, a low island, through which the canoes left on their voyage.

Ngatangiia also had its day in the sun in the early 1800s, when it was the headquarters of Charles Pitman, the missionary who came with the Rev. John Williams and later translated *Pilgrim's Progress* into Cook Islands Maori. Unlike many of his fellow missionaries, Pitman carefully avoided becoming involved in local politics or business, and he objected strongly when Williams forced the Cook Islanders to build the *Messenger of Peace.* The **courthouse** across from the church was the first one built in the Cook Islands.

The shore at Ngatangiia, with three small islands sitting on the reef beyond the lagoon, is one of the most beautiful parts of Rarotonga. An old stone **fish trap** is visible underwater between the beach and the islands. Such traps were quite common throughout eastern Polynesia: Fish were caught inside as the tide ebbed and flowed through Ngatangiia Passage.

South Coast　South of Ngatangiia begins magnificent **Muri Beach,** whose white sands stretch for 14km (8 miles) around the southeast corner of Rarotonga. Sailboats glide across the crystal-clear lagoon, the island's best for boating. A fine place to enjoy the beach and go for a swim in the lagoon is the **Rarotonga Sailing Club,** home of Sails Restaurant and the Boardwalk Cafe (see "Where to Dine," below).

Beyond The Little Polynesian hotel is the village of **Titikaveka.** The Cook Islands Christian Church here was built in 1841 of coral blocks hand-cut from the reef almost a mile away and carried to the building site. The lagoon at Titikaveka is the deepest on the island and the best for snorkeling.

From Titikaveka, the road runs along the south coast and passes another old stone fish trap just inside Avaavaroa Passage, and the late Albert Henry's white beachside home. **Mount Te Rua Manga,** the rock spire also known as "The Needle," can be seen clearly from the main road between the Liana's Restaurant and The Rarotongan Resort Hotel. You also will pass what looks like a modern ruin; it's the site of the aborted and highly controversial Sheraton Hotel.

West Coast   The road turns at The Rarotongan Resort and heads up the west coast to the low white walls of **Arorangi,** the coastal community founded as a peacemaking "Gospel Village" by the missionary Aaron Buzacott when a dispute over land boundaries broke out in 1828. Arorangi replaced the old inland village, Puaikura, where the Tahitian missionary Papeiha went to teach Christianity after he had converted all of Aitutaki. Papeiha is buried in the yard of Arorangi's Cook Islands Christian Church, which was built in 1849. According to Polynesian legend, the canoes that left Ngatangiia in the 1300s stopped in Arorangi before heading off west to New Zealand. There is no reef passage near Arorangi, but the story enables the people on both sides of Rarotonga to claim credit for colonizing New Zealand.

The flat-topped mountain behind Arorangi is **Mount Raemaru.** Another legend says that mighty warriors from Aitutaki, which had no mountain, stole the top of Raemaru and took it home with them. There is a steep and somewhat dangerous trail to the top of Raemaru.

The area north of Arorangi is well developed with hotels, restaurants, and shops. The shore just before the golf course is known as **Black Rock** because of the volcanic outcrop standing sentinel in the lagoon offshore. According to ancient Maori belief, the souls of the dead bid farewell to Rarotonga from this point before journeying to the fatherland, which the Cook Islanders called *Avaiki.*

There are two ways to proceed after passing the golf course. The main road continues around the west end of the **airport** runway (be careful; there are more road accidents on this sharp curve than anywhere else on Rarotonga). The airstrip was originally built by the New Zealand government during World War II. It was enlarged in the early 1970s to handle jumbo jets, and Queen Elizabeth II officially opened the new strip, which was renamed Rarotonga International Airport, on July 29, 1974. The **Parliament Building** is located on the shore about halfway along the length of the runway. Parliament meets from February to March and from July to September. Visitors can observe the proceedings from the gallery. The cemetery along the road just before town is the final resting place of cancer patients who came to Rarotonga in the 1970s to see Milan Brych, a controversial specialist who claimed to have discovered a cure. When Dr. Tom Davis became prime minister, he kicked Brych out of the country.

The other way to return to Avarua from Black Rock is to turn right on the first paved road past the golf course and then left at the dead-end intersection onto the **Ara Metua,** or "back road," as the section running from Black Rock to town is called. About halfway to town is **Tereora College,** established as a mission school in 1865. An international stadium was built on the college campus for the 1985 South Pacific Mini Games held on Rarotonga and is now the site of rock 'em, sock 'em rugby games on Saturday afternoons from June through August.

The short ride back to town concludes the circle island tour.

FLIGHTSEEING

Another way to see Rarotonga is by plane. **Air Rarotonga** (☎ 22-888) offers 20-minute sightseeing flights around the island for NZ$49 ($34.50) per person. Flights can be arranged at the customers' choice of time if two or more people fly. Departures are usually at 2pm, but try to go early in the morning before the clouds have built up over the mountains.

⭐ Frommer's Favorite Cook Islands Experiences

Cultural Touring. One of my fondest South Pacific memories was exploring Rarotonga with the entertaining and highly informative Exham Wichman. He told me much of what this chapter has to say about the Cook Islanders' lifestyle. Exham has retired from the tour business, replaced by the terrific Cook Islands Cultural Village, Pa's wonderful nature walks, and the round-island tours of Hugh Henry & Associates. Together, they make Rarotonga the best cultural experience of any island in the South Pacific.

Cook Islands Dancing. I never visit the Cook Islands without watching the hips swing at a traditional dance show. Take my word for it: Had the crew of H.M.S. *Bounty* seen the dancing on Rarotonga instead of Tahiti, even Captain Bligh might have stayed behind.

Pub Crawling. Rarotonga's infamous Banana Court Bar may have joined Quinn's of Papeete in history's graveyard, but like the Cook Islanders, I still crawl home from their lively pubs after a long night of partying on Fridays. The French could learn much about *joie de vivre* from the fun-loving Cook Islanders.

Aitutaki. Although physically not as awe-inspiring as Bora Bora over in French Polynesia, the Cooks' second-most-visited island still has a friendliness that is disappearing in some more visited parts of the South Pacific. Like many others, I plan my Aitutaki trips to include an island night at the Rapae Cottage Hotel and a meal and music at the Crusher Bar, one of the most charming eating and drinking establishments in the South Pacific.

10 Cultural Experiences

Given their use of English and their pride in their culture, the Cook Islanders themselves offer a magnificent glimpse into the lifestyle of eastern Polynesia. They are more than happy to answer questions put to them sincerely by inquisitive visitors. Some of them also do it for money, albeit in a low-key fashion, by offering some of the finest learning experiences in the South Pacific. Unless you sit on the beach and do nothing, you won't go home from the Cook Islands without knowing something about Polynesian culture, both of yesteryear and the present.

✪ **Cultural Tours**   One way to make a round-island tour a cultural experience is to go with **Hugh Henry & Associates** (☎ 25-320), a company founded by the late Hugh Henry, Sir Albert's son, and carried on expertly by his wife Helen and son Stuart. Their tours around the island cover local customs and traditions, marae and other prehistoric sites, fauna and flora, politics and history. The four-hour historic tour costs NZ$25 ($17.50).

✪ **Cook Islands Cultural Village**   For an examination of old Polynesian ways and skills, visit the Cook Islands Cultural Village (☎ 21-314), on the back road in Arorangi. The village consists of nine thatch huts, each one featuring a different aspect of life, such as the making of crafts, cooking, and even dancing. Guests are guided through the huts and then enjoy a lunch of island-style foods, music, and dancing. The gates open Monday to Saturday at 9:45am, with the tours beginning at 10am. Cost for the entire morning and lunch is NZ$36 ($25). The Cultural Village also does its own $1/2$-day circle island historical tour; it costs NZ$25 ($17.50) and includes lunch and the village tour. A full day combining the village tour, lunch, and a trip around the island costs NZ$55 ($38.50).

✪ **Pa's Nature Walks** While the cultural tours provide commentary on the history, lifestyles, and plants grown for domestic use, a blond, dreadlocked Cook Islander named Pa leads mountain and nature walks into the interior. Along the way he points out various wild plants, such as vanilla, candlenuts, mountain orchids, and the shampoo plant, and their everyday and medicinal uses in the days before corned beef and pharmacies. Either **Pa's Cross-Island Mountain Trek** or **Pa's Nature Walk** costs NZ$35 ($24.50) and requires good walking or running shoes and a bathing suit (for a dip in an ancient pool once used by warriors). The cross-island hike takes five hours and the nature walk, four hours. Reserve at any hotel activities desk, or call 21-079 or 20-270. You can also book at The Gallerie, Jillian Sobieska's little art gallery west of the traffic circle (she's Pa's wife).

Highland Paradise A steep road with great ocean views leads up to the remains of an ancient hill village, where the staff of **Highland Paradise** (☎ 20-610) explains the use of marae, the so-called killing and guillotine stones, and other aspects of old Polynesia. The park is open Monday to Friday from 9:30am to 4pm, with the first two-hour tour starting at 10am. Cost is NZ$20 ($14) per person, plus NZ$5 ($3.50) for round-trip transportation if needed. Reservations are essential.

Piri Puruto II To learn everything you ever wanted to know about the various uses of the coconut palm in old Polynesia, including a lengthy demonstration of old-time fire starting, catch a Piri Puruto's Show at the various hotels. Dressed in a loincloth and cap made of fibers from the top of a palm, Piri scales one of the tallest trees around and throws down several coconuts and various other materials for his fire-starting demonstration. He then whacks open the nuts with a bush knife and gives everyone a taste (the texture and flavor change with the age of each coconut). Look for one of Piri's brochures, or call 20-309 to find out where he's appearing. Some hotels charge non-guests to see his show; others don't.

Going to Church Nearly everyone in the Cook Islands puts on his or her finest white straw hat and goes to church on Sunday morning. Many visitors join them, for even though most sermons are in Maori, the magnificent harmony of Polynesian voices in full song will not soon be forgotten. Families have been worshipping together in the same pews for generations, but the ushers are accustomed to finding seats for tourists. Cook Islanders wear their finest to church, including neckties, but visitors can wear smart casual attire.

Sunday morning services at Rarotongan village churches usually begin at 10am; buses leave the hotels at 9:30am. Reserve at the activities desk, or just show up at any church on the island.

11 Where to Stay

Rarotonga may be a small island, but it's blessed with a wide range of accommodations. While all are comfortable, this is not the place to come for super-deluxe resorts like those in French Polynesia and Fiji. Most of the properties are small, owner-operated motels, whose friendly, hands-on management makes up for their lack of luxury. They call themselves "motels" because they're modeled after the typical New Zealand motel, in which each room has a small but quite complete kitchen, which compensates for the lack of restaurants on the premises. Whether motel or hotel, rooms in all except some of the least expensive establishments have electric "jugs" for making tea and coffee.

Accommodation here is grouped in three areas: the west coast, especially near Arorangi; the southeast, on or near Muri Beach; and in or near the town of Avarua. The west coast is somewhat drier than the other sides (it also can get hot during the summer months of December to March). It offers glorious sunsets. The west coast beach is fine, but the lagoon tends to be very shallow, especially at low tide. The southeast coast, on the other hand, boasts the marvelous Muri Beach and a lagoon that's wider, deeper, and better for snorkeling and sailing. The prevailing southeast trade winds, however, can make this area chilly during the austral winter months of June through August. By the same token, these same winds provide nature's air conditioning during the warmer summer months. The hotels on the north coast are near Avarua and its shops and restaurants, but the beaches are rocky and the lagoons perpetually shallow. Keep these factors in mind when making your choice.

Unless noted otherwise, every hotel or motel sits in a tropical garden setting complete with coconut palms and flowering plants. The government's 10% hotel tax is included in most rates quoted below, but you may want to ask to make sure.

HOTELS
EXPENSIVE

Manuia Beach Hotel

P.O. Box 700, Rarotonga (Arorangi, 8km [5 miles] from Avarua). ☎ **22-461**, or 800/448-8355. Fax 22-464. 20 rms. MINIBAR TV TEL. NZ$375–NZ$465 ($263–$325). Rates include a full breakfast. AE, DC, MC, V.

This little establishment bills itself as an intimate "boutique" hotel with an emphasis on comfort and service for an upscale adult clientele (no children under age 12 are accepted as guests). It unquestionably has the best service on Rarotonga, but the 20 rooms are in 10 duplex bungalows set rather close together on a narrow rectangle of beachfront land. Tropical foliage helps give the garden units some semblance of privacy, but the more expensive beachfront units definitely are the choice here. Ceiling fans send breezes down over cool, white tile floors in all units, and sliding glass doors lead to wooden verandas. Angled shower stalls in one corner and lavatories in another maximize space in rather small baths. The choice beachfront units have a view of the reef across a kidney-shaped swimming pool.

Dining/Entertainment: Although none of the rooms have kitchens, you can amble down to the Right on the Beach Bar and dig holes in its white sand floor while enjoying a bistro-style meal under a low-slung thatch roof. High tea is served every afternoon. The intimate Bounty Restaurant serves quality dinners amid nautical decor. There's entertainment three nights a week, including one island night with Cook Islands dancing.

Services: Laundry; evening turndown; twice daily maid service; sleeping attire (pareus); some outside restaurants and activities can be billed to clients' hotel account.

Facilities: Swimming pool, jacuzzi, free golf at Rarotonga Golf Club, snorkeling equipment, activities and car rentals, telephones and TV/videos in rooms on request.

The Pacific Resort

P.O. Box 790, Rarotonga (Muri Beach, 10.7km [6.4 miles] from Avarua). ☎ **20-427.** Fax 21-427. 46 units, 7 villas. MINIBAR (villas only) TV (villas only) TEL. NZ$240–NZ$345 ($168–$242) room; NZ$475–NZ$515 ($333–$360) villa. AE, DC, MC, V.

Sitting in a spacious coconut grove alongside the island's best beach and lagoon, this property comes closest of any Rarotonga hotel or motel to capturing the appearance and ambiance of French Polynesia's small resorts. In fact, it's luxurious seaside villas are considered by most observers to be at the top of Rarotonga's accommodations. These spacious houses have two bedrooms, private entertainment areas, full kitchens, laundry facilities, minibars, and TVs with video players. Each of the one- or two-bedroom motel-like units has a kitchenette in addition to ceiling fans, modern bath with shower, wicker furnishings, and its own patio or balcony. At best they are medium sized, however, and the wicker furniture in some is too big for the space available. Most units are in two-story buildings on either side of a tropical garden complete with a stream crossed by two foot bridges. More bungalow-like, the beachside and beachfront suites give the impression of having your own cottage.

Dining/Entertainment: The Barefoot Bistro Bar right on the beach offers breakfast, lunch, and snacks all day. In the same building, Sandals Restaurant serves breakfast and dinner at his open-air perch beside a stream. Island Night here usually is on Friday (see "Island Nights" below).

Services: Laundry, baby-sitting. Captain Tama's Water Sportz World on premises rents water sports equipment and teaches sailing and windsurfing.

Facilities: Swimming pool, volleyball court, children's playground, boutique, activities desk, rental cars and bikes.

Sokala Villas

P.O. Box 82, Rarotonga (Muri Beach, 10.4km [6.25 miles] from Avarua). ☎ **29-200.** Fax 21-222. 7 bungalows. TEL. NZ$295–NZ$395 ($207–$277). AE, DC, MC, V.

This unusual property sits in a small beachside casuarina-and-palm grove facing Motutapu islet across Ngantangiia Channel. Much of the thick vegetation has been left intact, obscuring the lagoon views but adding touches such as palms growing through the decks and tin roofs of some bungalows. Built entirely of New Zealand pine, they seem more like mountain cabins than tropical island retreats, with half-round log exteriors and knotty interior walls. Four two-story units have sleeping lofts opening to their own decks. The single-floor cabins have a separate bedroom. All have decks facing the beach, and five have their own little swimming pools. Each unit has a full kitchen equipped with microwave oven. Privacy is sparse, however, since the cabins are packed together on this small parcel of land. No children under 12 need apply.

Dining/Entertainment: There is no restaurant, but The Flame Tree (see "Where to Dine," below) is next door, and The Pacific Resort, Sails Restaurant, and the Boardwalk Cafe are short walks away.

Services: Laundry; morning papers delivered to each unit.

Facilities: Outrigger canoes.

MODERATE

Edgewater Resort

P.O. Box 121, Rarotonga (Arorangi, 6.8km [4 miles] from Avarua). ☎ **25-435.** Fax 25-475. 171 rms, 2 apts. A/C TV TEL. NZ$165–NZ$220 ($115–$154) room; NZ$300–NZ$350 ($210–$245) apt. AE, DC, MC, V.

In number of rooms, the Edgewater is the island's largest resort, and like The Rarotongan Resort (see below), it is often full of visitors on package tours. Although it's on a relatively small parcel of land—just four beachside acres—thick tropical foliage helps make the grounds seem less crowded. One of its two-story motel-style blocks of rooms was originally built as a clinic by the controversial cancer specialist Milan Brych, who was kicked out of the country in the 1970s after making a lot of money but curing no cancer. Several more concrete block structures have been added. Each room has a bougainvillea-draped patio or balcony. Rooms in the 400 and 500 blocks are closest to the beach and farthest from the restaurant–bar–swimming pool, which can be crowded and noisy when the house is full. The more expensive beachside executive suites are even farther removed, on the other side of the tennis courts, which makes them the pick here.

Rocks along the shoreline have been pushed back to create a sandy beach overlooked by the pool and expansive patio space for sunning and sitting. Opening to the pool, the Reef Restaurant serves three meals a day at moderate prices (this property has had a history of being unable to retain good chefs). The Spaghetti House on the main road is a better bet. Entertainment features a buffet and Cook Islands dance show two nights a week, usually Thursday and Saturday (one of the island's best troupes usually dances here on Saturday). Facilities include tennis courts, a Laundromat, video rentals, boutiques, and activities and car-rental desks.

✪ Lagoon Lodges

P.O. Box 45, Rarotonga (on southwest corner, near The Rarotongan Resort Hotel, 13.1km [7.8 miles] from Avarua). ☎ **22-020.** Fax 22-021. 17 units. TV TEL. NZ$135–NZ$165 ($95–$116) bungalows; NZ$375 ($263) executive villa for up to 7 persons. AE, MC, V.

Those who agree with me that bungalow living is the way to go in the South Pacific will find it at these lodges, which are within an easy walk of The Rarotongan Resort. Owners/managers Des and Cassey Eggelton have six studio units, each of which has a queen-size and a single bed, bath with shower, ceiling fan suspended from a peaked roof, kitchenette, dining table, and porch. Even though each cottage has two units, there is a feeling of privacy. In addition, six one-bedroom units and four two-bedroom cottages are like small houses with sizable verandas. They also have one real house: a three-bedroom villa with its own enormous veranda and private swimming pool, all set on a quarter of an acre of land. The spacious grounds of the bungalow complex contain a swimming pool, grass tennis court, and barbecue area, and the beach is just across the road.

The Little Polynesian

P.O. Box 366, Rarotonga (Titikaveka, 14.1km [8.5 miles] from Avarua). ☎ **24-280.** Fax 21-585. 9 units. MINIBAR. NZ$165–NZ$195 ($116–$137). AE, DC, MC, V.

Reminiscent of the small hotels on Moorea or Bora Bora but without the restaurant and bar, this establishment has an idyllic coconut grove location right on the beach and some of the deeper waters of Muri Lagoon. Owners/sisters Jeannine Peyroux and Dorice Reid have eight duplex units in four cottages, plus a "honeymoon" bungalow standing by itself beside the beach (it's not all that private, since other guests can walk right past its windows). Each unit has a king-size bed, ceiling fan in case the trades die down, and cooking facilities. The honeymoon bungalow also has its own veranda overlooking the beach. There's a small swimming pool surrounded by a rock ledge. Motor bike hires are available.

Moana Sands Hotel

P.O. Box 1007, Rarotonga (Muri Beach, 14.3km [8.6 miles] from Avarua). ☎ **26-189.** Fax 22-189. 14 rms. NZ$180 ($126). AE, DC, MC, V.

Right on the beach at the deepest part of Muri Lagoon, this two-story motel-like structure has six rooms upstairs and six on the ground level. Each has a balcony or patio facing the lagoon, ceiling fan, tiled shower-only bath, bright flower-print drapes and spreads, and pullman kitchen. A small dining room provides breakfasts (brought to your room if you wish) and two- or three-course fixed menu dinners (eaten under a beachside thatch pavilion if weather permits). No lunch is served, but guests have access to the dining room and "honesty" bar at all times. The guest lounge has a small library and games and other distractions for children. Guests can play golf and tennis at other facilities for free. Snorkeling equipment and sailboats are provided on site.

✪ The Muri Beachcomber

P.O. Box 379, Rarotonga (Muri Beach, 10.9km [6.5 miles] from Avarua). ☎ **21-022.** Fax 21-323. 18 units. NZ$150–NZ$175 ($105–$123). AE, DC, MC, V.

One of my favorites, this friendly motel is conveniently located near The Pacific Resort, the Rarotonga Sailing Club, and The Flame Tree restaurant, which more than makes up for the lack of on-site restaurant and activities. Spotlights illuminate the tropical foliage of the grounds at night, and the rising moon over the lagoon is a sight to see. One of two New Zealander couples who own the place—Helen and Peter Kemp or Lynley and Bill Tillick—is always available to lend assistance and advice. They have cars, scooters, and 12-speed bicycles to rent.

Ten of the one-bedroom, full-kitchen units are in five duplex units forming a courtyard fronting Muri Beach. Six more in two other buildings also have beach frontage. Two larger family units stand away from the beach but next to the swimming pool, making it easy for parents to keep an eye on the kids from their shady verandas.

Oasis Village

P.O. Box 2093, Rarotonga (Arorangi, 6.2km [3.8 miles] from Avarua). ☎ **28-213.** Fax 28-214. 4 bungalows. A/C. NZ$150 ($105). Rates include continental breakfast. AE, MC, V.

These four modern bungalows flank Teina Hosking's Oasis Village Steakhouse (see "Where to Dine," below) about 100 yards from the beach and within walking distance of other restaurants and the Edgewater Resort. Each has a peaked roof of shingles lined with New Zealand pine, sliding doors leading to decks, queen-size beds with mosquito nets, refrigerators, and large tiled shower-only baths. One bungalow is slightly larger than the others. The air-conditioning units are too small to cool the bungalows during the hottest summer days, and there are no ceiling fans to help out. Otherwise, this is a quiet, pleasant retreat with friendly owners and staff.

⊗ Puaikura Reef Lodges

P.O. Box 397, Rarotonga (southeast corner of island, 11.5km [6.9 miles] from Avarua). ☎ **23-537.** Fax 21-537. 12 units. NZ$113 ($79). AE, DC, MC, V.

Paul and Susan Wilson's comfortable motel units are situated in two one-story buildings facing a grassy lawn, swimming pool, and barbecue area. Half the units have a separate bedroom, and all have a double bed and two singles, tile bath with shower, clock radio, ceiling fan, kitchen, and patio with table and chairs. Rental cars and scooters are available, and a shady park with covered picnic tables is across the road along the beach.

The Rarotongan Resort Hotel

P.O. Box 103, Rarotonga (southwest corner of the island, 13km [8 miles] from Avarua). ☎ **25-800.** Fax 25-799. 151 rms. A/C TEL. NZ$125–NZ$165 ($75–$99) single or double. AE, DC, MC, V.

A renovation project has braked the slide of Rarotonga's flagship hotel, which was opened in 1977 and then went downhill when the government decided it wanted a Sheraton. With that project apparently placed on permanent hold, major improvements have been made here to the shingle-roofed, island-style central building that houses the reception and activities desks, boutique, restaurant, and poolside bar. Superbly situated by the beach on the island's southwest corner, the big building catches the cooling trade winds from one direction and a view of the setting sun from the other.

Most of the rooms in nine two-story buildings flanking the central complex should have been spiffed up by the time you arrive (remember, however, that The Rarotongan is not a luxury resort by today's standards). Some rooms face the beach; others look out on tropical gardens. Those on the upper floors have ceiling fans hanging from peaked ceilings; those downstairs have air conditioners and wall-mounted fans. All rooms have a double bed and a single one that serves as a settee, a radio, and a private balcony or patio beyond sliding glass doors. More spacious—and expensive—are 30 "Paradise Rooms," which are staggered to give the feel of individual bungalows. The decor throughout is tropical, with lots of varnished wood.

The Manava Terrace opening to the swimming pool serves as the hotel's coffee shop, while the White Sands Restaurant provides a setting for theme-night buffet dinners. The hotel usually stages its island-night buffet and dance show two nights a week, including Saturday. The resort has tennis courts, a well-stocked boutique, game and conference rooms, a swimming pool, and a host of daily activities.

✪ Rarotongan Sunset Motel

P.O. Box 377, Rarotonga (Arorangi, 6.3km [3.8 miles] from Avarua). ☎ **28-028** or 800/ 334-5623. Fax 28-026. 20 units. MINIBAR TV TEL. NZ$135–NZ$165 ($95–$116). AE, DC, MC, V.

New Zealand motelier Nigel Purdie's little place has come a long way since I spent my first night ever on Rarotonga here in the mid-1980s. Nigel was the first motelier to attract a North American clientele by installing an ice machine, a satellite dish feeding a TV in every room, and a swimming pool with adjacent bar. His units were furnished like a New Zealand motel when I first saw them; today tropical furniture makes them look like they belong on Rarotonga, not in Auckland. Each unit has a well-designed and -equipped kitchen and separate bedroom. Net curtains double as mosquito netting across the sliding glass fronts at night. In addition to videos and Rarotonga's broadcast TV station, the satellite dish brings in other programs, including occasional American sporting events. There are nine beachfront units, and most of the 11 garden units are situated to provide at least partial views of the beach and lagoon from the verandas (those with a view are filled first). The odd-shaped swimming pool has a bridge over it, with a shallow end for children; and the adjacent "Bird Cage Bar" has colorful wooden parrots suspended from its peaked ceiling. Nigel stages lively Sunday evening barbecues beside the pool. Rental cars and bikes are available. This is a very popular establishment, so book early.

INEXPENSIVE

Are-Renga Motel

P.O. Box 223, Rarotonga (Arorangi village). ☎ **20-050.** 20 units. NZ$40 ($28) double. No credit cards.

This good budget choice is located in the village of Arorangi and is popular with Canadian travelers. The entire property enjoys a beautiful view of the mountains, and a path leads to the beach through a churchyard across the road. The Estall family run a basic but clean establishment, and their units make up for a complete lack of frills with ample space. Nine units are in a newer, motel-like block at the rear of the property. An older building has six units in which the bedroom is separated from the living-cooking area by a curtain; the three upstairs apartments share a large veranda, while a patio does double duty for the three downstairs. All units have kitchen facilities. In addition, a small house has three bedrooms; houseguests share communal kitchen facilities, lounge, and veranda. Low-budget travelers can share a room or unit for NZ$15 ($10.50) each.

⑤ Kii Kii Motel

P.O. Box 68, Rarotonga (2.8km [1.6 miles] east of Avarua). ☎ **21-937.** Fax 21-450. 20 units. TV TEL. NZ$67–NZ$114 ($47–$80). AE, DC, MC, V.

Harry and Pauline Napa's motel is one of Rarotonga's better bargains if you don't need a great beach. They have eight units in a new building facing the lagoon and 12 older units—which are spotlessly maintained and spacious—only a few steps from the water. All units have full kitchens, including electric ranges with ovens, and they all face a swimming pool (which helps compensate for the absence of sand on the beach). The lower-priced budget rooms have the same amount of space as the newer units but do not have phones or TVs. There is no restaurant or bar on premises, but the Club Raro resort was under construction virtually next door during my recent visit and should be open by yours.

Paradise Inn

P.O. Box 674, Rarotonga (Avarua, east of traffic circle). ☎ **20-544.** Fax 22-544. 12 rms. NZ$66 ($46) regular room; NZ$82 ($57.50) family unit. AE, MC, V.

This is Rarotonga's most unusual accommodation, for until 1986 this warehouse-size pink building was a dance hall. Then American David Gragg divided it into 12 split-level rooms. Most have pullman kitchens, lavatories, large glass doors opening out to a narrow walkway alongside the hotel, and spiral staircases leading to sleeping lofts. Two small budget rooms have only one story; a lack of ventilation can make them hot and stuffy unless the outside door is left open. One family unit is more like an apartment. The common areas at the rear of the building are split level, with a bar and patio next to the beach and a guest lounge with honesty bar upstairs. Except for this common area, there are no grounds; the building occupies almost all the hotel's land. The Paradise is popular with business people and overseas volunteers serving in the Cook Islands.

HOSTELS

Backpackers' International Hostel

P.O. Box 878, Rarotonga (Arorangi, 12km [7.4 miles] from Avarua). ☎ and fax **21-847**. 20 rms, 8 dorm beds. NZ$20 ($14) per person in rooms; NZ$14 ($10) dorm bed. No credit cards.

This is the only establishment near the beach (it's less than a block inland) that caters exclusively to backpackers. Bill Bates and family have been so successful that they were constructing a new building when I was there recently. It will hold 20 simple rooms, all of which will share toilets and showers. The upstairs part of their existing building is being turned into a dormitory with eight beds; the open-air downstairs already had a TV lounge and communal kitchen. Breakfasts are available, and there's a weekly Cook Islands–style feast. Airport transfers cost NZ$2 ($1.40) each way.

Tiare Village Dive Hostel

P.O. Box 719, Rarotonga (on Back Road behind airport, 2km [1.2 miles] west of Avarua). ☎ **23-466**. Fax 20-969. 3 rms., 3 chalets. NZ$15 ($10.50) per person dorm bed; NZ$16 ($11.20) per person sharing room or chalet. Rates include airport transfers. MC, V.

Not just divers but low-budget backpackers are attracted by this hostel's location about equidistant from town and the beach. It has a guest house and three A-frame chalets in a thick tropical garden. The house does triple duty as lounge (usually on a large covered veranda), office, and communal kitchen. Each of the chalets has its own kitchen, small bath with shower stall, living room, and covered veranda downstairs, plus a bedroom with double platform bed, a tiny hallway with a single bed, and a half bath upstairs. The guest house has three bedrooms, one with a double bed for couples. Although basic, the establishment is clean and comfortable.

12 Where to Dine

If you sampled the fare at French Polynesia's fine restaurants, then you may be disappointed in the Cook Islands. Most of the cuisine here is cooked to New Zealand tastes, which means the chefs go easy with the spices. By and large, fresh ingredients are limited to local fruits and vegetables. Aitutaki supplies some lobster and lagoon fishes, but most of the fresh (as opposed to frozen) seafood on Rarotonga will be tuna caught outside the reef—and even that may be unavailable if the weather has kept the local fishing boats in port. The island also occasionally may lack some imported ingredients if a supply ship is late arriving (flour and butter have run out in recent years). You'll get good, substantial meals here, but don't expect gourmet quality anywhere except The Flame Tree and Portofino Restaurant (see listings below).

✪ **Island Feasts**   Like their counterparts throughout Polynesia, in pre-European days the Cook Islanders cooked all their food in an earth oven—known here as an *umu*—and they still do for special occasions. The food is as finger-licking good today as it was hundreds of years ago, although it's now eaten with knives and forks rather than fingers during **"Island Nights"** at Rarotonga's hotels, which include Cook Island dance shows (see "Island Nights," below). The hotels provide a wide assortment of salads and cold cuts for those who are not particularly fond of taro, arrowroot, and octopus cooked in coconut milk.

Get a schedule of island nights from the Cook Island Tourist Authority. Also check the daily *Cook Islands News* (especially the Thursday and Friday editions) or with the hotels to find out when the feasts are on. The buffets cost about NZ$35 ($24.50), and reservations are essential at all the establishments. Some of them may charge a small admission to see the dance show if you don't have dinner.

In addition to his coconut tree-climbing exhibitions, Piri Puruto (☎ 20-309) stages **Piri's Umukai Picnic** every Sunday at 10:30am at Piri's Place, his lagoonside home on the south coast, east of The Rarotongan Resort Hotel. Cost is NZ$30 ($21).

Money-Saving Tip   Some of the major restaurants have countered a steep rise in food costs in recent years by offering three-course, set-menu dinners at special prices. The main courses usually are of the sort that can be mass-produced or prepared cheaply, such as stews and stir-fries. These meals cost NZ$20 to NZ$25 ($14–$17.50) during my recent visit, a considerable savings over ordering à la carte.

EXPENSIVE

✪ The Flame Tree
Muri Beach, near The Pacific Resort (10.5km [6.3 miles] from Avarua). ☎ **25-123.** Reservations required. Main courses NZ$20–NZ$30 ($14–$21); special 3-course dinners NZ$25 ($17.50). AE, DC, MC, V. Tues–Sat 6:30–9:30pm, Sun 6–9pm. INTERNATIONAL.

Yachties-turned-restaurateurs Bill and Sue Curruthers showed up in Rarotonga a few years ago and immediately transformed the island's eating scene by opening Portofino (see below) and The Flame Tree. They have since gone their separate ways: Bill carries on at Portofino, and Sue operates The Flame Tree. It enjoys a convenient location within walking distance of The Muri Beachcomber, The Pacific Resort, and Sokala Villas. Calling on the cuisines of her native Kenya and other countries she visited during her extensive voyages, Sue whips together a wide range of selections, all displayed on a huge chalkboard menu, such as Thai ginger fish and an absolutely delightful East African dish of chicken served under a spicy tomato and peanut sauce. I particularly enjoyed one of her nightly specials: fresh parrot fish breaded, fried, and served over rice and under a mound of taro-top spinach sweetly cooked in coconut sauce. These and other recipes are in Sue's *The Flame Tree Cookbook,* available here and at bookstores in Avarua. Smoking is allowed only in outside seating, not inside the converted house.

Oasis Village Steakhouse
Arorangi, in Oasis Village. ☎ **28-213.** Reservations recommended. Main courses NZ$20–NZ$25 ($14–$17.50). AE, MC, V. Mon–Sat 6–9:30pm. STEAKS.

A New Zealander living on Rarotonga once said she appreciated the sacrifices of the Kiwis at home, since all their country's top-grade beef is exported rather than consumed at home. Some of these tender steaks end up at this open-air eatery under a peaked roof of exported New Zealand pine. Ideally it would be directly on the beach and not a half-block inland, but this convenient setting near the Edgewater Resort and Rarotongan Sunset Motel will do when you've tired of seafood and want an infusion of cholesterol chargrilled and served with a salad bar. Other offerings are chicken and a Polynesian seafood curry. Baked potatoes and other side dishes cost extra.

Ronnie's Bar & Restaurant

Avarua, west end of business district. ☎ **20-823.** Reservations recommended for dinner. Lunch NZ$7–NZ$15 ($5–$10.50); main courses NZ$21.50–NZ$38.50 ($15–$27). AE, MC, V. Mon–Sat 11am–2:30pm and 6–9:30pm. REGIONAL/MEXICAN.

Ronnie Siulepa came to Rarotonga from his native Western Samoa to play rugby and never went home. Now he and Cook Islander wife Janice own this friendly establishment in a colonial-style house that is almost below sea level on the land side of Avarua's main street. Lunches include nachos, tacos, enchiladas, seafood pasta, and spicy Indonesian-style beef satay. For dinner, a blackboard menu features selections with a heavy emphasis on chicken and fresh seafood prepared with island ingredients, especially fruit and coconut cream. I had a wonderful fish stewed in coconut cream and served in puff pastry over a bed of puréed taro leaves (known in the Cooks as *rukau).* An open-air bar opens to a shady courtyard to one side (it's a very popular watering hole, especially for sports fans addicted to Ronnie's satellite TV behind the bar).

Sails Restaurant

Muri Beach, in Rarotonga Sailing Club. ☎ **27-350.** Reservations recommended. Main courses NZ$20–NZ$28 ($14–$19.50). AE, DC, MC, V. Tues–Sun 6:30–9:30pm. SEAFOOD/ JAPANESE.

Reserve a table on the screened-in porch of this establishment above the Rarotonga Sailing Club, especially on moonlit nights when Muri Lagoon sparkles. Indeed, this is one of the more scenic restaurants on the island. The menu matches the setting, with nightly seafood offerings written on a chalkboard. The chef during my recent visit had come to Rarotonga from the Hamacho Japanese restaurant in The Regent of Fiji, so expect excellent sushi (and a curry or two) if he's still there.

Tumanu Tropical Restaurant & Bar

Arorangi, near Edgewater Resort. ☎ **20-501.** Reservations recommended. Main courses NZ$21–NZ$28 ($14.50–$19.50). AE, MC, V. Mon–Sat noon–2pm; daily 6–10pm; bar open to midnight. REGIONAL.

With its low-slung thatch roof and lush outdoor gardens, this is the only restaurant and bar on Rarotonga that genuinely looks like it belongs in the South Seas. Julie and Eric Bateman's cozy place has subdued lighting inside, dividers of driftwood separating the tables, foreign flags hanging on split bamboo walls, and various paraphanalia stuck around the bar area, including old license plates from Texas, Oregon, Iowa, and Alaska. Colorful tablecloths help spice up otherwise plain dining room furniture. The menu is heavy on seafood served braised or fried, but you can also get baked chicken or steaks in pepper or mushroom sauce. A special vegetarian platter comes with fruit salad, vegetables, and cheese omelet. A caution is in order: The humor can get raunchy at Eric's lively bar.

MODERATE

Kaena Restaurant and Bar

Arorangi, near The Rarotongan Resort Hotel. ☎ **25-433.** Reservations recommended. Main courses NZ$17–NZ$28 ($12–$19.50). AE, DC, MC, V. Mon–Sat 6–10pm. REGIONAL.

Tauei and Lynne Solomon's little place offers convenient dining for guests of the nearby Rarotongan Resort, Lagoon Lodges, and Puaikura Reef Lodges. In business since 1982, the Kaena shares a building with a mom-and-pop grocery; don't be misled by the outside appearance, for inside their restaurant is quite charmingly decorated. You can dine inside or in an enclosed veranda room with flowering vines growing under its tin roof. Main courses feature charbroiled steaks either plain or with sauce, chicken in fruit or coconut sauce, and seafood selections.

P.J.'s Cafe & Bar

Arorangi, near Edgewater Resort. ☎ **20-367.** Reservations not accepted. Burgers & sandwiches NZ$2.50–NZ$7 ($1.75–$5); main courses NZ$14–NZ$34 ($10–$24). AE, MC, V. Daily noon–2pm; Mon–Sat 6–10pm, Sun 6–9:30pm. Take-away counter Mon–Thurs and Sat noon–3pm and 6–11:30pm, Fri noon–2am, Sun noon–9:30pm. SANDWICHES/BURGERS/CANTONESE.

This popular establishment began life as a roadside take-away snack counter, but its location in the Arorangi hotel district has helped it grow into a lively sports bar with restaurant service and take-away counter. The counter is still there with picnic tables outside, dishing up sandwiches, burgers, and Cantonese dishes. These also are served to patrons of the sports bar, which has lots of memorabilia on its walls, the obligatory TVs, and a separate billiards room.

✪ Portofino Restaurant

Avarua, east of traffic circle. ☎ **26-480.** Reservations recommended. Main courses NZ$15–NZ$33 ($10.50–$23). AE, DC, MC, V. Mon–Sat 6:30–9:30pm. ITALIAN.

Bill Curruthers serves up the best homemade pastas and tomato sauce between Tahiti and Fiji in this cozy old clapboard store dressed up with a cross between Mediterranean and Polynesian decor. An open-air pavilion to one side makes room for a few fresh-air tables. Spaghetti or rigatoni is served with Neapolitan, bolognese, Florentine, or Alfredo sauces, either as a heavy appetizer or as a main course. Tender charbroiled New Zealand–bred steaks are cooked plain or under pizzaiola, garlic, or pepper sauce. Daily specials feature such tempting dishes as a seafood lasagna with fish, crabmeat, and smoked mussels. A money-saving feature here is an all-you-can-eat pasta dinner for NZ$18.50 ($13).

Trader Jack's Bar & Grill

Avarua, waterfront at traffic circle. ☎ **26-464.** Reservations recommended at dinner. Main courses NZ$13–NZ$26 ($9–$18). AE, DC, MC, V. Mon–Sat noon–2pm and 7–10pm; Sun 6–10pm. Bar Mon–Thurs and Sat 11am–midnight, Fri 11am–2am, Sun 6–10pm. REGIONAL.

"Trader Jack" Cooper spent a small fortune on this building with floor-to-ceiling windows on three sides facing the water and giving nearly everyone in the large bar and split-level dining area a view of the harbor, the reef, and the sea and sunsets beyond. One of Rarotonga's few restaurants actually beside the water, it's popular with local business and professional folk. There actually are three waterside decks, which can be packed at happy hour Monday to Friday and the rest of Friday night. The chalkboard menu featuring seafood, steaks, and pasta changes daily. Snacks are offered from 3 to 6pm.

INEXPENSIVE

Just as *les roulettes* offer some of the best food bargains in Papeete (see "Where to Dine" in the Tahiti chapter), Rarotonga has its own version of these popular food trucks. Known here as ✪ **food caravans,** they sit under the waterfront casuarina trees in Avatiu Market and offer everything from cold coconuts to slake a thirst to seafood platters to placate late-night hunger pangs. Most are open Monday to Saturday from 9am to 6pm. Some stay open Monday to Thursday until 9pm, Friday until 2am, and Saturday until midnight. Guess where everyone goes after crawling the pubs on Friday night.

K&M Takeaway has scrumptious seafood platters, fried fish, and *ika mata* (the local version of fish marinated in lime juice and mixed with coconut milk and raw vegetables) at prices ranging from NZ$4 to NZ$12 ($3 to $8.50).

Blue Note Café

Avarua, at the traffic circle. ☎ **23-236.** Breakfast NZ$3–NZ$10 ($2–$7); sandwiches, salads, and burgers NZ$4–NZ$10 ($3–$7). No credit cards. Mon–Fri 7am–4pm, Sat–Sun 8am–3pm. SNACK BAR.

A fine place to take a town break and watch the traffic along the waterfront, Tarita Hutchinson's snack bar occupies one end of the breezy veranda of the old Banana Court building. Breakfast is served all day, as are cappucino, fruit smoothies, home-made ice cream, milk shakes, and other refreshments. Sandwiches are made to order here.

Boardwalk Cafe

Muri Beach, in Rarotonga Sailing Club. ☎ **27-350.** Snacks NZ$7–NZ$10 ($5–$7); salads, burgers, baskets NZ$7.50–NZ$16.50 ($5.25–$11.50). MC, V. Daily 10am–4pm (lunch served 11am–2pm). SNACK BAR/SEAFOOD.

The daytime operation of Sails Restaurant (see above), this cafe on the beachside porch of the Rarotonga Sailing Club is a breezy retreat in which to have a snack or light lunch while watching everyone else play in Muri Lagoon. Snacks feature nachos, seafood chowder, and sandwiches. More substantial lunch fare includes burger platters and baskets of fried fish or chicken.

✪ Cook's Corner Cafe

Avarua, in Cook's Corner. ☎ **22-345.** Burgers and sandwiches NZ$2.50–NZ$8 ($1.75–5.50); meals and breakfasts NZ$6–NZ$10.50 ($4–$7.50). No credit cards. Mon–Fri 7am–4pm, Sat 7am–noon. SNACK BAR.

You will find me having a cooked breakfast and reading the *Cook Island News* at Maureen Young's little sidewalk cafe, where everyone waits for the bus (it begins its runs here). She also serves snacks, morning and afternoon teas, and light lunches, which include daily specials listed on a blackboard. They are purchased at a counter and eaten on the covered sidewalk of the small shopping center. I sometimes think Maureen sleeps wearing her ever-present flower crown.

The Flamboyant Place

Arorangi, between Edgewater Resort and Manuia Beach Hotel in Taio's Shopping Center. ☎ **23-958.** Breakfast NZ$4–NZ$8 ($3–$5.50); lunch NZ$2–NZ$10 ($1.50–$7); dinner NZ$7–NZ$15 ($5–$10.50). No credit cards. Mon–Thurs 8am–11pm, Fri–Sat 8am–2am, Sun 1–10pm. REGIONAL.

This clean little storefront establishment is the only non-hotel restaurant on the west coast offering cooked breakfasts every day except Sunday. Its lunches and meals feature local favorites such as fried fish and chicken, chow mein, ham steaks, and oysters. Take your meals away, or dine at wooden tables on the shopping center's sidewalk.

Mama's Cafe

Avarua, west of traffic circle next to Foodland. No phone. Sandwiches and pastries NZ$2–NZ$3.50 ($1.40–$2.50). No credit cards. Mon–Fri 8am–4:30pm, Sat 8am–12:30pm. SNACK BAR.

Look for Mama's clean cafeteria-style cafe at the big Foodland grocery store. Walk along the cafeteria line and choose from a variety of snacks in the cold or hot cabinets. Then, if you can find one vacant, eat at one of the plastic tables in the seating area pleasantly accented with potted plants. Best thing here: milk shakes from the ice cream bar at the front.

Ⓢ Metua's Cafe
Avarua, in Brown's Arcade, just east of traffic circle. ☎ **20-850.** Sandwiches and burgers NZ$2.50–NZ$5 ($1.75–$3.50); meals NZ$12.50–NZ$15.50 ($9–$11); breakfast NZ$5–NZ$9 ($3.50–$6.50). No credit cards. Mon–Thurs 7:30am–10pm, Fri 7:30am–2am, Sat 7:30am–midnight. REGIONAL/EUROPEAN.

Metua's is another good place for full American breakfasts, sandwiches and hamburgers, fish and chips, salads and soups, and hot meals, such as grilled scallops, steaks, or chops. Monday, Tuesday, and Wednesday dinners usually feature plain, New Zealand–style roasts for NZ$14 ($10). Friday night is barbecue night, with a band and Cook Islands dance show, all for NZ$13 ($9) a head.

13 Scuba Diving, Kayaking & Other Outdoor Activities

With tourism as its main business, Rarotonga has enough sporting and other outdoor activities to occupy the time of anyone who decides to crawl out of a beach chair and move the muscles. A few activities, such as Pa's Mountain Trek, are mentioned above in "Cultural Experiences."

FISHING If the sea is calm enough for them to leave Rarotonga's relatively unprotected harbors, charter boats start deep-sea fishing as soon as they clear the reef. There have been some world-class catches of skipjack tuna (bonito), mahi mahi, blue marlin, wahoo, and barracuda in Cook Islands waters. You can try your luck with **Seafari Charters** (☎ 20-328), **Pacific Marine Charters** (☎ 21-237), or **Beco Game Fishing Charters** (☎ 21-515). They like to have a day's notice. Standard cost for a day's fishing is less than NZ$100 ($70) per person, one of the lowest rates in the South Pacific. Don't expect to keep your catch; fresh fish are expensive in Rarotonga and will be sold by the boat operator. Bring a camera.

The **Cook Islands Game Fishing Club** (☎ 21-419) has its clubhouse beside the lagoon 1km (.6 mile) east of the traffic circle. Overseas guests are welcome to have snacks and drinks while taking in the view and swapping a few tall tales.

GOLF Visitors are welcome to take their shots at the radio towers and guy wires that create unusual obstacles on the nine holes of **Rarotonga Golf Club** (☎ 27-360). The course was once located on what is now the International Airport; club members had to move it when the runway was expanded. It now lies under Rarotonga's radio station antennae—balls that hit a tower or wire can be replayed. Greens fees are NZ$10 ($7). Rental equipment and drinks are available in the clubhouse. The club is open Monday through Saturday from 8am until dark.

HIKING There are a number of hiking trails on Rarotonga, but the most popular by far is the **Cross-Island Track** from Avarua to the south coast. It begins in the Avatiu valley and follows the stream high up to the base of Mount Te Rua Manga ("The Needle"). It's a very steep and often slippery climb, but the trail is well marked. Hundreds of visitors make the trek each year, most of them accompanied by a guide. **Hugh Henry & Associates** lead hikes over the Cross Island Track (see "Cultural Experiences," above), as does **Baker's Cross Island Adventures** (☎ 20-019). The walks cost NZ$35 ($24.50) per person. For do-it-yourselfers, the **Cook Islands Tourist Authority** distributes a brochure detailing the cross-island and other hikes, and it has helpful brochures published by the Cook Islands Natural Heritage Project, which explain what you will see.

HORSEBACK RIDING   They aren't actually horses, but **Aroa Pony Trek** (☎ 21-415) uses the smaller version for rides through plantations to a waterfall. Price for the trek is NZ$30 ($21).

LAGOON EXCURSIONS   Both **Captain Tama's Coral Cruizes** (☎ 23-810) and **Aquasports** (☎ 27-350), at The Pacific Resort and the Rarotonga Sailing Club, respectively, have glass-bottom boat and outrigger canoe excursions on Muri Lagoon. They cost NZ$35 ($24.50) including a barbecue lunch on a small island. Both also have sunset cruises for NZ$25 ($17.50).

LAWN BOWLS   The **Rarotonga Bowling Club** (☎ 26-277) has an international-standard bowling green on Moss Road in Avarua. Visitors are welcome, and there's a licensed bar on the premises.

RUNNING & JOGGING   The "Hash House Harriers" organization meets once a week for a fun run and sponsors an annual Round Rarotonga Road Run in November each year. Information is available from David Lobb (☎ 22-000). Really, all one has to do for a jog on Rarotonga is to run down the road or beach.

SAILING & KAYAKING   **Aquasports** (☎ 27-350) at the Rarotonga Sailing Club on Muri Beach, where the lagoon offshore is the island's best spot for boating, rents a variety of water sports equipment, including kayaks, sailboats, windsurfers, canoes, and snorkeling gear. Rental rates range from NZ$10 to NZ$40 ($7 to $28). Windsurfing and sailing lessons are available. Aqua Sports is open daily from 9am to 5pm.

Captain Tama's Water Sportz World at the nearby Pacific Resort (☎ 20-427) also rents kayaks, sailboards, canoes, and snorkeling equipment.

SCUBA DIVING   Rarotonga's lagoon is only 4 to 10 feet deep, but depths easily reach 100 feet outside the reef, and a drop-off starts at 80 feet and descends to more than 12,000 feet. There are canyons, caves, tunnels, and many varieties of coral. Visibility usually is in the 100- to 200-feet range. Two wrecks, and a 100-foot fishing boat and a 150-foot cargo ship, sit in depths of 80 feet and 60 feet, respectively.

Barry and Shirley Hill, owners of **Dive Rarotonga** (☎ 21-873), make dive trips daily. They charge NZ$40 ($28) per dive including tank, air, weight belt, and boat; and NZ$50 ($35), if you rent the rest of the equipment. Their office is roadside in Arorangi.

Greg Wilson of **Cook Island Divers**, P.O. Box 1002, Rarotonga (☎ 22-483), operates out of his house in Arorangi (watch for the roadside signs) and from the Mana Court Dive Shop in Avarua. He charges NZ$50 ($30) a dive including all equipment and teaches a four-day NAUI course for NZ$450 ($315) including all equipment.

Marineland Pacific Divers (☎ 22-450) on Muri beach charges the same per dive and teaches full PADI certification courses for NZ$420 ($294), or a three-hour resort course for NZ$60 ($42). This company is allied with Dive Rarotonga.

SQUASH   The **Edgewater Resort** (☎ 25-435) in Arorangi has the island's only squash courts. Rates are NZ$5 ($3.50) per person for outsiders; racquet rental is NZ$3 ($2.10). The courts are open Monday to Saturday from 9:30am to 7pm. Reservations are essential.

SWIMMING AND SNORKELING   Obviously, getting into the water has to have high priority during a visit to the South Pacific, and Rarotonga is certainly no exception. The lagoon is deep enough for snorkeling off most hotels at high tide, but you'll do better walking on the west coast reef when the tide's out. Only off The Little Polynesian and Moana Sands Beach Hideaway on the south coast is the lagoon deep enough for snorkeling at low tide (see "Where to Stay," below). Muri Beach has the best lagoon for boating, but its sandy bottom is not a good snorkeling spot.

Most hotels have snorkels, fins, and masks for their guests to use while snorkeling. The **Sports Centre** at the Edgewater Resort (☎ 25-435) rents them to non-guests. They also can be rented for NZ$3 ($2.10) per day from **Dive Rarotonga** (☎ 21-873) in Arorangi or from **Aqua Sports** (☎ 27-350) on Muri Beach. Aqua Sports also offers snorkeling tours of Muri Lagoon.

TENNIS   The **Rarotongan Resort Hotel** (☎ 25-800) allows non-guests to play on its tennis courts. Rates are NZ$10 ($7) per hour, and NZ$4 ($2.80) per hour for racquets. There are **public tennis courts** in Avarua and at Titikaveka College on the south coast, but ask your hotel reception desk before dashing off with racquet in hand; many Rarotongans take their tennis seriously and don't look kindly on tourists who hog the public courts.

14 Shopping

Thanks to the New Zealand dollar being valued less than its U.S. counterpart, Rarotonga offers some relatively good bargains for those of us carrying American bucks, especially on black pearls, native handcrafts, and silkscreened or tie-dyed cotton garments. For the most part, you can do your shopping during your visit to Avarua, for most shops line the town's waterfront on either side of the traffic circle.

HANDCRAFTS & ART

Cook Islanders may not produce island handcrafts in the same volume as Tongans, but there is a fine assortment to choose from, especially items made on the outer islands. Particularly good if not inexpensive buys are the delicately woven *rito* (white straw hats) the women wear to church on Sunday and the fine Samoan-style straw mats from Pukapuka in the Northern Group. Carvings from wood are plentiful, as is jewelry made from shell, mother-of-pearl, and pink coral. The most popular woodcarvings are small totems representing the exhibitionist Tangaroa—they may be more appropriate for the nightstand than the coffee table.

✪ **Beachcomber, Ltd.**
Avarua, east of traffic circle. ☎ **21-939.**

This upscale establishment is worth a stop just to see the beautiful renovation of its 1843-vintage coral-block school house (see "Walking Tour of Avarua," above). Owners Joan Rolls and husband David Gragg completely gutted the old roofless structure and turned it into Rarotonga's most picturesque shop. In addition to black pearls (see below), Joan sells some of the best handcrafts available, including woodcarvings, excellent black and pink coral jewelry, and exquisite rito hats. One section is devoted to paintings and other works by local artists, whose numbers include Joan herself.

Cook Islands Women's Handicraft Centre
Avatiu Market. ☎ **28-033.**

Although other shops now buy most of the best items directly from the producers, you should find some fine woven mats, grass skirts, straw hats, handbags, fans, brooms, headbands, purses made from coconut shells, woodcarvings, and jewelry.

The Gallerie
Avarua, west of traffic circle. ☎ **21-079.**

You can watch Jillian Sobieska working on some of her oil paintings in this little boothlike shop just west of the traffic circle. In addition to canvas, she paints landscapes, portraits, and florals on cards, T-shirts, and pareus.

Island Crafts
Avarua, in Centrepoint Building. ☎ **22-919.**

A must stop, this large shop is located on the main street, next to Westpac Bank. It has Rarotonga's largest selection of handcrafts—some from other parts of the South Pacific—and a wide selection of carved wooden Tangaroa tikis in various sizes. You can even buy a 9-karat gold pendant of the well-endowed god.

Manu Manea Fashions
Avarua, west of traffic circle. ☎ **25-527.**

Although primarily a clothing store (see below), this shop has tapa cloth from Fiji and some tie-dyed pareus. The **Kenwall Gallery** in the shop sells art supplies and the works of local artists such as Nga Vakapora, who paints sea life using water colors and acrylics on tapa cloth.

BLACK PEARLS
Manihiki and Penrhyn atolls in the Northern Group of the Cook Islands produce a fair number of pearls, many of them of the same black variety seen in French Polynesia (although most are more gray than black). Although they have yet to reach the quantity produced in the Tuamotus, in U.S. dollar terms, Cook Islands pearls can be somewhat less expensive. Shop around carefully, for top-quality pearls are not nearly so numerous here as in French Polynesia.

I strongly encourage anyone interested in buying pearls in the South Pacific to do some research beforehand, perhaps starting with an excellent article in the August 1985 issue of *National Geographic*. Also see "Best Buys" in the Tahiti chapter earlier in this book.

✪ Beachcomber Ltd.
Avarua, east of traffic circle. ☎ **21-939.**

In addition to carrying the handcraft items mentioned above, Joan Rolls also has an excellent selection of pearls (she's chairperson of the local Pearl Authority). Some are loose; others are set by a staff of jewelry designers in an atelier out back.

Island Crafts
Avarua, in Centrepoint Building. ☎ **22-919.**

In addition to this store's large collection of handcrafts, it carries some black pearls, especially set as pendants and earrings.

Goldmine
Avarua, west of traffic circle. ☎ **24-823.**

This modern yet colonial-style building next to Ronnie's Bar & Restaurant has a small offering of black pearls among a much larger selection of gold, silver, and shell jewelry, semi-precious stones, woodcarvings, leather goods, and ceramics.

✪ Pearls of Polynesia (The Pearl Shop)
Avarua, in Cook's Corner. ☎ **21-902.**

Mike and Marge Bergman helped to pioneer the pearl industry in the Cook Islands, and their shop is the place to see Rarotonga's largest selection, whether loose or incorporated into jewelry. Both they and Beachcomber Ltd. carry small pearls still attached to their gold-trimmed shells and sold as necklaces.

TROPICAL CLOTHING

The craze for tie-dyed or silkscreened clothing swept from Tahiti to Rarotonga, where local artisans make colorful cotton pareus, shirts, blouses, dresses, and other items. Some of their works are more artistically creative than those in French Polynesia, especially one-of-a-kind pareus and women's apparel.

Avatiu Market
Avatiu Harbour. No phone.

The shops in this waterfront park are the best places to look for tie-dyed bedspreads and tablecloths. They also have good prices on T-shirts, although some may be Chinese-made cottons that will shrink (buy a size larger than you usually wear).

Joyce Peyroux Garments
Arorangi. ☎ **20-202.**

The island's largest tropical clothing manufacturer and retailer, Mrs. Peyroux has her factory outlet on the ocean side of the road in Arorangi and her shops in the C.I.D.C. Building in the middle of Avarua.

Kristy & Kendrick Apparel
Avarua, in Cook's Corner. ☎ **28-223.**

This shop has pareus, shirts for men, blouses and dresses in tropical flower prints, and other quality items. The T-shirts have some clever designs, but be careful how you wash the shirts made in China; they may shrink.

Manu Manea Fashions
Avarua, west of traffic circle. ☎ **24-477.**

This shop has women's wear, including some silkscreened items. The company's factory and showroom between Avatiu Harbour and the airports is worth a look. They will alter their stock dresses for free or, for a reasonable price, make one for you from scratch.

TAV Ltd.
Avarua, on 2nd road inland behind Ronnie's Bar & Restaurant. ☎ **21-802.**

Check out TAV for one of the island's best selections of tie-dyed pareus, sundresses, and other items for men, women, and children. During my recent visit, it sold the pick of Rarotonga's colorful pareus. TAV's workshop will alter items for free or will make them for you from scratch.

Tuki's Pareu
Avarua, east of traffic circle. ☎ **20-537.**

In addition to pareus, this storefront shop carries T-shirts, aloha shirts, and other apparel. Pareus on thin, gauzelike cloth sell for NZ$12 ($8.50), while those on longer-lasting cotton cost NZ$16 ($11)—both good value.

Vina's Pona Pareu
Avarua, east of traffic circle. ☎ **26-240.**

Vina Reuther has a wide range of pareus and women's apparel in styles ranging from the traditional full-length "mu-mu" dresses to modern printed sundresses.

PERFUME & SOAPS

The Perfume Factory
Avarua, on the back road between the harbors. ☎ **20-964.**

John Abbott's factory produces delightful perfumes, soaps, body oils, and after-shave lotions made of local gardenia, jasmine, aloe vera, and coconut oils. He also makes coffee, coconut, and vanilla liqueurs.

Perfumes of Rarotonga
Matavera, 4.5km (2.7 miles) west of Avarua. ☎ **21-238.**

Travis Moore, an American who married a Cook Islander, produces a smaller selection of perfumes, soaps, and lotions than The Perfume Factory, but his pleasant shop is under a thatch pavilion in Matavera village east of Avarua. He has a snack bar and rest rooms on the premises. He has a small outlet in Avarua near the Cook Islands Tourist Authority at the traffic circle.

COINS AND STAMPS

For years the Cook Islands government has earned a considerable portion of its revenue from the sale of its stamps to collectors and dealers overseas. The **Philatelic Bureau,** at the Central Post Office in Avarua, issues between three and six new stamps a year. All are highly artistic and feature birds, shells, fish, flowers, and historical events and people, including the British royal family. For whatever reason—perhaps the remoteness of the islands or the beauty of the stamps—they are popular worldwide.

As noted earlier in this chapter, the Cook Islands government prints its own colorful notes and also mints some unusual coins, including the triangular $2 piece and the famous Tangaroa dollar. They have no value whatsoever outside the Cooks, but they do make interesting souvenirs. If you want to give someone special a suggestive hint, hand him or her a Tangaroa coin! You will get plenty of them in change, and there is no limit on how many you can take out of the Cook Islands.

15   Island Nights

Cook Islanders are some of the most fun-loving folks you will meet in the South Pacific, and you can easily catch their spirit. Every evening except Sunday seems to be a party night, and especially on Friday, when the pubs stay open until 2am (they close promptly when the Sabbath strikes at Saturday midnight). And like their Tahitian cousins, the infectious sound of the traditional drums starts every one dancing.

Cook Islands Dancing

No one should miss an "island night" Polynesian dance show on Rarotonga, for Cook Islanders are justly famous for their dancing. A New Zealander once told me in jest that all Cook Islanders are deaf because they grow up three feet from a drum whose beats you can hear from three miles away.

The hip-swinging *tamure* is very much like that in Tahiti, except it tends to be faster (which I found hard to believe the first time I saw it) and even more suggestive (which I had even more trouble believing). The costumes generally aren't as colorful as those in Tahiti but are more likely to be made in the traditional fashion, using natural materials as opposed to dyed synthetic fabrics.

Even though the dance shows at the hotels are tailored for tourists, the participants go at it with an enthusiasm that is too seldom seen in the French Polynesian hotel shows these days. Dancing is *the* thing to do in the Cook Islands, and it shows every time the drums start their tattoo.

Unadulterated Cook Islands dancing is best seen on the outer islands (I've known some travelers who have planned a side trip to Aitutaki around the Rapae Cottage Hotel's Friday island night) or when the outer islanders come to dance on Rarotonga during the annual Dance Week in April or during the Constitution Week celebrations in late July and early August.

In the absence of one of these celebrations, make do with a show or two at the hotels. There will be at least one performance every night except Sunday. A little detective work is required, but you'll easily find out where the next island night is being staged. Ask at your hotel tour desks or the Cook Islands Tourist Authority, which publishes a night-by-night listing of current evening entertainment and prices. Another source is the daily *Cook Islands News*.

PUB CRAWLING

When Rarotongans aren't dancing in a show, they seem to be dancing with each other at one or more of the most colorful bars in the South Pacific. No one ever explained to me why they call their tour-de-pubs a crawl. I assume it's because crawling is one method of travel after a few too many of the locally brewed Cook's Lagers.

For the less rowdy among us, the Friday night crawl begins about 10pm at **The Stair Case** (☎ 22-254), east of the traffic circle. At 11pm everyone seems to wander on down to **Metua's Cafe** (☎ 2-850), in Brown's Arcade near the traffic circle. After an hour there they proceed a few yards to **Trader Jack's** (☎ 26-464) at Avarua's old harbor. The crawl ends between 1 and 2am at **Ronnie's Bar & Restaurant** (☎ 20-823), on the west end of the business district. All these establishments have bands on Friday for dancing.

The young fisticuffs crowd, who once helped make the Banana Court infamous, is likely to be found at **Tere's Bar** (☎ 20-352), the thatch-roofed pub at Avatiu Harbour. Tere has rock-and-roll bands playing in her back yard.

Sometime before the bewitching hour of 2am Saturday morning, many crawlers head to the food caravans at Avatiu Market. Others drive around to Arorangi for a late bite at P.J.'s Cafe & Bar or the Flamboyant Place (see "Where to Dine," above).

If you don't have the courage to mingle on your own, **Steven Kavana's Nite-Life Tour** (☎ 21-583) will take you around to the pubs by minibus for NZ$48 ($33.50), including one drink at each stop. Reservations are essential.

16 An Easy Excursion to Aitutaki

The farther away visitors get from the South Pacific's international airports, the more likely they are to find an island and a way of life that have escaped relatively unscathed by the coming of Western ways—remnants of "old" Polynesia. This is certainly true of Aitutaki, the most frequently visited of the outer Cook Islands.

Lying 155 miles north of Rarotonga, Aitutaki is often referred to as "the Bora Bora of the Cook Islands" because it consists of a small, hilly island at the apex of a triangular barrier reef dotted with skinny flat islands. This reef necklace encloses one of the South Pacific's most beautiful lagoons, which appears at the end of the flight up from Rarotonga as a turquoise carpet spread on the deep blue sea. The view from the air is memorable.

The central island, only eight square miles in area, is dotted with the coconut, pineapple, banana, and tapioca plantations that are worked by most of the island's 2,500 residents. A few Aitutakians make their living at the island's hotels, but the land and the lagoon still provide most of their income. Aitutaki is a major supplier of produce and seafood to Rarotonga. Much of the fresh reef fish and lobsters consumed at Rarotonga's restaurants is harvested here.

The administrative center, most of the shops, and the main wharf are on the west side of the island at **Arutanga** village, where a narrow, shallow passage comes through the reef. Trading boats cannot get through the pass and must remain offshore while cargo and passengers are ferried to land on barges. A network of mostly unpaved roads fans out from Arutanga to **Viapai** and **Tautu** villages on the east side, and to the airport on a flat hook at the northern end of the island.

The uninhabited coconut-studded small islands out on the reef have white-sand beaches on their lagoon sides and pounding surf on the other; they're perfect for picnics and snorkeling expeditions, which are Aitutaki's prime attractions.

A Little History   Legend says that in the beginning Aitutaki was completely flat, but then its warriors sailed to Rarotonga and stole the top of Mount Raemaru. Pitched battles were fought on the way home, and parts of the mountain fell into the sea: Black Rock, on Rarotonga's northwest point; Rapota and Moturakau islands, in the south of Aitutaki's lagoon; and the black rocks along Aitutaki's west coast. In the end, the Aitutakian warriors were victorious, and the top of Raemaru is now **Mount Maungapu,** the highest point on Aitutaki at 407 feet. There's a walking trail to the top (see "Hiking," below).

According to another legend, the first Polynesians to reach Aitutaki came in through **Ootu Pass,** between the airport and **Akitua** island, site of the Aitutaki Lagoon Resort. They were led by the mighty warrior and navigator Ru, who brought four wives, four brothers, and a crew of 20 young virgins from either Tubai or Raiatea (the legend varies as to which one) in what is now French Polynesia. Akitua island, where they landed, originally was named Urituaorukitemoana, which means "where Ru turned his back on the sea."

The first European to visit Aitutaki was Capt. William Bligh, who discovered it in 1789 a few weeks before he was set adrift in Tonga by the mutinous crew of H.M.S. *Bounty.* Just south of the post office in Arutanga is the **Cook Islands**

Impressions

At last I came to Maungapu, the highest point on Aitutaki. At 407 feet high, Maungapu is no Everest, but it offered me a view that, I submit, could not have been improved upon by Everest itself.

—Lawrence Millman, 1990

Christian Church, the country's oldest, built in 1839 of coral and limestone. The monument in front is to John Williams, the exploring missionary who came to Aitutaki in October 1821, and to Papeiha, the Tahitian teacher who came with him and stayed for two years, during which he converted the entire island. Papeiha then went to Rarotonga and helped the missionaries do the same thing there. The interior of the church is unusual in that the altar is on one side rather than at one end. Worshippers from each village sit together during services, but visitors can take any vacancy during services at 10am on Sunday. An anchor suspended from the ceiling is a symbol of hope being a sure and steadfast anchor, as in Hebrews 6:19.

The volcanic part of Aitutaki is joined to the reef on the island's north end, and it was here that the American forces—with considerable help from the local residents—built the large airstrip during World War II. About 1,000 Americans were stationed at the strip, which was used as a refueling stop on the route between North America and New Zealand. Many present-day Aitutakians reportedly are the children and grandchildren of those American sailors. The war ended before the Americans could complete a navigable channel from Arutanga to deep water. Today all cargo must be unloaded offshore and brought to the wharf by barge.

The late Sir Albert Henry was born and raised on Aitutaki, and the divided road to the wharf is named for him and his wife Elizabeth (one lane for Sir Albert and one lane for Lady Elizabeth).

GETTING THERE

Air Rarotonga (☎ 22-888 on Rarotonga) has several flights a day from Monday to Saturday to and from Aitutaki. Round-trip fare is about NZ$285 ($200). It also has day trips to Aitutaki for about NZ$300 ($210), which includes round-trip air fare and a lagoon excursion with a barbecue lunch. The flight takes about 50 minutes.

Air-hotel packages to Aitutaki can vary in price but always represent a savings over do-it-yourself arrangements, so check with the travel agents in Avarua to see whether they have deals. **Island Hopper Vacations** (☎ 22-026), **Hugh Henry & Associates** (☎ 25-320), and **Stars Travel** (☎ 23-669) specialize in outer island trips.

Since Aitutaki's airport sits on the northeast corner of the island, you more than likely will fly over the lagoon on the approach; if possible, get a seat on the left side of the aircraft.

GETTING AROUND

The airport is about 7km (4 miles) from most hotels and guest houses. The airline provides **airport transfers** for NZ$5 ($3.50) each way. The minibuses pick up passengers from the hotels prior to departing flights. Ask the hotel desk to reconfirm your return to Rarotonga; otherwise, the bus won't stop for you. Air Rarotonga's office is in Ureia village just north of Arutanga.

There is no public transportation system on Aitutaki.

All hotels and guest houses can arrange scooter rentals.

FAST FACTS: AITUTAKI

Currency Exchange   Traveler's checks can be cashed at Westpac Bank's little agency or at the post office, both in Arutanga, Monday to Friday from 8am to 3pm.

Dentist/Doctor   See "Hospitals," below.

Drugstores   Some prescription drugs are available at the island's hospital near Arutanga. There is no private pharmacy on Aitutaki.

Emergencies   In case of emergency, contact your hotel staff. The police station is in Arutanga.

Hospitals   Medical and dental treatment are available at the island's hospital near Arutanga.

Liquor Laws   The post office in Arutanga houses the bond store, where liquor and beer can be purchased.

Post Office   The post office at Arutanga is open Monday to Friday 8am to 4pm.

Safety   The police station is in Arutanga. See the Fast Facts for Rarotonga earlier in this chapter for general warnings and precautions.

Telegrams/Telex/Fax   The communications counter at the post office is open Monday to Friday from 8am to 4pm. There's a Phonecard public phone outside the building.

Water   Visitors should not drink the tap water on Aitutaki unless they are sure it comes from a rainwater catchment. Ask first.

WHAT TO SEE & DO

The hotels all offer land tours of the small island, but most visitors come here for sports and outdoor activities, especially on the lagoon.

WHERE TO STAY

During my recent visit, new owners were in the process of taking over and renovating the **Rapae Cottage Hotel**, P.O. Box 4, Aitutaki (☎ 31-320, fax 31-3321). It may have reopened by the time you plan your trip; if so, it has a very convenient location on the beach, about 1km (.6) mile north of Arutanga. The government built it originally as an official guest house but operated it for many years as a hotel. It often is used as a reference point in giving directions, both by local residents and in the listings below. Its famous Friday island-night feasts and dance shows were continuing during renovations (see "Island Nights," below).

Aitutaki Lagoon Resort

P.O. Box 99, Aitutaki (on Akitua Island, 2km [1.2 miles] south of airport, 9km [5.4 miles] from Arutanga). ☎ **20-234.** Fax 20-990. Telex 62048. 25 bungalows. NZ$265–NZ$344 ($185–$241). AE, DC, MC, V.

Recent renovations have restored this bungalow-style resort as Aitutaki's premier establishment. A foot bridge crosses Ootu Passage to Akitua, a sandy motu south of the airport. Although the rates are high compared to similar establishments elsewhere in the South Pacific, this is the only resort in the Cook Islands that is modeled on the concept of scattering bungalows around a central building on a beach.

The ocean surf breaks on one side of this islet; the magnificent lagoon laps a white-sand beach on the other. Although the lagoon is too shallow for anything other than wading and skimming over in canoes or windsurfers, it's beautiful to look at. Although quite comfortable, the shingle-roof bungalows are close together and have large window-walls on both sides, which adds up to a lack of privacy. Although pricey, the beachfront units look out onto the lagoon instead of neighboring units, which makes them the choice here. All units have cane lounge furniture, and porches with entrances both to the main rooms and to large, shower-only baths.

In the large central building, the restaurant and bar open to the lagoon and swimming pool. Another bar on a pier over the lagoon offers both daytime snacks and dinners. Local entertainers strum and sing each evening, and one night a week usually sees an island dance show after dinner. Facilities include a boutique, tour desk, and some water sports equipment. Rental scooters are available on premises.

Aitutaki Lodges

P.O. Box 70, Aitutaki (east side of island, between Vaipai and Tautu villages). ☎ **31-334.** Fax 31-333. 6 bungalows. MINIBAR. NZ$145 ($102). AE, MC, V.

Two of your fellow readers, Tony Carter and Kathy Bisset of Whitehorse in Canada's Yukon, found Wayne and Aileen Blake's establishment before I did. I've seen it since, but here's what they accurately reported:

"Located on the east side of the island just south of Vaipai village, it is within a 10-minute drive of Arutanga village. Accommodations consist of six immaculate A-frame-style bungalows set into a hillside sloping to the edge of the lagoon. Each bungalow has a queen-size and single bed, bathroom with a shower, ceiling fan, full kitchen including a stocked minibar, and a porch offering spectacular views across the lagoon to the islands and the reef. They are quiet and private. Although the water in front of the hotel is too shallow to be considered good swimming, there is a launch available to take guests out on the lagoon."

Since Tony and Kathy were there, the Blakes have added a small thatch-roofed dining room and bar where guests have a grand view down a lawn to the lagoon. They serve three meals a day. Wayne will customize lagoon cruises to fit his guests' desires.

Maina Sunset Motel

P.O. Box 34, Aitutaki (on west coast, 6km [3.7 miles] from airport, 1km [.6 mile] south of Arutanga). ☎ **31-511.** Fax 331-611. 12 units, 1 apt. NZ$125–NZ$150 ($88–$105). AE, DC, MC, V.

Tauei and Lynn Solomon, owners of the Kaena Restaurant on Rarotonga but who intend to retire to Aitutaki, built this little motel on one of the prettiest stretches of beach on the island. Their beachside restaurant and bar enjoys a lovely view across the shallow lagoon to Maina Island out on the reef (hence, the motel's name). Their one-story motel units are built around a courtyard with small pool. Four of these have separate bedrooms; the others are like motel rooms with full kitchens (there's a grocery shop on the premises). All have verandas facing the pool, ceiling fans, and jalousie windows to permit ample cross-ventilation. The Solomons even installed their own supply of drinkable tap water.

Paradise Cove Guest House

P.O. Box 64, Aitutaki (1.5km [1 mile] north of Rapae Cottage Hotel). ☎ **31-218.** Fax 31-456. 6 bungalows, 5 rms (none with bath). NZ$40 ($22) double. MC, V.

Almost tentlike, the very basic beachside bungalows here are the only accommodations in the Cook Islands constructed of thatch and other natural materials. Low-slung thatch roofs cover just enough space for a bed and small refrigerator. They have electric lights and are fully screened. The rooms are in a European-style house that has a kitchen and large lounge. All guests share toilets and cold-water showers.

WHERE TO DINE

✪ The Crusher Bar

1.5km (1 mile) north of Rapae Cottage Hotel. ☎ **31-283.** Reservations required. Main courses NZ$15–NZ$18 ($10.50–$12.50). MC, V. Sat–Thurs 7:30–11pm; bar open Sat–Thurs 6:30pm–midnight. REGIONAL.

Along with English-born wife Lesley and children Dax, Asti, and Dane, owner Teariki "Ricky" Devon makes this the most charming South Seas restaurant-bar I have ever been in. An entertainer who made his mark in Australia and Europe, Ricky brought the family home to Aitutaki a few years ago and named this old-fashioned, thatch-roofed establishment after the gravel-maker at the rock quarry not far away. Dinners consist of a salad bar and local fish and New Zealand steaks. Saturday sees an island-style feast featuring roast pig. Though ample, the food is secondary to the music, for when enough guests are on hand, Ricky and children take to the stage and entertain the rest of the night. Said one guest recently, "Ricky isn't a bar owner, he's a first-rate blues musician." Don't miss an evening here.

Ralphie's Bar & Grill

Opposite Rapae Cottage Hotel. ☎ **31-418.** Reservations required for dinner. Lunches NZ$7.50–NZ$10.50 ($5.25–$7.50); main courses NZ$14–NZ$18 ($10.50–$12.50). MC, V. Sun–Thurs 10am–9pm, Fri 10am–2am, Sat 10am–midnight. REGIONAL.

Andrew and Moyra McBirney offer a variety of fare. To one side, they serve fish and chips, salads, and other light items at a counter. You can take it away or eat at picnic tables under a tin roof. Dinners served inside their modern octagonal building with shingle roof feature daily specials from a blackboard menu, usually fresh seafood and a mixture of grills, Chinese, and Italian dishes.

HIKING, LAGOON CRUISES & OTHER OUTDOOR ACTIVITIES

✪ **LAGOON EXCURSIONS**   The big attraction on Aitutaki is a day on the lagoon and one of the small islands out on the reef. The "standard" day trip begins at 9am and ends about 4pm. The boats spend the morning cruising and fishing on the lagoon. Midday is spent on one of the reef islands, where guests swim, snorkel, and sun while the crew cooks the day's catch and the local vegetables. The itinerary changes from day to day depending on the weather and the guests' desires.

A common destination is **Tapuaetai,** or "One Foot," island, and its adjacent sandbar known as Nude Island (for its lack of foliage, not clothes). According to Teina Bishop, who runs one of the lagoon excursions, this tiny motu got its name when an ancient chief prohibited his subjects from fishing there on pain of death. One day the chief and his warriors saw two people fishing on the reef and gave chase. The two were a man and his young son. They ran onto the island, the boy carefully stepping in his father's footprints as they crossed the beach. The son then hid in the top of a coconut tree. The chief found the father, who said he was the only person fishing on the reef. After a search proved fruitless, the chief decided it must have been rocks he and his men saw on the reef. He then killed the father. Ever since, the island has been known as Tapuaetai (in the local dialect, *tapuae* means footprint, and *tai* is one).

Those dark things that look like cucumbers dotting the bottom of the lagoon, by the way, are *bêches-de-mer* (sea slugs). Along with sandalwood, they brought many traders to the South Pacific during the 19th century because both brought high prices in China. Sea slugs are harmless—except in China, where they are considered to be an aphrodisiac.

Your hotel can book an excursion for you any day except Sunday. I had a marvelous time snorkeling and picnicking out at Tapuaetai with Teina Bishop of **Bishop's Lagoon Cruises** (☎ 31-009). In addition to his all-day outings, Teina offers sunset barbecue cruises. **Viking Lagoon Cruises** (☎ 31-180) tends to specialize in Maina Island, on the southwest corner of the lagoon near the wreck of the *Alexander,* a good snorkeling spot. Both firms charge NZ$40 ($28) per person for the all-day excursions. Viking Lagoon Cruises also will leave you alone on a deserted islet or take you on an educational cruise to three islets. *Note:* There are no lagoon cruises on Sunday.

The boats all have canopies, but bring a hat and plenty of sunscreen. The sun on the lagoon can blister even under a canopy.

SCUBA DIVING   Divers can contact Neil Mitchell of **Aitutaki Scuba,** P.O. Box 40, Aitutaki (☎ 31-103, fax 31-310), for underwater adventure over the edge of the reef. Neil operates from his home just south of the Rapae Cottage Hotel. He charges NZ$55 ($38.50) per one-tank dive and NZ$65 ($45.50) with equipment, and will teach a four-day PADI and NAUI certification course for NZ$450 ($315). Neil also can tell you how to go deep-sea fishing.

GOLF   Golfers who missed hitting the radio antennae and guy wires on the Rarotonga course can try again at the nine-hole course at the **Aitutaki Golf Club,** on the north end of the island between the airport and the sea. Balls hit onto the runway used to be playable, but broken clubs and increasing air traffic put an end to that. You can rent equipment at the clubhouse. The club has neither a phone

---

Readers Recommend

Atiu Motel, P.O. Box 79, Atiu Island (☎ 20-979). *"My wife and I chose to go to Atiu and had a wonderful long weekend. The Atiu Motel has only three units . . . We were the only foreigners on the island. We were treated royally and entertained well. On Saturday morning we were taken down to the shore and watched everyone fishing or gathering seafood. When we took off to the south coast, we walked beautiful sandy coral beaches for hours and saw no one all afternoon. Talk about Paradise. On Sunday it was a tour of the cave of the Kopeka birds—a fascinating experience. A visit to a tumunu is also a must. The locals sit in a circle at their bush bar and drink bush beer. When the half coconut shell of beer is passed to you, you are to drink it at once. They also hope that visitors will sing some songs with them. It's great to sit and listen to grown men sing nursery songs."* —Donald B. MacLeod, Porthill, Idaho.

(*Author's Note:* The island's only accommodation, the Atiu Motel, now has four units, all with kitchen and bath. Rates are NZ$100 [$70] for a double. Atiu has no restaurants.)

nor regular hours, but the hotels and guest houses can arrange rentals and a tee-off time. Members are more likely to volunteer to mow the greens between May and August than during the wetter summer months.

HIKING Hikers can take a trail to the top of **Mount Maungapu,** Aitutaki's highest point at 124 meters (410 feet). It begins about a mile north of the Rapae Cottage Hotel, across from the Paradise Cove Guest House. The trail starts under the power lines and follows them uphill for about a mile. The tall grass is sharp and can be soaked after a rain, but the track is usually well tramped and should be easy to follow. Nevertheless, wear trousers. The view from the top includes all of Aitutaki and its lagoon. Sunrise and sunset are the best times.

ISLAND NIGHTS

Other than whatever is going on at the Aitutaki Lagoon Resort, evening entertainment during the week consists of having dinner and listening to music (live or recorded) at **The Crusher Bar** (see "Where to Dine," above). As I said above, this is the most charming South Seas bar I have ever been in.

Assuming the new owners haven't ruined a good thing, Friday night at the **Rapae Cottage Hotel** (☎ 31-320) is why some people come to Aitutaki. Things kick off at 7pm with a buffet of island foods cooked in an umu. Once everyone has eaten, the show begins. The quality of the dance will depend on which troupe performs, but it always will be energetic. It seems that the entire island turns out once the drums start to beat. Dinner and show cost NZ$26.50 ($18.50) and is well worth it.

9

Introducing Fiji

If there is one thing every visitor remembers about Fiji, it's the enormous friendliness of the Fijian people. You'll see why as soon as you get off the plane, clear Customs and Immigration, and are greeted by a procession of smiling faces, all of them exclaiming an enthusiastic *"Bula!"* That one word—"health" in Fijian—expresses the warmest and most heartfelt welcome you'll receive anywhere.

Fiji is a relatively large and diverse country, and its great variety also will be immediately evident, for the taxi drivers who whisk you to your hotel are not Fijians of Melanesian heritage, but Indians whose ancestors migrated to Fiji to escape the shackles of poverty in places like Calcutta and Madras. Now slightly less than half the population, these "Fiji Indians" have played major roles in making their country the most prosperous of the independent South Pacific island countries.

The great variety continues to impress as you get around the islands, for in addition to Fiji's cultural mix, you'll find gorgeous white-sand beaches bordered by curving coconut palms, azure lagoons and colorful reefs offering some of the world's best scuba diving, green mountains sweeping to the sea, and a warm climate in which to enjoy it all.

For budget-conscious travelers, Fiji is an affordable paradise. Its wide variety of accommodations ranges from deluxe resorts nestled in tropical gardens beside the beach to down-to-basics hostels catering to the young and the young-at-heart. It has a number of charming and inexpensive small hotels and the largest and finest collection of remote, Robinson Crusoe-like offshore resorts in the entire South Pacific—if not the world. Regardless of where you stay, you are in for a memorable time. The Fijians will see to that.

1 Fiji Today

The Fiji Islands lie in the southwestern Pacific some 3,200 miles southwest of Honolulu and 1,960 miles northeast of Sydney. This strategic position has made Fiji the transportation hub of the South Pacific islands. **Nadi International Airport** is the main connection point for flights going to the other island countries, and Fiji's capital city, **Suva,** is one of the region's prime shipping ports.

The archipelago forms a horseshoe around the reef-strewn **Koro Sea,** a body of water shallow enough for much of it to have been dry

What's Special About Fiji

Beaches/Natural Spectacles
- More than 300 tropical islands with thousands of beaches.
- Rainbow Reef and the Great White Wall, scuba divers' heaven.
- The Great Sea Reef makes a water playground by enclosing a huge lagoon dotted with islands.

Cultures
- A fascinating if not entirely harmonious mix of Fijians and Indians.

Activities
- Cruising through protected waters to uninhabited islands.
- Train and boat rides, plus sightseeing, orchid, and cultural exhibitions.
- Some of the world's most famous scuba diving and snorkeling.

Great Towns/Villages
- The old capital Levuka looks much the same as a century ago.
- Savusavu evokes memories of South Seas copra-trading days.
- Suva still has touches of the British Empire.

TV & Film Locations
- The Yasawas, where two versions of *The Blue Lagoon* were filmed.

land during the last Ice Age some 18,000 years ago. There are more than 300 bits of land ranging in size from **Viti Levu** ("Big Fiji"), which is 10 times the size of Tahiti, to tiny atolls that barely break the surface of the sea. With a total land area of 7,022 square miles, Fiji is slightly smaller than the state of New Jersey. Viti Levu has 4,171 of those square miles, giving it more dry land than all the islands of French Polynesia put together.

Viti Levu and **Vanua Levu,** the second-largest island, lie on the western edge of Fiji. The **Great Sea Reef** arches offshore between them and encloses a huge lagoon dotted with beautiful islands. Many scuba divers think of the coral reefs in this lagoon, the **Astrolabe Reef** south of Viti Levu, and the **Rainbow Reef** between Vanua Levu and Taveuni as the closest places on earth—or below it—to paradise.

Government Fiji made the world's political pages in 1987 when the Fijian-dominated army stormed into parliament and overthrew a newly elected government that was dominated by Indians (see "A Look at the Past," below). Until then, Fiji was governed under a constitution adopted in 1970, when the British granted independence to its former colony. That document left control of most land with the majority Fijians, while giving the Indians a chance to gain political power. Indians outnumbered the indigenous Fijians by the mid-1980s, and in coalition with some of the more liberal Fijians, they gained the upper political hand in the 1987 elections. Their new government lasted just one month until the military coups

Impressions

There is no part of Fiji which is not civilized, although bush natives prefer a more naked kind of life.

—James A. Michener, 1951

of May 1987. A Fijian interim government ruled until 1990, when it promulgated a new constitution under which Fiji has a Fijian president and a hybrid, Westminster-style parliament in which Fijians always hold 37 of the 70 total seats. Regardless of their population, Indians have just 27 seats. One seat is reserved for Rotuma (a Polynesian island that is part of Fiji), and five are held by general electors (that is, Europeans, Chinese, or persons of mixed race). This arrangement permanently denies the Indians a chance at a majority and has been subject to much criticism. A commission had been appointed during my recent visit. It will try to come up with a new scheme acceptable to both sides.

Economy   Fiji is the most self-sufficient of the South Pacific island countries and the only one with a positive balance of trade. Tourism is its largest and most profitable industry; in fact, Fiji is the tourism Goliath among South Pacific island nations, getting twice as many visitors each year as French Polynesia.

Sugar is a close second to tourism. Grown by Indian farmers, the cane is milled by the Fiji Sugar Company, a government-owned corporation that bought out the private Colonial Sugar Refining Company in 1973 (you still will see the initials "CSR" on much of the company's equipment). Five sugar mills process the annual crop, one each in Lautoka, Ba, Tavua, Rakiraki, and Labasa. The mill at Rakiraki produces for domestic consumption; the rest is exported, primarily to Malaysia. There is no refining mill, so most of the sugar served in Fiji is brown, not white.

The Emperor Gold Mine on northern Viti Levu makes an important contribution, as do copra, timber, garments, furniture, and other consumer goods produced by small manufacturers (the Colgate toothpaste you buy in Fiji is made there). Fiji also is a major transshipment point for goods destined for other South Pacific island countries.

The economy nosedived into recession after the 1987 coups. Tourism dropped to a relative trickle, and unemployment became even more of a problem than it was before. Although tourism and the overall economy have returned to record levels, unemployment is a persistent problem. More than half the population is under the age of 25, and there just aren't enough jobs being created for the youngsters coming into the work force. A marked increase in burglaries and other property crimes has been linked to this lack of jobs.

2   A Look at the Past

Dateline

- 1500 B.C. Polynesians arrive from the west.
- 500 B.C. Melanesians settle in Fiji, push Polynesians eastward.
- A.D. 1300–1600 Polynesians, especially Tongans, invade from the east.
- 1643 Abel Tasman sights some islands in Fiji.
- 1774 Capt. James Cook visits Vatoa.

continues

Although the Dutch navigator Abel Tasman sighted some of the Fiji Islands during his voyage of discovery in 1642 and 1643, and Capt. James Cook visited Vatoa, one of the southernmost islands, in 1774, Capt. William Bligh was the first European to sail through and plot the group. After the mutiny on the *Bounty* in April 1789, Bligh and his loyal crew sailed their longboat through Fiji on their way to safety in Indonesia. They passed Ovalau and between Viti Levu and Vanua Levu. Large Fijian *druas* (speedy war canoes) gave chase near the Yasawas, but with some furious paddling, the help of a fortuitous squall, and the good luck to pass through a break in the Great Sea Reef,

Bligh and his ship made it to the open ocean. The druas turned back.

Bligh's rough, handmade charts were amazingly accurate and shed the first European light on Fiji. For a while, Fiji was known as the Bligh Islands, and the passage between Viti Levu and Vanua Levu still is named Bligh Water.

Like Bligh, the Europeans who later made their way west across the South Pacific were warned by the Tongans of Fiji's ferocious cannibals, and the reports by Bligh and others of reef-strewn waters only added to the dangerous reputation of the islands. Consequently, European penetration into Fiji was limited for many years to beach bums and convicts who escaped from the British penal colonies in Australia. There was a sandalwood rush between 1804 and 1813. Other traders arrived in the 1820s in search of *bêche-de-mer* (sea cucumber). This trade continued until the 1850s and had a lasting impact on Fiji, since along with the traders came guns and whisky.

Rise of Cakobau The traders and settlers established the first European-style town in Fiji at Levuka on Ovalau in the early 1820s, but for many years the real power lay on Bau, a tiny island just off the east coast of Viti Levu. With the help of Swedish mercenary Charlie Savage, who supplied the guns, High Chief Tanoa of Bau defeated several much larger confederations and extended his control over most of western Fiji. Bau's influence grew even more under Tanoa's son and successor, Cakobau. Monopolizing the *bêche-de-mer* trade and waging almost constant war against his rivals, this devious chief rose to the height of power during the 1840s. He never did control all the islands, however, for Enele Ma'afu, a member of the Tongan royal family, moved to the Lau Group in 1848 and quickly exerted Tongan control over eastern Fiji. Ma'afu brought along Wesleyan missionaries from Tonga and gave them a foothold in Fiji.

Even though Cakobau ruled much of western Fiji as a virtual despot, the chiefs under him continued to be powerful enough at the local level to make his control tenuous. The lesser chiefs, especially those in the mountains, also saw the Wesleyan missionaries as a threat to their power, and most of them refused to convert or even to allow the missionaries to establish outposts in their

- **1789** After mutiny on the *Bounty,* Capt. William Bligh navigates his longboat through Fiji, is nearly captured by a war canoe.
- **1804** Sandalwood rush begins on Vanua Levu.
- **1808** Swedish mercenary Charlie Savage arrives at Bau, supplies guns to Chief Tanoa in successful wars to conquer western Fiji.
- **1812** Cakobau, future king of Fiji, is born.
- **1813** Charlie Savage is killed; sandalwood era ends.
- **1822** European settlement begins at Levuka.
- **1835** Methodist missionaries settle on Lekeba in Lau Group.
- **1840** United States Exploring Expedition under Capt. John Wilkes explores Fiji and charts waters.
- **1848** Prince Enele Ma'afu exerts Tongan control over eastern Fiji from outpost in Lau Group.
- **1849** U.S. Consul John Brown Williams' home burned and looted during July 4th celebrations; he blames Cakobau.
- **1851** American warship arrives, demands Cakobau pay $5,000 for Williams' losses.
- **1853** Cakobau installed as high chief of Bau, highest post in Fiji.
- **1854** Cakobau converts to Christianity.
- **1855** American claims against Cakobau grow to $40,000; U.S. warship arrives, claims some islands as mortgage.
- **1858** Cakobau offers to cede Fiji to Britain for $40,000.

continues

- 1860 John Brown Williams dies, his claims still unsettled.
- 1862 Britain rejects Cakobau's offer.
- 1867 Unrest grows; Europeans crown Cakobau as King of Bau; Rev. Thomas Baker eaten.
- 1868 Polynesia Company buys Suva in exchange for paying Cakobau's debts.
- 1870 Hurricanes destroy cotton crop as prices fall.
- 1871 Europeans form central government at Levuka, make Cakobau king of Fiji.
- 1874 Cakobau's government collapses; he and other chiefs cede Fiji to Britain without price tag.
- 1875 Measles kills one-fourth of all Fijians; Sir Arthur Gordon becomes first Governor.
- 1879 First Indians arrive as indentured laborers.
- 1882 Capital moved from Levuka to Suva.
- 1916 Recruitment of indentured Indians ends.
- 1917 German Raider Count Felix von Luckner captured at Wakaya.
- 1917–18 Fijian soldiers support Allies in World War I.
- 1942–45 Fijians serve as scouts with Allied units in World War II; failure of Indians to volunteer angers Fijians.
- 1956 First Legislative Council established with Ratu Sir Lala Sukuna as speaker.
- 1966 Fijian-dominated Alliance Party wins first elections.
- 1969 Key compromises pave way for constitution and independence.

continues

villages. (During an attempt to convert the Viti Levu highlanders in 1867, the Rev. Thomas Baker was killed and eaten.)

Fall of Cakobau   Cakobau's slide from power is usually dated from the Fourth of July 1849, when John Brown Williams, the American consul, celebrated the birth of his own nation. A cannon went off and started a fire that burned Williams's house. The Fijians retrieved his belongings from the burning building and kept them. Williams blamed Cakobau and demanded $5,000 in damages. Within two years an American warship showed up and demanded that Cakobau pay up. Other incidents followed, and American claims against the chief totaled more than $40,000 by 1855. Another American man-of-war arrived that year and claimed several islands in lieu of payment; the U.S. never followed up, but the ship forced Cakobau to sign a promissory note due in two years. In the late 1850s, with Ma'afu and his confederation of chiefs gaining power and disorder growing in western Fiji, Cakobau offered to cede the islands to Great Britain if Queen Victoria would pay the Americans. The British pondered the offer for four years, then turned him down.

Cakobau worked a better deal when the Polynesia Company, an Australian planting and commercial enterprise, came to Fiji looking for suitable land after the price of cotton skyrocketed during the American Civil War. Instead of offering his entire kingdom, Cakobau this time tendered only 200,000 acres of it. The Polynesia Company accepted, paid off the American claims, and in 1870 landed Australian settlers on 23,000 acres of its land on Viti Levu, near a Fijian village known as Suva. The land was unsuitable for cotton and the climate too wet for sugar, so the speculators sold their property to the government, which moved the capital there from Levuka in 1882.

Fiji Becomes British   The Polynesia Company's settlers were just a few of the several thousands of European planters who came to Fiji in the 1860s and early 1870s. They bought land for plantations from the Fijians, sometimes fraudulently and often for whiskey and guns. Claims and counterclaims to landownership followed, and with no legal mechanism to settle the disputes, Fiji was swept to the brink of race war. Some Europeans living in Levuka clamored for a national government; others advocated turning the islands over to a colonial power. Things came to a head in 1870, when the bottom fell out of cotton prices, hurricanes destroyed the crops, and anarchy threatened. Within a year the Europeans established a national government at Levuka and named Cakobau king of Fiji. The situation continued to deteriorate, however, and three years later Cakobau was forced to cede the islands to Great Britain. This time there was no price tag attached, and the British accepted. The deed of cession was signed on October 10, 1874.

Britain sent Sir Arthur Gordon as the new colony's first governor. As the Americans were later to do in their part of Samoa, he allowed the Fijian chiefs to govern their villages and districts as they had done before (they were not, however, allowed to engage in tribal warfare) and to advise him through a Great Council of Chiefs. He declared that native Fijian lands could not be sold, only leased. That decision has to this day helped to protect the Fijians, their land, and their customs, but it has led to bitter animosity on the part of the land-deprived Indians.

In order to protect the native Fijians from being exploited, Gordon prohibited their being used as laborers (not that many of them had the slightest inclination to work for someone else). When the planters decided in the early 1870s to switch from profitless cotton to sugarcane, he convinced them to import indentured servants from India. The first 463 East Indians arrived on May 14, 1879 (see "The Fiji Indians," below).

- Provision guarantees Fijian land ownership.
- **1970** Fiji becomes independent; Alliance party leader Ratu Sir Kamisese Mara chosen first prime minister.
- **1987** Fijian-Indian coalition wins majority, names Dr. Timoci Bavadra as prime minister with Indian-majority cabinet; Col. Sitiveni Rabuka leads two bloodless military coups, installs interim government. Most Sunday activities banned outside hotels.
- **1991** New constitution guaranteeing Fijian majority is promulgated. Sunday ban eased.
- **1992** Rabuka's party wins election; he becomes prime minister.
- **1994** Second election cuts Rabuka's majority; he retains power in coalition with mixed-race general electors.
- **1995** Sunday ban survives by one vote; Rabuka appoints constitutional review commission.

The Count Confounded Following Gordon's example, the British governed "Fiji for the Fijians"—and the European planters, of course—leaving the Indians to struggle for their civil rights. The government exercised jurisdiction over all Europeans in the colony and assigned district officers (the "D.O.s" of British colonial lore) to administer various geographic areas.

As usual there was a large gulf between the appointed civil servants sent from Britain and the locals. An example occurred in 1917 when Count Felix von Luckner arrived at Wakaya Island off eastern Viti Levu in search of a replacement for his infamous World War I German raider, the *Seeadler,* which had gone aground in the Cook Islands. A local constable became suspicious of the armed foreigners and notified the district police inspector, who in turn was forbidden to arm his Fijian constables. Only Europeans—not Fijians or Indians—could use firearms. As it turned out, the inspector took his band of unarmed Fijians to Wakaya in a small cattle trading boat anyway. Thinking he was up against a much larger armed force, von Luckner unwittingly surrendered.

Ratu Sir Lala The British continued to rely on the Fijian chiefs at the village level. One, the highest-ranking, Ratu Sir Lala Sukuna, rose to prominence after World War I. (Like *tui* in Polynesian, *ratu* means "chief" in Fijian.) Born of the chiefly lineage of both Bau and the Lau Islands in eastern Fiji, Ratu Sukuna was educated at Oxford, served in World War I, and worked his way up through the colonial bureaucracy to the post of chairman of the Native Land Trust Board. Although dealing in that position primarily with disputes over land and chiefly titles, he used it as a platform to educate his people and to lay the foundation for the independent state of Fiji. As much as anyone, he was the father of modern, independent Fiji.

After the attack of Pearl Harbor began the Pacific war in 1941, the Allies first rushed to Fiji's defense in the face of the Japanese advance across the Pacific, then turned the islands into a vast training base. The airstrip at Nadi was built during this period, and several coastal gun emplacements can still be seen.

Heeding Ratu Sukuna's call to arms (and more than a little prodding from their village chiefs), thousands of Fijians volunteered to fight and did so with great distinction as scouts and infantrymen in the Solomon Islands campaigns. Their knowledge of tropical jungles and their skill at the ambush made them much feared by the Japanese. The Fijians were, said one war correspondent, "death with velvet gloves."

The war also had an unfortunate side: Although many Indians at first volunteered to join, they also demanded pay equal to the European members of the Fiji Military Forces. When the colonial administrators refused, the Indians disbanded their platoon. Their military contribution was one officer and 70 enlisted men of a reserve transport section, and they were promised they would not have to leave Fiji. Many Fijians to this day begrudge the Indians for not doing more to aid the war effort.

The Brits Quit   Ratu Sukuna continued to push the colony toward independence until his death in 1958, and although Fiji made halting steps in that direction during the 1960s, the road was rocky. The Indians by then were highly organized, in both political parties and trade unions, and they objected to a constitution that would institutionalize Fijian control of the government and Fijian ownership of most of the new nation's land. Key compromises were made in 1969, however, and on October 10, 1970—exactly 96 years after Cakobau signed the Deed of Cession—the Dominion of Fiji became an independent member of the British Commonwealth of Nations.

Under the 1970 constitution, Fiji had a Westminster-style Parliament consisting of an elected House of Representatives and a Senate composed of Fijian chiefs. For the first 17 years of independence, the Fijians maintained a majority—albeit a tenuous one—in the House of Representatives and control of the government under the leadership of Ratu Sir Kamisese Mara, the country's first prime minister.

Then, in a general election held in April 1987, a coalition of Indians and liberal Fijians voted Ratu Mara and his Alliance party out of power. Dr. Timoci Bavadra, a Fijian, took over as prime minister, but his cabinet was composed of more Indians than Fijians. Hard feelings immediately flared between some Fijians and Indians.

Rambo's Coups   Within little more than a month of the election, members of the predominantly Fijian army stormed into Parliament and arrested Dr. Bavadra and his cabinet. It was the South Pacific's first military coup, and although peaceful, it took nearly everyone by complete surprise.

The coup leader was then-Col. Sitiveni Rabuka (pronounced "Rambuka"), whom local wags quickly nicknamed Rambo. A Sandhurst-trained career soldier, the 38-year-old Rabuka at the time was third in command of Fiji's army. A Fijian of non-chiefly lineage and a lay preacher in the Methodist church, he immediately became a hero to his "commoner" fellow Fijians, who saw him as saving them from the Indians and preserving their land rights from a government dominated by Indians, who at the time slightly outnumbered the Fijians.

Rabuka at first installed a caretaker government, retaining Ratu Sir Penaia Ganilau as governor-general and Ratu Mara as prime minister. In September 1987, after the British Commonwealth suspended Fiji's membership, he staged another bloodless coup. A few weeks later he abrogated the 1970 constitution, declared Fiji to be an independent republic, and set up a new interim government with Ganilau as president, Ratu Mara as prime minister, and himself as minister of home affairs and army commander (he later gave up all cabinet posts but remained as head of the army).

The government instituted pay cuts and price hikes in 1987 after the Fijian dollar fell sharply on world currency markets. Coupled with the coups, the economic problems led to thousands of Indians—especially professionals, such as doctors, lawyers, accountants, and schoolteachers—fleeing the country.

Dr. Bavadra was released shortly after the coups. He died of natural causes in 1989. Ratu Penaia died in 1994 and was succeeded as president by Ratu Mara.

Rabuka's interim government ruled until 1990, when it promulgated a new constitution guaranteeing Fijians a parliamentary majority. His pro-Fijian party won the initial election, but he barely hung onto power in fresh elections in 1994 by forming a coalition with the European, Chinese, and mixed-race general electors. Although some of his more conservative backers advocated sending all Fiji Indians back to India, Rabuka has taken a more moderate stance. In 1995 he proposed lifting the Sunday ban altogether; it passed the house but lost by one vote in the more conservative Senate, which is dominated by Fijian chiefs of the Methodist persuasion.

He also appointed a three-person Constitutional Review Commission, made up of a New Zealander, a Fijian, and an Indian, to come up with a new scheme that will be fairer to the Indian minority. The commission had just began meeting as we went to press.

3 The Islanders

According to the latest census, Fiji's population in 1990 was 735,985. Indigenous Fijians made up 49.9%, Indians 46.2%, and other races—mostly Chinese, Polynesians, and Europeans—the remainder. Although the overall population has been rising slightly, the country has been losing about 5,000 Indians annually since the military coups of 1987.

It's difficult to imagine peoples of two more contrasting cultures living side by side. "Fijians generally perceive Indians as mean and stingy, crafty and demanding to the extent of being considered greedy, inconsiderate and grasping, uncooperative, egotistic, and calculating," writes Professor Asesela Ravuvu of the University of the South Pacific. On the other hand, he says, Indians see Fijians as "jungalis," still living on the land, which they will not sell, poor, backward, naive, and foolish.

Given that these attitudes are not likely to change any time soon, it is remarkable that Fijians and Indians actually manage to coexist. Politically correct Americans may take offense at some things they could hear said in Fiji, since racial distinctions are a fact of life here. While there is animosity between many Fijians and Indians, and even among Fijians of different classes and skin tones, not all racially connected comments are meant to be derogatory. A Fijian friend of mine once described a rugby star I was to meet as a "big, black fellow." He did not mean it as a racial slur. It was his quite accurate way of telling me to watch for a very big man with very black skin.

From a visitor's standpoint, the famously friendly Fijians give the country its laid-back South Seas charm while at the same time providing relatively good service at the hotels. Although a few of the industrious Indians can be aggravating at times, they make Fiji an easy country to visit by providing excellent maintenance of facilities and efficient and inexpensive services, such as transportation.

THE FIJIANS

When meeting and talking to the smiling Fijians, it's difficult to imagine that less than a century ago their ancestors were among the world's most ferocious cannibals. Today the only vestiges of this past are the four-pronged wooden cannibal forks sold in any handcraft shop (they make interesting conversation pieces when used at home to serve hors d'oeuvres). Yet in the early 1800s, the Fijians were so fierce that Europeans were slow to settle in the islands for fear of literally being turned into a meal—perhaps even being eaten alive. More than 100 white-skinned individuals ended up with their skulls smashed and their bodies baked in an earth oven. William Speiden, the purser on the U.S. exploring expedition that charted Fiji in 1840, long after Europeans had settled in Tahiti and elsewhere in the South Pacific, wrote home to his wife that "one man actually stood by my side and ate the very eyes out of a roasted skull he had, saying, 'Venaca, venaca,' that is, very good."

Cannibalism was an important ritualistic institution among the Fijians, the indigenous Melanesian people who came from the west and began settling in Fiji around 500 B.C. Over time they replaced the Polynesians, whose ancestors had arrived some 1,000 years beforehand, but not before adopting much of Polynesian culture and intermarrying enough to give many Fijians lighter skin than that of most other Melanesians, especially in the islands of eastern Fiji near the Polynesian Kingdom of Tonga. (This is less the case in the west and among the hill dwellers, whose ancestors had less contact with Polynesians in ancient times.) Similar differences occur in terms of culture. For example, while Melanesians traditionally pick their chiefs by popular consensus, Fijian chiefs hold titles by heredity, in the Polynesian fashion.

Impressions

Many of the missionaries were eaten, leading an irreverent planter to suggest that they triumphed by infiltration.

—James A. Michener, 1951

Societies that do not eat people are fascinated by those that do (or did).

—Ronald Wright, 1986

FIJIAN SOCIETY

Ancient Fijian society was organized by tribes, each with its own language, and subdivided into clans of specialists, such as canoe builders, fishermen, and farmers. Powerful chiefs ruled each tribe and constantly warred with their neighbors, usually with brutal vengeance. Captured enemy children were hung by the feet from the rigging of the winners' canoes, and new buildings sometimes were consecrated by burying live adult prisoners in holes dug for the support posts. The ultimate insult, however, was to eat the enemy's flesh. Victorious chiefs were even said to cook and nibble on the fingers or tongues of the vanquished, relishing each bite while the victims watched in agony.

Fijians wouldn't dream of doing anything like that today, of course, but they have managed to retain much of their old lifestyle and customs, including their hereditary system of chiefs and social status. Most Fijians still live in small villages along the coast and riverbanks or in the hills, and you will see many traditional thatch *bures,* or houses, scattered in the countryside away from the main roads. Members of each tribe cultivate and grow food crops in small "bush gardens" on plots of communally owned native land assigned to their families. More than 80% of the land in Fiji is owned by Fijians.

A majority of Fijians are Methodists today, their forebears having been converted by puritanical Wesleyan missionaries who came to the islands in the 19th century. A backer of Prime Minister Rabuka and a strong advocate of Fiji's Sunday Ban, the Methodist Church is a powerful political force in the country.

FIJIAN CULTURE

The Tabua   The highest symbol of respect among Fijians is the tooth of the sperm whale, known as a *tabua* (pronounced "tambua"). Like large mother-of-pearl shells used in other parts of Melanesia, tabuas in ancient times played a role similar to money in modern society and still have various ceremonial uses. They are presented to chiefs as a sign of respect, given as gifts to arrange marriages, offered to friends to show sympathy after the death of a family member, and used as a means to seal a contract or other agreement. The value of each tabua is judged by its thickness and length, and some of the older ones are smooth with wear. It is illegal to export a tabua out of Fiji, and even if you did, the international conventions on endangered species make it illegal to bring them into the U.S. and most other Western countries.

Fire Walking   Legend says that a Fijian god once repaid a favor to a warrior on Beqa island by giving him the ability to walk unharmed on fire. His descendants, all members of the Sawau tribe on Beqa, still walk across stones heated to white-

Impressions

A hundred years of prodding by the British have failed to make the Fijians see why they should work for money.

It is doubtful if anyone but an Indian can dislike Fijians. . . . They are one of the happiest peoples on earth and laugh constantly. Their joy in things is infectious; they love practical jokes, and in warfare they are without fear.

—James A. Michener, 1951

To Gag Is Gauche

Known as *kava* elsewhere in the South Pacific, the slightly narcotic drink Fijians call *yaqona* ("yong-gona") rivals the potent Fiji Bitter beer as the national drink. You likely will have half a coconut shell full of "grog" offered—if not shoved in your face—beginning at your hotel's reception desk. Fiji has more "grog shops" than bars.

Yaqona plays an important ceremonial role in Fijian life. No significant occasion takes place without an elaborate yaqona ceremony. Mats are placed on the floor, the participants gather around in a circle, and the yaqona roots are mixed with water and strained through coconut husks into a large carved wooden bowl, called a *tanoa*.

The ranking chief sits next to the tanoa during the welcoming ceremony. He extends in the direction of the guest of honor a cowrie shell attached to one leg of the bowl by a cord of woven coconut fiber. It's extremely impolite to cross the plane of the cord once it has been extended.

The guest of honor then offers a gift to the village (a kilogram or two of dried grog roots will do these days) and makes a speech explaining the purpose of his visit. The chief then passes the first cup of yaqona to the guest, who claps once, takes the cup in both hands, and gulps down the entire cup of sawdust-tasting liquid in one swallow. Everyone else then claps three times.

Next, each chief drinks a cup, clapping once before bolting it down. Again, everyone else claps three times after each cup is drained. Except for the clapping and formal speeches, everyone remains silent throughout the ceremony, a tradition easily understood considering kava's numbing effect on the lips and tongue.

hot by a bonfire—but usually for the entertainment of tourists at the hotels rather than for a particular religious purpose.

Traditionally, the participants—all male—had to abstain from women and coconuts for two weeks before the ceremony. If they partook of either, they would suffer burns to their feet. Naturally a priest (some would call him a "witch doctor") would recite certain incantations to make sure the coals were hot and the gods were at bay and not angry enough to scorch the soles.

Today's fire walking is a bit touristy but still worth seeing. If you don't believe the stones are hot, go ahead and touch one of them—but do it gingerly.

Some Indians in Fiji engage in fire walking, but it's strictly for religious purposes.

Etiquette   Fijian villages are easy to visit, but remember that to the people who live in them, the entire village is home, not just the individual houses. In your native land, you wouldn't walk into a stranger's living room without being invited, so find someone and ask permission before traipsing into a Fijian village. The Fijians are highly accommodating people, and it's unlikely they will say no; in fact, they may ask you to stay for a meal or perhaps stage a small yaqona ceremony in your honor. They are very tied to tradition, however, so do your part and ask first.

If you are invited to stay or eat in the village, a small gift to the chief is appropriate. The gift should be given to the chief or highest-ranking person present to accept it. Sometimes it helps to explain that it is a gift to the village and not payment for services rendered, especially if it's money you're giving.

Impressions

The question of what to do with these clever Indians of Fiji is the most acute problem in the Pacific today. Within ten years it will become a world concern.

—James A. Michener, 1951

Only chiefs are allowed to wear hats in Fijian villages, so it's good manners for visitors to take theirs off. Shoulders are covered at all times. Fijians go barefoot and walk slightly stooped in their bures. Men sit cross-legged on the floor; women sit with their legs to the side. They don't point at one another with hands, fingers, or feet, nor do they touch each other's heads or hair. They greet each other and strangers with a big smile and a sincere "Bula."

THE FIJI INDIANS

The Fiji Indians' version of America's *Mayflower* was the *Leonidas,* a labor transport ship that arrived at Levuka from Calcutta on May 14, 1879, and landed 463 indentured servants destined to work the sugarcane fields.

As more than 60,000 Indians would do over the next 37 years, these first immigrants signed agreements *(girmits,* they called them) requiring that they work in Fiji for five years; they would be free to return to India after five more years. Most of them labored in the cane fields for the initial term of their girmits, living in "coolie lines" of squalid shacks hardly better than the poverty-stricken conditions most left behind in India. After the initial five years, however, they were free to seek work on their own. Many leased small plots of land from the Fijians and began planting sugarcane or raising cattle on their own. To this day most of Fiji's sugar crop, the country's most important agricultural export, is produced on small leased plots rather than on large plantations. Other Indians went into business in the growing cities and towns, and, joined in the early 1900s by an influx of business-oriented Indians, thereby founded Fiji's modern merchant and professional classes.

Of the immigrants who came from India between 1879 and 1916, when the indenturing system ended, some 85% were Hindus, 14% were Muslims, and the remaining 1% were Sikhs and Christians. Fiji offered these adventurers far more opportunities than they would have had in caste-controlled India. In fact, the caste system was scrapped very quickly by the Hindus in Fiji, and, for the most part, the violent relations between Hindus and Muslims that racked India were put aside on the islands.

Life for the Indians was so much better in Fiji than it would have been in India that only a small minority of them went home after their girmits expired. They tended then—as now—to live in the towns and villages, and in the "Sugar Belt" along the north and west coasts of Viti Levu and Vanua Levu; Hindu and Sikh temples and Muslim mosques abound in these areas. Elsewhere the population is overwhelmingly Fijian.

4 Languages

Fiji has three official languages. To greatly oversimplify the situation, the Fijians speak Fijian, the Indians speak Hindi, and when they speak to each other, they speak English. Schoolchildren are taught in their native language until they are proficient in English, which thereafter is the medium of instruction. This means that English-speaking visitors will have little trouble getting around and enjoying the country.

There is one problem for the uninitiated, however: the unusual pronunciation of Fijian names. For instance, Cakobau is pronounced "Thak-om-bau." There are many other names of people and places that are equally or even more confusing.

FIJIAN

As is the case throughout Melanesia, many native languages are spoken in the islands of Fiji, some of them similar, others quite different. Fijians still speak a variety of dialects in their villages, but the official form of Fijian—and the version taught in the schools—is based on the language of Bau, the small island that came to dominate western Fiji during the 19th century.

Fijian is similar to the Polynesian languages spoken in Tahiti, the Cook Islands, Samoa, and Tonga in that it uses vowel sounds similar to those in Latin, French, Italian, and Spanish: *a* as in b*a*d, *e* as in s*a*y, *i* as in b*ee*, *o* as in g*o*, and *u* as in kangar*oo*.

Some Fijian consonants, however, sound very much different from their counterparts in English, Latin, or any other language. In devising a written form of Fijian, the early Wesleyan missionaries decided to use some familiar Roman consonants in unfamiliar ways. It would have been easier for English speakers to read Fijian had the missionaries used a combination of consonants—*th,* for example—for the Fijian sounds. Their main purpose, however, was to teach Fijians to read and write their own language. Since the Fijians separate all consonant sounds with vowels, writing two consonants together only confused them.

Accordingly, the missionaries came up with the following usages: *b* sounds like *mb* (as in re*m*e*mb*er), *c* sounds like *th* (as in *th*at), *d* sounds like *nd* (as in Su*nd*ay), *g* sounds like *ng* (as in si*ng*er), and *q* sounds like *ng* + *g* (as in fi*ng*er).

Here are some Fijian names with their unusual pronunciations:

Ba	mBah	**Labasa**	Lam-*ba*-sa
Bau	mBau	**Mamanuca**	Ma-ma-*nu*-tha
Beqa	*mBeng*-ga	**Nadi**	*Nan*-di
Buca	*mBu*-tha	**Tabua**	*Tam*-bua
Cakobau	Thack-*om*-bau	**Toberua**	Tom-*bay*-rua
Korotogo	Ko-ro-*ton*-go	**Tubakula**	Toom-ba-*ku*-la

You are likely to hear these Fijian terms used during your stay:

English	Fijian	Pronunciation
hello	bula	*boo*-lah
hello (formal)	ni sa bula	nee sahm *boo*-lah
good morning	ni sa yadra	nee sah *yand*-rah
good night	ni sa moce	nee sah *mo*-thay
thank you	vinaka	vee-*nah*-kah
thank you very much	vinaka vaka levu	vee-n*ah*-kah *vah*-ka *lay*-voo
house/bungalow	bure	*boo*-ray
tapa cloth	masi	*mah*-see
sarong	sulu	*sue*-loo

If you want to know more Fijian, look for A.J. Schutz's little book *Say It in Fijian* (Pacific Publications, Sydney), available at many bookstores and hotel boutiques.

FIJI HINDI

The common everyday language spoken among the Indians is a tongue peculiar to Fiji. Although it is based on Hindustani, in fact it is very different from that language as spoken in India. The Indians of Fiji, in fact, refer to it as Fiji Bat, or "Fiji talk," because it grew out of the need for a common language among the immigrants who came from various parts of the subcontinent and spoke some of the many languages and dialects found in India and Pakistan. Thus it includes words from Hindi, Urdu, Tamil Nadu, a variety of Indian dialects, and even English and Fijian.

Unlike the Fijians, who are likely to greet you with a "Bula," the Indians invariably address visitors in English. If you want to impress them, here are the greetings in Fiji Hindi:

English	Fiji Hindi	Pronunciation
hello and good-bye	namaste	na-*mas*-tay
how are you?	kaise?	ka-*ee*-say
good	accha	*ach*-cha
I'm okay	Thik hai	teak high
right or okay	rait	right

Jeff Siegel's slim handbook *Say It in Fiji Hindi* (Pacific Publications, Sydney) is available at many bookstores and hotel boutiques in Fiji.

5 Planning a Trip to Fiji

Given the size and diversity of the country, any trip to Fiji requires careful planning to avoid disappointment. Some visitors spend their entire vacation in Nadi, and while the tourism industry provides a host of activities to keep them busy, in my opinion those unfortunate souls miss the best parts of Fiji. After all, this is a country of more than 300 gorgeous islands, and not to experience more than one is a mistake. By and large, the main island of Viti Levu does not have the best beaches in Fiji, and where it does have good sands, the reef offshore is more walkable than swimmable, especially at low tide. In other words, look elsewhere for good beaches and the best diving.

THE REGIONS IN BRIEF

From a tourist's standpoint, Fiji is divided into several regions, each with its own special characteristics and appeal. Here's what each region has to offer.

Nadi Most visitors arrive at Nadi International Airport, a modern facility located among sugarcane fields on Viti Levu's dry western side. Known collectively as **Nadi,** this area is the focal point of much of Fiji's tourism industry, and it's where most tourists on package deals spend their time. There are a variety of hotels between the airport and hot, dusty, predominately Indian **Nadi Town,** whose main industry is tourism and where duty-free, souvenir, and handcraft merchants wait to part you from your dollars. None of the airport hotels is on the beach, and even at the Sheraton Fiji and The Regent of Fiji, the area's two large resorts, coastal mangrove forests make the beaches grey and the water offshore murky. There are many things to do in Nadi, but knowledgeable visitors with more than one or two days to spend in Fiji will consider it a transit stopover on the way to some-place else.

The Mamanucas Beckoning offshore, the **Mamanuca Islands** offer day cruises from Nadi and several offshore resorts of various sizes appealing to a broad spec-trum, from swinging singles to quieter couples and families. Generally speaking, they are in the driest part of Fiji, which means sunshine most of the time. Some are flat atolls so small you can walk around them in five minutes. Others are on hilly, grassy islands reminiscent of the Virgin Islands in the Caribbean. They are relatively close together, and most offer excursions to the others. They also are close to Nadi, so you don't have to spend much extra money or time to get there.

The Yasawas Other visitors join up with **Blue Lagoon Cruises** at its base in **Lautoka,** Fiji's second-largest city and its prime sugar-milling center. The cruises spend several days or a week in the **Yasawas,** a chain of gorgeous and unspoiled islands shooting off north of the Mamanucas. Like Moorea and Bora Bora in French Polynesia, the Yasawas are often used as movie sets. Two versions of *The Blue Lagoon* were filmed here, the latest starring Brooke Shields as the castaway schoolgirl. The Yasawas have two super-deluxe resorts and several establishments catering to backpackers.

The Coral Coast The **Queen's Road** runs around the south coast of Viti Levu through the **Coral Coast,** the first resort area in Fiji. This area has comfortable hotels, luxury resorts, and fire-walking Fijians, but the beaches here lead into very shallow lagoons, and most visitors staying on the "The Coast" these days prima-rily are package tourists from Australia. It's still a good choice for anyone who wants on-the-beach resort living while being able to see conveniently some of the country. Offshore, the island of **Vatulele** has one of the world's finest small resorts, and **Beqa** attracts divers from around the planet. Farther south, **Kadavu** and its Astrolabe Reef are becoming meccas for scuba divers.

Northern Viti Levu An alternative route to Suva, the **King's Road** runs from Lautoka through the Sugar Belt of northern Viti Levu, passing through the pre-dominately Indian towns of Ba and Tavua to **Rakiraki,** a Fijian village near the island's northernmost point and site of one of the country's few remaining colo-nial-era hotels. Jagged green mountains lend a gorgeous backdrop to the shoreline along the Rakiraki coast. Offshore, **Nananu-I-Ra Island** beckons with backpacker-style retreats and a moderately priced beach resort.

By the time you get there, all of the King's Road except about 30 miles through the central mountains should be paved. East of Rakiraki, it turns into deep, moun-tain-bounded **Viti Levu Bay,** one of the most beautiful parts of Fiji. From the head of the bay, the road then twists and turns its way through the mountains, following the Wainbuka River until it emerges near the east coast at Korovou. A left turn there takes you to Natovi Wharf; and a right, to Suva. In other words, it's possible to drive or take buses all the way around Viti Levu via the Queen's and King's Roads.

Suva The Queen's road goes on to **Suva** (pop. 85,000), Fiji's busy capital and one of the South Pacific's most cosmopolitan cities. Steamy Suva houses a fasci-nating mix of atmospheres and cultures. Remnants of Fiji's century as a British possession and the presence of so many Indians give the town a certain air of the colonial "Raj"—as if this were Agra or Bombay, not the boundary between Polynesia and Melanesia. On the other hand, Suva has modern high-rise buildings

Fiji Islands

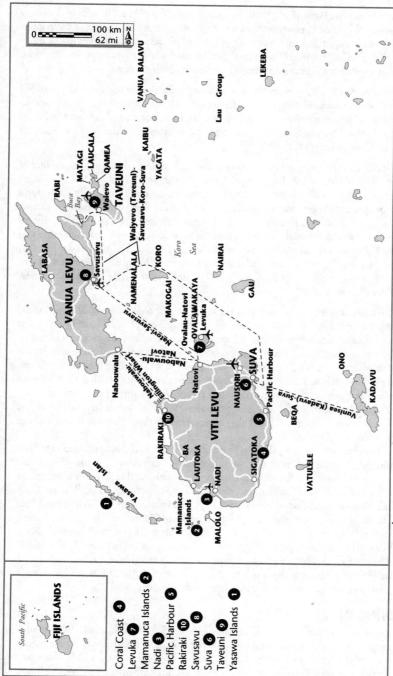

Airport ✈   Ferry - - -

1602

and lives at as fast a pace as will be found in the South Pacific west of Tahiti—
no surprise since in many respects it's the bustling economic center of the region.
The streets are filled with a melting-pot blend of Indians, Chinese, Fijians, other
South Pacific islanders, "Europeans" (a term used in Fiji to mean persons of white
skin regardless of geographic origin), and individuals of mixed race.

Ovalau & Levuka   From Suva, it's an easy excursion to the picturesque island
of **Ovalau** and its historic town of **Levuka,** which has changed little in appearance
since its days as a boisterous whaling port and the first capital of a united Fiji in
the 1800s. Few places in the South Pacific have retained their frontier facade as
has this living museum.

Northern Fiji   Vanua Levu, Taveuni, and their nearby islands are known locally
as "The North" since they comprise Fiji's Northern Province. Over on Vanua
Levu, a little town with the exotic name **Savusavu** lies nestled in one of the region's
most protected deep-water bays. It and the "Garden Isle" of **Taveuni** are throw-
backs to the old South Pacific, a land of copra plantations and small Fijian villages
tucked away in the bush. Travelers looking for a do-it-yourself soft adventure trip
into the past can take a local bus across Vanua Levu to Savusavu and a ferry on
to Taveuni. Both Savusavu and Taveuni have excellent places to stay, and there
are fine resorts off Vanua Levu and near Taveuni's north coast on **Matagi, Qamea,
Laucala,** and **Kaibu.**

Offshore Resorts   Fiji has one of the world's finest collections of offshore resorts,
small establishments with an island all to themselves. They all have lovely beach
settings and modern facilities, and without exception they are excellent places to
"get away from it all." The major drawback of any offshore resort, however, is that
you've done just that. You won't see much of Fiji while you're basking in the sun
on a tiny rock some 25 miles offshore. Consider them for what they have to
offer, but not as bases from which to explore the country. I have included the
offshore resorts in the following chapters along with the nearest large island. If you
decide to stay at one of them, I suggest you read all these chapters before making
your choice of resort.

Pay close attention to what I say about the owners and managers, and especially
the styles with which they run their operations. For example, if you don't enjoy
getting to know your fellow guests at sometimes raucous dinner parties, you might
not like Vatulele or Turtle Island resorts, but you might love The Wakaya Club
and Yasawa Island Lodge. If you like a large establishment with a lively, Club Med-
like ambience, you might prefer Mana Island and Plantation resorts. Many other
resorts offer peace, quiet, and few fellow guests. If you want to feel like a
houseguest at a rich person's private island, look no farther than Kaibu Island
Resort or Fiji Forbes. If you are taking the kids, Matagi Island is one of the best
small family resorts in the South Pacific, while nearby Qamea Beach Club doesn't
allow kids under 13 years old. In other words, choose carefully.

DIVING IN FIJI

Fiji is justly famous among divers as being the "Soft Coral Capital of the World"
because of its enormous number and variety of colorful soft corals. These species
grow well where moderate to heavy currents keep them fed. In turn, the corals
attract a host of fish. As one example, more than 35 species of angelfish and
butterfly fish swim in these waters.

Several of Fiji's most popular dive destinations are in Northern Fiji, especially the colorful Rainbow Reef and Great White Wall, both on Vanua Levu's barrier reef but within a few miles of Taveuni. The Great White Wall is covered from between 75 feet and 200 feet deep with pale lavender corals, which appear almost snow-white under water. Near Qamea and Matagi, off Taveuni, are the appropriately named Purple Wall, a straight drop from 30 to 80 feet, and Mariah's Cove, a small wall as colorful as the Rainbow Reef. Also in the north, Magic Mountain on the Namena barrier reef around Moody's Namena has hard corals on top and soft ones on the sides, which attract an enormous number of small fish and their predators.

Another popular site is Beqa Lagoon, easily reached by boat from Pacific Harbour, about 30 miles west of Suva. The soft corals in Beqa's Frigate Passage seem to fall over one another, and Side Streets has unusual orange coral.

The relatively undeveloped island of Kadavu is surrounded by the famous Astrolabe Reef, where holes in the coral attract volumes of fish and other sea life.

Even the heavily visited Mamanuca Islands off Nadi have their share of good sites, including The Pinnacle, a coral head rising 60 feet from the lagoon floor, and a W-shaped protrusion from the outer reef. A drawback for some divers is that they don't have the Mamanuca sites all to themselves.

All but a few resorts in Fiji have dive operations on site, as will be pointed out in the following chapters. Many of them have contacts in North America, as does the live-aboard dive ship *Matagi Princess II,* based in Northern Fiji.

THE BACKPACKERS' TRAIL

Fiji is the most popular destination in the South Pacific for young backpackers. The country is the least expensive of the island countries, and it offers a wide range of hostel accommodation, including establishments operated by Fijian villagers. After one night in a Nadi hostel, backpackers will have no trouble picking up the scent of the trail. In general, here's how it goes:

Popular side trips from Nadi are to Mana Island and Beachcomber Island Resort, both in the nearby Mamanucas, and longer excursions to Tavewa and Waya islands in the Yasawas. Mana and the Yasawas have become increasingly popular in recent years, since they offer basic accommodation in or near Fijian villages.

From Nadi, the traditional circuit swings around the north side of Viti Levu to Nananu-I-Ra, an island off Rakiraki that is equipped with basic accommodation (take your own food) and occasionally a shortage of water. After a few days on the lovely beaches there, take the ferry from Ellington Wharf to Nabouwalu on Vanua Levu, where you connect by bus to Labasa and on to Savusavu. From there, a bus-ferry combination goes to Taveuni, one of the hottest backpackers' destinations. From Taveuni, you can get a ferry to Suva. The city is interesting, but as a backpackers' destination, it pales in comparison to Levuka on Ovalau, reached by daily bus-ferry. There are no beaches on Ovalau, but you can stay on Leleuvia, a tiny islet between Ovalau and Viti Levu.

SUGGESTED ITINERARIES

These are *suggested* itineraries. I have designed them primarily with sightseeing in mind. Since Fiji is a relatively large country with much to see and do, your actual itinerary obviously will depend on your particular interests—water sports or cultural tours, lounging on a beach or sightseeing.

Many people stop in Fiji for a few days on their way to or from Australia or New Zealand. If you're one of them, don't cut your visit too short. Give yourself at least enough time to learn something about the islands and their peoples.

If your ambition is to rest on a tropical beach and not do much else, choose an offshore resort rather than staying on the "mainland" of Viti Levu. Frankly, their beaches are better than what you will find on the big island.

The usual "circuit" goes something like this: Nadi; Coral Coast; Suva; day trip to Levuka, Taveuni, or Savusavu; return to Nadi. An option in the dry season (May to September) is to drive from Nadi to Suva on the King's Road around northern Viti Levu, overnighting in Rakiraki, then return to Nadi via the Queen's Road.

If You Have 1 Day

Visit your hotel desk early to see what's happening. If nothing out of the ordinary catches your eye, spend the morning touring the Mamanuca Islands on the *Island Express*. Have lunch in Nadi Town, quickly shop for handcrafts, then take the open-air local bus to Lautoka. The bus stops at the market, so look there first for handcrafts. Stroll around the business district, including the duty-free shops. During the evening, take in a *meke*, the traditional Fijian feast and dance, at one of the Nadi hotels. (If shopping doesn't appeal, spend the entire day at a resort in the Mamanucas.)

If You Have 3 Days

Unless you can afford a room at the Regent or Sheraton, which are on Denaru Beach (see "Where to Stay" in the chapter on Nadi and Viti Levu), consider staying one night in Nadi and then moving to the Coral Coast. You'll be on the beach and closer to Suva.

Day 1 Take a day cruise to one of the Mamanuca resorts, where you can snorkel, swim, play with the water toys, and have lunch.

Day 2 Take a day trip to Suva, which usually includes stops at the cultural centers at Pacific Harbour or Orchid Island. Do your handcraft shopping in Suva, and don't miss the Fiji Museum.

Day 3 Take a land excursion from Nadi, such as the Nausori Highlands.

If You Have 7 Days
Blue Lagoon Cruise

Days 1–4 Take a Blue Lagoon Cruise through the Yasawa Islands.
You will see a meke and eat Fijian food, so on night four (back in Nadi), eat curry.

Day 5 Now that you're rested up, drive to Suva, stopping at either the Pacific Harbour or Orchid Island cultural centers on the way. Tour the town, including the Fiji Museum. Do your handcraft shopping. Overnight in Suva.

Day 6 Take a day trip to Levuka, Fiji's first capital.

Day 7 Morning flight back to Nadi, followed by a day of rest or one of the tours described in the chapter on Nadi and Viti Levu.

No Cruise

Day 1 Do what I recommend above for a one-day visit. Overnight in Nadi.

Day 2 Make your way by bus, taxi, or rental car to the Coral Coast. Overnight on the coast.

Day 3 Proceed on to Suva in the morning; tour the town and the Fiji Museum. Overnight in Suva.

Day 4   Take a day trip to Levuka, Fiji's first capital.

Days 5-7   Fly to Taveuni and spend the remainder of your holiday seeing the main island and relaxing at an offshore resort.

Day 7   Return to Nadi. If you have time, take one of the tours mentioned in the chapter on Nadi and Viti Levu.

Whirlwind

I actually did this seven-day whirlwind swing around Fiji once, so I know it can be done. You won't have much time to do much other than sightsee.

Day 1   Catch an early-morning flight from Nadi to Savusavu. Tour the town in the morning; spend the afternoon swimming and relaxing. Overnight in Savusavu.

Day 2   Morning flight to Taveuni (about 20 minutes). Tour the island and have lunch; then overnight on Taveuni or at one of the resorts on Matagi, Qamea, or Laucala.

Day 3   Morning flight to Suva. Tour the city. Overnight in Suva.

Day 4   Day trip to Levuka. Overnight in Suva.

Day 5   Drive the Coral Coast, stopping off at Orchid Island or Pacific Harbour Cultural Centre and Market Place. Overnight on the Coral Coast.

Day 6   Spend the morning resting on the Coral Coast, then drive to Nadi.

Day 7   Take the *Island Express* tour of the Mamanucas during the morning. Shop in Nadi Town or Lautoka during the afternoon.

If You Have 2 Weeks

Days 1-4   Take one of Blue Lagoon Cruises' short trips through the Yasawa Islands.

Day 5   Drive the Coral Coast, stopping off at Orchid Island or Pacific Harbour cultural centers. Overnight on the Coral Coast.

⭐ Frommer's Favorite Fiji Experiences

Cruising. One of my more pleasant tasks is to visit the offshore resorts in the lovely Mamanuca Islands; the best part is getting there on one of the cruise boats operating out of Nadi. Once I had the flu on a Blue Lagoon Cruise and still loved it.

Meeting the People. The Fijians are justly renowned for their friendliness to strangers, and the Indians are as well-educated and informed as anyone in the South Pacific. Together, these two peoples make for fascinating conversations at every turn.

Touring Levuka. Having grown up in Edenton, which still looks very much like it did as North Carolina's colonial capital in the 1700s, I feel almost nostalgic in Levuka, which hasn't changed much since it played the same role in Fiji.

The North. The old South Pacific of copra plantation and trading boat days still lives in Savusavu and Taveuni. True, it rains more up there in Fiji's "North," but that makes the steep hills lushly green. The diving and snorkeling here are absolutely world class.

Offshore Resorts. Nothing relaxes me more than running sand between my toes at one of Fiji's small get-away-from-it-all resorts. I am particularly fond of those in Northern Fiji, such as the moderately priced Matagi, Qamea, and Moody's Namenalala.

Day 6   Spend the morning resting on the Coral Coast, then drive to Suva (plan to arrive before dark).

Day 7   Tour Suva, including the Fiji Museum. Do your handcraft shopping.

Day 8   Take a day trip to Levuka, Fiji's first capital.

Day 9   Fly to Taveuni on a morning Air Fiji flight. Tour the island and overnight there or at Matagi, Qamea, or Laucala offshore resorts.

Day 10   Spend the day at leisure.

Day 11   Take a morning flight to Savusavu. Tour the town and overnight there.

Day 12   Spend the day at leisure.

Day 13   Fly to Nadi and overnight there.

Day 14   Take one of the Nadi tours mentioned and complete any unfinished handcraft shopping.

6 Visitor Information & Entry Requirements

VISITOR INFORMATION

The **Fiji Visitors Bureau,** G.P.O. Box 92, Suva, Fiji Islands, provides maps, brochures, and other materials from the bureau's head office in a restored colonial house at the corner of Thomson and Scott streets in the heart of Suva (☎ 302433, fax 300970) and at its small office in the international arrivals concourse at Nadi International Airport (☎ 722433).

Other "FVB" offices are:

United States and Canada, 5777 West Century Boulevard, Suite 220, Los Angeles, CA 90045 (☎ 310/568-1616 or 800/932-3454, fax 213/670-2318).

Australia, Level 12, St. Martins Tower, 31 Market St., Sydney, NSW 2000 (☎ 02/264-3399, fax 02/264-3060), and 620 St. Kilda Rd., Suite 204, Melbourne, VIC 3000 (☎ 03/525-2322, fax 03/510-3650).

New Zealand, 48 High St., 5th Floor, P.O. Box 1179, Auckland (☎ 09/373-2133, fax 09/309-4720).

Japan, NOA Building, 14th Floor, 3-5, 2 Chome, Azabuudai, Minato-ku, Tokyo 106 (☎ 03/3587-2038, fax 03/3587-2563).

Before you leave Nadi International Airport, drop in on the Fiji Visitors Bureau office and pick up a copy of *Spotlight on Nadi* and *Fiji Magic,* two informative publications aimed at the tourist market. They will tell you what is going on during your visit.

You can also call **Vodafone's Fiji** (☎ 902100), a 24-hour service providing the latest about accommodation, activities, restaurants, sporting events, transportation schedules, and other information. Each call costs F60¢ (42¢) a minute.

Warning: Some merchants and travel agents in Fiji are absolutely shameless when it comes to ripping off someone else's trade name or identity. When you see "Tourist Information Centre" in Nadi or elsewhere, it more than likely will be a travel agent or tour operator, whose staff invariably will steer you to their products. The only official, non-profit tourist information centers are operated by the Fiji Visitors Bureau, at the Suva and Nadi locations given above.

ENTRY REQUIREMENTS

Visitor permits good for stays of up to 30 days are issued upon arrival to citizens of Commonwealth countries, the United States, and most other Western nations, provided they have valid passports, onward or return airline tickets, and enough money or proof of finances to support them during their stay. Persons wishing to remain longer must apply for extensions from the Immigration Department, whose primary offices are at the Nadi International Airport terminal (☎ 722454) and in the Labour Department building on Victoria Parade in downtown Suva (☎ 211775).

Vaccinations are not required unless you have been in a yellow fever or cholera area shortly before arriving in Fiji.

Customs allowances are 200 cigarettes, two liters of liquor, beer or wine, and F\$50 (\$35) worth of other goods (which translates into a third liter of liquor) in addition to personal belongings. Pornography is prohibited. Firearms and nonprescription narcotic drugs are strictly prohibited and subject to heavy fines and jail terms. Pets will be quarantined. Any fresh fruits and vegetables must be declared and are subject to inspection and fumigation.

For more information, contact the **Embassy of Fiji,** Suite 240, 2233 Wisconsin Ave., NW, Washington, DC 20007 (☎ 202/337-8320, fax 202/337-1996), or the **Permanent Mission of Fiji to the United Nations,** One UN Plaza, 26th Floor, New York, NY 10017 (☎ 202/355-7316, fax 202/319-1896). Fiji also has diplomatic missions in London, England; Canberra and Sydney, Australia; Wellington and Auckland, New Zealand; Brussels, Belgium; Tokyo, Japan; Kuala Lumpur, Malaysia; and Port Moresby, Papua New Guinea. Check your local phone book.

7 Money

The national currency is the Fiji dollar, which is divided into 100 cents and trades independently on the foreign exchange markets. At the time of writing it was worth about U.S. 70¢. It has been worth within a few cents of the Australian dollar since the 1987 coups. The exchange rate is not published in American newspapers, but someone at the Fiji Visitors Bureau offices (see "Visitor Information," above) usually knows the approximate value.

What Things Cost in Fiji	U.S. $
Taxi from airport to Nadi Town	4.20
Taxi from airport to Sheraton & Regent resorts	10.50
Bus from airport to Nadi Town	.25
All-inclusive double room at Wakaya Club (very expensive)	875.00
Room at Regent of Fiji (expensive)	194.00
Room at Tanoa International Hotel (moderate)	112.00
Room at Sandalwood Inn (inexpensive)	24.00
Lunch for one at The Edge (moderate)	10.50
Lunch for one at Coffee Lounge (inexpensive)	3.20
Dinner for one at Chefs The Restaurant (expensive)	42.00
Dinner for one at Tiko's (moderate)	21.00
Dinner for one at Mama's Pizza Inn (inexpensive)	4.55
Beer	1.40
Coca-Cola	.70
Roll of ASA 100 Kodacolor film, 36 exposures	4.55

The Fiji & U.S. Dollars

At this writing, F$1 = approximately U.S. 70¢, the rate of exchange used to calculate the U.S. dollar prices given in the Fiji chapters. This rate may change by the time you visit, so use the following table only as a guide.

F$	U.S. $	F$	U.S. $
.25	.18	15.00	12.60
.50	.35	20.00	14.00
.75	.53	25.00	17.50
1.00	.70	30.00	21.00
2.00	1.40	35.00	24.50
3.00	2.10	40.00	28.00
4.00	2.80	45.00	31.50
5.00	3.50	50.00	35.00
6.00	4.20	75.00	52.50
7.00	4.90	100.00	70.00
8.00	5.60	125.00	87.50
9.00	6.30	150.00	105.00
10.00	7.00	200.00	140.00

The Fiji dollar is abbreviated "FID" by the banks and airlines, but I use **F$** in this chapter. A few establishments quote their rates in U.S. dollars, indicated here by **U.S. $**.

Like their islander counterparts elsewhere in the South Pacific, Fijians may take offense if you try to haggle over a price. On the other hand, most Fiji Indian merchants will expect you to do just that (see "Best Buys" in the "Nadi & Viti Levu" chapter).

The Fiji government instituted currency export controls in the wake of many Indians' fleeing the country after the 1987 coups. As a practical matter, the controls do not affect visitors from overseas as long as they do not try to smuggle large sums of money out of the country. If someone approaches you with such a proposition, turn and walk away.

How to Get Local Currency An ANZ Bank branch in the international arrivals concourse at Nadi International Airport is open 24 hours a day, seven days a week. It charges a F$2 ($1.40) fee for each transaction; neither ANZ's other branches nor any other bank charges such a fee.

ANZ Bank, Westpac Bank, National Bank of Fiji, and Bank of Baroda all have offices throughout the country where currency and traveler's checks can be exchanged. Bank of Hawaii has offices with ATM machines in Nadi Town and Suva (its operations are more American than the others, which subscribe to Australian and New Zealand banking practices). Banking hours nationwide are Monday to Thursday from 9:30am to 3pm and Friday from 9:30am to 4pm. Thomas Cook Travel Service, 21 Thomson St., Suva, will cash traveler's checks from 8:30am to noon on Saturday.

ANZ Bank, Westpac Bank, and Bank of Hawaii will make cash advances against MasterCard and Visa credit cards. All the banks can arrange international transfers of funds.

Credit Cards   American Express, Visa, Diners Club, and MasterCard are accepted by the larger hotels, car-rental firms, travel and tour companies, duty-free shops, and some restaurants.

8   When to Go

THE CLIMATE

During most of the year, the prevailing southeast trade winds temper Fiji's warm, humid, tropical climate. Average high temperatures range from 83°F during the austral winter (June to September) to 88°F during the summer months (December to March). Evenings are in the warm and comfortable 70s throughout the year.

The islands receive the most rain during the summer, but the amount depends on which side of each island the measurement is taken. The north and west coasts tend to be drier, and the east and south coasts wetter. Nadi, on the west side of Viti Levu, gets considerably less rain than does Suva, on the southeast side (some 200 inches a year). Consequently, most of Fiji's resorts are on the western side of Viti Levu. Even during the wetter months, however, periods of intense tropical sunshine usually follow the rain showers.

Fiji is in the heart of the South Pacific cyclone belt and receives its share of hurricanes between November and April. Fiji's Meteorological Service is excellent at tracking hurricanes and issuing timely warnings, and the local travel industry is very adept at preparing for them. I've been through the excitement of a few Fiji cyclones, and I never let the thought of one keep me from returning every chance I get.

EVENTS

The annual **Hibiscus Festival,** held in Suva during the first week of August, features a plethora of events, including traditional dance shows, parades, and the Hibiscus Ball. A similar **Bula Festival** is held in Nadi during the middle of July.

A colorful military ceremony marks the **changing of the guard** at Government House in Suva during the first week of each month.

Hindus celebrate the **Diwali,** or "Festival of Lights," in late October or early November, when they light their houses with oil lamps and candles.

HOLIDAYS

Banks, government offices, and most private businesses are closed for New Year's Day, Good Friday, Easter Saturday, Easter Monday, National Youth Day in March, the Monday closest to June 14 (in honor of Queen Elizabeth's Birthday), Ratu Sukuna Day (May 30), the Monday closest to October 10 (for Fiji Day, in honor of the country's independence), the Monday closest to November 14 (in honor of Prince Charles's Birthday), The Prophet Mohammed's Birthday (August 15), Diwali in late October or early November, Christmas Day, and December 26 (for Boxing Day). Some businesses may also close for various Hindu and Muslim holy days. Banks take an additional holiday on the first Monday in August.

SUNDAY IN FIJI

Prior to the 1987 coups, Fiji was relatively open on Sunday. One of the first things Colonel Rabuka did to curry favor with his Methodist minister and chiefly allies was to promulgate a tough Sunday decree, known as the Sunday Ban. The hotels and other tourist facilities were permitted to operate as usual, but the country was shut down as tight as Tonga from midnight Saturday to midnight Sunday. Needless to say, the non-Christian Indians didn't like it, nor did the many Fijians who had difficulty getting to church on time because no buses or taxis were running on Sunday morning.

The Sunday decree has since been relaxed so that most taxis can haul passengers. The buses in Nadi and Suva operate a truncated schedule. The airlines have full schedules of flights. Hotel restaurants and bars have been open all along; now restaurants licensed to sell alcoholic beverages can be open from noon to 10pm.

Moves are made from time to time to abolish the ban (a 1995 effort lost by one vote in the Fiji Senate). Things still move slowly on Sunday, and you should think of making it a time to stay around the hotel, take an excursion to an offshore resort, or be "in transit." During my recent visits, I have made it a practice to spend a Sunday driving from Nadi to Suva.

9 Getting There & Getting Around

GETTING THERE

Major airlines flying to Fiji from North America are **Air New Zealand** (☎ 310/642-0196 in Los Angeles or 800/262-1234); **Air Pacific** (☎ 800/227-4446); **Qantas Airways** (☎ 800/227-4500); and **Canadian Airlines International** (☎ 800/426-7000). Air New Zealand, Air Pacific, Polynesian Airlines, Royal Tongan Airlines, Solomon Airlines, Air Nauru, Air Marshall Islands, and Air Calédonie International all have regional services to other South Pacific islands.

Nadi International Airport Most international flights arrive at and depart from Nadi International Airport, about seven miles north of Nadi Town. A few flights arrive from Auckland, Western Samoa, and Tonga at Nausori Airport, some 12 miles from Suva on the opposite side of the island. Both airports are used for domestic flights. They are the only lighted airstrips in the country, which means you don't fly domestically after dark. Since many international flights arrive during the night, at least a one-night stay-over in Nadi likely will be necessary before leaving for another island.

Arriving passengers may purchase duty-free items at a shop in the baggage claim area before clearing Customs (imported liquor is expensive in Fiji, so if you drink, don't hesitate to buy three bottles).

A large sign on the wall behind the Immigration counters lists all the hotels in the Nadi area, their present room rates, and the taxi fares to get to them.

After clearing Customs, you emerge onto an open-air concourse lined on both sides by airline offices, travel and tour companies, car-rental firms, and a 24-hour-a-day branch of the **ANZ Bank.**

The **Fiji Visitors Bureau** has an office just to the left, and the friendly staff will give advice, supply information, and even make a hotel reservation for the cost of the phone call. Ask them for a map of Fiji and copies of *Spotlight on Nadi* and *Fiji Magic.* Brochures from every hotel and activity in Fiji are on display. The bureau's airport office is open during regular business hours (see "Fast Facts: Fiji," below) and for at least an hour after the arrival of all major international flights.

Touts for the inexpensive hotels will be milling about, offering free transportation to their establishments. The larger hotels will also have transportation available for their guests.

Taxis will be lined up to the right outside the concourse (see "Getting Around," below, for fares to the hotels).

Local buses to Nadi and Lautoka pass the airport on the Queen's Road every day; walk straight out of the concourse, across the parking lot, and through the gate to the road. Driving in Fiji is on the left, so buses heading for Nadi and its hotels stop on the opposite side, next to Raffles' Gateway Hotel; those going to Lautoka stop on the airport side of the road. You will see the covered bus stands.

The Nadi domestic terminal and the international check-in counters are to the right of the arrival concourse as you exit Customs (or to the left if you are arriving from the main road). An inexpensive **snack bar** can be found between the two terminals.

The Airport Security counter outside the snack bar provides **baggage storage** ("left luggage") for F$1 to F$2 (70¢ to $1.50) a day, depending on the size. The counter is open 24 hours every day. The hotels all have baggage-storage rooms and will keep your extra stuff for free.

A **post office,** in a separate building across the entry road from the main terminal, is open Monday to Friday from 8am to 4pm.

Departing   Passengers leaving the country must pay a **departure tax** of F$20 ($14)—in Fiji currency—at a desk to the right of the check-in counters (check in first, since you get your boarding pass stamped). There is no departure tax for domestic flights.

Once you have cleared Immigration, you enter the modern, air-conditioned international departure lounge, which has a bar, showers, and the largest duty-free shops in the South Pacific. Duty-free prices, however, are higher than you'll pay elsewhere in the country, and there is no bargaining.

Nausori Airport (Suva)   Suva is served by **Nausori Airport,** on the flat plains of the Rewa River delta about 12 miles from downtown. The small terminal has a snack bar but few other amenities. Taxis between Nausori and downtown Suva cost about F$16.50 ($11.50) each way. Nausori Taxi & Bus Service (☎ 477583) has regularly scheduled bus service between the airport and the city for F$2 ($1.40) per person each way. Look for the buses at the curb across from the baggage-claim platform. The company's Suva terminal is in the Suva Travelodge parking lot on Victoria Parade. Passengers departing on international flights must pay their F$20 ($14) departure tax to the check-in clerks. There is no tax on domestic flights. See "Getting There" in the "Suva & Levuka" chapter for more information.

GETTING AROUND

Fiji has an extensive and reliable transportation network of airlines, rental cars, taxis, ferries, and both long-distance and local buses. This section deals primarily with getting from one island or major area to another; see the "Getting Around" sections in the next chapters for details on transportation within the local areas.

BY PLANE   The government-owned **Air Pacific** (☎ 722499 from anywhere in Fiji) has a few flights between Nadi and Suva. The one-way fare is F$57 ($40) if purchased as part of an international ticket and F$63 ($44) if bought in Fiji. Air Pacific has an office in the international arrivals concourse at Nadi International

Airport. Its Suva office is in the CML Building on Victoria Parade (☎ 304388). It also has an office in Los Angeles (☎ 800/227-4446).

Air Fiji (☎ 722521 in Nadi, 313666 in Suva) flies from Nadi to most other destinations in the country. There is one morning and one afternoon flight between Suva and Levuka, making possible a day trip to the old capital. Air Fiji also has service from Suva to Savusavu and Taveuni. Air Fiji's main office is on Victoria Parade in Suva, next to the Pizza Hut. It also has an office in the international concourse at Nadi International Airport.

Air Fiji has a **"Discover Fiji Pass"** that permits visitors to fly on any four of its flights during a 30-day period for U.S. $199 and any five flights for U.S. $249. Restrictions apply. For information, see a travel agent or contact Air Promotion Services, Air Fiji's representative in Los Angeles (☎ 310/338-0708).

Sunflower Airlines (☎ 723016 in Nadi, 315755 in Suva, or 808/531-4496 in Honolulu) has flights from Nadi to the tourist destinations, including Malololailai (Plantation Island and Musket Cove resorts) and Mana Islands in the Mamanucas. One-way fare from Nadi to Malololailai is F$27.50 ($19); one-way to Mana Island is F$40 ($28).

One-way **fares** on both Air Fiji and Sunflower Airlines are F$66 ($46.20) between Nadi and Suva, F$96 ($67) between Nadi and Savusavu, and F$116 ($81) between Nadi and Taveuni.

Air Fiji and Sunflower flights from Nadi to Taveuni stop in Savusavu going and coming, so don't let an uninformed travel agent book you back to Nadi or Suva in order to get from Taveuni to Savusavu (it has been known to happen).

Turtle Airways (☎ 722988) flies small seaplanes from Nadi Bay to the offshore resorts all over Fiji, on a charter basis.

Baggage allowances may be 10kg (22 pounds) instead of the 20kg (44 pounds) allowed on international flights. Check with the airlines to avoid showing up with too much luggage.

Remember to **reconfirm** both your international and domestic return flights as soon as possible after arriving at your destination, and to check in when the airlines tell you to (the planes sometimes arrive and depart a few minutes early).

BY RENTAL CAR Rental cars are relatively expensive in Fiji. Each company has its own pricing policy, with frequent discounts, special deals, and some give-and-take bargaining over long-term and long-distance use. All major companies, and a few not so major, have offices in the commercial concourse at Nadi International Airport, so it's easy to shop around. Most are open seven days a week, some for 24 hours a day. Give careful consideration to how many kilometers you will drive; it's 197km (118 miles) from Nadi Airport to Suva, so an unlimited kilometer rate could work to your advantage.

All renters must be at least 21 years old, and a few companies require them to be at least 25.

Even though your home **insurance** policy may cover any damages that occur in Fiji, you must pay out of your own pocket and file a claim when you get home. Since that can be an enormous hassle, I strongly recommend local coverage when you rent a car. Give close attention to the insurance offered, however, for it may not cover damages that occur off the paved roads. Some policies even require you to pay the first F$500 ($350) or more of damages in any event.

I have found **Avis** (☎ 722233, or 800/331-1212 in the U.S. for reservations) to have the newest and best maintained fleet (the Toyota dealer is the local agent).

Rates start at F$55 ($38.50) a day plus F33¢ (23¢) per kilometer, or F$88 ($61.50) a day with unlimited kilometers. Add another F$18 ($12.50) a day for full insurance coverage. In addition to the office at Nadi Airport, Avis can be found in Suva (☎ 313833), Korolevu on the Coral Coast (☎ 530176), Nausori Airport (☎ 478936), and at several hotels.

Other international firms in Fiji are **Budget Rent-A-Car** (☎ 722735, or 800/527-0700 in U.S.); **Hertz** (☎ 723466 or 800/654-3131); and **Thrifty Car Rental** (☎ 722935 in Nadi or 800/367-2277 in the U.S.), which is handled in Fiji by Rosie The Travel Service.

Khan's Rental Cars (☎ 790617), the largest local company, is affiliated with Network Rentals of Australia. Other local operators include **Roxy Rentals** (☎ 722763), **Satellite Rentals** (☎ 721957), **Central Rent-A-Car** (☎ 722711), and **Sharmas Rent-A-Car** (☎ 701055).

Driving Rules   Your valid home driver's license will be honored in Fiji. Driving is on the **left-hand side** of the road, not on the right as in North America and Europe. **Seat belts** are mandatory. **Speed limits** are 80kmph (48 m.p.h.) on the open road and 50kmph (30 m.p.h.) in the towns and built-up areas.

Driving under the influence of alcohol or other drugs is a criminal offense in Fiji, and the police frequently throw up road blocks and administer Breathalyzer tests to all drivers.

You must **stop for pedestrians** in all marked crosswalks.

Most **roads** in Fiji are narrow, poorly maintained, and often crooked. Not all drivers are well-trained, experienced, or skilled, and some of them (including bus drivers) go much too fast for the conditions. Consequently, **drive defensively** at all times. **Always be alert** for potholes, landslides, hairpin curves, and various stray animals (cows and horses a very real danger, especially at night). Frankly, I try not to drive in Fiji after dark.

Also watch out for speed bumps known in Fiji as **road humps;** many villages have them, and most are poorly marked with small black and white roadside posts. You will be upon them before you see them. They are large enough to do serious damage to the bottom of your car, which no local rental insurance covers.

The Queen's Road is paved between Suva and Lautoka, and the King's Road is sealed except for a 30-mile stretch through the central mountains. Most other roads, including the unpaved portion of the King's Road, can be impassable during periods of heavy rain. Be very careful when coming down a hill on an unpaved road, as cars can easily skid on loose dirt and gravel.

Gasoline (petrol) is readily available, even on Sunday, at Shell, Mobil, and BP service stations in all the main towns. When I was there it was selling for F85¢ (60¢) a liter, or about $2.30 for an American-size gallon.

For information about road maps, see "Maps" under "Fast Facts: Fiji," below.

DISTANCES & TAXI FARES

Following are distances from Nadi International Airport via the Queens Road. The taxi fares are approximate; use the amounts given for guidance and bargaining.

From Nadi Airport to:	Km	Miles	Approx. Taxi Fare
Tanoa/Fiji Mocambo Hotels	1.3	.8	F$2.50 ($1.75)
Skylodge Hotel	3.3	2.0	F$3.00 ($2.10)

From Nadi Airport to:	Km	Miles	Approx. Taxi Fare
Dominion/Sandalwood Inn	5.2	3.1	F$4.00 ($2.80)
Regent and Sheraton	15.0	9.3	F$16.50 ($11.50)
Nadi Town	9.0	5.4	F$6.00 ($4.20)
Fijian Resort	60.0	36.0	F$40.00 ($28.00)
Sigatoka	70.0	42.0	F$45.00 ($31.50)
The Reef Resort	78.0	46.8	F$50.00 ($35.00)
Tambua Sands	88.8	53.2	F$50.00 ($35.00)
Hideaway Resort	92.0	55.2	F$50.00 ($35.00)
The Naviti	97.0	58.2	F$60.00 ($42.00)
The Warwick Fiji	104.0	62.4	F$60.00 ($42.00)
Pacific Harbour	148.0	88.8	F$85.00 ($59.50)
Orchid Island	182.0	109.2	F$90.00 ($63.00)
Suva	197.0	118.2	F$110.00 ($77.00)

BY BUS Buses are plentiful and inexpensive in Fiji, and it's possible to go all the way around Viti Levu on them. I did it recently by taking the Queen's Coach from Nadi to Suva one morning, an express to Rakiraki the next afternoon, then another express to Lautoka and a local back to Nadi.

Fiji Express (☎ 722811 in Nadi, 312287 in Suva) is the only air-conditioned "tourist class" express bus operating between Suva and Nadi Airport. It begins its daily runs at the Suva Travelodge at 8am, stops at the major hotels along the Queen's Road, and arrives at Nadi about 12:30pm. The return trip begins at 1:30pm, with arrival in Suva about 6pm. Fares run up to F$25 ($17.50), depending on how far you go. Book at any hotel tour desk or the UTC office at Nadi Airport.

Queen's Coach (☎ 477268 in Nausori) is a non-air-conditioned but comfortable express bus that leaves Nadi Airport daily at 7:30am, stops for pickups at the Nadi area hotels and for morning tea at the Hideaway Resort on the Coral Coast, and arrives in Suva about noon. It departs for the return trip from the Suva Travelodge at 4:10pm, from the seawall opposite the municipal handcraft markets at 4:30pm, with arrival back at Nadi about 8pm. Maximum one-way fare is F$12.50 ($9). Book at any hotel tour desk.

Sunset Express (☎ 720266 in Nadi, 322811 in Suva) has non-air-conditioned buses twice a day between Lautoka and Suva, with stops at Nadi Airport and Sigatoka. These usually leave Nadi Airport Monday to Saturday at 9:50am and 3:55pm, with arrival in Suva at 1:35 and 7:20pm. The return trips depart Suva at 8:45am and 4pm, getting back to Nadi Airport at 12:30 and 7:45pm. The Nadi–Suva fare is F$8 ($5.50). Sunset Express has an office on the second floor of the Nadi Airport arrivals concourse.

Pacific Transport Ltd. (☎ 700044 in Nadi, 304366 in Suva) has several express and local buses between Lautoka and Suva from Monday to Saturday via the Queen's Road. They all stop at the domestic terminal at Nadi Airport and the markets at Nadi Town, Sigatoka, and Navua. The Fiji Visitors Bureau usually has schedules at its offices. The express buses take about four hours between Nadi and Suva, compared to five hours on the local "stages." All these buses cater to local residents, do not take reservations, and have no air conditioning. The Nadi-to-Suva fare is about F$7 ($5), express or local.

Sunbeam Transport Ltd. (☎ 662822 in Lautoka, 382122 in Suva), **Reliance Transport Bus Service** (☎ 663059 in Lautoka, 382296 in Suva), and **Akbar Buses Ltd.** (☎ 694760 in Rakiraki) have express and local service between Lautoka and Suva via the King's Road. The Fiji Visitors Bureau may have their schedules. If not, ask around the local markets. The Lautoka–Suva fare is about F$10 ($7).

Fume-belching **local buses** use the produce markets as their terminals, but they'll stop anywhere if you signal the driver from the side of the road. Instead of glass, most have side windows made of canvas panels that are rolled down during inclement weather (they usually fly out the sides and flap in the wind like great skirts).

Buses run every few minutes along the Queen's Road between Lautoka and Nadi Town, passing the airport and most of the hotels and restaurants along the way.

BY TAXI Taxis are as abundant in Fiji as taxi meters are scarce outside of Suva. Some of the Nadi Airport taxi drivers have allegedly taken advantage of naive tourists, so make sure to settle on a fare to your destination before setting out. Some will complain about short fares and will badger you for more business later on during your stay; politely ignore these entreaties. In Suva, make sure the meter is turned on. See the distance chart for approximate taxi fares for destinations between Nadi Airport and Suva.

In Nadi and on the Coral Coast, you will see the same taxi drivers stationed outside your hotel every day. Usually they are paid on a salaried rather than a fare basis, so they may be willing to spend more time than usual showing you around.

"Share taxis" or "rolling taxis"—those not otherwise occupied—will pick up passengers at bus stops and charge the bus fare. They are particularly good value on long-distance trips. A taxi from Suva, for example, will stop by the Nadi Town market and pick up a load of passengers at the bus fare rather than drive back to the capital empty. Ask around the local market bus stops if share taxis are available. You'll meet some wonderful Fijians that way.

BY FERRY As an alternative to flying, you can take the *Drodrolagi* (☎ 661500 in Lautoka), a 60-passenger hydrofoil catamaran that virtually races at upwards of 40 knots from Lautoka to Savusavu. It departs Lautoka Monday to Saturday at 7:30am, arriving at Savusavu at 11:30, the return voyage leaves Savusavu at 5:30pm. One-way fares are F$55 ($38.50). Reservations are a very good idea. You can get away with pronouncing the boat's name "Dron-dro-langi," which means "Rainbow" in Fijian.

Consort Shipping Lines (☎ 302877 in Suva) has service between Suva, Koro, Savusavu, and Taveuni. Its roll-on, roll-off ferry normally leaves Suva at 5am on Wednesday and 10pm on Saturday for two-day runs out to Savusavu, stopping at Koro Island on the way. Once a week it goes on to Taveuni. It turns around at Savusavu or Taveuni and repeats the same stops in reverse order back to Suva. One-way deck-class fares from Suva are F$33 ($23) to Savusavu, and F$37.50 ($26) to Taveuni. Double the fares for round-trips. The company's main ticketing office is in the Dominion Arcade behind the Fiji Visitor's Bureau in downtown Suva.

Patterson Brothers Shipping Co. Ltd. (☎ 315644 in Suva, 661173 in Lautoka) operates Fiji Sea-Road Service, a combination of buses and ferries on three main routes. One goes by bus from Nadi to Ellington Wharf on northern Viti Levu, then by ferry to Nabouwalu on Vanua Levu. A second runs by bus from

Suva to Natovi Wharf on eastern Viti Levu, then by ferry to Nabouwalu. Buses connect Nabouwalu to Labasa. A third route is by bus from Suva to Natovi Wharf, then by ferry direct to Savusavu. A bus-ferry combination then goes on to Taveuni. One-way fare on these routes is about F$34 ($24) per adult. The company also connects Suva to Ovalau via Natovi Wharf. That fare is about F$19 ($13.50). Contact Patterson Brothers for more information. Its main ticketing office is in Suite ¹/₂, Epworth House, Nina Street, Suva.

Emosi's Express Shipping (☎ 313366 in Suva, 440057 in Levuka) provides service between Suva, the backpacker's resort on Leleuvia Island, and Levuka on Monday, Wednesday, Friday, and Saturday. Round-trip Suva–Leleuvia fare is F$30 ($21). Round-trip Suva–Levuka is F$36 ($25).

BY GUIDED TOUR   One way to see much of Fiji without having to make your own arrangements is to take an eight-day, seven-night Discover Fiji excursion with **Sun Tours** (☎ 722666, or 213/256-0647 in the U.S.), one of the country's largest tour operators. These trips by air-conditioned bus make a loop from Nadi around Viti Levu Nadi and include overnight stops at Rakiraki, Levuka, Suva, and the Coral Coast. Cost is about F$1,670 ($1,169) single and F$2,445 ($1,712) double, including transportation and hotel rooms.

FAST FACTS: Fiji

The following facts apply to Fiji generally. For more specific information, see the "Fast Facts" in the following chapters.

American Express   The full-service representative, Tapa International Ltd., has offices in Nadi and Suva. See "Fast Facts" in the "Nadi & Viti Levu" and "Suva & Levuka" chapters for details.

Area Code   The international country code for Fiji is 679. There are no area codes within Fiji.

Business Hours   Stores generally are open Monday to Friday from 8am to 4:30pm, although many close for lunch from 1 to 2pm. Saturday hours are from 8:30am to noon. Shops in many hotels stay open until 9pm. Government office hours are Monday to Thursday from 8am to 1pm and 2 to 4:30pm, Friday from 8am to 1pm and 2 to 4pm. Sunday business is restricted to hotels, airlines, taxis, buses, tourist-related activities such as tours and cruises, non-hotel licensed restaurants (which can open from noon to 10pm), and small "milk bar" grocery stores.

Camera/Film   Caines Photofast, the largest processor of Kodak films, has shops in the main towns.

Climate   See "When to Go," earlier in this chapter.

Clothing   Modest dress is the order of the day, particularly in the villages. As a rule, don't leave the hotel swimming pool or the beach in bathing suits or other skimpy attire. If you want to run around half naked, go to Tahiti where the French think it's all right. The Fijians do not. Do not enter a Fijian village wearing a hat or with your shoulders uncovered.

For their part, Fijian men and women wear *sulus,* the same wraparound skirts known as pareus in Tahiti and the Cook Islands and lavalavas in the Samoas. Fijian women wear *chambas,* or hip-length blouses, over their sulus. Many

Indian women prefer to wear colorful saris, six-foot lengths of cloth wrapped and pleated around the body.

Crime   See "Safety," below.

Currency Exchange   See "Visitor Information & Entry Requirements" and "Money," earlier in this chapter.

Doctor   Medical and dental care in Fiji is not up to the standards common in the industrialized world. The hospitals tend to be overcrowded and understaffed. Most hotels have private physicians on call or can refer one. Doctors are listed at the beginning of the White Pages section of the Fiji telephone directory under the heading "Medical Practitioners." See "Fast Facts" in the following chapters for specific doctors.

Drug Laws   One drive past the Suva Gaol will convince you not to smuggle narcotics or dangerous drugs into Fiji.

Drugstores   The main towns have reasonably well-stocked drugstores. Their medicines are likely to be from Australia or New Zealand. The large Morris Hedstrom department stores throughout Fiji carry a wide range of toiletries, including Coppertone, Colgate, and many other brands familiar to Americans. See "Fast Facts" in the following chapters for specific locations.

Electricity   Electric current in Fiji is 240 volts, 50 cycles. Many hotels have converters for 110-volt shavers, but these are not suitable for hairdryers. The plugs are the angled two-prong types used in Australia and New Zealand. Outlets have separate on-off switches mounted next to them.

Embassies and Consulates   The **U.S. Embassy** is at 31 Loftus St., Suva (☎ 314466). Major diplomatic missions in Suva are: **Australia,** 7th and 8th Floors, Dominion House, Thomson Street (☎ 312844); **New Zealand,** 10th Floor, Reserve Bank of Fiji Bldg., Pratt Street (☎ 311244); **Great Britain,** Victoria House, 47 Gladstone Rd. (☎ 311033); **Japan,** 2nd Floor, Dominion House, Thomson St. (☎ 302122); **France,** 1st Floor, Dominion House, Thomson St. (☎ 312925); **People's Republic of China,** 147 Queen Elizabeth Drive (☎ 311836); and **Israel,** 5th Floor, Parade Bldg., 69 Joske St. (☎ 303420). Others include **Papua New Guinea** (☎ 304244); **Republic of Korea** (☎ 300977); and **Malaysia** (☎ 312166).

Emergencies   The emergency telephone number for police, fire, and ambulance is 000 throughout Fiji.

Firearms   They are illegal in Fiji, and persons found with them could be fined severely and sentenced to jail.

Gambling   There are no casinos in Fiji, but you can play Tattslotto and a newspaper numbers game known as "Fiji Sixes."

Hitchhiking   Local residents seldom hitchhike, so the custom is not widespread. Women traveling alone should not hitchhike.

Insects   Fiji has no dangerous insects, and its plentiful mosquitoes do not carry malaria. The only dangerous animal is the bolo, a venomous snake that is docile and rarely seen.

Liquor Laws   Except in the hotels and licensed restaurants, alcoholic beverages may not be sold on Sunday. Both beer and spirits are produced locally and are considerably less expensive than imported brands, which are taxed heavily. If you drink quality brands of liquor, bring some with you. Fiji Bitter, the local beer, is sold both in bottles and on draft; the bottles are known as "Stubbies." Watch out for some Fijian bartenders: they keep pouring and bringing you new beers until you tell them emphatically to stop.

Maps The Sigatoka Bookshops chain publishes one of the best road maps of Fiji; it has stores in Sigatoka, Nadi, Lautoka, and Ba. Both *Spotlight on Nadi* and a free "How to Plan Your Fiji Vacation" published by the Fiji Hotel Association contain the same excellent map of the country; get copies at the Fiji Visitors Bureau.

Newspapers/Magazines Two national newspapers are published in English: the *Fiji Times* and the *Daily Post.* Both are tabloids and appear every morning except Sunday. They carry the latest major stories from overseas. The international editions of *Time* and *Newsweek* (the latter in the rear of *The Bulletin,* an Australian newsmagazine) and the leading Australian and New Zealand daily newspapers are available at some bookstores and hotel shops. The latter usually are several days old before they reach Fiji. Two magazines cover South Pacific regional news: the excellent *Islands Business Pacific* and *Pacific Islands Monthly,* both published in Suva.

Pets You will need advance permission to bring any animal into Fiji; if not, your pet will be quarantined.

Police The emergency phone number is 000 throughout Fiji. See "Safety," below.

Post Office All the main towns have post offices, and there is a branch at Nadi International Airport across the entry road from the terminal. Airmail connections between Fiji and North America are fairly rapid, but allow at least a week for delivery. Surface mail can take two months or more to reach the U.S. mainland. Airmail rates are F23¢ (16¢) for postcards and airgrams, and F63¢ (44¢) for letters. Post offices are open Monday to Friday from 8am to 4pm. Mail will move faster if you use the country's official name—Fiji Islands—on all envelopes and packages sent there.

Radio/TV The Fijian government operates three nationwide radio networks whose frequencies depend on the location of the relay transmitters. Radio Fiji 1 carries programming in Fijian. Radio Fiji 2 is Hindi. Radio Fiji 3 has mostly English programs and relays the world news from Radio Australia and the BBC several times a day. Radio Fiji 2 and 3 both carry full world, regional, and local news reports and weather bulletins daily at 7am and 6pm. English-language FM stations can be heard in Suva and Nadi.

Fiji has one broadcast TV channel, which can be received around Suva, Nadi, and Lautoka from noon to midnight. "The CBS Evening News with Dan Rather" is rebroadcast every night about 10pm. I say "about" because the published schedules, carried in the two newspapers, seldom are reliable.

Safety By and large, Fiji is a safe country in which to travel, although it has experienced a serious increase in property crime in recent years. A tourist's chances of being robbed or assaulted in Fiji are lower than in the centers of most large American cities, but caution is advised. Stick to the main streets after dark, and take a taxi back to your hotel if you're out late at night. Some of the smaller hotels in Suva lock their front doors at 11pm, and the large resorts have checkpoints to monitor who comes and who goes. Do not leave valuables in your hotel room or unattended elsewhere.

Women should not wander alone on deserted beaches and should be extremely cautious about accepting an offer to have a few beers outside a bar or to be given a late-night lift back to their hotel or hostel.

Taxes   Fiji imposes a 10% value added tax (VAT) on all goods and services. Businesses technically are required to include the tax in the prices they charge. These are known as "VAT Inclusive Prices," or VIP for short. Some still add it like a sales tax, however, and hoteliers need not include it in the rates they quote outside Fiji. Accordingly, be sure to ask whether a hotel room rate or other price includes the VAT.

Visitors leaving the country by air must pay a departure tax of F$20 ($14) in Fiji currency.

Telephone/Telex/Fax   International calls can be dialed directly into Fiji from most areas of the world. The international country code is 679.

The international long-distance carriers have access numbers their customers can call from within Fiji to reach their international networks: **AT&T** (☎ 00-48-901001); **MCI** (☎ 00-48-901002); **Sprint** (☎ 00-48-901003); **Hawaii Telecom** (☎ 00-48-901004); and **Teleglobe Canada** (☎ 00-48-901005). These numbers can be dialed toll free from any Phonecard public phone (see below).

International phone, telegram, and fax service also is available at all post offices and at Fiji International Telecommunications Ltd. (FINTEL), a colonial-style building on Victoria Parade in downtown Suva. See "Fast Facts" in the "Suva & Levuka" chapter for details.

The number for **directory assistance** in Fiji is 011.

Pay phones are located at all post offices. You can make local, domestic long-distance ("trunk"), or international calls without operator assistance from any of them.

They come in two types. One is an orange coin-operated model with a digital readout that tells you how much money you have left. To make a local call, lift the headset, listen for a dial tone, deposit a Fijian 20¢ coin, and dial the number. For long distance, dial 012 first, then deposit the money when the operator tells you to. You can reverse the charges or use your AT&T card from coin phones by dialing 010. AT&T cards must have international numbers on them. *Note:* The orange phones will take only Fiji coins minted prior to 1987; newer coins will be rejected.

The second type is silver and accepts only Fiji Telecom Phonecards, which post offices and many shops (including the gift shop in the Nadi Airport terminal) sell in denominations up to F$20 ($14). Lift the receiver and slip the card into the slot, picture side up. A digital readout will tell you how much money you have left on the card at all times during your call. Calls to the U.S. cost F$2.70 ($2) a minute when dialed directly. You *cannot* use your AT&T credit card from a Phonecard phone.

Most post offices provide fax service.

Time   Local time in Fiji is 12 hours ahead of Greenwich mean time. The country sits just west of the international date line, so it's one day ahead of the U.S. and shares the same day with Australia and New Zealand. Translated: When it's 5am on Tuesday in Fiji during standard time in the U.S., it's noon on Monday in New York and 9am on Monday in Los Angeles. (During daylight saving time, it's one hour earlier in the U.S.; thus it would be 11am on Monday in New York and 8am on Monday in Los Angeles.)

Tipping   Tipping is discouraged throughout Fiji unless truly exceptional service has been rendered. That's not to say the porter won't give you that where's-my-money look once he figures out you're an American.

Water   Except during periods of continuous heavy rain, the tap water in the main towns and at the resorts is safe to drink. Bottled "Fiji" spring water is widely available at shops and hotels.

Weights and Measures   Fiji is on the metric system.

Nadi International Airport was built in the sugarcane fields of Western Viti Levu because the relatively dry climate here ensures more reliable flying conditions than at Suva. This dry, warm climate immediately drew Australians and New Zealanders to one- or two-week vacations in the sun. To them, Fiji is like the Caribbean islands are to Americans. Along with a growing contingent of Europeans, Americans, and Japanese on package tours, the Aussies and Kiwis still flock to Nadi and the resorts in the nearby Mamanuca Islands. If you want a busy vacation, you'll get it in Nadi.

1 Nadi Today

Tourism has helped make Nadi the fastest growing area of Fiji, with new homes, department stores, and shopping centers popping up all along the 9km (5.4 miles) of the traffic-heavy Queen's Road between the airport and Nadi Town. The predominately Indian town has seen some improvement in recent years. Big new shops now offer fixed prices and gentle clerks, and a concerted civic effort (spurred by powerful Japanese interests) has even toned down most of the bargaining merchants who once would almost drag tourists off the sidewalks to look in their shops. It's cuisine once limited to curry shops, Nadi Town now even has one of the finest restaurants in Fiji. Nevertheless, it still is a tourist town that is in marked contrast to the genteel Lautoka 33km (20 miles) to the north.

But Nadi also is the gateway to more charming parts of Fiji. It's easy to hop over to the pleasant resorts out in the little Mamanuca Islands, which have the beaches and clear lagoons the mainland lacks. Farther out, the even more beautiful and less developed Yasawa Islands are the target of the low-keyed Blue Lagoon Cruises, one of the finest such operations in the world. South of Nadi along the Queen's Road, the Coral Coast has widely spaced resorts with gorgeous scenery and Fijian villages in between. To the north along the King's Road beckons Rakiraki and its charming old colonial-era hotel. And the airport gives easy access to Taveuni, Savusavu, and the rest of Fiji.

The airport lies midway on Viti Levu's west coast, between Fiji's second-largest city of **Lautoka** and **Nadi Town,** which is little more than a seven-block strip of the Queen's Road lined with a plethora of duty-free, handcraft, souvenir, and other small shops. Much of

---

Impressions

---

*The air smelled of blossoms and moistened earth; the hotel maids, who looked and dressed
rather like Africans, were singing in the corridors. Most surprising of all, the neatness
and tranquillity extended to the town outside the front door, and the countryside at the
back. The hotel did not seem to be an island built for foreigners in a sea of squalor.*
—Ronald Wright, 1986

Nadi's local shopping is quickly moving to new shopping centers north of town
in the areas known as **Martintar** and **Namaka.**

Most hotels are on or near the Queen's Road between the airport and Nadi
Town. None of these establishments is on a beach, and even if they were, runoff
from the mountains, hills, cane fields, and coastal mangrove swamps perpetually
leaves **Nadi Bay** murky, sometimes for several miles offshore.

Along the shore about 7km (4.3 miles) to the west of town, **Denarau Island**
is home to a huge, Japanese-financed real estate project that includes the Sheraton
Fiji and The Regent of Fiji (the country's finest big resort hotels), an 18-hole golf
course, a marina, and room for five more hotels and numerous residential lots.
Denarau is only technically an island, for a narrow, winding creek through a
mangrove forest is all that separates it from the mainland.

2 Getting Around Nadi

All of Fiji's major international and local **car-rental** firms have offices in the
international arrival concourse of Nadi International Airport.

Taxis gather outside the arrival concourse at the airport and are stationed at the
larger hotels. Ask the reception desk to call you one. The aggressive drivers will find
you in Nadi Town.

Local buses ply the Queen's Road between the markets in Nadi Town and
Lautoka, leaving each hour on the hour and on the half-hour between 6am and
8pm Monday to Saturday. The buses destined for Votualevu pass the Tanoa
International and Fiji Mocambo Hotels. Pay when you board. Tell the driver
where you're going; he'll tell you how much to pay. Fares vary according to the
length of the trip, but F35¢ (25¢) will get you around the Nadi area, and F90¢
(63¢) will take you from the airport to Lautoka.

A cream-and-blue **Denarau Island bus** is the only one between Nadi Town and
the Sheraton and Regent resorts, running every 30 minutes daily from 6:30am to
6:30pm. It does not go up the Queen's Road to the airport. One-way fare is F35¢
(25¢).

For more information, including approximate taxi fares in the Nadi area, see
"Getting Around" in the "Introducing Fiji" chapter.

FAST FACTS: Nadi

The following facts apply specifically to Nadi and Lautoka. For more information, see "Fast Facts: Fiji" in the "Introducing Fiji" chapter.

American Express   Tapa International Ltd. (☎ 722325) has full American
Express services at its office in the arrival concourse of Nadi International

Airport. The address is P.O. Box 9240, Nadi Airport, Fiji Islands. Open Monday to Friday from 8:30am to 4:30pm and Saturday from 8:30am to noon.

Bookstores Desai Bookshop on Queen's Road is the best place to shop for novels, magazines, and books about Fiji.

Camera/Film Caines Photofast has a film and one-hour processing shop on Queen's Road in Nadi Town. Most of the hotel gift shops also sell film and one-day processing.

Currency Exchange Bank of Hawaii, ANZ Bank, Westpac Bank, National Bank of Fiji, and Baroda Bank all have offices on the Queen's Road in Nadi Town and in Lautoka. Bank of Hawaii has an ATM machine. ANZ Bank's branch at Nadi International Airport is open 24 hours a day.

Dentist Ask your hotel staff to recommend a dentist in private practice. The government runs a dental clinic (☎ 700370).

Doctor Dr. Ram Raju, 36 Clay St., Nadi Town (☎ 700240 or 701769 after hours) has treated many visitors, including me.

Drugstores There are three drugstores on Queen's Road in Nadi Town. Budget Pharmacy is the best stocked. For toiletries go to any Morris Hedstrom department store.

Emergencies The emergency telephone number is 000.

Eyeglasses Try Opticare, 54 Naviti St. (near Vakabale Street and the market), Lautoka (☎ 663337).

Hairdressers/Barbers Several hotels have hairdressers.

Hospitals The main Western Province hospital is in Lautoka (☎ 663337). There is a government medical clinic in Nadi Town (☎ 701108).

Information The Fiji Visitors Bureau (☎ 722433) has an office in the arrivals concourse of Nadi International Airport. Other so-called Tourist Information Centres in reality are travel agents or tour operators.

Laundry/Dry Cleaning Northern Press Ltd. (722787), on Northern Press Road between the airport and Nadi Town, has one-day laundry and dry-cleaning service.

Libraries Nadi Town Council Library is in the town council shopping arcade, on the east side of the Queen's Road about midway through Nadi Town. It's open Monday to Friday 9am to 5pm and Saturday 9am to 1pm.

Police The Fiji Police have stations at Nadi Town (☎ 700222) and at the airport terminal (☎ 722222).

Post Office The Nadi Town post office is on Hospital Road near the south end of the market. There is a small airport branch across the main entry road from the terminal (go through the gates and turn left). Both are open Monday to Friday from 8am to 4pm.

Impressions

The buses in Fiji are like mobile balconies, with no glass in their windows.
—John Dyson, 1982

3 What to See & Do in Nadi

All but a few hotels have at least one tour desk that can make reservations or arrangements for all the activities mentioned below, and the reception-desk staffs of the others will do so. Like travel agents, the activities desks get a percentage of the proceeds; their services cost you nothing extra. Round-trip bus transportation from the Nadi area hotels is included in the price of the organized cruises and outings; a bus usually will pick you up within 30 minutes of the scheduled departure time. Children under 12 years of age pay half fare on most of the activities.

The major tour operators are United Touring Fiji (UTC) (☎ 722811), Road Tours of Fiji (☎ 722935), and Sun Tours of Fiji (☎ 722666). They have decades of experience, their vehicles are clean and air conditioned, and their staffs are knowledgeable.

Pick up copies of *Spotlight on Nadi* and *Fiji Magic*, which give up-to-date, detailed information (the latter has four full pages of small type devoted just to tours and cruises from Nadi).

Sightseeing Tours   Several companies operate tours on air-conditioned buses to various destinations near Nadi, on the Coral Coast, and to Suva. Their rates are about the same, but some shopping around could pay off. Talk to more than one hotel activities desk; since most desks are operated by the tour companies, they understandably will steer you to their trips. Here are some of the key attractions.

✪ **Coral Coast Railway**   The *Fijian Princess,* a restored sugarcane locomotive, pulls passengers from Shangri-La's Fijian Resort on the Coral Coast to lovely Natadola Beach, where they swim (bring your own towel) and have lunch at a restaurant on the beach. There's an evening tour to Sigatoka that includes cocktails, a village visit with a pottery-making demonstration, and a Fijian dance show. These outings cost about F$77 ($54) from the Nadi hotels and F$66 ($46) from those on the Coral Coast.

Flightseeing   Island Hoppers Fiji (☎ 720410) offers helicopter sightseeing excursions, starting with a 20-minute flight over Denarau Island, Nadi Bay, the Mamanucas, and Vuda Point north of Nadi for F$107 ($75). Turtle Airways (☎ 722389) has scenic flights using its seaplanes based at Wailoaloa Beach.

✪ **Garden of the Sleeping Giant**   This lovely orchid range was started in 1977 by actor Raymond Burr, of "Perry Mason" and "Ironside" fame, to house his private collection of tropical orchids (he once also owned Naitoba, a small island in the Lau Group). You can visit the collection on a tour or on your own by rental car or taxi. Look for the sign at Wailoko Road off the Queen's Road between Nadi and Lautoka. It's open Monday to Saturday from 9am to 5pm. Entrance fees are F$9.35 ($6.50) for one adult, F$17.60 ($12.30) for a couple, and F$22 ($15.50) for a family. A guide and a fruit drink are included. Burr's former home in the hills overlooking Saweni Bay north of Nadi is now owned by Don and Aileen Burness, who have a collection of Fijian artifacts. Call them for information about touring the home (☎ 662206).

Levuka   Sun Tours (☎ 722666) has a full-day trip via Air Fiji to Levuka, Fiji's old capital (see the chapter on Suva and Levuka). These excursions leave early in the morning and require a change of planes at Nausori Airport in both directions. Round-trip airfare and a town tour are included in the F$300 ($210) price.

Viti Levu & Ovalau

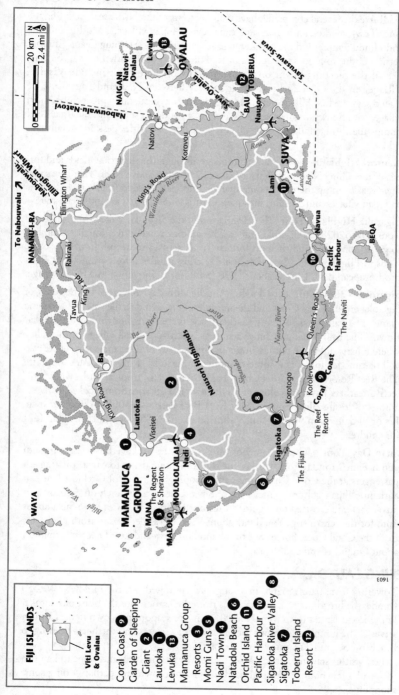

Airport ✈   Ferry - - -

1603

Nadi Area Several companies have half-day tours of the Nadi area, including the Nadi Town market, an Indian sugarcane farm, a Fijian village, a Muslim mosque and Hindu temple, and the orchid range at Garden of the Sleeping Giant. Another version of this tour goes to Lautoka instead of Nadi Town, with a stop at the Garden of the Sleeping Giant on the way. Many of these tours include **Viseisei Village,** on the Queen's Road about halfway between Nadi and Lautoka. One legend says the first Fijians settled here; today it's a typical, fairly prosperous Fijian village, with houses of concrete block and tin, a handcraft shop, and the usual road humps that bring traffic to a crawl. Ask your hotel activities desk for details and prices.

Nausori Highlands Several road tours go through the sugarcane fields and forests of the rolling Nausori Highlands, a cool 2,500 feet above Nadi. There are some fine vistas from up there, including many out to sea. These tours also include visits to Fijian villages and Muslim mosques. Cost is about F$35 ($24.50) per adult.

Sigatoka Highland Tour For a variation of the Sigatoka Valley trip, Highland Tours (☎ 520285 in Sigatoka) uses a 25-seat, four-wheel-drive, rough-terrain bus to go up the valley and then on forestry roads across the steep hills of the scenic Nausori Highlands to Nadi. The full-day trip includes information about Fiji's pre-European days. Price is about F$70 ($49), including lunch in a Fijian village.

Sigatoka Valley/Kula Bird Park Another full-day tour goes to the town of Sigatoka on the Coral Coast and the meandering river and fertile valley of the same name. The valley has so many market gardens that it is known as "Fiji's Salad Bowl." The tour usually includes a stop at Nadroga, a small village in the valley where Fijians still make pottery in the traditional way of their ancestors. There also will be time for lunch and some shopping in Sigatoka. Kula Bird Park, opposite The Reef Resort on the Coral Coast, has a collection of tropical birds, whose collective feathers have the colors of a rainbow, and an aquarium stocked with examples of local sealife. You can visit Kula Bird Park (☎ 500505) on your own. It's open daily from 9am to 4pm. Admission is F$7 ($5) for adults and F$3 ($2) for children.

Suva Day Tour The three major tour companies all have buses leaving Nadi about 8am Monday to Saturday for the four-hour drive to Suva, picking up passengers at the Coral Coast hotels and stopping for a tour of Orchid Island, an authentic Fijian cultural center west of Suva. Guests have lunch on their own in Suva, then are escorted on a guided tour of the city. The buses leave Suva about 4pm for the return trip. You'll pay about F$60 ($42) per person from Nadi, less from the Coral Coast hotels. See the chapter on Suva and Levuka for information about Orchid Island and the capital.

SEEING LAUTOKA

Towering royal palms march in a long, orderly row down the middle of Vitogo Parade, the broad main street that runs from the harbor into the heart of Lautoka, Fiji's second-largest town (pop. 30,000). A major seaport in its own right, Lautoka serves as the jumping-off point for Blue Lagoon Cruises and the boats heading to Beachcomber and Treasure Island Resorts.

Few visitors stay in Lautoka. Most make their base in Nadi and come to Lautoka to spend a few hours looking around the pleasant town and perhaps doing some shopping.

Dreaded Degei

The tour guides like to point out that Viseisei village between Nadi and Lautoka is where the great canoe *Kaunitoni* came out of the west and deposited the first Fijians some 3,000 years ago. From there, the legend goes, they dispersed all over the islands. The yarn is helped by the local district name Vuda, which means "our origin" in Fijian, and Viseisei, which means "to scatter."

Although it's clear today that the Fijians did indeed migrate from the west, no one knows for sure whether they landed at Viseisei, for like all Pacific Islanders, the Fijians had no written language until the missionaries arrived in the mid-19th century.

The most common oral legend has the great chiefs Lutunasobasoba and Degei arriving in the *Kaunitoni* on the northwest coast of Viti Levu. From there they moved inland along the Nakauvadra Range in Northern Viti Levu. Lutunasobasoba died on this trip, but Degei lived on to become a combination man, ancestor, and spirit—and an angry spirit at that, for he is blamed for causing wars and a great flood that washed the Fijians to all parts of the islands.

The dreaded Degei supposedly still inhabits a mysterious cave in the mountains above Rakiraki, but no one is about to go in there to find out.

Local buses leave the market in Nadi Town every half hour for the Lautoka Market from Monday to Saturday between 6am and 8pm. The fare is no more than F$1 (70¢), depending on where you get on. The one-way taxi fare to Lautoka is F$15 ($10.50) from Nadi airport and F$20 ($14) from Nadi Town.

If you're driving yourself, you will come to two traffic circles on the outskirts of Lautoka. Take the second exit off the first one and the first exit off the second. That will take you directly to the post office and the southern end of Vitogo Parade, the main drag with stores on one side, a row of royal palms down the center, and a park on the other.

The duty-free shops and other stores along **Vitogo Parade** mark the boundary of Lautoka's business district; behind them are several blocks of stores and the lively **Lautoka Market,** which doubles as the bus station and is second in size only to Suva's Municipal Market. Handcraft stalls at the front of the market offer a variety of goods, especially when cruise ships are in port. Shady residential streets trail off beyond the playing fields of Churchill Park on the other side of Vitogo Parade. The Hare Krishnas have their most important temple in the South Pacific on Tavewa Avenue.

Tourism may rule Nadi, but sugar is king in Lautoka. The **Fiji Sugar Corporation's** huge mill, one of the largest crushing operations in the southern hemisphere, was built by the Colonial Sugar Refining Company in 1903. The government-owned FSC bought it after Fiji became an independent nation. Free guided tours can be arranged by calling 660800 in Lautoka.

Where to Dine   Except on cruise ship days, tourism is a minor part of Lautoka's business, which translates into a shortage of good places to dine. Business people tend to congregate in the dining room of the Waterfront Hotel (☎ 664777) on Marine Drive, diagonally across the park at the south end of Vitogo Parade. By international standards, this clean, motel-style establishment is the city's prime place to stay. The dining room features a reasonably priced luncheon buffet.

In the business district, **Gopal's Vegetarian Restaurant,** on Vitogo Parade opposite the stadium (☎ 660938), is on a par with the excellent Hare Krishna Restaurants in Suva and the equally good Coffee Lounge in Nadi. Spicy vegetarian curries are served in spotlessly clean surroundings. Prices range from F$1.50 ($1) for one curry and rice to F$6 ($4.20) for *thali,* a sampler plate that will fill you up. The lounge is open Monday to Sat 11am to 2:30pm. The curry bar outside is open Monday to Saturday from 9am to 6pm. No credit cards are accepted.

Cultural Tours   Although several tours include brief visits to Fijian villages, and others stop at the Orchid Island cultural center near Suva, three trips give a more in-depth look at Fijian culture:

Navua River Tour

This full-day trip goes by bus to Navua, a rice-growing town near the mouth of the Navua River on Viti Levu's south coast. Guests then travel by outrigger canoe past waterfalls and through forests to Namuamua, a Fijian village that puts on a yaqona ceremony, a lunch of local-style foods, and a traditional dance show. Price is about F$80 ($56) from the Nadi hotels, less from those on the Coral Coast. Some companies call this their Jewel of Fiji tour; others call it Namuamua Inland Tour.

Pacific Harbour

These tours visit the cultural center at Pacific Harbour, a planned resort development 30 miles west of Suva. The center has a reconstructed Fijian village, with demonstrations of what Fijian life was like before the Europeans came. These are best done on a day when the Dance Theater of Fiji is performing (see "Nearby Attractions," in the "Suva & Levuka" chapter). The trips include time for shopping at Pacific Harbour's Marketplace. Prices are about F$65 ($45.50) from the Nadi hotels, less from those on the Coral Coast.

Sigatoka River

At least one tour company in Nadi has day trips by boat up the winding Sigatoka River and its flat valley. The cruises stop for visits to the ancient Tavuni Hill Fort, demonstrations of pottery making, a kava welcoming ceremony, and a Fijian feast. The boats then go downriver to the Sigatoka Sand Dunes (see "The Coral Coast," below). These cost about F$65 ($45.50).

4 Where to Stay in Nadi

The Sheraton and Regent resorts are on pancake-flat Denarau Island, which is separated from the mainland by a short bridge over a creek running through a mangrove forest 7km (4.3 miles) west of Nadi Town. This large Japanese-financed development, known in its entirety as Denarau Island Resort, also has Denarau Golf & Racquet Club and Denarau Island Marina, where most of the area's cruises are based. If you stay on Denarau, you will have to take a taxi to get anywhere else after 6:30pm, when the only bus stops running between there and Nadi Town. The one-way taxi fare from Denarau is F$8 ($5.60) to Nadi Town, F$11 ($7.70) to the Martintar hotel and restaurant district, and F$16.50 ($11.50) to the airport.

Along with Shangri-La's Fijian Resort (see "The Coral Coast," below), the Sheraton and Regent are Fiji's big resort hotels, boasting some 900 rooms among them. The Fijian Resort, 45 minutes south of Nadi, has a whiter beach and clearer lagoon than those at Denarau, but it lacks the convenience of having so many activities on its doorstep.

Nadi

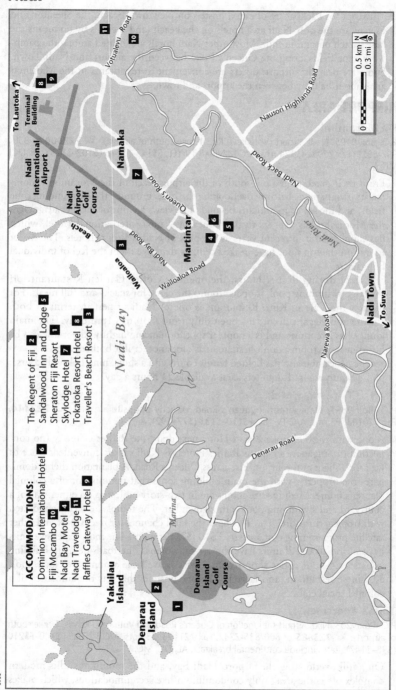

ACCOMMODATIONS:

Dominion International Hotel **6**
Fiji Mocambo **10**
Nadi Bay Motel **4**
Nadi Travelodge **11**
Raffles Gateway Hotel **9**

The Regent of Fiji **2**
Sandalwood Inn and Lodge **5**
Sheraton Fiji Resort **1**
Skylodge Hotel **7**
Tokatoka Resort Hotel **8**
Traveller's Beach Resort **3**

Except for backpacker-oriented hostels on Newtown Beach, the Sheraton and Regent are the only Nadi area hotels on the beach (and theirs is by no means the best stretch of sand in Fiji). Most other Nadi hotels are located among the patchwork cane fields along the Queen's Road between the airport and Nadi Town. Some are near the airport; others are convenient to restaurants in the Martintar area, about halfway between the airport and town.

AIRPORT AREA

Fiji Mocambo

P.O. Box 9195, Nadi Airport (Votualevu Rd., 1 mile south of airport). ☎ **722000** or 800/942-5050. Fax 720324. 124 rms. A/C MINIBAR TV TEL. F$145–F$176 ($102–$123). AE, DC, MC, V.

From their perch atop a hill south of the airport, each of the Mocambo's rooms has its own patio or balcony overlooking the hotel grounds, the surrounding cane fields, and the sea or mountains beyond. The views are one of the few advantages the Mocambo has over its rival, the nearby Tanoa International Hotel, which has supplanted it in recent years as the pick of Nadi's airport hotels. The newer rooms on the top floor have peaked ceilings that give them the feel of individual bungalows.

Except during dinner hours, the open-air Coffee Garden Restaurant, off the large swimming pool, is open around the clock for snacks and full meals. For dinner, the Vale ni Kuro Restaurant is one of Nadi's finest in terms of both cuisine and elegant decor; it's open only from 6:30 to 11pm daily. The main lounge has live music and is a popular spot for dancing nightly (the music can be heard in some rooms; don't hesitate to ask for another if it bothers you).

The Mocambo also has lighted tennis courts and a short, nine-hole golf course, plus a beauty salon. Room service is available 24 hours a day.

Raffle's Gateway Hotel

P.O. Box 9891, Nadi Airport (Queen's Road, directly opposite airport). ☎ **722444.** Fax 720163. 93 rms. A/C TV TEL. F$110–$131 ($77–$92). AE, DC, MC, V.

Along with the Tokatoka Resort Hotel next door, the Raffles Gateway (no connection to Singapore's famous Raffles Hotel) is Nadi's most convenient place to wait for a flight at the airport just across Queen's Road. A plantation theme dominates the property, with the main building somewhat reminiscent of a colonial planter's home. Medium-size rooms are in two-story buildings on either side of a courtyard and swimming pool with its own bar. The rooms are nicely appointed with tropical furniture. The TVs have the local channel for free; CNN and other satellite programming cost an extra F$10 ($7) per night. The more expensive units have sitting areas. All units have shower-only baths. The roadside main building houses a 24-hour coffee shop (room service is available around the clock, too), a Chinese restaurant, and large bar-lounge upstairs that has the ambiance of a colonial social club.

Tanoa Apartments

P.O. Box 9203, Nadi Airport (at junction of Queen's Road and Votualevu Roads, 1 mile south of airport). ☎ **723685** or 800/835-7742. Fax 721193. 23 apts. A/C TV TEL. F$140–F$210 ($98–$147). Rates include continental breakfast. AE, DC, MC, V.

On a hill overlooking the airport, Nadi Bay, and the mountains, this modern complex offers the area's only condominium-like accommodations, which makes it a good choice for longer-term stays or for families who don't need a restaurant on premises. Ranging in size from one- to three-bedroom, the spacious units have tropical furniture, TVs with the local channel, kitchens equipped with microwave ovens, large shower-only baths (not all bedrooms in the larger units have baths with showers). Top-floor apartments have sleeping lofts over the kitchens. Facilities include a hilltop swimming pool, spa, sauna, lighted tennis court, coin laundry, and a small bar that opens for houseguests only at 3pm daily. Guests can charge meals and use the facilities at the Tanoa International Hotel.

✪ Tanoa International Hotel

P.O. Box 9203, Nadi Airport (Votualevu Rd, 1¹/₂ mile south of airport). ☎ **720277** or 800/ 835-7742. Fax 720191. 114 rms. A/C MINIBAR TV TEL. F$160–F$170 ($112–$117). AE, DC, MC, V.

My favorite haunt, this former Nadi Travelodge has been turned into the pick of the airport hotels by the locally owned Tanoa Hotels, which put up the capital for renovations and installed excellent management to oversee a friendly, veteran staff. The service, cleanliness, and maintenance here are among the best in Fiji. You walk into a bright public area with reception, tour desk, comfortable bar and lounge with nightly entertainment, indoor-outdoor restaurant specializing in reasonably priced theme-night buffets, an air-conditioned coffee shop open 24 hours a day, a small duty-free emporium, and a well-stocked gift shop. These all open onto a lush garden with swimming pool, beside which big canvas umbrellas cover varnished wood tables and chairs for dining or relaxing.

The medium-size guest rooms are in two-story blocks linked to the public building by thatch-covered walkways. All recently refurbished, they have cool tile floors, bright spreads and tropical furniture, coffeemakers, TVs (the local channel, CNN, and two movies), a double and a single bed, and combination tub-shower baths with toiletries and hairdryers. A special Travelodge facility is a guest Laundromat. A new conference facility was being built during my recent visit. Services include baby-sitting, laundry and dry cleaning, and 24-hour room service.

Tokatoka Resort Hotel

P.O. Box 9305, Nadi Airport (Queen's Road opposite airport). ☎ **720222.** Fax 720400. 70 units. A/C TV TEL. F$127–$223 ($89–$156). AE, DC, MC, V.

This modern complex has Nadi's most varied mix of accommodations, ranging from hotel rooms to two-bedroom villas, which sit in a yard behind two buildings fronting the Queen's Road. The entire complex is equipped with pleasant, if somewhat utilitarian, tropical-style furniture. The highlight here is an unusual swimming pool-restaurant-bar complex at the rear of the property, which makes the Tokatoka a favorite of families with children. The youngsters can play to their heart's content on an S-shaped water slide streaming down into an angular pool, which is partially under the same steel-beam- and brick-supported roof covering the restaurant and bar. It's also a very popular spot for local families to spend lazy Sunday afternoons, and it's a fine place to kill time while waiting for a flight home. Open 24 hours a day, the Harvesters' Restaurant serves snacks all the time and goes heavy on barbecues and buffets for lunches and dinners. Evening entertainment is provided; when I was there recently, Fiji's top jazz guitarist played and sang every evening from an island in the pool.

DENARAU ISLAND

✪ The Regent of Fiji

P.O. Box 9018, Nadi Airport (Denarau Island, 4.3 miles west of Nadi Town). ☎ **750700** or 800/545-4000. Fax 750850. 291 rms, 9 suites. A/C MINIBAR TEL. F$280–F$380 ($196–$266) room; F$725 ($508) suite. AE, DC, MC, V.

This venerable establishment has been one of the finest hotels in the South Pacific since 1972, and it has considerably more Fijian charms than the newer and more modern Sheraton next door. Covered by a peaked wooden roof, The Regent's dark, breezy foyer opens to an irregular-shaped pool with thatch-covered, swim-up bar on one end (something the Sheraton's rectangular pool lacks). A grassy berm, built after cyclones damaged the beach a few years ago, separates the pool from the grey beach.

Like the Sheraton's, the rooms here are in a series of two-story, motel-style blocks grouped in "villages" surrounded by tropical gardens and linked by covered walkways to the central building. The spacious units are equipped with twin or double beds, large baths and wardrobes, dressing areas with twin vanities, refrigerators, radios, tea- and coffee-making facilities, and private patios or balconies. The furnishings are made of rattan or bamboo and are accented by tapa cloth and exposed timbers.

Dining/Entertainment: Although not up to the Sheraton's standards for cuisine, The Regent boasts that the choices at its three restaurants are so extensive that guests can remain on the premises for a month without eating the same dish twice. The dining rooms have barbecue buffets several nights a week and a Fijian feast with fire-walking once a week. Boasting fine and relatively expensive Japanese cuisine, Hamacho Restaurant (☎ 750177) sits on the Sheraton end of the property. There's another Hamacho branch on the Queen's Road in Martintar (☎ 720252). Reservations are essential at either Hamacho.

Services: Laundry, baby-sitting, 24-hour room service, business services.

Facilities: Shopping arcade with several boutiques; bank; beauty salon; sailboats, Windsurfers, paddleboats; private island across the lagoon where guests can swim, snorkel, and sunbathe; tour desk.

✪ Sheraton Fiji Resort

P.O. Box 9761, Nadi (Denarau Island, 4.3 miles west of Nadi Town). ☎ **750777** or 800/ 325-3535. Fax 750818. 300 rms. A/C MINIBAR TV TEL. F$415–F$605 ($290–$424). AE, DC, MC, V.

One of the world's busiest Sheratons, this 1987-vintage property is the most luxurious of Fiji's three big resorts. A fountain flows through a series of pools running down the center of its airy, off-white grand foyer, which opens to a large rectangular swimming pool and the beach beyond (there is no berm on the Sheraton end of Denarau Island). With the lawn-type umbrella tables of a cafe on one side and a series of glass-enclosed boutiques and shops on the other, the Sheraton's lobby is strongly reminiscent of a shopping mall back home (it does indeed have some very fine shops) and contrasts sharply with the dark-wood, handcraft-accented public areas of The Regent. In other words, the Sheraton could be put down in any tropical resort location, not necessarily in the South Seas.

Nevertheless, its spacious, tropically decorated rooms each have an ocean view, private terrace or balcony, two queen-size beds or one king-size bed, TVs with in-house movies and CNN, ceiling fans for days when the air conditioning is unnecessary, and the usual fridge and tea- and coffee-making facilities found in this part of the world.

Dining/Entertainment: Three bars and four food outlets (none of them inexpensive) include Ports O' Call, one of the country's finest restaurants. Enormous buffets in the poolside Verandah dining room feature one international cuisine each night. Fijians strum their guitars and sing island songs every evening. Planters Bar is a dimly lit pub with disco dancing after 9pm.

Services: Laundry, baby-sitting, 24-hour room service, business services.

Facilities: Shopping arcade with several boutiques; fitness center; sailboats, Windsurfers, and paddleboats; private island across the lagoon where guests can swim, snorkel, and sunbathe; activities desk.

MARTINTAR AREA

Dominion International Hotel

P.O. Box 9178, Nadi Airport (Queen's Road, 3.1 miles south of airport). ☎ **722255** or 800/448-8355. Fax 720187. 85 rms. A/C TEL. F$100–F$120 ($70–$84). AE, DC, MC, V.

The friendly, motel-like Dominion is one of the few establishments in Fiji at which you can park a car right next to your door or the stairs leading to your room. Two white, three-story buildings flank a lush garden with swimming pool. A central building with restaurant and bar sits at the Queen's Road end, completing the hotel's U shape. The rooms are very much motel-style, with tub-shower bathrooms at the entrance on one end and glass doors sliding to patios or bougainvillea-draped balconies on the other. All rooms have a queen and twin bed plus two chairs and a coffee table in a small sitting area. A few are equipped for disabled guests. A dining room under a dark, Fijian-style roof extracts a reasonable price for rather plain fare. Also on the premises are a tour desk, gift shop, hairdresser, and nine-hole putting course. As a brief layover when tropical charm doesn't matter, it's good value for the price.

Nadi Bay Motel

Private Bag NAP0359, Nadi Airport (Newtown Beach Rd., about 100 yards west of Queen's Rd., 3.2 miles south of airport). ☎ **723599**. Fax 720092. 23 rms (all with bath), 24 dorm beds. F$28–F$42 ($19.50–$29.50) room; F$8 ($5.50) dorm bed (10% discount for YHA members with cards). AE, DC, MC, V.

The rooms in this two-story concrete-block building are clean, spacious, and well if basically furnished, and have sliding glass doors opening onto a balcony or a patio. Eleven "deluxe" rooms have kitchens, separate sitting areas, and air conditioners; the other 10 rooms have no kitchens and are cooled by electric fans. Two dormitory rooms have 12 bunks each. The motel has a bar, a dining room specializing in inexpensive Indian curries and barbecues, a swimming pool, and a laundry room with coin-operated washing machines. Be prepared for roosters crowing outside your window and jets roaring overhead.

⑤ Sandalwood Inn

P.O. Box 9454, Nadi Airport (Martintar, near Queen's Road, 3.1 miles south of airport). ☎ **722553** or 800/223-9868. Fax 720103. 49 rms (44 with bath). A/C TEL. F$28 ($19.50) without bath; F$34–F$60 ($24–$42) with bath. AE, DC, MC, V.

John and Ana Birch's inn is a clean, comfortable establishment popular with New Zealanders, John's home country (Ana is a friendly Fijian). The top floor of their original two-story, concrete building houses spacious, air-conditioned rooms with telephones and large windows opening to balconies. The ground level holds a restaurant, small bar, and lounge. An older, one-story building on the opposite side of a swimming pool has smaller, non-air-conditioned rooms, some with their own small bathrooms, others sharing two toilets and two showers. The other rooms are in a modern complex called the Sandalwood Lodge, about 200 yards away on the same side road. They are New Zealand motel style, with kitchenettes.

Readers Recommend

Horizon Beach Resort, P.O. Box 1401, Nadi (Martintar, at Newtown Beach, 1 mile west of Queen's Road). ☎ 722832. Fax 720662. *"Having stayed at the Sandalwood Inn and Travellers Beach Resort, I was very impressed with the Horizon Beach Resort. This is located 100 yards from Travellers Beach Resort. Horizon is family run. The rates are better than the other two spots. The rooms are large and clean. Those with bathrooms are excellent value. The clientele is varied in age and nationality. The beers are always cold and refreshing. Food is excellent, and the bartender is very attractive. When I return to Fiji, I know where I'll be staying."*

—Mark I. Ghorayeb, Miami, Florida.

(*Author's Note:* In a two-story clapboard house across an open lot from the beach, this friendly establishment is owned by Gopi Chand, a retired government health inspector who keeps it spotless. Gopi and family have 11 rooms, all with bath, and 10 dorm beds. Some rooms are air-conditioned. Rates are F$29 to F$37.50 [$20.50 to $26] for rooms, and F$5.50 ($3.85) for a dorm bed. American Express, MasterCard, and Visa cards are accepted.)

⑤ Skylodge Hotel

P.O. Box 9222, Nadi Airport (Namaka, on Queen's Road, 2 miles south of airport). ☎ **722200** or 800/448-8355. Fax 720212. 53 rms. A/C TV TEL. F$90 ($63) without kitchen, F$125 ($87.50) with kitchen. AE, DC, MC, V.

The eclectic Skylodge was built as a crew base for Qantas Airways in the early 1960s, shortly after big jets started arriving at Nadi Airport two miles away, but it has been well maintained and still has South Pacific atmosphere. The preferable rooms are in four-unit bungalows scattered through 11 acres of tropical gardens; some of these have cooking facilities. The other, smaller rooms are in the original wooden lodge, which resembles one of those "temporary" structures built by the U.S. armed forces during World War II. Most of these are long and narrow and have rather small bathrooms. Some are next to the bar and swimming pool, where a band plays dance music every evening until midnight. The restaurant and bar are in a low, thatch-accented central building adjacent to the swimming pool. The restaurant offers well-prepared European, Fijian, and Indian dishes at moderate prices. Dining is inside or al fresco at the side of the pool. You can also play tennis and the pitch-and-putt golf.

Travellers Beach Resort

P.O. Box 700, Nadi (Martintar, at Newtown Beach, 1 mile west of Queen's Rd.). ☎ **723322.** Fax 720026. 32 rms (all with bath), 12 dorm beds. F$38–F$50 ($26.50–$35); F$11 ($7.70) dorm bed. AE, DC, MC, V. Follow Turtle Airways signs off Queen's Road.

Other than the luxury Regent and Sheraton resorts, this is the only Nadi accommodation right on a beach. In the Nadi Bay Beach Estates housing development, this establishment feels more like a pension than a hotel, since the original Indian owners built it by expanding onto their beachside home. Eight of the rooms are in a motel-style wing added to the house. The others are in a two-story building across the street. Two rooms on the beachfront are the most expensive. Each unit has at least two beds and a kitchenette. Twenty rooms are air conditioned; the others have fans. A swimming pool sits between the building and the beach, and a restaurant and bar provide reasonably priced meals and poolside libations.

5 Where to Dine in Nadi

Except for Chefs The Restaurant, reviewed below, Nadi's finer restaurants are all in the hotels described above, especially the Sheraton Fiji's excellent Ports 'O Call.

Most of the larger hotels devote at least one night a week to special meals, usually a poolside barbecue, a buffet of Indian curries, or a Fijian feast followed by traditional dancing. *Spotlight on Nadi* and *Fiji Magic* both list the schedules, or phone the hotels to find out.

The Fijian Meke   Like most South Pacific islanders, the Fijians in pre-European days steamed their food in an earth oven, known here as a *lovo*. They would use their fingers to eat the huge feasts *(mekes)* that emerged, then settle down to watch traditional dancing and perhaps polish off a few cups of yaqona.

The ingredients of a lovo meal are *buaka* (pig), *doa* (chicken), *ika* (fish), *mana* (lobster), *moci* (river shrimp), *kai* (freshwater mussels), and various vegetables, such as dense *dalo* (taro root), spinach-like *rourou* (taro leaves), and *lumi* (seaweed). Most dishes are cooked in sweet *lolo* (coconut milk). The most plentiful fish is the *walu*, or Spanish mackerel.

Fijians also make delicious *kokoda* ("ko-kon-da"), their version of fresh fish marinated in lime juice and mixed with fresh vegetables and coconut milk. Another Fijian specialty is *palusami*, a rich combination of corned beef or fish baked in banana leaves or foil with onions, taro leaves, and coconut milk.

Several Nadi hotels have mekes on their schedule of weekly events. The foods are cooked in a lovo on the hotel grounds and served buffet style, often beside the swimming pool if weather permits. Traditional Fijian dance shows follow the meals.

On the more authentic side, **Dratabu Village** near Nadi hosts a traditional feast complete with welcoming yaqona ceremony and meke dance performance. These took place on Tuesdays and Thursdays during my recent visit. Cost was F$52 ($36.50) per person. Book with Optional Tours of Fiji (☎ 722666).

Curry Etiquette   While you will see Fijian-style dishes on many menus, invariably they will have at least one Indian curry. Most curries in Fiji are prepared on the mild side, but you can ask for it extra spicy and get it so hot you can't eat it. Curries are easy to figure out from the menu: lamb, goat, beef, chicken, vegetarian. If in doubt, ask the waiter or waitress.

What's not so easy to figure out is how to eat curry, since it may not be put before you in the way we Westerners serve our meals. The entire meal may come on a round steel plate, with the curries, condiments, and rice in their own dishes arranged on the larger plate. It's perfectly all right to pick at the various small dishes with your fork as you would a European meal. The authentic method, however, is to dump the rice in the middle of the plate, add the smaller portions to it, then mix them all together. Sometimes you will see Indians eating their meals by picking up the curry with small pieces of bread held by the fingers of their right hands, but forks are more common in Fiji.

The key words to know are the names of those delicious Indian breads. *Roti* is the round, heavily leaden bread normally used to pick up your food (it is a hybrid of the round breads of India and Pakistan). *Puri* is a soft, puffy bread. *Papadam* is round, crispy, and chiplike; it's so tasty you will send back for more.

AIRPORT AREA

Chopsticks
Queen's Road, Namaka, in West Garden Hotel. ☎ **721788**. Reservations accepted. Main courses F$5.50–F$16.50 ($4–$11.50). AE, MC, V. Daily 10am–10pm. CANTONESE.

Don't stop at the Chinese take-away on the Queen's Road level, for on the second floor of this hotel is where brothers Colin and Moon Chan serve up a wide variety of surprisingly tasty Cantonese dishes. Their bright, clean, and air-conditioned dining room has simple decor with round wooden tables and pink woodwork. There's another convenient but less appealing branch on the Queen's Road in Nadi Town (☎ 700178).

Maharaja Restaurant
Queen's Road, Namaka, in K. Nataly & Sons Building. ☎ **722962**. Reservations not accepted. Main courses F$6–F$17 ($4–$12). MC, V. Mon–Sat 9am–10pm, Sun 7–10pm. INDIAN/EUROPEAN/CHINESE.

Kishore Nand's somewhat cramped storefront establishment offers Chinese and European selections, but his Indian dishes, including spicy curries of beef, lamb, goat, chicken, or vegetables, are the main attractions. They are well seasoned and clearly reflect Kishore's motto: "Good food at a good price." The Maharaja Banquet offers a sampling for F$20 ($14) per person. Lobster in butter sauce leads the European dishes, which otherwise lean toward plain but hearty grilled steaks, fish, and pork and lamb chops. The Chinese selections are prepared in the Cantonese style.

MARTINTAR AREA

The Bounty Restaurant
Queen's Road, Martintar. ☎ **720840**. Reservations accepted. Main courses F$12–F$17 ($8.50–$12). MC, V. Mon–Sat 9am–10pm, Sun 5–10pm. INTERNATIONAL/FIJIAN.

Brian and Veronica Smith always offer a daily Fijian special, such as palusami, at their pleasant storefront eatery within walking distance of the Martintar hotels. Their regular menu stars grilled tender local steaks from a butcher shop just down the Queen's Road, but the Bounty Special is a sweet combination of grilled chicken, onions, green peppers, and pineapple simmered in wine and served in a hollowed-out pineapple. Their straight-backed chairs are a bit uncomfortable, but candles and subdued lighting add a romantic atmosphere. A small bar and a New Zealand–style drinking table in the rear draw a very mixed clientele of tourists, resident expatriots, and parliamentarians. A Fijian band plays Monday to Saturday evenings and a jazz group plays on Sunday. Guests so inclined can dance in a small open area.

Valentino's
Kennedy Street, Martintar, behind Sia's Bar & Nite Club. ☎ **720640**. Reservations accepted. Main courses F$9–F$23 ($6.50–$16). AE, MC, V. Tues–Sun 6:30–10pm. ITALIAN.

A converted house with two dining rooms inside and an outdoor patio, this establishment is not your usual spaghetti house, for you won't get a bolognese sauce here. Instead, the menu includes spaghetti with sun-dried tomatoes, spinach ravioli, pan-fried octopus Napolitana, lemon fish, lobster prepared four ways, and a delicious brandied chicken. Arched doorways divide the two indoor dining rooms, which have small paintings of Italian scenes.

NADI TOWN

✪ Chefs The Restaurant

Sangayam Road, Nadi Town (behind Jack's Handicrafts). ☎ **703131.** Reservations advised. Main courses F$20–F$33 ($14–$23). AE, DC, MC, V. Mon–Sat 6–10pm. CONTINENTAL.

The chefs here are Josef Frankl and Eugene Gomes, who left the Sheraton Fiji to open the dining complex at Jack's Handicrafts (see The Edge and The Corner, below). Chefs The Restaurant is where they show off their culinary skill, which makes this one of the finest eateries in Fiji. A large, Sphinx-like statue and an aqua-and-coral color scheme dominate their modern, urban-style dining room. The service is extraordinarily attentive, and the cuisine very well presented. You won't soon forget the staff's rolling a trolley to your table loaded with monstrous wooden salt and pepper shakers. The changing menu leans toward continental cuisine, especially wiener schnitzel and other selections from Josef's native Germany. You might also find Hungarian goulash and Spanish paella. They always have grilled prawns, beef tenderloin, and rack of lamb to satisfy their Australian and New Zealand guests. Guests of the Sheraton Fiji can charge their bills here to their rooms.

⑤ Coffee Lounge Restaurant

Queen's Rd., Nadi Town, opposite Jack's Handicrafts. ☎ **701240.** Reservations not accepted. Snacks F50¢–F$1.50 (35¢–$1.05); curries F$2–F$3.50 ($1.40–$2.50). No credit cards. Mon–Sat 8am–6pm. INDIAN.

This immaculately clean and very popular vegetarian restaurant offers fresh fruit juices, refreshing ice creams, plain sandwiches, and delicious curries. If it's morning coffee you need, try their piping hot cappucino. The hot Indian items are displayed behind the glass of a hot table, so you can see what you're ordering. A three-course lunch special is served from noon to 2pm. At F$3.50 ($2.50), this is a remarkable value considering the quality and the cleanliness of this establishment.

The Corner

Queens Road, Nadi Town, opposite Jack's Handicrafts. Reservations not accepted. ☎ **703131.** Sandwiches, burgers, and hot dogs F$2.50–F$5 ($1.75–$3.50); meals F$5.50–F$9 ($4–$6.30). No credit cards. Mon–Sat 9am–6pm. SNACKS/PASTRIES/CANTONESE.

One of The Chefs' operations, this pleasant cafeteria-style establishment has an ice cream bar at the entrance offering tropical fruit selections in freshly baked cones. The cafeteria menu is varied: pastries and coffee, hot dogs and hamburgers, sandwiches and salads, roast chicken, and fish and chips. Most meals are Cantonese stir-fries, but a highlight here is a creamy Thai curry chicken that shows off chef Eugene Gomes's international experience with the Sheraton chain.

Curry Restaurant

Queen's Road, Nadi Town, opposite Mobil Station. ☎ **700960.** Reservations not accepted. Meals F$5.50–F$12.50 ($4–$8.75). No credit cards. Mon–Sat 8am–9:30pm, Sun 9am–9pm. INDIAN.

Don't come to this popular "curry shop" for anything except Nadi Town's best crab, prawn, goat, fish, chicken, lamb, and duck curries, all served with dhal soup, rice, roti, papadam, and a selection of chutneys. One alternative is *palau*, the multiflavored rice dish that is the staple at most Indian homes. Although crab and duck curries run up to F$12.50 ($8.75), most dishes cost about F$8 ($5.50).

The Edge

Sagayam Road, Nadi Town, behind Jack's Handicrafts. ☎ **703131.** Reservations not accepted. Burgers F$6.50 ($4.50); main courses F$9–F$15 ($6.30–$10.50). AE, DC, MC, V. Mon–Sat 9am–6pm. INTERNATIONAL.

The third dining establishment of chefs Josef Frankl and Eugene Gomes, this air-conditioned cafe is a more comfortable, upscale version of The Corner. It has an ice cream bar, a variety of hamburgers, and many of the same Asian stir-fries and Thai curry chicken offered at The Corner, but here they are served at your table. This cool, casual establishment is a fine place to take a shopping break over a cup of cappucino, espresso, or herbal tea.

ⓢ Mama's Pizza Inn

Queen's Road, Nadi Town, opposite Mobil Station. ☎ **701221.** Reservations not accepted. Pizzas F$4–F$21 ($3–$15); pastas F$5.50 ($4). MC, V. Mon–Sat 10am–11pm, Sun 11am–11pm. ITALIAN.

Travelers in need of a tomato sauce fix can follow the aroma of garlic to Robin O'Donnell's cozy establishment. Robin is a Fiji-born European, but her pizzas are worthy of an Italian upbringing. They range from a small plain model to a large deluxe version with all the toppings. She also has spaghetti, lasagna, and fresh salads. Order at what looks like a bar in a drinking establishment and take your meal at one of the picnic-style tables. There's another Mama's with the same menu, prices, and hours in the Colonial Plaza shopping mall on the Queen's Road in Namaka (☎ 720922).

6 Cruises, Island Escapes & Other Outdoor Activities

Nadi has a host of sporting and outdoor activities to suit almost every interest. Only a few of these are in the immediate vicinity of Nadi; most require a boat trip to the Mamanuca Islands or to other locations on Viti Levu. See "Resorts off Nadi" later in this chapter for more information about what these islands have to offer.

A DAY ON AN ISLAND The Great Sea Reef off northwest Viti Levu in effect encloses a huge lagoon whose usually calm waters surround the nearby Mamanuca and Yasawa island groups with speckled shades of yellow, green, and blue as the sea changes from shallow to deep. It's a fine place to go cruising for at least a day or longer. Most of the excursions mentioned below depart from Denarau Island Marina, although a few leave from Lautoka. Bus transportation from the Nadi area hotels is included in their prices.

Aqualand (☎ 700144) is a group of buildings on a tiny islet with little vegetation but lots of sand and a surrounding lagoon. Water sports enthusiasts can pay to play all day at a wide variety of activities, such as scuba diving, waterskiing, windsurfing, parasailing, and scooting around on small craft. Round-trip transfers cost F$44 ($31) including lunch and F$33 ($23) without a meal (you can order snacks à la carte). Most activities cost extra. There is no overnight accommodation at Aqualand.

Beachcomber Day Cruises (☎ 661500) sail from both Denarau Island Marina and Lautoka to youth-oriented Beachcomber Island Resort. Adults pay F$58 ($40.50) for bus transportation, the cruise, and an all-you-can-eat buffet lunch on Beachcomber Island. Snorkeling gear costs F$3 ($2) for two hours, plus a refundable F$40 ($28) deposit. It's a fine way to join the young folks frolicking in the sun without having to stay overnight. A few tops have been known to drop at Beachcomber, so if the sight of a woman's unclothed breasts offends, think twice before signing up for this one.

Captain Cook Cruises (☎ 701823) sails on the *Ra Marama,* a 110-foot square-rigged brigantine built in Singapore during the 1950s and used as the official yacht for Fiji's colonial governors-general. Now fully restored, it makes a day cruise through the Mamanuca Islands, including stops at Mystery Island and Plantation Island Resort. It costs F$54 ($38) per person.

Castaway Island Resort (☎ 722988) hosts day trippers who arrive by the ketch *Ariadne,* which stops at Daydream Island on the way (see below). A string band entertains during the one-hour voyage each way from Denarau Island Marina. The cruise and buffet lunch on Castaway Island cost F$66 ($46).

Daydream Island (☎ 723314) actually is Malama, a six-acre islet studded with palm trees and circled with white-sand beaches. The only inhabitants will be you and your fellow passengers, who will use Malama's only building, a thatch bure, for a barbecue lunch. Guests are taken to the island on the sailing ketch *Ariadne,* which goes on to Castaway Island Resort (see above). The F$66 ($46) price includes lunch.

Island Express (☎ 700144), a 300-passenger, diesel-powered catamaran, makes two trips a day through the hilly, picturesque Mamanucas. It primarily serves as a ferry for visitors who have too much luggage to fly to the Mamanucas. It departs Denarau Island Marina daily at 9am for Mana Island and stops briefly at Castaway Island, Club Naitasi, and Plantation Island resorts on the way back. Its second voyage begins at 1:30pm and goes over the same route in reverse order. You have two options for day trips. One, you can spend four hours sightseeing through the islands on the morning run for F$35 ($24.50) per person. You won't be able to luxuriate on any beaches, as the boat stops at each resort only long enough to put off and pick up passengers and their luggage. Two, you can take the morning trip, get off at **Castaway Island Resort** or **Mana Island Resort,** have a buffet lunch, swim and sunbathe, and catch the afternoon voyage back to The Regent. The Castaway Island excursion costs about F$59 ($41.50), and the Mana Island stop about F$69 ($48.50). Both include a buffet lunch.

Malololailai Island, nine miles offshore, can be visited by plane as well as on a day cruise. Sunflower Airlines (☎ 723016) has frequent flights from Nadi Airport to the little gravel strip separating Plantation Island and Musket Cove Resorts. Sunflower's special excursion round-trip fare is F$44 ($31). The trip includes free use of some facilities at Plantation Island Resort, but you pay for motorized water sports such as parasailing and waterskiing. Once on Malololailai, you can hang out at either resort, shop at Louis and Georgie Czukelter's Art Gallery on the hill above Musket Cove, and dine at Anandas Restaurant and Bar (☎ 722333) by the airstrip.

Seafari Cruise is what South Sea Cruises (☎ 701445) calls its rent-a-boat service at Denarau Island Marina. You design your own cruise to the Mamanuca Group, such as picnicking at a deserted beach or picking your own snorkeling spots. Prices depend on the size of the boat. The largest can hold up to 20 passengers.

FISHING The Regent of Fiji, the Sheraton Fiji, and all the resorts in the Mamanucas offer sports fishing as a pay-extra activity for their guests. On the mainland, **South Sea Cruises** (☎ 701445) has a fleet of fishing boats and guides based at Denarau Island Marina. Offshore, that same company operates under the name **Pleasure Marine** (same phone), with boats at Musket Cove Resort and Mana Island Resort. **Bay Cruises** (☎ 722676) also has fishing boats available.

GOLF & TENNIS   The 18-hole, 7,150-yard, par-72 links of **Denarau Golf & Racquet Club** (☎ 750477) sit on most of Denarau Island, opposite The Regent of Fiji and the Sheraton Fiji. The clubhouse has a restaurant and bar as well as showers and locker rooms. Greens fees are F$77 ($54) for guests of the two big resorts and F$85 ($59.50) for those of us who can't afford to stay there. The course is open daily from 7am to dark. The club has six all-weather tennis courts and six Wimbledon-standard grass courts. They are open from 7am to 7:30pm daily. They are free to guests of The Regent and Sheraton; everyone else pays F$17.50 ($12.50) an hour from 7 to 11am and 3 to 7:30pm, F$9 ($6.50) an hour from 11am to 3pm. Lessons are available. Proper tennis attire is required.

The hotel tour desks can arrange for you to play at the 18-hole **Nadi Airport Golf Club** (☎ 722148) near Newtown Beach, behind the airport. The 5,882-yard, par-70 course isn't particularly challenging, but the setting, on the shores of Nadi Bay, is attractive. Greens fees are F$11 ($7.70). Rental clubs are available. You must bring your own libation and pay a F$5 ($3.50) fee to use the clubhouse bar. The **Fiji Mocambo Hotel** (☎ 722000) has a short course for its guests. The South Pacific's best course is at **Pacific Harbour** (☎ 450022), in Deuba near Suva, some 89 miles from Nadi. Greens fees there are F$44 ($31).

HIKING   An arm of Rosie The Travel Service (☎ 722755), **Adventures Fiji** offers trekkers (as hikers are known in these parts) the chance to make a one-day walk some 2,000 feet up into the Nausori Highlands above Nadi. The trail crosses streams, where hikers can take a refreshing dip. Fijian villagers provide a local-style lunch. Cost is F$50 ($35) per person. The company also has four-, six- and 10-day hikes across central Viti Levu ranging in price from F$375 to F$900 ($262.50 to $630), including transfers, guide, accommodation, and meals provided by Fijian villagers along the way.

HORSEBACK RIDING   Groups of six riders can meander through the hills near Nadi Town with **Safe Riders** (☎ 703390). The tours cost F$50 ($35) per person, including transportation to the ranch.

JET BOATS   For a thrill-a-minute carnival ride afloat, **Shotover Jet Fiji** (☎ 750400) will take you twisting and turning through the mangrove-lined creeks behind Denarau Island. This is the company that pioneered jet-boating on the Shotover River in New Zealand, and its speedy "Big Red" boats go roaring around these Fijian waterways. Heart-stopping 360-degree turns are guaranteed to get the adrenalin flowing and the clothes wet. The half-hour rides depart every 15 minutes daily from Denarau Island Marina. A shuttle connects the nearby Sheraton and Regent; there are scheduled pickups from the airport area hotels, so call for reservations. Price is F$55 ($38.50) for adults and F$24 ($17) for children.

RIVER RAFTING   Travel videos and brochures seem always to feature tourists lazily floating down a Fijian river on a raft made of bamboo poles lashed together. In the old days, mountain-dwelling Fijians really did use *bilibilis*—flimsy bamboo rafts—to float their crops downriver to market. They would discard the rafts and walk home. Today you can ride your own bilibili down the Navua River, on the Coral Coast west of Suva. The full-day trips cost about F$70 ($49) from the Nadi hotels, less from the Coral Coast. Contact UTC (☎ 722811) for information and reservations.

For regular white-water adventures in rubber rafts, **Wilderness Fiji Tours** (☎ 386498 in Suva) and **Roaring Thunder** (☎ 702029 in Nadi) operate trips down the Ba River, the stream that flows swiftly through the Naloto Range and crosses a delta to Ba, a predominantly Indian town on Viti Levu's north coast. The amount of white water will depend on the amount of rain the area has received. The first two hours of the all-day trip are spent in a bus winding through the countryside and up into the hills. The trips cost F$70 ($49), including a riverside lunch. The trips are restricted to visitors between 15 and 45 years of age, unless they are "perfectly fit" and willing to sign a form releasing the company of liability. Bring bathing suits or shorts, lace-up athletic shoes, plenty of sunscreen, and insect repellent.

SAILING   Fiji's reef-strewn waters will not permit strictly "bareboat" yacht charters, but you can rent both boat and skipper or local guide for extended cruises through the islands.

Captain Cook Cruises (☎ 701823, fax 702045) has regularly scheduled, four-day, three-night "sailing safaris" on the *Rubaiyyat*, a ketch-rigged sailboat with clipper bow. Guests actually stay ashore in two-person tents pitched beside a deserted beach. Cost is about F$375 ($263) per person. The cruises include a stop at Beachcomber Island Resort.

The Moorings (☎ and fax 666710) has one of its South Pacific operations based at Musket Cove Resort in the Mamanucas. Boats ranging in size from 36 feet to 50 feet can be sailed through the Mamanucas and Yasawas, but you must be accompanied by a local guide. Prices range from U.S. $2,300 to U.S. $4,500 per week. If a boat is available, it can be rented for F$500 to F$990 ($350 to $693) a day. Provisions are extra. The Moorings also offers sailing lessons. Week-long charters should be booked before leaving home. For more information contact The Moorings, 19345 U.S. 19 North, Suite 402, Clearwater, FL 34624 (☎ 813/535-1446 or 800/535-7289).

Dulcinea, a 55-ketch, and ***Hobo,*** a 37-footer, both operate from Musket Cove Resort (☎ 662215) in the Mamanucas. Musket Cove's marina is a mecca for cruising yachts such as these, some of whose skippers hang around and take charters for a living. These two vessels have day cruises for F$35 ($24.50) per person and are available for longer cruises.

✪ ***Whale's Tale*** (☎ 722455, fax 720134), a luxury, 100-foot auxiliary sailboat owned by American Paul Myers, takes no more than 12 guests on day cruises from Denarau Island Marina through the Mamanucas. The F$160 ($112) per person cost may seem steep, but it includes a continental breakfast with champagne on departure; a buffet lunch prepared on board; and all beverages, including beer, wine, and liquor, and sunset cocktails. The *Whale's Tale* also is available for charters ranging from one day in the Mamanucas to three days and two nights in the Yasawas. Rates depend on the length of trip.

SCUBA DIVING & SNORKELING   Dive operators in the Nadi area include **Tropical Divers Fiji** (☎ 750777, ext. 189) at the Sheraton Fiji Resort, **South Sea Divers** (☎ 701455) at The Regent, and **Inner Space Adventures** (☎ 723883) at Wailoaloa Beach. All have dive guides and teach courses. Prices range from F$60 to F$80 ($42 to $56) for a one-tank dive. **H₂O Sportz** (☎ 720100) operates at Seashell Cove Resort south of Nadi. It charges F$66 ($46) for a two-tank dive, including all equipment.

7 Shopping in Nadi

Bargaining is not considered to be polite when dealing with Fijians. And although the better stores have gotten away from the practice, bargaining is quite acceptable when dealing with most Indian merchants. They will start high, you will start low, and somewhere in between will be found a mutually agreeable price. I usually knock 40% off the asking price as an initial counteroffer and then suffer the merchants' indignant snickers, secure in the knowledge that they aren't about to kick me out of the store. After all, the fun has just begun.

Caution: Fijians normally are extremely friendly people, but beware of so-called **sword sellers.** These are Fijian men who carry bags under their arms and approach you on the street. "Where you from, States?" will be their opening line, followed quickly by "What's your name?" If you respond, they will quickly inscribe your name on a sloppily carved wooden sword carried in the bag. They expect you to buy the sword, whether you want it or not. They are especially numerous in Suva, but they likely will come up to you in Nadi, too. The Fiji government discourages this practice but has had only limited success in stopping it. The easiest way to avoid this scam is not tell any stranger your name.

Duty-Free Shopping   Fiji has the most developed duty-free shopping industry in the South Pacific, as will be very obvious when you walk along the main thoroughfare in Nadi Town. One shop after another offers brand-name perfume, jewelry, watches, electronic equipment, cameras, liquor, cigarettes, and a plethora of other items.

The Fiji government charges a flat 10% import tax on merchandise brought into the country, so the stores aren't exactly "duty free." Accordingly, shop around carefully before leaving home if you are thinking of buying an expensive watch or camera. You likely will find better prices and selections at the larger-volume dealers at home, especially in the United States, Canada, Australia, and New Zealand. Find the item at home first so that you can compare the price in Fiji. Also compare the models offered in the duty-free shops with those available at home. Those sold in Fiji may not be the latest editions.

If you decide to make a purchase, follow this advice from the Fiji National Duty Free Merchants Association: Request receipts accurately describing your purchases. Make sure all guarantee and warranty cards are properly completed and stamped by the merchant. Examine all items before making payment. If you later find that the item is not what you expected, return to the shop immediately with the item and your receipt. As a general rule, purchases are not returnable and deposits are not refundable.

Personally, I pay for my duty-free purchases by credit card. That way, if something goes wrong after I'm back home, I can call for help from the large financial institution that issued my card.

To avoid the hassles of bargaining, visit **Jack's Handicrafts, Prouds,** and **Tappoo** the largest and most reputable merchants. They have well-stocked shops on Queen's Road in Nadi Town as well as in the shopping arcades of the larger hotels in Nadi and on the Coral Coast. Prouds and Tappoo also are in Sigatoka and downtown Suva. Jack's Handicrafts' upstairs rooms have clothing and leather goods. Tappoo carries a broad range of merchandise, including electronics, cameras, and sporting goods. Prouds concentrates more on jewelry, perfumes, and watches.

If you missed anything, you'll get one last chance at the huge shops in the departure lounge at Nadi airport.

Handcrafts   Fijians produce a wide variety of handcrafts, such as carved tanoa (kava) bowls, war clubs, and cannibal forks; woven baskets and mats; pottery; and masi (tapa cloth). Although generally not of the quality of those produced in Tonga, they are made in prolific quantities. Be careful when buying some wood-carvings, however, for many of today's items are machine-made. Only with masi can you be sure of getting a genuine Fijian handcraft.

On the other hand, virtually every shop now sells some very fine face masks and *nguzunguzus* ("noozoo noozoos"), the inlaid canoe prows carved in Solomon Islands, and some primitive art from Papua New Guinea. (Although you will see plenty hanging in the shops, the Fijians never carved masks in the old days.)

If you're going to Suva, wait until you've visited **Wolf's Boutique** (the top handcraft store in the country) and the **Government Handicraft Centre.** There you will see some of the best items, all of them authentic, and get a firm idea of the going prices. See the "Suva & Levuka" chapter, later in this book, for details.

The largest and best-stocked shop on Queen's Road is **Jack's Handicrafts** (☎ 700744), opposite the Morris Hedstrom department store. It has a wide selection of handcrafts, jewelry, T-shirts, clothing, and paintings by local artists. The prices are reasonable and the staff helpful rather than pushy. The Chefs restaurant complex is on premises (see "Where to Dine in Nadi," below). Jack's Handicrafts also has an outlet in the shopping arcade of the Sheraton Fiji Resort (☎ 701777) and in Sigatoka (☎ 500810).

Other places to look are **Nadi Handicraft Center** (☎ 780357), a block south of Jack's Handicrafts on the other side of Queen's Road, and **Nad's Handicrafts** (☎ 703588), near the north end of town. Nad's usually has the best selection of Fijian pottery.

In the Sheraton Fiji arcade on Denarau Island, the **General Store** (☎ 701585) has a small but excellent selection of handcrafts. The Sheraton's shops are open daily 9am to 9pm.

Nadi Handicraft Market (no phone) is a collection of stalls on the Queen's Road near the south end of Nadi Town. The best are operated by Fijian women who sell baskets and other goods woven of pandanus.

If you're going that way, check out the handcraft stalls in the **Lautoka Market** for shells and shell jewelry, mats, straw hats and purses, grass skirts, and tapa cloth. The wood carvings tend to be a bit touristy, since the stalls do most of their business on days when cruise ships put into Lautoka.

Tropical Clothing   Although not of the quality in other South Pacific countries, colorful tie-dyed clothing and sulus are for sale at most of the hotel boutiques and in the shops along Queen's Road in Nadi Town. **Sogo Fiji** (☎ 701604), on Queen's Road in Nadi Town, carries up-market designer dresses and beachwear. It has other outlets in Sigatoka and on Victoria Parade in Suva. **Tiki Togs** is the country's largest producer of resort wear; it has shops in most major hotels and on Victoria Parade in Suva. For the most unusual items, **Michoutouchkine Creations** (☎ 750158), in the shopping arcade of the Sheraton Fiji Resort, has the creations of Nicolai Michoutouchkine, the noted Vanuatu artist whose squiggly swirls distinguish each of his shirts, blouses, pants suits, and beach towels.

Impressions

Every resort seemed to have a platoon of insanely friendly Fijians.
—Scott L. Malcolmson, 1990

8 Island Nights in Nadi

The large hotels usually have something going on every night. As noted in "Dining Out in Nadi," above, this may be a special meal followed by a Fijian meke dance show. They also frequently have live entertainment in their bars during the cocktail hour. Check the *Spotlight on Nadi* and *Fiji Magic* tourist publication for what's happening.

Unlike the fast, hip-swinging, suggestive dancing of Tahiti and the Cook Islands, Fijians follow the custom of the Samoas and Tonga, with gentle movements taking second place to the harmony of their voices. Only in the spear-waving war dances do you see much action. Nevertheless, taking in a meke is a popular way to spend at least one evening in Nadi.

Popular watering holes—especially during the 6 to 7pm Monday to Friday happy hours—are **The Bounty Restaurant** (☎ 720840) in Martintar, **Mama's Pizza Inn** (☎ 701221) in Nadi Town, and the open-air bar at the **Tanoa International Hotel** (☎ 720277). The lounge bar in the **Fiji Mocambo Hotel** (☎ 722000) has music and dancing every evening, including Sunday.

9 Resorts off Nadi

Although I am placing Fiji's offshore resorts in the sections devoted to their jumping-off points, I suggest you review each of them carefully before making a choice. As I already have pointed out, offshore resorts are great places to relax or engage in water sports, but they are not in themselves bases from which to explore the country. Just because a resort is situated close to Nadi, therefore, doesn't necessarily mean it will have the features that will appeal to you. I recommend that you review all Fiji's offshore resorts carefully before making a decision. In particular, see The Wakaya Club and Toberua Island Resort in the "Suva & Levuka" chapter; and Moody's Namena, Qamea Beach Club, Matagi Island Resort, and Kaimbu Island Resort, all in the "Northern Fiji" chapter.

Most of the resorts off Nadi are in the Mamanuca Islands, a chain of small flat atolls and hilly islands ranging from four to 20 miles west of Nadi. Others are in the Yasawas, a similar but much less developed chain as much as 60 miles northwest of Nadi. Another is on Vatulele, a flat, raised coral island 30 miles south of Viti Levu but serviced from Nadi Airport.

Lt. Charles Wilkes, commander of the U.S. exploring expedition that charted Fiji in 1840, said the Yasawas reminded him of "a string of blue beads lying along the horizon," and they haven't changed much over the intervening century and a half. Fijians still live in small villages huddled among the curving coconut palms beside some of the South Pacific's most awesomely beautiful beaches.

The climate on all these islands is semiarid. Coupled with their proximity to Nadi Airport, this consistent sunshine made the Mamanuca Islands the first in Fiji to be opened to tourists back in the early 1960s. They still are very popular with Australians and New Zealanders on one- or two-week holidays. The younger resorts in the Yasawas and on Vatulele fall into the very expensive, super-deluxe category.

Getting There   The *Island Express* (☎ 700144) essentially provides ferry service from Denarau Island Marina to the Mamanuca resorts twice daily. Fares are F$30 ($21) one-way or F$54 ($38) round-trip to Plantation and Musket Cove Resorts, F$40 ($28) one-way or F$72 ($50.50) round-trip to Castaway or Mana Island. Backpackers going to the Mana Island hostel pay F$33 ($23) one-way or F$66 ($46) round-trip.

Beachcomber Island and Treasure Island Resorts are served by the *Tui Tai* from Lautoka and the *Stardust* from Denarau Island Marina (☎ 661500 for both).

Sunflower Airlines (☎ 723016) flies several times a day from Nadi Airport to both Mana Island and Malololailai, home of Plantation and Musket Cove resorts. **Turtle Airways** (☎ 722988) provides chartered seaplane service to Mana Island. **Island Hoppers** (☎ 720172) has charter helicopter service to the Sheraton Vomo, Mana Island, Treasure Island, and Castaway Island Resorts. **Pleasure Marine** (☎ 700144) provides water taxi service to the islands from Denarau Island Marina.

The Mamanuca, Yasawa, and Vatulele resorts will make transfer arrangements when you reserve with them.

VERY EXPENSIVE

Sheraton Vomo Island

P.O. Box 5650, Lautoka (Vomo Island, 20 miles northwest of Nadi Airport). ☎ **667955** or 800/325-3535. Fax 667997. 30 bungalows. A/C MINIBAR TEL. F$1,030–F$2,425 ($721–$1,698). Rates include champagne breakfast, first stocking of minibar, and round-trip helicopter transfers from Nadi Airport. AE, DC, MC, V.

The most interesting thing about this new resort is Vomo Island itself. This unusual clump of land has a steep, 550-foot-high hill on one end; the other consists of a perfectly flat, 200-acre shelf surrounded by a reef edged by brilliantly colorful corals. The resort, which is not managed by the Sheraton chain, is built along the western side, with bungalows either along a fine stretch of beach or climbing the hill to provide views of the reef and sea. You likely will have next-door neighbors here, since all but a few bungalows are in duplex buildings. The shiplap wooden units have beige tin roofs; screened porches (with coconut-shell "Do Not Disturb" signs); sitting areas with sofas, TVs, and multimedia sound systems; polished wooden floors with throw rugs; dressing areas with robes and slippers; and baths with both spa tubs and glass-enclosed showers.

Dining/Entertainment: Three restaurants, one of them in a central building with a bar, provide excellent cuisine, with an emphasis on fresh seafood. Outdoors, The Gazebo provides gourmet dining, while On the Rocks offers chargrilled seafood. The latter faces rocky Vomolailai (Little Vomo) Island, where guests can escape for private picnics. Fijian bands play for evening dining at all three venues.

Services: In-room dining; laundry and dry cleaning; evening turndown.

Facilities: Swimming pool; tennis courts; nine-hole, pitch-and-putt golf course; Windsurfers, catamarans, snorkeling gear, scuba diving, fishing (guests pay for diving and motorized water sports).

✪ Vatulele Island Resort

P.O. Box 9936, Nadi Airport (Vatulele Island, 30 miles south of Viti Levu, a 30-minute flight from Nadi). ☎ **720300** or 800/828-9146. Fax 720062. 15 bungalows. MINIBAR.

F$1,000–F$1,245 ($700–$872) double. Rates includes room, food, bar, all activities except scuba diving. Higher quoted rates apply April and May, July–October, December and January. Four-night minimum stay required. Round-trip transfers F$308 ($216) per person. AE, DC, MC, V.

When Australian TV producer Henry Crawford *(A Town like Alice)* and Fiji-born hotel manager Martin Livingston (formerly of Turtle Island Lodge, below) both turned 40 in the late 1980s, they decided to build the ultimate hideaway resort. They chose a 1km-long beach on Vatulele, a relatively flat island off the Coral Coast known for its unique red prawns (that is, shrimp that are red while alive, not just after being cooked). With an eye on the environment, they cleared just enough thick native brush to build 15 spacious bures and a central dining room-bar-lounge complex. Each bure faces the beach but is separated from its companions by lots of privacy-providing foliage and distance. In a fascinating blend of Santa Fe and Fijian native architectural styles, the bures and main building have thick adobe walls supporting tall Fijian thatch roofs. Each L-shaped bure has a lounge and raised sleeping areas under one roof, plus another roof covering an enormous bath that can be entered both from the bed/dressing area and from a private, hammock-swung patio. Each unit has a king-size bed with mosquito net suspended from the rafters. Although benchlike seats in the lounge can double as beds for children, kids under 12 are allowed only during certain weeks, usually coinciding with Australian school holidays.

Dining/Entertainment: Before they opened in 1990, Henry and Martin hired a gourmet chef away from The Regent, so the food is top-notch. Weather permitting, guests dine on a patio beside the central building. They can dine anytime and anyplace they want, but most meals are taken dinner-party-fashion with Martin acting as host (Henry spends most of his time in Australia). Frankly, dining at the same table with Martin Livingston is one reason to visit Vatulele, providing you can hold your own in razor-sharp conversation and don't mind a bit of raunchy humor. Although staff members play guitars and sing island songs, the nightly dinner parties *are* the entertainment at Vatulele, and they can go into the wee hours. (This style of dining is a major difference between Vatulele and other very expensive resorts, such as The Wakaya Club and Yasawa Island Lodge, where guests are left more to themselves.)

Services: Laundry; evening turndown.

Facilities: A Library with 2,000 volumes; scuba diving; wide array of non-motorized water sports equipment; tiny private island for secluded picnics; all-weather tennis court.

Turtle Island Lodge

P.O. Box 9317, Nadi Airport (Nanuya Levu Island, Yasawas, about 55 miles off Lautoka). ☎ **722921** or 800/826-3083. Fax 720007. 14 bungalows. MINIBAR. U.S. $770 per couple (all inclusive). Round-trip seaplane transfers U.S. $520 per couple. AE, DE, MC, V.

San Franciscan Richard Evanson graduated from Harvard Business School, married into a prominent Seattle, Wash., family, made a bundle in cable television, and then ran into alcoholism and divorce. In 1972 he bought hilly, 500-acre Nanuya Levu, one of the few privately owned islands in the Yasawas, and shortly thereafter founded this retreat for the rich and famous. Until the resorts on Vatulele, Wakaya, and Kaibu opened in 1990, he had the top-of-the-line market in Fiji all to himself (competition is tough now; some regular clients have followed Turtle's former manager, the highly entertaining Martin Livingston, to Vatulele).

Turtle's 14 spacious, thatch-roofed bures sit next to two of the island's 12 picturesque beaches, some of which were used as settings for the second making of *The Blue Lagoon*, starring Brooke Shields. The other 10 beaches on Nanuya Levu are deserted, as are four of the seven smaller islands nearby (one of which is owned by Blue Lagoon Cruises, which anchors its boats there and lets its guests play ashore; another is Taweva, home of two backpackers' paradises—see below). Turtle Island accommodates only "mixed adult couples" (translated: no children and no same-sex couples welcome; you don't have to be married, but you do need to be straight).

Dining/Entertainment: Excellent quality meals are served in the thatch-roofed, beachside dining room. As Martin does at Vatulele, Richard acts as dinner host most evenings; otherwise, guests can dine in their bungalows. Staff members strum guitars and sing island songs during cocktail hour and after the meals. Fijian mekes are staged some evenings.

Services: Laundry; guests names are carved on wooden plaques attached to their bures; evening turndown.

Facilities: A wide range of water sports activities and equipment, including scuba diving.

✪ Yasawa Island Lodge

P.O. Box 10128, Nadi Airport (Yasawa Island, 30-minute charter flight northwest of Nadi). ☎ **663364** or 800/441-6880. Fax 665044. 16 bungalows. A/C MINIBAR TEL. F$725–F$930 ($508–$683). Rates include room and all meals but no drinks. Round-trip transfers F$330 ($231) per person. AE, DC, MC, V.

This deluxe, informal resort sits in a small indention among steep cliffs lining the west coast of skinny, relatively dry Yasawa Island, northernmost of the chain. After arriving at a private dirt airstrip that reaches from shore to shore (one end actually goes uphill), guests are handed a fruit punch by charming managers Max and Dorothy Storck, and driven to the resort on the back of a "Bula Bus," a plodding World War II troop transport equipped with a thatch roof. There they find an airy octagonal main building whose tall, thatch-covered tin roof is held up by umbrella-like beams. Sitting next to a pool fed by chlorinated seawater (fresh water can be scarce in the Yasawas), it holds a spacious dining area and bar. The Great Sea Reef is so far offshore that surf slaps against shelves of black rock just off a nearby beach of deep white sand.

The large, air-conditioned guest bures come in two types. Most are long, 1,000-square-foot rectangular models with thatch roofs over white stucco walls (the style makes this resort physically reminiscent of Vatulele Island Resort). On one end, a row of potted tropical plants separates a raised sleeping area from a spacious living room with bar, table and chairs, divans built into a wall, and two ceiling fans. On the other, a bath has toiletries, a hairdryer, Japanese-style robes, and a monstrous shower with his-and-her heads. There's no shower curtain, so you can watch yourself cavort in the mirrors above two sinks across the room. A door leads from the shower to a private sunbathing patio. There's also a separate dressing area and walk-in closet equipped with iron and board. A few other one- and two-bedroom models are less appealing but are better arranged for families and have fine views from the side of the hill backing the property. Children are allowed here only at Christmas, Easter, and certain school holiday periods in June, July, and August.

Dining/Entertainment: Gourmet cuisine features local seafood such as lobster and "pretty ladies" (reef crabs). Guests are offered at least one meat and one seafood course for dinner. They all dine together for twice-weekly Fijian-style lovos, but otherwise they can choose their own spacious seating arrangements. Staff members play string instruments during cocktail hour and dinner, and nearby villagers come over to serenade. Activities included in the rates are tennis, croquet, fishing, snorkeling, sailing, hiking to a lookout with a 360-degree panoramic view, village visits, and picnics and shelling expeditions to deserted beaches. Guests pay extra for scuba diving and deepsea fishing.

Services: Laundry; baby-sitting; evening turndown.

Facilities: Tennis and croquet court; pool; Windsurfers.

EXPENSIVE

✪ Castaway Island Resort

Private Mail Bag, Nadi Airport (Qalito Island, 13 miles off Nadi). ☎ **661233** or 800/888-0120. Fax 665753. 66 bungalows. F$310–F$370 ($217–$259). Rates include breakfast buffet. AE, DC, MC, V.

Built in the mid-1960s of logs and thatch, without the use of heavy equipment, Castaway maintains its rustic, Fijian-style charm despite many improvements over the years. The central activities building, perched on a point with white beaches on either side, still has a thatch roof, and the ceilings of the bures are still lined with genuine tapa cloth. Fijian staff members mingle freely with guests, who can join them at their church on Sunday. Although the guest bures sit relatively close together in a coconut grove, their roofs sweep low enough to provide privacy. Each unit has a queen-size bed, two settees that can double as beds for children, and rattan table and chairs. In addition to the central lounge-dining-bar building, a beachside water sports shack has a "Sundowner Bar" upstairs, appropriately facing west toward the Great Sea Reef. Guests dine in the central building, usually at umbrella tables on a stone beachside patio. Sydney restauranteur Geoff Shaw, who owns Castaway, makes sure the food is good and substantial. Staff members entertain with Fijian songs. For children, the staff provides a wide range of activities, from learning Fijian to sack races.

Facilities include a swimming pool, tennis court, games room, medical center with nurse, well-stocked boutique, children's playroom, and nursery. The resort has a wide variety of water sports, including scuba diving, parasailing, jet- and waterskiing. Guests pay extra for most motorized sports.

Mana Island Resort

P.O. Box 610, Lautoka (Mana Island, 20 miles off Nadi). ☎ **661333**. Fax 662713. 32 rms, 128 bungalows. A/C TEL. F$320–F$365 ($224–$256) rooms; F$235–F$385 ($165–$270) bungalows. Rates include full American breakfast. AE, DC, MC, V.

The largest resort off Nadi, this Japanese-owned property attracts a mix of nationalities, from Japanese singles and honeymooners to Australian and New Zealand couples and families. Since it has the only pier big enough to land the *Island Express,* Mana is a popular day-trip destination from Nadi (see "Sightseeing Tours," above). Seaplanes, planes, and helicopters land here, and Pleasure Marine has its water taxi base at Mana, so both daytrippers and guests have a wide choice of ways to get here. The complex sits on a flat saddle between two hills and two beaches, which means guests have a calm place to swim and snorkel whichever way the wind is blowing.

Accommodation is in bungalows of European construction with Fijian-shaped tile roofs; standard units have been around a long time, but new deluxe models on the beach are by far the choice here. A relatively new block of 32 hotel rooms faces the beach; entry is via rear walkways with lashed log railings. The rooms and deluxe bungalows are air conditioned. The older bungalows have ceiling fans but still can be quite warm at midday.

Guests can dine either on European-style fare in a large central building that also has a bar, lounge, and nightclub; at a steak house; or in a small daytime snack bar. There's a wide range of water sports activities, with guests paying to use the motorized toys. Aqua Trek Ocean Sports Adventures, an American firm, has its scuba-diving operation here (☎ 702413 or 800/541-4334).

Musket Cove Resort

Private Mail Bag, Nadi Airport (Malololailai Island, 9 miles off Nadi). ☎ **722371.** Fax 720378. 24 bungalows, 6 villas. F$220–F$250 ($154–$175) bungalow; F$300 ($210) villa. AE, DC, MC, V.

One of three Australians who own Malololailai Island, Dick Smith founded this little retreat in 1977. Built of native materials and decorated accordingly, but considerably spiffed up in recent years, the older bures sit in a row across a coconut grove from the beach. They have full kitchens (there are two small groceries on the island). Newer, larger models are closer to the beach and have separate bedrooms and much larger baths than their older siblings; they have toasters but no cooking facilities. The new, luxury villas have a living room, full kitchen, and master bedroom downstairs and two bedrooms upstairs; each bedroom has its own private bath.

Dick's Place has been retained as the name of Musket Cove's pleasant open-air bar and restaurant next to the swimming pool and a large flame tree (poinciana) that bursts into bloom around Christmas. Cruising yachties call at Musket Cove's modern marina from June to September. The names of their boats are posted on a wall in the inside bar. The yachties also congregate at the Two Dollar Bar, under a thatch roof out on a tiny manmade island reached by the marina's pontoons. Musket Cove hosts the annual Fiji Regatta Week in September, when it's the starting line for the yacht race from Musket Cove to Port Vila (Vanuatu). The Moorings have their charter yachts based here, and at least two other boats are available for day sailing (see "Cruises, Island Escapes, & Outdoor Activities," above). Although a broad mud bank appears here at low tide, Dick dredged out a swimming beach area when he built the marina. It has Hobie Cats, Windsurfers, and rowboats. For a fee, guests can go scuba diving, rent boats, and make excursions to other islands.

⑤ Naitasi Resort

P.O. Box 10044, Nadi Airport (Malolo Island, 15 miles off Nadi). ☎ **723999** or 800/392-8213. Fax 720197. 28 bungalows, 10 villas. TEL. F$250 ($175) bungalow; F$350 ($245) villa. AE, DC, MC, V.

Although not a luxury resort, Naitasi has two things going for it: all units have kitchens, which makes it attractive to families, and it has one of the few deep-water lagoons where you can swim off the beach at any tide. A pleasant bar and water sports shack surrounded by a large deck speckled with bright lounge furniture sits right on this fine beach. Anyone who can't tolerate the magnificent lagoon can take a dip in a swimming pool, which is chiseled out of the base of a hill, up by the main building. Guests have breakfast and dinner in the dark dining room of this building, but the rest of their time likely will be spent by the water's edge. Activities there include sea kayaking, sailing, and canoeing. Guests can go to nearby Castaway Island Resort for parasailing, jet- and waterskiing, and scuba diving.

Accommodation is in 10 spacious two-bedroom villas and 28 one-room duplex bungalows. They all have kitchen facilities, adequate shower-only baths, their own porches, and except for the duplex units, are far enough apart to provide privacy. Natural log beams supporting tin roofs are accented with coconut sennit, adding island-style charm. The resort's boutique carries grocery items.

Plantation Island Resort

P.O. Box 9176, Nadi Airport (Malololailai Island, 9 miles off Nadi). ☎ **722444.** Fax 720260. 41 rms, 70 bungalows. F$154–F$187 ($108–$131) rooms; F$248–F$385 ($174–$270) bungalow. AE, DC, MC, V.

One of the largest and most diverse of the offshore resorts, Plantation attracts couples, families, and day trippers from Nadi, giving it a Club Med–style atmosphere of nonstop activity. The resort has four types of accommodations: duplex bures suitable for singles or couples, two-bedroom bungalows suitable for families, and rather dark, uninviting hotel rooms in a two-story building. My personal choice is one of the spacious duplex bures with two ceiling fans. A large central building beside the beach has a bar, dance floor, lounge area, coffee shop, and restaurant. Guests can also wander over to Ananda's, a barbecue-oriented restaurant near the airport, or to Musket Cove for a meal. Facilities include a freshwater swimming pool, tennis courts, a beach, and free nonpowered water sports. Waterskiing, parasailing, scuba diving, and coral viewing in a semisubmersible craft all cost extra. There's also a children's playroom with a full-time baby-sitter.

Treasure Island Resort

P.O. Box 2210, Lautoka (Eluvuka Island, 12 miles off Lautoka). ☎ **666999** or 800/521-7242. 66 rms. F$264 ($185). AE, DC, MC, V.

Treasure Island occupies a tiny atoll that barely breaks the surface of the vast lagoon, about an hour's boat ride from the port town of Lautoka. It's geared to couples and families rather than to the sometimes-raucous singles who frequent its neighbor, Beachcomber Island Resort. Treasure's 33 duplex bungalows hold 66 rooms. They have wood-paneled walls, rattan furniture, built-in vanities, shower-only baths, and three single beds, one of which serves as a settee. Each bungalow has a porch facing the emerald lagoon and white beach that encircles the island (a sandy stroll of 20 minutes or less brings you back to your starting point). Although the bungalows have steep tin roofs built to look Fijian, the interior ceilings are low, so the rooms can get hot during the blistering midday sun. The windows aren't screened, but fortunately a stiff sea breeze usually keeps mosquitoes away. A series of pathways through tropical shrubs joins the bures, several playgrounds for both adults and children, and swimming and spa pools set off by a row of red hibiscus from an airy central activities building. Three tasty meals a day are served in Treasure Island's pleasant dining room. Water sports include kayaking, parasailing, windsurfing, and scuba diving. Guests pay for motorized activities and to visit Beachcomber Island Resort.

INEXPENSIVE

Beachcomber Island Resort

P.O. Box 364, Lautoka (Tai Island, 12 miles off Lautoka). ☎ **661500** or 800/521-7242. Fax 664496. 40 dorm beds, 14 "lodge" rms (none with bath), 18 bures (all with bath). F$69 ($48.50) dorm bed; F$189 ($132) double lodge; F$242 ($169) double bure (including meals). AE, DC, MC, V.

Back in the early 1960s, Fiji-born Dan Costello bought an old Colonial Sugar Refining Company tugboat, converted it into a day cruiser, and started carrying tourists on day trips out to a little atoll known then as Tai Island. The visitors liked it so much that some of them didn't want to leave. Recognizing the market, Costello built a few rustic bures, a dining area and bar, and gave the little dot of sand and palm trees a new name: Beachcomber Island.

Today it still packs in the young and young-at-heart on a "deserted" island—deserted, that is, except for other like-minded souls in search of fun, members of the opposite sex, and a relatively inexpensive vacation (considering three all-you-can-eat meals a day is included in the rates). The youngest-at-heart cram into 20-bunk, coed dormitories. If you want more room, you can have or share a semi-private lodge (they have communal toilets and showers). And if you want your own bure with private bath, you have that, too—just don't expect luxury. Rates also include snorkeling gear, coral viewing in glass-bottomed boats, volleyball, and minigolf; you pay extra for sailboats, canoes, windsurfing, scuba diving, waterskiing, and fishing trips.

HOSTELS

Not only rich folks go offshore from Nadi. In the Mamanucas, the Fijian village on Mana Island welcomes young backpackers to stay in dormitories or simple houses for F$27 ($19) per person a day, including all meals. Guests are not allowed to use the facilities at Mana Island Resort, however. Book at any Nadi hostel, but make sure you ask for **Ratu Kini's village** (he's the friendly chief).

In the Yasawas, favorite backpacker destinations are **Coral View Resort** (formerly Uncle Robert's) and **David's Place,** both beside a long, gorgeous beach on Taweva Island near Turtle Island Resort. Both charge F$50 ($35) for a simple, Fijian-style bure; F$22 ($15.50) for a dorm bed; F$13 ($9) for a camp site (all including meals); and F$22 ($15.50) for trips to the famous Sawa-I-Lau Caves, featured in the *Blue Lagoon* movies. Most Nadi hostels will make reservations, or book Coral View Resort directly at the Cathay Hotel in Lautoka (☎ 660566), David's Place at the Lautoka Hotel (☎ 660388).

Two scuba diving bases on Waya Island in the Yasawas also are popular with backpackers: **Dive Trek Waya** (☎ 701823) and the German-operated **Octopus Club Fiji** (☎ 666337 in Lautoka). Dive Trek Waya charges F$30 ($21) per person, including meals. Accommodation is in rooms with shared toilets and showers. Octopus Club is a little more upscale, since its Fijian-style bures have their own showers and toilets. Octopus Club charges F$98 ($68.50) for two people, including breakfast and dinner. Both are in Fijian villages, so you will have a chance to soak up some culture while there.

Round-trip boat transfers to all Yasawa Island backpackers' establishments—a 3¹/₂-hour voyage each way—cost about F$66 ($46) per person.

10 Blue Lagoon Cruises

✪ **Blue Lagoon Cruises** is one of the best ways to see more than one of the Yasawa Islands. Started with a converted American crash vessel in the 1950s by the late Capt. Trevor Withers, this first-class operation has grown to include six ships. Its cruises are so popular with Australians, New Zealanders, and a growing number of Americans and Canadians that they're usually booked solid more than two months in advance of each daily departure from Lautoka.

Three of Blue Lagoon's vessels are identical, 126-foot-long ships capable of carrying 54 passengers in 22 air-conditioned cabins. Two others, the 181-foot-long *Yasawa Princess* and the 155-foot-long *Nanuya Princess,* carry up to 66 passengers in 33 staterooms and look as if they should belong to a Greek shipping magnate. Their accommodations may not quite be up to tycoon standards, but a new luxury cruiser slated to join the fleet in 1996 will be.

The ships cruise through the islands for four days and three nights or seven days and six nights. They all depart Lautoka at 3pm and arrive in the Yasawas in time for a welcoming cocktail party and dinner on board. They then proceed to explore the islands, stopping in little bays for snorkeling, picnics or lovo feasts on sandy beaches, and visits with the Yasawans in their villages. The ships anchor in peaceful coves at night, and even when they cruise from island to island, the water is usually so calm that only incurable landlubbers get seasick.

There are four cruises to choose from: a short "Popular Cruise" on one of the smaller boats; either a short or long "Club Cruise" on one of the larger ships; and a "Luxury" cruise, once the new vessel arrives. Guests on the Club Cruises are treated to a free captain's cocktail party and get wine with a meal and a souvenir gift package.

Rates range from F$670 to F$1,886 ($469 to $1,320) per person double occupancy per cruise, including all meals, activities, and taxes. Singles pay a hefty supplement.

For reservations or information, contact a travel agent or **Blue Lagoon Cruises,** P.O. Box 54, Lautoka (☎ 661622 or 661268, fax 664098).

11 The Coral Coast

Long before big jets began bringing loads of visitors to Fiji, many affluent local residents built cottages on the dry southwestern shore of Viti Levu as sunny retreats from the frequent rain and high humidity of Suva. When visitors started arriving in big numbers during the early 1960s, resorts sprang up among the cottages almost overnight, and promoters gave a new, more appealing name to the 50km (30-mile) stretch of beaches and reef on either side of the town of Sigatoka: the Coral Coast.

The appellation was apt, for coral reefs jut out like wide shelves from the white beaches that run between mountain ridges all along this picturesque coastline. In most spots the lagoon just reaches snorkeling depth at high tide, and when the water retreats you can put on your aqua sports or a pair of old running shoes and walk out nearly to the surf pounding on the outer edge of the shelf.

Frankly, the Coral Coast is now overshadowed by other parts of Fiji. Its large hotels host groups of tourists, primarily Australians. Nevertheless, it does have some dramatic scenery, and it's a central location from which to see both the Suva and Nadi "sides" of Viti Levu.

GETTING THERE: THE QUEEN'S ROAD

Visitors reach the Coral Coast from Nadi International Airport by the Queen's Road. After a sharp right turn at the south end of Nadi Town, the highway runs well inland, first through sugarcane fields undulating in the wind and then past acre after acre of pine trees planted in orderly rows, part of Fiji's national forestry program. The blue-green mountains lie off to the left; the deep-blue sea occasionally comes into view off to the right.

Momi Bay and Natadola Beach The Old Queen's Road branches off toward the coast and Momi Bay, 16km (10 miles) south of Nadi Town. This graded dirt road leads to the **Momi Guns,** the World War II naval batteries now maintained as a historical park by the National Trust of Fiji. To make this side trip, turn at the Momi intersection and follow the dirt road for 5km (3 miles) through the cane fields to a school, then turn right and drive another 4km (2¹/₂ miles) to the concrete bunkers. They command a splendid view over the water to the west. The park has toilets and drinking water.

Maro Road branches off the Queen's Road 35km (21 miles) south of Nadi and runs down to ✪ **Natadola Beach,** one of the prettiest in Fiji. A sign pointing to the village of Batiri marks the Maro Road intersection. Turn right on Maro Road and right again at the first intersection almost immediately after leaving the Queen's Road. This dirt track leads another 8km (5 miles) to a T-intersection. Turn left and look for sand pathways leading to the beach. There's a restaurant and small hotel at the beach. The easiest way to get there is on the *Fijian Princess,* a refurbished train that makes daily trips to Natadola Beach from Shangri-La's Fijian Resort (see "Sightseeing Tours," earlier in this chapter).

Sigatoka The pine forests on either side of the Queen's Road soon give way to rolling fields of mission grass before the sea suddenly emerges at a viewpoint above Shangri-La's Fijian Resort on Yanuca Island. Watch as you go under the railway bridge about 8km (5 miles) past the Fijian, for here begins the **Sigatoka Sand Dunes.** These high sand hills extend for several miles, separating the fields from the crashing—and dangerous—surf. Pieces of ancient pottery have been found among the dunes, but be warned: Removing them is against the law. To reach the dunes, turn right at the "National Park/Camping" sign. The dunes aren't a Fiji national park yet, but they may be someday.

The Queen's Road soon enters Sigatoka (pop. 2,000), a quiet, predominantly Indian town perched along the west bank of the **Sigatoka River,** Fiji's longest waterway. The broad, muddy river lies on one side of the main street; on the other is a row of duty-free and other shops.

The stoplight—one of the few in Fiji outside Suva—controls traffic across the long one-lane bridge precariously spanning the river. Drivers who cheat at the light run the risk of being met halfway across by a vehicle coming in the opposite direction. Wait your turn, for the resulting impasses have been known to turn into heated mid-river fistfights.

For a daytime meal, try the pleasant and very clean tearoom on the third floor of the large Tappoo store at the stoplight. For less expensive fare, drop into the coffee lounge in P. Makanju & Sons Supermarket on the Queen's Road next to Westpac Bank.

Sigatoka River Valley The Queen's Road turns right at the stoplight and crosses the bridge. The road straight ahead follows the west bank of the river as it meanders inland, flanked on both sides by a patchwork of flat green fields of vegetables that give the Sigatoka Valley its nickname: "Fiji's Salad Bowl." The pavement ends about a kilometer (half a mile) from the town; after that, the road surface is poorly graded and covered with loose stones.

The residents of **Lawai** village at 1.6km (1 mile) from town offer Fijian handcrafts for sale. Two kilometers (1.2 miles) farther on, a small dirt track branches off to the left and runs down a hill to **Nakabuta,** the "Pottery Village," where the residents make and sell authentic Fijian pottery. Tour buses from Nadi and the Coral Coast stop there most days.

If you're not subject to vertigo, you can look forward to driving past Nakabuta: the road climbs steeply along a narrow ridge commanding panoramic views across the large Sigatoka Valley with its quiltlike fields to the right and much smaller, more rugged ravine to the left. It then winds its way down to the valley floor and the **Sigatoka Agricultural Research Station,** on whose shady grounds some tour groups stop for picnic lunches. The road climbs into the interior and eventually to Ba on the northwest coast; it intersects the **Nausori Highlands** road leading back to Nadi, but it can be rough or even washed out during periods of heavy rain. Unless they have a four-wheel-drive vehicle or are on an organized tour with a guide, most visitors turn around at the research station and head back to Sigatoka.

Tavuni Hill Fortification   A sign on the east end of the Sigatoka River bridge points left to the Tavuni Hill Fortification, built by an exiled Tongan chief as a safe haven from the ferocious Fijian hill tribes living up the valley. Those highlanders fought constant wars with the coastal Fijians, and they were the last to give up cannibalism and convert to Christianity. When they rebelled against the Deed of Cession to Great Britain in 1875, the colonial administration sent a force of 1,000 men up the Sigatoka River. They destroyed all the hill forts lining the river, including Tavuni. Today the fort is a Fiji Heritage Project open to the public. There's a reception bure, with toilets and a refreshment stand, which has brochures and exhibits. Admission is F$6 ($4) for adults and F$3 ($2) for children.

GETTING AROUND

The larger hotels have car-rental desks as well as taxis hanging around their main entrances. Express buses between Nadi and Suva stop at Shangri-La's Fijian Resort, The Reef Resort, the Hideaway Resort, The Naviti, and The Warwick Fiji. Local buses ply the Queen's Road and will stop for anyone who flags them down. See "Getting Around" in the "Introducing Fiji" chapter for more information.

FAST FACTS: The Coral Coast

The following information applies to Sigatoka and the Coral Coast. If you don't see an item here, see the "Fast Facts" for Nadi earlier in this chapter and in the "Introducing Fiji" chapter.

Bookstores   Sigatoka Book Depot (☎ 500166) is on Market Place in Sigatoka. Boutiques in the larger hotels carry paperback novels and some Australian magazines.

Camera/Film   Caines Photofast has a shop on Market Road in Sigatoka (☎ 500877). Most hotel boutiques sell color print film and provide one-day processing.

Currency Exchange   ANZ Bank, Westpac Bank, and National Bank of Fiji have branches on Queen's Road in Sigatoka. The hotel desks will cash traveler's checks.

Drugstores   Patel Pharmacy (☎ 500213) is on Market Road in Sigatoka.

Emergencies   The emergency phone number for police, fire, and ambulance is 000.

Hospitals   Government-run Sigatoka Hospital (☎ 500455) can handle minor problems.

Police The emergency number is 000. The Fiji Police has posts at Sigatoka (☎ 500222) and at Korolevu (530322).

Post Office Post offices are in Sigatoka and Korolevu.

Telephone/Telegrams/Fax See "Post Office," above. Coral Coast telephone numbers are listed under Sigatoka in the Fiji directory.

WHAT TO SEE & DO

Excursions The hotel reception or tour desk can make reservations for many of the activities mentioned earlier in this chapter. These include tours of the Sigatoka Valley and day trips to Pacific Harbour and Suva. You may have to pay more for such Nadi-area activities as cruises in the Nadi area than if you were staying on the west coast. On the other hand, you are closer to Coral Coast activities, such as the *Fijian Princess* railroad, and you can more easily take advantage of the sights and activities at Pacific Harbour and in Suva. See the chapter on Suva and Levuka for more information.

Locally, **Bounty Cruises** (☎ 500963 or 500969) depart the Sigatoka Jetty, in town on the Queen's Road, at 10am Monday to Saturday for 2¹/₂ hours of cultural voyaging up the Sigatoka River. These cost F$20 ($14) per person. There's an all-day cruise on Tuesday, Thursday, and Saturday, which includes visits to Tavuni Hill Fortification, for F$48 ($33.50). You can get more information or make reservations at P. Makanju & Sons Supermarket on the Queen's Road next to Westpac Bank.

Water Sports & Other Outdoor Activities Most hotels have abundant sports facilities for their guests (see "Where to Stay," below). If yours doesn't, **The Reef Resort** (☎ 500044) rents its equipment to non-guests and allows them to use its golf course, tennis courts, and horses for reasonable fees (see "Where to Stay," below).

Seasports Ltd., based at The Fijian Resort (☎ 520155, ext. 823), serves all the Coral Coast hotels. One-tank dives cost F$52 ($36.50), F$120 ($84) with full equipment rental. You can take an introductory lesson for F$90 ($63) or a NAUI certification course for F$425 ($298). Book at any hotel activities desk.

The hotels will arrange horseback excursions to **Savu-na-matelaya waterfall** and its nearby hot springs, near the old Korolevu airstrip. The walk from the road to the waterfall takes about 20 minutes and fords seven streams. Bring canvas shoes for the hike, and a bathing suit and wraparound sulu if you want to take a dip in the cascade.

Shopping Although the larger hotels have shopping arcades with duty-free shops and clothing and handcraft boutiques, most visitors do their serious shopping in the town of Sigatoka. For handcrafts, **Jack's Handicrafts** and **Sigatoka Handicraft Centre,** both on the Queen's Road in Sigatoka, are well stocked and worth a look. **Korotongo Souvenir Centre,** opposite The Reef Resort, has fixed prices on its merchandise, as does **Baravi Handicrafts,** at Vatukarasa village 13km (8 miles) east of Sigatoka. **Prouds** and **Tappoo** both have shops in Sigatoka, as does **Sogo Fiji,** the purveyor of up-market resort- and beachwear.

Island Nights Night life centers around the hotels and whatever Fiji meke shows they are sponsoring. The famous **Fijian fire walkers** from Beqa, an island off the south coast (remember, it's pronounced "Mbengga," not "Beck-a"), parade across the steaming stones to the incantations of "witch doctors" at various hotels on the Coral Coast and at Nadi. The Warwick Fiji (☎ 530010) usually sponsors a performance at 7pm on Monday and Friday; The Reef Resort (☎ 500044) on Friday. Admission is F$9 ($6.50) per person at The Warwick, F$12 ($8.50) at The Reef.

WHERE TO STAY
EXPENSIVE

○ Shangri-La's Fijian Resort

Private Mail Bag, Nadi Airport (Yanuca Island, 36 miles from Nadi Airport, 6 miles west of Sigatoka). ☎ **520155** or 800/942-5050. Fax 520000. 436 rms, 4 bungalows. A/C MINIBAR TEL. F$250–F$365 ($175–$256) room; F$575–F$675 ($403–$473) bungalow. AE, DC, MC, V.

Fiji's largest hotel, this resort occupies all 105 acres of flat Yanuca Island, which is joined to the mainland by a short, one-lane causeway. The ocean side of Yanuca is lined with a coral-colored sand beach that is superior to those at the Sheraton Fiji and The Regent Fiji on Denarau Island near Nadi. Covered walkways wander through thick tropical foliage to link the hotel blocks to two main restaurant-and-bar buildings, both adjacent to swimming pools, shady lawns, and beaches. Blue road signs point the way, for it's easy to miss a turn in this sprawling complex. The Fijian is so spread out that a shuttle constantly runs around the property, and a trolley bar operates along the beach. Fijian artisans weave baskets and mats, carve war clubs, and string shell jewelry in a handcraft demonstration area near the hotel's entrance, a large bure set in a lush grove of banana and breadfruit trees. Near the reception desk, a bas-relief depicts scenes of Fijian village life.

The Fijian's spacious rooms, all equipped with comfortable wicker lounge furniture and colorful flower-print spreads, occupy 13 three-story buildings. All of them are on the shore of the island, so each room has a view of the lagoon and sea from its own private balcony or patio. Each has a refrigerator, tea- and coffee-making facilities, a radio, and piped-in music.

Dining/Entertainment: The Fijian's four restaurants have something for everyone's taste, if not necessarily for everyone's pocketbook. One of them is open 24 hours a day. Seven bars are ready to quench any thirst. Evening entertainment features buffet dinners followed by various Fijian dance demonstrations and fire walking.

Services: Laundry, baby-sitting, business services.

Facilities: Two swimming pools; six lighted tennis courts; a "Quiet Room" for reading or just getting away from your fellow tourists; games room for children; scuba diving, deep-sea fishing, and other water sports, most for a fee; nine-hole golf course; fitness center and gym.

The Warwick Fiji

P.O. Box 100, Korolevu (62 miles from Nadi Airport, 20 miles east of Sigatoka). ☎ **520555.** Fax 500555. Fax 520010. 250 rms. A/C MINIBAR TEL. F$190–F$270 ($133–$189) room; F$290–F$346 ($203–$242) suite. AE, DC, MC, V.

Once the Hyatt Regency Fiji, this large hotel has undergone extensive renovation in recent years. Sitting on a lovely palm-fringed beach, the complex appears to be little different from other tropical resorts when seen from the road. The interior of the central building, however, clearly reflects the distinctive architecture that is a legacy from its Hyatt days. A sweeping roof supported by natural wood beams covers a wide reception and lobby area bordered on either end by huge carved murals depicting Capt. James Cook's discovery of Fiji in 1779. Tall windows across the rear look out through towering palms to the sea. A curving staircase descends from the center of the lobby into a large square well, giving access to the dining and recreation areas on the beach level. A lounge and cafe open to a swimming pool bordered by palms and a sprawling poinciana tree.

The Warwick's comfortable but not overly large rooms (for more space, stay at The Naviti, The Warwick's sister hotel) are in two- and three-story blocks that flank the central building. Each room has its own balcony or patio with a view of the sea or the tropical gardens surrounding the complex. There are standard rooms and somewhat better-appointed "Warwick Club" models.

Dining/Entertainment: The sand-floored Wicked Walu, under a thatch roof on a tiny island offshore, features seafood selections and is the choice dining spot here. The open-air cafe appeals to the masses by offering a wide variety of cuisine and Fijian-style lovo feasts.

Services: Laundry, baby-sitting, business services. Guests can share facilities at The Naviti.

Facilities: Swimming pool with bar, water sports, tennis courts, volleyball, jogging paths, horseback riding, sports and fitness center, tour desks, beauty salon, boutique, drugstore.

MODERATE

⑤ Hideaway Resort

P.O. Box 233, Sigatoka (Queen's Road, 55 miles from Nadi Airport, 13 miles east of Sigatoka). ☎ **500177.** Fax 520025. 70 units. F$140 ($98) bungalow; F$165 ($116) family unit. AE, DC, MC, V.

Brothers Robert and Kelvin Wade bought this beachside property in the 1980s and have been enlarging and improving it ever since. During their early years it was famous as a young persons' hangout, with a large dormitory and mile-a-minute entertainment. The dormitory belongs to history now, but the Hideaway still attracts an active, younger clientele. The Wades have been expanding laterally along their narrow strip of land between the Queen's Road and the beach. They now have only 16 of their original, A-frame bungalows. They were planning to build a motel-like block of rooms during my recent visit, but in the meantime, all the rest of their units are in modern, duplex bungalows with tropical furnishings and shower-only baths equipped with hairdryers. The larger family units can sleep up to five persons.

The somewhat dark main building with dining, bar, and entertainment areas opens to a small swimming pool. Meals are plain European, Fijian, and Indian fare and feature buffets, barbecues, and Fijian lovos several nights a week. A band provides nightly entertainment and dancing in the main lounge. A host of activities includes tennis, horseback tours, trips to the mountains and waterfalls, snorkeling, scuba diving, windsurfing, glass-bottom boat rides, minigolf, kayaking, Fijian fish-drives, and on-site games such as crab races. Across the road is an aboveground pool with bumper boats. There's a fitness center under its own thatch roof.

The Naviti

P.O. Box 29, Korolevu (Queen's Road, 58 miles from Nadi Airport, 16 miles east of Sigatoka). ☎ **530444.** Fax 530344. 144 rms. A/C MINIBAR TEL. F$175 ($123). AE, DC, MC, V.

A sister of The Warwick Fiji (see above), The Naviti has some of Fiji's largest and most tastefully decorated rooms. They have bright floral-print drapes and spreads to complement blond tropical furniture and varnished natural-wood doors and trim. The site is spacious, too: 40 acres of coconut palms waving in the trade wind beside a lovely beach but very shallow lagoon, in which guests can wade to an islet offshore. That's plenty of room for a nine-hole golf course, five lighted tennis courts, and playgrounds for kids, which means The Naviti attracts golf and tennis buffs who want to vacation with the children (translated: lots of active Australian families). Three-story concrete block buildings hold the rooms and are joined to a central facility by double-deck covered walkways.

The central complex under several Fijian-shaped shingle roofs holds a coffee shop, a candlelit restaurant for evening dining, and a large lounge where a band plays for dancing every evening. Other facilities include a pool, golf course, tennis courts (F$10 [$7] per hour for night play), children's playground, games room, water sports (including scuba diving), deep-sea fishing, coral viewing, horseback and donkey riding, Laundromat, and tour and car-rental desks.

The Reef Resort

P.O. Box 173, Sigatoka (Queen's Road, 47 miles from Nadi Airport, 5 miles east of Sigatoka). ☎ **500044.** Fax 520074. 72 rms. A/C TEL. F$140–F$160 ($98–$112). AE, DC, MC, V.

Even if you don't stay here, this venerable if uninspired hotel is a good bet for a meal or some entertainment. Newer properties have stripped the Reef of its position as the Coral Coast's leading resort, but it's well maintained and provides all the facilities found at its larger and more expensive competitors. It also is well promoted in Australia as a reasonably priced destination, so it usually stays full of working-class Australian couples and families. The complex snuggles on a narrow strip of land between the Queen's Road and the shore, putting the main building and its restaurant, bar, lounge, and patio right on a small beach.

Of the Reef's spacious rooms, 48 are in a three-story, concrete-block building set perpendicular to the beach and separated from the activities building by the larger of two swimming pools. My personal choice, however, would be one of the 24 rooms in the older, two-story Korotogo Wing, which is a short, grassy crawl from the beach. These rooms are somewhat smaller and darker than those in the newer building and don't have bathtubs under their showers, but their private balconies or patios directly face the lagoon. Three somewhat larger rooms on the beach end of the newer wing cost slightly more than the other rooms.

The cuisine in the pleasant, air-conditioned Village Restaurant features a few interesting local specialties, but basically its fare is pitched to Australian tastes. The pleasant Palm Court Bar & Brasserie is open 24 hours a day for meals and snacks. A band plays every evening for dancing, and various Fijian-style shows are staged several nights a week. The hotel has a full range of water sports equipment, a nine-hole golf course, tennis courts, and horses to ride. Non-guests can pay reasonable fees to use all the facilities here.

INEXPENSIVE

Tambua Sands Beach Resort

P.O. Box 177, Sigatoka (Queen's Road, 53 miles from Nadi Airport, 11 miles east of Sigatoka). ☎ **500399.** Fax 530265. 31 units. F$88 ($61.50). AE, DC, MC, V.

This little Korean-owned resort appeals to those of us who prefer to stay in our own bungalow set in a grove of coconut palms beside a beach. The bungalows have high peaked ceilings with fans, large baths with showers, queen-size beds and two single beds, love seats, coffee tables, refrigerators, and coffee- and tea-making facilities. They are placed in a narrow palm grove between the Queen's Road and part of a three-mile-long stretch of truly gorgeous beach.

A wooden footbridge crosses a stream flowing through the grounds and connects the bungalows with a swimming pool and plantation-style bar-dining-lounge building. The open-air restaurant concentrates on dishes made from fresh local produce. Residents of a nearby Fijian village come over, prepare a Fijian-style meal in a lovo, and then perform traditional Fijian dances one night a week.

Tubakula Beach Bungalows

P.O. Box 2, Sigatoka (Queen's Road, 49 miles from Nadi Airport, 7 miles east of Sigatoka). ☎ **500097.** Fax 393056. 24 dorm beds, 23 bungalows (all with bath). F$11 ($7.70) dorm bed; F$48–F$55 ($33.50–$38.50) bungalow. AE, DC, MC, V.

This establishment (whose name is pronounced "toomb-a-koola") sits in a beachside coconut grove and will appeal to anyone who wants a dorm bunk or a basic bungalow with kitchen but none of the usual hotel facilities. The bungalows are A-frame cottages with simple furnishings. Downstairs has a lounge, kitchen, bath, and bedroom; upstairs is a sleeping loft. Each unit can sleep six persons, so sharing one represents good value. The dorm units are in European-style houses. No more than eight bunks are in any one room, and guests share communal kitchens, showers, and toilets. There is a swimming pool.

WHERE TO DINE

Many Coral Coast hotels have special nights, such as meke feasts of Fijian foods cooked in a lovo, served buffet style, and followed by traditional dancing. The specifics, including prices, are given in the tourist publication *Fiji Magic*.

Two storefront restaurants had just opened opposite The Reef Resort when I was there recently: **Something Fishy** and **Fasta Food** (☎ 520619 for both). Both were being operated by Julie Doyle, who has lived along the Coral Coast for many years. Obviously, Something Fishy specializes in seafood, particularly Fijian-style dishes like *ika vaka lolo* (fish with coconut milk). Main courses range from F$8.50 to F$13.50 ($5.50 to $9.50). Fasta Food has a cafeteria-style hot table with pizzas, chicken and chips, burgers, and sandwiches. Sandwiches and burgers cost about F$3 ($2); pizzas range from F$4 to F$25 ($3 to $17.50), depending on size and toppings.

Tom's Seafood Restaurant

Queen's Rd., Korotogo, 1¼ miles west of The Reef Resort. ☎ **520238** or 500744. Reservations recommended. Main courses F$3.50–F$27.50 ($2.50–$19). MC, V. Mon–Sat noon–3pm; daily 6–10pm. SEAFOOD/CANTONESE.

A chef at various Fiji hotels and restaurants since 1969, Tom Jacksam opened his own restaurant a few years ago and now puts his culinary skills to work on specialties such as lobster, prawns, mangrove crabs, and whole fish in garlic, black bean, or ginger sauce. Other dishes on his extensive menu are Cantonese, European, and Indian. Tom's pleasant dining room is on the first floor of this house on the mountain side of the Queen's Road. Service is friendly and efficient. Free rides back to Korotogo hotels are provided after 9pm.

✪ Vilisite's Seafood Restaurant

Queen's Road, between The Warwick and The Naviti. ☎ **500395.** Reservations required. Full meals F$18–F$32 ($12.50–$22.50). MC, V. Daily 8am–10pm. SEAFOOD.

Vilisite (sounds like "Felicity"), a friendly Fijian, operates one of the few places in Fiji where you can dine right by the lagoon's edge. Come in time for a sunset drink and bring a camera, for the westward view from her veranda down the Coral Coast belongs on a postcard. Her extraordinarily well-prepared cuisine is predominately fresh local seafood—fish, shrimp, lobster, octopus—in curry, garlic, and butter, or coconut milk (the Fijian way). She offers only five items on the dinner menu, and they are all full meals. If these won't do, she will adjust for individual tastes or diets. Lunch features inexpensive sandwiches, hamburgers, chop suey, and curry. Vilisite provides free rides for dinner parties of four or more from as far away as The Reef Resort. If you dine at only one restaurant in Fiji, have a meal here. You won't soon forget the view or this extraordinarily friendly Fijian, who certainly knows how to cook.

12 Northern Viti Levu

Few travelers will be disappointed by the scenic wonders on the northern side of Viti Levu. Cane fields climb hilly valleys to towering green mountain ridges. Cowpokes round up cattle on vast ranches. A stunning bay is bounded by dramatic cliffs and spires. A narrow mountain road winds along the rushing Wainibuka River, once called the "Banana Highway" because in pre-road days Fijians used it to float their crop downs to Suva on disposable bilibili rafts made of bamboo. A relatively dry climate beckons anyone who wants to catch a few rays. Offshore, Nananu-I-Ra Island more than makes up for a lack of beaches along the swampy, mangrove coast of the nearby "mainland."

GETTING THERE: THE KING'S ROAD

The only way to get there is via the King's Road, which runs for 290km (180 miles) from Nadi Airport around the island's northern side to Suva—93km (57¹/₂ miles) longer than the Queen's Road to the south. All but about 50km (31 miles) of the King's Road (the stretch along the Wainibuka River Valley through the central mountains) is paved. Since the unsealed portion is slow going, most visitors who drive the King's Road spend at least a night in Rakiraki, on Viti Levu's northern point, about halfway between Nadi and Suva.

Scheduled local and express buses run the entire length of the King's Road, as do unscheduled share taxis (see "Getting Around" in the "Introducing Fiji" chapter). From the Nadi side, the buses depart from the Lautoka Market. The hotels and backpacker's resorts in Rakiraki and on Nananu-I-Ra Island provide their guests with transport from Nadi (see "Where to Stay," below).

The King's Road officially begins at Lautoka. To reach it by car from Nadi, follow the Queen's Road north and take the second exits off both traffic circles in Lautoka.

Ba and Tavua   From Lautoka, the King's Road first crosses a fertile plain and then ascends into hills dotted with cattle ranches before dropping to the coast and entering the gorgeous **Ba Valley,** Fiji's most productive sugar-growing area. With some 65,000 residents, most of them Indians, this valley of steep hills is second only to Suva in both population and economic importance. Many of the country's most successful Indian-owned businesses are headquartered in the town of **Ba,** a prosperous farming community on the banks of the muddy Ba River. Indeed, while most Fiji towns have the air of the British Raj or Australia, the commercial center of Ba is a mirror image of many towns in India. Ba has one of Fiji's five sugar mills. Gravel roads twisting off from town into the valley offer some spectacular vistas. One of these roads follows a tributary into the central highlands and then along the Sigatoka River down to the Coral Coast. You can explore the Ba Valley roads in a rental car, but take the cross-island route only if you have a four-wheel-drive vehicle and a good map.

From Ba, the King's Road continues to **Tavua,** another predominately Indian sugar town backed by its own much smaller valley reaching up to the mountains.

Rakiraki   The enchanting peaks of the Nakauvadra Range keep getting closer to the sea as you proceed eastward toward Rakiraki. Legend says the mountains are home to Degei, the prolific spiritual leader who arrived with the first Fijians and later populated the country. As the flat land is squeezed between foothills and sea, cane fields give way to the grasslands and mesas of the 17,000-acre Yaqara Estate, Fiji's largest cattle ranch. Offshore, conelike islands begin to dot the aquamarine lagoon.

Although everyone calls this area Rakiraki, the chief commercial town actually is **Vaileka,** about 1km ($^1/_2$ mile) off the King's Road. Just before you reach the well-marked junction, look on the right for the **Grave of Udre Udre.** Legend says the stones at the base of the tombstone represent every one of the 900 men this renowned cannibal chief had for dinner.

Vaileka itself is home to the **Penang Mill,** the only sugar mill in Fiji producing solely for domestic consumption. There also is a nine-hole **Penang Golf Course** near the mill, which visitors may play (arrange at the Rakiraki Hotel; see "Where to Stay," below).

Rakiraki itself is a Fijian village (with the usual car-destroying road humps) on the King's Road, about 1km ($^1/_2$ mile) past the Vaileka junction. It's home of the *Tui Ra,* the high Fijian chief of Ra district, which encompasses all of northern Viti Levu. You may see him driving around in his sporty blue Cadillac sports model, which he keeps parked under a shed next to his modest home in the village. He also likes to stroll across the road to the Rakiraki Hotel, on the village's eastern boundary.

After the village, a paved road leads to **Ellington Wharf,** jumping-off point for **Nananu-I-Ra,** a semiarid island about 15 minutes offshore, which has a good moderately priced resort and four backpackers' retreats (see "Where to Stay," below). A ferry leaves Ellington Wharf for Nabouwalu on Vanua Levu every day except Sunday.

Rakiraki to Suva   From Ellington Wharf, the King's Road rounds the island's north point into **Viti Levu Bay,** whose surrounding mountains topped with basaltic cliffs, thumbs, and spires give it a tropical splendor similar to Moorea's. About 15km (9.3 miles) from Rakiraki stands **St. Francis Xavier Church,** home of the unique *Naiserelagi,* or Black Christ mural painted by artist Jean Charlot in 1963. From the head of the bay, the road begins to climb through rice paddies and more cattle country to the head of the winding **Wainibuka River.** This "Banana Highway" is a major tributary of the mighty Rewa River that eventually flows into the sea through a broad, flat delta northeast of Suva. The cool, often cloudy highlands of the Wainibuka Valley is old Fiji, a land of few Indians and many traditional Fijian villages perched on the slopes along the river. If you're driving, be careful on the many switchback curves above the river. There are no shoulders to pull off on, and you suddenly come upon several one-lane wooden bridges that can be icy slick during frequent rains. And watch out for the huge buses that regularly ply this route, taking up the entire road as they rumble along at break-neck speeds.

You leave the Wainibuka and enter the dairy-farming region of eastern Fiji, source of the country's fresh milk and cheeses (be alert for cows on the road!). The small town of **Korovou**, 107km (66 miles) from Rakiraki, is the major junction in these parts. Turn right for Nausori and Suva at the dead end (a left turn will take you to Natovi Wharf).

From Korovou, the King's Road goes directly south for 25km (15¹/₂ miles) until it joins the **Rewa River**, now a meandering coastal stream. You soon come to bustling Nausori, the delta's main town. Turn right and cross the steel-girdered bridge to reach Suva.

WHERE TO STAY
RAKIRAKI

✪ Rakiraki Hotel

P.O. Box 31, Rakiraki (Rakiraki village, on King's Road, 1¹/₂ miles east of Vaileka, 82 miles from Nadi Airport). ☎ **694101** or 800/448-8355. Fax 694545. 46 rms. A/C TEL. F$38.50–F$90 ($27–$63) room; F$12 ($8.50) dorm bed. AE, DC, MC, V.

This venerable establishment is one of the few remaining colonial-era hotels in Fiji, and that means lots of charm unhurried by the pace of modern tourism. The two clapboard roadside buildings were built as guesthouses when American soldiers were stationed nearby during World War II. One houses a tongue-and-groove paneled bar and dining room, where guests enjoy the homecooked meals. The other has an old-fashioned hall down the middle with five rooms to either side. Two are air conditioned, the others have ceiling fans, and all have private baths. Two of these rooms have four beds each, which are rented on a dormitory basis. Out in the back yard, three modern two-story motel blocks have 36 rooms outfitted to international standards, with quiet air-conditioning units, phones, and tiled shower-only baths. These rooms flank a pool, tennis court, games area under a thatch roof, and championship-caliber bowling green. Behind all is an extensive garden full of tropical fruits and vegetables, which the chef raids daily. The friendly staff will arrange excursions to Vaileka and to Fijian villages, horseback riding, golfing, scuba diving, and treks into the highlands.

NANANU-I-RA ISLAND

Hilly, anvil-shaped Nananu-I-Ra, a 15-minute boat ride from Ellington Wharf, has long been popular as a sunny retreat for local Europeans who own beach cottages there (the island is all freehold land). In recent years, it has become increasingly popular with young backpackers, who stop off for a few days on their way by bus and ferry from Nadi to Savusavu and Taveuni. All that sunshine has a price, for Nananu-I-Ra is semiarid between May and September, when water shortages can occur. Accordingly, backpackers usually bring extra drinking water as well as their own groceries.

Of the backpackers' resorts, European-managed **Kon Tiki Island Lodge,** P.O. Box 340, Rakiraki (☎ 694290), on the island's isolated western end, and **Charlie's Place,** P.O. Box 407 Rakiraki (☎ 694676), near the other two on the more developed south end, are less restrained. **Betham's Beach Cottages,** P.O. Box 5, Rakiraki (☎ 694132) and **Nananu Beach Cottages,** P.O. Box 140, Rakiraki (☎ 694633), have more the flavor of a relaxing but polite visit to grandma's (translated: no loud parties or topless sunbathing). All have dorm beds for about F$12 ($8.50) per person and cottages ranging from about F$25 to F$45 ($17.50 to $31.50) single or double. Express minibuses run daily from Nadi to Ellington Wharf for about F$22 ($15.50) per person. Boat transfers from the wharf are F$12 ($8.50). These properties all promote heavily at Nadi's inexpensive hotels and hostels, so you will have no trouble getting the full details.

Mokusigas Island Resort

P.O. Box 268, Rakiraki (Nananu-I-Ra Island, 15 minutes by boat from Ellington Wharf). ☎ **720755** or 800/348-3436. Fax 720579. 20 bungalows. F$220–F$240 ($154–$168). AE, DC, MC, V.

Physical fitness is the theme at this resort on the narrowest part of Nananu-I-Ra. It takes physical effort just to climb concrete pathways from either of two beaches to the guest bungalows, which sit near a main building atop a saddle of land with breathtaking views of the sea and the mountains of nearby Viti Levu. If that's not enough to get your heart pumping, the resort has a fully equipped gym, and its other activities emphasize scuba diving and world-class windsurfing before the stiff trade wind. The colonial-style main building is surrounded by a porch, where guests enjoy the views while ordering drinks and dining from a blackboard menu featuring fresh seafood. Built of pine, 10 duplex bungalows hold the 20 guestrooms, all of which have a double bed, sitting area, sliding doors opening to decks, and shower-only baths with lots of natural wood accents (the decks have minimal railings, so Mokusigas is not recommended for children under six years of age). A long pier runs from one beach out to a gazebo over deep water, where a mobile bar serves sunset cocktails. The other beach is a magnificent line of sand stretching for more than a mile. Only Mokusigas guests may use the resorts facilities, so backpackers cannot wander in from the island's other properties.

11 Suva & Levuka

This chapter could easily be called "A Tale of Two Capitals," for Suva and Levuka are the former and present seats of Fiji's government. Sitting on the beautiful island of Ovalau some 20 miles east of Viti Levu, Levuka was the original center of European presence in Fiji and served as Great Britain's colonial capital from the Deed of Cession in 1874 until the government pulled up stakes and moved to Suva in 1882. The old town of Levuka still looks very much as it did in those days, and it's a wonderful excursion from Suva.

Neither the likelihood of frequent showers nor the chance of an occasional deluge should discourage anyone from visiting the modern, vibrant capital city of Suva. Grab your umbrella and hit the sidewalks. Wander through narrow streets crowded with Fijians, Indians, Chinese, Europeans, Solomon Islanders, Rotumans, Tongans, Samoans, and people of various other ancestries. Stroll among grand public buildings, broad avenues, and orderly parks and parade grounds—souvenirs of Fiji's 96 years as a British Crown Colony.

1 Suva Today

Suva sprawls over a hilly, 10-square-mile peninsula jutting like a thumb from the southeastern coast of Viti Levu. To the east lies windswept **Laucala Bay** and to the west, Suva's busy harbor and the suburbs of **Lami Town** and **Walu Bay.** Jungle-draped mountains rise to heights of 4,000 or more feet on the "mainland" to the north, high enough to condense moisture from the prevailing southeast trade winds and create the damp climate that cloaks the city in lush green foliage all year round.

Modern Suva began in 1870, when the Polynesia Company, having bought the land in exchange for paying Chief Cakobau's foreign debts, sent a group of Australian settlers to the area. They established a camp on the flat, swampy, mosquito-infested banks of **Nubukalou Creek,** on the western shore of the peninsula. When the settlers failed to grow first cotton and then sugar, speculators obtained the land and in 1875 convinced the new British colonial administration to move the capital from Levuka. The move was approved in 1877, and the government shifted to Suva in 1882.

The business heart of the city still sits near Nubukalou Creek, and visitors can see most of the city's sights and find most of its shops, interesting restaurants, and lively nightspots within a 10-block area of downtown.

2 Getting There & Getting Around

GETTING TO SUVA

BY PLANE   Suva is served by **Nausori Airport** 12 miles northeast of downtown near the Rewa River town of Nausori. Taxis between there and Suva cost F$16.50 ($11.50) each way. Nausori Taxi & Bus Service (☎ 477583 in Nausori, or 312185 in Suva) has regularly scheduled bus service between the airport and the city for F$2 ($1.40) per person each way. Look for the buses at the curb across from the baggage-claim platform. The company's Suva terminal is in the Suva Travelodge parking lot on Victoria Parade. Buses leave there for the airport at 6, 9, 10, and 11:15am, and 1:45 and 3pm daily.

BY CAR   If you're driving from the Nadi side, don't leave without a good map of Suva, whose maze of streets can be confusing, especially at night (I try never to drive in Suva after dark). If you can find it in a Nadi or Lautoka bookstore, the best map is *Suva and Lami Town* (No. FSM-1), published by the Fiji Department of Lands & Surveys.

GETTING AROUND SUVA

Hundreds of **taxis** prowl the streets of Suva. Licensed taxis have meters, but occasionally a driver without one will claim to be a "private car" or "limousine." Official fares are F50¢ (35¢) at the flag fall and F60¢ (42¢) for each kilometer, but you will have to negotiate anything over 10 (6.2 miles). Make sure the driver drops the flag. I have been very satisfied with **Black Arrow Taxis** (☎ 300139 or 300541 in Suva, 477071 in Nausori) and **Nausori Taxi & Bus Service** (☎ 477583 in Nausori, or 304178 in Suva), which is based at the Suva Travelodge parking lot. The main **taxi stands** are on Central Street, behind the Air Pacific office in the CML Building on Victoria Parade (☎ 312266), and on Victoria Parade at Sukuna Park (no phone). Other taxis gather at the Suva Municipal Market.

Local **buses** fan out from the municipal market from before daybreak to midnight Monday to Saturday (they have limited schedules on Sunday). The fares vary but should be no more than F50¢ (35¢) to most destinations in and around Suva. The excellent *Suva City and Lami Town* map mentioned above shows the bus routes by color-coding the streets.

See "Getting Around Fiji" in the "Introducing Fiji" chapter for the phone numbers of the major **car-rental** firms.

FAST FACTS: Suva

The following facts apply to Suva. If you don't see an item here, see "Fast Facts: Fiji" in the "Introducing Fiji" chapter.

American Express   Tapa International Ltd. (☎ 302333) has an office on the 4th floor of the ANZ House, 25 Victoria Parade. Hours are Monday to Friday from 8:30am to 5pm, Saturday from 9am to noon. Personal check cashing is available only from 9:30am to 3pm weekdays, since you have to take your approved check to the ANZ Bank downstairs. The mailing address is G.P.O. Box 654, Suva.

Bookstores Dominion Book Centre, in Dominion Arcade, Thomson Street (behind the Fiji Visitors Bureau), has the latest newsmagazines, local and Australian newspapers, and books on the South Pacific. Desai Bookshops, at the corner of Thomson and Pier Streets (opposite the Fiji Visitors Bureau), has a large selection of books about Fiji. The large Morris Hedstrom department store on Thomson Street and the Prouds shop in the Suva Travelodge carry novels and magazines. The *Fiji Times,* 177 Victoria Parade, sells maps and books, including Albert J. Schütz's *Suva: A History and Guide* (Sydney, Pacific Publications, 1978), to which I am indebted for much of the walking tour in this chapter.

Currency Exchange Bank of Hawaii, Westpac Bank, ANZ Bank, National Bank of Fiji, and Bank of Baroda have offices on Victoria Parade, south of the Fiji Visitors Bureau. Bank of Hawaii has an ATM machine. The Thomas Cook office on Victoria Parade near the Fiji Visitors Bureau cashes travelers checks Monday to Friday from 8:30am to 5pm and Saturday from 8:30am to noon.

Dentist Ask your hotel staff for a recommendation.

Doctor Most expatriot residents go to the private Gordon Street Medical Centre, 98-100 Gordon St. (☎ 313355). It's open 24 hours a day. The clinic has Fiji's only recompression chamber facility.

Drugstores Gordon Street Medical Centre (see "Doctor," above) has a pharmacy, as does the Morris Hedstrom department store on Thomson St.

Embassies/Consulates See "Fast Facts: Fiji" in the "Introducing Fiji" chapter.

Emergencies Phone 000.

Eyeglasses Two companies sell complete lines of eyewear, including contact lenses: Jekishan & Jekishan, Epworth House, Victoria Parade; and Asgar & Co. Ltd., Queensland Insurance Centre, Victoria Parade.

Hairdressers/Barbers Cut Above Salon, Honson Arcade, Thomson Street, next to Canadian Airlines International.

Hospitals Colonial War Memorial Hospital, end of Ratu Mara Road at Brown Street, is the public hospital, but see "Doctor," above, for a private clinic.

Information The Fiji Visitors Bureau (☎ 302433) has its headquarters in a restored colonial house at the corner of Thomson and Scott Streets, in the heart of Suva. The bureau has both *Fiji Magic* and *What's On In Suva,* an informative local tourist publication.

Libraries Suva City Library on Victoria Parade (☎ 313433) has a small collection of books on the South Pacific. It's open Monday, Tuesday, Thursday, and Friday from 9:30am to 6pm; Wednesday from noon to 6pm; and Saturday from 9am to 1pm. The library at the University of the South Pacific (☎ 313900) has one of the largest collections in the South Pacific. The university is on Laucala Bay Road.

Maps *What's On In Suva,* available at the Fiji Visitors Bureau and many hotel desks, contains maps of downtown. Desai Bookshops, corner of Thomson and Pier Streets, opposite the Fiji Visitors Bureau, may have the excellent *Suva and Lami Town.* If not, it's published by the Department of Lands & Surveys, whose main sales office is in the Government Buildings on Victoria Parade.

Impressions

The English, with a mania for wrong decisions in Fiji, built their capital at Suva, smack in the middle of the heaviest rainfall. . . . Yet Suva is a superb tropical city.
  —James A. Michener, 1951

Photographic Needs Caines Photofast, corner of Victoria Parade and Pratt Street, sells a wide range of film and provides one-hour processing of color-print film.

Police Fiji Police's Central Station is on Joske Street, between Pratt and Gordon Streets (☎ 311222).

Post Office The General Post Office is on Thomson Street, opposite the Fiji Visitor's Bureau. It's open Monday to Friday from 8am to 4:30pm, Saturday from 9am to noon.

Safety The downtown area around Victoria Parade is relatively safe during the evenings, but many areas of town are not. Don't take chances anywhere in Suva. Stick to the main, well-lighted streets after dark, and take taxis if you're out late at night. See "Safety" in the Fast Facts: Fiji in the "Introducing Fiji" chapter.

Telephone/Telegrams/Fax International phone, telegram, fax, and telex service is provided by Fiji International Telecommunications Ltd. (FINTEL) at its colonial-style building on Victoria Parade. It's open Monday to Saturday from 8am to 8pm. You may reverse the charges or put the call on an AT&T credit card, which *must* have an international number on it. Otherwise, you must deposit enough cash in advance to cover the cost of the call, or buy a FINTEL Phonecard at the counter (Fiji Telecom Phonecards won't work). Stand by for a short wait if paying cash, for the operator will place your call and ring you when the connection is made. A typical station-to-station call from Fiji to the U.S. will cost F$3.00 ($2.10) per minute. Person-to-person calls cost extra.

The General Post Office on Victoria Parade and the Telecommunications Services shop across Edward Street (it's quieter and less crowded) have both coin and Telecom Phonecard pay phones.

For more information, see "Fast Facts: Fiji" in the "Introducing Fiji" chapter.

3 What to See & Do in Suva

Too many visitors spend only a day in Suva, which is hardly enough time to do justice to this fascinating city. Two or three days can easily be spent walking through its streets, seeing its sights, and poking your head into its multitude of duty-free and handcraft shops.

WALKING TOUR
Suva

Start: The Triangle.
Finish: Government House.
Time: 2¹/₂ hours.
Best Time: Early morning or late afternoon.

Worst Time: Midday, or Saturday afternoon and Sunday, when the market and shops are closed and downtown is deserted.

Begin at the four-way intersection of Victoria Parade, Renwick Road, and Thomson and Central Streets. This little island in the middle of heavy traffic is

1. **The Triangle.** Now the center of Suva, in the late 1800s this spot was a lagoon fed by a stream that flowed along what is now Pratt Street. A marker in the park commemorates Suva's becoming the capital, the arrival of Fiji's first missionaries, the first public land sales, and Fiji's becoming a colony. Three of the four dates are slightly wrong. From The Triangle, head north on Thomson Street, bearing right between the Fiji Visitors Bureau and the old Garrick Hotel (now the Sichuan Pavilion Restaurant), whose wrought-iron balconies recall a more genteel but non-air-conditioned era. Continue on Thomson Street past the Morris Hedstrom department store to

2. **Nubukalou Creek.** The Polynesia Company's settlers made camp beside this stream and presumably drank from it. A sign on the bridge warns against eating fish from it today—with good reason, as you will see and smell. Morris Hedstrom's picturesque covered walkway along the south bank gives the creek its nickname: The Venice of Fiji. Across the bridge, smiling Fijian women wait under a flame tree in a shady little park to offer grass skirts and other handcraft items for sale. Pass to the left of them for now, and head down narrow

3. **Cumming Street.** This area, also on reclaimed land, was home of the Suva market until the 1940s. Cumming Street was lined with saloons, yaqona "grog" shops, and curry houses known as "lodges." It became a tourist-oriented shopping mecca when World War II Allied servicemen created a market for curios. When import taxes were lifted from electronic equipment and cameras in the 1960s, Cumming Street merchants quickly added the plethora of duty-free items you'll find there today. When you've finished browsing, return to Thomson Street, turn right and then left on Usher Street, which takes you past the intersection at Rodwell Road and Scott Street to the

✪ 4. **Municipal Market,** the largest and most lively produce market in the South Pacific and Suva's main supply of food. A vast array of tropical produce is offered for sale, and if they aren't too busy, the merchants will appreciate your interest and answer your questions about the names and uses of the various fruits and vegetables. The market teems on Saturday morning, when, it seems, the entire population of Suva shows up to shop and select television programs for the weekend's viewing. Few sights say as much about urban life in the modern South Pacific as does that of a Fijian carrying home in one hand a bunch of taro roots tied together with pandanus, and in the other a collection of rented videocassettes stuffed into a plastic bag. Big ships from overseas and small boats from the other islands dock at Princes Wharf and Kings Wharf beyond the market on Usher Street. The bus station is behind the market on Rodwell Road; on the other side of this busy street is the popular Suva Flea Market. Have a look there for whatever Suva residents want to sell or swap. We will follow wide Stinson Parade back across Nubukalou Creek and along the edge of Suva's waterfront to the large parking garage on the left. Downstairs is the

5. **Municipal Curio and Handicraft Centre.** In yet another bit of cultural diversity, you can haggle over the price of handcrafts at stalls run by Indians but not at those operated by Fijians. Wait until you have visited Wolf's Boutique and the Government Handicraft Centre, however, before making a purchase

Walking Tour—Suva

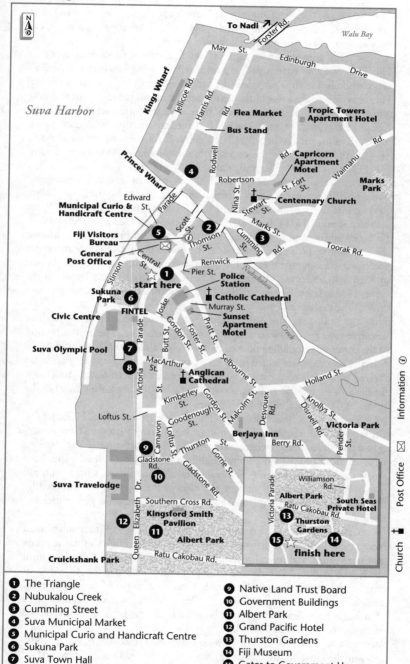

1. The Triangle
2. Nubukalou Creek
3. Cumming Street
4. Suva Municipal Market
5. Municipal Curio and Handicraft Centre
6. Sukuna Park
7. Suva Town Hall
8. Suva City Library
9. Native Land Trust Board
10. Government Buildings
11. Albert Park
12. Grand Pacific Hotel
13. Thurston Gardens
14. Fiji Museum
15. Gates to Government House

(see "Best Buys," below). Continue on Stinson Parade past Central Street. The gray concrete building on the corner is the YWCA. When you get there, cut diagonally under the palms and flame trees across

6. **Sukuna Park,** named for Ratu Sir Lala Sukuna, founding father of independent Fiji. This shady waterfront park is a favorite brown-bag lunch spot for Suva's office workers. On the west side is the harbor and on the east, Victoria Parade. For many years only a row of flame trees separated this broad avenue from the harbor, but the shallows have been filled and the land extended into the harbor by the width of a city block. The large, nondescript auditorium standing south of the park is the Suva Civic Centre. Head south on the seaward side of Victoria Parade, pass the cream-colored colonial-style headquarters of FINTEL, the country's electronic link to the world, to

7. **Suva Town Hall,** a picturesque old building with an intricate, ornamental wrought-iron portico and a sign proclaiming it now to be the Ming Palace Restaurant. Built as an auditorium in the early 1900s and named Queen Victoria Memorial Hall, this lovely structure later was used as the Suva Town Hall (city offices are now in a modern building adjacent to the Civic Centre on the waterfront). The stage still stands at the rear of the restaurant. At this point you can take a shopping break at the Government Handicraft Centre, in the rear of Ratu Sukuna House, the tall office building across Victoria Parade at the corner of MacArthur Street (see "Best Buys," below). Afterwards, continue south on Victoria Parade until you come to the

8. **Suva City Library.** The American industrialist and philanthropist Andrew Carnegie gave Fiji £1,500 sterling to build this structure. The central portion of the colonnaded building opened in 1909 with an initial collection of 4,200 books. The wings were added in 1929. Books on Fiji and the South Pacific are shelved to the left of the main entrance. (See "Fast Facts: Suva," above, for the library's hours.) Keep going along Victoria Parade past Loftus Street to the corner of Gladstone Road, where sits the

9. **Native Land Trust Board Building.** This site is known locally as Naiqaqi (The Crusher) because a sugar-crushing mill sat here during Suva's brief and unsuccessful career as a cane-growing area in the 1870s. A small statue of Ratu Sukuna stands in front of the modern office building that now occupies the site. Ratu Sukuna served as chairman of the Native Land Trust Board, whose main job is to collect and distribute rents on the 80% of the country that is owned by the Fijians. Across Gladstone Road you can't miss the imposing gray edifice and clock tower of the

10. **Government Buildings.** Erected between 1937 and 1939 (they look much older), these British-style gray stone buildings house the High Court, the prime minister's office, and several government ministries. Parliament met here until 1987, when Colonel Rabuka and gang marched in and arrested its leaders (it now meets in a new complex on Ratu Sukuna Road in the Muanikau suburb). The clock tower is known as "Fiji's Big Ben." When it works, it chimes every 15 minutes from 6am to midnight. Now walk past the large open field on the south side of the building, which is

11. **Albert Park,** named for Queen Victoria's consort, Prince Albert. The pavilion opposite the Government Buildings, however, is named for Charles Kingsford Smith, the Australian aviator and first person to fly across the Pacific. Smith was unaware that a row of palm trees stretched across the middle of Albert Park, his intended landing place. A local radio operator figured out Smith's predicament,

and the colonial governor ordered the trees cut down immediately. The resulting "runway" across Albert Park was barely long enough, but Smith managed to stop his plane within a few feet of its end on June 6, 1928. Opposite the park on Victoria Parade stands the

12. Grand Pacific Hotel, which was closed during my recent visit, pending a long-delayed, complete renovation. The Union Steamship Company built it in 1914 to house its transpacific passengers during their stopovers in Fiji. The idea was to make them think they had never gone ashore, for rooms in the "GPH" were designed like first-class staterooms, complete with saltwater baths and plumbing fixtures identical to those on an ocean liner. All rooms were on the second floor, and guests could step outside on a 15-foot-wide veranda overlooking the harbor and walk completely around the building—as if they were walking on the "deck." When members of the British royal family visited Fiji, they stood atop the wrought-iron portico, the "bow" of the Grand Pacific, and addressed their subjects massed across Victoria Parade in Albert Park. Continue south on Victoria Parade to the corner of Ratu Cakobau Road, and enter

13. Thurston Gardens. Originally known as the Botanical Gardens, this cool, English-like park was renamed in 1976 for its founder, the amateur botanist Sir John Bates Thurston. He started the gardens at another location in 1881; they were moved to this present site in 1912. Henry Marks, scion of a family who owned a local trading company, presented the drinking fountain in 1914. After G.J. Marks, a relative and lord mayor of Suva, was drowned that same year in the sinking of the S.S. *Empress* in the St. Lawrence River in Canada, the Marks family erected the bandstand in his memory. Children can climb aboard the stationary *Thurston Express,* a narrow-gauge locomotive once used to pull harvested cane to the crushing mill. Walk to the southeast corner of the gardens, where you will find the fascinating

✪ **14. Fiji Museum,** one of the South Pacific's finest. Although some of the museum's artifacts were damaged by Suva's humidity while they were hidden away during World War II, a marvelous collection of war clubs, cannibal forks, tanoa bowls, shell jewelry, and other Fijian relics remains. Exhibits in the rear of the building explain Fiji's history. On display is the rudder and other relics of H.M.S. *Bounty,* burned and sunk at Pitcairn Island by Fletcher Christian and the other mutineers in 1789 but recovered by the National Geographic Society in the 1950s. The museum (☎ 315944) is open Monday to Friday from 8:30am to 4:30pm and Saturday from 9am to 4:30pm. Guided tours are conducted on the hour between 10am and 3pm. Admission is F$3.30 ($2.30) for tourists, free for school-age children. Guided tours cost an extra F$2.50 ($1.75). Backtrack through the gardens to Victoria Parade and head south again until, just past the manicured greens of the Suva Bowling Club on the harbor, you arrive at the big iron gates of

15. Government House, the home of Fiji's president, which is guarded like Buckingham Palace by two spit-and-polish, sulu-clad Fijian soldiers. The original house, built in 1882 as the residence of the colonial governor, was struck by lightning and burned to the ground in 1921. The present rambling mansion was completed in 1928 and opened with great fanfare. It is closed to the public, but a colorful military ceremony marks the changing of the guard during the first week of each month. Ask the Fiji Visitors Bureau whether a ceremony will take place while you're there. From this point, Victoria Parade becomes Queen Elizabeth Drive, which skirts the peninsula to Laucala Bay. With homes

My Word!

Before the Government Buildings on Victoria Parade were erected between 1937 and 1939, the land under them was a swampy area called Naiqaqi, or Crusher, for the sugar mill that operated from 1873 to 1875 where the Native Lands Trust Board Building now stands. Naiqaqi was populated by shacks, some of them houses of ill-repute.

Local residents tell of a sailor who often visited the shacks while his ship was in port. He left Suva in 1931 for a long voyage, carrying with him fond memories of Naiqaqi—and, in particular, of one of its residents, a beautiful young woman named Annie.

The sailor's next visit to Suva came in 1940. Instead of a swamp, he found an imposing gray stone building standing where the old, familiar shacks had been. "My word," he exclaimed upon seeing the great new structures, "Annie has done well!"

and gardens on one side and the lagoon on the other, it's a lovely walk or drive. The manicured residential area in the rolling hills behind Government House is known as The Domain; an enclave of British civil servants in colonial times, it now is home to the Fiji parliament, government officials, diplomats, and affluent private citizens.

Guided Tours The easiest way to see the residential suburbs as well as downtown Suva is on a guided tour. **United Touring Fiji (UTC),** which has a tour desk in the lobby of the Suva TraveLodge (☎ 312287), charges F$20 ($14) per person for the two-hour tour.

NEARBY ATTRACTIONS

✪ **Orchid Island** A self-described "living museum" 9km (5¹/₂ miles) west of Suva on the Queen's Road, Orchid Island (☎ 361128) gives a glimpse into Fijian life in the days before Europeans arrived on the islands. The world's largest drua (war canoe) and a 50-foot-high "spirit house"—the first such thatch temple constructed since Christianity conquered Fiji more than a century ago—dominate the replica of a traditional village, which was built on a small island in the crook of a river, with help from the Fiji Museum. Fijians go about the routines of life as did their forebears: preparing food, building fires, plaiting rope from coconut fibers, making handcrafts for everyday use. A "mini museum" explains the country's history, and a small zoo houses turtles, mongooses, vividly colored parrots, monkeys, and the rare crested iguana, a species found only in Fiji. The village and surrounding area are made lush—and educational—by examples of all the various plants found in the islands.

Two-hour guided tours begin Monday to Saturday at 10:30am. Admission is F$10 ($7) for adults and F$4 ($2.80) for children. Taxi fares from Suva are about F$12 ($8.50) each way. The hotel activities desks can make arrangements for tours and transportation.

Pacific Harbour Although it never really took off, Pacific Harbour was begun in the early 1970s as a recreation-oriented, luxury residential community and resort 30 miles west of Suva on the Queen's Road (translated: a real estate development). Today Pacific Harbour is noted primarily for its excellent golf

Impressions

The balcony I recognized from Derek's reminiscences on many a Canadian winter night. When it was thirty or forty below zero outside, we would open a bottle of brandy, watch his Fiji slides, and talk quietly of warm tropical evenings. But here in Suva it was still rush hour, and we had to shout above the roar of Leyland buses. One of the things I always forget about the Third World is the noise.

—Ronald Wright, 1986

course, as a jumping-off point for diving in the Beqa Lagoon offshore (see "Golf, Tennis & Other Outdoor Activities," below), and the shopworn but still interesting Cultural Centre and Marketplace of Fiji.

The **Marketplace** is a shopping center of colonial-style clapboard buildings joined by covered walkways. You can wander through its boutiques and handcraft shops (open Monday to Saturday from 9am to 5pm), perhaps have some refreshment at one of two restaurants or a snack bar, and poke through a small museum. You don't have to pay for anything so far except the meal.

It will cost, however, to visit the **Culture Centre** on "Sacred Island," across a lake behind the Marketplace. Boats paddled by muscular young Fijian men dressed in traditional costumes leave a wharf at the end of a covered walkway for tours of the island with its replica of an ancient Fijian village. As on Orchid Island, a tall "spirit house" dominates the other thatch-roofed buildings in the village, and Fijians demonstrate age-old skills, such as fire-walking and handcraft making. The boats leave for hour-long guided tours of the island every 15 minutes Monday to Saturday from 9:30am to 1:30pm.

If you missed them on the Coral Coast, Beqa Islanders perform their **fire-walking ceremony** here at 3pm on Tuesday and Saturday. An announcer explains what's going on—which may not happen during fire-walking performances at the hotels.

The ✪ **Dance Theatre of Fiji,** dedicated to preserving ancient dances and rituals, performs at 3:30pm on Monday, Wednesday, Thursday, and Friday. You're not likely to see more authentic Fijian dancing.

Tickets for either the guided tour, fire-walking ceremony, or dance show cost F$15 ($10.50) for adults and F$7.50 ($5.25) for children between 5 and 15 years old. A combination ticket for any two events costs F$28 ($19.50) for adults and F$9 ($6.30) for children.

The telephone number at the Marketplace and Cultural Centre is 450177.

United Touring Fiji (UTC) (☎ 312287) has round-trip bus excursions from the Suva Travelodge to Pacific Harbour for F$24 ($17), plus the entrance fees. **Wilderness (Fiji) Tours** (☎ 386498) has an all-day tour that includes a stop at the Suva Municipal Market, Orchid Island, and Pacific Harbour. Cost is F$69 ($48.50) adults and F$45 ($31.50) children.

Colo-I-Suva Forest Park At a 400- to 600-foot altitude, the Fiji Forestry Department's Colo-I-Suva Forest Park provides a cool, refreshing respite from the heat, if not the humidity, of the city below. Picnic at tables in thatch pavilions with fire grates, or hike the well-marked system of trails through the heavy indigenous forests and stands of mahogany to one of several lovely waterfalls that cascade into swimming holes. Bring walking shoes with good traction because the trails are covered with gravel or slippery soapstone. The park is best visited on a clear day, since Colo-I-Suva gets twice as much rain as Suva, and even under the best of conditions the thick overhanging foliage blocks out as much as 90% of the sunlight reaching the treetops (holding the high temperature to 70°F on most days). The creeks can flood quickly during periods of heavy rains, so be careful in the park. And don't dive into the swimming holes unless you know how deep they are.

Colo-I-Suva is open every daily from 8am to 5:30pm. The entrance is just beyond Tamavua village on the Prince's Road, about 11 km (6.6 miles) from Suva. Signs at intersections in the area show the way to the park. It's a long walk from the bus stop at the Colo-I-Suva Forest Station to the pools, but you can get there on the Sawani bus—one leaves Suva Municipal Market every hour. The fare is about F50¢ (35¢).

Wilderness (Fiji) Tours (☎ 386498) has daily tours to the park for F$40 ($28) per person.

4 Where to Stay in Suva

MODERATE

Best Western Berjaya Inn

P.O. Box 112, Suva (Corner of Gordon and Malcolm Sts.). ☎ **312300** or 800/528-1234. Fax 301300. 50 rms. A/C MINIBAR TV TEL. F$134–F$146 ($94–$102). AE, DC, MC, V.

Even sans balcony, you will have a commanding view over Suva, the harbor, and the south coast of Viti Levu from this curving, eight-story building, the former Suva Courtesy Inn. All the rooms face the harbor; even though the rates for the rooms are the same for each floor, the rooms on the sixth, seventh, and eighth floors have the best views. The neighborhood is quiet and residential, yet the hotel is a mere three-block walk from the shops on Victoria Parade. A Malaysian restaurant shares a room on the building's second floor with a bar that features quiet jazz music on weekend nights. The lobby has a coffee shop with patio seating. Facilities include a swimming pool (unfortunately on the shady side of the building), beauty salon, and tour desk. There's 24-hour room service.

Raffles Tradewinds Hotel

P.O. Box 3377, Lami Town (Queen's Rd. at Bay of Islands, a 10-min. drive west of Suva, 40-min. west of Nausori Airport). ☎ **362471.** Fax 361464. 108 rms. A/C TV TEL. F$135 ($94.50). AE, DC, MC, V.

If you don't mind being on the outskirts of town, this hotel offers a location right on the picturesque Bay of Islands, Suva's yacht harbor. In fact, international cruising yachts tie up right alongside the hotel's bulkhead. Comfortable rooms are in two waterfront wings on either side of the main building. Those on the Suva side are smaller and have angled balconies. Those on the Nadi side are larger and have balconies facing directly to the bay. About half of the 108 rooms have TVs. An attractively appointed lounge, bar, and restaurant open to the bay. Patrons also can dine on a covered barge moored to the dock. Facilities include a small bayside pool, tour desk, and large conference center across the Queen's Road. There's 24-hour room service.

Suva Travelodge

P.O. Box 1357, Suva (Victoria Parade, opposite Government Buildings). ☎ **301600** or 800/835-7742. Fax 300251. 134 rms. A/C MINIBAR TEL. F$176 ($123). AE, DC, MC, V.

The city's unofficial gathering place, this hotel's waterfront location couldn't be better: Suva Harbour laps one side, the stately Government Buildings sit across

Victoria Parade on the other, and the business district is a three-block walk away. The balconies or patios of the Australian-style rooms look out from two-story buildings onto a tropical garden and a boomerang-shaped swimming pool by the water's edge. The rooms have no cross-ventilation, which means they can become musty in Suva's heat and humidity. The central building has a very pleasant coffee shop, a more formal restaurant, and a bar with comfortable chairs and a view through floor-to-ceiling windows to the pool and harbor. Poolside barbecues on Sunday afternoons are popular with locals. Facilities include a United Touring Fiji (UTC) activities desk and conference rooms. The Travelodge has seven non-smoking rooms and one equipped for disabled guests.

INEXPENSIVE

✪ Capricorn Apartment Hotel

P.O. Box 1261, Suva (top end of St. Fort St.). ☎ **314799.** Fax 303069. 34 rms. A/C TV TEL. F$75–F$105 ($52.50–$73.50). AE, DC, MC, V.

Although a steep, two-block walk uphill from Cumming Street, Mulchand Patel's establishment is popular with Australians and New Zealanders who like to do their own cooking. The three-story, L-shaped building looks out on Suva Harbour and down the mountainous coast. Private balconies off each apartment share the view, as does a pear-shaped swimming pool on the Capricorn's grounds. The furniture in the older, inexpensive units is on the plain side, but Mulchand keeps these roomy efficiencies spotless. A dozen modern, condolike units are luxuriously furnished and much better outfitted than the older apartments. They are the more expensive units here and are on a par with any accommodation in Suva. Each unit has an air conditioner, although windows on both sides of the building let the cooling trade winds blow through. There's no restaurant, but the reception staff will sell you canned goods from its small on-premises store or have "Dial-A-Meal" deliver to your room. The maids will wash and dry your laundry for F$10 ($7) per load.

Sunset Apartment Motel

P.O. Box 485, Suva (Corner of Gordon and Murray Streets). ☎ **301799.** Fax 303466. 16 apts, 12 dorm beds. A/C. F$55 ($38.50) with kitchen; F$44 ($31) without kitchen; F$77 ($54) family unit; F$9 ($6.30) dorm bed. AE, DC, MC, V.

Manager Violet Matalau keeps a tight rein at this apartment building, which is popular with Pacific Islanders. Nine larger units have two bedrooms each—one with a double bed, one with two single beds—and full kitchens off their living rooms. Of six other one-room units, two have kitchens and four don't. Each unit has a sliding glass door leading to a private balcony. One unit is family size, and another has dormitory beds. The furniture is dated but adequate. Just a block off Victoria Parade, the location is very convenient, although passing buses make it noisy.

Tropic Towers Apartment Hotel

P.O. Box 1347, Suva (Robertson Rd., above Cumming and Marks Streets). ☎ **304470.** Fax 304169. 37 units. A/C TEL. F$62–F$88 ($43.50–$61.50). AE, MC, V.

Another establishment popular with islanders, this four-story concrete-and-glass building in a quiet residential neighborhood offers small, budget rooms and two- and three-bedroom apartments. Recently renovated, the units have blond wood trim, tile floors, tiled shower-only baths, and full kitchens. Although a bit utilitarian, they all are very clean. There's a pool, bar, tour desk, and small grocery shop on the premises.

HOSTELS

South Seas Private Hotel
P.O. Box 157, Suva (Williamson Rd. off Ratu Cakobau Rd., behind Albert Park). ☎ **312296.**
42 dorm beds, 34 rms (one with bath). F$18 ($12.50) double room; F$8 ($5.60) dorm bed.
No credit cards.

This large barracks-like wooden structure with a long sun room across the front
(it can be hot in the afternoons) could be cleaner, but it's a friendly establishment
and usually is packed with young people on the go. It has dormitories, basic rooms,
a rudimentary communal kitchen, and laundry facilities. Bed linen is provided, but
bring your own towel or pay F$3 ($2.00) deposit to use one of theirs. Showers have
both hot and cold water. The rooms have fans, but they operate only from 6pm
to 6am.

5 Where to Dine in Suva

EUROPEAN RESTAURANTS

✪ Old Mill Cottage
49 Carnavon St., near corner of Loftus St. ☎ **312134.** Reservations not accepted. Breakfasts
F$2–F$4 ($1.50–$3); meals F$2.50–F$5.50 ($3–$4). No credit cards. Mon–Fri 7am–6pm, Sat
7am–5pm. FIJIAN/INDIAN/EUROPEAN.

One of the few remaining late 19th-century homes left in Suva's diplomatic-
government section, this charming, two-room clapboard cottage is one of the best
places in the South Pacific to get consistently good home cooking. Walk past the
tables on the front porch and in the former living room to the counter near the
rear of the house. Order there from a selection of daily specials such as Fijian
palusami, mild Indian curries, or European-style mustard-baked chicken with real
mashed potatoes and peas. Diplomats (the U.S. Embassy is out the back door) and
government executives pack the place at midday. Saturday's menu is geared toward
Fijian seafood dishes. Breakfast is served next door in another cottage at 47
Carnavon St. These charming old cottages will someday give way to a high-rise,
so hurry.

✪ Swiss Tavern
16 Kimberly St. ☎ **303233.** Reservations essential. Main courses F$16–F$280 ($11–$19.50).
AE, DC, MC, V. Mon–Fri noon–2pm; Mon–Sat 6–10pm. CONTINENTAL.

Hans Kehrli, former chief chef at Shangri-La's Fijian Resort, specializes in the
cuisine of his native Switzerland at this house, which he remodeled into one of
Fiji's finest restaurants. Both a downstairs bar and upstairs dining room are
completely paneled in blond Fiji pine. If veal in heavy Zurich-style sauces doesn't
appeal, try the delicious Fijian-style bouillabaisse, with local seafood cooked the
Marseille way.

✪ Tiko's Floating Restaurant and Steakhouse
Stinson Parade at Sukuna Park. ☎ **313626.** Reservations recommended. Main courses F$7–
F$27 ($5–$19). AE, DC, MC, V. Mon–Fri noon–2pm; Mon–Sat 6–10pm. SEAFOOD/STEAKS.

Founder-owner-manager Tiko Eastgate describes himself as a fourth-generation
English-Fijian, since two of his ancestors were Fiji's first English magistrate and
the Fijian woman he married in the 1870s. After nearly 20 years with Shangri-La's
Fijian Resort, Tiko bought this ship for scrap-metal prices, replaced everything
below deck, and opened the restaurant and bar in 1985. His menu on the top deck

features nicely prepared fresh local seafood, such as *walu* (Spanish mackerel) and *pakapaka* (snapper). One level down, choose a steak and pay by the gram to have it broiled over charcoal. The service is attentive, and a terrific jazz musician-singer usually provides dinner music. The engine-room-level bar is a popular spot for after-work drinks.

INDIAN RESTAURANTS

Curry House
255 Victoria Parade, in Old Town Hall. ☎ **313000.** Reservations not accepted. Main courses F$2–F$7 ($1.40–$5). No credit cards. Mon–Wed 9am–9:30pm; Thur–Sat 9am–10pm. INDIAN.

This clean eatery displays its curries cafeteria-style at the front of the building and has booths and formica-top tables inside. All curry meals are served with dhal soup, potato and eggplant curry, chutney, and choice of two rotis or rice.

❸ Hare Krishna Restaurant
16 Pratt St. and 37 Cumming St. ☎ **314154.** Reservations not accepted. Curries F$1–F$6.50 (70¢–$4.50). No credit cards. Dining room Mon–Sat 11am–2:30pm, Fri 6–9pm; downstairs snack bar Mon–Thurs 9am–8pm, Fri 9am–9pm, Sat 9am–3:30pm. VEGETARIAN INDIAN.

This very popular restaurant specialize in a wide range of vegetarian curries— eggplant, cabbage, potatoes and peas, okra, and papaya to name a few—each seasoned delicately and differently from the others. Interesting pastries, breads, side dishes, and salads (such as cucumbers and carrots in yogurt) cool off the fire set by some of the curries. If you can't decide what to order, check the items on display in a cafeteria-like steam table near the entrance to the second-floor dining room, or get the *thali* sampler and try a little of everything—it's the most expensive item on the menu and will tingle your taste buds. Downstairs has an excellent yogurt and ice cream bar; climb the spiral stairs to reach the dining rooms. The Hare Krishnas allow no alcoholic beverages or smoking. There's another branch at 37 Cumming St. (☎ 312259).

CHINESE RESTAURANTS

✪ Great Wok of China
Bau St. at Laucala Bay Rd., Flagstaff. ☎ **301285.** Reservations recommended. Main courses F$7–F$27 ($5–$19). AE, DC, MC, V. Mon–Fri noon–2pm; Mon–Sat 6:15–10:45pm. SICHUAN.

Get to Suva's top Chinese restaurant early enough to order a cold beer and a serving of *kwai me far sing;* you'll need the beer to wash down these mouth-watering, spicy roasted peanuts. Otherwise, you won't go wrong ordering any of the Sichuan offerings, especially the whole crispy fish big enough to feed at least two persons. The dining room has an understated elegance, with blond wooden chairs, white linen table cloths, floral centerpieces, soft jazz on the sound system, and air conditioning.

❸ Lantern Palace
10 Pratt St. ☎ **314633.** Reservations recommended. Main courses F$5–F$10 ($3.50–$7). AE, DC, MC, V. Mon–Sat 11:30am–2:30pm and 5–10pm. CANTONESE.

Another popular establishment, this occupies a storefront on the same block of Pratt Street as the Hare Krishna Restaurant. It has the usual assortment of Chinese letters on the wall and lanterns hanging overhead, but the tables are draped with white linen cloths that contribute to a quiet, upscale atmosphere. You can choose from a wide range of excellent Cantonese dishes. By all means have the honey chicken.

Ming Palace

Victoria Parade in Old Town Hall. ☎ **315111.** Reservations recommended. Main courses F$7.50–F$11.50 ($5–$8). AE, DC, MC, V. Mon–Sat noon–2pm and 6–10pm. CANTONESE.

The owners here completely refurbished the auditorium of the Old Town Hall, which we passed during our walking tour of Suva. A huge Chinese dragon and bird now hang above the stage, and lanterns dangle from long poles reaching down from the high, arch-supported ceiling. Screens separate the tables to keep you from feeling as if you're dining in a meeting place, and the service is attentive and efficient. The menu includes Cantonese-style dishes of beef, chicken, pork, prawns, and crayfish lobster.

ITALIAN RESTAURANTS

Leonardo's

207 Victoria Parade, at MacArthur St. ☎ **312968.** Reservations recommended. Main courses F$6.50–F$16 ($4.50–$11). AE, DC, MC, V. Mon–Fri noon–2pm, Mon–Sat 6–10pm, Sun 7–10pm. ITALIAN/CONTINENTAL.

From mechanical drawings to the Mona Lisa, prints of Leonardo DaVinci's works line the stairs leading to this second-floor establishment above the Pizza Hut (see below). This classical introduction is a prelude to a refined dining room, in which a vase of flowers on every table is softly illuminated by a tiny ceiling spotlight. Soft jazz and classical background music adds to the ambience. The regular menu has a few pizzas and pastas, and nightly specials always offer a pasta, such as spaghetti under a Naples-style tomato sauce heavy on capers. Otherwise, the menu and daily specials lean more to continental and regional fare. I enjoyed a perfectly chargrilled slice of fresh mahi mahi with a fresh herb sauce.

Pizza Hut

207 Victoria Parade, at MacArthur St. ☎ **311825.** Reservations recommended on weekends. Pizzas F$4.50–F$16 ($3–$11); pastas F$5.50–F$6 ($3.85–$4.20). AE, DC, MC, V. Mon–Sat 11am–10:30pm, Sun 7–10pm. PIZZA/PASTA.

This is not related to the American chain by either quality or ownership (the proprietor of the Pizza Hut, Leonardo's, O'Reilly's, and a nightclub on this corner building is Irishman Liam Hindle). Nevertheless, it still has reasonably good pizza and pasta. Pies range from small and plain ones to large ones with prawns. Also on the menu: salads, spaghetti, and lasagna. You can dine in a cozy, brick-accented dining room or eat and drink in a comfy bar while listening to the music of blues stars whose photos hang on the walls.

SNACK BARS

Bentley's Fish & Chips

Thomson St. in Harbour Centre Arcade. ☎ **314980.** Reservations not accepted. F80¢–F$4 (55¢–$3). No credit cards. Mon–Thur 9:30am–4:30pm, Fri 9:30am–7pm, Sat 10am–1pm. FRIED SEAFOOD.

Australians say the fried fish and chips (french fries) here are as good as back home. Order at the blue tile counter of this clean, modern shop on the Thomson Street side of the Harbour Centre Arcade behind the Fiji Visitors Bureau. Other items include sausages, mussels, squid and onion rings, and fish or lamb burgers. Add vinegar for spice.

Palm Court Bistro
Victoria Parade, in the Palm Court Arcade, Queensland Insurance Centre. ☎ **304662.**
Reservations not accepted. Breakfasts F$2.50–F$7 ($1.75–$5); sandwiches, meat pies,
burgers, fish and chips F$1.50–F$3.50 ($1–$2.50). No credit cards. Mon–Fri 7am–6pm, Sat
7am–3pm. SNACK BAR.

You can partake of excellent cooked breakfasts and a variety of other snacks and
light meals at this walk-up carryout in the open-air center of the Palm Court
Arcade. Order at the counter and then eat at plastic tables under cover, or go sit
in the shade of the namesake palm in the middle of the arcade.

6 Golf, Tennis & Other Outdoor Activities

Suva is no Nadi when it comes to recreation, but many city folk are avid golfers
and tennis players. There are no beaches in or near the city, but there is a picnic
cruise to an islet out on the reef, and Suva is a base for scuba-diving and snorkeling expeditions to the fine Beqa Lagoon.

FISHING   The waters off southern Viti Levu are renowned for their big game
fish, and **Ocean Pacific Club,** P.O. Box 3229, Lami Town (☎ 303252, fax
300732), caters to anyone who is serious about fishing. Located on a peninsula
about 15 miles west of Suva, the Club has a fleet of boats, comfortable accommodations, a restaurant, and a bar.

GOLF   One of the South Pacific's finest courses is at **Pacific Harbour Golf and
Country Club** (☎ 450022), the centerpiece of the planned resort community on
Queen's Road, 30 miles west of Suva. The 18-hole, par-72 course was designed
by Robert Trent Jones, Jr. Some of the fairways cross lakes; others cut their way
through narrow valleys surrounded by jungle-clad hills. Visitors are welcome to use
the links: greens fees are F$44 ($31). A full range of equipment can be rented
at the pro shop. The links here are in much better shape than the shopworn
clubhouse, which has a restaurant and bar.

Closer to town, the less challenging 18-hole course of the **Fiji Golf Club**
(☎ 382872) lies along Rifle Range Road, on the eastern side of the peninsula.
Contact the club's secretary for more information or to schedule a tee-off time.

RIVER TRIPS   **Wilderness (Fiji) Tours** (☎ 386498) operates a popular, full-
day trip on the Navua River west of Suva. A bus or car picks you up at 8am for a
two-hour drive through fields, forests, and villages to the upper reaches of the river.
You then spend the rest of day canoeing down the river, navigating over cascades
in the hills, and then meandering through rice paddies in the flat valley below. A
bus or car brings you back to Suva from the river's mouth 39km (23 miles) west
of the city on the Queen's Road. Cost for the full day, including lunch beside the
river, is F$55 ($38.50) per person.

Wilderness Adventures runs similar bus-and-boat half-day trips to roaring
Wairoro Falls, up the Rewa River east of Suva. These popular tours include a visit
to a Fijian village for a cup of yaqona. These cost F$50 ($35) per person for a full
day, F$35 ($24.50) for half a day.

SCUBA DIVING   **Beqa Divers** (☎ 361088) takes snorkelers along on a variety of scuba-diving expeditions from its base at the marina at the Tradewinds
Hotel, about four miles west of town on the Bay of Islands. Most dives on the reefs
in the immediate Suva area take half a day, but the company also has full-day trips
to the gorgeous, unspoiled Beqa lagoon from an auxiliary base at Pacific Harbour.

Two-tank Beqa dives cost F$130 ($91) and snorkelers pay F$61 ($42.50), including equipment and lunch. Beqa Divers does not take snorkelers on its night-dive trips.

Ocean Pacific Divers (☎ 303252) and **Dive Connections** (☎ 450371) also have dive expeditions to Beqa Lagoon from their respective bases at Ocean Pacific Club, about 15 miles west of Suva, and at Pacific Harbour.

SWIMMING & SNORKELING　One easy way to get to a beach for swimming and snorkeling is with **Coral Sea Cruises** (☎ 321570), which goes to Nukulau Island, a tiny atoll used as a quarantine station when Indians were brought to Fiji as indentured laborers. Fresh fruit and morning tea are served on the way out, and Fijian divers hand-feed the fish beneath glass observation panels in the hull. The boats leave daily at 9:30am and return at 3:30pm. The fare is F$40 ($28) per person, including hotel transfers and lunch on the island.

To the rear of the Old Town Hall on Victoria Parade, the **Suva Olympic Pool** is open to all comers Monday to Friday from 10am to 6pm and Saturday from 8am to 6pm during the winter months (April to September); in summer (October to March), it's open Monday to Friday from 9am to 7pm and Saturday from 6am to 7pm. Admission is F$1.10 (77¢) for adults and F55¢ (39¢) for children. Lockers rent for F22¢ (15¢) plus a refundable F$2 ($1.40) key deposit.

TENNIS　Suva has lighted, hard-surface **public tennis courts** in Albert Park on Victoria Parade and in Victoria Park on Disraeli Road. Telephone 313428 to make a reservation.

7 Shopping in Suva

If you took the walking tour of Suva, you already have a good idea of where to shop for handcrafts and duty-free merchandise. Most of the city's best shops are along **Victoria Parade** and on **Cumming Street.** The two largest and most reliable merchants are the large **Morris Hedstrom** department store on Thomson Street at Nubukalou Creek; **Prouds,** at the Triangle near the Fiji Visitors Bureau and at the corner of Thomson and Cumming Streets; and **Tappoo,** which has a large store at the corner of Thomson and Usher Streets. The prices are fixed at Morris Hedstrom, Prouds, and Tappoo, but bargaining is the order of the day in Suva's so-called duty-free shops. Before you buy at the small stores, read the discussion of duty-free shopping in "Best Buys in Nadi," in the chapter on Nadi and Viti Levu.

Suva has some fine tropical clothing outlets, several of them on Victoria Parade near the Regal Theatre. **Tanya Whiteside Creations,** at the corner of Sukuna Park, has the most unusual dresses, all of them personally designed by talented proprietor Tanya Whiteside. **Tiki Togs,** which specializes in bright colors, has a shop at 199 Victoria Parade and another at 38 Thomson Street. The up-market resort- and beachwear specialist **Sogo Fiji** is on Victoria Parade opposite the theatre.

Stamp collectors will find colorful first-day covers from Fiji and other South Pacific island countries at the **Philatelic Bureau,** on the first floor of the General Post Office. It's open Monday to Thursday from 8am to 1pm and 2 to 4pm, Friday to 3:30pm. American Express, Diner's Club, MasterCard, and VISA cards are accepted.

Warning: Suva is crawling with the **sword sellers** I warned you about under "Best Buys in Nadi," in the chapter on Nadi and Viti Levu. The government requires these scam artists to stay in Thurston Park near the Fiji Museum, but you could be approached anywhere. Avoid them!

HANDCRAFTS

Government Handicraft Centre

Corner of Victoria Parade and MacArthur St., in rear of Ratu Sukuna House. ☎ **211306.**

Before buying Fijian handcrafts elsewhere, you should browse through the merchandise here. Operated by the Ministry of Trade and Commerce, the centre was founded in 1974 to continue and promote Fiji's handcrafts. Special attention is given to rural artisans who cannot easily market their works. Although Wolf's Boutique (see below) has the highest quality merchandise, you will see fine wood-carvings, woven goods, pottery, and tapa cloth, and you will learn from the fixed prices just how much the really good items are worth. The Fijian staff is friendly and helpful. Open Monday to Thursday from 8am to 4:30pm, Friday from 8am to 4pm and Saturday from 9am to noon.

Municipal Curio and Handicraft Centre

Municipal Car Park, Stinson Parade, on the waterfront. ☎ **313433.**

Having checked out the government center, you can visit these stalls and bargain with the Indian merchants (but not with the Fijians) from a position of knowl-edge, if not strength. Be careful, however, for some of the work here is mass produced and aimed at cruise ship passengers who have only a few hours in Fiji to do their shopping.

✪ Wolf's Boutique

Thomson St., opposite Fiji Visitors Bureau. ☎ **302320.**

Wolf Walter and Emele Naivaurua have the highest quality handcrafts, not only from Fiji but from other South Pacific island countries as well, including some excellent *nguzunguzus* (inlaid canoe prows) from the Solomon Islands. Prices for Fijian-carved war clubs and figurines are very reasonable for the excellent quality. Look also for straw hats, baskets, and mats; tapa cloth; shell jewelry; and works by local artists, such as drawings on tapa cloth by Alifereti Malai (whose exquisite works are easily carried home in your luggage).

8 Island Nights in Suva

Fijian-style meke feast-and-dance nights are scarce in Suva. The Suva Travelodge, Victoria Parade (☎ 301600), usually has one a week. Otherwise, nocturnal activi-ties in Suva revolve around sharing drinks with friends, then "polishing the floors" (dancing) until the wee hours on Friday, the biggest night out.

Most of the action is along Victoria Parade, especially at **Lucky Eddie's** and the **Urban Jungle,** both over the Pizza Hut (☎ 312968). Entrance to both clubs is up a stairwell posted ONLY SOBER AND WELL-BEHAVED PEOPLE ADMITTED. They appeal to a younger set who like ear-shattering rock and disco music. Lucky Eddie's side of the house is slightly more restrained. The Urban Jungle has street signs, parking meters, and graffiti everywhere. Lucky Eddie's is open Monday to Friday from 7pm to 1am and Saturday from 7:30 to 11:30pm. The Urban Jungle is open Thursday and Friday from 7pm to 1am and Saturday from 7:30 to 11:30pm. Admission ranges from F$2 ($1.40) weeknights to F$4 ($3) on Friday and Saturday.

These two pubs are part of Irishman Liam Hindle's restaurant and nightclub empire, so it's not surprising that he also built **O'Reilly's,** a genuine Irish pub on MacArthur Street just around the corner (☎ 312968). The big square bar serves

Guiness stout and has the obligatory sports TVs. Guests can also play darts and billiards. Open Monday to Friday from 11:30am to 2:30pm and 6pm to 1am, and Saturday from 6 to 11:30pm.

Other popular watering holes are **Tingle's Bar,** in Tiko's Floating Restaurant and Steakhouse on Stinson Parade at Sukuna Park (☎ 313626); **Trap's Bar,** 305 Victoria Parade, two blocks south of the Pizza Hut (☎ 312922); and the blues bar in the **Pizza Hut** (☎ 311825).

9 Resorts off Suva

Although guests can get there from Nadi, Suva is the usual jumping-off point to two small offshore resorts, including one of most expensive in Fiji. One is on Toberua, a tiny atoll off Viti Levu's east coast. The other is on Wakaya, in the Lomaviti (Central Fiji) group of islands, where Count Felix von Luckner was captured in 1917.

○ Toberua Island Resort

P.O. Box 567, Suva (Toberua Island, 12 miles off Viti Levu). ☎ **479177** or 302356 in Suva, or 800/354-7471, ext. 3434. Fax 302215. 14 bungalows. MINIBAR. F$352 ($246). Transfers F$23.50 ($16.50) per person from Nakelo landing, near Nausori Airport. Meals F$81 ($58) per person per day. AE, DC, MC, V.

Reached by 45-minute taxi-and-boat trip from Suva, Michael Dennis's resort is one of the oldest in Fiji but still going strong. He has comfortable bures and a main building on his tiny palm-dotted and beach-encircled atoll. The island is too flat to draw moisture from the sky; therefore, it isn't in the "rain belt" created by the mountains behind Suva. Guests enjoy such an easygoing lifestyle that they are warned to take at least four days to slow down and grow accustomed to the pace. Actually, there's plenty to do: sunbathe, swim, snorkel, scuba dive, collect shells, sail, windsurf, visit nearby Fijian villages and uninhabited islands (including one with a protected booby colony), fish in the lagoon, or play a round of "reef golf" (which is exactly what it sounds like: holes and fairways are out on the reef at low tide). Anyone who gets "bure fever" after a few days on this small atoll can charter the *Adi Toberua,* a cross between a cabin cruiser and a comfortable houseboat, for trips to nearby destinations such as Levuka. Rates are F$415 ($291) per day for boat, skipper, and meals. The boat can sleep three guests.

Toberua's large, Fijian-style bures are constructed of native materials. Each has its own modern bath with indoor and outdoor entrances. Their minibars are stocked with beer and wine. A few units are available to time-share owners.

Dining/Entertainment: The waterside dining room features excellent cuisine, with an emphasis on fresh seafood. Meal plans are required, since there is no other place to eat. A separate bar is a popular gathering spot. Fijians strum guitars and sing at night.

Services: Laundry, baby-sitting.

Facilities: Saltwater swimming pool; sailboats, Windsurfers, fishing equipment for free; excursions, fishing trips, and scuba diving cost extra.

○ The Wakaya Club

P.O. Box 15424, Suva (Wakaya Island, Lomaviti Group). ☎ **302630** or 212/644-7100. Fax 302714 or 212/644-7916. 8 units. MINIBAR. U.S. $875 double. Rates include meals, bar, and all activities. Round-trip transfers U.S. $780 from Nadi, U.S. $390 from Suva. AE, DC, MC, V.

A 20-minute flight away by private plane from Nausori Airport, 50 minutes from Nadi, this super-deluxe facility belongs to Canadian entrepreneur David Gilmour, who acquired the island in the 1970s. He had an interest in the Pacific Harbour development back then; as he did there, Gilmour is selling off pieces of Wakaya for deluxe getaway homes (his own Japanese-influenced mansion—the largest private residence in Fiji—sits high on a ridge overlooking the resort). Wakaya is an uplifted, tilted coral atoll with cliffs falling into the sea on its western side and beaches along the north and east. There are still relics of a Fijian fort on the cliffs; a chief and all his men once leaped to their deaths from there rather than be roasted by a rival tribe. The spot is known as Chieftain's Leap.

More recent famous events have included visits by actress Cheryl Ladd (who poses—without being identified—on Wakaya's brochure) and supermodel Christie Brinkley, who brought along her daughter and nanny but not then-husband Billy Joel. In fact, Hollywood and Beverly Hills types feel right at home in Wakaya's 1,500-square-foot, deluxe rectangular bungalows. On one end they have large living rooms with wet bars. Separate entrances off spacious decks lead to bedrooms with built-in desks and monstrous closets. Baths on the far end have oversized tubs, separate shower stalls, three sinks each, toilets, and bidets. Crabtree and Evelyn toiletries are imported from England.

Compared to Vatulele, Turtle Island, and other deluxe resorts, where a party atmosphere often prevails, the management and excellent and unobtrusive Fijian staff here leave the guests alone.

Dining/Entertainment: The food is of gourmet quality and outstandingly presented. Guests dine in a huge thatch-roofed beachside building or outside, either on a patio or under two gazebo-like shelters on a deck surrounding a swimming pool with its own waterfall.

Services: Laundry, anything else you need. Management leaves most guest contact to a highly efficient, unobtrusive Fijian staff.

Facilities: Nine-hole golf course, tennis and croquet courts, sailing, fishing.

10 Levuka

In Levuka, Fiji's first capital on the ruggedly beautiful island of Ovalau, you may think you've slipped into the "Twilight Zone" as you stroll down historic Beach Street along the town's curving waterfront. Everything here seems to be from a century earlier: ramshackle dry-goods stores with false fronts, clapboard houses with tin roofs to keep them dry and shaded verandas to keep them cool, and round clocks in the baroque tower of Sacred Heart Catholic Church. Where the regular streets end, "step streets" climb to more houses up near the base of the jagged cliffs towering over the town.

Not that Levuka hasn't changed at all since its 19th-century days as one of the South Pacific's most notorious seaports. All but one of the 50 or more hotels and saloons that dispensed rum and other pleasures disappeared long ago. The sole survivor—the Royal Hotel—is now a quiet, family-run establishment. The fistfighting whalers and drifting beach bums went the way of the square-rigged ships that once crowded the blue-green harbor beyond the row of glistening ficus trees and park benches along Beach Street. Gone, too, are the pioneering merchants and copra planters who established Levuka as Fiji's first European-style town in the 1830s and who for years carried guns to protect themselves from its ruffians.

There appeared to be a rowdy devil-may-care sort of look about the whole of them; and the great part of the day, and the night too, seemed to be spent in tippling in public house bars. I dare say that of the row of houses that make Levuka, fully half are hotels or public houses. The amount of gin and water which is consumed must be amazing, for the bars are always crowded, and the representatives of white civilization always at it.
— Robert Philp, 1872

But Levuka still looks much the same as it did in 1882, when the colonial administration moved to Suva. The 1,200-foot-tall walls of basalt, which caused the demise of Levuka by preventing expansion, create a soaring backdrop that puts Ovalau in the big leagues of dramatic tropical beauty.

Despite its history, beauty, and extremely hospitable residents, Levuka is relatively off the beaten tourist track. The volcano that created Ovalau has eroded into such rugged formations that it has very little flat land and only one decent beach; therefore, the island has not attracted resort or hotel development. All of Levuka's accommodations are basic and fall in the low-budget category. Unless you're willing to put up with very little in the way of comforts and amenities, make Levuka a day trip from Suva or Nadi.

GETTING THERE & GETTING AROUND

GETTING THERE   **Air Fiji** (☎ 313666 in Suva, 722251 in Nadi) has early-morning and late-afternoon flights to Ovalau's unpaved airstrip at Bureta, on the island's west coast. One-way fares are F$33 ($23) from Suva and F$96 ($67) from Nadi. Levuka is halfway around Ovalau on the east coast. An unpaved road circles the island along its shoreline and makes the bus ride from airport to town a sightseeing excursion in its own right. Airport bus transfers cost F$3.30 ($2.30) each way.

More adventurous souls can watch Ovalau's jagged green peaks go by from one of the **ferries** that run between Viti Levu and Levuka. Most boats land on the northwest coast, a 30-minute bus or taxi ride from Levuka.

Sun Tours (☎ 722666) has day trips from Nadi to Levuka via Air Fiji. These cost F$300 ($210), including round-trip airfare and a town tour.

For more information, see "Getting Around" in the "Introducing Fiji" chapter earlier in this book.

GETTING AROUND   Levuka is a small town, and your feet can get you to most places in 25 minutes.

For **taxis,** call **Vuniba Taxis** (☎ 440322), **Levuka Taxis** (☎ 440147), or **B. Murgan Transport Co.** (☎ 440180). Fares are F$1 (70¢) in town plus F50¢ (39¢) per kilometer thereafter; F$17 ($12) to the airport; F$25 ($17.50) to Lovoni; and F$50 ($35) around Ovalau. Be sure you and the driver agree on a fare before departing.

Local **buses** depart for the outlying villages from Beach Street about four times a day. They don't run after dark, so make sure you find out from the driver when—and whether—he returns to Levuka at the end of the day. Fares should be no more than F$1.50 ($1). Buses to Lovoni leave at 7:30am, noon, and 5pm. They leave Lovoni for Levuka at 6:30am, 8:30am, and 5pm.

FAST FACTS: LEVUKA

The following facts apply to Levuka and Ovalau. If you don't see an item here, look in "Fast Facts: Fiji" in the "Introducing Fiji" chapter.

Currency Exchange   Westpac Bank and National Bank of Fiji have offices near the Levuka Community Centre (old Morris Hedstrom store). Hours are Monday to Thursday from 9:30am to 3pm and Friday from 9:30am to 3:30pm.

Emergencies   The emergency phone number is 000.

Hospitals   The government maintains a small hospital in Levuka (☎ 440105).

Information   The best source is the Café Levuka (see "Where to Dine in Levuka," below). The staff at the Levuka Community Center (☎ 440356) can provide information. The Centre is open Monday to Friday from 9am to 5pm and Saturday from 9am to 1pm.

Libraries   The Community Center has a small library. You pay a F$5 ($3.50) registration fee to use the library, and you make a refundable F$10 ($7) deposit to check out books.

Police   The Fiji Police station is opposite the Masonic Lodge (☎ 440222).

Post Office   The post office is behind the Café Levuka. Open Monday to Friday from 8am to 1pm and 2 to 4pm.

Safety   See "Police," above.

Telephone/Telegrams/Fax   Public phones are scarce on Ovalau. Place long-distance and international calls at the post office.

WHAT TO SEE & DO

A walking tour of Levuka should take about two hours. Begin at the **Levuka Community Centre,** across the street from the Air Fiji office, which occupies the quaint old **Morris Hedstrom** store built by Levukans Percy Morris and Maynard Hedstrom in 1878. The trading company they founded, now one of the South Pacific's largest department store chains, pulled out of Levuka entirely a century later. After the company donated the dilapidated structure to the National Trust of Fiji, the Levuka Historical and Cultural Society raised money throughout the country to restore the structure and install a small branch of the Fiji Museum, a public library, a meeting hall, a crafts and recreational center, and a small garden. The furniture is made of timbers salvaged from the rotting floor. Mrs. Dora Patterson, matriarch of the Patterson Brothers Shipping Company family, donated the museum's waterside garden; she could oversee the project from her colonial-style mansion on the hill above Levuka. From the Community Centre head south.

Nasova and the Deed of Cession   The post office stands at the entrance to the **Queens Wharf** on the south side of the museum. The drinking fountain in front marks the site of a carrier-pigeon service that linked Suva and Levuka in the late 1800s. The Queens Wharf is one of Fiji's three ports of entry (Suva and Lautoka are the others), but along with domestic cargo, it now handles primarily exports from the Pacific Fishing Company's **tuna cannery,** established by a Japanese firm in 1964. You can follow your nose to the cannery in the industrial buildings south of the pier.

Keep going to **Nasova,** a village on the shore of the little bay about half a mile south of the cannery. Chief Cakobau signed the deed that ceded Fiji to Great Britain here. The site is now marked by three stones in the center of a grassy park at the water's edge. Plaques commemorate the signing ceremony on October 10, 1874; Fiji's independence exactly 96 years later; and the 1974 centennial celebration of the Deed of Cession. A Fijian-style thatch meetinghouse stands across the road.

South of Nasova, the **Old Levuka Cemetery** is tended to perfection by prison inmates.

Beach Street Backtrack to the weathered storefronts of Levuka's three-block-long business district along **Beach Street.** Saloons no longer line Beach Street; instead, the Indian- and Chinese-owned stores now dispense a variety of dry goods and groceries. On the horizon beyond the ficus trees and park benches lie the smoky-blue outlines of Wakaya, Makogai, and other members of the Lomaiviti ("Central Fiji") group of islands. The green cliffs still reach skyward behind the stores, hemming in Levuka and its narrow valley. Walk along the waterfront, and don't hesitate to stick your head into the dry-goods stores.

After the last store stands the **Church of the Sacred Heart,** a wooden building fronted by a baroque stone tower. It was built by the Marist Fathers who came to Levuka in 1858. In case you missed the number of chimes marking the time, the clock in the tower strikes once on the hour—and again, for good measure, one minute later. Across Beach Street stands a **World War I monument** to the Fijian members of the Fiji Labour Corps who were killed assisting the British in Europe.

Walk on across Totoga Creek to low **Niukaubi Hill,** on top of which is another World War I monument, this one to Levukans of English ancestry who died fighting as British soldiers in that conflict. Parliament House and the Supreme Court building sat on this little knoll before the capital was moved to Suva. They had a nice view across the town, the waterfront, and the reef and islands offshore. At the bottom of the hill is the **Levuka Club,** a colonial-era drinking establishment.

Keep going north on Beach Street, which soon passes the 1904-vintage Anglican church before arriving in the original Fijian village known as **Levuka.** The Tui Levuka who lived here befriended the early European settlers. Later, Chief Cakobau worshipped in the Methodist church built on the south side of the creek in 1869. John Brown Williams, the American consul, is buried in the village's Old Cemetery near the church. (Remember, good manners dictate that you have permission before entering a Fijian village.)

To the north, **Gun Rock** towers over Levuka village. In order to show the chiefs just how much firepower it packed, a British warship in 1849 used this steep headland for target practice. Beach Street now runs under the overhang of Gun Rock, where the Marist Fathers said their first mass. There was no road then, only a shingly beach where the sea had worn away the base of the cliff.

Inland Beyond Gun Rock lies the village of **Vagadaci,** where the Duke of York—later King George V—and his brother, the Duke of Clarence, once played cricket, but I usually turn around at Gun Rock and return to the first street inland south of the hospital. It leads to the **199 steps** that climb Mission Hill from the Methodist church to the collection of buildings that comprise Delana Methodist School. For the energetic, the view from the 199th step is worth the climb.

From the church, cut down Chapel Hill Road and Langham Street past the Royal, the South Pacific's oldest operating hotel. Keep going south along the banks of Togoga Creek to the Roman-style **Polynesia Masonic Lodge,** which was founded in 1875. The **Town Hall,** next door, was built in 1898 in honor of Queen Victoria's 50 years on the British throne; it still houses most of Levuka's city offices. The nearby **Ovalau Club** is the oldest drinking club in the South Pacific, a reminder of the social clubs where the Old Boys of the British Empire gathered to escape the heat, drink gin, and play snooker (billiards). The Ovalau Club today has a racially diverse membership that welcomes clean-cut visitors from overseas. Behind the lodge, club, and Town Hall, **Nasau Park** provides the town's rugby and cricket field, bowling green, and tennis courts.

Now head uphill along the creek until you get to the lovely white Victorian buildings with broad verandas of **Levuka Public School,** Fiji's first educational institution (opened in 1879) and still one of its best. A row of mango and sweet-smelling frangipani trees shade the sidewalk known as Bath Road between the school and the rushing creek. Walk up Bath Road, which soon turns into a "step street" as it climbs to a waterfall and concrete-lined swimming hole known as The Bath. Cool off at this refreshing spot before heading back down the steps to Beach Street.

Guided Tours   The **Levuka Community Centre** (☎ 440356) provides guided tours of the town, sometimes led by entertaining Lord Mayor George Gibson, for a F$5 ($3.50) per person donation. Reserve at the Centre at least a day in advance. All-day bush walks across the mountains to Lovoni village in the center island, with a swim and return by local bus, cost F$15 ($10.50). Half-day climbs to Ovalau's highest peak cost F$3 ($2).

EXCURSIONS FROM LEVUKA

Some villages on Ovalau offer attractions in their own right, but remember to ask permission before entering a Fijian village, don't wear a hat or have bare shoulders, and don't visit on Sunday except to go to church.

Lovoni, a picturesque Fijian village in the crater of Ovalau's extinct volcano, is a popular day trip by guided hike or via local bus. In pre-colonial days, Lovoni was the home of ferocious warriors who stormed down to the coast and attacked Levuka on several occasions. Chief Cakobau settled that problem by luring them into town to talk peace; instead, he captured them all and deported them to other parts of Fiji. Today's Lovonians have seen so many travelers wandering around their village that most are adept at pleasantly smiling while ignoring you. The houses are of wood with corrugated iron roofs. See "Getting Around" and "Guided Tours," above, for more information.

Waitovu village, about a 50-minute walk north of town (look for its mosque), has the nearest waterfall to town. Ask permission, and ask the residents to show the way. You can dive into the top pool from the rocks above.

Rukuruku village has a waterfall and Ovalau's sole swimming beach.

OFFSHORE ISLANDS

Tiny **Leleuvia Island,** an atoll between Viti Levu and Ovalau, has become a favorite backpacker retreat in recent years. Guests stay in a mix of dormitories, thatch bures, and European cottages. They can sunbathe (topless if desired) on the islet's gorgeous beaches and swim and snorkel over some lovely reefs. A small shop sells beer and some groceries, and the staff prepares basic meals. Rates, including three meals, are F$18 ($12.50) for a dorm bed, F$21 ($14.70) per person in bures without bath, F$36 to F$52 ($25 to $36.50) in European cottages with bath, and F$15 ($10.50) per person for campsite (bring your own tent). Transportation is by Emosi's Express Shipping, which leaves Levuka at 9am Monday to Saturday. The boat ride costs F$15 ($10.50) each way, but you can go from Leleuvia on to Suva for another F$18 ($12.50). Book in Levuka at the Old Capitol Inn on Convent Street (☎ 440057) or in Suva with Emosi's Ferry Service (☎ 313366).

Caqueli Island (pronounced Than-*kay*-lee) also has camping and primitive bures. Owned by the local Methodist church, it's more peaceful, a lot more restrained, and gets less visitors than nearby Leleuvia. Rates are less than at Leleuvia. Book at Paak Kum Loong Restaurant (☎ 440382) on Beach Street.

Lost Island, or Yanuca Taitai, is large enough for bush walks ("hikes" in American English) by guests who go for the day. It's run by villagers who prepare lovo-style lunches on a beach, provided five or more guests attend. Inquire at the Levuka Community Center (☎ 44356) at least a day in advance.

Naigani Island Resort (☎ 300925, fax 300539) is total luxury when compared to the other islets off Levuka. It sits beside a gorgeous half-moon bay on hilly Naigani Island, northwest of Ovalau about halfway to Natovi Wharf on Viti Levu. It has 12 deluxe villas, each of which will sleep up to eight persons. Regular rates are about F$180 ($126), but the resort has a special four-night backpacker package deal from Levuka for F$149 ($104) per person, including dorm bed, all meals, and transfers.

WHERE TO STAY IN LEVUKA

Mavida Lodge

P.O. Box 91, Levuka, Ovalau (Beach Street). ☎ **440477.** 5 rms (none with bath), 21 dorm beds. F$12 ($8.50) per person. Rates include cooked breakfast. No credit cards.

Rosie Patterson of the Patterson Brothers Shipping family recently bought these two late 19th-century clapboard cottages and gave them a scrubbing and a coat of paint. Both houses have charming, enclosed veranda rooms with long rows of double-hung windows facing the lagoon across Beach Street. There's a covered patio between them for lounging. One house has private rooms, some with antique beds whose mosquito nets sweep down from seven-foot-tall headboards. The other has 21 beds jammed into every possible position in its rooms, none of them private. All guests share baths and a communal kitchen. Dinners are available at a very reasonable F$4 ($3) per person.

Old Capitol Inn I & II

P.O. Box 50, Levuka, Ovalau (Convent St. and Beach St.). ☎ **440057.** 19 bunks, 15 rms (none with bath). F$7 ($5) dorm bed; F$26 ($18) double. Rates include breakfast. No credit cards.

The start of Emosi Yee Shaw's shipping and Leleuvia Island backpackers empire, these two facilities cater to anyone who wants absolutely no frills and little charm. The Old Capitol Inn I is Emosi's original storefront establishment on Convent Street just off Beach Street. It has three rooms and four dorm beds upstairs, a Chinese restaurant and bar downstairs (which can be noisy). The Old Capitol Inn II is a clapboard house on Beach Street. It has 12 rooms and 15 dorm beds, all flanking a central hallway leading to a communal kitchen, bath, and showers. It has a pleasant sitting room on the front facing the lagoon.

Ovalau Resort

P.O. Box 113, Levuka, Ovalau (2 miles north of town). ☎ **440329.** Fax 440019. 5 bungalows. F$35 ($24.50) bungalow; F$7.50 ($5.25) dorm bed. No credit cards.

Ovalau's only accommodation in a coconut grove beside a beach, albeit a rocky one, Steve and Sokula Diston's little place has five bungalows with kitchens.

There's nothing tropical about them, being constructed and furnished in a New Zealand style. They do have a charming bar, in an old whaler's cottage on the property.

○ Royal Hotel

P.O Box 47, Levuka, Ovalau (Beach Street). ☎ **440024.** 14 rms (none with bath), 3 cottages. F$26 ($18) room; F$55 ($38.50) cottage; F$7 ($5) dorm bed. No credit cards.

This establishment rates a star as an attraction, for even if you don't stay at the South Pacific's oldest operating hotel, have a look at its public rooms. It was built about 1852 and "modernized" in the 1890s (except for stringing an electric light to each room, little has been done to it since). Not much imagination is required to picture W. Somerset Maugham or Robert Louis Stevenson relaxing in the comfortable rattan chairs of the Royal's charming lounge, slowly sipping gin-and-tonics at its polished bar, or playing a game of snooker at its antique billiard table. One of Levuka's fine old families, the Ashleys, has run the Royal for more than half a century with such attentive care that it seems more like a pension full of antiques than a hotel. In contrast to the ancient and very basic rooms, the three modern cottages are the pick of Levuka's lodgings. The Ashleys serve three meals a day in the dining room, but book in advance.

WHERE TO DINE IN LEVUKA

Café Levuka

Beach St., next to Levuka Community Centre. ☎ **440095.** Reservations not accepted. Sandwiches and burgers F$5–F$6 ($3.50–$4); meals F$4.50–F$8 ($3–$5.50). No credit cards. Daily 7am–8pm. REGIONAL.

This storefront cafe is the town's most popular gathering spot for locals and travelers alike. Guests show up not just for cappuccino, espresso, fresh fruit juices, cooked breakfasts, sandwiches, burgers, and meals such as fish in lolo, but to have a look at the cafe's information book, which has the latest on Levuka and Ovalau. It should be your first stop.

Whale's Tale Restaurant

Beach St., middle of town. ☎ **440235.** Reservations not accepted. Sandwiches and snacks F$2–F$5.50 ($1.40–F$4); dinner F$5–F$7 ($3.50–$5). No credit cards. Daily 11:30am–9pm. REGIONAL.

Australian Julia Ditrich, daughter Liza, and Fijian partner Susana Rakala renovated one of Beach Street's old storefronts and opened this cramped but pleasant eatery. Their lunch menu includes sandwiches, burgers, and daily specials. At night they put cloths on the tables and offer three-course meals from a chalkboard menu, which always includes a vegetarian selection.

12 Northern Fiji

If you're going to spend the money to come to Fiji, then you may as well shell out a few extra dollars to visit the northern part of the country, for these pristine islands are what the old South Seas are all about. Compared to populated and relatively developed Viti Levu, the islands of Vanua Levu and Taveuni take us back to the old days of copra planters, of Fijians living in small villages in the hills or beside crystal-clear lagoons.

The rolling plains of northern Vanua Levu, the country's second-largest island, are devoted to sugarcane and are of little interest to anyone who has visited Nadi. But on Vanua Levu's south side, rugged mountains drop to coconut plantations, to an old trading town with the sing-song name Savusavu, and to villages where smiling people go about life at the ageless pace of tropical islands everywhere. And on Taveuni, Fiji's lush "Garden Isle," with the country's largest population of indigenous plants and animals, things are even more like they used to be.

The North is where visitors come to experience the natural wonders of Fiji—to "eco-tour" in today's vogue terminology. It's also where they come for some of the world's best scuba diving, for the strong currents in and around the Somosomo Strait between Vanua Levu and Taveuni feed a vast collection of colorful soft corals. Other South Pacific locations have more abundant sea life, but Northern Fiji is unsurpassed for coral viewing. Diving here is at its best from late May through October, when visibility reaches 120 feet and more. Because of the strong currents, however, dives to the outer reefs can be strenuous any time of the year.

1 Savusavu

A spine of volcanic mountains runs lengthwise down the center of Vanua Levu, trapping moisture from the prevailing southeast trade winds and giving the rolling hills and deltas of the north shore an ideal climate for growing sugarcane. Consequently, the area around the predominately Indian town of **Labasa** is one of Fiji's prime sugar-producing regions.

On the south coast, however, the usually cloud-topped mountains quickly give way to narrow, well-watered coastal plains, ideal for copra plantations. Until the Great Depression of the 1930s,

Northern Fiji

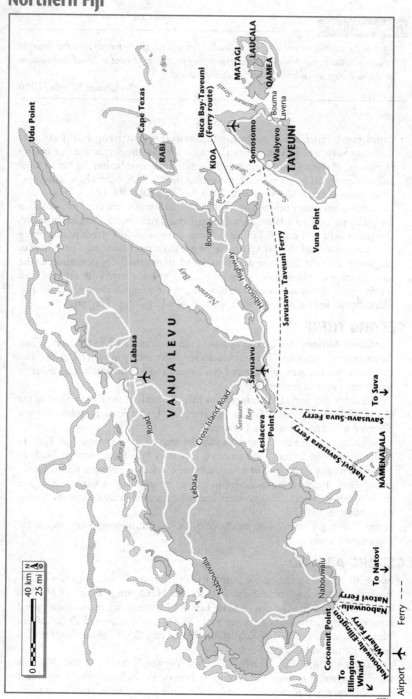

Airport ✈   Ferry – – –

9091

| **Impressions** |

By now I was drowsy; the warm air blowing freely through the windowless bus brought smells of flowers, damp earth, and copra-drying fires, that seemed to blend and thicken as the day lengthened and colours became enriched.

—Ronald Wright, 1986

copra production made picturesque **Savusavu** a thriving European settlement. Savusavu is Vanua Levu's major sightseeing attraction, primarily because of its volcanic hot springs and magnificent scenic harbor—a bay so large and well protected by surrounding mountains that the U.S. Navy chose it as a possible "hurricane hole" for the Pacific Fleet during World War II.

Savusavu sits snugly behind a small island in the southeastern corner of Savusavu Bay. The paved Cross-Island Road from Labasa runs along the eastern shore, through town, and out to Lesiaceva Point at the end of a peninsula forming the southern side of the bay and protecting it from the Koro Sea. The **Hibiscus Highway** starts at Savusavu and cuts south across the hilly peninsula to the airport before continuing along the south shore to Buca Bay. This unpaved road is neither a highway nor lined with hibiscus, but it does run along a picturesque, island-dotted lagoon through the heart of Vanua Levu's copra region.

GETTING THERE

Sunflower Airlines and **Air Fiji** fly from both Nadi and Suva to Savusavu. Their flights between Nadi and Taveuni usually stop here briefly in each direction. The tiny Savusavu airport is on Vanua Levu's south coast. The hotels send buses to meet guests who have reservations.

The super-fast ferry *Drogrolagi* from Lautoka lands at the Copra Shed in the center of Savusavu from Monday to Saturday. Other inter-island ferries use the main wharf on the west end of town.

Adventurous travelers can make a two-day trip all the way from Viti Levu to Taveuni without flying. First comes a bus-ferry trip from Suva or Nadi to Nabouwalu on Vanua Levu. From there, buses connect to Savusavu via the Cross-Island Road, a sightseeing excursion in its own right. From Savusavu, a bus goes to Buca Bay on Vanua Levu's eastern end, where a small ferry crosses the Somosomo Strait to Taveuni.

See "Getting There & Getting Around" in the "Introducing Fiji" chapter for more information.

GETTING AROUND

Some 30 **taxis**—an incredible number for such a small place—gather by the market in Savusavu when not hauling passengers. **Hot Springs Taxis** (☎ 850226) are radio dispatched. The cars of **Shiu Taxis** (☎ 850624) are in reasonably good condition. Fares from Savusavu are F$2 ($1.40) to the airport, F$5 ($3.50) to Namale Resort, F$10 ($7) to Kontiki Resort, and F$5 ($3.50) to the Cousteau Fiji Islands Resort on Lesiaceva Point.

Budget (☎ 850700), **Thrifty** (☎ 850256), and **Kahn's** (☎ 850580) have car-rental agencies in Savusavu. If you rent a car on Vanua Levu, bear in mind that even the few paved roads can be washed out during heavy rains, and that gasoline stations exist only in Labasa and Savusavu.

Local buses fan out from the Savusavu market to various points on the island. Most of them make three or four runs a day to outlying destinations, but ask the drivers when they will return to town. The longest runs should cost no more than F$6 ($4), with local routes in the F55¢ to F$1 (39¢ to 70¢) range.

FAST FACTS: SAVUSAVU

The following facts apply to Savusavu. If you don't see an item here, check the Fast Facts in the "Introducing Fiji" chapter.

Bookstore   Bula Bookshop in the Copra Shed on the waterfront has newspapers, magazines, and books on Fiji. It also has color print film processing, but it takes 48 hours.

Currency Exchange   Westpac Bank, ANZ Bank, and National Bank of Fiji have offices on the main street.

Dentist   See "Hospital" below.

Doctor   The nearest private practitioners are in Labasa.

Drugstores   See "Hospital" below.

Emergencies   Phone 000.

Hospitals   The government hospital (☎ 850800) is east of town in the government compound.

Police   The police station (☎ 850222) is east of town.

Post Office   The post office is east of town.

Safety   Savusavu generally is a safe place to visit, but don't tempt the mortals. Keep an eye on your personal property.

Telephone/Telegrams/Telex   Go to the post office. There's a Phonecard public phone in the Copra Shed.

WHAT TO SEE & DO

For practical purposes, there is only one street in Savusavu, and that runs along the shore for about a mile. The modern **Copra Shed,** an old warehouse that has been turned into modern shops and a cafe, stands about midway along the shore. It and the market are the centers of activity.

Highlights of a stroll along the bay-hugging avenue are the gorgeous scenery and the volcanic **hot springs.** Steam from underground rises eerily from the rocky beach on the west end of town, and you can see more white clouds floating up from the ground beyond the sports field behind the Shell station. To reach the springs, go inland at the Shell station, then bear left at the oil storage tanks. A concrete pot has been built to make a natural stove in which local residents place meals to cook slowly all day. Overlooking the springs and bay, the **Hot Springs Hotel** has great views.

WHERE TO STAY
RESORTS

✪ Cousteau Fiji Islands Resort

Post Office, Savusavu (Lesiaceva Point, 3 miles west of town). ☎ **850118** or 800/246-3454. Fax 850340. 20 bungalows. MINIBAR. F$374–F$612 ($262–$428). Rates include airport transfers, breakfast, and all activities except scuba diving. AE, MC, V.

On the verge of opening during my recent visit, this joint venture between the deluxe Post Ranch Inn of Big Sur, Calif., and Jean-Michel Cousteau, son of the famous Jacques Cousteau, had extensively upgraded the former Na Koro Resort, which looks like an old-time Fijian village set in a flat palm grove beside the bay on Lesiaceva Point. The new establishment is an "environmentally correct" resort, with extensive use of solar power and recycling programs.

The large, comfortable bures are built to one side of two central buildings, in which reception and the resort's bar are under a large roof built like a chief's bure. The dining room is covered by a taller and more impressive roof constructed to resemble a priest's bure. These two areas, joined for the convenience of guests, sit next to a deck-surrounded swimming pool just steps from one of the best beaches in the area. The luxurious thatch-roof bures have ceiling fans to augment the natural breezes flowing through floor-to-ceiling louvered windows that make up the front and rear walls.

There is a host of water sports activities available here, including snorkeling, kayaking, and windsurfing, but the emphasis is on environmentally oriented activities as part of Jean-Michel Cousteau's Project Ocean Search. An on-site marine biologist gives lectures and leads birdwatching expeditions and visits to Fijian villages. Scuba diving is with guides skilled in marine biology. The resort has a custom-built dive boat capable of reaching the famous Namena Reef, which surrounds Moody's Namena (see "A Resort off Savusavu," below), in about one hour.

Kontiki Resort

Private Bag, Savusavu (Hibiscus Highway, 10 miles east of town). ☎ **850262.** Fax 850355. 16 bungalows. MINIBAR TEL. F$165 ($116). AE, MC, V.

Tony and Joyce Hoskins' pleasant resort attracts divers, fishing enthusiasts, and golfers, since it has no beach on the premises but does sport a marina blasted into the reef and a short nine-hole golf course beneath the coconut palms of an old plantation. The Hibiscus Highway runs through the property, separating the lagoon from a pool, tennis court, bungalows, and a thatch-roofed building with bar and restaurant. The land turns quickly from flat coastal shelf to hills, where some of the guest bungalows are perched, thus commanding views through the palms to the sea. All bungalows have peaked, thatch-covered roofs, sliding doors opening to porches, ceiling fans, a king-size and a single bed, and tiled shower-only baths. A short nature walk across the golf course and through tropical forest leads to the resort's own refreshing cascades and the site of an ancient Fijian village. Guests can visit a modern-day Fijian village, whose residents come to the resort for mekes once a week. Another excursion goes to an 1860s planters house hand-built of super-hard *vesi* (local teak). If you want to buy a piece of this paradise, lots are for sale in the hills above the resort.

Namale Resort

P.O. Box 244, Savusavu (Hibiscus Highway, 7 miles east of town). ☎ **850435** or 800/ 727-3434. Fax 850400. 10 bungalows. MINIBAR. F$525–F$700 ($368–$490). Rates include meals, bar, all activities except scuba diving. AE, DC, MC, V.

Owned by toothy American motivational author and speaker Anthony Robbins, who vacations and holds some of his high-priced seminars here, this resort sits on a narrow headland jutting out into Naidi Bay. The rest of the property has been a working copra plantation since the 1860s, when an Englishman bought it from the local chief for 10 guns. Robbins recently tore down the charming old plantation house and replaced it as the main building with a soaring thatch Fijian-style bure, which has a bar and library area. Guests can dine inside the big building, but the majority of meals are taken on a deck commanding an excellent view from the point jutting out into the bay.

The guest bures are widely scattered in the blooming tropical gardens surrounding the main house, thus affording honeymoon-like privacy if not a setting directly on the beach (this area has been geologically uplifted, so all buildings are on a shelf 10 feet to 20 feet above sea level). They have either one or two bedrooms and are attractively appointed with rattan furniture and tropical spreads and drapes. The honeymoon and oceanfront units have large baths whose glass-walled showers look out to the sea (passing boats can get an eyeful). Although the windows in all units are screened, the staff drops romantic mosquito nets over the beds at turndown. There is a pool, a tennis court, a gym, water sports equipment including kayaks and paddleboards, and a fully equipped dive shop with instructor. Robbins reserves the Wave-runners for himself.

HOSTELS

David's Holiday House
P.O. Box 65, Savusavu (in town behind Shell station). ☎ **850216** or 850149. 6 rms (none with bath). F$20.50 ($14.50) room, F$10 ($7) dorm bed. Rates include tax and breakfast. No credit cards.

For guesthouse living, David Lal has clean and totally unpretentious rooms with table fans, two nightstands, and coffee tables. Guests share the communal kitchen, toilets, and showers. The dormitory is in a separate building. David has bicycles and a boat for rent, and will arrange pig hunts and guided hikes. If the house and dorm are full, you can pitch a tent in the yard. Airport transfers are free for stays of five days or longer.

WHERE TO DINE

Savusavu may someday have some fine eating establishments outside its resorts, but for now the choices are extremely limited. There are a few basic "curry shops" scattered among the shops in the business district, but only two restaurants stood out during my recent visit:

Captain's Cafe (☎ 850511), in the Copra Shed, is a pleasant place for an outdoor meal, with seating inside or outside on a deck over the bay. The name and nautical decor may be misleading, however, for when I was there only fish and chips came from the briny deep. Other offerings were sandwiches, burgers, pizzas, side salads, and garlic bread. Fish, burgers, and sandwiches cost from F$2 to F$5 ($1.40 to $3.50). The pies range from F$6 to F$24 ($4 to $17). Open Monday to Thursday from 9am to 9:30pm, Friday and Saturday from 9am to 9pm, and Sunday from 3 to 9pm.

Most meals at **Wing Yuen** (☎ 850108), next to the National Bank of Fiji, cost from F$2.50 to F$7 ($2 to $5), but for a real treat, try the prawn special at F$9.50 ($6.50). Hours are daily from 8am to 2pm and 6 to 9pm.

FISHING, SCUBA DIVING & OTHER OUTDOOR ACTIVITIES

Curly and Liz Carswell of **Eco Divers,** P.O. Box 264, Savusavu (☎ 850122 or 800/599-5507; fax 850344), arrange not only diving but accommodation and excursions on Vanua Levu. Originally from New Zealand, Curly and Liz have lived in Savusavu for many years and are now Fiji citizens. During my recent visit, they were developing a series of outdoor adventures, which should be up and running by the time you arrive. One was to go by four-wheel-drive vehicle to a Fijian village with an ancient fortification and its own hot springs. Return was to be by bilibili bamboo raft down a river. Another excursion was to be to a large waterfall and to a pool with red prawns. Vanua Levu is one of only three places in Fiji with shrimp that are red before cooking (Vatulele and Kaibu islands are the others). These red prawns are found only in Fiji and the Philippine Islands. Other tours include a visit to a coconut plantation, a hike through a rainforest, and a cross-island visit to Labasa. Check with Eco Divers early in your visit, for these tours require advance arrangements. Their office is in the Copra Shed on the waterfront.

FISHING With rich waters rising from the super-deep Tonga Trench just to the east, Northern Fiji has marvelous game fishing. **Kontiki Resort** (☎ 850262) has a fully equipped, 33-foot Power Cat game fishing boat that can accommodate up to four guests fishing for a day or on extended expeditions. Cost for the entire boat is F$750 ($525) a day. Contact the resort for the best seasons for fishing (see "Where to Stay," above).

SCUBA DIVING Most of the resorts have complete diving facilities, as noted in "Where to Stay," below. The dive shop at **Kontiki Resort** (☎ 850262) welcomes non-guests for diving and instruction.

At the Copra Shed, the environmentally conscious **Eco Divers** (☎ 850122) offers two-tank dives for F$94 ($66), with a third dive of the day for F$55 ($39). It uses many of the same buoyed sites as the Cousteau Fiji Island Resort, many of them on the Rainbow Reef between Vanua Levu and Taveuni. Full equipment rental is available.

SWIMMING & SNORKELING The nearest beach is a wonderfully shady stretch of sand on Lesiaceva Point just outside the Cousteau Fiji Islands Resort, about three miles west of town, which is the end of the line for west-bound buses leaving Savusavu market.

There also is a lovely half-moon beach at Naidi Bay, an extinct volcanic crater, just west of Namale Resort on the Hibiscus Highway. The road skirts the bay, but the beach is not easy to see. Take a taxi or ask the bus driver to let you off at Naidi Bay—not Naidi village or nearby Namale Resort. The bar and restaurant at Namale Resort are not open to walk-in customers, so bring something to drink and eat.

ISLAND NIGHTS

The expensive resorts provide nightly entertainment for their guests. Otherwise, there's not much going on in Savusavu after dark. Visitors are welcome at the **Planter's Club** (☎ 850233) in a clapboard building near the west end of town. This friendly holdover from the colonial era has a "snooker" pool table and a pleasant bar. It's open Monday to Saturday from 10am to 10pm. Closed Christmas and Good Friday. Admission is free (bona fide visitors are asked to sign in). **Savusavu Yacht Club** (no phone), upstairs in the Copra Shed overlooking the harbor, also welcomes visitors. It's open Monday to Friday from noon to 8pm and Saturday from 10am to 9pm.

2 A Resort off Savusavu

Tom and Joan Moody (she pronounces her name "Joanne") left western Pennsylvania in the 1960s to work at various resorts in the Florida Keys and the Caribbean. They scraped together some capital and in 1974 opened a small, isolated resort in Panama's San Blas Islands, catering to serious scuba divers and others who just wanted a total escape. Terrorists attacked their peaceful outpost in 1981, however, shooting and nearly killing Tom and tying Joan up. Fortunately, Tom survived, but they soon sold out and left Panama.

After searching the South Pacific, they settled on dragon-shaped Namenalala, little more than a rocky ridge protruding from the Koro Sea and covered with dense native forest and bush. The huge Namena barrier reef sweeps down from Vanua Levu and creates a gorgeous lagoon in which Tom can indulge his passion for diving. The Moodys have designated most of Namenalala as a nature preserve in order to protect a large colony of boobies that nest on the island, and sea turtles that climb onto the beaches to lay their eggs from November through February. In other words, the setting is remote and interesting. So is their little resort:

Moody's Namena

Private Mail Bag, Savusavu. ☎ **813764.** Fax 812366. 5 bungalows. F$214 ($150) (including fishing, and snorkeling trips). F$80 ($55) per person a day for meals, including wine at dinner. AE, MC, V. Closed March and April.

The Moodys perched all but one of their comfortable bungalows up on the ridge so that each has a commanding view of the ocean but not of one another. Each of the hexagonal structures resembles a treehouse; in fact, the huge trunk of a tree grows right through the balcony surrounding one of the bures. Surely this was how Robinson Crusoe would have preferred to live.

A lack of fresh ground water and electricity adds to the effect. The "his and her" toilets in each bungalow are flushed with seawater, and rainwater takes care of drinking and bathing. Propane provides both lights and refrigeration (you will find a cigarette lighter in your room to ignite the gaslights at dusk). The entire walls of the bungalows slide back to render both views and cooling breezes, so you will sleep under a mosquito net. Instead of treading sandy paths among palm trees, you climb rocky pathways along the wooded ridge to the central building, where the Moodys provide excellent meals and ice upon which to pour the booze you bought at the duty-free store (they do not have a liquor license). After one day in their care, these "hardships" matter not at all.

Scuba diving among the colorful reefs and sea turtles costs extra. Tom does not teach scuba diving, so you must be certified in advance.

The least expensive way to get to Namenalala is on the fast ferry _Drogrolagi_ from Levuka or Savusavu. The trip takes about 30 minutes from Savusavu and four hours from Lautoka. It costs about F$25 ($17.50) each way from Savusavu and about F$80 ($56) from Lautoka. The Moodys also will arrange to charter Turtle Island Airways' four-passenger seaplane for the one-hour flight from Nadi. That costs about F$975 ($683) round-trip, but the Moodys try to schedule their guests' arrivals and departures so that two couples share the cost.

3 Taveuni

Cigar-shaped Taveuni, Fiji's third-largest island, lies just four miles from Vanua Levu's eastern peninsula across the Somosomo Strait, one of the world's most famous scuba-diving spots. Although the island is only six miles wide, a volcanic ridge down Taveuni's 25-mile length soars to more than 4,000 feet, blocking the southeast trade winds and pouring as much as 30 feet of rain a year on the mountaintops and the island's rugged eastern side. Consequently, Taveuni's 9,000 residents (three-quarters of them Fijians) live in a string of villages along the gently sloping, less rainy but still lush western side. They own some of the country's most fertile and well-watered soil—hence Taveuni's nickname: "The Garden Isle."

Thanks to limited land clearance and the absence of the mongoose found in such profusion on the cane-growing islands, Taveuni still has all the plants and animals indigenous to Fiji, including the unique Fiji fruit bat, the Taveuni silktail bird, land crabs, and some species of palm that have only recently been identified. The **Ravilevu Nature Preserve** on the east coast and the **Taveuni Forest Preserve** in the middle of the island are designed to protect these rare creatures.

Taveuni's most famous sight is **Lake Tagimaucia,** home of the rare tagimaucia flower that bears red blooms with white centers. A shallow lake whose sides are ringed with mud flats and thick vegetation, it sits among the clouds in a volcanic crater at an altitude of more than 2,700 feet.

Bouma Falls are among Fiji's finest and most accessible, and the area around them is now an environmental park. Past Bouma at the end of the road, a coastal hiking track begins at **Lavena** village and runs through the Ravilevu Nature Reserve.

Fiji's last governor-general and first republican president, the late Ratu Sir Penaia Ganilau, called Taveuni's **Somosomo** village his home. A big new meetinghouse was built in this "chiefly village" for the 1986 gathering of Fiji's Great Council of Chiefs.

The main village of **Waiyevo** sits halfway down the west coast. Half a mile south, a brass plaque marks the **180th Meridian** of longitude. This would have been the international date line were it not for its slicing of the Aleutians and Fiji in two and for Tonga's wish to be on the same day as Australia. The village of **Waikiki** sports both a "Meridian Cinema" and a lovely 19th-century Catholic mission built to reward a French missionary for helping the locals defeat a band of invading Tongans.

In stark contrast to the rest of unspoiled Taveuni, the paved roads, uninhabited condominiums, and often shaggy golf course of **Soqulu Plantation** south of Waikiki stand as a reminder that not all real estate developments work. A few expatriots have homes here, but the project never really got off the ground in the 1980s.

Off Taveuni's northeastern end are the small, rugged islands of **Qamea, Matagi,** and **Laucala,** homes of three very fine offshore resorts. Forty miles to the southeast in the Lau Group, **Kaibu Island** has one of Fiji's most expensive resorts. From there you can see **Naitoba,** once owned by Raymond Burr and now headquarters of an exotic American cult.

GETTING THERE

Both **Sunflower Airlines** and **Air Fiji** fly to Taveuni from Nadi, and Air Fiji has direct service from Nausori Airport near Suva. Taveuni's airport is at its northern tip. The hotels send buses or hire taxis to pick up their guests.

Impressions

They passed the kava cups around and drank deep of the milky, slightly stupefying grog. They chatted quietly under the starlight. They laughed, one would propose a song, and then they would break into chorus after chorus, in perfect harmony, of some of the great Fijian folk songs, songs that told of sagas of long ago and far away, and always of war and peace, of love, and of triumph over disaster.

—Simon Winchester, 1990

The ferries land—and most commerce takes place—at Waiyevo. The Patterson Brothers Shipping Company's *Yabula* ferry (☎ 850161 in Savusavu) runs across the Somosomo Strait between Waiyevo and Buca Bay on Vanua Levu. A bus connects Savusavu to the ferry wharf at Buca Bay.

For more information, see "Getting Around" in the "Introducing Fiji" chapter.

GETTING AROUND

Taxis are reasonably plentiful, but they don't regularly ply the roads. The only taxi stand is outside Lesuma Supermarket in Waiyevo. Your hotel staff can hail one within a few minutes, or you can phone 880442 or 880424. Negotiate for a round-trip price if you're going out into the villages and having the driver wait for you. None of the taxis have meters, but the fare from the airport to Navakoca (Qamea) Landing should be about F$12 ($8.50); to Dive Taveuni, F$1.50 ($1); to Waiyevo, F$12 ($8.50); and to Bouma, F$15 ($10.50). Taxis will take you anywhere and back for about F$12 ($8.50) an hour.

Local **buses** fan out from Waiyevu to the outlying villages about three times a day from Monday to Saturday. For example, one of them leaves Waiyevu for Bouma at 8:30am, 12:15pm, and 4:30pm. The one-way fare to Bouma is no more than F$2 ($1.50). Contact Pacific Transport (☎ 880278) opposite Kaba's Supermarket in Nagara, the predominately Indian village next to Somosomo.

Kaba's Rentals (☎ 880233), in Kaba's Supermarket, Nagara, rents jeeps and sedans, but Taveuni's roads are rough, winding, narrow, and at places are carved into sheer cliffs above the sea. Also, many local drivers—including bus drivers—roar along at top speed. There can be very little room to get off the road to avoid them. If you want to risk your life, rent a car. I hire a taxi and driver.

FAST FACTS: TAVEUNI

The following facts apply to Taveuni. If you don't see an item here, see "Fast Facts: Fiji" in the "Introducing Fiji" chapter.

Currency Exchange Westpac Bank has an office at Nagara. National Bank of Fiji is at Waiyevo. The hotels will cash traveler's checks.

Doctor See "Hospital" below.

Emergencies Phone 000.

Hospitals The government hospital (☎ 880222) is in the government compound in the hills above Waiyevo, but it has only nurses on its staff. To get there, go uphill on the road opposite the Garden Island Resort, then take the right fork.

Police The police station (☎ 880222) is in the government compound.

Post Office It's in the government compound (see "Hospital," above).

Safety Taveuni is relatively safe, but exercise caution if out late at night.

Telegrams/Telex See "Post Office," above. There's a Phonecard public phone at Lesuma Supermarket in Waiyevo.

WHERE TO STAY

In addition to the resorts, hostel, and campgrounds mentioned below, visitors can rent modern cottages complete with kitchens from three Americans who live near the airport on the northwest shore. Audrey Brown of **Audrey's By the Sea** (☎ 880039) has a bungalow next to her own home on 14 acres of tropical gardens. Ronna Goldstein of the **Coconut Grove Cafe** (☎ 880328) has a bure set above a beach next to her restaurant, which is named for her hometown in Florida. And Scott Suit of **Little Dolphin Sports Rentals** (☎ 880130) has a more basic "tree house" next to his equipment rental and pizza business. These units all have sea views. Dorothy and Ronna charge F$65 ($45.50) a night for their units. Scott charges F$45 ($31.50) from January to April, and F$55 ($38.50) from May to December. The mailing address of all three is Postal Agency Matei, Taveuni.

Dianne and Warwick Bain, who often are away on their charter yacht *Seax of Legra,* have a two-bedroom unit below their own home known as **Ki Kelekele Apartment,** P.O. Box 89, Waiyevo, Taveuni (☎ 880141). The Bains live near Prince Charles Beach south of the airport. They charge U.S. $75 a night and do not allow smoking in the apartment.

None of these owners accepts credit cards.

⑤ Garden Island Resort

P.O. Box 1, Waiyevo, Taveuni (Waiyevo village, 7 miles south of airport). ☎ **880286.** Fax 880288. 28 rms (all with bath), 8 dorm beds. TEL. F$77 ($54) room, F$18 dorm bed. AE, DC, MC, V.

Built as a Travelodge motel in the 1960s, this hotel has been considerably spiffed up in recent years by owner Daniella Prym Waga, an American who married a Fijian. Most of the clientele are divers looking for less expensive accommodation than elsewhere on Taveuni and its nearby resorts (this is the closest to the White Wall and Rainbow Reef). The motel-style rooms have the original furniture made brighter with paint. Ten rooms are air conditioned; the others have ceiling fans. Some have telephones. Two rooms are used as dorms with four beds each. Opening to a strait-side swimming pool (there's no beach here), the dining room serves plain meals at reasonable prices. As noted above, Rainbow Reef Divers operates from here.

Kaba's Motel and Guest House

P.O. Box 4, Waiyevo, Taveuni (Nagara village, north of Waiyevo). ☎ **880233.** Fax 880202. 5 rms (none with bath), 6 motel units (all with bath). TV TEL. F$25 ($14) double guesthouse; F$38 ($26.50) double motel unit. AE, MC, V.

The motel at this establishment in the predominantly Indian village of Nagara, next to Somosomo, is surprisingly modern, comfortable, and very clean. The units are airy and have kitchens, tiled floors, ceiling fans, radios, and even video movies at night. Rooms in the hostel-like guesthouse next door also are quite clean if basic. The little complex is owned by the Kaba family, who run Kaba's Supermarket nearby, the island's largest trading store. There is no dining room.

Maravu Plantation Resort

Post Office, Matei, Taveuni (¹/₂ mile south of airport). ☎ **880555.** Fax 880600. 10 bungalows (all with bath). F$200 ($140). AE, DC, MC, V.

Anyone expecting to stay on a beach will be disappointed here, for this unusual retreat really is set among the palms of a working copra plantation (with some cocoa, coffee, and vanilla thrown in for diversification). The bures—three of which have outdoor showers—are laid out among grounds carefully planted with bananas, papayas, and a plethora of ginger plants and wild orchids brought down from the mountains. The dining room and bar are under a high thatch roof of the central building, which looks out to a lawn with swimming pool surrounded by an expansive deck. The guest bungalows have thatch-covered tin roofs and reed or mat accents to lend a tropical ambience. Two have outdoor showers. Non-guests should call ahead for dinner reservations. I should point out that Ormond Ayre, the delightful founder of this resort, died a few years ago. His partners were trying to sell when I was there recently.

CAMPING

Campers who like to sleep by the sea can find a beautiful (if not insect-free) site at **Beverly Campground** (☎ 880381), on the beach about a mile south of the airport. Large trees completely shade the sites and hang over portions of the lagoon-lapped shore. The ground has rustic bures (they are little more than thatch tents with double beds), flushing toilets, and a rudimentary beachside kitchen. Per person rates are F$10 ($7) in the bures or for a site with rental tent, F$6 ($4) for a tent site if you bring the tent. The campground rents kayaks. **Lisi's Camping** (880194) nearby has two bures made of leaves and tent sites in the large lawn surrounding Lisi's home, in which campers can share the toilets, cold-water showers, and kitchen. The property is across the road from a beach. Rates there are F$20 ($14) for the bures, F$5 ($3.50) per person for camping. Bring your own tent. Meals are available.

WHERE TO DINE

Except at the resorts, Taveuni has little to offer in the way of restaurants. One exception is the **Coconut Grove Cafe** (☎ 880328), where American Ronna Goldstein offers a variety of local seafood dishes and Thai and Fijian curries. Dining is on Ronna's front porch, which has a great view of the little islands off Taveuni, making it a fine place to wait for a flight. Main courses range from F$11 to F$14 ($8 to $10). Open daily from 8am to 3pm and 6 to 9pm. Ronna does not accept credit cards.

Down the road, **Audrey's Sweet Somethings** (☎ 880039) really isn't a restaurant but American Audrey Brown's front porch. Audrey is known as Taveuni's best baker, and she offers her pastries, cakes, and Fiji coffees for F$5 ($3.50) per serving. Open Wednesday to Monday from 10am to 6pm and Tuesday from 4 to 6pm. Audrey takes no credit cards.

A little farther down the road from the airport, Scott Suit's **Little Dolphin** (☎ 880130) has pizzas for about F$14 ($10), but call before 3pm to order a pie for pick-up between 4:30 and 6:30pm. Again, no credit cards.

HIKING, SAILING & OTHER OUTDOOR ACTIVITIES

The hotels and resorts can arrange sightseeing tours to all of the sights mentioned in the introduction to this section, but tourism here is devoted to outdoor activities.

HIKING One attraction on everyone's list are the ✪ **Bouma Falls,** in the Bouma Environmental Tourism Project on Taveuni's northeastern end, 11 miles from the airport, 23 miles from Waiyevo. The government of New Zealand provided funds for the village of Bouma to build trails to the three levels of the falls. It's a flat, 15-minute walk along a road bed from the park entrance to the lower falls, which plunge some 600 feet into a broad pool. From there, a trail climbs sharply to a lookout with a fine view of Qamea and as far offshore as the Kaibu and Naitoba islands east of Taveuni. The trail then enters a rain forest to a second falls, which are not as impressive as the lower cascade. Hikers must ford slippery rocks across a swift-flowing creek while holding onto a rope (a sign says "Best Wait for Flood"—it means don't cross during a flood). This 30-minute muddy climb can be made in shower sandals, but be careful of your footing. A more difficult track ascends to yet a third falls, but I've never followed it, and people who did have told me it wasn't worth the effort. The park is open Monday to

Saturday from 8am to 5pm. Admission is F$5 ($3.50) per person. See "Getting Around," above, for information about how to get there.

At the end of the road past Bouma, the village of Lavena is on one of Taveuni's best beaches. From there, the **Lavena Coastal Walk** runs for 5km (3 miles) along the coast, then climbs to **Wainibau Falls.** The last 20 minutes or so of this track are spent walking up a creek bed, which can be flooded during heavy rains. The creek water is safe to drink, but you might want to bring your own supplies. Admission to the village and walking track is F$5 ($3.50) per person.

Another track leads to **Lake Tagimaucia,** home of the famous flower that blooms from the end of September to the end of December. This crater lake is surrounded by mud flats and filled with floating vegetation. The hike to the lake takes about eight hours round-trip up and down an often muddy, slippery path. Only hikers who are in shape should make the full-day trek to see the lake and back, and then only with a guide. An alternative is to take a four-wheel-drive vehicle up Des Voeux Peak for a look down at the lake. Since the Taveuni mountains get more rainfall than any other part of Fiji, the drive is best done early in the morning. The Garden Island Resort (see "Where to Stay," above) will make arrangements for a guide or vehicle.

SAILING Warwick and Dianne Bain (☎ 880141) base their 45-foot steel-hull ketch *Seax of Legra* in Taveuni and take charter parties through the colorful waters around the island and nearby Vanua Levu. For a full week's worth of sailing, count on U.S. $4,500 for two persons and U.S. $5,000 for four, including meals. They will rendezvous at the resorts for scuba diving. For more information, write them at P.O. Box 89, Waiyevo, Taveuni. They have no phone on board. They do not allow smoking on the yacht. By the way, Warwick's greying blond beard makes him look every inch the proper English gentleman he is.

✪ SCUBA DIVING The swift currents of the Somosomo Strait feed the soft corals on the Rainbow Reef and the White Wall between Taveuni and Vanua Levu, making them two of the world's most colorful and famous scuba-diving sites. The Rainbow Reef is only four miles off Waiyevo, so the Garden Island Resort is the closest dive base, with Dive Taveuni second closest. In addition to the operators mentioned here, Matagi, Qamea, and Fiji Forbes resorts off Taveuni (see below) specialize in diving equally great locations off Taveuni's eastern end.

Because of the strong currents, dives on Taveuni's most famous sites must be timed according to the tides. Accordingly, you can't count on making the dives you want if the tides are wrong when you're here. A very good friend of mine spent 10 days in the area and never did get to the Rainbow Reef.

One very good way to be out there at the right tide is on the live-aboard dive ship *Matagi Princess II,* which operates out of Matagi Island Resort off Taveuni to all the popular sites plus many others out of reach of small boats, such as the Rennell Reefs about 50 miles east of Taveuni. This 85-foot luxury vessel can accommodate 12 divers in six cabins, each with its own air-conditioning unit. The main lounge has a bar, sound system, and video players, and there's a darkroom on board. Rates are U.S. $265 a night per person for divers, including meals and diving. For more information, contact Matagi Island Resort, P.O. Box 83, Waiyevo, Taveuni (☎ 880260 or 800/362-8244; fax 880274).

New Zealanders Ric and Do Cammick can accommodate up to 10 experienced divers at their **Dive Taveuni,** Postal Agency Matei, Taveuni (☎ 880441, fax 880466). Their six bures surround their own home, which commands a magnificent view of the strait from a bluff one mile south of the airport and directly across the road from Maravu Plantation Resort (see "Where to Stay," above). They charge U.S. $145 per person a day for a bed in one of the bungalows and three meals. Ric runs two dives a day to the Rainbow Reef, White Wall, and other spots around Taveuni at a cost of U.S. $85 a day. Bring your own regulators, wetsuits, masks, fins, and snorkels. He supplies the weight belts, backpacks, and tanks.

Dave Dickenson's **Rainbow Reef Divers,** based at the Garden Island Resort (☎ 880286), is the closest operator to the Rainbow Reef and Great White Wall, both a 20-minute boat ride across the Somosomo Strait from Waiyevo. Prices start at F$100 ($70) for a two-dive excursion. PADI learn-to-dive courses cost F$440 ($308).

SWIMMING & SNORKELING   Since Taveuni is a relatively new island in geological terms, it does not have a great number of good swimming beaches. One of the best is at Lavena village at the far end of the north shore road (see "Hiking," above). A more convenient place to swim and snorkel is **Prince Charles Beach,** about a mile south of the airport. **Little Dolphin Sports Rentals** (☎ 880130), east of the airport on the north shore, has a wide range of sporting equipment for rent, including snorkeling gear, kayak-style paddle boats, outrigger canoes, boogie boards, surfboards, fishing rods, and mountain bikes. This company is run by Marylander Scott Suit, who has lived in Fiji off and on for several years. Scott's paddle boats can be taken out to three little islands off the airport end of the island. The Garden Island Resort (see "Where to Stay," above) can arrange trips out to **Korolevu,** a rocky island in the Somosomo Strait off Waiyevo.

4 Resorts off Taveuni

The northern end of Taveuni gives way to a chain of small, rugged islands that are as beautiful as any in Fiji. Their steep, jungle-clad hills drop to rocky shorelines in most places, but here and there little shelves of land and narrow valleys are bordered by beautiful beaches. The sheltered waters between the islands cover colorful reefs, making the area a hotbed of scuba diving and snorkeling. Except for a few Fijian villages and the three resorts that follow, these little gems are undeveloped and unspoiled.

✪ Fiji Forbes' Laucala Island

P.O. Box 9952, Nadi Airport (Laucala Island, 25 minutes by boat from Taveuni). ☎ **880077** or 719/379-3263. Fax 880099 or 719/379-3266 in U.S. 7 bungalows. A/C (bedrooms only) MINIBAR TEL. U.S. $2,100 per person per week. Rates include room, food, bar, transfers, all activities except scuba-diving instruction and equipment rental. No credit cards on island; must be prepaid. Minimum four-night stay required.

The late publisher Malcolm S. Forbes, Sr., bought 3,000-acre Laucala Island in 1974 and grew to love it so much that his ashes are buried there. Guests can visit the crypt, use the swimming pool outside his hilltop home, and enjoy the stunning, 360-degree view of Laucala and surrounding islands and reefs. Laucala is a plantation worked by Fijians who live in a modern village Forbes built for them. In fact, the ambiance here is more like being a plantation houseguest than a customer at a resort. The 1920s clapboard planter's home serves as a gathering place for guests, who live in comfortable one- or two-bedroom bungalows scattered in a coconut grove beside a beach. There are no planned activities; guests are on their own to use a wide range of playthings, such as fishing boats and canoes. They can go scuba diving and on hiking and birdwatching expeditions.

Dining/Entertainment: Staff members prepare breakfasts in the bungalows' own kitchens. Lunches are served picnic-style at various points (such as a ridgetop retreat overlooking the islands or a unique treehouse perched above its own private beach). Dinners are taken in the planter's home.

Services: Laundry, baby-sitting, turndown.

Facilities: Swimming pool, tennis court, gift shop, wide range of water sports.

✪ Kaimbu Island Resort

Postal Agency Kaibu, Kaibu Island (40 miles southeast of Taveuni). ☎ **880333** or 800/ 473-0332. Fax 880334, or 714/730-0827. 3 units. MINIBAR. U.S. $995 per couple a day; U.S. $2,500 a day for whole island (including bungalow, food, bar, all activities, round-trip flights from Suva or Taveuni). No credit cards on island (must be prepaid).

American Jay Johnson made a mint by inventing the chopper gun, which revolutionized the fiberglass industry. He and wife Margie bought 800-acre Kaibu Island in 1969 as a vacation retreat. Rather than be bored after moving here full time in the 1980s, they built three deluxe, 1,000-square-foot bungalows and a cliff-top central building to entertain paying guests. A 50-minute charter flight from Suva, the remote location has attracted the likes of actors Goldie Hawn and Kurt Russell, who find themselves treated like houseguests on a private island. Jay and Margie now spend most of their time in Virginia's horse country, leaving the resort to their radio-voiced son Scott and his charming wife Sally, the New Zealander daughter of Dive Taveuni's Ric Cammick.

Since a teenager, Scott has explored the uplifted coral island's mysterious caves and played in the gorgeous lagoon formed by a 14-mile-around barrier reef enclosing Kaibu and its larger neighbor, hat-shaped Yacata Island. The resort faces Yacata, which has one of the finest collections of gorgeous, deserted beaches anywhere. Scott and his Fijian helpers, most from Yacata's only village, pick up guests from their own beach and take them waterskiing, scuba diving, and sailing, or deposit them on their own secluded islands for romantic champagne picnics. On Kaibu itself, guests can take "gentle jungle treks" to the caves, one of which contains the bones of ancient warriors. Another is one of three known locations of Fiji's red prawns.

The three guest bungalows are virtually identical hexagonal structures with tall peaked roofs made of timber. Most of the walls are sliding glass doors, and plant dividers mounted behind long built-in sofas separate the living areas from king-size beds and large baths with glass showers opening to outside patios. The honeymoon bure has a large deck overlooking the lagoon and Yacata; a hammock outside is completely surrounded by tropical foliage, and a path leads down to its own beach.

Kaibu is pronounced "Kaimbu," which explains the phonetic spelling of the resort's name. Only adult couples are allowed as guests unless they rent the entire resort. A six-night minimum stay is required.

Dining/Entertainment: Guests can choose when and where to dine, but most meals are served in the central restaurant. The cuisine features fresh seafood except for one dinner a week, when the chef prepares filet mignon of grass-fed Taveuni beef. The resort grows many of its vegetables and fruits. A Fijian string band plays every evening, and the staff stages a meke once a week.

Services: Laundry; turndown.

Facilities: Sailing, waterskiing, Windsurfers, sport fishing, golf driving range on the airstrip. Kaimbu has 110-volt electric current.

✪ Matagi Island Resort

P.O. Box 83, Waiyevo, Taveuni (Matagi Island, 20 minutes by boat from Taveuni). ☎ **880260** or 800/362-8244. Fax 880274. 11 bungalows. MINIBAR. U.S. $120–U.S. $200. U.S. $40 round-trip transfers from Taveuni. U.S. $55 per person a day for meals. AE, DC, MC, V.

It's unfortunate that geography places this resort next to last in my coverage of Fiji, for Matagi is one of the best values in Fiji—which is one reason it's also one of the most popular (book early, for it's usually full). Another reason is owners Noel and Flo Douglas. Of English-Fijian descent, Flo's family owns all of hilly, 260-acre Matagi, a horseshoe-shaped remnant of a volcanic cone, where in 1987 they built their resort in a beachside coconut grove on the western shore (gorgeous sunset views of Qamea and Taveuni). At first they catered to low-budget Australian divers, but as their business grew, their clientele shifted to a mix of diving and non-diving Americans, plus a few Australians and Europeans. For divers who bring their children, the Douglases send the grown-ups out in the boats for two morning dives, while the staff keeps the kids busy building sand castles on the shady beach. This arrangement makes Matagi one of the South Pacific's top family resorts. But by the same token, honeymooners can escape to their own romantic bure 20 feet up in a shady Pacific almond tree, or be taken to a half-moon beach in aptly named Horseshoe Bay for a secluded picnic.

Except for the tree-house honeymoon bure, Matagi's bungalows are round, in the Polynesian-influenced style of eastern Fiji. Umbrellalike spokes radiating from hand-hewn central poles support reed-lined conical roofs. Reed dividers separate sitting areas with single bed-settees from sleeping areas to the rear of the units. Although somewhat small, the tiled shower-only baths are adequate. All of the units are furnished in island styles and have round, thatch-roof front porches. One bure is equipped for disabled guests.

Dining/Entertainment: Guests dine in a relatively small but comfortable central building with bar and lounge area. The menus are limited, but the staff will cater to all tastes on request. Staff members entertain at night.

Services: Laundry, baby-sitting, turndown.

Facilities: World-famous scuba diving (for which guests pay extra); wide range of water sports equipment.

✪ Qamea Beach Club

P.O. Matei, Taveuni (Qamea Island, 15 minutes by boat from Taveuni). ☎ **880220** or 800/392-8213. Fax 880092. 11 bungalows. MINIBAR. F$315 ($221). F$78 ($55) per person per day for meals. F$60 ($42) per person round-trip transfers from Taveuni. AE, DC, MC, V.

This is another property I regret coming to last, for American Jo Kloss has some of the most stunning bures and main building of any resort in Fiji, and the value-for-dollar here is excellent. In the proverbial coconut grove, this entire property shows remarkable attention to American-style comfort and Fijian detail. Qamea's centerpiece is a soaring, 52-foot-high priest's bure supported by two huge tree trunks. Rope made of coconut fiber and some well-disguised nuts and bolts hold the poles and sweeping thatch roof together. Orange light from kerosene lanterns hung high under the roof lends incredibly romantic charm at twilight, when guests wash their bare feet in giant clam shells and then sit on the surrounding veranda to sip cocktails and recap their days of scuba diving, snorkeling, visiting Fijian villages, trekking to the Bouma Falls on Taveuni, or doing absolutely nothing except sleeping in hammocks.

Guests relive the old South Seas days and nights in my favorite of all Fijian bures. If I were to build a set for a South Seas movie, it would feature these bungalows covered by a foot-thick layer Fijian thatch. Spacious and rectangular, they have old-fashioned screen doors leading out to a porch complete with hammocks strung between two posts. Reed-lined, each bure is large enough to swallow the king-size bed, two sitting chairs, coffee table, and several other pieces of island-style furniture exquisitely handcrafted by the staff.

While Matagi gets its share of children, nearby Qamea is aimed at couples, accepting no children under 13 years old.

Dining/Entertainment: Gourmet-quality meals are served in the big central bure, as is silver-service afternoon tea. The staff entertains several nights a week, including a Fijian meke dance show. Three tables are set aside for honeymooners to dine in relative privacy.

Services: Laundry, turndown.

Facilities: Swimming pool; snorkeling gear, Hobie Cats, canoes for free; guests pay extra for scuba dives and lessons.

Western Samoa   13

The scenic 19-mile drive from Faleolo Airport into the historic capital of Apia provides a fitting introduction to Western Samoa, a cultural storehouse where the old Polynesian lifestyle known as *fa'a Samoa*—The Samoan Way—remains very much alive and well. On one side of the road lies the lagoon; on the other, coconut plantations climb gentle slopes to the volcanic ridge along the middle of Upolu, the main island. Along the shore sit hundreds of Samoan *fales* (houses), their big turtle-shaped roofs resting on poles, their sides open to the breeze and to the view of passersby. Their grass carefully trimmed and their borders marked with boulders painted white, expansive village lawns make the entire route seem like an unending park. Samoans wrapped in *lavalavas* shower under outdoor faucets and sit together in their fales. Only the dim glow of television screens coming from beneath tin roofs rather than thatch remind us that a century has passed since Robert Louis Stevenson lived, wrote, and died in Western Samoa.

Even the town of Apia harkens back to those bygone South Seas days. White clapboard stores and government buildings sleep along Beach Street, just as they did when Stevenson stepped ashore here in 1889. Compared with the hustle and bustle of Papeete in French Polynesia, or with the congestion and tuna canneries of Pago Pago in nearby American Samoa, life in Apia is slow and easy.

If you go with an eye to exploring the culture as well as visiting some of the South Pacific's most beautiful and undeveloped beaches, Western Samoa will enchant you just as it did Robert Louis Stevenson, W. Somerset Maugham, and Margaret Mead, who found plenty here to write home about.

Advice: Although American ways have made a serious impact in neighboring American Samoa (see the next chapter), the people there share fa'a Samoa with their relatives in Western Samoa. Much of the background information in this chapter, therefore, applies equally to both countries. American Samoa suffers a serious lack of accommodation, while Western Samoa is blessed with comfortable and charming hotels and a first-class beach resort. Even if you plan to visit American Samoa, I recommend you make Apia your base of operations and treat American Samoa as a brief excursion—even a day trip— from Western Samoa.

What's Special About Western Samoa

Beaches
- Return to Paradise Beach, so lovely it was used for Gary Cooper's 1951 movie *Return to Paradise.*
- Vavau, an incredible site where you actually can snorkel in the shade.

Literary Shrines
- Now a museum to his memory, Robert Louis Stevenson's home Valima looks exactly as it did when he died there in 1903.
- Stevenson's grave, overlooking Apia, with the author's famous requiem carved in stone.

Great Towns/Villages
- Century-old clapboard buildings give Apia the old South Seas look.

Cultures
- Fa'a Samoa (The Samoan Way): Polynesia's oldest culture continues its ancient ways into the present and future.

Natural Spectacles
- Now dormant, volcanoes have left lava fields with tunnels on Savai'i, the country's largest island.

1 Western Samoa Today

Western Samoa is located in the central South Pacific some 1,200 miles west of Tahiti and 2,600 miles southwest of Hawaii. Its nine islands are part of a 300-mile-long archipelago that Western Samoa shares with American Samoa.

A series of volcanoes on a line running roughly east to west formed the main island of **Upolu,** which is about 39 miles long and 13 miles wide. Although Upolu is considerably smaller than **Savai'i,** 13 miles to the west, some 75% of Western Samoa's population lives there. On the other hand, Savai'i in many ways is the most "old Polynesia" of any island covered in this book; there are no towns there, and the villagers live very much by fa'a Samoa.

Apolima and **Manono,** the tops of two small volcanos, sit in the Apolima Strait between the two main islands. Locals like to claim that James A. Michener was inspired by Apolima and Manono to create the mysteriously romantic island of "Bali Hai" in his *Tales of the South Pacific* (Michener once said in a television interview that he got the idea from a cloud-draped island off Espiritu Santo in Vanuatu, where he spent much of World War II).

Geography   The nine islands of Western Samoa have a land area of 1,090 square miles, 703 of which are on Savai'i, the largest Polynesian island outside Hawaii and New Zealand. Upolu, the most heavily populated, is about the size of Tahiti. With the exceptions of Savai'i and Upolu, the other islands are the small tops of volcanoes that seem to have given up the ghost and quit growing early in life.

With few exceptions, all of the Samoa Islands are high and volcanic, lush, and well watered. Geologically they are younger than the islands in French Polynesia. Volcanoes on Savai'i erupted as recently as 1911. Consequently, the islands are fringed with coral reefs that have had time to enclose few deep lagoons; the surf pounds directly on black volcanic rocks in many places. In others there are small bays with some of the most picturesque beaches in the South Pacific.

Government   An independent nation since 1962, Western Samoa is ruled by a Parliament made up of 47 members, of whom 45 are *matais,* or chiefs. Only matais could vote for candidates for these seats until 1991, when universal suffrage was enacted. The other two members are elected by non-Samoans living in the country. There are two political parties: the Human Rights Protection party and the Christian Democratic party.

The titular head of state is Malietoa Tanumafili II, one of Western Samoa's four paramount chiefs and a descendant of the Malietoa who sided with the Germans in 1889–89 during the lead-up to Western Samoa's becoming a German colony in 1890 (see "A Look at the Past," below). Malietoa Tanumafili II will hold the job for life, which in effect makes Western Samoa a constitutional monarchy. Under the constitution, Parliament will choose his successor from among Western Samoa's four paramount chiefs. That person will serve not for life but for a term of five years.

Economy   Western Samoa is the poorest country covered in this book. Once a large exporter of fresh bananas to New Zealand, it lost that market to Ecuador and other Latin American countries in the 1980s. A freak series of hurricanes in 1990 and 1991 devastated all crops in the islands, and that disaster was followed by a taro blight, which wiped out the country's other major export earner. The largest export now is coconut oil. There is some light manufacturing, including cigarettes and beer (try a German-style Vailima brew while you're there), but the industrial sector is in its infancy. Furthermore, the country's exclusive fishing zone is one of the smallest in the Pacific. Only foreign aid and remittances sent home by Samoans living in American Samoa or overseas keep the country out of bankruptcy.

To correct its huge trade imbalance, the Western Samoan government imposes heavy duties on most imports. To avoid the "price shocks" if their prices were quoted in local currency, Western Samoa's hotels, car-rental firms, and some tour operators quote their rates in U.S. dollars. Although expensive by local standards, most prices in Western Samoa are among the least expensive in the South Pacific for travelers using U.S. dollars.

A majority of the work force is employed by the government. Even in those jobs, wages are so low that several thousand Western Samoans regularly live and work in the much more prosperous American Samoa.

2 A Look at the Past

Archaeologists believe that Polynesians settled in the Samoan Islands about 3,000 years ago, after migrating from Southeast Asia through Melanesia and Fiji. Some 1,000 years later, voyagers went on to colonize the Marquesas, Society, and other island groups farther east in the great triangle known today as Polynesia. Thus the Samoas are known as the "Cradle of Polynesia."

The universe known by the early Samoans included Tonga and Fiji, to which they regularly journeyed, often waging war. Tongan invaders

Dateline

- **3,000 B.C.** Polynesians arrive from the west, settle the Samoa Islands.
- **2,000 B.C.** Samoans venture south and west, colonize Tonga, Marquesas, Society, and other island groups.

continues

- A.D. 950 Tongans invade, conquer Samoans, and rule until 1250.
- 1722 Dutch explorer Jacob Roggeveen is first European to sight the Samoan Islands.
- 1768 After finding Tahiti, de Bougainville sails through the Samoas but does not land; names them the Navigator Islands.
- 1787 Thirty-nine Samoans and 12 members of French exploring team under Jean La Pérouse killed during skirmish at Massacre Bay on Tutuila in American Samoa.
- 1830 Rev. John Williams lands first missionaries at Leone on Tutuila, American Samoa. European-style settlements soon established at Apia and Pago Pago.
- 1850s Germans start plantations on Upolu.
- 1872 American Navy negotiates treaty with Tutuila chiefs for American coaling station at Pago Pago.
- 1887 German residents on Upolu stage a coup, set off an argument between U.S., Britain, and Germany.
- 1888 Ousted chief Mataafa leads bloody rebellion at Apia but loses to German-backed chief Malietoa.
- 1889 Warships arrive at Apia to back claims of Western powers; hurricane sinks four, drives two aground, kills 146 sailors. Treaty of Berlin is negotiated and signed. Robert Louis Stevenson settles in Apia.

continues

ruled the Samoas for some 300 years between A.D. 950 and A.D. 1250.

The first European to see the Samoas was Dutchman Jacob Roggeveen, who in 1722 sighted the Manu'a Islands in what is now American Samoa. After visiting Tahiti in 1768, the Frenchman Antoine de Bougainville sailed through the Samoas and named them the Navigator Islands because of the natives he saw in canoes chasing tuna far offshore. The first Europeans to land in Samoa were part of a French expedition under Jean La Pérouse in 1787. They came ashore on the north coast of Tutuila in American Samoa and were promptly attacked by Samoan warriors. Twelve members of the landing party and 39 Samoans were killed during the skirmish.

To the Samoans, the great ships with their white sails seemed to have come through the slit that separated the sky from the sea, and they named the strange people sailing them *papalagi,* "sky busters." Shortened to *palagi,* the name now means any Westerner with white skin.

The Rev. John Williams, who roamed the South Pacific in *The Messenger of Peace,* discovering islands and preaching the Gospel, landed the first missionaries in Samoa in 1830. Shortly afterward came traders—including John Williams, Jr., the missionary's son. European-style settlements soon grew up at Apia on Upolu and on the shores of Pago Pago Harbor on Tutuila. By the late 1850s German businessmen had established large copra plantations on Upolu. When steamships started plying the route between San Francisco and Sydney in the 1870s, American businessmen cast an eye on Pago Pago. The U.S. Navy negotiated a treaty with the chiefs of Tutuila in 1872 to permit the U.S. to use Pago Pago as a coaling station. The U.S. Congress never ratified this document, but it served to keep the Germans from penetrating into Eastern Samoa, as present-day American Samoa was then known.

The Germans Take Over　Meanwhile, German, British, and Americans jockeyed for position among the rival Samoan chiefs on Upolu, with the Germans gaining the upper hand when they staged a coup in 1887, backed up (unofficially) by German naval gunboats. They governed through Malietoa, one of the island's four paramount chiefs, who had thrown in his lot with them. One of his rivals, Mataafa, lost a bloody rebellion in

1888, during which heads were taken in Samoan style. Mataafa subsequently was exiled to the German Marshall Islands.

Continuing unrest turned into a major international incident—fiasco is a better word—when the U.S., Britain, and Germany all sent warships to Apia. Seven vessels arrived, anchored in the small and relatively unprotected harbor, and proceeded to stare down each other's gun barrels. It was March 16, 1889, near the end of the hurricane season. When one of the monster storms blew up unexpectedly, only the captain of the British warship *Calliope* got his ship under way. It was the sole vessel to escape. In all, four ships were sunk, two others were washed ashore, and 146 lives were lost despite heroic efforts by the Samoans on Upolu, who stopped their feuding long enough to pull the survivors through the roaring surf. Of the three American warships present, the *Trenton* and the *Vandalia* were sunk, and the *Nipsic* was beached. Another beached ship, the Germans' *Adler,* rested half-exposed until the reef was covered by landfill 70 years later. (A newspaper story of the time is mounted in the lounge of Aggie Grey's Hotel in Apia.)

Cooler heads prevailed after the disaster, and in December 1889 an agreement was signed in Berlin under which Germany was given Western Samoa, the U.S. was handed the seven islands to the east, and Britain was left to do what it pleased in Tonga (it created a protectorate). After many years of turmoil, the two Samoas were split apart and swept into the colonial system.

The German flag was raised in Apia on March 1, 1900, after which several stern governors sent more of Mataafa's followers and other resisters into exile. Malietoa remained as the chosen chief, and the Germans residing in Western Samoa proceeded to make fortunes from their huge, orderly copra plantations.

A Kiwi Backwater German rule came to an abrupt end with the outbreak of World War I in 1914, when New Zealand sent an expeditionary force to Apia and the German governor surrendered without a fight. The Germans in Samoa were interned for the duration of the war, and their huge land holdings were confiscated. The plantations are still owned by the Western Samoa Trust Estates Corporation (WSTEC), a government body whose name you will see all over the country.

- **1890** Treaty goes into effect giving Western Samoa to Germany, Eastern Samoa to U.S., free hand in Tonga to Britain.
- **1894** Robert Louis Stevenson dies at Vailima, his home above Apia; is buried at end of "Track of Loving Hearts."
- **1900** Germany officially establishes colony of Western Samoa, raises its flag at Apia. U.S. negotiates treaty with Tutuila chiefs to cede their island; U.S. flag raised at Pago Pago.
- **1905** Chief of Manu'a finally cedes his islands to the U.S., completing American possession of Eastern Samoa.
- **1914** New Zealand expeditionary force seizes Western Samoa from Germany at outbreak of World War I, confiscates German lands.
- **1920** League of Nations establishes New Zealand trusteeship over Western Samoa.
- **1929** New Zealand constables put down Mau rebellion, killing nine Samoans. U.S. Senate ratifies treaties of 1900 and 1905 turning Eastern Samoa over to U.S.
- **1942–45** Allied troops use both Samoas as training bases for World War II battles in central and southwestern Pacific. Aggie Grey starts her hot dog and hamburger business in Apia.
- **1949** New Zealand creates local legislative assembly in Apia, grants Western Samoa limited internal self-government.

continues

- **1951** U.S. Government transfers administration of American Samoa from Navy to Interior Department.
- **1960** Western Samoas vote for independence, draft a constitution.
- **1961** *Reader's Digest* criticizes American Samoa as "America's Shame in the South Seas." U.S. aid starts flowing to Pago Pago.
- **1962** Western Samoa becomes first South Pacific colony to gain independence.
- **1977** American Samoans choose first locally elected governor.
- **1991** Universal suffrage comes to Western Samoa after 30 years of only chiefs voting for Parliament.

New Zealand remained in charge until 1962, first as warlord, then after World War I as trustee, initially under the League of Nations and then under the United Nations. The New Zealand administrators did relatively little in the islands except keep the lid on unrest, at which they were generally successful. In 1929, however, the Mau Movement under Tupua Tamasese Lealofi III created an uprising. The movement was crushed when the New Zealand constables fired on Tamasese and a crowd of his followers gathered outside the government building in Apia, killing him and eight others.

Twenty years later, after opposition to colonialism flared up in the United Nations, a Legislative Assembly of matais was established to exercise a limited degree of internal self-government. A constitution was drafted in 1960, and the people approved it and their own independence a year later by referendum (the only time until 1991 that all Samoans could vote). On January 1, 1962, Western Samoa became the first South Pacific colony to regain its independence from the Western powers.

For most of its life as a colony and trusteeship territory, Western Samoa remained in the backwaters of the South Pacific. Only during World War II did it appear on the world stage, and then solely as a training base for thousands of Allied servicemen on their way to fight the Japanese in the islands farther west and north. Tourism increased after the big jets started landing at Pago Pago in the early 1960s, but significant numbers of visitors started arriving only after Faleolo Airport was upgraded to handle large aircraft in the 1980s.

3 The Samoan People

About 190,000 people live in Western Samoa, the vast majority of them full-blooded Samoans. They are the second-largest group of pure Polynesians in the world, behind only the Maoris of New Zealand.

Although divided politically in their home islands, the Western Samoans and American Samoans share the same culture, heritage, and, in many cases, family lineage. Despite the inroads that Western influences have made—especially in American Samoa—they are a proud people who fiercely protect their old ways.

"Catch the bird but watch for the wave" is an old Samoan proverb that expresses the basically cautious approach followed in the islands. This conservative attitude is perhaps responsible for the extraordinary degree to which Samoans have preserved fa'a Samoa while adapting it to the modern world. Even in American Samoa, where most of the old turtle-shaped thatch fales have been replaced with structures of plywood and tin, the firmament of the Samoan way lies just under the trappings of the territory's commercialized surface.

The Teller of Tales

The salvage crews were still working on the hulks of the British, American, and German warships sunk by a hurricane in 1889 when a thin, tubercular writer arrived from Scotland.

Not yet 40 years old, Robert Louis Stevenson already was famous—and wealthy—for such novels as *Treasure Island* and *Dr. Jekyll and Mr. Hyde*. He arrived in Samoa after traveling across the United States and a good part of the South Pacific in search of a climate more suitable to his ravaged lungs. With him were his wife, Fanny (an American divorcée 11 years his senior), his stepmother, and his stepson. His mother joined them later.

Stevenson intended to remain in Apia for only a few weeks while he caught up on a series of newspaper columns he was writing. He and his entourage stayed to build a mansion known as Vailima up on the slopes of Mount Vaea, overlooking Apia, where he lived lavishly and wrote more than 750,000 published words. He learned the Samoan language and translated into it "The Bottle Imp," his story about a genie. It was the first work of fiction translated into Samoan.

Stevenson loved Samoa, and the Samoans loved him. Great orators and storytellers in their own right, they called him Tusitala, the "Teller of Tales."

On December 3, 1894, almost five years to the day after he arrived in Apia, Stevenson was writing a story about a son who had escaped a death sentence handed down by his own father and had sailed away to join his lover. Leaving the couple embraced, Stevenson stopped to answer letters, play some cards, and fix dinner. While preparing mayonnaise on his back porch, he suddenly clasped his hands to his head and collapsed. He died not of tuberculosis but of a cerebral hemorrhage.

More than 200 grieving Samoans hacked a "Track of Loving Hearts" up Mount Vaea to a little knoll below the summit, where they placed him in a grave with a perpetual view overlooking Vailima, the mountains, the town, the reef, and the sea he loved. Carved on his grave is his famous requiem:

> *This be the verse you grave for me:*
> *Here he lies where he longed to be;*
> *Home is the sailor, home from the sea,*
> *And the hunter home from the hill.*

THE AIGA

The foundation of Samoan society is the extended family unit, or *aiga* (pronounced "ah-eeng-ah"); unlike the Western family, it can include thousands of relatives and in-laws. In this basically communal system, everything is owned collectively by the aiga; the individual has a right to use that property but does not personally own it. As stated in a briefing paper prepared for the government of American Samoa by the Pacific Basin Development Council, "the attitude toward property is: if you need something which you don't have, there is always someone else who has what you need." This notion is at odds with Western concepts of private ownership, and visitors may notice the difference directly when a camera or other item left unattended suddenly disappears.

At the head of each of more than 10,000 aigas is a matai ("mah-tie"), a chief who is responsible for the welfare of each member of the clan. Although the title of matai usually follows bloodlines, the family can choose another person—man or woman—if the incumbent proves incapable of handling the job. The matai settles family disputes, parcels out the family's land, and sees that everyone has enough to eat and a roof over his or her head.

Strictly speaking, all money earned by a member of an aiga is turned over to the matai, to be used in the best interest of the entire clan. Accordingly, the system has been threatened as more and more young Samoans move to the U.S. or New Zealand, earn wages in their own right, and spend them as they see fit. Nevertheless, the system is still remarkably intact in both Samoas. Even in Samoan outposts in Hawaii, California, Texas, and Auckland (which collectively have a larger Samoan population than do the islands), the people still rally around their aiga, and matais play an important role in daily life.

As is true throughout the South Pacific, landownership is a touchy subject. In Samoa land is held by the aiga, not by individuals. There are very strict laws prohibiting non-Samoans from owning land, although it is possible for them to lease property under certain circumstances.

ORGANIZATION & RITUAL

Above the aiga, Samoan life is ruled by a hierarchy of matais known in English as high talking chiefs, high chiefs, and paramount chiefs, in ascending order of importance. The high talking chiefs do just that: talk on behalf of the high chiefs, usually expressing themselves in great oratorical flourishes in a formal version of Samoan reserved for use among the chiefs. The high chiefs are senior matais at the village or district level, and the paramount chiefs can rule over entire island groups. The chiefly symbol, worn over the shoulder, is a short broom resembling a horse's tail.

The conduct and relations between chiefs are governed by strict rules of protocol. Nowhere is ritual more obvious or observed than during a *kava* (pronounced 'ava in Samoan) ceremony. This slightly narcotic brew is made by crushing the roots of the pepper plant *Piper methysticum.* In the old days the roots were chewed and spit into the bowl by the virgin daughter of a chief. That method of kava preparation has disappeared in the face of modern notions of disease control. Coconut shells are scooped into a large wooden bowl of the grey liquid (which tastes of sawdust) and passed around. Each participant holds out the cup, spills a little on the mats covering the floor, and says *"Manuia"* ("Good health") before gulping it down. It's all a show of respect to host and honored guest. Kava works on the lips like Novocain, which must do wonders for the conversation that follows.

Although some Samoans can become unruly after imbibing too much of potions containing not kava but alcohol, the showing of respect permeates their life. They are by tradition extremely polite to guests, so much so that some of them tend

Impressions

All life is to be seen on the stage of the Samoan fale. *In the evening, when television sets as well as electric lights are switched on, the scene is surreal.*

—Ron Hall, 1991

How impossible it would be for us, with our notions of so-called civilization and style, to exist in our northern city suburbs with open spaces for walls and the camouflage of the night our only privacy. Yet here it seemed the most natural thing in the world, a picture of harmony and a vivid example of what they call fa'a Samoa, the Samoan Way.
—John Dyson, 1982

to answer in the affirmative all questions posed by a stranger. The Samoans are not lying when they answer wrongly; they are merely being polite. Accordingly, visitors who really need information should avoid asking questions that call for a yes or no answer.

MISSIONARIES & MINISTERS

Like other Polynesians, the Samoans in pre-European days worshipped a hierarchy of gods under one supreme being, whom they called Le Tagaloa. When the London Missionary Society's Rev. John Williams arrived in 1830, he found the Samoans willing to convert to the Christian God. Williams and his Tahitian teachers brought a strict, puritanical Christianity. His legacy can be seen both in the large white churches that dominate every settlement in both Samoas and in the fervor with which the Samoans practice religion today.

The majority of Samoans are members of the Congregational Christian church, a Protestant denomination that grew out of the London Missionary Society's work. Western Samoa almost closes down on Sunday, and even in more Westernized American Samoa things come to a crawl on the Sabbath. Swimming is tolerated in both countries only at the hotels and, after church, at beaches frequented by overseas visitors.

Christianity has become an integral part of fa'a Samoa, and every day about 6:30pm each village observes *sa,* 10 minutes of devotional time during which everyone goes inside to pray, read Scripture, and perhaps sing hymns. A gong (usually an empty acetylene tank hung from a tree) will be struck, once to announce it's time to get ready, a second time to announce the beginning of sa, and a third time to announce that all's clear. It is permissible to drive on the main road during sa, but it's not all right to turn off into a village or to walk around.

Even if you can't understand the sermon, the sound of Samoans singing hymns in harmony makes going to church a rewarding experience.

MISS MEAD STUDIES SAMOAN SEX

Despite their ready acceptance of much of the missionaries' teaching, the Samoans no more took to heart their puritanical sexual mores than did any other group of Polynesians. In 1928 anthropologist Margaret Mead published her famous *Coming of Age in Samoa,* which was based on her research in American Samoa. She described the Samoans as a peaceable people who showed no guilt in connection with ample sex during adolescence, a view that was in keeping with practices of Polynesian societies elsewhere. Some 55 years later, New Zealand anthropologist Derek Freeman published *Margaret Mead and Samoa: The Making and Unmaking of an Anthropological Myth,* in which he took issue with Mead's conclusions and argued instead that Samoans are jealous, violent, and not above committing rape. The truth may lie somewhere in between.

The Samoans share with other Polynesians the practice of raising some boys as girls, especially in families short of household help. These young boys dress as girls, do a girl's chores around the home, and often grow up to be transvestites. They are known in Samoan as *fa'afafines*.

RULES OF CONDUCT

Visitors should be aware of several other customs of this conservative society. The briefing paper prepared by the Pacific Basin Development Council for the American Samoan Office of Tourism gives some guidelines that may be helpful.

- In a Samoan home don't talk to people while standing, and don't eat while walking around a village.
- Avoid stretching your legs straight out in front of you while sitting. If you can't fold them beneath you, then pull one of the floor mats over them.
- If you are driving through a village and spot a group of middle-aged or elderly men sitting around a fale with their legs folded, it's probably a gathering of matais to discuss business. It's polite not to drive past the meeting place. If going past on foot, don't carry a load on your shoulders or an open umbrella (even if several of Pago Pago's 200 inches of annual rainfall are pouring on you).
- If you arrive at a Samoan home during a prayer session, wait outside until the family is finished with its devotions. If you are already inside, you will be expected to share in the service. If you go to church, don't wear flowers.
- If you are invited to participate in a kava ceremony, hold the cup out in front of you, spill a few drops on the mat, say "Manuia," and take a sip. In Samoa you do not bolt down the entire cup in one gulp as you would in Fiji; instead, save a little to pour on the floor before handing back the empty cup. And remember, this is a solemn occasion—not a few rounds at the local bar.
- Whenever possible, consult Samoans about appropriate behavior and practices. They will appreciate your interest in fa'a Samoa and will take great pleasure in explaining their unique way of life.

To those guidelines, I would add: Don't wear bathing suits, short shorts, halter tops, or other skimpy clothing away from the beach or hotel swimming pool. Although shorts of respectable length are worn by some young Samoan men and women, it is considered very bad form for a Samoan to display his or her traditional tattoos, which cover many of them from knee to waist. Even though Samoan women went barebreasted before the coming of Christianity, that is definitely forbidden today. Traditional Samoan dress is a wraparound lavalava, which reaches below the knee on men and to the ankles on women.

Finally, should you be invited to stay overnight in a Samoan home, let them know at the beginning how long you will stay. Upon leaving, it's customary to give a small gift known as a *mea alofa*. This can be money—between $5 and $10 a day per person—but make sure your hosts understand it is a gift, not a payment.

Impressions

Imagine an island with the most perfect climate in the world, tropical yet almost always cooled by a breeze from the sea. No malaria or other fevers. No dangerous snakes or insects. Fish for the catching, and fruits for the plucking. And an earth and sky and sea of immortal loveliness. What more could civilization give?

—Rupert Brooke, 1914

Most Samoan villages have adopted the practice of charging small "custom fees" to visitors who want to use their beaches or swim under their waterfalls. These usually are a dollar or two and are paid by local residents from other villages as well as by tourists.

In all cases, remember that almost everything and every place in the Samoas is owned by an aiga, and it's polite to ask permission of the nearby matai before crossing the property, using the beach, or visiting the waterfall. They will appreciate your courtesy in doing so.

4 The Samoan Language

Although English is an official language in both countries and is widely spoken, Samoan shares equal billing and is used by most people for everyday conversation. It is a Polynesian language somewhat similar to Tahitian, Tongan, and Cook Islands Maori, but with some important differences.

The vowels are pronounced not as in English (*ay, ee, eye, oh,* and *you*) but in the Roman fashion: *ah, ay, ee, oh,* and *oo* (as in kanga*roo*). All vowels are sounded, even if several of them appear next to each other—although there have been some modern corruptions. The village of Nu'uuli in American Samoa, for example, is pronounced New-oo-lee. The apostrophe that appears between the vowels indicates a glottal stop—a slight pause similar to the tiny break between "Oh-oh!" in English. The consonants *f, g, l, m, n, p, s, t,* and *v* are pronounced as in English with one major exception: the letter *g* is pronounced like "ng." Therefore, *aiga* is pronounced "ah-eeng-ah." Pago Pago is pronounced "Pango Pango" as in "pong."

Here are some words that may help you win friends and influence your hosts.

English	Samoan	Pronunciation
hello	talofa	tah-*low*-fah
welcome	afio mai	ah-*fee*-oh my
good-bye	tofa	*tow*-fah
good luck	manuia	mah-*new*-yah
please	fa'amolemole	fah-ah-*moly*-moly
man	tamaloa	tah-mah-*low*-ah
woman	fafine	fah-*fini*
transvestite	fa'afafine	fah-fah-*fini*
thank you	fa'afetai	fah-*fee*-tie
kava bowl	tanoa	tah-*no*-ah
good	lelei	*lay*-lay
bad	leaga	lay-*ang*-ah
happy/feast	fiafia	fee-ah-*fee*-ah
house	fale	*fah*-lay
wraparound skirt	lavalava	lava-lava
dollar	tala	tah-lah
cent	sene	say-nay
high chief	ali'i	ah-*lee*-ee
small island	motu	*mo*-too
white person	palagi	pah-*lahng*-ee

Many words in Samoan—as in most modern Polynesian languages—have European roots. Take the word for corned beef, *pisupo* (pee-soo-poh). The first Western canned food to reach Western Samoa was pea soup. Pisupo, the Samoan version of pea soup, was adopted as the word for corned beef, which also came in cans. It was and still is much more popular than pea soup.

5 Visitor Information & Entry Requirements

VISITOR INFORMATION

The friendly staff of the **Western Samoan Visitors Bureau**, P.O. Box 2272, Apia, Western Samoa (☎ 20-878 or 20-180, fax 20-886), have free brochures and other publications available at their office in a handsome Samoan fale on the harbor side of Beach Road east of the Town Clock. They also sell a map of Western Samoa. The Bureau's hours are 8am to noon and 1 to 4:30pm Monday through Friday, 8am to 12:30pm on Saturday.

The tour desks just inside Aggie Grey's Hotel (see "Where to Stay," below) also have brochures and other information.

ENTRY REQUIREMENTS

No **visa** or entry permit is required for visitors who intend to stay 30 days or less and who have a valid passport, a return or ongoing airline ticket, and a place to stay in Western Samoa. As a practical matter, however, your passport will be stamped for the length of stay you request, up to 30 days or the date of your flight out, whichever is earlier. Those who wish to stay longer must apply, prior to arrival, to the Immigration Office, Government of Western Samoa, Apia, Western Samoa (☎ 20-291).

Vaccinations are not necessary unless arriving within six days of being in an infected area.

Customs exemptions for visitors are 200 cigarettes, either a 26-ounce or a 40-ounce bottle of liquor, and their personal effects. Firearms, ammunition, illegal drugs, and indecent publications are prohibited—so leave your *Playboy* magazine in Pago Pago. Plants, live animals, or products of that nature, including fruits, seeds, and soil, will be confiscated unless you have obtained prior permission from the Western Samoa government's Department of Agriculture and Forest.

6 Money

Western Samoa uses the *tala* (the Samoans' way of saying "dollar"), which is broken down into 100 *sene* ("cents"). Although most people will refer to them as dollars and cents when speaking to visitors, you can avoid potential confusion by making sure they mean dollars and not talas. The official abbreviation for the currency is SAT, but I have used **WS$** in this chapter. As noted in Chapter 7, Western Samoa's major hotels and most car-rental firms quote their prices in U.S. dollars. Their U.S. dollar prices are given in this chapter as **U.S. $.**

At presstime the **exchange rate** was about WS$2.40 for each U.S. $1 (that is, WS$1 equals U.S. 40¢).

Since the tala is worthless outside Western Samoa, you won't be able to buy any before arriving there. Remember, too, to change your talas back to another currency before leaving Western Samoa. There is no quick way of finding out in

What Things Cost in Western Samoa	U.S. $
Taxi from airport to Apia	12.00
Bus from airport to Apia	2.40
Room at Aggie Grey's Hotel (expensive)	85.00
Room at Le Godinet Beachfront Hotel (moderate)	55.00
Room at Samoan Outrigger Hostel (inexpensive)	26.50
Lunch for one at Gourmet Seafood Grille (moderate)	8.50
Lunch for one at The Town Clock Cafe (inexpensive)	4.50
Dinner for one at Apia Inn (expensive)	29.00
Dinner for one at Le Godinet Restaurant (moderate)	17.50
Dinner for one at Giodano's Pizzeria (inexpensive)	9.50
Beer	1.40
Coca-Cola	.60
Roll of ASA 100 Kodacolor film, 36 exposures	7.50

The Tala & U.S. Dollar

At this writing, WS$1 = approximately U.S. 40¢, the rate of exchange used to calculate the U.S. dollar prices given in this chapter. This rate may change by the time you visit, so use the following table only as a guide.

WS $	U.S. $	WS $	U.S. $
.25	.10	15.00	6.00
.50	.20	20.00	8.00
.75	.30	25.00	10.00
1.00	.40	30.00	12.00
2.00	.80	35.00	14.00
3.00	1.20	40.00	16.00
4.00	1.60	45.00	18.00
5.00	2.00	50.00	20.00
6.00	2.40	75.00	30.00
7.00	2.80	100.00	40.00
8.00	3.20	125.00	50.00
9.00	3.60	150.00	60.00
10.00	4.00	200.00	80.00

advance the exchange rate that will be in effect when you arrive. A travel agent may be able to give you an approximate figure.

How to Get Local Currency   The Bank of Western Samoa and the Pacific Commercial Bank both have main offices on Beach Road in Apia. Banking hours are Monday through Friday from 9:30am to 3pm. No bank fees are charged to exchange foreign currency or traveler's checks, but you will have a few seni deducted for stamp tax. The banks have offices at Faleolo Airport, which are open when international flights arrive and depart. You can get cash advances against your MasterCard or Visa cards at the banks. There were no ATM machines in Western Samoa during my recent visit.

Credit Cards　American Express, Visa, MasterCard, and Diner's Club credit cards are accepted by the major hotels and car-rental firms. Elsewhere, carry enough cash to cover your anticipated expenses.

7　When to Go

THE CLIMATE

Both Samoas enjoy a humid tropical climate, with lots of very intense sunshine even during the wet season (December to May). Average daily high temperatures range from 83°F in the drier and somewhat cooler months of June through September to 86°F from December to April, when midday can be hot and sticky. Evenings are usually in the comfortable 70s all year round.

EVENTS

The **Arts and Crafts Fair** during the third week in March is dedicated to reviving the ancient handcrafts. **Easter Week** sees various religious observances, including hymn singing and dramas. The **Independence Celebrations** in early June are the biggest event here, featuring dances, outrigger-canoe races, marching competitions, and horse racing. Samoans living overseas are invited to come home and perform in the **Musika Extravaganza** on the last weekend in July. The **Teuila Tourism Festival** during the first week of September displays a variety of entertainment, including canoe races, dance competitions, traditional games, and a beauty pageant. The second Sunday in October is observed as **White Sunday,** during which children go to church dressed in white, lead the services, and are honored at family feasts. **Christmas week** is celebrated with great gusto.

In addition to the manmade holidays and events, late October or early November will see hundreds if not thousands of Samoans out on the reefs with lanterns and nets to snare the wiggly *palolo,* a coral worm that comes out to mate on the seventh day after the full moon. Palolo are considered by Pacific Islanders to be the caviar of their region.

The Western Samoa Visitors Bureau can tell you the precise dates and the schedules for these events (see "Visitor Information & Entry Requirements" and "Money," above).

HOLIDAYS

Offices and schools are closed both January 1 and January 2 for New Year's; Easter Monday; ANZAC Day on April 25, as a memorial to those who died in the two World Wars; the Monday after the second Sunday in May as Mothers Day of Samoa; June 1 through June 3, for the annual Independence Celebrations; Arbor Day on the first Friday in November, to encourage the planting of trees and appreciation of conservation; Christmas Day; and Boxing Day (December 26).

8 Getting There & Getting Around

GETTING THERE

Air New Zealand has direct service between Los Angeles and Apia, with a brief stop in Los Angeles. Those flights go on to Tonga and Auckland. **Polynesian Airlines,** Western Samoa's national carrier, links Apia to Australia, New Zealand, Tonga, and the Cook Islands. **Air Pacific** has service between Apia and Fiji. **Royal Tongan Airlines** links Apia to Tonga.

A less desirable way to get to Apia is on **Hawaiian Airlines,** which flies between several West Coast cities and Honolulu, thence to Pago Pago in American Samoa. Connections can then be made on either **Polynesian Airlines** and **Samoa Air,** both of which fly small aircraft between Pago Pago and Apia.

Flights into and out of the Samoas are often packed with Samoans leaving and returning to the islands, so reserve your seat as soon as possible.

For more information, see the "Getting There" section in Chapter 3.

ARRIVING   Unless you're coming from Pago Pago, your flight will arrive at **Faleolo Airport,** on the northwest corner of Upolu, about 19 miles from Apia. **Fagali'i Airstrip** near Apia is used only for flights between Western Samoa and Pago Pago.

Both the Bank of Western Samoa and Pacific Commercial Bank have small booths at Faleolo Airport where you can change money while waiting to clear Customs.

Transportation from the airport is by taxi or by a relatively small Polynesian Airlines bus that meets all international flights (you will be astounded by how many passengers and their baggage can be crammed into one of these vehicles). The bus ride costs WS$6 ($2.40) each way. The government-regulated taxi fare into town is WS$30 ($12). Transportation from Fagali'i Airstrip is by taxi only (the fare into downtown Apia is about WS$8 ($3.20)).

The airline buses also transport passengers from the Apia hotels to the airports for departing international flights. They arrive at the hotels two hours before departure time. Be sure to reconfirm your flight (even if Air New Zealand says you don't have to) and tell your hotel what flight you are leaving on; otherwise, the bus could leave you behind. If you drive a car to the airport, you will be hit with a WS50c (20¢) parking fee at the gate.

When leaving the country, get your boarding pass and then pay WS$20 ($18) **departure tax** at a booth to the right of the check-in counters (to the check-in clerk at Fagali'i Airstrip).

There is no bank in the departure lounges of either airport, so change your leftover talas before clearing Immigration at Faleolo, or in town before leaving for Fagali'i. Remember, Western Samoan currency cannot be exchanged outside the country, even in American Samoa.

GETTING AROUND

Polynesian Airlines flies between Fagali'i Airstrip and Maota on Savai'i, and the ferry *Lady Samoa* runs between Mulifanua Wharf on Upolu's western end and

Salelologa on Savai'i southeastern corner. Privately owned boats shuttle between Mulifanua Wharf and Manono Island, and between Apolima-uta and Apolima Island. For details, see "Getting There" in the section on Savai'i at the end of this chapter.

BY RENTAL CAR   The car-rental firms will arrange to pick you up at the airport if you have reservations. Most of them quote their rates in U.S. dollars, and all accept American Express, Diner's Club, MasterCard, and Visa credit cards. Insurance policies do not cover damage to the vehicles' undercarriages, which may occur on some rocky, unpaved roads. Don't count on buying gasoline outside of Apia. Depending on your own insurance policies, you may also want to buy optional personal accident coverage, which covers you and your passengers.

Although a road-paving program has greatly improved most of the main roads on Upolu, some are still rocky and muddy. Accordingly, I highly recommend a four-wheel-drive Jeep for a full tour of the island.

Budget Rent-A-Car has an office in the National Provident Fund building opposite the Town Clock in Apia (☎ 20-561, or 800/527-0700 in the U.S.). Rates range from U.S. $48 to U.S. $57 a day, including unlimited miles. There's a mandatory U.S. $7 per day for insurance on all models. As with all of Apia's car-rental firms, Budget will not allow you to take its vehicles on the ferry to Savai'i, nor can you drive them on unpaved roads. You pay for the gasoline; bring it back full. Gasoline cost WS$2 (80¢) per liter during my recent visit, or about $3 for a U.S. gallon.

Avis (☎ 20-486, or 800/831-2847) has an office east of Aggie Grey's Hotel. It also operates in American Samoa and will reserve a car for you in Pago Pago at no extra charge.

Le Car Rentals (☎ 22-754) is a local firm that specializes in four-wheel-drive vehicles. Other local companies are **Funway Rentals** (☎ 22-045), **Pavitt's U-Drive** (☎ 21-766), **Billie's Car Rentals** (☎ 21-724), and **G&J Rentals** (☎ 21-078). Their rates could be less than Budget's or Avis's, but be sure to look their cars over carefully before agreeing to a contract.

Driving Rules   You drive on the right-hand side of the road in the American fashion, stopping for pedestrians in crosswalks, and not exceeding the speed limits of 35 m.p.h. on the open road or 25 m.p.h. in Apia and the villages. Western Samoans and their dogs, chickens, and pigs have a habit of walking in the middle of the roads that pass through their villages, so proceed with care. Even if the way is clear, local courtesy dictates that you slow down when going through the villages so as not to kick up a lot of dust. Special care is required on Sundays, when Samoans usually lounge around the village after going to church.

Visitors technically are required to get a local **driver's license** from the police department traffic office on Ifi'ifi Street. You neglect this cumbersome procedure at your own risk; that having been said, I've never bothered to get one, nor do I know anyone who has. The car-rental firms will ask to see your home driver's license.

BY MOTORCYCLE   **Tulei Rentals** (☎ 24-145) in Kava Kavings Handicraft shop on Beach Road rents motorcycles for WS$50 ($20) a day. If you don't have a MasterCard or Visa, you must pay by cash or traveler's check in advance and leave a WS$200 ($80) refundable deposit. You buy the fuel. You must wear a helmet when riding on a motorcycle.

Samoa Islands

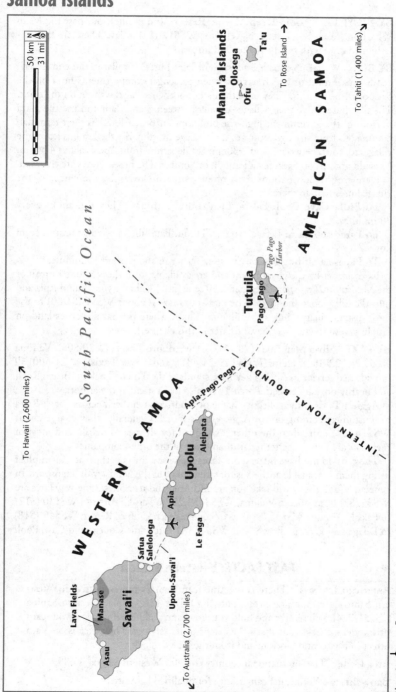

BY BICYCLE **Palolo Deep Marine Reserve** (no phone), out past the Main Wharf on Beach Road, rents bicycles for WS$12 ($5) a day. These are the old-fashioned kind with peddle brakes and no gears.

BY BUS Western Samoa has a system of "aiga buses" (similar to those in American Samoa), most of which have wooden passenger compartments built on the back of flatbed trucks. They have the names of their villages written on the front. The first buses leave their villages usually between 5 and 7am and use the plaza in front of the government high-rise buildings on Beach Road as their terminal, fanning out from there to return to their villages. Ordinarily the last bus leaves the villages for town between 2 and 2:30pm; last departure from Apia is about 4:30pm. They do not run on Saturday afternoon or Sunday. The buses always are crowded.

Here are the destinations most often visited, followed by the names of the village buses that go there:

To Piula Cave Pool: Falefa, Luatuanuu, Lufilufa. They run about every 30 minutes.

To Paradise Beach: Lefaga, Safata, Si'umu, Falealili. They run about once an hour.

To Papase'a Sliding Rocks: Se'ese'e. They run about every 30 minutes.

Fares are set by the government and are available from the Visitor's Bureau or the Ministry of Transport. In general, 50 sene (20¢) will take you around Apia and into the hills above the town. The maximum fare is about WS$4 ($1.60) to the most distant villages and to Mulifanua Wharf, where the Savai'i ferries land on Upolu's western end (see "Savai'i" later in this chapter).

BY TAXI **Silver Star Taxis** (☎ 21-770), **Marlboro Taxis** (☎ 20-808), **Vailima Taxis** (☎ 22-380), **Heini Taxis** (☎ 24-431), and **Town Taxis** (☎ 21-600) all provide taxi service in Apia. They have stands at the Town Clock on Beach Road and nearby on Vaea Street. **Town Taxis** also has a stand at the airport.

Aggie's Taxis is the collective name of cabdrivers who wait across Beach Road for customers coming out of Aggie Grey's Hotel. Generally, they charge about WS$1 (40¢) more than the other taxis, but they all speak English, and most of their cars are kept in better repair than those of the other companies.

The cabs do not have meters, but **fares** are set by the government. A pamphlet listing them is available at the Visitor's Bureau or at the Ministry of Transport. In general, WS$2 (80¢) will take you around Apia and its hotels. One-way fares are WS$5 ($2) from Apia to Vailima; WS$8 ($3.20) to Fagali'i Airstrip; WS$30 ($12) to Faleolo Airport; WS$35 ($14) to Coconuts Beach Club & Resort; WS$45 ($18) to Lefaga and Paradise Beach; and WS$25 ($10) to Piula College and Cave Pool.

FAST FACTS: Western Samoa

American Express There is no American Express representative in Western Samoa. Retzlaff Travel & Tours, P.O. Box 1863, Apia, Western Samoa (☎ 21-724), will receive and hold your mail and will help if you lose your card or traveler's checks, but that's the extent of its services. The office is on Vaea Street in the second block inland from the Town Clock.

Area Code The international country code for Western Samoa is 685.

Baby-sitters Your hotel can arrange for qualified babysitters.

Bookstores Aggie's Gift Shop (☎ 22-880), next to Aggie Grey's Hotel on Beach Road, carries books on Samoa and the South Pacific and a few paperback novels. Le Moana Cafe (☎ 24-828), in the Lotemau Centre at Vaea and Convent Streets, has the latest editions of *Time* and *Newsweek,* the latter in *The Bulletin.*

Business Hours Most shops and government offices are open Monday to Friday from 8am to noon and 1:30 to 4:30pm, Saturday from 8am to noon. Except for the major hotels, the only businesses open on Sunday are the scores of mom-and-pop grocery shops in Apia and some villages.

Camera & Film Quantity and selection of film available in Western Samoa are limited, so bring some with you from home or from Pago Pago. Try Aggie's Gift Shop or the photo shop in Forsgren's, just west of the Town Clock.

Clothing Lightweight, informal summer clothing is best throughout the year, although a light sweater or wrap could come in handy for evening wear from June through September. Men can wear shorts and shirts almost anywhere, but women should stick to dresses away from the hotels and should never wear bathing suits or skimpy clothing away from the beach or swimming pool. Topless or nude bathing is outlawed. Outside Apia most Samoans still wear wraparound lavalavas, which come well below the knees of men and to the ankles on women.

Dentist Ask your hotel staff for a recommendation.

Doctor There are doctors with private clinics in Apia; ask your hotel staff to recommend one. For American-trained doctors, you will have to go to the Lyndon B. Johnson Tropical Medical Clinic in American Samoa (see the next chapter). Also see "Hospital," below.

Drugstores Samoa Pharmacy (☎ 22-595) and Apia Pharmacy (☎ 22-703) are both on Beach Road west of the Town Clock. They carry cosmetics, nonprescription remedies, and prescription drugs—most of New Zealand or Australian manufacture.

Electrical Appliances Electricity in Western Samoa is 240 volts, 50 cycles, and most plugs have angled prongs like those used in New Zealand and Australia. Aggie Grey's Hotel and the Tusitala Hotel supply 110-volt current for electric shavers only; you will need a converter and adapter plugs for other American appliances.

Embassies/Consulates The U.S. Embassy (☎ 21-631) is in the John Williams Building on Beach Road at Falealili Street (the Cross Island Road). Hours are Monday to Friday from 9:30am to 12:30pm. New Zealand and Australia both have high commissions on Beach Road.

Emergencies The emergency phone number for police, fire, and ambulance is 999.

Eyeglasses Try the National Hospital (see "Hospitals" below); if they can't be fixed there (replacements must be ordered from New Zealand), try the Lyndon B. Johnson Tropical Medical Center in Pago Pago.

Gambling There are no casinos, but you can play the local lottery at its office on Vaea Street.

Hairdressers/Barbers Aggie Grey's Hotel has a beauty parlor (☎ 23-277).

Hospital The National Hospital, on Ifi'ifi Street in Apia (☎ 21-212), has an outpatient clinic open daily from 8am to noon and from 1 to 4:30pm. If you have something seriously wrong, however, head for the Lyndon B. Johnson Tropical Medical Center in Pago Pago.

Insects   There are no dangerous insects in Western Samoa, and the plentiful mosquitoes do not carry malaria. Bring a good insect repellent with you, and consider burning mosquito coils at night.

Libraries   Nelson's Public Library, opposite the Town Clock on Beach Road, is open from 9am to 5pm on Monday, Tuesday, and Thursday; 8am to 8pm on Wednesday; from 8am to 4pm on Friday; and from 9am to noon on Saturday.

Liquor Laws   Except for a prohibition of Sunday sale of alcoholic beverages outside the hotels or licensed restaurants, the laws are fairly liberal. Bars outside the hotels can stay open Monday to Saturday to midnight. Spirits, wine, and beer are sold at private liquor stores. Try Samoa Wine & Spirits Ltd., three blocks inland on Vaea Street.

Lost Property   Report to the Police Station (☎ 22-222) on Ifi'ifi Street, a block inland behind the Prime Minister's office.

Luggage Storage/Lockers   There are none in Western Samoa. The hotels will store your extra gear.

Maps   The Western Samoa Visitors Bureau sells a one-sheet collection of maps of Upolu, Savai'i, and Apia town. See "Visitor Information & Entry Requirements" and "Money," above.

Newspapers/Magazines   The daily *Samoa Observer* carries local and world news. Check Aggie's Gift Shop at Aggie Grey's Hotel and Le Moana Cafe for copies of the international news magazines (see "Where to Stay" and "Where to Dine," below).

Police   The police station (☎ 22-222) is on Ifi'ifi Street, inland from the Prime Minister's office.

Post Office   The Chief Post Office is located on Beach Road, east of the Town Clock. Airmail letters to North America cost 90 sene (36¢), and postcards and airgrams, 85 sene (34¢). Hours are Monday to Friday from 9am to 4:30pm.

Radio/TV   Western Samoa's government owns the only broadcast television station in the country, and cable TV hasn't gotten here yet. The government channel has New Zealand programming daily from 5 to 11pm (earlier or later if there's a rugby game on). Many homes on Upolu's north shore can receive the American Samoan channels, one of which has CNN during the mornings. The government also operates two AM radio stations, on which most programming is in Samoan. The world news is rebroadcast from Radio Australia and Radio New Zealand several times a day. A privately owned FM station broadcasts lots of music on FM 98.8. American Samoa's AM station, WVUV, can be picked up fairly well on Upolu's north shore.

Safety   Thefts have been on the increase in Western Samoa in recent years, so don't leave valuables in your hotel room. Remember that the communal property system still prevails in the Samoas, and items such as cameras and bags left unattended may disappear. Street crime has not been a serious problem, but be on the alert if you walk down dark streets at night. Women should not wander alone on deserted beaches. Western Samoans take the Sabbath seriously, and there have been reports of local residents tossing stones at tourists who drive through some villages on Sunday. If you plan to tour by rental car, do it during the week.

Taxes   Western Samoa imposes a 10% General Services Tax, which is included in hotel, restaurant, and bar bills and is added to the cost of some other items.

Also, an airport departure tax of WS$20 ($8) is levied on all passengers leaving Western Samoa at both Faleolo and Fagali'i airports. No such tax is imposed on domestic flights or on the ferry to Pago Pago (see the chapter on American Samoa).

Telephone/Telex/Fax   International calls can be directly dialed into Western Samoa from most parts of the world. The international country code is 685.

Domestic long-distance and international calls may be placed at the International Telephone Bureau just inside the Chief Post Office on Beach Road. You place your call with the clerk at the central booth and wait to be paged to one of the side booths. The bureau does not accept credit cards; you must reverse the charges or pay cash in advance of having your call placed. Station-to-station calls to North America cost WS$13.50 ($5.40) for the first three minutes, then WS$4.50 ($1.80) a minute thereafter. Calls to Australia and New Zealand cost about half that amount. The bureau is open daily from 8am to 10pm, but fax services are available daily from 8am to 4pm.

Pay telephones are in post offices in the villages. They are the same red phones used in Fiji and are operated by lifting the handset from its cradle atop the device, depositing a 20-sene coin, and dialing your call.

The number for directory assistance is 933; for the international operator, 900; and for the domestic long-distance operator, 920.

Time   Local time in Western Samoa is 11 hours behind GMT. That means it's three hours behind Pacific standard time (four hours behind during daylight saving time). If it's noon standard time in California and 3pm in New York, it's 9am in Apia. During daylight saving time, it's 8am in Western Samoa.

The islands are east of the international date line; therefore, they share the same date with North America and are one day behind Tonga, Fiji, Australia, and New Zealand. That's worth remembering if you are going on to those countries or will be arriving in Western Samoa from one of them.

Tipping   There is no tipping in Western Samoa except for extraordinary service, and the practice is discouraged as being contrary to the traditional way of life, fa'a Samoa. One exception is the practice of throwing money on the dance floor to show appreciation of a show well performed.

Water   All tap water should be boiled before drinking. Safe bottled water is produced locally.

Weights and Measures   Western Samoa officially is on the metric system, but in their everyday lives, most residents still calculate distances by the British system used in American Samoa and in the U.S. Speed limits are posted in miles per hour, and the speedometers of many local vehicles (all of which have the steering wheels on the left side in the American and European fashion) are calculated in miles.

9 What to See & Do in Apia & Upolu

The town of Apia sits midway along the north coast of Upolu, which makes it a centrally located base from which to explore the main island. The Cross Island Road runs 14 miles from town across the range of extinct volcanoes that form Upolu, thereby bringing the south coast within easy reach of town.

Frommer's Favorite Western Samoa Experiences

Stevenson's Museum & Grave. Anyone who has ever put words on paper will feel a sense of awe when reading Robert Louis Stevenson's requiem carved on his grave up on Mount Vaea overlooking Apia. The climb isn't easy, but it's worth it if you have a single literary bone in your body. The museum is one of the finest literary shrines I've ever seen: you almost expect Stevenson to walk in at any second, so much does Vailima look like it did when he was alive.

Paradise Beach. Although the beach at Vavau is more spectacular in most respects, a Sunday afternoon spent at this beautiful spot is a highlight of any trip to Western Samoa. This is what all beaches should be like: surf breaking around black rock outcrops, palm trees draped over white sand. Gary Cooper must have loved it.

Fiafia Night at Aggie Grey's. The dancing is more suggestive in French Polynesia and the Cook Islands, but there is a warmth and charm to Aggie's fiafia nights that no other establishment comes close to matching.

Walking in Apia. A Hollywood set designer would be hard pressed to top Apia as an old South Seas town. I love to dodge the potholes and storm drains along the perfect half-moon curve of Beach Road and let the old churches and clapboard government buildings tell me how things used to be.

Touring Savai'i. The best way to see the desolate lava fields of Savai'i is with retired Australian geologist Warren Jopling. Having lived on Savai'i for many years, he also is an expert on Samoan customs and lifestyles (everyone on the island knows him). Touring with Warren is like having your own personal guide through a living geological and cultural museum.

✪ ROBERT LOUIS STEVENSON MUSEUM

When Robert Louis Stevenson and his wife, Fanny, decided to stay in Samoa in 1889, they bought 314 acres of virgin land on the slopes of Mount Vaea above Apia and named the estate **Vailima**—or "Five Waters"—because five streams crossed the property. They cleared about eight acres and lived there in a small shack for nearly a year. The American historian Henry Adams dropped in unannounced one day and found the Stevensons dressed in lavalavas, doing dirty work about their hovel. To Adams, the couple's living conditions were repugnant. Their Rousseauian existence didn't last long, however, for in 1891 they built the first part of a mansion that was to become famous throughout the South Pacific.

When completed two years later, the big house had five bedrooms, a library, a ballroom large enough to accommodate 100 dancers, and the only fireplace in Samoa. The Stevensons shipped 72 tons of furniture out from England, all of which was hauled the three miles from Apia on sleds pulled by bullocks. A piano sat in one corner of the great hall in a glass case to protect it from Samoa's humidity. There were leather-buttoned chairs, mahogany tables, a Chippendale sideboard, Arabian curtains of silver and gold, paintings by the masters, a Rodin nude given them by the sculptor, a damask tablecloth that was a gift from Queen Victoria, and a sugar bowl that had been used by both Robert Burns and Sir Walter Scott.

The Stevensons' lifestyle matched their surroundings. Oysters were shipped on ice from New Zealand, Bordeaux wine was brought by the cask from France and bottled at Vailima, and 1840 vintage Madeira was poured on special occasions. They dressed formally for dinner every evening—except for their bare feet—and were served by Samoans dressed in tartan lavalavas, in honor of the great author's Scottish origins.

Vailima and this lavish lifestyle baffled the Samoans. As far as they could tell, writing was not labor; therefore, Stevenson had no visible way of earning a living. Yet all this money rolled in, which meant to them that Stevenson must be a man of much mana. He was also a master at one of their favorite pastimes—storytelling—and he took much interest in their own stories, as well as their customs, language, and politics. When the followers of the defeated Mataafa were released from prison, they built a road from Apia to Vailima in appreciation for Stevenson's support of their unsuccessful struggle against the Germans. And when he died in 1903, they cut the "Track of Loving Hearts" to his grave on Mount Vaea overlooking Vailima.

Stevenson's wife, Fanny, died in California in 1914, and her ashes were brought back to Vailima and buried at the foot of his grave. Her Samoan name, Aolele, is engraved on a bronze plaque.

Western Samoa's head of state lived in Vailima until hurricanes severely damaged the mansion in 1990 and 1991. Since then, an extraordinary renovation has turned it into the **Robert Louis Stevenson Museum.** It now appears as it did when Stevenson lived there. A sitting room matches exactly that seen in a photo made of Fanny on a chair. Another photo of Stevenson dictating is hung in his library where he stood at the time.

Vailima is three miles south of Apia on the cross-island road (turn off Beach Road at the high-rise John Williams Building in Apia and go straight). The museum is open Tuesday to Friday from 9am to noon and 2 to 3:30pm, Saturday from 9am to noon. Guided tours take place Tuesday to Friday at 1pm. Admission is WS$15 ($6) for adults and WS$5 ($2) for children up to 12 years old. For more information, call 20-842.

The "Track of Loving Hearts" leading to **Stevenson's Grave** passes a lovely cascade, which Stevenson turned into a swimming pool. A short, rather steep walking track to the grave takes about 30 strenuous minutes; a longer but easier path takes about one hour. Mount Vaea is best climbed in the cool of early morning.

A WALKING TOUR OF APIA

Like most South Pacific towns, Western Samoa's capital and only town has expanded from one small Samoan village to include adjacent settlements and an area of several square miles, all of which is now known collectively as Apia (the name of the village where Europeans first settled). The town now has a population approaching 40,000. For the visitor, most points of interest lie along **Beach Road,** the broad avenue that curves along the harbor, the water on one side and churches, government buildings, and businesses on the other.

Be careful as you walk along Beach Road, whose uneven sidewalks and open storm drains can easily sprain an ankle, or worse.

We start our walking tour of downtown at **Aggie Grey's Hotel,** on the banks of the Vaisigano River. This famous hotel and its founder are stories unto themselves, which I have recounted in "Where to Stay," below. From Aggie's, head west, or to the left as you face the harbor.

Our place is in a deep cleft of Vaea Mountain, some six hundred feet above the sea, embowered in a forest, which is our strangling enemy, and which we combat with axes and dollars.

—Robert Louis Stevenson, 1890

The two large churches on the left are both Protestant, legacies of the Rev. John Williams, for whom the modern high-rise office building at the corner of Falealili Road is named. On the waterfront across Beach Road is a memorial to this missionary who brought Christianity to Samoa and many more South Pacific islands. Williams's bones are reputedly buried beneath the clapboard **Congregational Christian Church,** directly across Beach Road from the memorial. The missionary was eaten after the natives did him in on Erromango in what now is Vanuatu; the story has it that his bones were recovered and brought to Apia.

During business hours there's usually a line outside the **New Zealand High Commission** office, just beyond the church, as Western Samoans wait to apply for visas. Like their American Samoan cousins who flock to the U.S., they migrate to Auckland for better jobs and higher pay. Unlike them, however, Western Samoans do not have unrestricted access to the larger country and must apply for visas to enter New Zealand, their former "Mother Country."

The clapboard, colonial-style **Courthouse** on the next corner formerly housed the Supreme Court and Prime Minister's office before they moved into the big high-rise buildings across the road. In colonial times, it was headquarters of the New Zealand trusteeship administration, and site of the Mau Movement demonstration and shootings in 1929.

The Marist Brothers' Primary School is on the banks of Mulivai Stream. Across the bridge stands **Mulivai Catholic Cathedral,** begun in 1885 and completed some 20 years later. Farther along, the imposing **Matafele Methodist Church** abuts the shops in the **Wesley Arcade.** According to a monument across Beach Road, Chief Saivaaia of Tafua in Tonga brought Methodism to Samoa in 1835. The Methodist Church of Australia had responsibility for the Samoas from 1859 until an independent conference was established in Western Samoa in 1964.

The remains of the German warship *Adler* are buried under the reclaimed land, now the site of two huge, fale-topped government office buildings. Built in the mid-1990s with foreign aid from China, the huge structures house the prime minister's offices, government departments, and the central bank. On the water side of Beach Road stands a memorial to the Western Samoans who fought alongside the New Zealanders during World War II.

The center of modern Apia's business district is the **Town Clock,** the World War I memorial at the foot of Vaea Street. Behind the clock stands a large Samoan fale known as Pulenu'u House, where local residents can be seen lounging or eating their lunches. Next to the clock on the water side is **Nelson Memorial Public Library,** which has a collection of South Pacific literature in the Pacific Room, to the right after you enter. The clock and library were gifts from the family of Olaf Nelson, a Swede who arrived in 1868 and built a sizeable trading empire.

Beyond lies the sprawling **Old Apia Market.** Once the vegetable market, this large covered space is now home to stalls selling a wide range of items, from

Apia

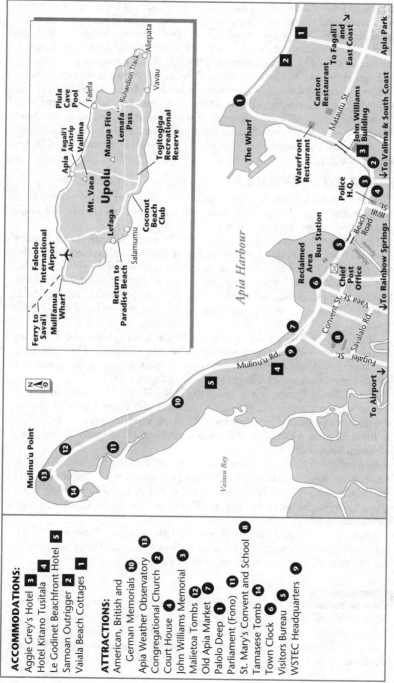

ACCOMMODATIONS:

Aggie Grey's Hotel **3**
Hotel Kitano Tusitala **4**
Le Godinet Beachfront Hotel **5**
Samoan Outrigger **2**
Vaiala Beach Cottages **1**

ATTRACTIONS:

American, British and
  German Memorials **10**
Apia Weather Observatory **13**
Congregational Church **2**
Court House **4**
John Williams Memorial **3**
Malietoa Tombs **12**
Old Apia Market **7**
Palolo Deep **1**
Parliament (Fono) **11**
St. Mary's Convent and School **8**
Tamasese Tomb **14**
Town Clock **6**
Visitors Bureau **5**
WSTEC Headquarters **9**

Post Office ⊠

8091

sandals to toothpaste. One area is devoted to handcraft vendors, and you can stop and watch local women weaving pandanus mats, hats, and handbags. This is a good place to shop for woodcarvings and tapa cloth. I haven't had the stomach for such local fare since my days as a young backpacker, but the food stalls along the market's water side are the cheapest (and dirtiest) places in town to get a meal.

Fugalei Street, which leaves Beach Road across from the market, goes to the airport and west coast. Walk down it a block, and turn left and go east on Convent Street past picturesque **St. Mary's Convent and School.** At the next corner, turn right on Saleufi Street and walk inland two blocks to the **New Market,** a modern, tin-roofed pavilion where Samoan families sell a wide variety of tropical fruits and vegetables, all of which have the prices clearly marked (there is no bargaining).

THE MULINU'U PENINSULA

Beyond the market, Beach Road becomes Mulinu'u Road, which runs about a mile to the end of Mulinu'u Peninsula, a low arm separating Apia Harbor to the east and shallow Vaiusu Bay on the west.

Just beyond the market on the left is the **Western Samoan Trust Estates Corporation,** which took over ownership of the copra plantations when the Germans were kicked out of the islands at the beginning of World War I. The WSTEC building was originally headquarters of the German firms that owned and managed the plantations. The Kitano Tusitala Hotel just up the way was built where once stood a boarding house for the German employees of the original company.

About halfway out on the peninsula are the **German, British, and American Memorials,** one dedicated to the German sailors who died in the 1889 hurricane, one to the British and American sailors who were drowned during that fiasco, and one to commemorate the raising of the German flag in 1900.

The Mulinu'u Peninsula is home of the **Fono,** Western Samoa's parliament. The new Fono building sits opposite a memorial to Western Samoa's independence, the two separated by a wide lawn. The Fono's old home is next to the road in the same park. A tomb on the lawn holds the remains of Iosefa Mataafa, one of the paramount chiefs.

Beyond the Apia Yacht Club stand the tombs of the Malietoa family of paramount chiefs, which makes this the **burial grounds** of Western Samoa's incumbent "royalty." At the end of the paved road, a dirt path goes left past a gravel quarry to the tombs of Tuimalaeali'ifano and Tupua Tamasese, two other paramount chiefs.

At the end of the peninsula you'll find the **Apia Weather Observatory,** originally built by the Germans in 1902 (they apparently learned a costly lesson from the unpredicted, disastrous hurricane of March 1889).

Impressions

Many an English village is bigger by far than Apia. And the whole place had an air of faded obsolescence, as if somebody had decided that it was hardly worth nailing the buildings to the ground or giving them a lick of paint because the inevitable hurricane was bound to blow them away.

—John Dyson, 1982

SEEING UPOLU

To travel along the roads of Upolu away from Apia is to see Polynesia relatively unchanged from the days before the Europeans arrived in the islands. There are very few road signs in Western Samoa, so make sure you buy a map from the Western Samoa Visitors Bureau (see "Visitor Information & Entry Requirements" and "Money," above). Also ask someone about the condition of the roads. A recent paving project has vastly improved most of the main routes, but some over the mountains can be virtually impassable at times.

Sightseeing Tours   Based at Aggie Grey's Hotel, **Samoa Scenic Tours** (☎ 22-880) offers a different tour of the island each day. Most stop along the way for photographs and a swim at beautiful beaches and waterfalls, and full-day tours include a beachside barbecue lunch (beers and soft drinks, too). Prices range from U.S. $14 for half-day trips to U.S. $35 for full-day trips. Each day's offerings are scrawled on a notice board in the lobby at Aggie's.

Other companies to call are **Annie's Tours** (☎ 21-550 or 20-744), **Gold Star Tours** (☎ 20-466), **Janes Tours** (☎ 20-942), and **Retzlaff's Tours** (☎ 21-724). Among them you will find something interesting, especially for Sunday, which, except for church services, will be a slow day in Samoa.

You can also negotiate with the taxi drivers who gather at Aggie Grey's Hotel.

For a bird's-eye view, **Pacific Helicopters** (☎ 20-047 or 20-595) has scenic flights from the helipad opposite Aggie Grey's Hotel. Prices start at U.S. $200 for a 16-minute pass over Apia and environs.

Environmental Tours   The sightseeing tours don't go to the remote areas visited by Dr. Steve Brown and his Samoan wife Lumaava of **Eco-Tour Samoa** (☎ 25-993 or 25-323). The Browns have a number of tours that explore the wildlife and fauna of such places as the Mount Vaea rain forest, remote Fagaloa Bay, the south coast estuaries and wetlands, and Lake Lanotoo, a crater lake in the center of Upolu that should be seen only with a guide. They also have expeditions to Savai'i. Transportation is by four-wheel-drive bus or outrigger canoe. Prices range from U.S. $15 to U.S. $150. Call them for more information, or contact the Western Samoa Visitors Bureau (☎ 20-878) or Island Hoppers Vacations on Vaea Street (☎ 22-026).

From Apia to Aleipata   One of the most popular sightseeing tours makes a loop from Apia to the long white beaches of Aleipata District on Upolu's eastern end. Most of Upolu is a volcanic shield that slopes gently to the sea, but since the east is older—and therefore more eroded and rugged than the central and western portions—this area has the island's most dramatic scenery. Serrated ridges come down to the sea, giving the eastern third of the island a tropical beauty reminiscent of Moorea in French Polynesia.

The East Coast Road follows the shore for 16 miles to the village of Falefa, skirting the lagoon and black-sand surf beaches at Lauli'i and Solosolo. Look for **Piula College,** a Methodist school on a promontory overlooking the sea about two miles before Falefa. Cut into the cliff below the church on the school grounds is the freshwater ✪ **Piula Cave Pool.** You can use snorkeling gear to swim through an underwater opening at the back of the pool into a second cave. The cave pool is open from 8am to 4:30pm Monday through Saturday; admission is WS$1 (40¢), and there are changing rooms for visitors. No alcoholic beverages are allowed on the grounds.

To the left of the bridge beyond Falefa village lie **Falefa Falls,** impressive during the rainy season. The road then slowly climbs toward 950-foot-high **Le Mafa Pass** in the center of the island, with some great views back toward the sea. Another rugged, winding road to the left just before the pass deadends at picturesque **Fagaloa Bay,** once a volcanic crater that exploded to seaward, leaving a mountain-clad bay cutting deep into the island. The Fagaloa road should be traveled only in a four-wheel-drive vehicle—and even then with the utmost caution.

Once over the pass, the main paved road crosses a bridge. Just beyond, an unpaved and unmarked road goes to the right and cuts through the forests down to the south coast. We will come back this way, road conditions permitting, but for now go straight ahead on the **Richardson Track.** Once a bush path, this paved road crosses a refreshingly cool high plateau and skirts **Afulilo Lake,** formed by the country's hydroelectric dam. From there it gently descends to ✪ **Aleipata,** a picturesque district whose villages sit beside gorgeous white-sand beaches. Four small islands offshore enliven the view, and on a clear day you can see the jagged blue outline of American Samoa on the horizon.

On the south coast, a cliff-like escarpment leaves a narrow shelf of land bordered by a long beach. There's not enough space here for villages, but on these sands stands a collection of rustic **beach fales** available for camping (see "Where to Stay," below). Stop here any day except Sunday for refreshment at Taufua Beach Bar.

Keep going along the southeast shore, then turn into ✪ **Vavau Beach Fales** (see "Where to Stay," below) for a visit to one of the South Pacific's great beaches. Rocky outcrops along the shore create a natural pool where you can actually snorkel in the shade.

From Vavau, the unpaved Le Mafa Pass Road climbs up the forested slopes back to the bridge at the pass, where it rejoins the main paved road. Le Mafa Pass Road has been a very rough route in recent years, virtually impassable during periods of heavy rain. If it's closed (your car-rental company will advise), then turn around and go back to Apia the way we came.

If it's open, Le Mafa Pass Road will take you to a viewpoint overlooking 175-foot-high **Sopo'aga Falls.** The villagers have built a small park atop the deep and narrow gorge, complete with picnic tables and toilets. They charge WS$2 (80¢) per vehicle. The spectacular sight is more than worth that small amount.

The Cross Island Road The Cross Island road runs for 14 miles from the John Williams Building on Beach Road in Apia to the village of Si'umu on the south coast. Along the way it passes first Vailima and then the modern, nine-sided **House of Worship,** one of six Baha'i Faith temples in the world. Open for meditation and worship, the temple was dedicated in 1984. An information center outside the temple makes available materials about the Baha'i Faith.

After passing the temple, the road winds its way through cool, rolling pastures and then starts its descent to the east coast. Watch on the right for a parking area overlooking **Papapai-tai Waterfalls,** which plunge 300 feet into one of the gorges that streams have cut into central Upolu's volcanic shield. Of the many waterfalls on Upolu, Papapai-tai is the most easily seen.

The Southwest Coast A left turn at the end of the Cross Island Road in Si'umu village on the south coast leads to **O Le Pupu-Pue National Park** and the **Togitogiga National Forest.** The park contains the best remaining tropical rain forest on Upolu, but you'll have to hike into the valley to reach it. Some 51 species of wildlife live in the park: 42 species of birds, five of mammals, and four

Western Samoa is different. Of all the Polynesian nations, it is the one with the most peculiar life-style, the strangest customs, the greatest resistance to foreign encroachment; and yet, paradoxically, it is the nation that offers itself most proudly for public inspection.

—Ron Hall, 1991

of lizards. Lovely **Togitogiga Falls** are a short walk from the entrance, from where a trail to **Peapea Cave** also begins. It's a two-hour round-trip hike to the cave. Another walking trail leads seaward to arches cut by the surf into the south coast. **Mount Le Pu'e,** in the northwest corner of the park, is a well-preserved volcanic cinder cone. The park and reserve are open during the daylight hours seven days a week, and there's no admission fee.

Heading west from Si'umu, the road soon passes the Coconuts Beach Club & Resort and then the nearby **Togo Mangrove Estuary,** a tidal waterway alive with birds, flowers, bees, and other wildlife. Coconut Watersports, based at Coconuts Beach Club & Resort, rents kayaks for exploring the waterways through this enchanting, swamp-like preserve (see "Water Sports, Golf & Other Outdoor Activities," below).

Some of Upolu's most beautiful beaches are on the southwest coast, particularly in the Lefaga district. One of these is at the village of **Salamumu.** Farther on the south coast road, Matautu village boasts ✪ **Return to Paradise Beach,** one of the most gorgeous coves in the South Pacific. Palms hang over a sandy beach punctuated by large boulders that confront the breaking surf. It gets its name from the movie starring Gary Cooper, which was filmed here in 1951. The WS$5 ($2) per-person custom fee charged by Matautu village is well worth it.

From Matautu the main road winds across the center of the island to the north coast.

10 Where to Stay

Western Samoa has seen an explosion of **beach fales** in recent years. Although included in many accommodation listings, these rustic little structures belong in the camping category. Most are miniature Samoan fales, with oval thatch roofs covering open-air platforms. Most provide mosquito nets, foam mattresses, and pull-down canvas or colorful plastic sides to afford some privacy and protection against the elements. Guests share communal toilets and showers in separate buildings. The best of the lot are in Aleipata, 1¼ hours by car from Apia on Upolu's southeastern corner. I say "best" not because of the quality of the accommodation, but because they sit right on one of Western Samoa's best beaches. Of these, **Tafua Beach Fales** (☎ 20-180) has a restaurant and bar across the road. **Litia Sini's Beach Fales** (☎ 24-327) actually has wood sides on four of its fales. Others within an easy walk are **Sieni's Beach Fales** and **Romeo's Beach Fales** (both ☎ 20-878). Rates at all four are WS$15 ($6) per person, cash only.

EXPENSIVE

✪ Aggie Grey's Hotel

P.O. Box 67, Apia (Beach Road, on the waterfront). ☎ **22-880** or 800/448-8355. Fax 23-626. 169 rms. A/C TV TEL. U.S. $85–$125. AE, DC, MC, V.

The late Aggie Grey's son Alan Grey, his wife Marina, and daughter Tonya are making sure that the hotel has the same warm, family feeling instilled by Aggie when she opened it in 1943 to cater to U.S. Marines training here. The fire marshal made Alan tear down the charming old clapboard hotel a few years ago, but he replaced it with a beautiful building housing the reception area, an air-conditioned restaurant, an open-air bar facing the harbor, and two floors of modern rooms and suites with private verandas overlooking the water, the curve of Beach Road, and the town of Apia. Most impressively, the Victorian-style building looks like it belongs on Apia's historic waterfront, with siding that looks like clapboard, a roof of corrugated tin, and verandas trimmed in gingerbread fretwork.

The new facility hasn't changed the relaxed atmosphere back in the large, exquisite fale beside the swimming pool with a palm tree growing in the middle. Guests can still take their meals under the great turtle-shaped roof or wander over to the bar for a cold Vailima beer and a chat with friendly strangers. A group of Samoans still strums guitars and sings in the bar after sundown. The efficient staff prepares feasts and barbecues in which the quantity of food dished out is, as always, astounding. And Alan, Marina, and Tonya maintain Aggie's tradition of circulating among their guests. Marina Grey now dances the siva on fiafia nights.

Most rooms here are in modern, stone-accented, two-story buildings rambling through a garden so thick with tropical vegetation that it's easy to get lost trying to find your way from one room to another. Although Alan is in the process of slowly turning the older rooms into cookie-cutter-like replicas of modern hotel rooms, those that haven't been renovated virtually ooze old South Seas charm. They are comfortable, and although air conditioned, have good natural ventilation (fans swing from the ceiling or oscillate from a wall to help out the usual breeze). They have old-fashioned touches like fold-down ironing boards, irons mounted in their own wooden holders, and comfy, bent rattan furniture. Each has a veranda or balcony where guests can sip their morning tea or coffee made right in the rooms.

Individual "VIP fale suites" are scattered around the other buildings, each of enormous size and bearing the name of one of Aggie's famous past guests, such as actors Gary Cooper, William Holden, and Marlon Brando.

Dining/Entertainment: No one goes hungry at Aggie's. Hearty breakfasts—either continental or a 1943 version of bacon and scrambled eggs—are served in the big fale. Sandwiches, hamburgers, and other light items are available at the bar for lunch, but they can disappear by 1pm.

Traditionally on Wednesday, fiafia nights feature an enormous buffet of European, Chinese, and Samoan selections (look the table over before going through the line, and watch for the Samoan dishes along the front). A similar spread, plus charbroiled steaks, chicken, and sausages is laid out on Sunday barbecue night, when many restaurants in Apia are closed. The all-you-can-eat fiafias and barbecues cost about WS$40 ($16).

On other evenings, you can order from the à la carte menu. Dinner reservations are essential at Le Tamarina, the Grey's formal restaurant overlooking the harbor (see "Where to Dine," below). Non-guests are welcomed at all meals, but men must wear long trousers and shirts with collars, and women skirts or slacks, in the bar and dining areas after 6pm.

Coconuts Beach Club & Resort

P.O. Box 3684, Apia (in Si'umu, 30 minutes south of Apia). ☎ **24-849.** Fax 20-071. 15 rms, 2 bungalows. A/C MINIBAR. U.S. $110–$165 rooms; U.S. $215–$240 bungalows. AE, DC, MC, V. Turn right at end of cross-island road.

Former Hollywood show-biz lawyers Barry and Jennifer Rose developed Upolu's first luxury beachside resort on a piece of land abutting the Togo Mangrove Estuary (mosquitos can be plentiful at times here). They chopped down enough of this dense growth for two bungalows, each with its own patch of beach and private garden, and a two-story, motel-style block of eight rooms reached by tree-house-like stairs. The spacious thatch-roofed, clapboard-sided bungalows (one has two bedrooms) have a rustic look without giving up luxuries. They have outdoorsy screened baths with showers pouring down rock walls into sunken tubs. In the rooms, you can step from oval bathtubs directly onto 24-foot-long covered patios or balconies. Lots of natural wood creates unusual accents, such as tree limbs used as posts for the king-size beds, towel racks in the baths, and legs for coffee tables. Another European-style building holds seven less-charming standard units whose separate bedrooms are air conditioned.

Dining/Entertainment: A bearded, former Hawaii restaurateur named Mika holds forth under a thatch pavilion with a friendly beachfront bar. He specializes in fresh seafood, especially local lobster and mud crabs from the nearby mangrove estuary. A string band plays evenings, and Wednesday usually is fiafia night.

Roger and Gayle Christman's Coconuts Watersports provides a host of activities, most of which cost extra (see "Water Sports, Golf & Other Outdoor Activities," below). A lava wall runs offshore, creating a good snorkeling area.

Hotel Kitano Tusitala

P.O. Box 101, Apia (Beach Road, Mulinu'u Peninsula). ☎ **21-122** or 800/448-8355. 96 rms. A/C TV TEL. U.S. $85–$140. AE, DC, MC, V.

Built in 1974 by the government and named simply the Tusitala in honor of Robert Louis Stevenson, this hotel was going downhill until purchased in 1991 by Kitano, a Japanese construction company. The modern structure is similar in appearance to the Rainmaker Hotel in Pago Pago in that its three main buildings are under huge turtle-shaped thatch roofs. They ring a tropical garden featuring a children's wading pool, from which water falls down two levels into a larger adult swimming pool. Nearby are two hard-surface tennis courts. The hotel also has a hair salon and gift shop.

The rooms are all in five two-story buildings grouped beyond the swimming pools. Those facing the pool have been renovated and refurnished. The rest have been repainted but still show their age. They have typical Australian and New Zealand features: a double bed with a single bed serving as a settee, tropical-style lounge chairs, bath with shower, refrigerator, tea- and coffee-making facilities, and sliding glass door opening onto either a private patio or balcony. They are air conditioned, but you won't feel any cross-ventilation unless you leave the back door open. Only the renovated "deluxe" rooms have TVs.

Dining/Entertainment: A bar and lounge in an open-air Samoan fale stands next to the pool, as does the Apaula Snackbar, open throughout the day. One of the three big common buildings houses Stevenson's Restaurant (with portraits of R.L.S. himself). The Tusitala usually has its fiafia night on Thursday. A band plays on Sunday evening.

MODERATE

Hotel Insel Fehmarn

P.O. Box 3272, Apia (on Cross Island Road, 1¼ miles uphill from Beach Road). ☎ **23-301.** Fax 22-204. 54 rms. A/C TV TEL. U.S. $75. AE, DC, MC, V.

This modern establishment sits on the side of the hill above Apia, affording it's motel-style rooms with views of town and the offshore reef from their balconies, especially those on the third (top) floor. Each identical room in this beige modern structure has two double beds, chairs, table, tiled shower-only bath, and kitchenette. There is a dining room and bar on the premises, as well as a convenience store, two tennis courts, and a pool.

⑤ Vaiala Beach Cottages

P.O. Box 2025, Apia (Vaiala Beach, 1 mile east of Main Wharf). ☎ **22-202.** Fax 22-008. 7 bungalows. U.S. $75. V.

When I'm not at Aggie's, I stay in one of Helen Mihaljevich's seven comfortable, modern, and airy bungalows, which share a yard with frangipani, crotons, and other tropical plants and are across the street from Vaiala Beach. Helen's sister, by the way, played Gary Cooper's daughter in the 1951 production of *Return to Paradise*, and her own daughter was a Miss Western Samoa.

Except for the tropical furnishings and decor, such as cane furniture and woven floor mats, the bungalows are all identical: a full kitchen with stainless-steel sink, a bedroom with either one double or two twin beds, a spacious bath with a shower and very hot water, and a narrow balcony off a bright living room. They were built in 1984 of New Zealand–treated pine, including the varnished interior walls. The living rooms have ceiling fans hanging over the sitting area, but the large, screened, louvered windows and sliding doors leading to the balconies usually allow the trade winds to cool the house without such assistance. Reservations are advised.

INEXPENSIVE

⑤ Le Godinet Beachfront Hotel

P.O. Box 9490, Apia (Beach Road, Mulinu'u Peninsula). ☎ **23-690.** 10 rms. A/C TEL. U.S. $55. DC, MC, V.

Derec Godinet returned to his native Apia after an entertainment career in Honolulu, Los Angeles, and Las Vegas to open this comfortable little establishment on the Mulinu'u Peninsula waterfront. Actually, the white two-story building, which looks more like a home than a hotel, sits on the land side of Beach Road, but it has a tiny sliver of beach on Apia Harbour. The 10 long, rather narrow but very clean rooms are lined up along one side of the building's second story. Their doors open to a breezeway, as do a set of louvered windows in each. They all have desks and long, benchlike tables along one wall. Small baths have showers. There are no closets, so storage space is at a premium. The room at the front of the building has large windows facing the harbor; it is by far the choice here. A common area on the upstairs breezeway has a fridge and tea- and coffee-making facilities.

A spacious restaurant with a small bar in one corner opens both to the harbor in front and to a carport along one side of the building. The food here is so good that I have included the restaurant separately in "Where to Dine," below. Island dance shows here usually are on Monday and Friday nights.

HOSTELS

✪ The Samoan Outrigger Hotel

P.O. Box 4074, Apia (Vaiala Beach, 1/2 mile east of Main Wharf). ☎ **20-042.** Fax 23-880. 7 rms (2 with bath), 24 dorm beds. WS$55–WS$88 ($22–$35) rooms, WS$27.50 ($11) dorm bed (including tropical breakfast). No credit cards.

Readers Recommend

Vavau Beach Fales (c/o Janes Tours, P.O. Box 70, Apia. ☎ 20-954. Fax 22-680). *"We would like to highly endorse Vavau Beach Fales as the perfect place to stay for at least one or two nights. We managed to reduce the price to allow four backpackers their first night in real paradise. We would recommend any honeymooners to put this as their number one accommodation."* —Lesley-Ann and Kathleen Brown, Wylam, England.

(Author's Note: Built by the Tourism Council of the South Pacific as a pilot project in village hotel management, these six bungalows stand on a fabulous beach with a natural swimming hole at Vavau village, 1 1/2 hours southeast of Apia. They are not typical of the tentlike beach fales common here. Each has living and sleeping areas as well as a full kitchen under a turtle-shaped roof. They are fully screened, have ceiling fans, and are attractively furnished. The shower-only baths are adequate if you don't need hot water. The project never got fully off the ground, so there is no restaurant or bar on the premises, and maintenance hasn't been what it could have been. Bring plenty of provisions. Rates are U.S. $65 per bungalow. Janes Tours does not accept credit cards.)

Claus Hermansen liked what he saw so much during a visit to Western Samoa that he gave up a banking career in Denmark to give one of the 1894-vintage colonial homes lining Vaiala Beach a thorough painting and turn it into one of the best backpackers' hostels in the South Pacific. Once the American consulate here, this tin-roofed house has a large central room with sea view. Claus installed a bar there so that his guests could sip a cold Vailima beer and enjoy the sunsets from the front stoop. Another room to the side serves as reading area and TV lounge, and to the rear is a pleasant communal kitchen and dining area. The choice guest room here is on the front, where it catches the breezes off the lagoon. It and another room have their own toilets and showers. Other guests share five showers, four toilets, and laundry facilities. This establishment was spotlessly clean throughout during my recent visit.

11 Where to Dine

Like other islanders, the Samoans gave up the use of pottery at least a thousand years before the Europeans arrived in the South Pacific. As did their fellow Polynesians, they cooked their foods in a pit of hot stones, which the Samoans call an *umu*. When it had all steamed for several hours, they threw back the dirt, unwrapped the delicacies, and sat down to a ✪ **fiafia.** Favorite side dishes were fresh fruit and *ota* (fish marinated with lime juice and served with vegetables in coconut milk, in a fashion similar to poisson cru in Tahiti). If you happen to be in Samoa on the seventh day after the full moon in late October or early November, the meal may include the coral worm known as *palolo.*

Aggie Grey's Hotel (☎ 22-880) and the **Hotel Kitano Tusitala** (☎ 21-122) each have at least one fiafia a week for about WS$40 ($16) per person. Guests pass a long buffet table loaded with European, Chinese, and Samoan dishes. After stuffing down the food, they watch a show of traditional Samoan dancing. Check with the hotels to find out when they have their fiafia nights.

EXPENSIVE

Apia Inn

Beach Road at Ifi'ifi Street, in John Williams Bldg. ☎ **21-010.** Reservations recommended. Main courses WS$29–WS$37 ($11.50–$15). V. Mon–Fri noon–2pm; Mon–Sat 6–9pm. CONTINENTAL.

When you enter chef Stefan Stedegi's restaurant, you'd swear that you just walked into a fine restaurant in New York or Sydney, not a small South Seas outpost. Linen, crystal, and silverware grace the 15 tables, and the service is attentive and efficient (no "island time" here). Stefan's specialties are fish soup in a light, spicy broth with a hint of curry and red pepper; Swiss-style pork schnitzel with ham, tomato, and cheese; and beef medallions Tyrol style with tomato, onion rings, and bearnaise sauce. He also offers steaks with a variety of sauces, such as hot tomato or cognac cream; pork filets in Bombay curry-cream sauce served with pineapple and baked banana; and local lobster thermidor, which is superb.

Le Godinet Restaurant

Beach Road, on Mulinu'u Peninsula, in Le Godinet Beachfront Hotel. ☎ **23-690.** Reservations recommended. Main courses WS$22–WS$36 ($9–$14.50). DC, MC, V. Daily 6:30–10am, noon–2pm, and 6:30–10pm. SEAFOOD.

Derec Godinet's restaurant is worth a visit even if you don't stay in his house-cum-hotel. Occupying his spacious first floor, the dining room has stucco walls and heavy exposed beams of dark wood. The tables, all with frangipani as their centerpieces and some with a queen buri chair at their heads, are scattered among large potted plants. Fans hanging from the ceiling augment the breeze coming through large windows from the harbor just across the road. Locals come here for seafood, especially lobster moray and a shellfish combination mixed with homemade pasta. Samoan dance shows usually are on Monday and Friday nights.

Le Tamarina Restaurant

Beach Road, in Aggie Grey's Hotel. ☎ **23-626.** Reservations advised. Main courses WS$30–WS$36 ($12–$14.50). AE, DC, MC, V. Mon–Sat noon–2pm and 7–10pm. INTERNATIONAL.

Tropical plants and furnishings lend appropriate atmosphere to this elegant, air-conditioned dining room with a view of Apia from the ground floor of Aggie's. Guests can wear shorts for buffet lunches, but slacks and dresses are required for evening meals, which feature local and New Zealand produce in a variety of preparations. Fresh lobster was prepared with a tasty herb sauce during my recent visit, while T-bone steak periperi had a spicy, Asian flavor from a marmalade of chili, black pepper, soy, garlic, ginger, and sherry.

MODERATE

Canton Restaurant

Matautu Street (east coast road, 50 yards inland from Aggie Grey's Hotel). ☎ **22-818.** Reservations recommended on weekends. Main courses WS$9–WS$22 ($3.50–$9), crabs and lobster at market price. No credit cards. Mon–Sat 11:30am–2pm; daily 6–9pm. CANTONESE.

I'm sure glad one of your fellow readers, Genevieve Glass of Chicago, Ill., found this gem because it's one of the best places to get those large crustaceans known in these parts as mud crabs. In fact, it's often difficult to hear yourself think in this plain but pleasant restaurant over the sound of shells being cracked. Harvested in the shallow estuary on Upolu's south shore, the creatures are best eaten here under black bean sauce. Otherwise, the menu includes a variety of Cantonese with some spicy Szechuan dishes, all of them well prepared. Manager Ricky Wong, who attended university in San Francisco, serves up Samoan-sized portions.

INEXPENSIVE

Daphne's Coffee Shop

Beach Road at Ifi'ifi Street, in John Williams Bldg. ☎ **22-400.** Breakfast WS$5–WS$14 ($2–$5.50); salads, sandwiches, and burgers WS$5.50–WS$10 ($2–$4). No credit cards. Mon–Fri 6am–5pm, Sat 7am–12:30pm. SNACK BAR.

You'll find me at Daphne's pleasant place with large windows looking to the harbor, scarfing up a hearty cooked breakfast at a fraction of the hotels' prices. The menu also features omelettes, soups, burgers, sandwiches, tuna salads, and—if your sweet tooth can stand a piece—yummy passion fruit pie with homemade ice cream.

✪ Giodano's Pizzeria

Cross Island Road, opposite Hotel Insel Fehmarn. ☎ **25-985.** Reservations not accepted. Pizzas WS$9–WS$28 ($3.50–$11); pasta WS$16–WS$18 ($6.50–$7). No credit cards. Tues–Wed 3–10pm, Thurs–Sat 11am–10pm, Sun 5–9pm. PIZZA/PASTA.

Walk around the take-away counter to Alex Stanley's pleasant courtyard where patio tables with kerosene lanterns sit amid frangipani, papaya, and other tropical trees. Small- or large-size pizzas come with a choice of several toppings. Pasta dishes, which all cost the same, consist of lasagna with beef sauce or spaghetti under bolognaise, marinara, carbonara, or a hot vegetarian sauce. With jazz on the speaker system, this is a very popular establishment with local expatriot residents.

⑤ Gourmet Seafood & Grille

Convent Street, 1 block behind Central Post Office. ☎ **24-625.** Sandwiches and burgers WS$2–WS$10 (80¢–$4); main courses WS$6–WS$21 ($2.50–$8.50). No credit cards. Mon–Sat 7am–10pm. SEAFOOD/STEAKS.

You can start your day with fresh fruit pies and muffins at this popular local establishment, which would win all awards for charm in the inexpensive-restaurant category anywhere. Large tree trunks hold up the roof, under which fishnets form a ceiling. Buoys and other nautical items add to the atmosphere. There's nothing gourmet about the substantial home cooking, but you can get your fill of fish and steaks, plus stir-fries and curries from a hot table at midday. A steak bar offers chargrilled beef from 6 to 10pm. Order at the counter; they will call your number.

✪ Le Moana Cafe

Vaea Street at Convent Street, in Lotemau Centre. ☎ **24-828.** Breakfast WS$6.50–WS$10 ($2.50–$4); sandwiches, burgers, and snacks WS$4–WS$7.50 ($1.50–$3); meals WS$8.50–WS$10 ($3.50–$4), weekend dinners WS$20–WS$40 ($8–$16). Mon–Thurs 7am–4pm, Fri 7am–3pm and 6:30–9:30pm, Sat 7am–1pm and 6:30–9:30pm, Sun 9am–1pm. SNACK BAR.

Downtown's most popular spot for a quick lunch, this spotlessly clean, air-conditioned cafe in the modern Lotemau Centre mall has cafeteria-style service featuring fresh fruit, sandwiches, hot meat pies, and two daily specials such as beef curry or roast chicken. Dinner on Friday and Saturday sees a changing menu, with wine and beer offered. No smoking is allowed inside, but you can puff or not on an outside terrace.

The Town Clock Cafe

Vaea Street, off Beach Road at Town Clock. ☎ **20-941.** Sandwiches and light meals WS$5–WS$11 ($2–$4.50). No credit cards. Mon–Fri 8:30am–4:30pm, Sat 8am–12:30pm, Sun 5–9pm. SNACK BAR.

Don't be fooled by the center-of-town storefront appearance, for Roger and Adele Rasmussen's air-conditioned cafe has several tables pleasantly appointed with small flower bouquets. Full cooked breakfasts will get you started, and huge, fresh sandwiches (the bread is baked on the premises) go well after a morning walking around Apia. For something hot, try the daily meat pie special. Sunday evening is New Zealand–style roast night. Roger and Adele will prepare dinners upon request.

12 Water Sports, Golf & Other Outdoor Activities

Apia is not a beach destination, and at presstime, Upolu had only one resort actually on the beach: Coconuts Beach Club & Resort near Si'umu village on the south coast (see "Where to Stay," above). That's where Americans Roger and Gayle Christman of **Coconuts Watersports** (☎ 24-849) offer a host of activities to resort guests and non-guests alike, including scuba diving, fishing charters, snorkeling trips, kayak rentals and guided tours, and sunset cruises. Roger and Gayle will pick up guests in Apia for the 15-mile drive across the mountains to Coconuts Beach Club & Resort.

FISHING   Coconut Watersports (☎ 24-849) has deep sea fishing charters for U.S. $24 per person per hour. They will pick up guests in Apia. In town, **Samoa Marine** (☎ 22-271) near the Main Wharf has game fishing charters.

GOLF   The **Royal Samoan Golf Club** has a nine-hole course at Fagali'i, on the eastern side of Apia, and visitors are welcome to use the facilities. Call the club's secretary (☎ 20-120) for information and starting times. The Samoa Open Golf Championship tournament is played each year in August.

KAYAKING   Rentals and self-guided tours are available from **Coconut Watersports** (☎ 24-849). One tour goes through the Togo Mangrove Estuary, whose entrance is a short paddle west of Coconuts Beach Club & Resort. Another goes east to lava walls and arches along the coast near the Togitogiga National Forest. Kayaks cost WS$22 ($9) per hour. Each will hold one or two persons.

SCUBA DIVING   Coconut Watersports (☎ 24-849; fax 20-071) will pick up divers in Apia for PADI courses and individual dives on the south coast rocks and reefs. Costs are U.S. $50 per dive, U.S. $90 for a short resort course, and U.S. $350 for a certification course. In Apia, **Samoa Marine** (☎ 22-721) near the Main Wharf is primarily a commercial dive operation but will guide recreational divers on one-tank excursions for U.S. $55, two-tank outings for U.S. $65. Tank hires and refills also are available.

SWIMMING & SNORKELING   Just east of the main wharf in Apia, canyons in the reef at ❂ **Palolo Deep Marine Reserve** (no phone) make for good snorkeling without having to leave town. The reserve is open daily during the daylight hours, and has changing rooms; a bar; and snorkeling gear, reef shoes, and bicycles for hire. A contribution of WS$2 (80¢) to the preservation fund is required.

A short walk beyond Palolo Deep is sandy **Vaiala Beach;** the swimming isn't that good there, but there are picnic tables in a grassy coconut grove between the road and the beach.

Some people think a trip to **Papase'a Sliding Rocks** is a highlight of a trip to Apia. You of strong bottom can slide down this waterfall into a dark pool. Take a taxi or the Se'ese'e village bus. The rocks are about two kilometers (1.2 miles) from the paved road; the bus driver may go out of his way to take you there, but you will have to walk back to the bus route. The villagers extract WS$5 ($2) custom fee per person.

Another popular outing away from Apia is to **Piula Cave Pool** and the outlying beaches. See "Seeing Upolu," above, for details.

On the south coast, **Coconut Watersports** (☎ 24-849) has guided snorkeling expeditions. Trips cost WS$35 ($14) without equipment, WS$45 ($18) with gear, both including transportation from Apia.

TENNIS, SQUASH & LAWN BOWLS   Public tennis courts were built in **Apia Park** prior to the 1983 South Pacific Games. They're open Monday to Saturday. Each player pays a small fee. Just east of town (turn right past Aggie Grey's Hotel), 40-acre Apia Park originally was a racetrack built in German times. The property was confiscated from its German owner during World War I and is now used as a multipurpose recreation facility. Rugby and soccer games draw huge crowds on Saturdays from May to September. An open-air gymnasium houses basketball and volleyball courts.

Channel College (☎ 21-821) in Moamoa and the **All Saints Anglican Church** (☎ 21-498) in Leififi'i both have private tennis courts, which can be reserved and used for small donations. Non-guests also can play at **Hotel Insel Fehmarn** (☎ 20-301), on the Cross Island Road 1¼ miles uphill from Beach Road. Cost there is WS$4 ($1.60) per person per hour. Rental racquets are available.

Apia Squash Centre, opposite the main wharf on Beach Road (☎ 23-780), welcomes visitors. It's open Monday to Friday from noon to 1:30pm and 4 to 9pm, Saturday from 3 to 6pm, and has gear for rent.

Apia Bowling Club has lawn-bowling greens (☎ 22-254) next to the Tusitala Hotel on the Mulinu'u Peninsula.

13 Shopping

Economic hard times and encouragement by local dealers has led to an increase in quantity and quality of Samoan handcrafts in recent years: baskets, sewing trays, purses, floor mats, napkin rings, placemats, and fans woven from pandanus and other local materials, plus some woodcarvings.

By and large, your stroll along Beach Road will take you past most of the shops worth poking your head into. In addition to those listed below, some of the Samoan families who have booths in the **Old Apia Market** on Beach Road sell handcraft items.

Aggie's Gift Shop
Beach Road, next to Aggie Grey's Hotel. ☎ **22-880.**

The hotel's gift shop has a wide range of handcrafts and Samoan products such as sandalwood soap, small bags of kava, and watercolors by local artists. The handcrafts include shell and black coral jewelry and tapa cloth *(siapo* in Samoan), carved wooden war clubs, ceremonial kava bowls, and high talking chiefs' staffs (known as *tootoo).* Among clothing items are hand-screened lavalavas, T-shirts, shorts, and dresses. The shop also carries books about the Samoas and has a snack bar just inside the front door.

Amy's Gift Shop
Vaea Street, in Leung Wai Arcade. ☎ **22-092.**

Hot Dogs & Hamburgers

Back in 1919, a young woman of British and Samoan descent named Agnes Genevieve Grey started the Cosmopolitan Club on a point of land where the Vaisigano River flows into Apia Harbor. It was just a small pub catering to local businessmen and tourists who climbed off the transpacific steamers stopping in Apia.

And then the U.S. Marines landed.

That was in 1942, when thousands of American servicemen arrived in Western Samoa to train for the South Pacific campaigns against the Japanese. Aggie Grey started selling them much-appreciated hot dogs and hamburgers. Quickly her little enterprise expanded into a three-story clapboard hotel, with a bar at ground level, a dining room on the next, and rooms to rent on the third. Many of those young Marines, including future U.S. Secretary of State George Shultz, left Samoa with fond memories of Aggie Grey and her hotel.

Another serviceman who came to Aggie's was a U.S. naval historian named James A. Michener. Everyone in Western Samoa believes Michener used Aggie as the role model for Bloody Mary, the Tonkinese woman who provided U.S. servicemen with wine, song, and other diversions in his *Tales of the South Pacific*.

Although her hotel grew after the war to include more than 150 rooms, Aggie always circulated among her guests, making them feel at home. Everyone sat down family-style when taking a meal in the old clapboard building on Beach Road, and afterward moseyed over for coffee in the lounge. Afternoon tea was a time for socializing and swapping gossip from places far away. And on *fiafia* nights, when the feasts were laid out, Aggie herself would dance the graceful Samoan *siva*.

Like Robert Louis Stevenson before her, Aggie Grey was revered by the locals. They made her the only commoner ever to appear on a Western Samoan postage stamp. And when she died in 1988 at the age of 90, Head of State Malietoa Tanufafili II and hundreds of other mourners escorted her to her final resting place in the hills above Apia.

Some local artists are now using original tapa boards as inspiration for Samoan motif designs. One of these is Kalolo Steffany, who often can be found in his own little shop across the walkway from this one, which is owned by his mother, Amy Leung Wai. She carries his designs as well as tie-dyed jumpsuits, dresses, blouses, and aloha shirts. The arcade is in the second block inland on Vaea Street.

Island Styles
Beach Road, in the Wesley Arcade. ☎ **21-850.**

Island Styles is Apia's largest producer of South Pacific–style silkscreened and tie-dyed dresses, skirts, and lavalavas. In addition to this small shop near the Methodist church, it has a warehouse showroom on the Cross Island Road in Vailima. If you want to bring home a little taste of Samoa, consider a bottle of **Talofa Wine** made from passion fruit, banana, mango, or papaya, or Talofa chocolate liqueur made from locally grown cacao; you can sample them at the Island Styles in Vailima.

✪ Janes Handicrafts
Vaea Street, in Leung Wai Arcade. ☎ **20-954.**

Sharing space with Janes Tours, this shop has a wide array of handcrafts from Western Samoa, Tonga, and Fiji. Other items offered here include baskets, mats, handbags, carved wooden bowls, coconut ukeles, spears and war clubs, and jewelry made of shell and black coral.

✪ Kava Kavings Handicraft
Beach Road, west of John Williams Building. ☎ **24-145.**

Harry Paul has been encouraging Western Samoans to resume making handcrafts, and he carries some of the resulting works: bone fishhooks, carved war clubs, spears, and orator's staffs and "horses tails" of the type carried by high talking chiefs, hair clasps and ukeleles made from coconut shells, and many other items. He also has imported handcrafts from Tonga, Fiji, and other South Pacific islands. Kava Kavings will pack and ship your purchases home.

Perenise Handicrafts
Vaea Street at Convent Street, in Lotemau Centre. ☎ **26-261.**

This small shop in the modern Lotemau Centre mall has a selection of tapa, fans, mats, serving trays, and carved wooden bowls and war clubs. It also has some pandanus goods from Tonga and Tokelau (the latter is a small Polynesian island governed by New Zealand from Apia).

14 Island Nights

Samoan Dance Shows   Western Samoa is no different from the other Polynesian countries in that watching a traditional dance show as part of a fiafia night is a highlight of any visit. Samoan dance movements are graceful and emphasize the hands more than the hips; the costumes feature more tapa cloth and fine mats than flowers. While the dances are not as lively nor the costumes as colorful as those in Tahiti and the Cook Islands, they are definitely worth seeing.

✪ **Aggie Grey's Hotel** (☎ 22-880) consistently has the best fiafia night in town, and the show just keeps getting better. Recent additions include a rousing "We Are Samoa" number in which Aggie's staff performers wear costumes representing the many occupations present in Western Samoa. This isn't a Las Vegas floor show, but the fire dance around the swimming pool is nothing short of spectacular for these parts. Aggie's fiafia night traditionally is on Wednesday at 7pm and costs about WS$40 ($16) for dinner and show.

Hotel Kitano Tusitala (☎ 21-122) usually has its show in one of its huge fales on Thursday at 7pm. The dinner and show costs WS$45 ($18).

Le Godinet Restaurant (☎ 23-690) had a dance show after dinner on Monday and Friday nights during my recent visit. Admission was the price of your meal.

Margrey-Ta's Lagoon Beer Garden (☎ 25-395), on Beach Road near the Main Wharf, actually is a tropical garden, albeit with a concrete patio floor (the better to wipe up spilled beer at this popular local drinking establishment). Recorded disco dancing occupies most evenings here, but one night a week (Thursday during my recent visit) features a Polynesian dance show staged by the owner's family and friends. There's a WS$5 ($2) cover charge on performance nights.

Pub Crawling   Other than the dance shows, nightlife in Apia centers on several pubs, which attract local clientele. Most of these have live bands on Friday (the biggest night) and Saturday. Thanks largely to citizens outraged by bars opening in residential neighborhoods, pubs legally must close at midnight throughout the week (none are open on Sunday). As a practical matter, some of them keep right on going into the wee hours.

Pub crawling in Apia essentially is along Beach Road, beginning with **Margrey-Ta's Lagoon Beer Garden** (☎ 25-395) near the Main Wharf, then proceeding west around the harbor. Although you would never believe it by the slapped-together facade and worse-than-plain furniture on its sidewalk terrace, the most popular with local expatriot residents is **Otto's Reef** (☎ 22-691). Nearby is **The Loveboat** (☎ 24-065) and the air-conditioned **Don't Drink the Water** (☎ 20-093). These three are near the Catholic Cathedral.

The crawl then skips past the Town Clock to the **RSA Club** (☎ 20-171) and the **Hotel Kitano Tusitala** (☎ 21-122), which turns one of its big fales into a dance floor. Most folks end the night at the **Beach Bar** (☎ 20-248) on Mulinu'u Peninsula, another spot particularly popular with expatriot residents.

The young set end their night at the **Mount Vaea Club** (☎ 21-627) on Vaitele Street near Tofafuafua Road. Don't expect much charm here, just loud music, much talk, a packed house of young Samoans, and an occasional fight around midnight on Friday and Saturday. Women should exercise caution if visiting this South Seas joint alone.

15 Savai'i

You may wish you had stayed longer on Savai'i, whose green mountains rise out of the sea and into the clouds across the 13-mile-wide Apolima Strait. Savai'i is half again as large as Upolu, yet it has only a third as many people as its smaller and more prosperous sister, and they live in villages mainly along the east and south coasts. Elsewhere, Savai'i is made up of practically deserted lava fields and forests. It's 470 volcanic craters are considered to be dormant (the last major eruption occurred in 1911).

On Savai'i, rural Samoan life has changed less than on any other island, and travelers can visit picturesque villages sitting on the edge of the lagoon.

On the trip over, you will see the picturesque islands of **Manono** and **Apolima** sitting in the Apolima Strait between Upolu and Savai'i. Apolima is a small volcanic crater. The beachside village of Apolima-tui sits on the shore where the crater collapsed on one side. Small boats shuttle between Apolima Island and the village of Apolima-uta on Upolu's western end. Boats to Manono leave from Mulifanua Wharf. There are no hotels or restaurants on either island, but **Samoa Scenic Tours** (☎ 22-880) at Aggie Grey's Hotel operates popular day trips to Manono and its beautiful surrounding reef.

GETTING THERE

You can organize a trip to Savai'i yourself, but the easiest way is to contact one of the tour operators in Apia (see "What to See & Do in Apia & Upolu," earlier in this chapter). For example, **Oceania Tours** (☎ 24-443) has a two-day, one-night package starting at U.S. $160, including round-trip transportation, transfers, and a half-day tour of Savai'i. Oceania's day trips to Savai'i cost U.S. $105.

Eco-Tour Samoa (☎ 25-993 or 25-323 in Apia) has two- and three-day expeditions around Savai'i, with an emphasis on exploring the volcanic craters, lava fields, wetlands, and rain forests. These cost from U.S. $150 to U.S. $300 per person, including transportation and accommodation.

Polynesian Airlines (☎ 21-261 or 22-172) flies several times a day between Fagali'i Airstrip near Apia and Maota Airstrip, near Salelologa on the southeast corner of Savai'i (the island's only airstrip). The Fagali'i–Savai'i fares are WS$31 ($12.50) one way, WS$55 ($22) round trip.

The *Lady Samoa,* a passenger and automobile ferry, operates three times daily between Mulifanua Wharf on Upolu and Salelologa on Savai'i. The one-way fare is WS$6 ($2.50). Local buses leave regularly from the Apia market and pass Mulifanua Wharf on their way to Pasi O Le Vaa. Bus fare to the wharf is WS$1.40 (56¢). For more information, check the bulletin board in the Visitors Bureau or contact the **Western Samoa Shipping Corporation** (☎ 20-935), at Vaea and Convent Streets.

GETTING AROUND

Taxis meet the planes and ferry. One-way fare from Maota Airstrip to the "hotel district" around Safua on the east coast is WS$15 ($6). From the ferry wharf to the hotels costs WS$10 ($4) one way. The fare is WS$100 ($40) one way to Asau village, 55 miles away on the opposite side of Savai'i.

Local **buses** operate frequently along the east coast. Those headed to Puapua and Tuasivi pass the hotels. The fare is WS60¢ (24¢). Long-distance buses leave Salelologa shortly after each ferry arrival. It's possible to take a bus as far as Asau and back.

Savai'i Car Rentals (☎ 51-206, or 51-295), rents Jeeps for WS$110 ($44) a day. A deposit of WS$100 ($40) is required, and this company did not accept credit cards during my recent visit. It is part of **Savai'i Travel & Tours,** at the intersection of the wharf and main roads in Salelologa. They can assist with reconfirming your return flight on Polynesian Airlines. Most car-rental companies in Apia frown on customers taking their vehicles on the ferries.

The east coast road is paved to Sasina on the north shore. This paved portion crosses the Matavanu Lava Fields on the northeastern corner of Savai'i but not the larger flows on the north shore, where the road can be rugged going. The scenic south-coast road is paved all the way to Asau but misses the lava fields.

WHAT TO SEE & DO

Unless you have a week or more and plenty of energy, take a tour of this large and sparsely populated island with so little public transport and few road signs.

✪ **Safua Tours,** based at the Safua Hotel (☎ 51-271), offers excursions, usually guided by Warren Jopling, a retired Australian geologist who has lived on the island many years. I went with Warren recently and found him to be a font of information, especially about the desertlike lava fields. He will tailor any tour to suit your interests. It will take a full day to see most of the sights, with half the day spent going along the east and north coasts, the other half along the south shore. Each half-day tour costs US$35 with lunch, US$20 without lunch.

In addition to its two- and three-day round-island expeditions, **Eco-Tour Samoa** (☎ 25-993 or 25-323 in Apia) offers two day trips, one to the Satoalepai Wetlands and one to the Mount Matavanu Craters. The wetlands trip costs U.S. $15 per person; the more difficult trip up Mount Matavanu costs U.S. $40 per person.

THE EAST AND NORTH COASTS

Leaving the Safua Hotel, the east coast road soon passes a memorial to the Rev. John Williams, then goes up a rise to **Tuasivi,** the administrative center of the island and site of the hospital and police station. From there it drops down to **Faga** and **Siufaga,** two long, gorgeous beaches. Many villages along this stretch have bathing pools fed by fresh water running underground down from the mountains. Only the south side of Savai'i has rivers and streams. Rainwater seeps into the porous volcanic rock elsewhere and reappears as springs along the shoreline.

Mount Matavanu last erupted between 1905 and 1911, when it sent a long lava flow down to the northeast coast, burying villages and gardens before backing up behind the reef. Today the desertlike **Matavanu lava field** is populated primarily by primitive ferns. The flow very nearly inundated the village of **Mauga,** which sits along the rim of an extinct volcano's cone. The villagers, who play cricket on the crater floor, charge WS$5 ($2) per vehicle to look around their fertile outpost in this barren black plain. Past Mauga there is the **Virgin's Grave,** a hole left around a grave when the lava almost covered a nearby church. The steeple still sticks out of the twisted black mass. It will cost another WS$5 ($2) to visit the grave.

The north-coast road past the lava fields is picturesque but holds little of interest other than gorgeous tropical scenery. A drink at **Le Lagoto Bar,** between Fagamalo and Lelepa, or lunch at **Stevenson's at Manase,** just west of Manase village, makes a nice refueling stop if you get that far (see "Where to Stay & Dine," below).

The paved road goes on Safune, halfway along the north shore. From there a rough road crosses the lava fields caused by a 1760 eruption to Asau, but all north-shore buses end at Safune.

THE SOUTH COAST

On the south coast near Vailoa, on the Letolo Plantation, stands the ancient **Pulemelei Mound,** a collection of rocks similar to the ceremonial temples, or maraes, in French Polynesia and the Cook Islands. It's the largest archaeological ruin in Polynesia: A 2-tiered pyramid 240 feet long, 193 feet wide, and 48 feet high. This one is so old, however, that the Samoans no longer have legends explaining their original function. The side road, which passes Afu'a'au Waterfall, ends some 1¹/₂ miles from the mound. A steep and often muddy track leads down to the waterfall.

From the mounds, the south-coast road continues to Gautavai Waterfall, a lovely black-sand beach at Nu'u, and geyser-like blowholes at Taga on the island's southernmost point.

WHERE TO STAY & DINE

Like Upolu, Savai'i has seen a growth of beach fales during the past few years. The pick here is Kuki and Sara Retzlaff's **Le Lagoto Beach Fales,** P.O. Box 34, Fagamalo (☎ 24-325), on the north coast between Fagamalo and Lelepa village. The Retzlaffs have four cottage-like fales equipped with double beds, mosquito nets, toaster ovens, refrigerators, fans, and shower-only baths. Although simple, they are comfortable, and they have beautiful sunset views from their beachside perches *(lagoto* means sunset in Samoan). Sara will prepare meals at Le Lagoto Bar next door. They charge U.S. $55 a night per bungalow and accept MasterCard and Visa credit cards.

Safua Hotel

Private Bag, Salelologa, Savai'i (in Safua village, 4 miles north of wharf). ☎ **51-271.** Fax 51-272. 10 fales (all with bath). U.S. **$88.** Rates include three meals. No credit cards.

This somewhat rustic hotel is known not so much for the quality of its accommodations as for its owner, Moelagi Jackson, who holds two chiefly titles in her own right. Her main fale holds a bar and dining room, where family-style meals feature Samoan favorites such as chicken curry and whole fish in ginger. The fales scattered about her lawn are of clapboard construction, with front porches, screened windows, basic electric lights, and baths with cold-water showers. Don't be surprised to hear a cat fight or the grunts of pigs running loose at night. The Safua will arrange village accommodation for U.S. $25 per person, including meals.

The Savaiian Hotel

P.O. Box 5082, Salelologa, Savai'i (in Safua village, 4 miles north of ferry wharf). ☎ **51-296** or 51-206. Fax 51-291. 6 rms (all with bath). A/C. WS$115 ($46) double. No credit cards.

Opened in 1992, this lagoonside establishment is the most modern and up-to-date accommodation on Savai'i. There's a restaurant here, and the Safua Hotel is virtually across the road. A large main building often hosts official functions on weekend evenings (the owner was serving as Western Samoa's prime minister when I was there recently). The six identical rooms are in three duplex, concrete block structures with peaked tin roofs. They all have sliding doors opening to porches with views of the lagoon. They come with double beds, kitchenettes, and adequate shower-only baths with hot water.

Siufaga Beach Resort

P.O. Box 8002, Tuasive, Savai'i (in Faga village, 8 miles north of ferry wharf). ☎ **53-518.** Fax 53-535. 6 bungalows (all with bath). U.S. $40 double. No credit cards.

Dr. Peter Cafarelli, an Italian who has lived on Savai'i since the late 1960s, actually owns the seven acres of lawn under his six Samoan-style fales facing Faga Beach and an emerald lagoon speckled with coral heads. Guests can sit under an open fale and enjoy the view. Although somewhat basic, the tin-roofed guest fales are cooled by the trade winds (they have electric fans just in case). Each has a kitchenette equipped with a small refrigerator and hotplate (the village store is next door). Only two of the fales have hot water coming from their shower-only baths.

Stevenson's at Manase

P.O. Box 210, Apia (at Manase village, 30 miles north of ferry wharf). ☎ **58-219.** Fax 58-219 or 24-166. 19 rms (all with bath). A/C. U.S. $55 room; U.S. $30 dorm bed. MC, V.

Situated on a lovely beach just west of Manase village, this establishment boasts two stunning thatch-roofed, sawdust-floored buildings holding Fanny's Restaurant and the Admiral Benbow Bar. Unfortunately the small, basic, motel-style rooms don't hold up their end of the South Seas charm quotient. They almost appear to be constructed of surplus shipping containers, and their mat-lined walls and outdoor showers don't overcome this first impression. Backpackers can share beach fales on a dormitory basis. Stevenson's is a popular local beach on weekends. (The Stevenson here actually is owner Trevor Stevenson, an Apia lawyer who was born in New Zealand.)

Vaisala Hotel

P.O. Box 570, Apia (at Vaisala, 55 miles from ferry wharf). ☎ **53-111** on Savai'i or 22-557 on Apia. Fax 23-396. 27 rms (18 with bath). U.S. $58. AE, MC, V.

This Samoan-owned hotel has a lovely location on a hill overlooking a white sandy beach and Vaisala Bay near Asau. Manager Papu Vaal has 18 rooms with their own kitchenettes, bathrooms, and tea- and coffee-making facilities, and nine rooms that share common toilets and showers. One of the two bars stays open all day and evening. A restaurant on a long balcony overlooking the bay serves three meals a day. The Vaisala rents vans for tours of the island, with the cost depending on the number of persons going along.

14 American Samoa

Contrasts between Western Samoa and American Samoa become evident on the seven-mile ride from the airport at Tafuna into Pago Pago. Instead of following a gentle shoreline like the west coast road on Upolu, here it twists and turns along a gorgeous rocky coastline of one of the South Pacific's most dramatically beautiful islands, Tutuila. At places it rounds the cliffs of headlands that come down to the sea; at others it curves along beaches in small bays backed by narrow valleys. All the way, the surf pounds on the reef. When you make the last turn at Blount's Point, there before you are the green walls of fabled Pago Pago Harbor. The physical beauty of this little island competes with the splendor of Moorea and Bora Bora in French Polynesia.

But you notice right away that this is an American place, for the roads are crowded with automobiles and buses, and you may well hit a traffic jam before you get into Pago Pago. Big police cruisers, their drivers bedecked with revolvers, patrol the streets. A huge, air-conditioned shopping warehouse, which could be in Honolulu or Los Angeles, sits in marked contrast to the small shops and clapboard stores in other South Pacific countries, including Western Samoa just 80 miles to the west. Only the slightly dilapidated old shops in Pago Pago remain from the South Seas of yesteryear. The view across the fabled harbor toward two smelly tuna canneries is obscured in places by a veritable mountain of rusting shipping containers. It's little wonder many visitors see American Samoa as ruined by modern commercialism—as crowded, littered, seedy, run-down.

Yet others find charm in its blend of American and Samoan cultures, for despite the inroads of Western ways, the local residents still hang on to *fa'a Samoa,* the ancient Samoan way of life. While many young American Samoans wear Western clothes and speak only English—with a pronounced Hawaiian or Californian accent—out in the villages the older folk still speak Samoan and abide by the old ways.

For information about the early history of the Samoas, the unique culture of the islands, and the common Samoan language, see Chapter 13, "Western Samoa."

Advice: The Samoan culture is best experienced in Western Samoa. The main attraction of American Samoa is its great natural beauty, which can easily be seen on a day trip from Western Samoa.

Given the territory's lack of suitable accommodation, plan to stay in Apia and make Pago Pago a possible excursion.

1 American Samoa Today

The seven islands of American Samoa are located on the eastern end of the 300-mile-long Samoan Archipelago. Together they comprise a land area of 77 square miles, 53 of which are on **Tutuila**, the slender remains of an ancient volcano. One side of Tutuila's crater apparently blew away, almost cutting the island in two. Thus was created the long, bent arm of Pago Pago Harbor, one of the South Pacific's most dramatically scenic spots.

American Samoa is the only United States territory south of the equator. Legally, it is an "unincorporated territory," meaning that certain provisions of the U.S. Constitution may be subservient to those of the treaties under which the U.S. governs the islands. For example, ownership of most land is restricted to persons of American Samoan ancestry. If American Samoa were a state, such a racially discriminatory restriction would be on shaky Constitutional grounds.

American Samoans are nationals, not citizens, of the United States. They often refer to the islands—not to the United States—as their "country." Although they carry American passports, have unrestricted entry into the U.S., and can serve in the U.S. armed forces, they cannot vote in American presidential elections.

At the present time, only half as many American Samoans live in their home islands as reside in the U.S., where a number of them have made names for themselves as college and professional football players. They have been replaced at home by Western Samoans and some Tongans, who have swelled the population to some 55,000, up from 30,000 just a few years ago.

Government   The United States Department of the Interior in Washington has jurisdiction over American Samoa, but the territory has considerable say over its local affairs. The territorial government is patterned on that of the United States, with some important local wrinkles. In addition to an executive branch and the courts, there's a bicameral legislature known as the Fono. Members of the Fono's lower House of Representatives are elected by universal suffrage, while senators are chosen in accordance with Samoan custom by the matais. Although both the Interior Department and the governor have veto power over the laws it passes, the Fono has authority over the budget and local affairs. Local government is organized by counties and villages under a secretary of Samoan affairs, a position traditionally held by a ranking matai. The High Court of American Samoa has a special branch that deals exclusively with landownership and matai titles.

American Samoans choose their leaders every four years. They also elect a nonvoting delegate to the U.S. House of Representatives.

The American Samoan government's annual budget is considerably larger than that of Western Samoa, which has a population four times larger than American

Impressions

The melancholy irony of this smug little island is that American Samoa epitomises the state of comfortable dependence on cash and Western goods to which so many aspire.
                                                                            —John Dyson, 1982

Samoa's. It receives about half its revenue from the U.S. federal government, but like its counterpart in Washington, still manages to run in the red. Some 80% of the taxes raised locally go to pay about 46% of the local work force.

Economy   Federal aid money from Washington and the tuna canneries in Pago Pago are the major sources of income. The canneries employ some 4,000 workers, most of them Western Samoans, and produce about $300 million of canned fish a year. They have faced increased competition from Asian canneries in recent years, however, and lower protective tariffs have reduced their advantage in selling to the U.S. mainland. How much longer they will continue to operate was in question at presstime.

Most other workers are employed by retail establishments, a few small manufacturers, and service businesses, especially shipping companies, which have made Pago Pago a major trans-shipment point (the Budweiser beer sold in Western Samoa and Tonga is shipped through Pago Pago).

With so many American Samoans living in the U.S. rather than in their home islands, at least a third of the work force is made up of Western Samoans, Tongans, and other Pacific Islanders who have come to Pago Pago to take their place and to earn much higher incomes than at home. For example, minimum wages in American Samoa are about $3 an hour, nearly triple those in Western Samoa.

2   A Look at the Past

As friendly as American Samoans are today, their ancestors did anything but warmly welcome a French expedition under Jean La Pérouse, which came ashore in 1787 on the north coast of Tutuila. Samoan warriors promptly attacked, killing some 12 members of the landing party, which in turn killed 39 Samoans. The site of the battle is known as Massacre Bay. La Pérouse survived that incident, but he and his entire expedition later disappeared in what is now Solomon Islands.

Even before the Germans attempted to make Western Samoa one of the Kaiser's colonies a century later, American businessmen cast an eye on Pago Pago. The U.S. Navy negotiated a treaty with the chiefs of Tutuila in 1872 to permit the U.S. to use Pago Pago as a coaling station. The U.S. Congress never ratified this document, but it helped keep the Germans out of Eastern Samoa, as present-day American Samoa was then known.

In 1900, the U.S. entered into a treaty with the chiefs on Tutuila, who ceded control of their island. Another five years went by before the Tu'i Manu'a, the paramount chief of the Manu'a Group of islands east of Tutuila, entered into a similar agreement. The Tu'i Manu'a was so distraught over what he had done that he willed that his title go to the grave with him. To this day it has not been revived.

Finally ratified by the U.S. Senate in 1929, those treaties are the legal foundation for the U.S. presence in American Samoa. "Presence" is the accurate term, for under those treaties the U.S. does not "possess" American Samoa as it does, say, the U.S. Virgin Islands, which it literally bought from Denmark during World War I. Instead, the U.S. is present in American Samoa subject to the conditions of the treaties, one of the most important of which is a U.S. obligation to preserve the system of matais and to retain the traditional ways of fa'a Samoa, including the communal ownership of Samoan land.

Unfriendly Fire

Except during World War II, the United States Navy did very little during its half century in control of American Samoa. When the war with Japan broke out, Tutuila became a major forward training base for the U.S. Marine Corps. The Marines installed shore batteries in the hills above the entrance to Pago Pago Harbor and built concrete pillboxes along Tutuila's shoreline. Many of them can be seen still standing.

Thousands of American Samoans joined the Marines during the war, and thousands of others formed a home guard militia. Enlisting in the United States armed services—especially the Marines—is to this day considered an honorable undertaking for American Samoans.

The home guard militia had only one chance to see action during World War II. That occurred when a Japanese submarine surfaced offshore and lobbed a few shells toward Tutuila. Ironically, their target was a store owned by Frank Shimasaki, the island's only resident of Japanese descent.

Anchors Aweigh   Unlike Western Samoa, which has ample land suitable for large copra plantations, the American islands are small, rugged, and comparatively unproductive. There was little reason, therefore, for American planters to invade or for the U.S. government to take much interest in the islands except to keep a coaling station at Pago Pago.

From 1900 until 1951, American authority in Samoa rested with the U.S. Navy, which maintained the refueling station at Pago Pago and for the most part left the local chiefs alone to conduct their own affairs in their own fashion. Tutuila became a training base for U.S. servicemen during World War II, but things quickly returned to normal after 1945. The islands lost their global strategic value during the Cold War, and control of the territory was shifted from the navy to the U.S. Department of the Interior. American Samoa now has little military value to the United States.

On the Dole   The Interior Department did little to change things in American Samoa until 1961, when *Reader's Digest* ran a well-publicized article about "America's Shame in the South Seas." The story took great offense at the lack of roads and adequate schools, medical care, water and sewer service, and housing. What the magazine actually described was a virtually untouched Polynesian society, complete with thatch houses, subsistence farming, smiling faces, and few motor vehicles. By contemporary American standards, that was a "shame."

The U.S. federal government reacted by building sealed roads, an airstrip capable of handling intercontinental airliners, water and electrical systems, the modern Rainmaker Hotel and nearby convention center, and revamping the school system. A mile-long cable was strung across Pago Pago Harbor to build a television transmitter atop 1,610-foot Mount Alava, from which education programming was beamed into the schools. The territory's duty-free status and relatively low wages enticed American firms to build the two tuna canneries at Pago Pago. More money came in the form of Great Society social programs.

For fear of losing all that federal money, American Samoans were reluctant to tinker with their political relationship with Washington during the 1960s and

1970s, when other South Pacific colonies were becoming independent. The United States offered to let them have local autonomy, but they refused. That attitude finally changed in the mid-1970s, when an appointed governor turned out to be very unpopular. After twice previously having turned down the proposal, American Samoans voted in 1976 to elect their own governor, and in 1977 chose Peter Tali Coleman, a federal official of part-Samoan descent and a former appointed governor of the territory.

3 Visitor Information & Entry Requirements

VISITOR INFORMATION

The **American Samoan Office of Tourism,** P.O. Box 1147, Pago Pago, AS 96799 (☎ 633-1091, fax 633-1094), has offices next to the High Court. They also act as booking agents for the *Fale, Fala Ma Ti,* or homestay program (see "Where to Stay," below).

The Delegate from American Samoa to the U.S. Congress also dispenses some tourist information. The address is U.S. House of Representatives, Washington, D.C. 20515 (☎ 202/225-8577).

ENTRY REQUIREMENTS

Visas are not required for stays of up to 30 days. Technically, U.S. citizens need only proof of citizenship (such as a birth certificate) to enter American Samoa. They will need valid passports to enter Western Samoa, however, and having them speeds reentry into the U.S. Citizens of other nations must have passports to enter American Samoa. Everyone must possess a ticket for onward passage.

Immunizations are required only if a person has been in an infected yellow fever or cholera area within 14 days of arrival at Pago Pago.

Customs allowances (you pay no duty) are one gallon of liquor or wine and either 200 cigarettes, 50 cigars, or one pound of tobacco. Illegal drugs and firearms are prohibited, and pets will be quarantined. Returning American citizens get larger customs allowances for purchases made in American Samoa, provided they have been in the territory for at least 48 hours. See "Best Buys" in Chapter 1, "The Best of the South Pacific."

4 Money

U.S. bank notes and coins are used in American Samoa. Western Samoan currency is not accepted, nor can it be exchanged in American Samoa. There is no bargaining over prices.

How to Get Local Currency   The Bank of Hawaii and the Amerika Samoa Bank in Fagatogo are open Monday to Friday from 9am to 3pm. Transacting business with them is virtually the same as doing business with a bank on the U.S. mainland. You can get cash advances against your MasterCard or Visa cards at the banks. The Bank of Hawaii has an ATM machine mounted on the sidewalk outside its office.

Credit Cards   American Express, Visa, MasterCard, and Diners Club credit cards are accepted by the hotels, car-rental firms, and airlines. Otherwise, it's best to carry enough cash to cover your anticipated expenses.

What Things Cost in American Samoa	U.S. $
Taxi from airport to Pago Pago	10.00
Room at Motu O Fiafianga (moderate)	60.00
Room at Herb & Sia's Motel (inexpensive)	45.00
Lunch for one at Pago Pago Bay Restaurant (moderate)	12.00
Lunch for one at Pizza Time (inexpensive)	7.00
Dinner for one at Sadie's Restaurant (expensive)	40.00
Dinner for one at Pago Pago Bay Restaurant (moderate)	24.00
Dinner for one at Pizza Time (inexpensive)	9.00
Beer	3.00
Coca-Cola	.85
Roll of ASA 100 Kodacolor film, 36 exposures	6.00

5 When to Go

"It did not pour, it flowed," wrote W. Somerset Maugham in his 1921 short story "Rain," the famous tale of prostitute Sadie Thompson, who seduces a puritanical missionary while stranded in American Samoa. This description, however, applies mainly to Pago Pago, which, because of its location behind appropriately named Rainmaker Mountain, gets an average of over 200 inches of rain per year. For the most part, American Samoa enjoys a typically tropical climate, with lots of very intense sunshine even during the wet season from December to April. Average daily high temperatures range from 83°F in the drier and somewhat cooler months of June through September to 86°F from December to April, when midday can be hot and sticky. Evenings are usually in the comfortable 70s all year round.

EVENTS & HOLIDAYS

The biggest celebration is on April 17, when **Flag Day** commemorates the raising of the Stars and Stripes over Tutuila in 1900. The second Sunday in October is observed as **White Sunday,** when children attend church dressed in white and later are honored at family feasts.

American Samoa observes the normal U.S. holidays plus one big one of its own: New Year's Day, President's Day (the third Monday in February), Good Friday, Flag Day (April 17), Memorial Day (the last Monday in May), the Fourth of July, Labor Day (the first Monday in September), Columbus Day (the second Monday in October), Veteran's Day (November 11), Thanksgiving (the fourth Thursday of November), and Christmas Day.

6 Getting There & Getting Around

GETTING THERE

From Western Samoa   Some travel agents in Apia offer packages for day trips from Western Samoa to Pago Pago. For example, **Oceania Tours** (☎ 24-443 in Apia) offers one-day tours for $190 per person, including round-trip airfare, a guided tour of Pago Pago, and lunch. Oceania Tours' offices are on Beach Road, on the Mulinu'u Peninsula in Apia.

Polynesian Airlines (☎ 21-261 in Apia, or 633-4331 in Pago Pago) and **Samoa Air** (☎ 22-321 or 22-901 in Apia, 633-4331 in Pago Pago) both shuttle back and forth between Fagali'i Airstrip near Apia and Pago Pago several times a day. Round-trip fares on both airlines are WS$176 ($70) if purchased in Apia, $95 if bought in American Samoa. In other words, thanks to an exchange rate of better than two-to-one for the Western Samoan tala against the U.S. dollar, it is less expensive to fly from Apia to Pago Pago and return than the other way around. That's one more reason to make your Samoan base in Apia.

For the adventurous, a relatively modern **ferry,** the *Queen Salamasina,* makes the eight-hour voyage between Pago Pago and Apia once a week, usually leaving the main wharf in Apia about 10pm on Wednesday and departing Pago Pago's marine terminal the following afternoon. Tickets should be bought at least a day ahead of time. One-way fare is WS$30 ($12) if purchased in Apia but $20 in Pago Pago. The *Queen Salamasina* is operated by the Western Samoa Shipping Corporation, whose ticket office is at the corner of Vaea and Convent Streets in Apia (☎ 20-935). The American Samoa agent is Polynesia Shipping Services (☎ 633-1211), whose office is opposite Sadie's Restaurant in Pago Pago. Since the trade winds prevail from the southeast, the trip going west with the wind toward Apia is usually somewhat smoother.

From Other Countries   The only international carrier serving American Samoa at presstime was **Hawaiian Airlines,** which flew from several West Coast cities to Pago Pago, with a change of planes at its base at Honolulu. Otherwise, you can fly to Faleolo Airport in Western Samoa on **Air New Zealand, Air Pacific,** or **Polynesian Airlines,** then connect on to Pago Pago. For more information, see "Getting There" in Chapter 3.

GETTING AROUND

The runways at **Pago Pago** International Airport extend for half their length on landfills over the reef near the village of Tafuna, about seven miles west of The Rainmaker Hotel. Taxi fare is $10 from the airport to Pago Pago. Local buses shuttle along the Tafuna road, which is about a half-mile from the terminal. The bus fare to town is 50¢.

There is no departure tax on passengers leaving Pago Pago.

BY RENTAL CAR   The only international car-rental firm in American Samoa is **Avis** (☎ 699-4408, or 800/331-1212), which rents air-conditioned cars for $50 a day including unlimited mileage, plus $8 for insurance. The Avis office in Apia (☎ 20-486) will reserve a car in Pago Pago for you. Local firms include **Royal Samoan Car Rental** (☎ 633-2017 or 633-4545) and **Pavitt's** U-Drive (☎ 633-1456).

Driving Rules: Your valid home driver's license will be honored in American Samoa. Driving is on the right-hand side of the road, and traffic signs are the same as those used in the U.S. Speed limits are 15 m.p.h. in the built-up areas and 25 m.p.h. on the open road.

BY BUS   It sometimes seems that every extended family on Tutuila owns an "aiga bus," since so many of these gaily painted vehicles prowl the roads from early in the morning until sunset every day except Sunday, when they are put to use to haul

Pago Pago

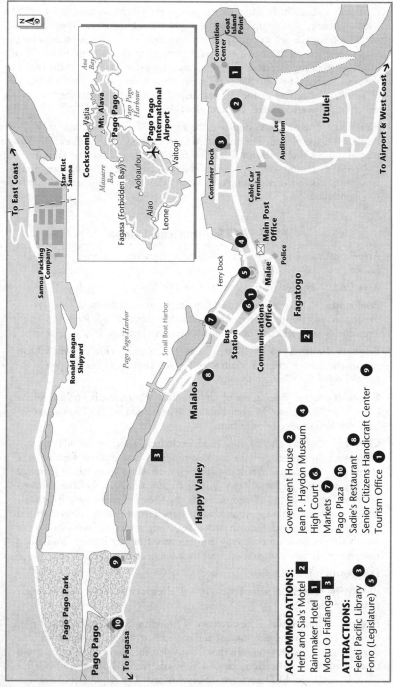

ACCOMMODATIONS:

Herb and Sia's Motel **2**
Rainmaker Hotel **1**
Motu O Fiafianga **3**

ATTRACTIONS:

Feleti Pacific Library **3**
Fono (Legislature) **5**
Government House **2**
Jean P. Haydon Museum **4**
High Court **6**
Markets **7**
Pago Plaza **10**
Sadie's Restaurant **8**
Senior Citizens Handicraft Center **9**
Tourism Office **1**

6091

the family to church. Basically they run from the villages to the market in Pago Pago and back, picking up anyone who waves along the way. To get off, push the button for the bell as you approach your destination. Some buses leave the market and run to Fagasa on the north coast or to the east end of the island; others go from the market to the west. None goes from one end of the island to the other, so you'll have to change at the market in order to do a stem-to-stern tour of Tutuila. The drivers are friendly and helpful, so just ask how far they go in each direction. Fares are between 25¢ and $1 a ride.

BY TAXI　There are **taxi stands** at the airport (☎ 699-1179) and at the Pago Pago market (no phone). The taxi companies are **Aeto Cab** (☎ 633-2366), **Black Ace** (☎ 633-5445), **Island Taxi** (☎ 633-5645), and **Samoa Cab Service** (☎ 633-5870 or 633-5871). None of the taxis has a meter, so be sure to negotiate the fare before driving off. As a starting point for your discussions, the fares should be about $1 a mile.

FAST FACTS: American Samoa

American Express　There is no American Express representative in American Samoa.

Area Code　The international country code is 684.

Bookstores　Transpac, in Nu'uli Shopping Center on the main road west of the airport, and the gift shop in The Rainmaker Hotel in Pago Pago both carry a reasonably wide selection of paperback books and current U.S. magazines.

Business Hours　Normal shopping hours are Monday to Friday from 8:30am to 5pm and Saturday from 8:30am to noon. Government offices are open Monday to Friday from 7:30am to 4pm.

Camera/Film　A wide variety of film is available at reasonable prices. Samoa Photo Express, opposite the Fono building in Fagatogo (☎ 633-2374), has one-hour developing of color print film.

Clothing　Lightweight, informal summer clothing is appropriate all year, with perhaps a light sweater or wrap for evenings from June through September. I always carry a folding umbrella or plastic raincoat, since it can rain any time of the day or night in Pago Pago. Young American Samoans have adopted Western-style dress, including blue jeans and shorts of respectable length, although the traditional wraparound lavalava still is worn by many older men and women. In keeping with Samoan custom regarding modesty, visitors should not wear bathing suits or other skimpy clothing away from the hotels. This is not a French territory, so women must wear their bikini tops.

Drugstores　See "Hospital," below.

Electricity　American Samoa uses 110-volt electric current and plugs identical to those in the U.S.

Embassies/Consulates　The governor of American Samoa is a consular official of the U.S. federal government and can issue temporary passports to U.S. citizens and nationals who lose theirs, provided they have some other proof of citizenship. Applications should be made to the Immigration Office (☎ 633-4203), in the Department of Legal Affairs. The Republic of Korea has a consulate, and the Republic of China (Taiwan) maintains a liaison office in

Pago Pago, primarily to assist the Korean and Taiwanese crews of the tuna boats unloading their catches at the tuna canneries.

Emergencies The emergency telephone number for the police, fire department, and ambulance is 911. The emergency room at the Lyndon B. Johnson Tropical Medical Center (☎ 633-5555) in Faga'alu is open 24 hours a day.

Firearms They are tightly controlled, and permits will be required.

Gambling There are no casinos or other organized forms of gambling in American Samoa except for slot machines in some stores and private clubs. Money also is wagered at very popular bingo games.

Hospital The Lyndon B. Johnson Tropical Medical Center in Faga'alu west of Pago Pago (turn off the main road at Tom Ho Chung's store) may be a classic example of socialized medicine, but it's one of the better hospitals in the South Pacific. The outpatient clinic is open 24 hours a day. The medical center's main phone number is 633-1222. The emergency line is 633-5555.

Insects There are no dangerous insects in American Samoa, and the plentiful mosquitoes do not carry malaria.

Libraries Feleti Pacific Library, north of The Rainmaker Hotel, has a good collection of books about the South Pacific.

Liquor Laws There are no unusual laws to worry about. Most of the beer consumed is imported from the U.S.

Maps The American Samoa Office of Tourism distributes a one-sheet set of maps of the islands.

Newspapers/Magazines American Samoa has two tabloid newspapers that carry local news: the weekly *Samoa Journal* and the daily *Samoa News*. Both papers' coverage of local events can be quite colorful. See "Bookstores," above.

Post Office The United States Postal Service's main post office is in Fagatogo. U.S. postage rates apply, which means that your first-class letters will go to the U.S. via air for 32¢. Unless you pay the first-class priority mail rate, parcel post is sent by ship and will take several weeks to reach the U.S. The main post office is open Monday to Friday from 8am to 4pm and Saturday from 8am to noon. The ZIP Code for American Samoa is 96799.

Radio/TV Those transmitters atop Mount Alava are used during the day to send educational TV programs to the territory's public schools and to transmit CNN and live sporting events. At night they broadcast three channels of U.S. network entertainment programs that were taped a week earlier off the Honolulu stations and flown to Pago Pago (you may already have seen the same shows at home). The broadcasts can be seen 80 miles away in Western Samoa.

The territory has one FM and one AM radio station, both of which transmit American network news broadcasts on the hour.

Safety Street crime is not a serious problem in American Samoa except late at night around Pago Pago Harbor. Fa'a Samoa and its rules of communal ownership are still in effect, however, so it's wise not to leave cameras, watches, or other valuables lying around unattended.

Taxes The government of American Samoa charges no sales tax; however, an import tax of 5% is imposed on most merchandise (it's much stiffer on tobacco and alcoholic beverages). There is no airport departure tax.

Telephone/Telex/Fax   Telephone calls can be dialed directly into American Samoa from most parts of the world. The international country code is 684.

The local telephone system is identical to that in the U.S. The pay telephones are the same type used in phone booths throughout the U.S. The number for directory assistance is 411. For emergencies, dial 911.

Visitors can place overseas calls from the International Communications Office, which is diagonally across the Fagatogo *malae* (village green) from the Fono building. Station-to-station calls to the U.S. mainland cost about $7 for the first three minutes and $1 for each additional minute. The office accepts AT&T credit cards, or you can pay cash in advance or reverse the charges.

Time   Local time in American Samoa is 11 hours behind Greenwich mean time. That's three hours behind Pacific standard time (four hours behind during Daylight Saving Time). In other words, if it's noon standard time in California and 3pm in New York, it's 9am in Pago Pago. If daylight saving time is in effect, it's 8am in American Samoa. American Samoa is east of the international date line and shares the same date with North America, one day behind Tonga, Fiji, Australia, and New Zealand.

Tipping   Although this is an American territory, there is no tipping in American Samoa.

Weights and Measures   American Samoa is the only country or territory in the South Pacific whose official system of weights and measures is the same as that used in the U.S.: pounds and miles, not kilograms and kilometers.

7 What to See & Do

SEEING TUTUILA

As a Day Trip from Apia   In brief, here's how to see American Samoa in one day as a side trip from Western Samoa. Fly early in the morning from Fagali'i Airstrip in Apia to Pago Pago, then ride a taxi to The Rainmaker Hotel. Take the walking tour of Pago Pago described below, then stop for lunch. If you haven't rented a car, grab an aiga bus at the market for a ride out to the east end, followed by another bus ride to the west end. On the way back, you can get off and call a taxi, catch a Tafuna aiga bus, or walk the 1½ miles from the main road to the airport for a late-afternoon return flight to Apia.

See "Getting There & Getting Around," above, for information about Apia travel agents' day trips.

A WALKING TOUR OF PAGO PAGO

Although the actual village of Pago Pago sits at the head of the harbor, everyone refers to the built-up area on the south shore of the harbor, including Fagatogo, the government and business center, as Pago Pago. The harbor is also called the Bay Area. Despite development that has come with economic growth of the territory, Pago Pago still has much of the old South Seas atmosphere that captivated W. Somerset Maugham when he visited and wrote "Rain" in the 1920s.

We'll begin our tour at **The Rainmaker Hotel** on the east end of the inner harbor, actually in the village of Utulei. Just across the main road from the hotel, a set of concrete steps climbs to **Government House,** the clapboard mansion built in 1903 to house the governor of American Samoa. Unless you have business with the governor, the mansion is not open to the public. There is a nice view, however, from the top of the steps looking back over the hotel and across the harbor to flat-top Rainmaker Mountain.

Back on the main road heading north toward town, we pass a mountain of shipping containers standing idle on the main wharf before we reach **Feleti Pacific Library,** which has a good collection of books on the South Pacific. Beyond the busy port terminal is the **Jean P. Haydon Museum,** featuring exhibits on Samoan history, sea life, canoes, kava making, and traditional tools and handcrafts, including the finely woven mats that have such great value in Samoa and Tonga. The old iron-roofed building housing the museum was once the U.S. Navy's commissary. The museum is open Monday to Friday from 10am to 3pm, except on holidays. Admission is free.

Every Samoan village has a **malae,** or open field, and the area across from the museum is Fagatogo's. The chiefs of Tutuila met on this malae in 1900 to sign the treaty that officially established the U.S. in Samoa. The round modern building across the road beside the harbor is the **Fono,** American Samoa's legislature; the visitors' galleries are open to the public. The ramshackle stores along the narrow streets on the other side of the malae were for half a century Pago Pago's "downtown," although like any other place under the Stars and Stripes, much business now is conducted in suburban shopping centers. On the malae, the **American Samoa Archives Office** occupies the old stone jail built in 1911.

Just beyond the malae on the main road, the big white clapboard building with columns, which from its colonial style looks as if it should be in South Carolina rather than the South Pacific, is the **Judicial Building,** home of the High Court of American Samoa (everyone calls it the Court House). Across the road on the waterfront stands **Fagatogo Plaza,** a modern shopping center anchored by Ted of Samoa's department store. In marked contrast are the **produce and fish markets** a few yards farther on. They usually are poorly stocked, and when they do have produce, it most likely comes by ferry from Western Samoa. The markets also serve as the bus terminal.

Continuing north along the harbor, we soon come to the **Sadie Thompson Building,** a large wooden structure now housing Sadie's Restaurant and the Transpac store. This was the rooming house where W. Somerset Maugham was marooned during a measles epidemic early in this century. It provided the grist for his famous short story "Rain."

The Oriental-style building across the playing fields at the head of the harbor may look like a Chinese restaurant, but in reality it is **Korea House,** a hospitality center for the Korean sailors who man many of the boats that bring tuna to the canneries. The canneries are in the large, industrial buildings on the north side of the harbor at the base of Mount Alava. No need to go around there; turn around and repeat your steps.

TOURING TUTUILA

The North Coast An unmarked paved road turns off the main highway at Spenser's Store in Pago Pago village and leads up **Vaipito Valley,** across a ridge, and down to Fagasa, a village huddled beside picturesque Fagasa, or **Forbidden**

Bay, on Tutuila's north shore. The road is steep but paved all the way, and the view from atop the ridge is excellent. The track up Mt. Alava begins on the saddle (see "Hiking," below). Legend says that porpoises long ago led a group of three men and three women to safety in Fagasa Bay, which has long been a porpoise sanctuary.

The East Side   The 18-mile drive from Pago Pago to the east end of Tutuila skirts along the harbor, past the canneries and their fishy odor, and then winds around one headland after another into small bays, many of them with sandy beaches and good swimming holes over the reef. Watch particularly for **Pyramid Rock** and the **Lion's Head,** where you can wade out to a small beach.

From Aua, at the foot of Rainmaker Mountain, a switch-backing road runs across Rainmaker Pass (great views from up there) to the lovely north shore village of **Vatia,** on a bay of the same name. World War II pillboxes still dot the beach here. At the north end of Vatia Bay sits the skinny, offshore rock formation known as **The Cockscomb,** one of Tutuila's trademarks.

Another paved road leaves Faga'itua village and climbs to a saddle in the ridge, where it divides. The left fork goes down to Masefau Bay; the right goes to Masausi and Sa'ilele villages. Near the east end, a road from Amouli village cuts across Lemafa Saddle to **Aoa Bay** on the north coast.

Aunu'u Island will be visible from the main road as you near the east end of Tutuila. Aunu'u is the top of a small volcanic crater and has a village near a famous quicksand pit. Motorboats leave for it from the small-boat harbor at Au'asi on the southeast coast.

Alao and **Tula** villages on the east end of Tutuila are the oldest settlements in American Samoa. They have long, gorgeous surf beaches, but be careful of the undertow from waves driven by the prevailing southeast trade winds.

The West Side   You probably saw some of Tutuila's rugged coast on the drive in from the airport west of Pago Pago, including the **Flower Pot,** a tall rock with coconut palms growing on its top sitting in the lagoon. About halfway from the airport to the Rainmaker Hotel is a road inland (at Tom Ho Chung's store) leading to the **Lyndon B. Johnson Tropical Medical Center** in the Faga'alu Valley. If you feel like a hike, take the left fork in the road past the medical center, and when the pavement ends, follow the track to **Virgin Falls.** It's not the easiest walk, but the falls have a nice pool beneath them. Give yourself several hours for this sweaty outing.

The **airport** sits on the island's only sizable parcel of relatively flat land, and the main road from there west cuts through rolling hills and shopping centers until emerging on the rugged west end.

At Pava'ia'i village a road goes inland and climbs to the village of A'oloaufou, high on a central plateau. A hiking trail leads from the village down the ridges to the north coast; from here it drops to A'asutuai on **Massacre Bay,** where Samoans attacked the La Pérouse expedition in 1787. The French have put a monument there to the members of the expedition slain by Samoan warriors.

Back on the main road, head west and watch for a sign on the left marking the turn to the villages of Illi'ili and Vaitogi. Follow the signs to **Vaitogi,** and once in the village, bear right at the fork to the beach. Take the one-lane track to the right along the beach, past some graves and the stone remains of an old church, and up a rocky headland through pandanus groves. When you reach the first clearing on the left, stop the car and walk over to the cliff. According to legend, Vaitogi once experienced such a severe famine that a blind old woman and her granddaughter jumped off this cliff and were turned into a shark and a turtle. Today the villagers reputedly can chant their names and the turtle and the shark will appear. You may not be lucky enough to see them, but the view of the south coast from **Turtle and Shark Point,** with the surf pounding the rocks below you, is superb.

The picturesque village of **Leone,** which sits on a white sand beach in a small bay, was chosen by the Rev. John Williams as his landing place on Tutuila in 1830, and it became the cradle of Christianity in what was to become American Samoa. There is a monument to Williams in the village. The road beside the Catholic church leads about a mile and a half to **Leone Falls,** which has a freshwater pool for swimming (but never on Sunday).

The road from Leone to the western end of the island is quite scenic, as it winds in and out of small bays with sandy beaches and then climbs spectacularly across a ridge to Poloa village on the northwest coast.

8 Where to Stay

The lack of accommodations, and the apparent lack of interest by the government or anyone else to do anything about it, is a major reason you should consider making Pago Pago a day trip from Apia instead of staying here.

Most package tours put visitors up at **The Rainmaker Hotel,** P.O. Box 996, Pago Pago, AS 96799 (☎ 633-4241; fax 633-5959). This establishment was built with government backing in the 1960s, and under government management has gone steadily downhill ever since. It originally had 184 rooms; no more than 40 are serviceable today. If you stay at The Rainmaker, demand an upstairs room in the Beach Wing. Avoid any attempt to put you in the Harbor Wing. Even in the Beach Wing, inspect the room thoroughly before moving in. Make sure that the air conditioner works, the night latches engage properly, the plumbing actually does what it's supposed to do, and the sheets and towels are clean. Do not hesitate to go back to the front desk and insist on another room. You won't be the first person they've heard make such a request, nor will you be the last. Leave absolutely no valuables in your room, and lock the safety latch when you're inside. A restaurant, snack bar, beauty salon, and tour desks are on the premises. If you must stay there, rooms cost $85 (an exorbitant amount compared to what you get at Aggie Grey's Hotel in Apia for the same price).

Given this situation, the American Samoa Office of Tourism matches visitors seeking inexpensive accommodation with local families willing to take in paying guests. This **homestay program** is known as Fale, Fala Ma Ti. Prices vary from $25 to $40 a night, depending on the homes. Some are Western-style houses; others are Samoan fales. All of them have modern toilets and showers. Some homes also have space for campers who bring their own tents. The Samoan hospitality will more than make up for the simple accommodation. Prior arrangements are required. Contact the Office of Tourism, P.O. Box 1147, Pago Pago, AS 96799 (☎ 633-1092, fax 633-1094).

The following establishments offer a roof over your head. Period.

Herb and Sia's Motel

P.O. Box 430, Pago Pago, AS 96799 (Fagatogo, up the street directly behind the Communications Office). ☎ **633-5413.** 9 rms (3 with showers, none with toilet). A/C. $45. No credit cards.

New Zealand-born Herb Scanlon and his American Samoan wife, Sia, built a rather dark bedroom for each of their nine children in their hillside house in Fagatogo. The children are grown now, so Sia rents the rooms to visitors. Six of them share two baths and don't have windows; the other three are on the outside of the building and have their own shower but share toilets. The rooms have small refrigerators, but only one is air conditioned.

Motu O Fiafianga

P.O. Box 1554, Pago Pago, AS 96799 (on main road near head of harbor in Pago Pago). ☎ **633-7777.** Fax 633-4767. 12 rms (none with bath). A/C TV. $60 single or double, $50 single or double for stays of 3 days or more (including continental breakfast). AE.

Evalani Pearson Viena's little place perched at the foot of a cliff next to her cabaret doesn't look like much from the outside, since entry is through a dusty ground-level workshop and storage area. The inside is bit gaudy, with brass light fixtures and lots of paintings of James Dean and Marilyn Monroe. Nevertheless, this is the most modern place to stay in American Samoa, provided you don't need a private bath nor mind staying next to Evalani's Cabaret next door. The 12 rooms, all off a narrow hallway, share four toilets and showers, two each for men and women. Guests can use a common lounge with a bar, an exercise room, and a sauna. Each room has a queen-size bed, a writing desk, an open closet, and a small table with two chairs. Five rooms have TVs.

9 Where to Dine

Sadie's Restaurant

Pago Pago, west of market in Malaloa area. ☎ **633-5981.** Reservations recommended. Lunch $7–$9; main courses $10–$27. AE, MC, V. Mon–Sat 11am–2pm and 6–10pm. AMERICAN.

Appropriately located upstairs in the old building where W. Somerset Maugham stayed and set his short story "Rain," Sadie's has in recent years taken on that elegantly deteriorating look which Maugham would have loved. That is, it's seen just enough wear and tear to its cut-glass-and-mauve style to look the South Seas outpost part. The best seats are on the refurbished front porch with a commanding view of the harbor, but reserve early or the local palagis and affluent American Samoans will beat you to those tables. Lunches offer a wide variety of sandwiches, diet plates, and seafood and chicken platters. Dinners see seafood, steaks, and chicken in various styles.

Pago Pago Bay Restaurant

Pago Pago, near head of harbor. ☎ **633-4197.** Reservations not needed. Lunch $5.50–$16.50; main courses $9–$28. AE, V. Mon–Sat 7am–11:30pm. AMERICAN/CANTONESE.

This restaurant sits right on the bay, with excellent water and mountain views from its large dining room, which is popular with civic groups as a place for luncheon meetings. The menu features a selection of burgers and sandwiches, a Samoan-size New York steak, and a variety of Chinese dishes, all of which are available throughout the day.

Pizza Time

Fagatogo, behind Tedi of Samoa in Fagatoga Square. ☎ **633-1199.** Reservations not accepted. Pizzas $5.50–$15; chicken, sandwiches, burgers, and hot dogs $1.50–$6. No credit cards. Mon–Sat 7am–11pm; Sun noon–8pm. PIZZA/SNACK BAR.

An extensive menu at this waterfront fast-food establishment offers pizzas, barbecue rib platters, fried chicken, sandwiches, hamburgers, hot dogs, nachos, *lumpia* (Philippine-style egg rolls), and ice cream. It's not as fast as it could be, since all items are cooked to order. Even if you don't eat here, stop by for a cold soda and enjoy the magnificent view of the harbor.

10 Water Sports & Other Outdoor Activities

FISHING & SCUBA DIVING   Mahi mahi, wahoo, sailfish, blue marlin, barracuda, and yellowfin, dogtooth, and skyjack tuna abound in Samoan waters. And if you know where to go, the fringing reefs beckon to serious scuba divers. Chuck Brugman of **Dive Samoa, Inc.,** P.O. Box 3927, Pago Pago, AS 96799 (☎ 633-2183), takes guests on fishing and diving expeditions.

GOLF   The **Lava Lava Golf Course** has 18 holes rambling across the relatively flat land between the airport and village of Illi'ili. For a starting time, call 699-9366 or 633-1191. Equipment is available to rent at the clubhouse, which has a restaurant and bar. The course is open seven days a week.

HIKING   Several exciting trails await adventurous hikers. One is the often-slippery track to the Mt. Alava summit, where another trail drops down to Vatia on the north shore. Also from the Pago Pago–Fagasa Pass, a difficult track leads to the summit of Matafao Peak, at 2,143 feet the highest point on Tutuila. Another more-often-used track descends from A'asufou village high in the interior down to A'asutuai village and the French monument at Massacre Bay. Some of these will eventually be included in a national park, but for now, ask for directions at the America Samoa Office of Tourism (see "Information, Entry Requirements & Money," above).

11 Shopping

American Samoa is famous in the South Pacific as *the* place to shop for American goods and products ranging from Best Foods mayonnaise to large Coleman picnic coolers. The prices are barely more than Americans pay at home. The huge, air-conditioned **Cost-U-Less** warehouse in Tafuna near the airport is the best-stocked store between Hawaii and New Zealand.

The best buys for many visitors are **Reebok shoes,** but only if you come from Australia, New Zealand, or another country where they are exorbitantly expensive (they cost about the same in Pago Pago as in the U.S.). **Tedi of Samoa,** the waterfront department store opposite the High Court in Pago Pago, usually carries a good selection.

The best place to shop for handcrafts is **Luana's South Sea Curios** (☎ 633-1850) in the Samoa News Building between The Rainmaker Hotel and the post office. Look for baskets, shell necklaces, woodcarvings, and polished shells. Luana's hours are Monday to Friday from 9am to 5pm and Saturday from 10am to 2pm.

Harry Paul of Apia has a branch of his **P&H Karvings 'n' Things** (☎ 633-7870) on the hill behind the Fagatogo malae. Look for wood carvings, tapa cloth, and pandanus baskets and mats from Western Samoa and Tonga.

The **Senior Citizens Handicraft Market** on the Fagatogo malae (no phone) has a worthy goal of keeping alive the old arts and making some money for senior citizens while doing it. It's busiest when a cruise ship is in port.

15 Tonga

Thanks to a quirk of humankind and not of nature, the International Date Line swings eastward from its north-south path down the Pacific Ocean just enough to make the last Polynesian monarch the first sovereign to see the light of each new day.

When King Taufa'ahau Tupou IV of Tonga greets the morning and looks out on his realm from the veranda of his whitewashed Victorian palace, he sees a country of low but extremely fertile islands, of gorgeous sandy beaches, of colorful coral reefs waiting to be explored, and of Polynesian faces whose infectious smiles make it immediately obvious why Capt. James Cook named tiny Tonga "The Friendly Islands."

His is a nation protected but never ruled by a Western power. Like Western Samoa to the north, Tonga has managed to maintain its Polynesian culture in the face of modern change. As the Tonga Visitors Bureau says, the kingdom "still remains far away from it all; still different, still alone, and to the joy of those who find their way to her—essentially unspoiled."

While this description is true of the perfectly flat main island Tongatapu, it is especially applicable to Vava'u, a group of hilly islands whose fjordlike harbor makes it one of the South Pacific's most popular yachting destinations. Not only is it pleasing to the eye, but visiting Vava'u is like traveling back in time to the old South Seas.

1 Tonga Today

In other Polynesian languages, the word *tonga* means "south." It stands to reason that Tonga would be so named because the kingdom lies south of Samoa, the first islands permanently settled by Polynesians and presumably the launching site for the colonization of Tonga and the rest of Polynesia. But to the Tongans the name means "garden," and when you drive from the airport into **Nuku'alofa,** the nation's capital, you can see why. It seems that every square yard of the main island of **Tongatapu** ("Sacred Garden") not occupied by a building or by the road is either under cultivation or lying fallow but ready for the next planting of bananas, tapioca, taro, yams, watermelons, tomatoes, and a plethora of other fruits and vegetables. Crops grow in small plots under towering

What's Special About Tonga

Beaches
- Vava'u has tiny islets surrounded by white sand beaches and emerald lagoons.

Natural Spectacles
- Unique in the South Pacific, Vava'u is a collection of islands split apart by narrow, nearly landlocked waterways.
- Blowholes—the surf spouts geysers on Tongatapu's south shore.

Cultures
- King Taufa'ahau Tupou and 33 Nobles of the Realm rule the last pure Polynesian chiefdom.

Ancient Monuments
- Ha'amonga Trilithon—without wheels, the Tongans managed to put the 35-ton stone on top in A.D. 1200.
- Ancient terraced tombs have given way to graves trimmed with beer bottles.

Great Towns/Villages
- Neiafu—curving around Port of Refuge on Vava'u, this little gem evokes the South Seas of yesteryear.
- Dusty or muddy, the nation's capital, Nuku'alofa, has rough-around-the-edges charm.

Sunday Selections
- The Sabbath is sacred, but having a good time on Sunday is not as difficult as it may seem in this fundamentalist bastion.

Shopping
- The South Pacific's great trove of tapa, anything made of pandanus, and black coral.

Festivals
- *Heilala,* when Tongans do just about everything they can think of to have a good time around the King's Birthday in July.

coconut palms so numerous that this flat island appears to be one huge copra plantation. The Tongans are generally poor in terms of material wealth, but they own some of the South Pacific's most fertile and productive land.

There just isn't much of it. The kingdom consists of 170 islands, 36 of them inhabited, scattered over an area of about 100,000 square miles, an area about the size of Colorado. The amount of dry land, however, is only 269 square miles—smaller than New York City.

The largest island in the kingdom, Tongatapu has about a third of the country's land area and about two-thirds of its population. It's a flat, raised atoll about 40 miles across from east to west and 20 miles across from north to south at its longest

Impressions

Nature, assisted by a little art, no where appears in a more flourishing state than at this Isle.

—Capt. James Cook, 1773

Impressions

What could the Tongan people do? "Not much," he reflected. "All we can do is resign ourselves to our lot, become very religious, and pray that there will be more land available in Heaven."

—John Dyson, 1982

and widest points. In the center is a sparkling lagoon now unfortunately void of most sea life.

The government and most businesses and tourist activities are in Nuku'alofa (pop. 22,000), but there is much to see outside of town, including some of the South Pacific's most important and impressive archaeological sites.

There are three major island groups in the country. Tongatapu and the smaller **'Eua** comprise the southernmost group. About 96 miles north are the islands of the **Ha'apai Group,** and about 67 miles beyond them is the beautiful **Vava'u Group.** Even farther north, and definitely off the beaten path, are the **Niuas Islands.** The most frequently visited islands are Tongatapu and the sailor's paradise of Vava'u.

The Natural Environment   Tonga lies roughly north-south along the edge of the Indo-Australian Plate. The Tonga Trench, one of the deepest parts of the Pacific Ocean, parallels the islands to the east where the Pacific Plate dips down and then under the Indo-Australian Plate. The resulting geological activity puts Tonga on the "Ring of Fire" that encircles the Pacific Ocean. One of Tonga's islands, Tofua, is an active volcano, and the entire country experiences frequent earth tremors. Legend says that earthquakes are caused when the Polynesian goddess Havea Hikule'o moves around underground; consequently, Tongans customarily stomp the shaking ground to get her to stop whatever she's doing down there.

Most of the islands are raised coral atolls. The exceptions are the Niuas and, in the Ha'apai Group, the active volcano Tofua and its sister volcanic cone, Kao. Geologists say that the weight of the growing Ha'apai volcanoes has caused the Indo-Australian Plate to sag like a hammock, thereby raising Tongatapu and 'Eua on the south end of the Tongan chain and Vava'u on the north end. As a result, the sides of Tongatapu and Vava'u facing Ha'apai slope gently to the sea, while the sides facing away from Ha'apai end in cliffs that fall into the ocean.

Government   Although Tonga is a constitutional monarchy, the king in reality is head of a system of hereditary Polynesian chiefs who happen to have titles derived from England. He picks his own Privy Council of advisors and appoints seven cabinet members and the governors of Ha'apai and Vava'u. With few exceptions they all are nobles. The cabinet members and the governors serve until they retire, and they hold 12 of the 30 seats in Parliament—in effect, for life. Of the 16 other members of the Parliament, the nobles choose 9 from among their ranks, leaving 9 to be elected by the taxpaying commoners.

The king's brother is prime minister. His son, Crown Prince Tupouto'a, is both minister of foreign affairs and minister of defense. It would be an understatement to say that the royal family has a hand in every important decision made in Tonga; in fact, very little gets done without its outright or tacit approval or involvement. Foreigners doing business in the country must have Tongan partners, and it's not surprising that many such partners are of royal or noble blood.

With more and more Tongans living abroad, and those at home being exposed more and more to news of the world, the monarchy has been under increasing pressure to move to a democracy. This is not likely to happen as long as King Taufa'ahau Tupou IV is on the throne. What happens after he dies was very much up in the air during my recent visit (see "A Look at the Past," below).

Economy   Tonga has few natural resources other than its fertile soil and the fish in the sea within its exclusive economic zone; and the world markets for its major exports—vanilla, kava, bananas, coconut oil, pineapples, watermelons, tomatoes, and other vegetables—has been unstable and even depressed at times in recent years. The country imports far more than it exports.

In addition, the kingdom has run out of land to apportion under the rule that gives each adult male $8^{1}/_{4}$ acres for growing crops. As a result, many thousands of Tongans have left the country and now live overseas. Money sent home by them is a major source of foreign exchange for the country.

For the commoners who remain behind, labor unions are illegal, and the primary chance for economic advancement is in small businesses, which are flourishing when compared to those of other South Pacific island countries. Even there, however, the king can get involved when leases or permits are required from the government.

2 A Look at the Past

Dateline

- 500 B.C. Polynesians from Samoa settle in Tonga.
- 950 A.D. By legend, supreme god Tangaloa comes to earth, fathers a son by beautiful virgin, thus founds Tui Tonga dynasty.
- 1642 Dutchman Abel Tasman is first European to set foot in Tonga.
- 1777 Captain Cook is feted by Finau I in Ha'apai, names them "The Friendly Islands," leaves as Finau plans to kill him.
- 1781 Spaniard Francisco Mourelle discovers Vava'u.
- 1789 Mutiny on the *Bounty* takes place off Ha'afeva in Ha'apai Group.
- 1798 First missionaries land in Ha'apai Group during Tongan wars; two are killed, and the rest flee to Australia.

continues

Legend has it that the great Polynesian god Maui threw a fishhook into the sea from Samoa and brought up the islands of Tonga. He then stepped on some of his catch, flattening them for gardens. Tofua and Kao in the Ha'apai Group and some of the Niuas were left standing as volcanic cones.

Polynesian settlers found and settled these gardens sometime around 500 B.C. on their long migration across the South Pacific. Around A.D. 950, according to another myth, the supreme god Tangaloa came down to Tongatapu and fathered a son by a lovely Tongan maiden named Va'epopua. The son, Aho'eitu, thus became the first Tui Tonga—King of Tonga—and launched one of the world's longest-running dynasties. Under subsequent Tuis, Tonga became a power in Polynesia; its large war canoes loaded with fierce warriors conquered and dominated the Samoas and the eastern islands of present-day Fiji.

The first Tuis Tonga ruled from the village Niutoua on the northwest corner of Tongatapu. They moved to Lapaha on the shore of the island's interior lagoon about 800 years ago, apparently to take advantage of a safer anchorage for the large, double-hulled war canoes they used to extend their empire as far as Fiji and Samoa. At that time, a deep passage linked the lagoon to the sea; it has been slowly closing as geological forces raise the

- 1806 Chief Finau II captures the *Port au Prince,* slays all its crew except young Will Mariner, who becomes the chief's favorite, later writes a book about his adventures.
- 1823 Wesleyan missionaries settle on Lifuka in Ha'apai Group; Chief Taufa'ahau begins his rise to power.
- 1831 Taufa'ahau converts to Christianity, names self George, with missionary help launches wars against his rivals.
- 1845 Taufa'ahau conquers all of Tonga, proclaims self King George.
- 1860 Rev. Shirley Baker arrives, exercises influence over Tonga for next 30 years.
- 1862 King George I frees commoners, makes his chiefs "Nobles of the Realm," establishes Privy Council, gives land to every male.
- 1875 King George I adopts Constitution, including "Sabbath-is-sacred" clause, essentially shutting Tonga down on Sunday.
- 1890 Under Treaty of Berlin, Great Britain establishes protectorate over Tonga, kicks out Rev. Baker, straightens out kingdom's finances.
- 1893 King George I dies, ending reign of 48 years. King George II assumes throne.
- 1900 King George II turns Tonga's foreign affairs over to Great Britain, preventing further colonial encroachments.
- 1918 King George II dies, Queen Salote begins 47-year reign during which

continues

island and reduce the entrance to the present shallow bank.

Over time, the Tui became more of a figurehead, and his power was dispersed among several chiefs, all of them descendants of the original Tui. For centuries the rival chiefs seemed to stop warring among themselves only long enough to make war on Fiji and Samoa. One of the domestic wars was in full swing when missionaries from the London Missionary Society arrived in 1798 and landed on Lifuka in the Ha'apai Group. Two of the missionaries were killed. The rest fled to Sydney, leaving Tonga to the warring heathens.

Europeans Arrive   Tongatapu and Ha'apai had been sighted by the Dutch explorers Schouten and Lemaire in 1616, and the Dutchman Abel Tasman had landed on them during his voyage of discovery in 1643. The missionaries knew of the islands, however, from the visits of British Captains Samuel Wallis, James Cook, and William Bligh in the late 1700s. During his third voyage in 1777, Captain Cook was feted lavishly on Lifuka by a powerful chief named Finau I. Cook was so impressed by this show of hospitality that he named the Ha'apai Group "The Friendly Islands." Unbeknownst to Cook, however, Finau I and his associates apparently plotted to murder him and his crew, but they couldn't agree among themselves how to do it before the great explorer sailed away. The name he gave the islands stuck, and today Tonga uses "The Friendly Islands" as its motto.

Captain Bligh and H.M.S. *Bounty* visited Lifuka in 1789 after gathering breadfruit in Tahiti. Before he could leave Tongan waters, however, the famous mutiny took place near the island of Ha'afeva in the Ha'apai Group.

Some 20 years later Chief Finau II of Lifuka captured a British ship named the *Port au Prince,* brutally slaughtering all but one member of its crew, stealing all of its muskets and ammunition, and setting it on fire. The survivor was a 15-year-old Londoner named Will Mariner. He became a favorite of the chief, spent several years living among the Tongans, and was made a chief. Mariner later wrote an extensive account of his experiences, telling in one of the four volumes how the Tongans mistook 12,000 silver coins on the *Port au Prince* for gaming pieces they called *pa'angas.* The national currency today is known as the pa'anga.

The arrival of the Wesleyan missionaries on Lifuka in the 1820s coincided with the rise of Taufa'ahau, a powerful chief they converted to Christianity in 1831. With their help, he won a series of domestic wars and by 1845 had conquered all of Tonga. He made peace with Fiji, took a wife of the incumbent Tui Tonga as his own, and declared himself to be the new Tui Tonga. The deposed Tui, last of the direct descendants of the original Tui Tonga, lived on until 1865.

Royalty Arrives Meanwhile, Taufa'ahau took the Christian name George and became King George I of Tonga. In 1862 he made his subordinate chiefs "nobles," but he also freed the commoners from forced labor on their estates and instituted the policy of granting each adult male a garden plot and house lot. He created a Privy Council of his own choosing and established a legislative assembly made up of representatives of both the nobles and commoners. This system was committed to writing in the Constitution of 1875, which still is in effect today, including its "Sabbath-is-sacred" clause. The legislative assembly is known now as Parliament.

King George I was dominated during his later years by the Rev. Shirley W. Baker, a missionary who came to Tonga from Sydney in 1860 under the auspices of the Wesleyan Church. Over the next 30 years he held almost every important post in the king's government. When the British established their protectorate over Tonga according to the terms of the 1889 Berlin treaty, which also divided the Samoas between Germany and the U.S., they found the kingdom's finances to be in a shambles. In cleaning up the mess, they arranged to have Baker deported to New Zealand, where he stayed for 10 years. Baker returned to Tonga in 1900 as a lay reader licensed by the Anglican church and died there in 1903. His children erected a large statue of his likeness at his grave on Lifuka, in the Ha'apai Group.

King George I died in 1893 at the age of 97, thus ending a reign of 48 years. His great-grandson, King George II, ruled for the next 25 years and is best remembered for signing a treaty with Great Britain in 1900. The agreement turned Tonga's foreign affairs over to the British and prevented any further encroachments on Tonga by the Western colonial powers. As a result, the Kingdom of Tonga is one of the few Third World countries never to have been colonized.

Tonga remains a backwater.

- 1953 Queen Salote comes to world attention by going bareheaded during rainstorm at coronation of Queen Elizabeth II in London.
- 1965 Queen Salote dies; new King Taufa'ahau Tupou IV begins opening Tonga to tourists.
- 1967 King Taufa'ahau Tupou IV crowned among pomp and circumstance; International Dateline Hotel opens.
- 1970 King ends treaty with Great Britain; Tonga resumes own foreign affairs.
- 1989 Commoner members of Parliament begin push for more accountability from King's government.
- 1990 Passport scandal rocks the government.
- 1992 Pro-democracy conference calls for new elections.
- 1993 New elections bring same old results.

Impressions

The good natured old Chief interduced me to a woman and gave me to understand that I might retire with her, she was next offered to Captain Furneaux but met with a refusal from both, tho she was neither old nor ugly, our stay here was but short.

—Capt. James Cook, 1773

Impressions

The people were hospitable and, as you sailed in, local boats really did come alongside as they did in voyagers' tales, to invite you to their villages for a feast. Only when arrangements were finalised does the awful truth dawn: it is not natural hospitality being pressed so warmly upon you, but salesmanship.

—John Dyson, 1982

King George II died in 1918 and was succeeded by his daughter, the six-foot-two-inch Queen Salote (her name is the Tongan transliteration of "Charlotte"). For the next 47 years Queen Salote carefully protected her people from Western influence, even to the extent of not allowing a modern hotel to be built in the kingdom. She did, however, come to the world's attention in 1953, when she rode bareheaded in the cold, torrential rain that drenched the coronation parade of Queen Elizabeth II in London (she was merely following Tongan custom of showing respect to royalty by appearing uncovered in their presence).

King Taufa'ahau Tupou   Queen Salote died in 1965 and was succeeded by her son, the present King Taufa'ahau Tupou IV. Trained in law at Sydney University in Australia, the new king—then 49 years old—set about bringing Tonga into the modern world. On the pretext of accommodating the important guests invited to his elaborate coronation scheduled for July 4, 1967, the modern International Dateline Hotel was built on Nuku'alofa's waterfront, and Fua'amotu Airport on Tongatapu was upgraded to handle jet aircraft. Tourism, albeit on a modest scale, had finally arrived in Tonga.

The king ended the treaty of protection with Great Britain, and in 1970 Tonga reassumed her small role on the world's stage. This enabled her to acquire aid from other countries with which to make further improvements.

Although not as tall as his mother, the king stands above six feet and once weighed on the order of 460 pounds (the large statue of him beside the old terminal at Fua'amotu Airport is only a slight exaggeration of his former size). He has slimmed down in recent years to just over 300 pounds, thanks in part to an exercise program including bicycling and rowing, his bodyguards puffing along behind. He has been seen wearing ski goggles and a motorbike helmet when flying from island to island. Watching him arrive at an airport should not be missed.

Democracy Doesn't Arrive   The king and his government have had their problems in recent years, thanks to more and more of his commoner subjects going overseas to work in the Western democracies, and to those at home becoming better educated and more aware of what's going on both in Tonga and in the world. In the late 1980s a group of commoners founded *Kele'a,* a newspaper published without the king's input. The paper created a ruckus almost from its first issue by revealing that some government ministers had rung up excessive travel expenses on trips abroad.

Then came news that the government had stashed millions of dollars in U.S. banks, money earned from selling Tongan passports to overseas nationals (most of them Hong Kong Chinese but including Imelda Marcos, wife of the deposed Philippine dictator). For $20,000 the buyers received a passport declaring them to be "Tongan protected persons." The documents didn't allow the person to live

Let's Make a Date

One of diplomacy's great contributions to the geography of the Pacific Ocean (and to the eternal confusion of travelers) is the international date line. Established by international agreement in 1884, this imaginary line marks the start of each calendar day. Theoretically, it should run for its *entire length* along the 180th Meridian, halfway around the world from the Zero Meridian, the starting point for measuring international time.

If it followed the 180th Meridian precisely, however, most of the Aleutian Islands would be a day ahead of the rest of Alaska, and Fiji would be split into two days. To solve these problems, the date line swings west around the Aleutians, leaving them in the same day as Alaska. In the South Pacific, it swerves east between Fiji and Western Samoa, leaving all of Fiji a day ahead of the Samoas.

Since Tonga and Western Samoa lie east of the 180th Meridian, both countries logically should be in the same day. But Tonga wanted to have the same date as Australia and New Zealand, so the line was drawn arbitrarily east of Tonga, putting it one day ahead of Western Samoa.

To travelers, it's even more confusing, since Tonga and Western Samoa are in the same time zone. When traveling from one to the other, therefore, only the date changes, not the time of day. For example, if everyone is going to church at 10am on Sunday in Tonga, everyone's at work on Saturday in Samoa.

Tonga's Seventh-Day Adventists, who celebrate the Sabbath on Saturday but work on Sunday, have taken advantage of this abnormality to avoid running afoul of Tonga's tough Sunday blue laws. In God's eyes, they say, Sunday in Tonga really is Saturday. Accordingly, Tonga is the only place in the world where Seventh-Day Adventists observe their Sabbath on Sunday.

in Tonga, however, so other nations refused to recognize them. To compound the problem, the Tongan High Court ruled the sales to be unconstitutional. Rather than refund the money, Parliament held a special session in 1991 and amended the constitution—a document that had not been significantly changed since 1875. It also raised the price to $50,000. The new passports also allow the holders to live in Tonga.

Incensed, several hundred Tongans marched down Nuku'alofa's main street in a peaceful protest. Nothing like that had ever happened in Tonga before, but it was just the beginning. When the king kept on selling passports, the leaders held a pro-democracy conference in late 1992. That led to fresh elections in 1993— with the same old results. It was difficult at presstime to predict what future course Tongan politics would take. Many observers believe the monarchial system will stay intact as long as King Taufa'ahau Tupou, now about 80 years old, is in power. The crown prince has indicated that some changes eventually will occur, but those aren't likely to be known until Tonga gets a new king.

Whether the crown prince gets the job seemed to be in doubt during my recent visit. The same age as President Bill Clinton, he has never married and has a widespread reputation as a playboy. The king's second son married a commoner, so he is out of the line of succession. His third son is favored by many Tongans to become king, since he married the daughter of a baron and is said to be devoted to the church.

3 The Tongans

The population of Tonga is estimated at somewhere around 100,000 (no one knows for sure). Approximately 98% of the inhabitants are pure Polynesians, closely akin to the Samoans in physical appearance, language, and culture.

As in Samoa, the bedrock of the Tongan social structure is the traditional way of life—*faka Tonga*—and the extended family. Parents, grandparents, children, aunts, uncles, cousins, nieces, and nephews all have the same sense of obligation to each other as is felt in Western nuclear families. Although Tongans are poor by Western standards, the extended-family system makes sure that no one ever goes hungry or without a place to live. Little wonder, therefore, that they are an extremely friendly and hospitable people who are quick to smile, laugh, and welcome strangers to their country.

The Tongan System   The extended family aside, some striking differences exist between Tonga, Samoa, and the other Polynesian islands. Unlike the others, in which there is a certain degree of upward mobility, Tonga has a rigid two-tier caste system. The king and 33 "Nobles of the Realm"—plus their families—make up a privileged class at the top of society. Everyone else is a commoner, and although commoners can hold positions in the government, it's impossible for them to move up into the nobility even by marriage. Titles of the nobility are inherited, but the king can strip members of the nobility of their positions if they fail to live up to their obligations (presumably including loyalty to the royal family).

The king owns all the land in Tonga, which technically makes the country his feudal estate. Tonga isn't exactly like the old European feudal system, however, for although the nobles each rule over a section of the kingdom, they have an obligation to provide for the welfare of the "serfs" rather than the other way around. The nobles administer the villages, look after the people's welfare, and apportion the land among the commoners.

Under Tonga's constitution, each adult male is entitled to a garden plot of $8^1/_4$ acres and a site for a house in the village. Unfortunately, the population has outstripped the amount of available land, but this system is primarily responsible for the intensely cultivated condition of Tongatapu and the other islands and for the abundance of food in the country.

Foreigners are absolutely forbidden to own land in Tonga, and leases require approval of the Cabinet, which for all practical purposes means the king.

Tongan Dress   Even traditional Tongan dress reflects this social structure. Western-style clothes have made deep inroads in recent years, especially among young persons, but many Tongans still wear wraparound skirts known as *valas*. These come to well below the knee on men and to the ankles on women. To show their respect for the royal family and to each other, traditional men and women wear finely woven mats known as *ta'ovalas* over their valas. Men hold these up with waistbands of coconut fiber; women wear decorative waistbands known as *kiekies*. Tongans have ta'ovalas for everyday wear, but on special occasions they will break out mats that are family heirlooms, some of them tattered and worn. The king owns ta'ovalas that have been in his family for more than 500 years.

Tongan custom is to wear black for months to mourn the death of a relative or close friend. Since Tongan extended families are large and friends numerous, the black of mourning is seen frequently in the kingdom.

In keeping with Tonga's conservatism, it's against the law for men as well as women to appear shirtless in public. While Western men can swim and sunbathe shirtless at the hotel swimming pools and beaches frequented by visitors, you will see most Tongans swimming in a full set of clothes.

Religion   Wesleyan missionaries gained a foothold in Tonga during the early 1820s and by 1831 had converted Taufa'ahau, the high chief of the Ha'apai Islands. As happened with the converted chief named Pomare in Tahiti, Taufa'ahau then used missionary support—and guns from other sources—to win a series of wars and become king of Tonga. Tonga quickly became a predominantly Christian nation—apparently an easy transition, as Tongan legend holds that their own king is a descendant of a supreme Polynesian god and a beautiful earthly virgin.

When Taufa'ahau instituted a constitution in 1862, a clause in that document declared, "The Sabbath Day shall be sacred in Tonga forever and it shall not be lawful to work, artifice, or play games, or trade on the Sabbath." The penalty for breaking this stricture is a T$10 ($8) fine or three months in the slammer at hard labor. Although there now is some flexibility that allows hotels to cater to their guests on Sunday, almost everything else comes to a screeching halt on the Sabbath. Taxis don't run, airplanes don't fly, most restaurants other than those in the hotels don't open. Tongans by the thousands go to church, then enjoy family feasts and a day of lounging around in true Polynesian style.

About half of all Tongans belong to the Free Wesleyan Church of Tonga, founded by the early Methodist missionaries and headed by the king. The Free Church of Tonga is another local Protestant denomination. There are also considerable numbers of Roman Catholics, Anglicans, Seventh-Day Adventists, and Mormons. Church services usually are held at 10am on Sunday, but very few of them are conducted in English. St. Paul's Anglican Church, on the corner of Fafatehi and Wellington Roads, usually has communion in English on Sunday at 8am. The royal family worships at 10am in the Free Wesleyan Church on Wellington Road, a block behind the Royal Palace.

The red national flag has a cross on a white field in its upper corner to signify the country's strong Christian foundation.

The Mormon church has made inroads in Tonga. Gleaming white Morman temples have popped up in many Tongan villages, along with modern schools that offer quality education and the chance for students to go on to Mormon colleges in Hawaii and Utah. Many Tongans have joined the church, reportedly for this very reason, and there are now sizable Tongan communities in Honolulu and around Salt Lake City, headquarters of the Mormon church. Unlike the Samoans and Cook Islanders, Tongans do not have unlimited access to a larger Western country such as the U.S. or New Zealand, and the promise of Mormon help in settling in America is an appealing prospect in light of the population pressures at home.

Tongans of all religions bury their dead in unique cemeteries set in groves of frangipani trees. The graves are sandy mounds decorated with flags, banners, artificial flowers, stones, and seashells. Many of them are bordered by brown beer bottles turned upside down.

As was the case throughout Polynesia, the Tongans accepted most of the puritanical beliefs taught by the early missionaries but stopped short of adopting their strict sexual mores. Today Tongan society is very conservative in outlook and practice in almost every aspect of life except the sexual activities of unmarried young men and women.

The people stay home on Sundays and entertain each other with good food, even if they have to semi-starve all week.

—John Dyson, 1982

In keeping with Polynesian custom described earlier in this book, Tongan families without enough female offspring will raise boys as they would girls. They are known in Tongan as *fakaleitis* ("like a woman") and live lives similar to those of the mahus in Tahiti and the fa'afafines in the Samoas. In Tonga they have a reputation for sexual promiscuousness and for persistently approaching Western male visitors in search of sexual liaisons.

4 The Tongan Language

The official language is Tongan, but English is taught in the schools and is widely spoken in the main towns.

Tongan is a Polynesian language similar to Samoan. One major difference between them is the enormous number of glottal stops (represented by an apostrophe in writing) in the Tongan tongue. These are short stops similar to the break between "Oh-oh" in English.

Every vowel is pronounced in the Latin fashion: *ah, ay, ee, oh,* and *oo* (as in kangar*oo*) instead of *ay, ee, eye, oh,* and *you* as in English. The consonants are sounded as they are in English.

An extensive knowledge of Tongan will not be necessary for English-speakers to get around and enjoy the kingdom, but here are a few words you can use to elicit smiles from your hosts and to avoid the embarrassment of entering the wrong rest room. Here are a few helpful words and phrases:

English	Tongan	Pronunciation
hello	malo e lelei	*mah*-low ay *lay*-lay
welcome	talitali fiefia	tah-lay-*tah*-lay fee-ay-*fee*-ah
how do you do?	fefe hake?	*fay*-fay *hah*-kay?
fine, thank you	sai pe, malo	*sah*-ee pay, *mah*-low
good-bye	'alu a	ah-*loo* ah
thank you	malo	*mah*-low
how much?	'oku fiha?	*oh*-koo *fee*-hah?
good	lelei	lay-*lay*-ee
bad	kovi	*koh*-vee
woman	fefine	fay-*feen*-ay
man	tangata	tahn-*got*-ah
house	fale	*fah*-lay
transvestite	fakaleiti	fah-ka-*lay*-tee

For more information, the Friendly Islands Bookshop on Taufa'ahau Road carries language books, and the Tonga Visitors Bureau on Vuna Road distributes a brochure of Tongan phrases.

5 Visitor Information & Entry Requirements

VISITOR INFORMATION

The friendly staff have many brochures, maps, and other materials available at the **Tonga Visitors Bureau,** P.O. Box 37, Nuku'alofa, Kingdom of Tonga (☎ 21-733, fax 22-129). The office is on Vuna Road near the International Dateline Hotel. Especially good are the bureau's brochures on Tongan dancing, handcrafts, archaeology, construction skills, and a walking tour of central Nuku'alofa. A stop by the "TVB" is a must before setting out to see the country. Hours are Monday to Friday from 8:30am to 4:30pm and Saturday from 9am to 1pm.

Other sources of information are:

North America: Tonga Consulate, 360 Post Street, Suite 604, San Francisco, CA 94108 (☎ 415/781-0365, fax 415/781-3964).

Australia: Tonga Visitors Bureau, 642 King Street, Newton, NSW 2042 (☎ 02/550-4711, fax 02/519-9419).

New Zealand: Tonga Visitors Bureau, P.O. Box 24-054, Royal Oak, Auckland (☎ 09/634-1519, fax 09/636-8973).

United Kingdom: Tonga High Commission, 36 Molyneux Street, London W1H 6AB (☎ 724-5828, fax 723-9074).

Once you're in Tonga, be on the lookout for *'Eva: Your Holiday Guide to Tonga,* a slick bimonthly tabloid full of news about Tongan tourism and advertisements for the hotels, restaurants, and nightclubs. It's carried as a supplement in *Matagi Tonga,* an excellent local magazine.

ENTRY REQUIREMENTS

Visas are not required for bona fide visitors to enter Tonga; they are permitted to stay for up to 30 days provided they have a valid passport, an onward air or sea ticket, proof of adequate funds, and relevant health certificates. As a practical matter, your initial permit will likely be limited to the number of days you request on your entry form or the date of your return or onward ticket, whichever is earlier. Expect to have your tickets examined.

Applications for stays of longer than 30 days must be made to the principal immigration officer in Nuku'alofa.

Vaccinations are required only if a traveler has been in a yellow fever or cholera area within two weeks prior to arrival in Tonga.

Customs   Visitors are allowed to bring in 200 cigarettes and one liter of alcoholic beverage, as well as personal belongings in use at the time of arrival. Pets, dangerous drugs, firearms, and ammunition are prohibited, and foodstuffs must be declared and inspected. Arriving visitors can buy duty-free merchandise at Fua'amotu Airport after clearing Immigration but before going through Customs.

6 Money

The Tongan unit of currency is the **pa'anga,** which is divided into 100 **seniti.** The pa'anga is abbreviated in this book as **"T$."**

The value of the pa'anga is determined by a basket of currencies, but as a practical matter, it usually is worth a few cents more than the Australian dollar. At the time of writing, T$1 was worth about U.S. 80¢. The equivalent U.S. dollar prices given in parentheses are based on this rate of exchange.

What Things Cost in Tonga	U.S. $
Taxi from airport to Nuku'alofa	9.50
Bus from airport to Nuku'alofa	5.00
Room at International Dateline Hotel (expensive)	75.00
Room at Pacific Royale Hotel (moderate)	66.00
Room at Sela's Guest House (inexpensive)	24.00
Lunch for one at Davina's (moderate)	12.00
Lunch for one at Fred's Restaurant (inexpensive)	5.00
Dinner for one at the Seaview (expensive)	32.00
Dinner for one at The Italian Restaurant (moderate)	19.50
Dinner for one at Akiko's (inexpensive)	8.00
Beer	2.50
Coca-Cola	1.20
Roll of ASA 100 Kodacolor film, 36 exposures	7.00

The Pa'anga & The U.S. Dollar

At this writing, T$1 = approximately $.80, the rate of exchange used to calculate the U.S. dollar prices given in this chapter. This rate may change by the time you visit, so use the following table only as a guide.

T $	U.S. $	T $	U.S. $
.25	.20	15.00	12.00
.50	.40	20.00	16.00
.75	.60	25.00	20.00
1.00	.80	30.00	24.00
2.00	1.60	35.00	28.00
3.00	2.40	40.00	32.00
4.00	3.20	45.00	36.00
5.00	4.00	50.00	40.00
6.00	4.80	75.00	60.00
7.00	5.60	100.0	80.00
8.00	6.40	125.00	100.00
9.00	7.20	150.00	120.00
10.00	8.00	200.00	160.00

Most Tongans will refer to "dollars" and "cents" when doing business with visitors, meaning pa'angas and senitis.

Tongan coins bear the likeness of the king on one side and such items as bananas, chickens, and pigs on the other.

How to Get Local Currency   The Bank of Tonga has an office at the waterfront end of Taufa'ahau Road, Nuku'alofa's main street. It is open Monday to Friday from 9am to 3:30pm and Saturday from 8:30 to 11:30am. ANZ Bank has its office at the corner of Railway and Salote Roads, near the market. It is open Monday to Friday from 9am to 4pm and Saturday from 8:30 to 11:30am. You will need your passport in order to exchange currency or traveler's checks. The International Dateline Hotel and the Pacific Royale Hotel will change money at a rate lower than you will get at the banks.

You can get cash advances using your MasterCard and Visa at either bank. There were no ATM machines in Tonga during my recent visit.

Credit Cards   The major hotels, car-rental firms, travel agencies, and Friendly Island Airways accept American Express, Diners Club, MasterCard, and Visa credit cards. Most restaurants and other businesses, however, do not. It's a good idea to ask first if you want to put your purchases on plastic.

7 When to Go

THE CLIMATE

Like Rarotonga in the Cook Islands to the east and New Caledonia to the west, Tongatapu is far enough south of the equator to have cool, dry, and quite pleasant weather during the austral winter months (July to September), when temperatures range between 60°F and 70°F. However, the ends of occasional cold fronts from the Antarctic and periods of stiff southeast trade winds can make it seem even cooler during this period. During the summer (December to March), the high temperatures can reach above 90°F, with evenings in the comfortable 70s. A sweater, jacket, or wrap will come in handy for evening wear at any time of the year. The islands get about 70 inches of rainfall a year (compared to 200 inches in Pago Pago, American Samoa), the majority of it falling during the summer months. Vava'u to the north tends to be somewhat warmer and slightly wetter than Tongatapu.

Tonga is in the southwestern Pacific cyclone belt, and hurricanes are possible from November to April. Rest assured, however, that there will be ample warning if one bears down on the islands while you're there. The Tongans have seen enough hurricanes to ensure their guests' safety.

EVENTS

The largest annual festival is ✪ **Heilala,** which coincides with the King's Birthday on July 4. Nuku'alofa goes all out for a week of dance and beauty competitions, parades, sporting matches, band concerts, marching contests, yacht regattas, parties, and the lovely Night of Torches on the waterfront. Tongans living overseas like to come home for Heilala, so hotel reservations should be made well in advance. Vava'u stages its own version of Heilala early in May.

The Tongan version of a state fair is the **Royal Agricultural Show.** One show is held in each of the island groups during late August or early September. His Majesty visits them all and examines the best of the crops and handcrafts.

Other festivals are **Red Cross Week** in May, the **opening of Parliament** early in June, and the **Music Festival** early in December.

The Tonga Visitors Bureau keeps track of when the festivals will occur each year.

HOLIDAYS

Public holidays in Tonga are New Year's Day, Good Friday and Easter Monday, ANZAC (Memorial) Day (April 25), Crown Prince Tupouto'a's birthday (May 4), Emancipation Day (in honor of King George I, June 4), the King's Birthday (July 4), Constitution Day (November 4), King Tupou I Day (December 4), Christmas Day, and Boxing Day (December 26).

8 Getting There & Getting Around

GETTING THERE

Air New Zealand flies between Los Angeles and Tonga at least once a week, with brief stops in Honolulu and Western Samoa. Those flights go on to Auckland and return over the same route. **Air Pacific** connects Tonga to its flights from Los Angeles to Fiji. **Polynesian Airlines** also flies to Tonga from Auckland, Sydney, Western Samoa, and the Cook Islands. **Royal Tongan Airlines** has Auckland–Tonga and Nadi–Tonga service, and it may have direct flights between Nadi and Vava'u by the time you plan your trip. **Samoa Air,** based in American Samoa, flies its small planes between Pago Pago and Vava'u.

There are no flights into, out of, or in Tonga on Sunday, when the local airports are closed.

For more information, see "Getting There" in "Planning a Trip to the South Pacific" (Chapter 3).

GETTING AROUND

Except for the few international flights destined for Vava'u, most land at **Fua'amotu Airport** on Tongatapu, 24km (14 miles) from Nuku'alofa. Built with Japanese aid, the new terminal has a bank, duty-free shop, and small handcraft outlet. International passengers can purchase duty-free liquor and cigarettes after clearing Immigration but before going through Customs.

Transportation from the airport into Nuku'alofa is by hotel minibuses or taxi. The bus ride to town costs T$6 ($5). The one-way taxi fare into Nuku'alofa is about T$12 ($9.50); the drivers will be happy to take U.S., New Zealand, or Australian currency.

A departure tax of T$15 ($12) is charged of all passengers leaving on international flights. You pay it in Tongan currency at Fua'amotu Airport, at a separate booth outside Immigration. There is no departure tax for domestic flights.

BY PLANE   The kingdom's only domestic carrier, **Royal Tongan Airlines** (☎ 23-414) has a monopoly on air travel within the country, providing at least three round-trip flights a day between Tongatapu and Vava'u. Daily service is also provided between Tongatapu, 'Eua, and Ha'apai. The round-trip fare from Tongatapu to Vava'u is about T$240 ($192); to 'Eua, T$34 ($27); and to Ha'apai, T$120 ($96).

It's always a good idea to book your flights as far in advance as you can. Always reconfirm your return flight as soon as possible after arriving on an outer island.

The airlines' offices are in the Royco Building on Fatafehi Road at Wellington Road.

BY FERRY   It's not for everyone, but the **Shipping Corporation of Polynesia** (☎ 21-699) operates weekly ferry service from Nuku'alofa to Ha'apai and Vava'u, using the M.V. *Olovaha,* a car-ferry with a few passenger cabins. It usually leaves

Nuku'alofa

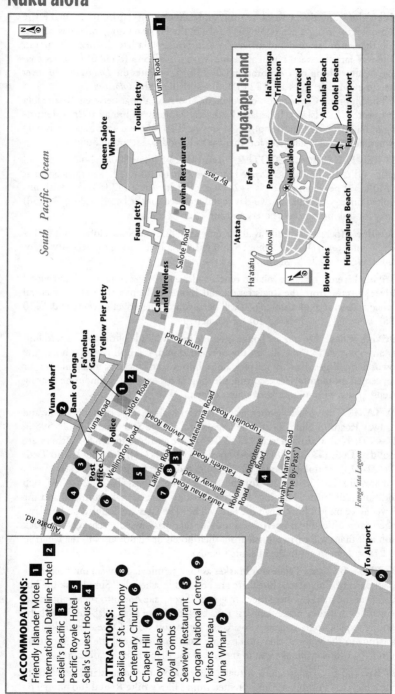

ACCOMMODATIONS:
Friendly Islander Motel **1**
International Dateline Hotel **2**
Lesieli's Pacific **3**
Pacific Royale Hotel **5**
Sela's Guest House **4**

ATTRACTIONS:
Basilica of St. Anthony **8**
Centenary Church **6**
Chapel Hill **4**
Royal Palace **3**
Royal Tombs **7**
Seaview Restaurant **5**
Tongan National Centre **9**
Visitors Bureau **1**
Vuna Wharf **2**

⊠ Post Office

South Pacific Ocean

Tongatapu Island

'Atata
Fafa
Pangaimotu
Ha'amonga Trilithon
Terraced Tombs
Anahula Beach
Oholei Beach
Fua'amotu Airport
Nuku'alofa
Kolovai
Ha'atafu
Hufangalupe Beach
Blow Holes

Vuna Road
Touliki Jetty
Queen Salote Wharf
Faua Jetty
Davina Restaurant
By Pass
Salote Road
Cable and Wireless
Yellow Pier Jetty
Fa'onelua Gardens
Bank of Tonga
Vuna Wharf
Police
Post Office
Tungi Road
Salote Road
Vuna Road
Wellington Road
Laifone Road
Lavinia Road
Mateialona Road
Fatafehi Road
Taufa'ahau Road
Railway Road
Holomui Road
Longoteme Road
Tupoulahi Road
A Laivaha Mama'o Road ("The By-Pass")
Alipate Rd.
Fanga 'uta Lagoon
To Airport

0191

Nuku'alofa one day a week at 6pm and takes about 16 hours to make the 163-mile trip to Vava'u, stopping at Lifuka in the Ha'apai Group on the way. The ship then turns around and arrives back in Nuku'alofa late the next afternoon. One-way fares between Nuku'alofa and Vava'u are T$42 ($33.50) for deck passage. **Walter Shipping Corporation** (☎ 23-855) operates the *Lotoha'amgana* over the same route. Its fares are T$2 ($1.60) less than on the *Olovaha*.

The Shipping Corporation of Polynesia also runs a boat between Nuku'alofa and nearby 'Eua Island. It departs Faua jetty Monday to Friday at 2pm, returning to Nuku'alofa the next morning. Fares are T$6 ($5) one way. Small, privately owned boats leave Faua jetty for 'Eua around midday, except on Sunday.

BY RENTAL CAR & SCOOTER   Avis (☎ 23-344, or 800/331-1212 in U.S.) has an office in the Pacific Royale Hotel on Taufa'ahau Road. The rates begin at T$40 ($32) per day plus T15¢ (12¢) per kilometer, or T$47 ($37.50) with unlimited mileage (minimum two-day rental required for the latter). Add T$10 ($8) a day for full insurance. Scooters rent for T$26 ($21) a day.

Gasoline   (petrol) is readily available only at stations in Nuku'alofa, so fill up before leaving town. It cost about T$1.60 ($1.28) a liter during my recent visit, or about $4.90 for a U.S. gallon.

Driving License   Before you can officially drive in Tonga you must obtain a local driver's license from the Registration and Licensing Department at the Central Police Station in Nuku'alofa. You will need your home driver's license and T$10 ($8) for rental cars, T$4 ($3.20) for scooters.

Driving Rules   Driving in Tonga is on the left-hand side of the road. Speed limits are 65kmph (39 m.p.h.) on the open road and 40kmph (24 m.p.h.) in the towns and villages. Be alert for pigs, dogs, horses, and chickens, and pull over for policemen on motorcycles escorting the king in his long black limousine bearing license plates with no numbers, only a crown.

BY TAXI   Taxis usually gather near Talamahu Market at the corner of Salote and Railway Roads in Nuku'alofa. The largest firm is **Five Star Taxis** (☎ 21-595 or 21-429). **Nuku'alofa Taxis** (☎ 22-624) are radio dispatched. Others are **Holiday Taxis** (☎ 21-858), **One-Way Taxis** (☎ 21-741), **Friendly Island Taxis** (☎ 21-023), **Malolala Taxis** (☎ 22-500), and **City Taxis** (☎ 22-734).

Fares are T$1.50 ($1.20) for the first kilometer plus T30¢ (24¢) for each additional kilometer, but since the taxis have no meters, make sure you and the driver agree on just how much the fare will be. The fares are doubled on Sundays, when taxis officially are permitted only to take passengers to church and back (some of them will carry tourists from their hotels or guesthouses to the wharf in order for them to get to the offshore islands).

BY BUS   Buses use **Talamahu Market** as their terminal. They fan out from there to all parts of Tongatapu, but there are no reliable schedules. Simply ask the bus drivers at the market where they are going. If you take one into the countryside, remember that they make their last runs back to Nuku'alofa at about 3pm daily, in time to pick up passengers who are just getting off work. Once they make their last runs to the villages, they don't come back to town until the next morning. About T$1 (80¢) will take you to the end of the island in either direction.

BY BICYCLE   Tongatapu is virtually flat, making it an ideal island on which to ride a bicycle. "Pushbikes" can be rented from **Niko's Bike Rental** (no phone) on the Vuna waterfront near the International Dateline Hotel. One-speed models cost T$2 ($1.60) per hour or T$6 ($4.80) for a full day.

FAST FASTS: Tonga

American Express   American Express has no representative in Tonga.

Area Code   The international country code is 676.

Bookstores   Friendly Islands Bookshop (☎ 23-787), on Taufa'ahau Road near the Pacific Royale Hotel, carries greeting cards made from tapa cloth, paperback books, postcards, international news magazines, week-old Australian newspapers, books about Tonga and the South Pacific, and a sheet of maps of Tonga.

Business Hours   In general, Tonga's shops are open Monday to Friday from 8am to 1pm and 2 to 5pm, Saturday from 8am to noon. Government offices are open Monday to Friday from 8:30am to 12:30pm and 1:30 to 4:30pm.

Camera/Film   Color film and color print film processing are available at a number of shops in Nuku'alofa, including the gift shop at the International Dateline Hotel.

Clothing   Summer clothing is in order during most of the year, but a sweater, jacket, or wrap should be taken for evening wear throughout the year. Tongans are very conservative, and visitors should not wear bathing suits or skimpy attire away from the hotel pools or beaches frequented by foreigners. In fact, appearing in public without a shirt is a punishable offense for both men and women, as is nudity of any degree.

Dentist   Vaiola Hospital (☎ 21-200) provides dental service in Nuku'alofa; the outpatient clinics are open from 8:30am to 4:30pm daily.

Doctor   German-trained Drs. Helga Schäfer-Macdonald and Bruno Blersch (☎ 22-736) practice on Wellington Road at Fatafehi Road.

Drug Laws   Don't even think about bringing illegal narcotics or dangerous drugs into Tonga.

Drugstores   The Nuku'alofa Pharmacy Clinic (☎ 21-007) is on Salote Road in the block west of Taufa'ahau Road. Hours are Monday to Friday from 9:30am to 5pm and Saturday 9am to noon. For toiletries, go to the big Morris Hedstrom department store on Salote Road near the market.

Electricity   Electricity in Tonga is 240 volts, 50 cycles, and the plugs are the heavy, angled type used in Australia and New Zealand. You will need a converter and adapter plug to operate American appliances.

Embassies and Consulates   The nearest U.S. embassy is in Suva, Fiji. There is an office of the United States Peace Corps in Nuku'alofa (☎ 21-467). Consular offices in Tonga are the Australian High Commission (☎ 21-244), the British High Commission (☎ 21-021), the New Zealand High Commission (☎ 21-122), the Embassy of the Republic of China (Taiwan) (☎ 21-766), the Honorary Consulate of France (☎ 21-830), the Honorary Consulate of West Germany (☎ 21-477), and the Honorary Consulate of Nauru (☎ 22-109).

Emergencies   The emergency telephone number for the police, fire department, and hospital is 911.

Eyeglasses   Vaiola Hospital is the only place to get glasses fixed or replaced. See "Hospital," below.

Firearms   They are illegal in Tonga.

Gambling   There is no casino or other form of organized gambling in Tonga.

Hitchhiking   It's not against the law, but Tongans are not particularly accustomed to picking up strangers.

Hospital   Vaiola Hospital (☎ 21-200) provides medical, dental, and optical service, but it's considerably below Western standards. The outpatient clinics are open from 8:30am to 4:30pm daily.

Insects   There are no dangerous insects in Tonga, and the mosquitoes do not carry malaria. Vava'u, warmer and more humid than Tongatapu, tends to have more mosquitoes and has tropical centipedes that can inflict painful stings if touched; watch your step if walking around with bare feet.

Library   'Utue'a Public Library, on the ground floor of Basilica of St. Anthony of Padua on Taufa'ahau Road, usually is open Monday to Friday from 3 to 9pm and Saturday from 10am to 3pm.

Liquor Laws   Licensed hotels can sell alcoholic beverages to their guests seven days a week; otherwise, sale is prohibited from midnight Saturday to midnight Sunday.

Maps   Free maps of Nuku'alofa, Tongatapu, and Vava'u are available at the Tonga Visitors Bureau. Friendly Islands Bookstore, on Taufa'ahau Road near the Pacific Royale Hotel, sells a sheet of maps of Tonga.

Newspapers/Magazines   The *Tonga Chronicle* is a government-owned weekly newspaper appearing on Friday. It carries local news in both Tongan and English, but there are so many stories about the king and his family that many locals facetiously call it the "Royal Diary." For a different view, look for *Matangi Tonga,* a fine monthly magazine edited by the noted Tongan writer and publisher Pesi Fonua. It carries features about the kingdom and its people.

Police   The main station is Salote Road at Railway Road. The emergency phone number is 911.

Post Office   The Nuku'alofa Post Office is at the corner of Taufa'ahau and Salote Roads. It's open Monday to Friday from 8:30am to 4pm. Air mail letters to the U.S. cost T80¢ (64¢); postcards are T45¢ (36¢). Tongan stamps, some of which are in the shape of bananas and pineapples, are collectors' items. They are available at the post office counters or upstairs in the Philatelic Bureau, which is open Monday to Friday from 8:30am to 12:30pm and 1:30 to 4:30pm.

Radio/TV   The government-owned radio station, A3Z or "Radio Tonga," broadcasts in both the AM and FM bands. Most programming on the AM station is in Tongan, although the music played is mostly American, Australian, or British popular tunes. The news in English is relayed from the BBC or Radio Australia several times a day. Some programming is provided by the Voice of America. There is a private AM and FM station that broadcasts Christian programs.

Tonga has two television channels—one government-owned, one Christian-owned—which are on the air daily from 5 to 11pm.

Safety Although crimes against tourists have been rare in Tonga, remember that the communal property system still prevails in the Kingdom. Items such as cameras and bags left unattended may disappear, so take the proper precautions. Street crime is not a problem, but it's a good idea to be on the alert if you walk down dark streets at night. Women should not wander alone on deserted beaches.

Taxes The government imposes a 5% sales tax on all items purchased in Tonga, $7^{1}/2\%$ on hotel rooms. The tax is added to some bills in the American fashion and included in others. All passengers on international flights pay a departure tax of T$15 ($12).

Telephone/Telex/Fax Calls can be dialed directly into Tonga from most areas of the world. The international country code is 676.

International calls, telegrams, and telex messages can be placed from your hotel or at the office of Cable and Wireless Ltd., on Salote Road at the corner of Takaunove Road, open 24 hours a day, seven days a week. Station-to-station phone calls to the U.S. cost T$9.50 ($7.60) for the first three minutes, T$12 ($9.60) for person-to-person. The rates to Australia and New Zealand are about half those amounts. Cable and Wireless accepts MasterCard, Visa, and AT&T credit cards.

Public pay telephones are at the airport and post offices, and in red, English-style booths in a few villages. You lift the receiver, listen for a dial tone, deposit a Tongan 20-seniti coin, and dial the number. The number for directory assistance is 910 or 919; for emergencies, 911; and for the international operator, 913.

Time Local time in Tonga is 13 hours ahead of Greenwich mean time. Translated, Tonga is three hours behind the U.S. West Coast during standard time (four hours behind during daylight saving time)—and one day ahead. If it's noon on Tuesday in Tonga, it's 3pm pacific standard time on Monday in Los Angeles and 6pm eastern standard time on Monday in New York.

Tipping Although it has gained a foothold, tipping is officially discouraged in Tonga because it's considered contrary to the Polynesian tradition of hospitality to guests. One time it is encouraged is during Tongan dance shows, when members of the audience rush up to the female dancers and stick notes to their well-oiled bodies.

Water The tap water in Nuku'alofa is drinkable, but the same cannot be said about the water in the rest of the kingdom. Bottled water is available at most groceries in Nuku'alofa. When outside of town, make sure to ask whether the drinking water is from a rainwater catchment.

Weights and Measures Tonga uses the metric system of weights and measures.

9 What to See & Do

This quaint little kingdom has a lot for visitors to see and do six days a week. **Sunday in Tonga** is more of a challenge, since nearly everyone goes to church, followed by a family feast and an afternoon of lounging around. You can worship with the royal family at 10am in the Centenary Church on Wellington Road. Tongan men wear neckties, but tourists get by without if they're neatly dressed. Women should wear dresses that cover the shoulders and knees. When I was there recently, **Paea Tours** (☎ 21-103) was offering a special Sunday outing that began with church, then a tour of eastern Tongatapu, a stop for a traditional lunch with a Tongan family, and a tour of the island's western side. It was a good value at T$35 ($28) per person. Many of us visitors—and a good many Westernized Tongans, too— head for one of the offshore resorts (see "Island Excursions, Water Sports & Other Outdoor Activities," below), where we can get a meal, some libation, and a legal swim.

For a broadening cultural experience, the Tonga Visitors Bureau operates a complimentary **home visit system** that pairs overseas visitors with Tongan families willing to have them into their homes and show them the Tongan way of life. You can request families whose members are engaged in particular professions or occupations. Contact the TVB for procedures (see "Information, Entry Requirements & Money," above). Applications must be made at least a day in advance of when you wish to visit.

✪ TONGAN NATIONAL CENTER

Anyone with the slightest interest in native cultures should make a point to visit the **Tongan National Center** (☎ 23-022), one of the South Pacific's best exhibitions. Located on the lagoon shores across from Vaiola Hospital, about a mile south of Nuku'alofa on Taufa'ahau Road, the center's fale-style buildings house displays of Tongan history, geology, and handcrafts. In fact, artisans work daily on their crafts and sell their wares to visitors (no packing and shipping). In other words, you can see how Tonga's remarkable handcrafts are made, which should help as you later scour the local shops for good buys. The exhibition hall is open from Monday to Friday from 9am to noon. Regular admission is T$2 ($1.60). A lunch of Tongan food is followed by special displays from 2 to 4pm featuring demonstrations of carving, weaving, tapa making, food preparation, a kava ceremony, and dance demonstration. The price is T$12 ($9.50) for lunch and

---

✪ Frommer's Favorite Tonga Experiences

Seeing the King. Being an American and therefore not particularly enamored of royalty, I nevertheless enjoy watching King Taufa'ahau Tupou being chauffeured around his kingdom—sometimes in the back seat of a stretched pickup truck— and being given the royal treatment whenever he arrives somewhere.

Sunday on an Islet. I usually stay very busy revising this guide, but I am forced by law to put it aside and relax on Sunday in Tonga. I like to spend my day doing nothing at one of the little resorts off Nuku'alofa.

Watching the Blow Holes. Having crossed the Pacific several times in U.S. Navy ships and sailed across it once in a small boat, I am acutely aware of the power of the sea. It's strangely comforting to watch it explode through the Blow Holes on Tongatapu's south coast. Maybe it's because I know those waves can't get me up there on dry land.

Exploring Vava'u. There are a lot of South Pacific places where I would like to stay just a little longer, and beautiful Vava'u is at the top of the list. Visiting this boating paradise is a very different experience than visiting Tongatapu. The main village of Neiafu is a trip even farther back in time than Nuku'alofa.

tour, T$8 ($6.50) for tour only. A travel agent or hotel tour desk will make reservations for you.

A highlight in the history section is the long robe Queen Salote wore at the coronation of Queen Elizabeth II in 1953, and the carcass of Tui Malila, the Galapagos tortoise Capt. James Cook reputedly gave the Tui Tonga in 1777. The beast lived until 1968.

A WALKING TOUR OF NUKU'ALOFA

Before you start out to see Nuku'alofa, drop by the Tonga Visitors Bureau office on Vuna Road near the International Dateline Hotel and pick up a copy of the excellent brochure, "Walking Tour of Central Nuku'alofa." A morning's stroll around this interesting town will be time well spent, for in many respects it's a throwback to times gone by in the South Pacific. Although there are no street-name posts, the visitors bureau has put up signs giving general directions to the main sights. In addition, Nuku'alofa more or less is laid out on a grid, so you shouldn't have trouble finding your way around. It's also flat, with no hills to climb.

Teta Tours (☎ 21-688) offers a guided tour of Nuku'alofa for just T$8 ($6.50) per person. If you do it yourself, here is a truncated version of the visitors bureau tour that hits the highlights of Nuku'alofa.

Start at the **Tonga Visitors Bureau** and walk west along Vuna Road toward the heart of town. The park on the left as you leave the Visitors Bureau is known as **Fa'onelua Gardens.** The modern three-story building before Railway Road houses the government ministries of works, agriculture, health, education, lands and survey, and civil aviation. As a resident of the Washington, D.C., area, every time I see this building I think of my own nation's capital, where it takes several huge buildings and hundreds of acres of land to house that many departments of the U.S. government.

Turn left on Railway Road. The small colonial-era wooden structure on the left in the first block serves as both the **Court House** and **parliament** when it meets from June to September. Both court and parliament sessions are open to the public. Now return to Vuna Road and turn left.

Vuna Wharf, at the foot of Taufa'ahau Road, Nuku'alofa's main street, was built in 1906, and for some 60 years most visitors to Tonga debarked from ships that tied up here. It became less trafficked when Queen Salote Wharf was erected east of town in 1966 to handle large ships, and a major earthquake in 1977 damaged Vuna Wharf so extensively that it has been used since only in emergencies. A railroad once ran through town along Railway Road to transport copra and other crops to Vuna Wharf. Meat and seafood are sold at **Vuna Market** to the east of the wharf.

Directly across Vuna Road from the wharf is the low **Treasury Building.** Constructed in 1928, it's a fine example of South Pacific colonial architecture. Early in its life it housed the Tongan Customs service and the post office as well as the Treasury Department.

The field to the west of the wharf is the **Pangai,** where royal feasts, kava ceremonies, and parades are held. Overlooking the Pangai and surrounded by towering Norfolk pines is the ✪ **Royal Palace,** a white Victorian building with gingerbread fretwork and gables under a red roof. The palace was prefabricated in

New Zealand, shipped to Tonga, and erected in 1867. The second-story veranda was added in 1882. You can get a good view over the low white fence built of coral blocks (the best spot for photographs is on the east side, so save some film until we get around there). The king and queen usually live on a large spread west of town.

Now walk up Taufa'ahau Road past the huge rain tree in front of the modern Bank of Tonga (a local gathering place). Across the street stands the colonial-style **Prime Minister's Office** with its quaint tower.

Turn right at the post office on Salote Road. The **Nuku'alofa Club** on the left, about halfway down the block, is another holdover from the old South Pacific: It's a private club where Tonga's elite males gather to relax over a game of snooker and a few Australian beers. The next block of Salote Road runs behind the Royal Palace. You can look over the backyard fence and observe the royal geese. Turn right on Vaha'akolo Road and walk along the west side of the palace toward the sea. The highest point on Tongatapu, **Chapel Hill** (or Zion Hill) to the left, part of the Royal Estate, was a Tongan fort during the 18th century and the site of a missionary school opened in 1830 and a large Wesleyan church built in 1865. The school is now located four miles west of Nuku'alofa and is known as **Sia'atoutai Theological College.** The church has long since been torn down.

When you get to the water, look back and take your photos of the palace framed by the Norfolk pines.

Picturesque **Vuna Road** runs west from the palace, with the sea and reef on one side and stately old colonial homes on the other. The house at the end of the first block was the home of a Tongan noble who on several occasions in the 1800s went to England, where he stayed with friends in Newcastle; accordingly, he named the house **Niukasa.** The British High Commissioner's residence, in the second block, sports a flagpole surrounded by four cannons from the *Port au Prince,* the ship captured and burned by the Tongans at Ha'apai in 1806 after they had clubbed to death all its crew except young Will Mariner. King George I had two wives—not concurrently—and both of them are buried in casuarina-ringed Mala'e'aloa Cemetery, whose name means "tragic field." The clapboard house in the next block is known as **Ovalau** because it was built in the 1800s at Levuka, the old capital of Fiji on the island of Ovalau, and was shipped to Tonga in the 1950s.

Turn inland at the corner, walk two blocks on 'Alipate Road, take a left on Wellington Road, and walk two blocks west to **Centenary Church.** The mansion just before the church was reputed to have been built about 1871 by the Rev. Shirley W. Baker, the missionary who had so much influence over King George I. Now it's the home of the president of the Free Wesleyan Church of Tonga. Centenary Church was built by the Free Wesleyan Church of Tonga between 1949 and 1952. Most of the construction materials and labor were donated by members of the church. While construction was going on, the town was divided into sections that fed the workers three meals a day on a rotating basis. The amount of money spent on the building was about T$80,000 ($72,000); the actual value of the materials and labor was many times that amount. The church seats about 2,000 persons, including the king and queen, who worship there on Sunday mornings.

Turn right past the church and proceed inland on Vaha'akolo Road. On the right behind the Centenary Church is the old **Free Wesleyan Church of Tonga,** built in 1888 and an example of early Tongan church architecture. Past the old

We had come to see the island and the islanders had come to see us and both sides were having a fine time.

—John Dyson, 1982

church is **Queen Salote College,** a girls' school named for a wife of King George I and not for his great-great-granddaughter, the famous Queen Salote.

Turn left at the first street, known as Laifone Road, and walk along a large open space to your right. Since 1893 this area has been known as the ✪ **Royal Tombs,** and King George I, King George II, Queen Salote, and most of their various wives and husbands are buried at the center of the field. For many years the rest of the area was used as a golf course; today, however, the king's cattle keep the grass mowed. On Taufa'ahau Road, behind this open expanse stands the modern **Queen Salote Memorial Hall,** the country's national auditorium, which opened in 1994.

On the other side of Taufa'ahau Road, opposite the Royal Tombs, rises the tent-shaped **Basilica of St. Anthony of Padua,** the first basilica built in the South Pacific islands. On the ground level are the Loki Kai Cafeteria (more commonly known as Akiko's Restaurant) and the 'Utue'a Public Library.

Now follow **Taufa'ahau Road** toward the waterfront. This is Nuku'alofa's "main street," and you'll pass shop after shop, some of them carrying handcrafts and clothing. Between Wellington Road and Salote Road is an old house that now is the home of the **Langa Fonua Women's Association Handicraft Center** (see "Best Buys," below). The clapboard house was built by William Cocker, a local merchant, for his five daughters, who lived in New Zealand but spent each winter in Nuku'alofa.

Turn right on the next street—Salote Road—and walk past the police station on the left to **Talamahu Market** in the second block, where vendors sell a great variety of fresh produce ranging from huge taro roots and watermelons to string beans and bananas. Tongatapu's climate is just cool enough during the winter months that both European and tropical fruits and vegetables grow in great bounty. Several stalls carry handcraft items, such as tapa cloth and straw baskets and mats.

After looking around the market and perhaps munching on a banana or sipping a fresh young coconut, continue walking east. In the next block is the park known as Fa'onelua Gardens; walk through it to the Tonga Visitors Bureau, where we began our tour and where we end it.

SEEING TONGATAPU

Most visitors see Tonga's main island in two parts: first the eastern side and its ancient archaeological sites, then the western side for its natural spectacles. You can see the island with **Paea Tours** (☎ 21-103), which has some of the best sightseeing bargains: T$20 ($16) for a tour of the whole island, T$10 ($8) for a half-day tour of Tongatapu's western side, and T$25 ($20) for half-day on the eastern side. **Teta Tours** (☎ 21-688) charges a bit more for its out-of-town sightseeing excursions. Prices jump appreciably if only one person takes a tour.

The Eastern Tour Take Taufa'ahau Road out of Nuku'alofa, making sure to bear left on the paved road. If you want to see tropical birds in captivity, watch for the signs on the right-hand side of the road directing you to the bird exhibit at the **Tongan Wildlife Centre,** and follow the dirt track about 3km. There you will find a park with a small collection of birds from Tonga and other South Pacific islands kept in cages carefully planted with native vegetation. Admission is free, although donations are accepted. The exhibit is open Wednesday to Sunday from 10am to 5pm.

Now backtrack to the main road and turn right toward the airport. Keep left, especially at Malapo (where the road to the airport goes to the right), and follow the Tonga Visitors Bureau's excellent signs, which will show you the way to **Mu'a.** When the road skirts the lagoon just before the village, watch for a grassy area beside the water where Capt. James Cook landed and rested under a large banyan tree in 1777. Cook came ashore to meet with Pau, the reigning Tui Tonga, and attended the traditional presentation of first fruits marking the beginning of the harvest season. The banyan tree is long gone; in its place is a stone-and-brass monument commemorating **Captain Cook's Landing Place.**

The next village is ✪ **Lapaha,** seat of the Tui Tonga for six centuries beginning about A.D. 1200. All that remains of the royal compound is a series of *langa,* or ancient terraced tombs, some of which are visible from the road. A large sign explains how the supreme Polynesian god, Tangaloa, came down from the sky about A.D. 950 and sired the first Tui Tonga. The last Tui Tonga, who died in 1865 after being deposed by King George I in 1862, is buried in one of the tombs. The 28 tombs around Lapaha and Mu'a are among the most important archaeological sites in Polynesia, but none of them has been excavated. Walk down the dirt road near the sign to see more of the tombs.

From Lapaha, follow the scenic paved road along the coast until reaching the ✪ **Ha'amonga Trilithon,** near the village of Niutoua on the island's northeast point, 32km (19 miles) from Nuku'alofa. This huge archway, whose lintel stone is estimated to weigh 35 tons, is 16 feet high and 19 feet wide. Tradition says it was built by the 11th Tui Tonga about A.D. 1200, long before the wheel was introduced to Tonga, as the gateway to the royal compound. The present King Taufa'ahau Tupou IV advanced a theory that it was used not only as a gateway but also for measuring the seasons. He found a secret mark on top of the lintel stone and at dawn on June 21, 1967, proved his point. The mark pointed to the exact spot on the horizon from which the sun rose on the shortest day of the year. You can stand under this imposing archway and ponder just how the ancient Tongans got the lintel stone on top of its two supports; it's the same sense of mysterious wonderment you feel while looking at Stonehenge in England or contemplating the great long-nosed heads that were carved and somehow erected by those other Polynesians far to the east of Tonga, on Easter Island.

The paved road ends at **Niutoua,** but a narrow dirt track proceeds down the east coast. **Anahulu** is a cave with limestone stalactites near the village of Haveluliku. A gorgeous sand beach begins here and runs to **Oholei Beach.** 'Eua Island is visible on the horizon.

On the way back to Nuku'alofa you can take a detour to **Hufangalupe Beach** on the south coast for a look at a large natural bridge carved out of coral and limestone by the sea.

The Western Tour   Proceed out of Nuku'alofa on Mateialona Road and follow the Visitors Bureau signs to the ✪ **blowholes** near the village of Houma on the southwest coast. At high tide the surf pounds under shelves, sending geysers of seawater through holes in the coral. These are the most impressive blowholes in the South Pacific, and on a windy day the coast for miles is shrouded in mist thrown into the air by hundreds of them working at once. They perform best on a day when the surf is medium—that is, just high enough to pound under the shelves and send water exploding up through holes in them. Lime sediments have built up terraces of circles, like rice paddies, around each hole, and the local women come just before dusk to gather clams in the shallow pools formed by the rings. There is a park with benches and a parking area at the end of the road near the blowholes, but you'll need shoes with good soles to walk across the sharp edges of the top shelf to get the best views. This area once was an underwater reef, and corals are still very much visible, all of them now more than 50 feet above sea level. (Look for what appear to be fossilized brains; they are appropriately named brain corals.) The blowholes are known in Tongan as *Mapu'a a Vaea,* "the chief's whistle."

From Houma, proceed west to the village of Kolovai and watch for the trees with strange-looking fruit. The sounds you hear and the odors in the air are coming from what appear to be black fruit hanging on the trees. In reality, these are the **Flying Foxes of Kolovai,** a type of bat with a foxlike head found on many islands in the Pacific. They are nocturnal creatures who spend their days hanging upside down from the branches of trees like a thousand little Draculas awaiting the dark, their wings like black capes pulled tightly around their bodies. They don't feed on blood but on fruit; hence they are known as fruit bats. On some islands they are considered a delicacy. In Tonga, however, where they live in trees throughout the villages of Kolovai and Ha'avakatolo, they are thought to be sacred, and only members of the royal family can shoot them. Legend says that the first bats were given to a Tongan navigator by a Samoan princess.

A road from Kolovai goes about a mile west of **Kolovai Beach** and the Good Samaritan Inn, a good place to sip a drink while watching the sun set or to enjoy a picnic on Sunday afternoons. Near the end of the island is **Ha'atafu Beach,** site of an offshore reef preserve.

The first missionaries to land in Tonga came ashore at the end of the peninsula on the northwest coast, and a sign now marks the spot at the end of the road. They obviously got their feet wet—if they were not inadvertently "baptized"—wading across the shallow bank just offshore.

You've now toured Tongatapu from one end to the other. Turn around and head back to town.

10 Where to Stay

Let's put it this way: if an expensive, super-luxurious vacation or honeymoon is your primary reason for coming to the South Pacific, go to Fiji or French Polynesia, not to Tonga. There are no large luxury resorts at all in Tonga, although there are comfortable—though far from deluxe—hotels and island hideaways to choose from.

That's not to say some establishments here don't have considerable charm, especially Tonga's **offshore resorts,** those little hideaways sitting all by themselves on small islands off Tongatapu's north shore. Go there to rest, relax, sunbathe, swim, snorkel, dive, dine, get drunk, or do whatever comes naturally in a romantic South Seas bungalow. On the other hand, don't spend your entire holiday at an offshore resort if you want to see much of the country or to sample exciting nightlife, since to get anywhere else requires a rather lengthy boat ride. Consider spending a weekend out in the islands, since everyone else will be there on Sunday anyway.   •

HOTELS

Friendly Islander Motel

P.O. Box 142, Nuku'alofa (Vuna Road, on the waterfront two miles east of downtown Nuku'alofa). ☎ **23-810.** Fax 24-199. 26 units. A/C TEL. T$60–T$95 ($48–$76). No credit cards.

Papiloa Foliaki, once Tonga's only female member of Parliament, started this motel in 1980 with 12 comfortable, self-contained units. She has added a swimming pool, restaurant, nightclub, bar, and 14 bungalows. The older units are in a two-story building facing the sea on one side and a courtyard full of tropical plants on the other. Those on the ocean side are small suites with separate bedrooms and sitting areas. All rooms have kitchenettes, tile baths, wall-mounted fans, radios, and sliding glass doors leading either to a patio on ground level or to a balcony on the second story. Built of modern materials but in the oval shape of Tongan fales, the new bungalows are across a side street or behind the main complex. Eight of them have one room; the others have a separate bedroom and are called "Family Fales." All bungalows have shower-only baths and both air conditioners and ceiling fans.

A dining room specializes in dishes featuring fresh local produce. The establishment also is home to the 'Ofa Atu Nightclub, but it's open only on Friday.

International Dateline Hotel

P.O. Box 39, Nuku'alofa (Vuna Road at Tupoulahi Road, on the waterfront). ☎ **23-411.** Fax 23-410. 76 rms. A/C TEL. T$94–T$120 ($75–$96). AE, DC, MC, V.

Built prior to the king's coronation in 1967, this is Tonga's most widely known place to stay. It has undergone a much-needed renovation in recent years, but some of the rooms and their spartan furnishings still remind me of those 1960s motels that line the old federal roads back in the U.S., having been bypassed by the Interstate highway system. In other words, the Dateline is an older but clean hotel. The property enjoys a choice location facing the harbor across Vuna Road on Nuku'alofa's waterfront, a few blocks from downtown, and it's the only hotel on Tongatapu with spacious grounds featuring a riot of tropical plants surrounding a swimming pool.

In good weather, the Tu'imalila Dining Room has tables and plastic chairs outside and some form of entertainment after dinner each evening, including traditional Tongan dance shows. The food is plain but adequate. Even if you don't eat there, drop by for a drink at the bar and a dance show. The activities desk will tell you what's on during your stay.

Lesieli's Pacific

P.O. Box 2432, Nuku'alofa (on Taufa'ahau Road, opposite Queen Salote Memorial Hall). ☎ **21-099.** Fax 21-069. 8 units. A/C TV TEL. T$90–T$110 ($72–$88). AE, DC, MC, V.

John and Elizabeth Botica—he's a New Zealander, she's Tongan—built and opened Nuku'alofa's most modern establishment in 1995. They have six motel-style rooms and two apartments lined up beside their restaurant, which serves huge cooked breakfasts, has a cafe menu for lunch, and specializes in Polynesian-style meals for dinner. The units are of New Zealand–style construction, with lean-to tin roofs. Each is comfortably furnished and has a satellite-fed TV with CNN, ESPN, and Television New Zealand. The motel rooms have tea and coffee facilities; the two- and three-bedroom apartments come with full kitchens and sleeping lofts. All units have shower-only baths.

Pacific Royale Hotel

P.O. Box 74, Nuku'alofa (Taufa'ahau Road, in center of business district). ☎ **21-344.** Fax 23-833. 60 rms. A/C TEL. T$75–T$104 ($60–$83). AE, DC, MC, V.

The first time I saw the then-Ramanlal Hotel in the mid-1980s, I wondered whether I had made a serious blunder in making a reservation there. The entrance was through a covered alley between two stores in the third block from the water on Taufa'ahau Road, and I had to look hard to find the name of the hotel written near the top of the building. Once through the dusty alley, however, I came upon a small, lush tropical garden surrounding a small swimming pool. Beyond stood two blocks of hotel rooms, all comfortable and modern and with balconies overlooking this surprising and quite incongruous sight in the middle of Nuku'alofa's busy shopping district.

Since then Joe and Soane Ramanlal—sons of an Indian father from Fiji and a Tongan mother—have rebuilt the street-front building to include a modern reception area paneled from floor to ceiling. Upstairs is the Café Palmiers, a bright dining room with lounge offering soft music during the evenings. To the rear, a small thatch-roofed bar sits at the edge of the garden. Beyond is another Tongan-style fale serving as a small dining room by the pool. They have converted the second and third stories of the streetfront commercial building into 30 spacious hotel rooms, including a two-bedroom executive suite and a penthouse apartment. Granted, the Pacific Royale is an in-town commercial hotel rather than a resort, but it is perfectly comfortable and convenient as a base from which to tour the kingdom.

GUESTHOUSES & HOSTELS

Good Samaritan Inn

P.O. Box 306, Nuku'alofa (Kolovai Beach, 11 miles west of Nuku'alofa). ☎ **41-022.** 12 units (4 with bath). T$20 ($16) without bath; T$40 ($32) with bath. MC, V.

Run by Irene Mo'ungaloa, wife of the king's deputy secretary, this establishment is a popular Sunday retreat because of its pleasant dining room, bar, and concrete terrace perched right on Kolovai Beach. Accommodation is in very basic bungalows suitable for backpackers and others who seek no frills whatsoever. All units have electric lights, and all private and communal showers have hot water. A very comfy beachside lounge is available for guests use only. A cyclone damaged the beach here in 1993, so you will have to walk a short distance for swimming and snorkeling. Cars, bicycles, and snorkeling gear can be rented on premises.

Sela's Guest House

P.O. Box 24, Nuku'alofa (Longoteme Lane, between Fatafehi and Tupoulahi Roads). ☎ **21-430.** 14 rms (8 with bath), 5 dorm beds. T$20 ($16) without bath; T$30 ($24) with bath; T$8 ($6.50) dorm bed. No credit cards.

Sela launched her establishment in 1974 by providing room and board for U.S. Peace Corps volunteers training in Nuku'alofa prior to serving on the outer islands. She now has 12 double and 2 single rooms in the main part of her house and in a wing that she subsequently added to the rear. Eight of the rooms have their own baths; the others share four toilets and two showers (one with hot water). Guests have their own communal kitchen, but home-cooked meals are available. This is an excellent place to experience Tongan family life.

Toni's Guesthouse

P.O. Box 3084, Nuku'alofa (corner of Railway and Mateialona Roads). ☎ **21-049.** 6 rms (none with bath). T$11 ($8.80) per person. No credit cards.

Englishman Toni Matthias manages this simple, basic establishment popular with backpackers. The rooms here are in a long building fronted by a communal kitchen and covered gathering area on the carport. Toni does a kava ceremony each evening and runs island tours in his own truck for T$50 ($40) per load. Bicycles can be hired for T$5 ($4) a day. Airport transfers cost T$10 ($8) per load.

OFFSHORE RESORTS

Fafa Island Resort

P.O. Box 1444, Nuku'alofa (Fafa Island, 6 miles off Nuku'alofa). ☎ **22-800,** or 800/448-8355 in U.S. Fax 23-592. Telex 66222. 16 units. T$70–T$130 ($56–$104). Meal plans T$55 ($44) per person per day. Round-trip transfers T$15 ($12) per person. AE, DC, MC, V.

German Rainer Urtel has stocked his little resort with bungalows made entirely of local materials: coconut timbers and shingles and lots of thatch. Although rustic and definitely not for anyone looking for all the comforts of home, they have Robinson Crusoe charm that has attracted a largely European clientele. He started out with eight very basic fales circling a central building, all set in the center of this 17-acre, atoll-like island studded with coconut palms. He has replaced his original central fale with a much-improved version right on the beach and added eight much larger guest bungalows, also on the beach. These new models have porches; over one of them is a romantic "honeymoon" sleeping loft with a lagoon view. An unusual feature has the toilets and lavatories on rear porches and showers actually sitting in the middle of fenced-enclosed courtyards. The push-out windows aren't screened, so each of the platform beds has its own mosquito net.

The beachside central building houses a bar and a restaurant that features excellent German and Tongan seafood specialties. Guests can use Windsurfers, snorkeling gear, and surf skis for free; they pay extra for Hobie Cats.

Royal Sunset Island Resort

P.O. Box 960, Nuku'alofa ('Atata Island, 6 miles off Nuku'alofa). ☎ **24-923.** Fax 21-254. 26 bungalows. T$108–T$150 ($86.50–$120) double. Round-trip transfers T$40 ($32) per person. AE, DC, MC, V.

David and Terry Hunt's resort shares small 'Atata Island with a native Tongan village. A gorgeous beach swings around their end of the island, but the surrounding lagoon offers the real attraction for swimmers, snorkelers, scuba divers, and anyone who loves to fish (see "Island Excursions, Water Sports & Other Outdoor Activities," below). Two large shingle-roofed fales house a dining room and sunken bar. A swimming pool outside sports a deck dotted with lawn tables and umbrellas.

Each of the resort's bungalows sits behind privacy-providing foliage just off the beach. About half face the prevailing southeast trade winds; these can be chilly from June to August but provide nature's air conditioning during the warmer months of December to March. The other units facing the lagoon have a much better beach. Of modern construction, they all have their own spacious baths with hot and cold water, kitchenettes, ceiling fans in both rooms, and large, fully screened windows. A few bungalows are "mini-suites" with sitting areas and minibars.

Sun Island Resort

Private Bag 44, Nuku'alofa (2¹/₂ miles off Nuku'alofa). ☎ **32-335.** Fax 24-699. 4 bungalows (3 with bath), 5 dorm beds, 80 tent sites. T$20-T$60 ($18-$48) bungalow; T$20 ($18) dorm bed; T$10 ($8) per tent site. Round-trip transfers T$10 ($8). No credit cards.

This resort was intended to be a time-share operation, but when it failed in the mid-1990s, Americans Annemarie and Earl Markham took it over and began attracting a Sunday crowd with inexpensive meals. Those are eaten on a deck extending over a white sand beach that is excellent for swimming and snorkeling. The bungalows are on the rustic side, with concrete floors, wood plank walls, and thatch over tin roofs. Their windows are screened, but they have mosquito nets over their beds. One bungalow does not have its own bath; it and the dormitory and campground share communal toilets and showers. An expansive lawn in the center of the island is used as a campground. The dining room features inexpensive lunch and dinner specials. Guests have free use of snorkeling gear, Windsurfers, and paddle boats; day-trippers must pay. *Note:* The Markhams may accept credit cards by the time you visit.

Tongan Beachcomber Island Village

P.O. Box 740, Nuku'alofa (Pangaimotu Island, 2 miles off Nuku'alofa). ☎ **23-579.** Fax 23-759. 4 bungalows (all with bath). T$55 ($44) bungalow; T$15 ($12) dorm bed. Round-trip transfers T$10 ($8). MC, V.

Usually referred to as "Pangaimotu Island Resort," Earle Emberson's lively little retreat is usually packed on Sunday afternoons when it becomes the playground of tourists, local expatriot residents, and Westernized Tongans (the bachelor crown prince is a frequent Sunday guest). The charm here is the rickety-looking main building where Earle plays jazz compact discs at the bar while the staff whips up full meals or burgers and sandwiches served on an adjacent sundeck hanging over a lovely beach. All meals feature fresh local seafood. Guests can use kayaks on one of the safest swimming lagoons in Tonga. The four basic but comfortable guest fales are built of natural materials. They have separate sitting and sleeping areas, platform double beds with mosquito nets, and their own simple baths with hot-water showers. All face the beach. Dorm beds are in a larger communal fale.

11 Where to Dine

Nuku'alofa is blessed with a few restaurants that serve continental cuisine of remarkably high quality for such a small and unsophisticated town. But first, consider a Polynesian-style feast.

Tongan Feasts Like most Polynesians, the Tongans in the old days cooked their food over hot rocks in a pit—an *umu*—for several hours. Today they roast whole suckling pigs on a spit over coals for several hours (larger pigs still go into the umu). The dishes that emerge from the umu are similar to those found elsewhere in Polynesia: pig, chicken, lobster, fish, octopus, taro, taro leaves cooked with meat and onions, breadfruit, bananas, and a sweet breadfruit pudding known as *faikakai-lolo,* all of it cooked with ample amounts of coconut cream. Served on the side are fish *(ota ika)* and clams *(vasuva),* both marinated in lime juice.

The **Tonga National Centre** (☎ 23-022) stages a full Tongan-style feast complete with traditional kava welcoming ceremony and dance show Tuesday and Thursday at 7:30pm. Cost is an incredibly reasonable T$15 ($12). Book by 4:30pm.

EXPENSIVE

Davina's Restaurant and Bar

Vuna Road, at Faua Jetty. ☎ **23-385.** Reservations recommended at dinner. Sandwiches and snacks T$3–T$10 ($2.50–$8); main courses T$15.50–T$25.50 ($12.50–$20.50). MC, V. Mon–Sat 9am–11pm (breakfast all day, lunch noon–3pm, snacks 3–6pm, dinner 6–11pm). REGIONAL.

The name Davina is derived from David Foy and Gina Greguhn, who with silent partner Princess Pilolevu own this pleasant establishment in a pink stucco-over-cinderblock house. David is English; Gina is Tongan. Together they keep the place open all day for breakfast, lunch, afternoon snacks, and dinners. You can take your afternoon tea on the front porch or under a small Tongan fale in the front yard. Other meals are eaten in a dining room attractively furnished with cane. Ceiling fans whirring overhead add to the tropical atmosphere. Most main courses feature fish, chicken, and local lobsters. A long bar on the front porch is a favorite drinking spot for expatriot residents, and David's satellite TV draws a crowd during rugby games.

Seaview Restaurant

Vuna Road, 3 blocks west of Royal Palace. ☎ **23-709.** Reservations essential. Main courses T$19.50–T$24 ($15.50–$19). AE, DC, MC, V. Mon–Fri 6–10pm. CONTINENTAL.

This extremely pleasant establishment is in an old colonial clapboard house tastefully decorated inside with tapa cloth and mats to give the dining room an appropriately tropical atmosphere. Daily specials depend on the availability of fresh lobster and quality meats imported from New Zealand. Some items that might appear are filet mignon wrapped in bacon and grilled, pepper steak, fresh lobster, or fish "Polynesia." Start with a lobster cocktail and finish with homemade German pastries for dessert. Try to get a table on the breezy front porch.

Sunrise Taloa Restaurant

Vuna Road, 5 blocks west of Royal Palace. ☎ **22-141.** Reservations recommended. Main courses T$15–T$23 ($12–$18.50). DC, MC, V. Tues–Fri noon–2pm and 6–10pm, Sat 6–10pm. CONTINENTAL.

I always have a meal under the ceiling fans on the veranda-like front room of this pleasant colonial-era house and enjoy the culinary skill German chef Friedel Pott. He prepares beef, pork, chicken, and venison in German, French, and Swiss sauces, plus some with island influences. If your taste buds have gone comatose eating too much island food, revive them with Freidel's super spicy peppercorn soup. Nightly specials feature an appetizer, choice of main courses, dessert, and coffee for T$18.50 ($15).

MODERATE

Fakalato Chinese Restaurant

Wellington Road, 1 block east of Taufa'ahau Road. ☎ **22-101.** Reservations not accepted. Main courses T$4–T$13 ($3.50–$10.50). No credit cards. Mon–Fri 11am–2pm and 5:30–10pm; Sat 5:30–10pm. CANTONESE.

This well-decorated, upstairs establishment actually is Tongan-owned, but the chef is imported from China. His extensive menu contains 16 ways of preparing fresh fish and 10 different sauces for local lobster. They are the most expensive dishes offered, but you can easily make a budget meal of fried noodles or rice. The portions, however, tend to be on the smallish size, and you pay T80¢ (64¢) extra for an order of plain rice.

Fred's Restaurant

Salote Road, in block east of Cable & Wireless. ☎ **22-100.** Reservations not accepted. Lunch specials T$5 ($4); main courses T$9.50–T$21.50 ($7.50–$17). No credit cards. Mon–Fri noon–2pm and 7–10pm. GERMAN.

Like the Seaview and Sunrise Taloa restaurants, Fred's is owned by a chef who immigrated from Germany. Fred has been here longer than most other German residents, as the dusty lampshades and tapa cloth decorating his colonial clapboard house will attest. Some of us think this slightly run-down condition lends a seedy South Seas charm. At least he doesn't gouge us pricewise so he can live in luxury. Fred's best bargain is his lunch special, usually steak or fish with a German sauce and fresh market vegetables. For dinner, he offers wienerschnitzel and other main courses from the home country. I stick with the fresh spiny lobster, of which Tonga is one of the South Pacific storehouses. Try it cooked Polynesia-style with tomatoes, papaya, and garlic. Seating is in the old home's dining room, on the front porch, and under a Tongan fale in the front yard.

The Italian Restaurant

Vuna Road, 1 block west of International Dateline Hotel. ☎ **22-289.** Reservations not accepted. Sandwiches T$2.50–T$3.50 ($2–$3); pizza and pasta T$8–T$16 ($6.50–$13); main courses T$8–T$19 ($6.50–$15). V. Mon–Sat 11:30am–2pm; daily 6:30–10pm. SOUTHERN ITALIAN.

Umberto Mottini and crew serve up tasty homemade pizzas, pastas, and a few meat and seafood dishes under the carport-like, lean-to roof beside the Fasi-Moe-Afi Guest House. His authentic offerings are helped considerably by pastas and many other ingredients he imports from his native Italy. His carbonara, mushroom, basil, clam, bolognese, and napoli sauces over spaghetti, tagliatelle, penne, macaroni, gnocchi, or tortellini will tingle your taste buds. He also serves up excellent salads. Sandwiches are available only at lunch.

INEXPENSIVE

Akiko's Restaurant (Loki Kai Cafeteria)

Taufa'ahau Road, in Basilica of St. Anthony of Padua. No phone. Reservations not accepted. Lunch specials T$3–T$4 ($2.50–$3.50); main courses T$5–T$8 ($4–$6.50). No credit cards. Mon–Fri 11:30am–2pm and 6:30–8pm. EUROPEAN/JAPANESE/CHINESE.

Although a sign may still say "Loki Kai Cafeteria" on the ground floor of the Basilica, this extraordinarily popular eatery is known locally as Akiko's, in honor of its former Japanese owner. This plain but spotlessly clean establishment provides a selection of European, Chinese, and—yes—Japanese selections that are marvelous bargains. Local expatriots flock here for dinner when they don't want to dress up. No alcoholic beverages are served.

12 Island Excursions, Water Sports & Other Outdoor Activities

✪ ISLAND EXCURSIONS   Water sports activities are concentrated in the huge lagoon on Tongatapu's north shore. There is no beach resort on the mainland, however, so most visitors head for the small islets off Nuku'alofa. In fact, the most popular way to spend a day—particularly a very slow Sunday in Tonga—is swimming, snorkeling, sunbathing, dining, or just hanging out at the flat, small islands of Pangaimotu, Sun Island, Fafa, or 'Atata, each of which has a resort just a few miles off Nuku'alofa. These little beachside establishments have water sports activities, restaurants, and bars.

Tongan Beachcomber Island Village (☎ 24-923) on Pangaimotu is the oldest and closest of the offshore resorts. Its boat usually leaves Faua Jetty on Vuna Road at 10am, 11am, and noon. Round-trip fare is T$10 ($8). Once there, a chalkboard menu offers burgers and sandwiches, and kayaks may be rented. There's a children's playground.

Sun Island Resort (☎ 23-335) runs its own boat from Faua Jetty Monday to Saturday at 10am. On Sunday, Stuart and Frances Bollam's 40-foot catamaran *Hakula* departs Faua Jetty for Sun Island at 10am. Round-trip fare any day is T$10 ($8). Americans Annemarie and Earl Markham, Sun Island's managers, were offering a T$5 ($4) lunch special during my recent visit.

Fafa Island Resort (☎ 22-800), a German-owned Robinson Crusoe–like establishment, operates its own sailboat from Faua Jetty daily at 11am. Round-trip transfers and lunch cost T$27 ($21.50).

Royal Sunset Island Resort (☎ 21-155) on 'Atata, the most modern and comfortable of the resorts, welcomes day-trippers only on Sunday. Cost there is T$30 ($24), including transfers and lunch.

See "Where to Stay," below, for more information about these offshore resorts.

FISHING   Based at Royal Sunset Island Resort on 'Atata Island, **Royal Sunset Sportfishing** (☎ 21-254) has the 55-foot live-aboard M.V. *Zeus,* the personal pride of New Zealander hosts Dave and Melita Mair. This luxury craft appeals to experienced fishers who want to venture in search of skipjack, yellowfin tuna, sailfish, blue marlin, and other deep-sea species living on the great seamounts between Tongatapu and Ha'apai. Cost is T$770 ($616) a day plus T$65 ($52) per person for provisions.

GOLF   You won't be playing any golf on Sunday, but you can every other day at the flat, nine-hole **Manamo'ui Golf Course,** home of the Tonga Golf Club. The tour desk at the International Dateline Hotel (☎ 21-411) can arrange equipment rentals and tee-off times on this somewhat-less-than-challenging course, which is on the main road between the airport and town.

SAILING   Another operation based on 'Atata Island, **Royal Sunset Cruising** (☎ 21-254) has the 41-foot sloop *Summer Breeze* available for charter. This crewed craft sleeps four guests. Cost is T$660 ($528) a day, including skipper, crew, and provisions.

SCUBA DIVING & SNORKELING   Although diving off Tongatapu must play second fiddle to Vava'u, the reefs offshore have some colorful coral and a great variety of sealife. **Beluga Diving & Watersports Centre** (☎ 23-576), on Vuna Road at Faua Jetty, has close-in dives and more distant excursions to Hakaumana'o and Malinoa Reef Reserves, two protected underwater parks. Cost for dives ranges from T$80 ($64) for one tank close-in to T$105 ($84) for two tanks farther out. The company also teaches PADI advanced and open water courses for T$300 ($240) and T$400 ($320), respectively. Snorkelers can go on the close-in dive trips for T$21 ($17) and on the longer excursions for T$26 ($21), including equipment.

13 Shopping

Tonga is the best place to shop for extraordinary Polynesian handcrafts, such as tapa cloth, mats, carvings, shell jewelry, and other exquisite items. Your large laundry basket will take at least three months to get home via ship if you don't send it by air freight or check it as baggage on your return flight, but the quality of its craftsmanship will be worth the wait.

Tapa cloth and finely woven pandanus mats are traditional items of clothing and gifts in Tonga, and the women of the kingdom have carried on the ancient skills, not only out of economic necessity but also out of pride in their craft. Collectively they produce thousands of items a day, every one made by hand and no two exactly alike. The sounds of hammers beating tapa cloth from the bark of the paper mulberry tree is a familiar sound in many Tongan villages.

For an excellent description of how tapa cloth is made and the process by which the women weave baskets, mats, and other items from natural materials, pick up a copy of the Tonga Visitors Bureau's brochure "Tongan Handicrafts."

A few artisans have shops on Vuna Road next to the Tonga Visitors Bureau, where they sell jewelry they have made from shells and black coral. The quality of some items is quite good, especially at Miki's Curio Shop, reviewed below.

There are handcraft stalls in **Talamahu Market** on Salote Road, where occasionally you can find an excellent basket or other item.

Important advice: I recommend you purchase items already made and on display rather than ordering for future production and delivery after you have left Tonga.

Except for tobacco products and liquor, Tonga has little to offer in the way of duty-free shopping. Get your booze and smokes at the airport, or order them at least one day prior to departure at Leiola Duty Free Shop in the International Dateline Hotel.

Kalia Handicrafts
Fatafehi Rd. at Salote Rd. ☎ **23-155.**

The retail outlet of the Friendly Islands Marketing Cooperative (FIMCO) is the place to start looking for handcrafts in Nuku'alofa, since this organization gets the best and largest variety of baskets, mats, tapa, shell jewelry, and other handcrafts. You can pay with American Express, MasterCard, and Visa credit cards, and the staff will pack and ship your purchases home. The shop is open Monday to Friday from 8:30am to 6:30pm and Saturday from 8:30am to 12:30pm. There's a small branch on Taufa'ahau Road near the Pacific Royale Hotel.

Langa Fonua Women's Association
Taufa'ahau Rd, second block inland. ☎ **21-104.**

Before FIMCO came along, this shop in the colonial house on Taufa'ahau Road was the place to look. Queen Salote founded the association in 1953 in order to preserve the old crafts and provide a market. It still has an excellent collection, and some items may be priced somewhat lower than elsewhere.

Miki's Curio Shop
Vuna Road, next to the International Dateline Hotel. ☎ **32-083.**

This small emporium is run by veteran carver Mickey Guttenbeil and his family, who export their black coral, mother-of-pearl, wood, bone carvings, and scrimshaw to other South Pacific and Hawaiian shops.

Tongan National Centre
Taufa'ahau Road, 1 mile south of Nuku'alofa. ☎ **23-022.**

Artisans at this fine cultural center reviewed in "Seeing Tongatapu," above, actually make traditional handcrafts before your eyes, then put them up for sale at the centre's gift shop.

14 Island Nights

Tongan Dance Shows   As in Samoa, traditional **Tongan dancing** emphasizes fluid movements of the hands and feet instead of gyrating hips, as is the case in French Polynesia and the Cook Islands. There also is less emphasis on drums and more on the stamping, clapping, and singing of the participants. The dances most often performed for tourists are the *tau'olunga,* in which one young woman dances solo, her body glistening with coconut oil; the *ma'ulu'ulu,* performed sitting down by groups ranging from 20 members to as many as 900 for very important occasions; the *laklaka,* in which rows of dancers sing and dance in unison; and the *kailao,* or war dance, in which men stamp the ground and wave war clubs at each other in mock battle.

The ✪ **Tonga National Centre** (☎ 23-022) stages a full Tongan-style feast complete with traditional kava welcoming ceremony and dance show Tuesday and Thursday evenings. Cost is T$15 ($12). Book by 4:30pm. You'll also have a chance to see Tongan dancing in Nuku'alofa at the **International Dateline Hotel** (☎ 23-411), where floor shows start about 9pm after buffet-style dinners (the nights and prices change, so check with the hotel).

Pub Crawling   Since all pubs and nightclubs must close at the stroke of midnight Saturday, Friday is the busiest and longest night of the week in Tonga. That's when some establishments stay open until 2am or even 5am. Many Tongans start their weekends at one of the local bars, then adjourn to a nightclub for heavy-duty revelry.

The **International Dateline Hotel** (☎ 21-411) had a string band playing in its lounge bar on Friday and Saturday evenings when I was there recently. The comfortable, refined Café Palmiers upstairs at the **Pacific Royale Hotel** (☎ 21-344) may have piano jazz on Friday nights. The front porch bar at **Davina's Restaurant,** on Vuna Road at Faua Jetty (☎ 23-385), is a popular after-work watering hole for local expatriot residents. Davina's also is packed anytime a rugby game is on TV.

The **Ambassador Nite Club,** on Taufa'ahau Road on Fanga'uta Lagoon near the hospital (☎ 23-338), is a pleasant lagoonside pavilion with a bar, dance floor, meeting areas, and a fast-food restaurant. A band plays Monday to Saturday from 8pm onward, and special performances frequently occur, especially if a successful Tongan singer or band is home from overseas. Expect to pay a cover charge, depending on who's entertaining.

The **'Ofa Atu Nite Club** in the Friendly Islander Motel (☎ 23-810) features lively music from either a live band or disc jockey. The club is open only Friday from 8pm to 4am.

Joe's Tropicana Hotel, on Salote Road at Tungi Road (☎ 21-544), serves as Nuku'alofa's quintessential South Seas pub, consistently drawing throngs of young Tongans in search of cold brews and members of the opposite sex. This four-story concrete building has a sometimes rowdy bar at the ground level and a more reserved version on the roof.

15 Vava'u

Approximately 163 miles north of Tongatapu lies enchanting Vava'u, the second-most-visited group of islands in the kingdom and one of the South Pacific's most unusual destinations.

Often mispronounced "Va-vow," the group consists of one large, hilly island shaped like a jellyfish, its tentacles trailing off in a myriad of waterways and small, sand-ringed islets. In the middle is the magnificent fjord-like harbor known as **Port of Refuge,** one of the finest anchorages and most popular yachting destinations in the South Pacific. From its picturesque perch above the harbor, the main village of **Neiafu** (pop. 5,000) evokes scenes from the South Pacific of yesteryear.

Vava'u has its own unique history. The first European visitor was Spanish explorer Francisco Antonio Mourelle, who happened upon the islands in 1781 on his way to the Philippines from Mexico. He gave Port of Refuge its name. At the time, Vava'u was the seat of one of three chiefdoms fighting for control of Tonga. Finau II, who captured the *Port au Prince* in 1806, built a fortress at Neiafu and kept Will Mariner captive there until the young Englishman became one of his favorites. Two years later the brutal Finau won a major victory by faking a peace agreement with rival chiefs. He then tied them up and let them slowly sink to their deaths in a leaky canoe.

Finau II's successor, Finau 'Ulukalala III, converted to Christianity but died before his successor was old enough to rule. Before dying he asked George Taufa'ahau, who was then chief of Ha'apai, to look after the throne until the young boy was old enough. George did more than that; he took over Vava'u in 1833. Twelve years later he conquered Tongatapu and became King George I, ruler of Tonga.

To the south of Neiafu, the reef is speckled with 33 small islands, 21 of them inhabited. The others are spectacularly beautiful little dots of land that fall into the Robinson Crusoe category of places to escape from it all for a day. The white beaches and emerald surrounding lagoon are unsurpassed in their beauty.

Vava'u is heaven for water-sports enthusiasts and sailors. Getting out on the water for a day is easy. When you see these protected waterways, you'll know why cruising sailors love Vava'u. If you like walking on unspoiled white sandy beaches on uninhabited islands, swimming in crystal-clear water, and taking boat rides into mysterious caves cut into cliffs, you'll like Vava'u, too.

Vava'u is the most seasonal destination in the South Pacific. It virtually comes alive during the yachting season from May to October, when more than 100 yachts can be in port at any one time. In the offseason, Vava'u reverts to a sleepy back-water port.

Impressions

Despite the lack of green fields and church spires, in the pearly dawn from the ship's bridge the Vava'u Group had the appearance of a lump of Cornwall or Brittany that had been dropped on a hard surface from a height just sufficient to scatter the thirty-four fragments and create deep channels, scarcely wider than rivers, between them. As the ship wandered among the scrub-covered limestone tableaux I thought it was the nearest thing in cruise-liner terms to cross-country driving.

—John Dyson, 1982

I recommend that side trips to Vava'u be made early in a visit to Tonga in order to allow a day or two leeway in case you can't get back to Nuku'alofa on the day planned. As with Savai'i in Western Samoa, you will wish you had stayed longer in this most beautiful and enchanting part of Tonga.

GETTING THERE

Lupepa'u Airport is on the north side of Vauau'u, about 7km (4 miles) from Neiafu. The strip is paved, and a new terminal opened in 1995, thanks to European Union aid.

Royal Tongan Airlines (☎ 23-414 in Nuku'alofa) has several flights a day from Tongatapu to Vava'u, and plans were in the works during my recent visit to start direct service from Nadi in Fiji. **Samoa Air** flies very small planes between Pago Pago and Vava'u twice a week. For more information, see "Getting There," earlier in this chapter.

The Paradise Hotel's bus provides airport transfers to its guests for free and T$4 ($3.20) to anyone else, or you can take one of the island's few taxis to Neiafu for about T$7 ($5.50).

Don't forget that it's imperative to reconfirm your return flight to Tongatapu as soon as possible after arriving on Vava'u. The staff at your hotel can take care of this for you, or you can visit the office of Royal Tongan Airlines, on the main street in Neiafu.

The ferries from Nuku'alofa land at Uafu Lahi, the Big Wharf, in Neiafu. From there you can walk or take a taxi ride to your hotel or guesthouse. If on foot, turn right on the main street to reach the center of town and the accommodations.

The road from the airport dead-ends at a T-intersection atop the hill above the wharf. The main street runs from there in both directions along the water, with most of the town's stores and government offices flanking it. The government used convicted adulteresses to help build this road; hence, its Tongan name is Hale Lupe (Road of the Doves). There are no street signs, but the Tonga Visitors Bureau's helpful signs point the way to most establishments and points of interest.

GETTING AROUND

Public transportation on Vava'u is limited. If you book an excursion, ask about the availability of transportation to and from the event. **Taxis** are not metered, so be sure you determine the fare before getting in. Leopote Taxis (☎ 70-136), Paradise Taxis (☎ 70-083), and Ikahihifo Taxi (☎ 70-129) are available for about T$10 ($8) per hour or T$25 ($20) a day, but be sure to negotiate a fare in advance. **Buses** and pickup trucks fan out from the market in Neiafu to various villages, but they have no fixed schedule. If you take one, make sure you know when and whether it's coming back to town.

Bicycles are rented by the Chanel College Scouts for T$10 ($8) a day. Look for the sign on the caged-in building on the school grounds between town and the Paradise Hotel.

FAST FACTS: VAVA'U

If you don't see an item here, check the "Fast Facts: Tonga" earlier in this chapter, or just ask around. Vava'u is a very small place where nearly everyone knows everything.

Bookstores Friendly Islands Bookshop has a branch on the main street.

Currency Exchange   The Bank of Tonga office, on the main street in Neiafu, is open Monday to Friday from 9:30am to 3:30pm and Mbf [sic] Bank nearby is open Monday to Friday from 9am to 3:30pm and Saturday from 9 to 11:30am. When they are closed, traveler's checks can be exchanged at the Paradise Hotel.

Doctor & Dentist   Dr. Alfredo Carafa (70-519), an engaging Italian, has a private clinic with two doctors and a dentist in Toula village, 2km (1¹/₄ miles) south of the Paradise Hotel. Open Monday to Friday from 8:30am to noon.

Hospital   The government has a 40-bed hospital with dental service in Neiafu. Take my advice and call "Dr. Alfredo" at his clinic.

Police   The telephone number for the police is 70-234.

Post Office/Telephone/Telex/Fax   The post office opposite the wharf is open Monday to Friday from 8:30am to 12:30pm and 1:30 to 3:30pm. Local calls can be made at the post office, which has the island's only public telephone.

Telephone   Tonga Telecom next to the post office is open 24 hours a day, seven days a week for domestic and long-distance calls.

Tourist Information   The Tonga Visitors Bureau (☎ 70-115) has an office on the main road in Neiafu. Check there for lists of local activities while you're in town. The staff can also help arrange road tours of the island and boat tours of the lagoon. The office is open Monday to Friday from 8:30am to 4:30pm. The address is P.O. Box 18, Neiafu, Vava'u.

WHAT TO SEE & DO

You can take a walking tour of Neiafu, the picturesque little town curving along the banks of Port of Refuge. The Tonga Visitors Bureau (☎ 70-115) might also be able to organize a walking tour for a small group.

For sure, make the walk along Port of Refuge from the Paradise Hotel into town, a stroll of about 15 minutes.

The flat top mountain across the harbor is **Mo'unga Talau,** at 204 meters (675 feet) the tallest point on Vava'u. A hike to the top takes about two hours round-trip. To get there, turn inland a block past the Bank of Tonga on the airport road, then left at Sailoame Market. This street continues through the residential area and then becomes a track. The turnoff to the summit starts as the track begins to head downhill. It's a steep climb and can be slippery in wet weather.

Both the Paradise Hotel (☎ 70-211) and the Tonga Visitors Bureau (☎ 70-115) will arrange **sightseeing tours** of the island with Soane's Bus Tours. Cost is T$25 ($20) per person, with a minimum of three required. You will see lovely scenery of the fingerlike bays cutting into the island, visit some beautiful beaches, and take in the sweet smell of vanilla—the principal cash crop on Vava'u—drying in sheds or in the sun.

For a bird's-eye view, take a flight in a tiny "air boat" with Peter Goldstern of **Vava'u Amphibian Air** (☎ 70-193 or 70-541). Cost is U.S. $200 an hour if you take off and land on ground, slightly more for a water takeoff or landing. Peter also

---

Impressions

If I could repeat just one of my excursions in Polynesia, it would be that spent in a fast little jet-boat, exploring this maze of beaches, cliffs, caves, reefs, and lagoons—or at least, what small proportion of it could be fitted into a single day.

—Ron Hall, 1991

flies right into **Tofua Crater,** atop Tofua Island in the Ha'apai Group. That trip costs U.S. $525, including a barbecue lunch on the lake's deserted shores.

WHERE TO STAY

Vava'u had become the "hot" destination in Tonga during my recent visit, and several European expatriots living in Nuku'alofa were making plans to open small resorts or restaurants on the many small offshore islets. There may be several of these by the time you get to Vava'u. One had just opened when I was there: **Papa'o Village Resort,** c/o General Delivery, Neiafu, Vava'u (☎ **70-303,** fax 70-522), a 1¼-hour boat ride from Neiafu. This is the longtime dream of Hans Schmeiser, who immigrated from Switzerland and spent many years running a successful backpackers' hostel in Neiafu. Accommodation on Papa'o is in seven simple thatch-roofed Tongan fales, one of which has four dormitory beds. Guests share toilets and rainwater "bucket baths" (there is no well water or electricity on the island), and they cook their meals Tongan-style in a central building. There is a small bar. Rates range from T$8 to T$38 ($6.50 to $30.50), depending on the type of bungalow and length of stay. No credit cards are accepted.

Although the government does not encourage **camping,** it is possible to take a tent, sleeping gear, supplies, *and plenty of water* to one of the little uninhabited islands and spend some time there. You will need permission, however, from the villagers who own the island or the island council. Contact the Tonga Visitors Bureau.

HOTELS

✪ Paradise Hotel

P.O. Box 11, Neiafu, Vava'u, Tonga (east end of Neiafu). ☎ **70-211.** Fax 70-184. 49 rms. A/C TEL. T$42-T$90 ($33.50–$72). AE, DC, MC, V.

Perched on a grassy ridge overlooking Port of Refuge and a short walk from Neiafu, this is far and away the most comfortable hotel in Tonga. Kentuckian Carter Johnson, who made his fortune in building pipelines in the U.S. and Australia, bought the Paradise at auction in 1981 as "something to do" during an early retirement. What he has done is create an unusual property whose blocks of humongous rooms are joined by covered walkways sided with white pipe railings (a testament to his abilities with a welding torch). A large central building houses the reception area, a gift shop, bar, restaurant, and dance area. Next to it on a grassy lawn is a swimming pool with a panoramic view of the harbor below. A path leads down to the water's edge, where the hotel has its own pier, a popular spot for "yachties" from May to October, who congregate in the bar and contribute to a very friendly, informal atmosphere. Incidentally, the airplane engine hanging near the bar once was part of the hotel's aircraft that Carter crash-landed in 1985. Fortunately, no one was seriously injured.

The large, American-size rooms are in one- and two-story buildings. The best—and most expensive—have unimpeded views of Port of Refuge. A few older "economy" rooms have ceiling fans but no air conditioners, tea- and coffee-making facilities, hot water, or harbor views.

The dining room opens to the hilltop pool. Carter is notorious in these parts for not keeping chefs in his employ for very long, so I hesitate to comment on what fare you will find. The hotel has a game room in which video movies are shown in the evenings, and a local musical group plays in the dance area off the bar beginning at 8pm Monday to Saturday during the sailing season. The reception staff can tell you what's happening while you're there and also arrange tours and boat trips.

Tongan Beach Resort

P.O. Box 104, Neiafu, Vava'u (on 'Utungake Island, 5¹/₂ miles from Neiafu, 9¹/₂ miles from airport via dirt road and causeway). ☎ and fax **70-380**. 12 rms. T$100 ($80). Round-trip airport transfers T$20 ($16). MC, V.

Dietre and Senikau Dyck's isolated resort sits beside a lovely narrow channel south of Port of Refuge, giving guests their own swimming beach and jumping off point for scuba diving, kayaking, and other water sports. The main building here is an open Tongan fale housing a restaurant, whose menu varies each day depending on the catch, the emphasis being on fresh seafood. A sand-floored bar has its own fale next door. The comfortable, motel-like guest rooms flank the main complex. They are of New Zealand–style construction and furnishings. All have tile floors, ceiling fans, dressing areas, one queen and one single bed, and shower-only bath.

GUESTHOUSES

Hamana Lake Guesthouse

C/o General Delivery, Neiafu, Vava'u (west of town overlooking Port of Refuge). ☎ **70-507**. Fax 70-200. 6 rms (none with bath). T$30–T$35 ($24–$28). No credit cards.

Isiah and Pisila Tu'pulotu's modern but simple home seems to hang from a cliff, where it has a gorgeous view of Port of Refuge and Neiafu. The choice room here is Number 3, on the corner of the house where it has windows on two sides. Two more lower-level rooms have one-window views. A wall in another downstairs room actually is the hill, into which a double bed has been carved. Neither of the two upstairs rooms has a view. Some rooms have fans; others do not. The best views of all are from the communal kitchen.

Vava'u Guest House

P.O. Box 148, Neiafu, Vava'u (east end of Neiafu, opposite Paradise Hotel). ☎ **70-300**. 5 rms (none with bath), 4 bungalows (all with bath). T$13 ($10.50) room; T$25 ($20) bungalow. No credit cards.

You can get a room or stay in your own bungalow at this convenient establishment owned by Mikio Filitonga and his family. The four Tongan-fale bungalows are quite comfortable (albeit with cold-water showers). A European-style house on the property contains 10 rooms sharing two baths. A restaurant offers a mix of Chinese and Tongan dishes. Full dinners cost T$8 ($6.50); guests should book by 3pm.

WHERE TO DINE IN VAVA'U

If you missed a Tongan feast in Nuku'alofa, or just liked it so much you want to try again, **Isiah's Lisa Beach Feast** takes place Wednesday and Saturday on lovely Lisa Beach. **Matato's Feast** is on equally pretty Ano Beach on Saturday. Both cost about T$20 ($16) per person. Inquire at the Paradise Hotel or the Tonga Visitors Bureau.

Bounty Bar

Neiafu, main street in heart of town. ☎ **70-576**. Reservations accepted for dinner. Breakfast T$2–T$4 ($1.60–$3.20); snacks and meals T$4–T$6 ($3.20–$5). No credit cards. June–Aug, Mon–Fri 8:30am–7pm; Sept–May, Mon–Fri 8:30am–10pm. SNACKS/REGIONAL.

With its great view overlooking Port of Refuge, Lyn Bowe and daughter Amber have a very popular establishment with visitors and even locals, who take their morning tea here. The Bowes offer cooked breakfasts, burgers and sandwiches, and meals of sashimi, fried rice, and fresh local fish. They also provide full meals and live entertainment on Friday during the yachting season from June to August, but you must reserve in advance for the 7pm seating.

✪ Ocean Breeze Restaurant & Bistro Bar

Neiafu, on the Old Harbor. ☎ **70-582.** Reservations required in dining room. Sandwiches and burgers T$3.50–T$8 ($3–$6.50); main courses T$10.50–T$26.50 ($8.50–$21). No credit cards. Dining room Mon–Sat 6–10pm all year. Bistro Bar daily 11am–8pm, later from May–Oct. Sun dinner by reservation only. REGIONAL.

Born in Tonga, Amelia Dale lived for 15 years in England, where she met and married husband John. Now back in Vava'u, she and John have converted their living room into a restaurant, where she cooks up curry specialties. I had her lobster with banana, pineapple, and Bombay potatoes, which was right up there with any curry I've had anywhere, and that includes India and Pakistan. Ask her to turn down the chilies if you have a tender tongue! The Dales have their Bistro Bar out on the lawn overlooking the Old Harbour. There they serve breakfast all day and offer barbecued fish, burgers, kebabs, and ploughman's lunches. You can walk across the peninsula from Port of Refuge and the Paradise Hotel, but the trail is narrow and can be muddy. Take a cab for T$2 ($1.60) each way.

ISLAND TOURS, WATER SPORTS & OUTDOOR ACTIVITIES

As noted above, Vava'u has a very busy yachting season from May to October. Some of the activities mentioned below, especially sailing and fishing boats, operate only during this period, then clear out of Tonga entirely during the hurricane season from November to April. It's best to inquire in advance whether any particular activity is available when you will be in Vava'u.

✪ **BOAT TOURS**   The thing to do in Vava'u is to get out on the fabulous fjords for some swimming, snorkeling, and exploring of the caves and uninhabited islands.

The typical boat tour follows Port of Refuge to **Swallows Cave** on Kapa Island and then to **Mariner's Cave** (named for Will Mariner, the young Englishman captured with the *Port au Prince* in 1806) on Nuapapu Island. Both of these have been carved out of cliffs by erosion. Boats can go right into Swallows Cave for a look at the swallows flying in and out of a hole in its top. Swimmers with snorkeling gear and a guide can dive into Mariner's Cave. Both caves face west and are best visited in the afternoon, when the maximum amount of natural light gets into them. Most trips also include a stop at one of the small islands for some time at a sparkling beach and a swim over the reefs in crystal-clear water.

Soki Island Tours hits the high spots and includes lunch and a swim at an uninhabited islet. The trip costs T$20 ($16) per person. Inquire at the reception desk of the Paradise Hotel (☎ 70-211) or the Tonga Visitors Bureau (☎ 70-115).

John Dale at the Ocean Breeze Restaurant (☎ 70-582) will take up to four persons on full-day speedboat tours for T$125 ($100) per group, including lunch.

New Zealander Allan Bowe of **Phoenix Charters** (☎ 70-576) was gearing up for whale-watching cruises during my recent visit. Humpback whales regularly breed in the waters off Vava'u from June to October. Allan was going to take guests out to snorkel among these huge animals for T$50 ($40) per person a day. He also goes on nature-watch trips when sea birds breed on Maninita Island from November to June. Those trips cost T$75 ($60) per person. Book at the Bowe family's Bounty Bar in Neiafu.

The fastest way to see the caves and small islands is on a jet boat with Peter Goldstern of **Vava'u Watersports** (☎ 70-193 or 70-541). They cost T$49 ($39) per person.

Kayaks can be rented from the Paradise Hotel (☎ 70-211) or from **Friendly Islands Kayak Company** at the Tongan Beach Resort (☎ 70-380) during the yachting season from May to October.

FISHING The *Kiwi Magic* (☎ 70-441) takes visitors offshore for a full day of sports fishing for T$500 ($400) per day, with a maximum of three persons on board, or half-day's light tackle fishing in the lagoon for T$30 ($24) per person, with a four-person minimum. At least two snorkelers can go along for T$30 ($24) apiece.

Kitty Vane Charters and **Delray Charters,** both based at the Tongan Beach Resort (☎ 70-380), charge about T$550 ($440) per boat for a day's sports fishing, with a maximum of four persons. They operate only from May to October.

Scuba Diving The clear, sheltered waters of Vava'u are excellent for scuba diving, particularly since divers don't have to ride on a boat for several hours just to get to a spot with colorful coral and bountiful sea life. In Port of Refuge, divers can explore the wreck of the copra schooner *Clan McWilliam,* sunk in 1906.

When he isn't flying his amphibian, New Zealand–born and American-raised Peter Goldstern of **Vava'u Watersports,** Private Bag, Neiafu, Vava'u (☎ and fax 70-193), charges T$80 ($64) for a two-tank dive. He also teaches PADI open water courses for T$375 ($300).

During the yachting season from May to October, **Dolphin Pacific Diving** (☎ 70-507, or 619/728-4200 in the U.S.), which has an office in Neiafu and its base at the Tongan Beach Resort, offers two-tank dives for T$85 ($68) and a short resort course for T$120 ($96). Instructor Patty Vogan also teaches NAUI courses and rents Windsurfers and takes guests waterskiing.

SAILING The Florida-based company **The Moorings** (☎ 70-016), which pioneered charter sailboats in the Caribbean, has one of its South Pacific operations in Neiafu. Boats range in length from 37 feet to 51 feet and in price from U.S. $2,300 to U.S. $4,400 a week per boat for bareboat charters (that is, you hire the "bare" boat and provide your own skipper and crew). If a boat is available, day rates are range from U.S. $354 to U.S. $629. The Moorings requires that its clients be qualified to handle sailboats of the size it charters, and the staff will check out your skills before turning you loose. A skipper or guide is available at extra cost. The Moorings will do your shopping and have the boat provisioned with food and drink when you arrive. For more information, contact the Moorings, 19345 U.S. 19 North, Suite 402, Clearwater, FL 34624 (☎ 813/535-1446 or 800/535-7289).

American Vern Kirk provides cruises on his trimaran sailboat *Orion.* He charges T$35 ($28) per person for a full day's cruise around the lagoon, with a T$90 ($72) minimum. Bring your own lunch. Find him or book the *Orion* at the Paradise Hotel (☎ 70-211).

Americans sailmakers Andy and Sandy Peterson, who have lived in Vava'u since 1989, take guests out day sailing on their 56-foot Sparkman & Stephens yacht *Jakaranda* for T$50 ($40) per person. Longer cruises are available. Book at the Paradise Hotel (☎ 70-211).

New Zealanders John Beauchamp and Julia Matheson of **Sailing Safaris** (☎ 70-441) go day sailing on the 50-foot gaff-rigged ketch *Melinda* for T$45 ($36) per person. Longer voyages cost T$380 ($304) per boat, plus T$20 ($16) per person a day for food.

SHOPPING

If you depart Vava'u directly for Pago Pago or Nadi, you can buy some **duty-free merchandise** at the Tonga Visitors Bureau office on the main street.

As noted earlier in this chapter, Vava'u produces some of the finest handcrafts in Tonga. The establishments listed below will pack and ship your purchases home. Also look in the small jewelry shops along the main street for items of black coral and shell.

Friendly Islands Marketing Cooperative (FIMCO)
Main Street, opposite The Moorings. ☎ **70-242.**

The Vava'u branch of FIMCO has some good items, but most of the best is shipped to the main store in Nuku'alofa for sale. Open Monday to Friday from 8:30am to 4:30pm (to 5pm June through November) and Saturday 8:30am to noon.

Langa Fonua Handicrafts
Main Street, in Tonga Visitors Bureau. ☎ **70-356.**

The Vava'u branch of Langa Fonua, the women's handcraft organization founded by Queen Salote, has a shop in a Tongan fale adjacent to the Tonga Visitors Bureau. It has a good variety of baskets, mats, wood carvings, and other items at reasonable prices. Open Monday to Friday 8:30am to 4pm.

Paradise Hotel Gift Shop
Main Street, in the Paradise Hotel. ☎ **70-211.**

As with FIMCO's branch, you might find an unusual or high-quality piece here, although chances are that you will more likely be successful at Langa Fonua. Since you likely will either stay at the Paradise or visit it, stop in and have a look. Unlike the others, they do not pack and ship your purchases.

ISLAND NIGHTS

A dance band usually plays from 8pm nightly in the **Paradise Hotel** bar (☎ 70-211) during the busy yachting season from May to October, on Fridays and Saturdays during the rest of the year. Otherwise, there's not much to do except hang out with all the expatriots playing billiards, drinking, and gossiping at the **Neiafu Club** (☎ 70-566) overlooking the harbor on the main road between the Paradise Hotel and town. Members are affluent local businessmen, many of them expatriots, who welcome overseas visitors to use their rustic lounge with shelf of books and bar. The club is open daily from 3pm to 11pm, including all holidays, and it will stay open later if those still present ante up T$4 ($3.20) apiece to pay the bartender. Otherwise, admission is free.

Index

Now Save Money on All Your Travels by Joining

Frommer's
TRAVEL BOOK CLUB

The Advantages of Membership:

1. Your choice of any **TWO FREE BOOKS.**

2. Your own subscription to the **TRIPS & TRAVEL** quarterly newsletter, where you'll discover the best buys in travel, the hottest vacation spots, the latest travel trends, world-class events and festivals, and much more.

3. A **30% DISCOUNT** on any additional books you order through the club.

4. **DOMESTIC TRIP-ROUTING KITS** (available for a small additional fee). We'll send you a detailed map highlighting the most direct or scenic route to your destination, anywhere in North America.

Here's all you have to do to join:

Send in your annual membership fee of $25.00 ($35.00 Canada/Foreign) with your name, address, and selections on the form below. Or call 815/734-1104 to use your credit card.

Send all orders to:

FROMMER'S TRAVEL BOOK CLUB
P.O. Box 473 • Mt. Morris, IL 61054-0473 • ☎ 815/734-1104

YES! I want to take advantage of this opportunity to join Frommer's Travel Book Club.

[ ] My check for $25.00 ($35.00 for Canadian or foreign orders) is enclosed.
   All orders must be prepaid in U.S. funds only. Please make checks payable to Frommer's Travel Book Club.

[ ] Please charge my credit card: [ ] Visa or [ ] Mastercard

   Credit card number: _____

   Expiration date: ___ / ___ / ___

   Signature: _____

   Or call 815/734-1104 to use your credit card by phone.

Name: _____

Address: _____

City: _____ State: _____ Zip code: _____

Phone number (in case we have a question regarding your order): _____

Please indicate your choices for TWO FREE books (*see following pages*):

   Book 1 - Code: _____ Title: _____

   Book 2 - Code: _____ Title: _____

For information on ordering additional titles, see your first issue of the *Trips & Travel* newsletter.

Allow 4–6 weeks for delivery for all items. Prices of books, membership fee, and publication dates are subject to change without notice. All orders are subject to acceptance and availability.

AC1

The following Frommer's guides are available from your favorite bookstore, or you can use the order form on the preceding page to request them as part of your membership in Frommer's Travel Book Club.

FROMMER'S COMPLETE TRAVEL GUIDES

(Comprehensive guides to sightseeing, dining and accommodations, with selections in all price ranges—from deluxe to budget)

FROMMER'S $-A-DAY GUIDES

(Dream Vacations at Down-to-Earth Prices)

FROMMER'S COMPLETE CITY GUIDES

(Comprehensive guides to sightseeing, dining, and accommodations in all price ranges)

FROMMER'S FAMILY GUIDES

(Guides to family-friendly hotels, restaurants, activities, and attractions)

FROMMER'S WALKING TOURS

*(Memorable strolls through colorful and historic neighborhoods,
accompanied by detailed directions and maps)*

FROMMER'S AMERICA ON WHEELS

*(Guides for travelers who are exploring the U.S.A. by car, featuring a brand-new
rating system for accommodations and full-color road maps)*

FROMMER'S SPECIAL-INTEREST TITLES

Arthur Frommer's Branson!	P107	Frommer's Where to Stay U.S.A.,	
Arthur Frommer's New World		11th Ed.	P102
of Travel (avail. 11/95)	P112	National Park Guide, 29th Ed.	P106
Frommer's Caribbean Hideaways		USA Today Golf Tournament Guide	P113
(avail. 9/95)	P110	USA Today Minor League	
Frommer's America's 100 Best-Loved		Baseball Book	P111
State Parks	P109		

FROMMER'S BEST BEACH VACATIONS

(The top places to sun, stroll, shop, stay, play, party, and swim—with each beach rated for beauty, swimming, sand, and amenities)

California (avail. 10/95)	G100	Hawaii (avail. 10/95)	G102
Florida (avail. 10/95)	G101		

FROMMER'S BED & BREAKFAST GUIDES

(Selective guides with four-color photos and full descriptions of the best inns in each region)

California	B100	Hawaii	B105
Caribbean	B101	Pacific Northwest	B106
East Coast	B102	Rockies	B107
Eastern United States	B103	Southwest	B108
Great American Cities	B104		

FROMMER'S IRREVERENT GUIDES

(Wickedly honest guides for sophisticated travelers and those who want to be)

Chicago (avail. 11/95)	I100	New Orleans (avail. 11/95)	I103
London (avail. 11/95)	I101	San Francisco (avail. 11/95)	I104
Manhattan (avail. 11/95)	I102	Virgin Islands (avail. 11/95)	I105

FROMMER'S DRIVING TOURS

(Four-color photos and detailed maps outlining spectacular scenic driving routes)

Australia	Y100	Italy	Y108
Austria	Y101	Mexico	Y109
Britain	Y102	Scandinavia	Y110
Canada	Y103	Scotland	Y111
Florida	Y104	Spain	Y112
France	Y105	Switzerland	Y113
Germany	Y106	U.S.A.	Y114
Ireland	Y107		

FROMMER'S BORN TO SHOP

(The ultimate travel guides for discriminating shoppers—from cut-rate to couture)

Hong Kong (avail. 11/95)	Z100	London (avail. 11/95)	Z101